Building Your Financial Fortress

The Step-by-Step Guide to Passive Income

By Markus Heitkoetter

 ISBN 978-1-7373018-0-6

Information within this publication contains "forward-looking statements" within the meaning of Section 27A of the Securities Act of 1933 and Section 21B of the Securities Exchange Act of 1934. Any statements that express or involve discussions with respect to predictions, goals, expectations, beliefs, plans, projections, objectives, assumptions or future events or performance are not statements of historical fact and may be "forward-looking statements." Forward-looking statements are based on expectations, estimates, and projections at the time the statements are made that involve a number of risks and uncertainties which could cause actual results or events to differ materially from those presently anticipated. Investing involves the risk of loss as well as the possibility of profit. All investments involve risk, and all investment decisions of an individual remain the responsibility of that individual. Option and stock investing involves risk and is not suitable for all investors. Past performance does not guarantee future results. No statement in this book should be construed as a recommendation to buy or sell a security. The author and publisher of this book cannot guarantee that the strategies outlined in this book will be profitable and will not be held liable for any possible trading losses related to these strategies.

All information provided within this publication pertaining to investing, options, stocks, and securities is educational information and not investment advice. Rockwell Trading is not an investment advisor and recommends all readers and subscribers to seek advice from a registered professional securities representative before deciding to invest in stocks and options featured within this publication. None of the material within this publication shall be construed as any kind of investment advice. Readers of this publication are cautioned not to place undue reliance on forward-looking statements, which are based on certain assumptions and expectations involving various risks and uncertainties that could cause results to differ materially from those set forth in the forward-looking statements. Please be advised that nothing within this publication shall constitute a solicitation or an invitation to buy or sell any security mentioned herein. The author of this publication is neither a registered investment advisor nor affiliated with any broker or dealer.

Although every precaution has been taken in the preparation of this publication, the publisher and author assume no liability for errors and omissions. This publication is published without warranty of any kind, either expressed or implied. Furthermore, neither the author nor the publisher shall be liable for any damages, either directly or indirectly arising from the use or misuse of the book. Users of this publication agree to indemnify, release and hold harmless Rockwell Trading, its members, employees, agents, representatives, affiliates, subsidiaries, successors and assigns (collectively, "The Companies") from and against any and all claims, liabilities, losses, causes of actions, costs, lost profits, lost opportunities, indirect, special, incident, consequential, punitive, or any other damages whatsoever and expenses (including, without limitation, court costs and attorneys' fees) ("Losses") asserted against, resulting from, imposed upon or incurred by any of The Companies as a result of, or arising out of this agreement and/or your use of this publication. This publication is designed to provide accurate and authoritative information in regard to the subject matter covered. It is sold with the understanding that the author and publisher are not engaged in rendering legal, accounting, or other professional services. If legal advice or other expert assistance is required, the services of a competent professional person should be sought. Use of the material within this publication constitutes your acceptance of these terms.

HYPOTHETICAL PERFORMANCE RESULTS HAVE MANY INHERENT LIMITATIONS, SOME OF WHICH ARE DESCRIBED BELOW. NO REPRESENTATION IS BEING MADE THAT ANY ACCOUNT WILL OR IS LIKELY TO ACHIEVE PROFITS OR LOSSES SIMILAR TO THOSE SHOWN. IN FACT, THERE ARE FREQUENTLY SHARP DIFFERENCES BETWEEN HYPOTHETICAL PERFORMANCE RESULTS AND THE ACTUAL RESULTS SUBSEQUENTLY ACHIEVED BY ANY PARTICULAR TRADING PROGRAM.

ONE OF THE LIMITATIONS OF HYPOTHETICAL PERFORMANCE RESULTS IS THAT THEY ARE GENERALLY PREPARED WITH THE BENEFIT OF HINDSIGHT. IN ADDITION, HYPOTHETICAL TRADING DOES NOT INVOLVE FINANCIAL RISK, AND NO HYPOTHETICAL TRADING RECORD CAN COMPLETELY ACCOUNT FOR THE IMPACT OF FINANCIAL RISK IN ACTUAL TRADING. FOR EXAMPLE, THE ABILITY TO WITHSTAND LOSSES OR TO ADHERE TO A PARTICULAR TRADING PROGRAM IN SPITE OF TRADING LOSSES ARE MATERIAL POINTS WHICH CAN ALSO ADVERSELY AFFECT ACTUAL TRADING RESULTS. THERE ARE NUMEROUS OTHER FACTORS RELATED TO THE MARKETS IN GENERAL OR TO THE IMPLEMENTATION OF ANY SPECIFIC TRADING PROGRAM WHICH CANNOT BE FULLY ACCOUNTED FOR IN THE PREPARATION OF HYPOTHETICAL PERFORMANCE.

Table of Contents

BEFORE YOU READ A SINGLE CHAPTER

Claim Your Free Bonus Resources

[illegible]

Chapter 1: My Story

I was once where you are now.

In fact, I struggled for years with feeling stuck and unable to truly increase my net worth.

In case you don't know me already, my name is Markus Heitkoetter.

I was born and raised in Germany, pursuing the traditional career path of studying hard and beginning to work for a big company. And after doing it for a few years, I realized that THIS wasn't my true passion, so in 2002 I decided to take a leap of faith. I quit my job at IBM and moved from Munich, Germany, to Austin, TX, to become a professional trader and investor.

I came to America with only $30,000 in my pocket and now I am proud to say that I have built something out of nothing, achieving great success as a trader and investor. Today, I am a multi-Millionaire.

Now I wasn't always so successful.

This is going to be the full story of how I went from a desperate corporate worker for IBM to living the life I'm living now.

And I'm not leaving any details out of this.

There's no sugarcoating.

No editing to make it more friendly.

It's the exact way it happened ... and I hope that what I've learned along this bumpy road will help you reach your goals in a fraction of the time it took me.

My Career Path and Aha Moment

You see, when I was growing up, I followed all the rules:

Good grades in school. ✓

College degree. ✓

Corporate job with IBM .✓

At first, things were great. My hard work paid off quickly and in no time at all I'd risen to new heights within their organization. The money came pouring in, more than enough for me to live comfortably, and my coworkers praised me for my dedication and ambition.

I had it all:

The car. ✓

The fancy office with a view. ✓

I was living what I thought would be my ideal life. Except for one thing …

I wasn't happy.

Sure, there were moments of joy, like when I landed that next promotion or closed that important deal, but overall, something felt … off.

Every day felt like a chore. I was spinning my wheels and yet not getting anywhere. I played by their rules no matter how much it

drained me inside or how little satisfaction it brought me in return … because I hoped that one day it would get better.
One day, I wouldn't have to work so hard anymore.
One day, I would have more time.
One day …

I will never forget the day when everything changed for me.

As I sat in the dark, staring out of the hotel window at a city that was supposed to be my home for the next few weeks during a work project, my heart suddenly felt heavy. All of these years I'd been doing exactly what everyone had said was right, working hard on a corporate job and climbing the corporate ladder, but where had it gotten me?

Back home my friends were celebrating a birthday. And they didn't even invite me! Probably because whenever they asked, I always replied, "I'm too busy."

My chest tightened as a wave of loneliness washed over me. For the first time, I questioned why I was so dedicated to my job and was it really worth it?

So I made a drastic decision …

I left my job at IBM and moved from Munich, Germany, to Austin, Texas, with the goal of becoming a professional trader. The moment I hit the submit button and sent my resignation email to IBM, a wave of both excitement and fear washed over me. It wasn't easy leaving behind the safety of my job in Munich but I knew that this was what I had to do if I wanted to take my life back and make my dreams come true!

Moving to the US and Getting Started as an Investor/Trader

So there I was in America, a new country full of possibilities but also risks. I had $30,000 in my pocket. I set aside $10,000 for living expenses and put $20,000 in my trading account with the hope of turning it into millions … or so I thought!

Early Failures and Lessons Learned

It turns out trading isn't as easy as they say it is. Within months, due to inexperience combined with bad luck (and maybe even some careless trades), my $20,000 quickly dwindled down to just $8,000. I was very discouraged. And I was afraid that I might have to go back to IBM, tail between my legs, and begging for a job again.

But then I finally "got it." I realized what I did wrong. I used to believe the hype. That trading was all about making huge, life-changing profits in a matter of days or weeks. I watched videos of traders who made 286% in three days and turned a $500 account into $100,000 in less than a year. It seemed too good to be true! I realized I was chasing unicorns.

And then, something changed inside me. I realized that maybe this kind of thinking wasn't sustainable, that chasing after quick "windfall" profits is often a fool's errand and can lead you down some dangerous paths if you're not careful.

So instead, I decided to focus on what I call, **SRC Profits**: Systematic, Repeatable, and Consistent profits.

It was going slow at first. Every gain seemed insignificant compared to the ones promised by all those get-rich-quick schemes out there. But soon enough, my patience began paying off as little by little my account balance started increasing. And like a snowball, it started gaining momentum.

But the best part? Thanks to this new approach, the risk per trade has decreased significantly, and trading has become less stressful and more rewarding than ever before!

If I could turn it around, you can easily do the same.

What if I told you that many readers who read the very words you are reading now are building a passive income machine that never runs out of money and builds financial security for yourself and your family … simply by leveraging the concepts and strategies in this book that allow them to create a second and third income stream through smart trading and investing.

Think about it like building a financial fortress.

A fortress is built with strong walls and foundations to protect its inhabitants. Similarly, creating additional income streams through trading and investing helps you establish a solid financial foundation that can withstand economic ups and downs. With a well-built financial fortress, you will enjoy greater security and freedom in your life.

Listen, I get it if this sounds too good to be true. And it';s only normal to feel a bit skeptical.
Because the ugly truth is …

The Odds Are Against You Unless You Really Get This

To understand why, we need to differentiate between ***active*** and ***passive*** income.

Active Income relies on you actively working to earn money, whether you're an employee trading hours for dollars or a business owner working long hours to serve customers.

The problem? No matter how hard you work, there are only so many hours in a day.

That's why the legendary Robert Kiyosaki introduced the concept of the Cashflow Quadrant in his seminal book, Rich Dad Poor Dad.

The Cashflow Quadrant splits people into 4 categories based on their income source:

- **E** for Employee
- **S** for Self-Employed
- **B** for Business Owner
- **I** for Investor

Most people fall into the **E** and **S** quadrants — they work for money as an employee or in their own small business. Their income is directly tied to their efforts: If you want to make more money, you have to work harder.

The wealthy live in the **B** and **I** quadrants because they make money work for them.

In theory, business owners in the **B** quadrant leverage systems and teams to generate income.

But the reality is that most business owners work extremely long hours, think 60-80+ hour workweeks. Even big company CEOs like Steve Jobs and Elon Musk are known to work 6-7 days a week and 10+ hours per day. They may build large businesses but those businesses still rely heavily on their personal effort day to day.

So while having a business can be profitable, it rarely leads to true passive income.
Passive income is the key to true wealth, not just ordinary income generated by personal effort.

The only quadrant capable of generating substantial passive income is the **I** quadrant. Investors who make money while they sleep through assets like real estate, stocks, options and ETFs that produce cash flow whether they are actively working or not. As Warren Buffet says: ***If you don't find a way to make money while you sleep, you will work until you die.***

Most people remain stuck in the active income quadrants, trading time for money and never achieving true passive income. They are playing a game rigged against them.

I don't know if you're aware of this, however ...

... 59% of Americans said they will have to keep working longer, while 36% now believe they will never have enough money to be able to retire, according to the latest data from the Natixis Global Retirement Index.

... not to mention according to a study of the Board of Governors of the Federal Reserve System from 2022, only 45% of those aged 45 to 59 and only 52% of those 60 and over felt prepared for retirement.

Plus, retirement experts recommend that you need 10-12 times your annual salary to retire. So if you make $200,000 per year before retirement, you should aim to have at least $2,000,000 - $2.400,000 in your retirement account.

You really start to grasp how dire the situation really is.
I'm not saying this to scare you ...

I just want you to see how important having an edge truly is.

The No. 1 Goal You Should Have Is ...

To make money while you sleep and have multiple income streams so you can be secure in your finances, no matter what life throws at you and break the vicious cycle of working hard and long hours to have more time for yourself, your family and your friends.

Sound good?

And you will also want ALL of this:

- **with clarity and certainty**
- systematically
- **with confidence ...**
- while you inspire your friends and family
- **and while enjoying the process**

This Is More Crucial Than You Believe!

Because what you will discover in this book will make a stunning impact on your net worth and passive income streams.
By leveraging the strategies in this book, you can break free from this cycle and start generating the assets and investment income millionaires use to grow wealthy.

All you have to do to achieve this is to simply keep reading and take action.

Imagine Your Life Without Struggles

Picture yourself experiencing:

More time for yourself, family, and friends.

True financial independence and having the freedom to do whatever you want with your time and money … or even true financial independence, with multiple streams of income and reliable sources of passive income that don't require you to work anymore!

You can achieve these results as well ... like so many of my clients do after they implemented what I have to share with you today.

And I truly believe that by following my advice, you can build multiple streams of passive income to make money while you sleep and increase your net worth, systematically and consistently.

I can say that with quite a bit of confidence because thousands of people just like you are increasing their net worth, systematically, consistently, and building multiple streams of income to make money while they sleep.

Chapter 2: Why Now is the Time

When I was still working for IBM, I hoped that if I kept working hard, someday, I wouldn't have to work so hard anymore. And I wasn't alone.

Many of my co-workers hoped that if they kept their heads down and stayed loyal, eventually it would pay off.

We all hoped that at some point in the distant future, we would be able to relax and enjoy life.

The problem? Hope is not a strategy. Hoping and wishing for a better future is usually little more than a fantasy unless you take concrete actions to make it a reality.

I knew that without a solid wealth building strategy, the day I was waiting for would never come. Or it may come far too late.

Life is unpredictable. Economic conditions change. Market crashes happen. Industries evolve. Companies experience layoffs. Skills become outdated. Health deteriorates.

Nothing is guaranteed.

This is why it's absolutely critical that you take control of your financial future now, while you still have time on your side.

Because the sooner you start taking the right steps, the faster you can escape the rat race and begin living life on your own terms.

And yes, I can already hear the objections:

I'm too busy right now.
I'll start saving more next year when things will turn around.

Let me focus on this big project for work first, then I'll have more time.

I've heard them all. And I get it — life is busy. There are so many demands on your time.

But every day that goes by is a lost opportunity. Time waits for no one. I wish I would have started earlier!

Because the truth is … there is no perfect time to start. There will always be some fire to put out, some deadline to chase.

But if you keep waiting for that mythical "right moment," it may never arrive. Or the window to take full advantage could close. The time is now. Trust me. Your future self will thank you.

Here are five reasons it's absolutely essential to take action TODAY:

1. The sooner you start, the faster you can achieve financial freedom. Every day you delay is another day you remain stuck trading time for money. But if you start now, you can start growing your 2nd and 3rd income stream and expedite your path to freedom. Imagine finally being able to quit your job years earlier than expected, all because you took action now instead of waiting.

2. Time is your most valuable asset — use it wisely. We all get 24 hours in a day. You can't "save time" — make the most of it now by taking action. Once the day is gone, that time is lost forever. So maximize this precious resource - time — by taking action today.

3. Start now to maximize compound growth. Compounding works wonders but it takes time. The earlier you begin investing, the more your money can work for you, and the sooner you can achieve financial freedom.

4. Take control of your financial future before it's too late! As the saying goes, the best time to plant a tree was 20 years ago. The second best time is today. Don't look back with regret.

5. Early action provides more time to recover from mistakes. You will make mistakes starting out. It's normal. If you wait until later in life to start, a single mistake could derail your progress. Starting early gives you room to correct your course.

The key is to just begin.
Stop waiting.
Stop hoping.
Stop doubting yourself.

Take that first step and gain momentum!

But you already know that, right?

So why do most people fail to take action and remain stuck trading time for money? Why do they keep delaying and hoping instead of implementing a solid wealth-building strategy?

There is ONE primary psychological cause behind this inaction:

Asset Anxiety

"Asset Anxiety" is when you feel worried and stressed about how to handle your money, especially when it comes to investments.

Asset Anxiety comes in 3 forms:

Greed

First, there's greed. And YES, I absolutely support the statement,"Greed is good," from the fictional character, Gordon Gekko, in the famous movie, Wall Street.

Because it means that you're hungry, hungry for more.
More than just the measly returns that you see on your retirement account.
More than just the single-digit returns on life policies, money market accounts, or bonds.
More than the less than mediocre returns that Sean, your financial advisor, is generating for you.

And that's good!

Because you shouldn't be happy with mediocre returns!

Have you heard about the "Rule of 72"?
This rule tells you how long it will take for your money to double.

Here's how it works:

$$\textbf{Doubling time (number of years)} = \frac{\textbf{72}}{\textbf{Annual interest rate}}$$

So if you're currently getting 8% per year on your returns, it would take 72 / 8 = 9 years to double your account.

And let's say you're 45 years old and have saved $100,000.

Based on the "Rule of 72", you would have $200,000 when you're 54 years old.

And you would have $400,000 when you're 63 years old.
At 72 years old, you would have $800,000.

And let me tell you, that's not enough!

That's why it's good to be hungry for more.

Because in this book, you will learn strategies that can help you to achieve a return of 30% per year!
Based on the "Rule of 72," it means that your money will double every 72 / 30 = 2.4 years

So here's a table that illustrates the difference:

	8% Annual Return	**30% Annual Return**
$100,000	45 years old	45 years old
$200,000	54 years old	47.5 years old
$400,000	63 years old	50 years old
$800,000	72 years old	52.5 years old
$1,600,000	81 years old	55 years old
$3,200,000	90 years old	57.5 years old

Which scenario do you like better?
Obviously, the 30% return, right?

Like I said — greed is good!

Fear

But here's the other side of the coin: You are afraid to lose money!

You are scared about what happens with your investment when the economy tanks. You get nervous when the stock market goes up and down.

And these feelings lead to …

Insecurity

Let me guess: You feel stuck because on the one hand you want more but on the other hand you don’t want to lose your hard-earned money, right?

Does any of this sound like you?

If so, you suffer from asset anxiety, which can lead to the following problems:

Lazy Money Syndrome (LMS)

The "Lazy Money Syndrome (LMS)" is a reality that all too many people can relate to.

You know you need to invest in order to build wealth and secure your financial freedom but the abundance of information out there is overwhelming – not just because it's a lot of data to process, but because of all the uncertainties and "fear of losing money" associated with it.

I get it. You're worried about taking risks, scared of losing your hard-earned money, and you don't know where to find reliable resources or strategies that could help you make wise investments.

So instead of putting your money to work, you leave it to the "professionals" or it's just sitting in your account doing nothing.

But think of it this way:
You are coming home from work feeling exhausted and drained. You are a hard worker and always give 110% but no matter how much effort you put in, it never seems to be enough.

And when you get back home, there he is, your lazy boyfriend (a.k.a. your money) sitting on the couch playing video games like he doesn't have a care in the world. You have asked him a million times to contribute but he just keeps lounging on the couch while you cook dinner, clean up the house, and do all the chores.

You feel angry and frustrated but you don't know how to get your boyfriend (a.k.a your money) to work and deep inside you are also afraid that if you put him to work, you might lose him.

If you notice any of these symptoms, you're probably suffering from LMS:

- Avoiding looking at retirement account statements because you feel frustrated at the lack of growth.
- Pulling money out of investments at the first sign of volatility and then ...
- Stashing cash into a savings account earning minimal interest rather than investing.
- Failing to dedicate time to learn about investing options.

Muddled Investment Strategies Syndrome (MISS)

Muddled Investment Strategies Syndrome (MISS) is another common problem for busy professionals and business owners like you. It means there's either no comprehensive strategy for building passive income in place, or that investment decisions are based on fear, greed and emotions.

Here's what typically happens:
At some point you might realize you *should* do something about your investments. These thoughts typically occur on the weekend since your weekdays are incredibly busy.

So you dedicate a few hours of *research* on the weekend and either jump into some investments right away, e.g. buying some crypto or ETFs or dividend stocks, etc. Usually these investments are a poor choice since the decision was made in a rush.

Another possibility is that you realize you need more time to *do it right* and put the project on your already full to-do list. And with everything else going on in your life, it never gets done, until you find some time on a weekend, and the vicious cycle continues.

This often leads to confusion and frustration resulting in an *investment strategy* that's all over the place and doesn't get you anywhere. Worst case, it leaves you worse off than you were before.

Think of it this way ...

Let's say you want to lose a few pounds and you decide to do some research about the best way to do it on a weekend when you have some time. You might read about Keto and intermittent fasting and then also look into some exercises like HIIT, yoga, resistance bands, *muscle confusion* and all the other methods out there.

After a few hours, you feel smarter but you haven't lost any weight yet. So you decide to "start tomorrow," and "tomorrow' is a busy day, like every weekday.

So maybe you try to eat a little bit healthier, you might take the stairs instead of the escalator. But as your busy days go on, you don't really have time to "do all this" and you decide to really get serious about it next week or next month.

But you never find the time to actually do it; therefore, these few pounds that you wanted to lose are still there.

The same is true for your finances!

So, if you notice any of these symptoms, you're probably suffering from MISS:

- Trying new investments based on tips from friends or media hype.
- Getting excited about a strategy but dropping it after a short time.
- Making investment decisions without research.
- Constantly changing strategies instead of sticking to a plan.

Conclusion

The time to take control of your financial future is now. Every day that passes is a missed opportunity.
Come on.
No more hoping and waiting for the perfect time.
No more excuses that you're too busy today and will get to it someday. Someday may never come unless you take action now.

If you've been procrastinating up until this point, one of the reasons could be that you're suffering from Lazy Money Syndrome

(LMS) or Muddled Investment Strategy Syndrome (MISS) that we discussed earlier.

But don't worry – in the coming chapters, we will provide the cure to these challenges once and for all. I will give you a clear roadmap and wealth-building blueprint that will help you put your money to work for you instead of you working hard for your money.

With the right strategies and mindset shifts, you can overcome the psychological hurdles of LMS and MISS. I will guide you step-by-step towards building your financial fortress brick–by-brick.

This is your wake up call. Time and tide wait for no one. The key to building wealth is consistency over long periods of time. Maximize your most precious resource … time. The day you start taking action is the day everything changes. Your future self is cheering you on!

Let's start building your financial fortress today!

Chapter 3: Demystifying Wealth Building Myths

Let me guess ...

You want to start building your wealth through trading and investing. You know it's important. But there are all these doubts and fears holding you back.

Sound familiar? I've been there too. And I get it.

All the myths and misconceptions floating around are enough to make your head spin! It's downright confusing.

"They" say:

Trading is WAY too risky.

You need some insider secrets to succeed.

Don't even bother. The wealthy have all the advantages

I've heard it all.

And for too long, I bought into these myths too. They kept me from doing what I needed to do. They forced me to keep "playing it safe." But here's the truth. Most of what you've heard about trading, investing and building true wealth is dead wrong.

Often these myths are spread by financial advisors and other "consultants" who want you to trust THEM with your money so that they can charge you hefty fees for mediocre results.

It's time to break free!

In this chapter, we will take down some of the biggest and baddest wealth-building myths so you can see the truth clearly. No more confusion, no more excuses. You deserve to have the REAL facts to make smart decisions with confidence. I want to motivate you to take that first step toward the financial freedom you desire and deserve.

Let's debunk these myths together and separate fact from fiction once and for all!

Mistaken Beliefs Debunked

Myth 1: Trading Terror

Look, I get it. When you first start learning about trading, it can seem super risky and dangerous. The warnings are everywhere:

Be careful or you'll lose it all!
Trading is just glorified gambling!

I remember when I first started, I was terrified too.

"What if I lose everything?"

And you might have heard horror stories about people who tried it and lost it all. But here's the reality no one talks about ...

Trading only feels scary when you don't have a proven strategy.

Of course, it's dangerous to just guess and gamble without a plan!

But when you trade like a calculated, serious business person with tested methods, the risk decreases dramatically.

I used to chase quick windfalls too when I was starting out. And I got burned badly more than once. But once I got smarter and shifted my focus to systematic, repeatable, and consistent profits ... everything changed. With the right education, the right tools, and proper risk management, trading became way LESS risky, even less risky than traditional investing.

And yes, you CAN be in control. You can take measures to reduce the risk, and I will show you how.

Myth 2: Pricey Planners

Another common myth is that you must hire financial advisors if you want to succeed with trading and investing. Supposedly, only these advisors have the insider expertise to help you profit. They perpetuate this myth to make you feel helpless without their guidance.

But the reality is quite different ...

The truth about most financial advisors is far from the glossy image they present. In many cases, "advisor" is just a fancy title for a salesperson.

According to Glassdoor, in 2023, the average base salary for a financial advisor is around $70,000. But advisors can earn $41,000 or more in commissions by selling investment products like annuities, life insurances, ETFs, and mutual funds to you!

So it's in their interest to make you feel lost without their help.

And think about it: If a financial advisor really knew how to create wealth, would he be working a nine to five job that pays less than $120,000 per year? If these advisors really had some secret wealth-building formula, why would they waste time cold calling for new clients? They'd be enjoying their millions on a beach somewhere!

You have more knowledge and capability than you realize. Don't fall for the myth that you need to pay exorbitant fees for basic investment guidance.

In this book, you will learn the strategies, tools, and techniques that can help you to run circles around these "financial advisors."

Fun fact: A few of our Mastermind Members have been doing so well that their financial advisors begged them to show how they are generating these profits!

Myth 3: Misguided Mindset

Let me guess, you don't think you're "smart enough" to trade or invest successfully?

Maybe you got intimidated by a banker in a fancy suit who tried to make you feel like a dummy?

I've been there too. I used to think you had to be a math genius to make money in the markets. And all the technical jargon made my eyes glaze over.

But here's the truth no one talks about. Investing is NOT rocket science. Seriously, it's not.

At its core, successful investing is simply about making more good decisions than bad.
That's it.

NOBODY will be able to pick bottoms and tops consistently.
NOBODY wins all the time.

It's about making informed decisions and I'll show you how to do just that.

Billionaire investors like Warren Buffet have proven you don't need advanced degrees in finance. As he says:

> *You don't need to be a rocket scientist. Investing is not a game where the guy with the 160 IQ beats the guy with the 130 IQ.*

The "experts" try to make it sound complex so you keep relying on them. But with the right teacher and a hunger to learn, you will be able to identify opportunities others are missing. You've got a bright mind with way more potential than you realize. It's time to start believing in yourself. Don't let the misguided mindset myth steal one more minute of your success.

Myth 4: Time Trap

I'm sure you've heard this myth before:

Building wealth through trading and investing takes WAY too much time and energy.

After all, researching investments, monitoring the markets, executing trades, it certainly SOUNDS time-consuming.

I remember thinking there was no way I could find the hours needed with my busy schedule. The Time Trap myth had me convinced it wasn't even worth trying.

But here's the reality no one talks about ...

Investing Takes Less Time Than You Think

You do NOT need to spend all day glued to your screens.

Seriously, you don't.. I spend no more than 30 minutes a day and sometimes I don't even look at the markets for days!

Once you have proven strategies and the right tools, a lot of the heavy lifting is done for you. You can identify opportunities and execute trades efficiently without getting bogged down in analysis paralysis. In fact, getting stuck over-analyzing everything is exactly what you want to avoid. With the right approach, investing takes LESS time than you think.

Don't let the Time Trap myth stop you from your first trade. You CAN make it work within your busy life.
I'll show you how.

Myth 5: Insider Illusion

Here's another big myth that keeps most people paralyzed:

You need insider secrets and advantages if you want to succeed in the markets.

Supposedly, only the wealthy and Wall Street guys have all these unfair advantages and it's hopeless to try competing as an outsider. I remember thinking I could never reach their level without expensive data or exclusive access. The Insider Illusion myth had me convinced I was doomed from the start.

But the truth reveals a very different story ...

Knowledge is the Only True Advantage.
There are zero magic shortcuts only available to the ultra-rich. Secrets don't make billionaires.

What sets the super successful investors apart is experience and continuing education, not insider access. Warren Buffet spends 80% of his day reading and learning. By constantly developing his knowledge, any perceived "advantages" become available to him.

Don't fall for the Insider Illusion myth. You can absolutely compete at the highest level, because the right knowledge and the right tools are the great equalizer.

Myth 6: Analytical Anxiety

Let's tackle another common myth:

You need complex analytics and endless research to make smart investment decisions.

This myth gave me major analytics anxiety starting out. All the metrics and terms were overwhelming. I didn't know where to begin! But in reality, you absolutely can succeed without spending days crunching numbers and staring at charts. I know it sounds cliche but …

Keep it simple!

Here's the key no one talks about:

Avoid overcomplicating things.

Investment success isn't about getting lost in complex charts or dozens of indicators.

I personally don't read through any financial statements or earnings reports. I don't use any indicators. In fact, I just draw rectangles on the chart. You'll see exactly what I do in later chapters.

Keep in mind that complexity is often just a smokescreen designed to confuse you with the goal that you will give up trying to do it yourself and leave it to the “experts”.

Stay focused on core fundamentals rather than chasing analysis paralysis. I'll show you how step-by-step.

You've got this! Don't let Analytical Anxiety stop you from taking your first steps to financial freedom.

Myth 7: Random Riches

Here's one final big myth we often hear:

Successful investors just got lucky. They happened to be in the right place at the right time.

We see the mansions, the fancy cars, the yachts, the status symbols, and it's tempting to think it was all just some stroke of luck. No real strategy involved.

I remember thinking the wealthy were just born under some magic money-attracting star. The Random Riches myth had me convinced their success was out of reach.

But when we look closer, the truth reveals something quite different...

True Wealth is Created Through Discipline and Perseverance

Billionaire investors like Warren Buffet did NOT stumble into their fortunes on some accidental twist of fate. Their success was hard-earned through years of discipline and perseverance.

Yes, there might be somebody who just got "lucky" but most millionaires and billionaires will tell you that they made their fortune through discipline and perseverance.

You might have heard the saying:

Luck is What Happens When Preparation Meets Opportunity.

And that's why you are here. That's why you are reading this book:

To get ready.

So don't let the Random Riches myth fool you. With focused education and commitment to excellence, you can achieve success!

Alright, we've covered some serious ground in this chapter. We've taken a hard look at the 7 biggest myths and misconceptions that keep people from building wealth through trading and investing.

We've exposed, shattered and busted these myths, and there's one overarching lesson to take away from this chapter:

Don't let these common myths and misconceptions hold you back from pursuing your financial dreams.

You have everything you need to succeed as an investor and trader, right here, right now. You don't need to be a genius, you don't need to have some unfair advantage, and you certainly don't need to fall for the hype and the lies that keep so many people stuck on the sidelines.

So let's leave these myths in the rearview mirror where they belong. It's time to shift our focus to what real success as a trader and investor looks like.

And that's exactly what we're going to do in the next chapter. We're going to paint a vivid picture of the kind of life that becomes possible when you master the skills of wealth building.

We're going to explore the mindset shifts, the lifestyle upgrades, and the incredible freedom and flexibility that come with true financial independence.

So if you're ready to get inspired, if you're ready to start thinking bigger about what's possible for your future, then let's dive in.

Chapter 4: What Real Success Looks Like

The Illusion of the Rat Race

Let me take you back a few years. Back then, my weeks were a blur of endless work. Picture this: Work 50-60 hours a week, come home in the evenings, collapse in front of the TV, and then head to bed, only to repeat it all over again.

Or, I'd be on the road for almost the entire week, get home late Friday, spend all of Saturday trying to recover, and Sunday? That was for chores and packing, preparing for another exhausting week. Whether at home or traveling, I was too drained for anything else — friends, family, you name it.

Now, let's fast forward to today. My life couldn't be more different.

Right now, as I'm writing these words to you, I'm sitting on our sprawling 3000 sq ft deck.

The view? It's nothing short of breathtaking, overlooking the grandeur of Sunset Canyon.

Just a few hours ago, I had the pleasure of meeting my daughter for lunch — those moments, they're priceless.

And later? Well, the plan is to hop on my Harley and feel the wind against my face as we cruise down to our favorite local brewery. It's this little gem just down the road, where the pizza is as good as the company.

You see, these aren't just random events, they're the essence of my new life. A life where my next 'appointment' is not a meeting in a stuffy office room but the opening of the markets tomorrow at 8:30 AM.

And guess what? I'll be 'working', if you can call it that, for just about 30 minutes. That's it.

The rest of my day? It's a canvas waiting to be painted with activities I love.

Maybe I'll decide to meet some friends for lunch or perhaps I'll find a cozy nook to settle into with a good book.

The truth is, I don't have to know right now. That's the beauty of it. This freedom, this ability to choose how I spend each hour of my day, it's more than just liberating … It's exhilarating.

But let's get one thing clear: this transformation wasn't overnight magic. It was a journey – a tough one, I won't lie. But oh, so worth it.

So, why am I telling you this? Because, like many, I was caught up in the “rat race” illusion. While working at IBM, I chased after what I thought was “success.” You know the kind — a BMW 5-series as a company car, business-class flights, reserved parking spots and those big bonuses.

All material things.

And I thought, *This is it. This is success.*

But here's the kicker. I was working hard to climb a ladder that, it turns out, was leaning against the wrong wall!

It's a common trap, isn't it? We hustle and bustle, believing that the next promotion, the next pay raise, is what success looks like. But at what cost? I was too exhausted to spend quality time with the people I cared about. And all those material successes? They felt hollow.

Then, a realization hit me. It wasn't about climbing some corporate ladder or collecting status symbols. It was about finding real success and that meant redefining what success looked like to me. I needed to step out of the rat race and look at the bigger picture.

This chapter isn't just my story. It's a mirror reflecting a reality many of us live in, chasing after an illusion. It's about understanding that what we often chase isn't real success. It's about peeling back the layers to discover what truly matters. And trust me, it's not the next big promotion or that flashy company car.

So, buckle up.

We're about to dive into a journey of redefining success, transforming our priorities, and understanding what it really means to be financially free.

And who knows? By the end of this, you might just find yourself rethinking what success means to you too.

How Priorities Shift with Financial Independence

Let's talk about change. Not just any change but the profound shift in priorities that comes with financial independence. It's like stepping into a new world where the rules you once lived by no longer apply.

When I first embraced financial independence, the most significant shift I noticed was in how I viewed personal growth and memory-making. You see, in the rat race, we're so consumed with "making it" that we often forget to live. But now, it's a whole different ball game.

I've come to realize that life's richness isn't measured in bank statements but in the wealth of experiences we make. And so, I started investing — not just in markets but in myself and in experiences.

And no, I'm not all about becoming "woo-woo" but I love the idea of becoming the best version of ourselves we can be. So YES, I like the idea of investing in personal growth.

But it's not all about me.

More Quality Time for Family and Friends

Here's something close to my heart: It's all about creating lasting memories with family and friends. Believe me, these moments are the real treasures of life.

My kids, for example, are passionate sailors. About eight years ago, I made a decision that changed our lives. I bought an RV. Why? So we could travel across the country from Florida to California to New England participating in sailing regattas. Imagine this ... sometimes, we were on the road for two whole months. We drove from Austin, Texas to Long Beach, California, and then across the country to Rhode Island for the next regatta, soaking in new experiences and bonding over shared adventures. It was more than a vacation, it was a journey of connection and discovery.

And it's not just about my kids. It's about seizing every opportunity to spend meaningful time with my parents, my friends, before life takes us down different paths. It's about being there for the big moments and the small ones, creating memories that will last long after we're gone.

Flexibility Over How Time and Resources Get Allocated

Initially, my journey to financial independence was all about money. But once that was no longer a concern, my focus shifted dramatically … it became all about time. How do I use this precious, finite resource? The answer was clear. Maximize every moment with the people I care about most.

Now my decisions revolve around how best to use my time. Whether it's an impromptu trip with my kids, visiting my parents in Germany, or catching up with old friends, these moments are my new currency. It's a flexibility that money alone can't buy — the ability to be present, to participate actively in the lives of those I love.

In this journey of financial independence, it's crucial to understand that priorities will shift. It's a natural progression from a life focused on earning to a life centered around living. And trust me, this new focus on personal growth, quality time with loved ones, and the flexibility to enjoy life's pleasures … all of this is a trade-off you'll never regret.

Why You MUST Get Rich!

Let me lay it out straight: you MUST get rich.

And it's not about living in luxury or flaunting wealth. It's about something far more crucial, your mental well-being and YES, even your marriage!

Reducing Money Worries That Fuel Anxiety and Depression

First, let's face the cold hard facts. According to the American Psychological Association (APA), a whopping 66% of people are stressed about money. It's the highest number recorded since 2015. And it's not just a few worried souls, it's a sweeping trend affecting generations. If you are a "Gen-Xer" (between the ages of 43-58) or a Baby Boomer (between the ages of 59-77), then you're probably feeling the heat: 68% of Gen Xers and 79% of Baby Boomers say that they are stressed about their finances (Source: https://www.bankrate.com/banking/money-and-financial-stress-statistics/).

But it gets more personal. If you're married, the picture gets even more grim. Did you know that 42% of married couples argue about money more than chores, time together, or even sex? And these aren't just occasional fights: 27% of couples say they are fighting over money every week! (https://www.fool.com/the-ascent/personal-finance/articles/these-are-the-5-most-common-reasons-couples-fight-about-money/) (Source: Daly, L. (2023, March 13) These are the 5 Most Common Reasons Couples Fight About Money.The Motley Fool.

It's no wonder that money disagreements top the charts as the number one reason for fights and, sadly, divorces. Don't let that happen to you!

Regaining Mental Clarity and Creative Energy

Now, let's talk about the mental toll. When you're caught in the vice-grip of financial worries, it's like wearing blinders. All you can see is the next bill, the next paycheck. I remember those days at IBM, working my fingers to the bone just to make ends meet. Reading a book to improve myself? Please, I was too tired to even think straight.

Fast forward to now and my world has transformed. I invest 40-60 days a year in seminars and high-level Masterminds, diving deep into various aspects of life. And reading? I devour books and courses, spending roughly 2,000 hours a year, that's about 80 days of expanding my knowledge and skills. This kind of growth, this kind of exploration … it was unthinkable in my previous life, bogged down by a 50-60 hour workweek.

Now, let's be clear. I'm not telling you this to impress you. I'm sharing this with you so that you see first-hand what happens when you achieve financial success.

Breaking Free of Office Politics and Petty Power Struggles

Let's not forget one of the most soul-sucking aspects of the traditional work environment — office politics and petty power struggles. It's a draining, demoralizing game that many of us get trapped in. I've been there, stuck in the daily grind of navigating egos and agendas and let me tell you, it's exhausting.

But here's the beauty of financial freedom. You get to escape that. Now, I have my trusted companions for my *work* : my computer and my trading tools. No backstabbing, no gossiping, just you, your strategy, and the freedom to make your own choices.

The Bottom Line

So, why must you get rich? It's not about the glitz or the glamor. It's about reclaiming your mental peace, having time for your loved ones, and liberating yourself from the petty battles of office life. It's about having the space to grow, learn, and be truly present in your life.

In this pursuit of wealth, remember, it's not just about filling your bank account, it's about enriching your life in every sense. It's about creating a life where stress and conflict don't hold the reins, where your mental energy is spent on growth and creativity, not on worrying about the next paycheck.

As we delve deeper into this book, keep this in mind: Getting rich is not just a luxury; it's a necessity for a life of fulfillment, peace, and true freedom.

The Four Levels of Freedom Unlocked

Freedom.
It's a word that gets thrown around a lot, isn't it? But let's pause and think. What does it really mean?

For me, after breaking free from the rat race, I've come to realize that freedom operates on four distinct levels.

Let's dive into each one.

WHAT: Choosing Your Path

The first level of freedom is all about choice. The choice of WHAT you do. It's a powerful thing, you know. In the old days, my boss or clients dictated my every move. Every. Single. Day. It was like being a puppet on strings, dancing to someone else's tune.
But now? It's a whole different story. I choose what I want to do each day. Whether it's exploring new investment opportunities, reading a book, or simply deciding to take the day off and enjoy it with family and friends — it's all up to me. This level of freedom means being the master of your own destiny, and let me tell you, it feels amazing.

WHEN: Mastering Your Time

Next up is the freedom of WHEN. It's all about timing — mastering your own schedule. Remember the 9-5 grind? Scratch that. Now my "work" happens on my terms.

I prefer trading in the first 15-30 minutes after the markets open but that's only because it fits my lifestyle the best. I could trade anytime during the day. And if I decide to take a Wednesday off just because I can, that's my freedom.

This level is about breaking free from the conventional concept of office hours. It's about living life in sync with your internal clock, not someone else's schedule. Trust me, there's nothing quite like the freedom of owning your time.

WHERE: The Liberty of Location

Then we have the WHERE. Imagine this: Working from anywhere you choose. A beach in Bali? Sure. A café in Paris? Why not? Your own back deck overlooking the sunset? Absolutely. Winter in

Florida and summer in Colorado? Why not? In the world of trading and investing, your office is wherever you want it to be.

This level of freedom tears down geographical boundaries. It's about the liberty to move, to explore, and to find inspiration in the most unexpected places. It's about not being chained to a single location but having the world as your playground.

WITH WHOM: Surrounding Yourself with Positivity

Last, but definitely not least, is the freedom of WITH WHOM. It's about the people you surround yourself with. In the corporate world, you don't get to choose your company. But now, I choose to be around those who uplift and inspire me, not those who drain my energy.

This level of freedom is about cultivating a circle of positive, like-minded individuals who support and encourage each other. It's about leaving behind the naysayers and the negative influences, and embracing a community that fuels your growth and happiness.

So, there you have it — the four levels of freedom. It's not just about financial independence, it's about a complete transformation of your life. It's about the freedom to choose your path, own your time, roam the world, and surround yourself with positivity.

As you read this, I hope you start to see that these levels of freedom aren't just a distant dream. They are achievable, tangible realities!

Conclusion

As we wrap up this chapter, I want you to pause for a moment. Think about everything we've discussed. The transformation from the rat race to true financial freedom isn't just a fancy concept, it's a real, attainable goal. And now, it's your turn to take that first, crucial step towards your own journey of freedom.

Remember, this isn't just about money. It's about reshaping your entire life, about gaining the freedom to choose what you do, when you do it, where you do it, and with whom you share these moments. It's about liberating yourself from the constraints that once held you back and stepping into a world brimming with possibilities.

Let's recap the key lessons:

1. **Redefining Success**: Understand that real success is more than just material wealth, it's about quality of life.
2. **Priorities Shift with Financial Independence:** Focus on personal growth, family, and the flexibility to enjoy life's true riches.
3. **The Necessity of Wealth:** Wealth is essential not just for comfort but for mental peace and creative freedom.
4. **The Four Levels of Freedom:** Embrace the freedom to choose your path, your time, your location, and your companions.

I cannot stress enough how worthwhile this journey is. Yes, it requires effort, dedication, and sometimes, stepping out of your comfort zone. But the rewards? They are immeasurable. You'll find yourself living a life filled with purpose, joy, and fulfillment. A life where YOU call the shots.

This is your moment, your opportunity. Don't let it slip away. The road to financial freedom is open, waiting for you to take the first step. And when you do, you'll wonder why you didn't start sooner.

Chapter 5: Who This Book Is For

Before we dive into the Rockwell Wealth Building System in the next chapter, let's talk about who this book is for and who will benefit most from reading it.

Let's talk about …

The 4 Stages of Financial Success

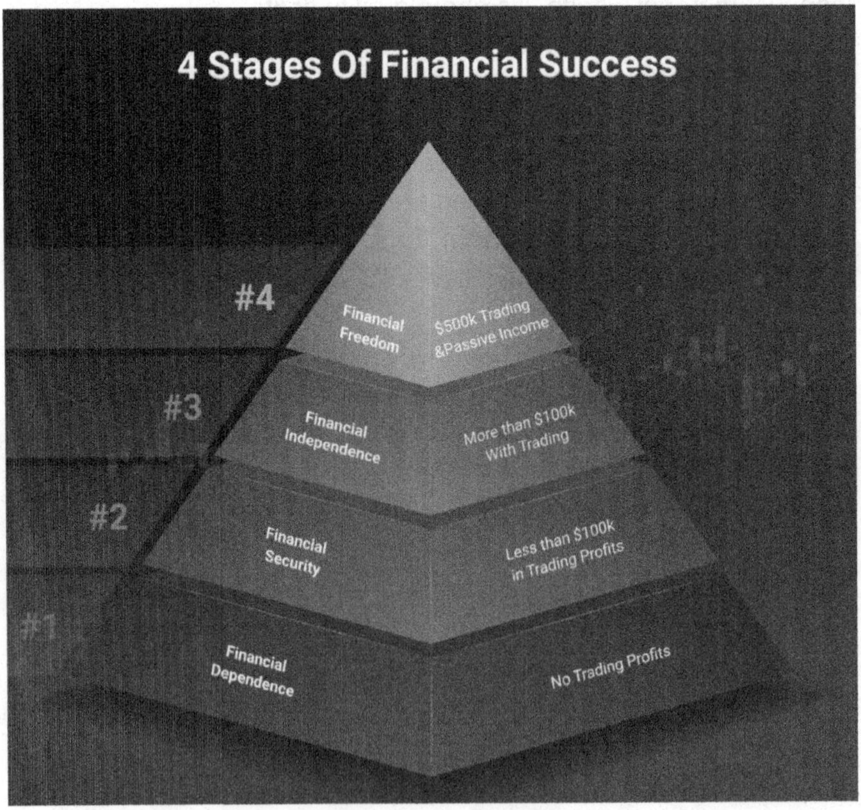

Stage 1: Financial Dependence

That's where we all start. When you are in this stage you are living paycheck to paycheck and have no savings or minimal savings.

I remember when I started my first job after college. It was exciting to see the money coming in but it wasn't much.

It always seemed that in the final days of the month, I needed to use credit cards to bridge the time until the next paycheck. And yes, I knew that I should save some money but it seemed impossible.

And whenever I was able to save a few hundred or even a few thousand dollars, an emergency came up like a broken appliance or car and I had to drain my savings account again.

And to be honest … sometimes, I simply used the money to go on a well-deserved vacation!

Do you remember those times? I'm sure you have been there too.

Anyhow, people who are in this stage should not be trading for a very simple reason: You should only trade with money that you can afford to lose and people who are in Stage 1 can definitely not afford to lose the money they save.

The best course of action for this stage is to either make a budget and save some money or find a way to make extra money.

But when you are in this stage, you shouldn't be trading.

Stage 2: Financial Security

In this stage you're no longer living paycheck to paycheck, and you already have some money in a savings or retirement account. However, it is not growing fast enough.

I remember being in this stage when I was working long hours at IBM.

I was no longer living paycheck to paycheck. I had some savings and a retirement account. But no matter how much I contributed, the balance barely budged.

And during the “dot-com bubble” in the beginning of 2000, my retirement account balance started to drop at an alarming rate.

At work, I felt overwhelmed and burnt out from the endless grind. I was the dancing bear, afraid that if I stopped dancing, the money would stop coming in.

Whenever I finally had some time off, I felt too exhausted and drained for simple pleasures like socializing or hobbies. It seemed like there was no escape from this cycle of overwork.

I'd stare at my retirement account balances and feel frustrated and disappointed that they weren't growing faster. I cringed thinking about how little was in there despite all my efforts.

That’s when I decided to take matters into my own hands. I was done leaving it to the “professionals.” Apparently, they didn’t know how to grow my accounts.

So I started to trade, at first with a rather small account of $20,000. And as you have read in the beginning of the book, it didn’t go well.

If you're in this stage, then you might or might not yet trade. If you do, your trading profits are less than $100,000.

So if you are in this stage and want to get to the next one, the key is to learn strategies to generate "SRC Profits" and get a proven trading plan that can help you to make $100,000 in profits.

Stage 3: Financial Independence.

When you've reached this stage, you've built up your skills and account enough that your trading income can replace a decent chunk or even all of your current income.

This means that you don't need to work to maintain your lifestyle at the same level you are now.

In this phase, you're also making more than $100,000 with trading and have joined the "100k Club."

Your trading profits are now "SRC Profits" - systematic, repeatable and consistent.

The key to getting to the next stage is to learn how to treat your trading as a business and to learn how to generate passive income.

Stage 4: Financial Freedom

This is the ultimate stage. When you are in this stage you have a passive income system in place that will never run out of money.

This means that you're generating at least $500,000 with trading and passive income combined.

Now you can enjoy life with less stress, more time, more freedom and make an impact.

Your Path

The ultimate goal is to get to stage 4: Financial Freedom.

Right now, as you're reading this book, you're probably in stage 2 or stage 3, and that's ok.

In this book, you will learn how exactly you get to the top of the pyramid.

Chapter 6: Overview of the Rockwell Wealth Building System

Let me tell you a little story from back in my corporate days that you might relate to ...

There I was, working crazy hours at IBM, grinding day and night to climb that corporate ladder. I thought it would lead me to "The Good Life," ya know?

The paychecks kept rolling in. I got all the trophies — fancy office, expensive car, team of my own. All the stuff you are rewarded with when you work 60-80 hours per week.

Colleagues called me ambitious. Driven. A model employee.

But even with all the status symbols, something just felt ... off. I couldn't enjoy it.

Long days bled into nights, nights bled back into days. I barely saw my family or friends. No time for hobbies I loved.

And then it finally hit me … I wasn't building MY fortress, I was building theirs.

IBM reaped the rewards while I sacrificed everything.

As they say, *If you're not rich, you're making somebody else rich.* That was me!

That's when I decided that something needed to change.

The problem: I didn't know how to build my own financial fortress.

However, there's ONE thing that I learned at IBM:

The Power of SYSTEMS and PROCESSES to Produce Results

Everything at IBM followed their step-by-step system. Like a well-oiled machine.

Didn't matter if you were in sales, IT, consulting, they had the playbook. The blueprint.

Sure, being a small cog in this machine wasn't fun. But seeing how a rock-solid system churns out success flipped a switch for me.

Got me thinking ... if IBM has a process for dominating the biz world, why not design my OWN system for dominating personal wealth?
Lightbulb!

So over the past few years, I developed my 9-step Wealth Building System — the blueprint for generating lasting wealth through smart trading and investing

It's got the same systematic approach as IBM's market-crushing process.

Carefully optimized.
Battle-tested.

And in this chapter, I want to share this blueprint with you.

Let's Start Building your Financial Fortress!

When you think "financial fortress," think solid as a 500-year-old castle, not a sandcastle washed away by the tide.

Let me tell you about this majestic fortress called *Castillo de Manzanares el Real*, towering in the mountains near Madrid since the 1400s.

I just sent you a text and an email with a picture of this fortress so that you can envision it.

Over 500 years old and still standing tall!

Now that's a fortress built to last generations.

And believe me, it's endured everything — wars, weather, sieges.

Our goal is to build a FINANCIAL FORTRESS that can weather any storm the economy can brew up: recessions, debt ceiling crisis, rising interest rates, banking crisis, stock market volatility etc.

Important: We're NOT building a sandcastle!

Think about it:

How long will it take you to build this sandcastle?
Maybe an hour.

And that's ok.

Because after a few hours or maybe the next day it will look like this:

A sandcastle might be fun for an afternoon but the next wave will flatten it.

But we're NOT building a sandcastle.

Think about it: Do you need a 9-step blueprint for building a sandcastle?

Of course not! Because a sandcastle is not built to last.

But I assume you're here because you want to build a financial fortress.

A fortress that lets you sleep at night, no matter what economic storms are brewing.
A fortress that will survive you.
A fortress that's built for generations to come!

Obviously, you can't build this in an hour.
You can't even build it in a few days. It will take time.

But you already know this, right?

That's why you're here and I can assure you, you're in the right place.

So let's take a look at the system.

The 3 Phases Of The Wealth Building System

Alright, now that you have the vision of our fortress, let's talk about how we actually build this.

Here's the blueprint — the Rockwell Wealth Building System.

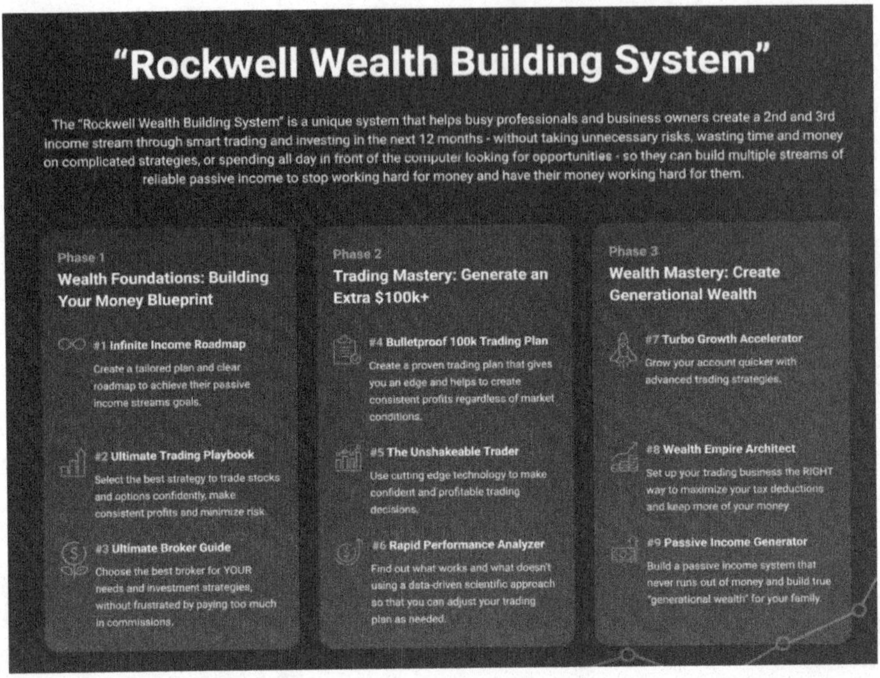

It's a step-by-step guide with 3 phases:

Phase 1: Wealth Foundations

The first phase is Wealth Foundations — this is the planning phase.
You'd never just start building a fortress without a plan, right? Same goes for your financial fortress.

Phase 1 is about creating your wealth building blueprint, laying the groundwork before construction begins.
It includes 3 steps:

Step 1 is the **Infinite Income Roadmap** — this outlines WHAT we want to build. It's the overarching blueprint defining your investing goals and passive income targets. It outlines how wide and tall your financial fortress will be and how many people can live in it.

Step 2 is the **Winning Strategy Selector** — the HOW. Here you will learn profitable trading strategies and techniques required to build your fortress and you will select the one that's best for YOU in terms of your goals, your account size, your risk tolerance, your time constraints, etc.

Step 3 is the **Ultimate Broker Guide** — the WHO. This is finding the ideal broker based on the strategy that you chose in step 2. Think about it like finding the best supplier to get the materials you need to build your fortress.

As you can see, Phase 1 establishes the strong foundation that we need for constructing your financial fortress in the next two phases.

Got it?

Here is a draft explanation of Phase 2, Trading Mastery, using the metaphor of erecting the fortress walls.

Phase 2: Trading Mastery

This is where we start erecting the walls of your financial fortress.

Phase 2 focuses on developing your daily processes and skills for actively building wealth through trading.

It contains 3 steps:

Step 4 is creating your **Bulletproof 100k Trading Plan** — your DAILY ACTION PLAN.

Think about this as the daily routine and strategies for constructing your fortress walls. It's a bulletproof trading plan that helps you make money regardless of market conditions. After all, you want to make progress when building your walls whether it's sunny or stormy weather. You can't just wait for sunshine to keep building. You need to learn how to grow your account in bull, bear, and sideways markets.

Step 5 is becoming an **Unshakeable Tech-Powered Trader** — your HEAVY MACHINERY. Keep in mind: The farmer with the tractor will always outperform the farmer with a plow, no matter how hard the farmer with a plow works. In this step, you will learn how to utilize powerful technology to accelerate construction and build the walls much faster than others would. While others take years to build their fortress, you will use powerful technology to achieve the same in months!

Step 6 is the **Rapid Performance Analyzer** — MAKING ADJUSTMENTS. Here you'll use data-driven insights to modify and strengthen your daily plan. Your broker statement doesn't give you the numbers you need to make rapid improvements. You will learn the key metrics to really need to adjust your trading strategy as needed.

After Phase 2 you'll have thick, impenetrable, fortress walls generated by optimized daily trading processes using powerful tools.

Now it's time to move on to Phase 3.

Phase 3: Wealth Mastery

In the final phase, we finish construction and add features to maximize protection and security.

It contains 3 steps:

Step 7 is the **Turbo Growth Accelerator**— BUILDING MORE WALLS. You'll deploy advanced tactics to rapidly grow your accounts, surrounding your fortune with more layers of protection.

Step 8 is the **Wealth Empire Architect** — BUILDING A MOAT. Here you'll optimize your trading tax structure to keep more of your money. It's like building a moat around your castle to keep intruders (like the IRS) out!

Step 9 is the **Passive Income Machine** — FINISHING TOUCHES. The final step is building a passive income system that never runs out of money and creates generational wealth for the family.. It's like adding the flags and banners that make your fortress a monument for eternity.

After Phase 3, your financial fortress will be complete — fortified from all angles with advanced features to sustain and grow your wealth for generations.

Patience + Discipline = Results

Now you might be wondering … do I need to follow this blueprint in order?

Absolutely! Just like at IBM, the power is in the process.

See, everything at IBM followed their step-by-step system. Didn't matter if you were in sales, IT, or consulting, they had the blueprint.

And you couldn't just skip around or reorder the steps randomly based on how you felt that day. IBM's process was calculated for maximum efficiency and results.
Same goes for constructing your financial fortress. You need to lay the foundation before building the walls and roof.

Let's consider these scenarios:

What if you started building the roof first without any walls or foundation? The entire structure would collapse!

What if you waited until after completing the fortress to plan how large you wanted it to be? That makes no sense!

The carefully engineered sequence of the 9-step blueprint is designed to take you from financial security step-by-step up to financial freedom.

Each phase builds on the previous one, like stacking bricks, one row at a time.

Now, you may be wondering … how do the phases line up with the stages of financial success we discussed earlier?

If you are currently at Stage 2 of the 4 Stages of Financial Freedom, where you have some money in your retirement account but make less than $100,000 with trading, then Phase 1 will provide the foundation to get you to Stage 3, in which you can replace most of your income with income from trading

Once you reach Stage 3, you are ready for Phase 2 "trading mastery" to propel you to Stage 4.

Think of it as constructing each level of your fortress in sequence:

Phase 1 of the Wealth Building Blueprint lays the groundwork to move from Stage 2 (Financial Security) to Stage 3 (Financial Independence).

And the steps in Phase 2 will help you to actually go from Stage 2 to Stage 3

Phase 3 will then help you to get from Stage 3 (Financial Independence) to Stage 4 (Financial Freedom).

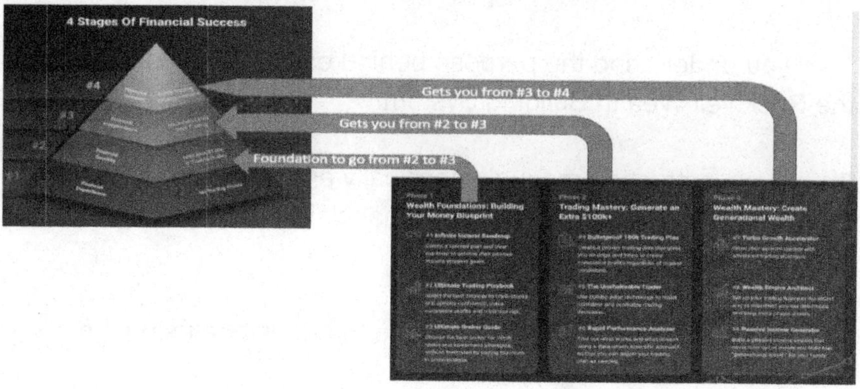

That's why the **Infinite Income Roadmap** comes first, because you must define the vision before making investment decisions.

Only after establishing strong trading processes can we apply advanced tactics to accelerate growth and lock in passive income.

I've spent years rigorously testing and optimizing to perfect this sequence for the best results.

While the steps work in harmony, you must remain disciplined and not jump ahead.

Trust the process from start to finish.

Patience and commitment are required but going step-by-step in order provides the path of least resistance on the journey to financial freedom.

Conclusion

And there you have it — the complete 9-step blueprint for systematically building your financial fortress and achieving true wealth mastery.

Now you understand the purpose behind each phase and step in the Rockwell Wealth Building System.

It's like an instruction manual specifically engineered to take you from financial security to complete financial freedom — if followed in order with patience and discipline.

The key is to begin laying that first foundation stone using the **Infinite Income Roadmap**.

Once underway, persist in working through each phase without skipping ahead. Progress one step at a time.

Stay committed to the path and the results will come. With the proper blueprint, your financial fortress is inevitable.

Now let's dive into each component of the system in detail, starting with Phase 1.

In the next chapter, we'll walk through the Infinite Income Roadmap — the first step in constructing your wealth creation blueprint.

Chapter 7: Step 1: Infinite Income Roadmap

Let me tell you a quick story about the lightbulb moment I had on a long haul from Texas to a sailing regatta in California with my daughter, Vivian, in the summer of 2021.

We were cruising down an empty highway for 1,347 miles. After hours of tumbleweeds and mammoth truck stops, my mind started wandering.

I started to think back to a book I read years ago called, "The 7 Habits of Highly Successful People," by Stephen Covey.

One habit still sticks with me: "Begin with the end in mind." Got me thinking ...

Did I really have a clear "end" for my trading journey?
A definite destination in mind?
An exit plan?

At that point, I was trading a $250,000 account.

And I was wondering:
Is this enough?
Or should I build up the account to $500,000? Or maybe $1,000,000? Even more?

And to be honest, I felt lost.
Overwhelmed.
Just trading without a real sense of direction.

Never knowing if I was "there" yet.

Glancing at the GPS navigation gave me an idea. We could see exactly how much road was left to reach our destination.

That's what my trading needed! Milestones to work towards. A personalized roadmap guiding me to the peak.

Otherwise, I was just roaming around aimlessly like in the middle of a desert.

But a concrete vision would make decisions easier and progress clearer.
Trading with intention.

So on that long, endless drive, I invented the RPIC Index you'll learn about shortly.

My North Star to point the way!
In this chapter, we'll get you a roadmap too so you know exactly where you're headed.

Clarity changes everything!

And remember, the first step to building your financial fortress starts with a solid plan.

So let's get started.

Action Step 1: Calculate Your RPIC Index

Remember: The ultimate goal is to generate enough passive income to cover all of your living expenses. This way, you will never tap into your principal, i.e. the money in your account. This means that now you have a passive income machine that never runs out of money.

So let's calculate your target passive income number using the RPIC Index.

First, what does RPIC stand for?

RPIC stands for **"Reliable Passive Income Coverage".**

It's calculated by taking your passive income divided by monthly expenses and multiplying by 100.

For example, if your reliable monthly passive income is $5,000 and your expenses are $10,000, your RPIC would be:

$5,000 (Income) ÷ $10,000 (Expenses) x 100 = 50

This means that you're currently covering only 50% of your expenses through passive income.

The RPIC Index gives you a numeric benchmark for when your passive income is sufficient to support your current lifestyle.

Anything under 100 means you need to tap into savings to cover costs.

100-119 is adequate but still a bit vulnerable because life happens, e.g.

— One of your investments is no longer producing.
— Something happens and your monthly expenses increase.
— Maybe you choose to support someone, e.g. one of your kids or your parents.

That's why the sweet spot is 120 or above — that's true passive income freedom!

Now, what exactly constitutes "passive" income for this calculation?

Passive income, as Warren Buffet says, means money rolling in that requires ZERO effort on your part. As he puts it:

If you don't find a way to make money while you sleep, you will work until you die.

Look at the table below:

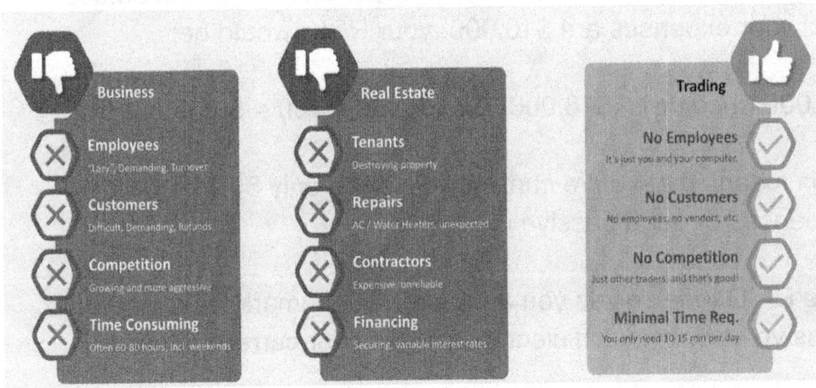

Running a business is work, not passive income.

Managing real estate properties is work.

YES, trading IS much better but you also have to be in front of the computer, even if it's just 10-15 min per day.

True passive income is cash flow on absolute autopilot, income generated from assets like stocks, royalties, and dividends that keep paying regardless of how many hours you put in.

The RPIC focuses on this hands-off income so you know exactly how much is needed to achieve complete financial freedom.

Let me give you an example:

Right now, my current RPIC is 180.
This means that for every $100 in expenses, I'm making $180.

Of course, this could change but right now, I generate more than enough passive income to cover all my living expenses.
And everything that's left over at the end of the month remains in the passive income account so that it can grow!

Knowing your exact RPIC number provides clarity on your "enough" amount to reach your definition of financial independence.

You can recalculate it annually as your lifestyle and desired level of freedom evolves. But for now, let's determine your initial target.

First, we need to determine your cost of living. Again, it's subject to change but in order to get a target, let's use your current cost of living.

There are 2 ways to determine it:

Calculation 1: Rough Estimate

This is the quickest and easiest way.

You simply take your current gross income and then deduct any amount you put away for savings or retirement right now. Why? Well, because you now ARE retired and don't need to save anymore for retirement.

Then you take a moment and think about any expenses that you *could* reduce. And I'm not talking about Suze Orman's famous "*Stop buying your Starbucks Latte*". I'm talking about real expenses, e.g. do you still need two cars when you're retired?

Or maybe you're paying a few hundred dollars for kids activities right now like sports or dance and you won't have those expenses anymore in a few years?

Again, your cost of living will change in a few years, but we need a number to get started.

Here's an example:

	Monthly	Annual	Calculated Annual
1 Your gross income		120000	$120,000.00
2 How much do you put away for savings?	$500.00		$6,000.00
3 COULD you reduce any expenses if you had to? How much?	$200.00		$2,400.00
		You need to make at least THIS amount ==>	**$111,600.00**

You might be wondering:
What about taxes?
Well, you're paying taxes right now, don't you?
So if you can make the same amount of money you're generating now, you will have enough to pay your taxes.

Don't make it more complicated than it has to be.

If you want to be more accurate, you could choose method 2:

Calculation 2: Budget

Making a budget is more work and some people hate it. However, there's also enough people out there who love it.

Here's a budget spreadsheet that we use in our "Income Machine Calculator".
You can download this spreadsheet under https://rockwell.rocks/incomecalculator

	Monthly	Annual	Calculated Annual
1 Rent or house payment			0
2 Real property taxes (if not included above)		$9,000.00	$9,000.00
3 Residence maint. (repairs, yard)	$350.00		$4,200.00
4 Homeowner's / Renter's Insurance (if not included above)	$200.00		$2,400.00
5 Utilities - Gas			0
6 Utilities - Electric and water	$200.00		$2,400.00
7 Mobile Phone & Internet	$200.00		$2,400.00
8 Utilities - Garbage service	$75.00		$900.00
9 Groceries and Household items	$1,600.00		$19,200.00
10 Meals away from home	$500.00		$6,000.00
11 School lunches			0
12 Dental and orthodontia			0
13 Medical and Prescriptions			0
14 Maid/Cleaning Services			0
15 Car payment			0
16 Gas and vehicle maintenance		$2,500.00	$2,500.00
17 Clothing and shoes	$200.00		$2,400.00
18 Insurance - Car	$235.00		$2,820.00
19 Insurance - Life			0
20 Insurance - Health (omit if payroll deduction)	$580.00		$6,960.00
21 Child care			0
22 Children's activities (EDP, Summer Camp)	$500.00		$6,000.00
23 Entertainment	$100.00		$1,200.00
24 Personal Care, Haircuts, etc.	$100.00		$1,200.00
25 Cable TV and newspaper			0
26 Dues/Licenses			0
27 Support or alimony payments to the another person			0
28 Tolls/Parking			0
29 Pets and Vet Expenses			0
30 Charitable Donations		$2,000.00	$2,000.00
31 Gifts		$2,000.00	$2,000.00
32 Travel	$3,000.00		$36,000.00
33 Monthly payment on debt (below)			0
Subtotal:			$109,580.00
	Tax Bracket	0.22	**$140,487.18** <
	Legal Status	Marrie...	

When you use a budget to calculate your monthly expenses, then you need to consider taxes.

In the example above, we assumed that this person is living in the United States and is married.
In this case, she would have to pay 22% in taxes.

Obviously, you need to adjust this to YOUR situation but you get the idea.
Now that you know your cost of living, let's talk about how exactly we generate the passive income you need to achieve and RPIC Index of 120 and higher.

Action Step 2: Define Your Ideal Investment Mix

Let me ask you: when it comes to growing your wealth, have you felt confused about whether to focus on active trading or long-term investing? I've been there myself!

Both seem to have pros and cons but how do you know what's right for YOU?

Here's the key — you need a blend of both trading AND investing as part of your wealth creation blueprint.

Let's break down the differences:

	Trading	Investing
Time needed	Active: 10-30 min per day	Passive: No actions needed
Return	30-60% per year	8 - 12% per year
Risk	30-60% drawdown	8 - 12% drawdown
Goal	Trading for Growth	Investing for Income
Account Size	25k - 50k	500k and more

See the difference?

Trading generates bigger returns but requires more active involvement.
Investing throws off passive income but at a lower rate of return.

Now, you're probably wondering ... which is better?

Well, here's the thing:

There's no definitively "right" choice. It depends on where you are in your wealth journey.
Let me explain ...

When you're just getting started, trading enables you to grow your capital faster. Those double digit returns add up quickly! But the drawdown can be larger too.
Once you've built up your account, emphasizing investing provides steady passive income. And you've got enough buffer to weather the volatility.

See how they each have a role? It's about finding the right MIX tailored to your situation.

And in the next Action Step, you will discover how you find the best mix for YOU.

Over time, as you achieve different milestones, you can adjust the blend. But having both engines running is the key.

Trading will help you accumulate assets faster early on.
Later, investing will generate the hands-off income you need.

Find the right fusion and your wealth building really takes off!

Now that you understand the key differences between trading and investing, and the benefits of utilizing both, let's look at how you can determine the ideal mix for your specific situation, goals and risk tolerance.

In the next section, I'll walk you through using the Income Calculator to create a tailored wealth creation roadmap just for you.

Action Step 3: Create Your Personalized Roadmap

Alright, you now understand the differences between trading and investing and why you need both.

But how do you determine the perfect blend for your specific goals and risk appetite?

This is where my **Income Calculator tool** comes in — your key to creating a tailored wealth creation roadmap unique to YOU.

You can download it here: https://rockwell.rocks/incomecalculator

This proprietary calculator allows you to input your current financial details like expenses, account size and time horizon.

You can easily adjust the trading vs investing mix and see projected outcomes.

The Income Calculator crunches the numbers behind the scenes. It will reveal how to allocate your capital between trading and investing to maximize returns while minimizing risk.

With your personalized blueprint, you can trade and invest with clarity and confidence. The guesswork is gone.
Now let's dive in and I'll walk you through how to leverage this powerful tool.

As you can see, there are only 4 steps:

Settings			
	--> Fill out all fields that are highlighted in yellow		
Step 1	How would you like to determine your "cost of living"?		
	Rough Estimate ▾	**<<= Select a method first!**	
Step 2	Cost of Living (see "Budget Tab)		**$111,600**
Step 3	**How much do you have currently in your retirement account?**		**$250,000**
Step 4	**What account size are you comfortable trading?**	$400,000	
	i.e. at what level will you stop growing your account and startuilding your income machine?		
	Suggested:	$390,600	

And the good news:

We already did Step 1 and Step 2 of this income calculator in **Action Step 1** in the previous chapter.

For Step 3, you just need to fill in how much money you have in your retirement account right now. In this example, we're using $250,000. But don't worry ... after you download the Income Calculator Tool, you can fill in YOUR values.

Step 4: Based on your living expenses, the tool will suggest an optimal trading account size. In this example, it's $390,600. So we chose $400,000 for Step 4.

But let me guess:
You don't have $400,000 in your trading account right now, right?

That's the magic of the Income Calculator Tool:
Based on these inputs, it will now calculate the optimal mix of trading and investing for you.

Let's say you have $100,000 right now to put into your trading account.
Again ... don't worry about it if you have more or less.

Just download the Income Machine Calculator Tool and you can fill in your own values.

But for this example, let's say the trader has $100,000 in her trading account:

Phase 2: Building Your Financial Fortress

Beginning of Year	Trading Account	Goal per Year	Trading Profits	Cash added to Trading Account	Excess Profits
2024	$100,000	30%	$30,000		0
2025	$130,000	60%	$78,000		0
2026	$208,000	60%	$124,800		0
2027	$332,800	60%	$199,680		$132,480
2028	$400,000	60%	$240,000		$240,000
2029	$400,000	60%	$240,000		$240,000
2030	$400,000	60%	$240,000		$240,000
2031	$400,000	60%	$240,000		$240,000
2032	$400,000	60%	$240,000		$240,000
2033	$400,000	60%	$240,000		$240,000
2034	$400,000	60%	$240,000		$240,000

For the first year, I recommend a conservative goal of 30% per year.

If you choose to be more aggressive or conservative, you can adjust this percentage but based on my experience, I recommend 30% as a goal.

If everything is going according to plan, you would make $30,000 in trading profits and your trading account grows to $130,000.

Now that you have been trading for a year you can get more aggressive.
That's why I recommend setting your trading goal to 60% per year but again ... ultimately, it's YOUR decision how conservative or aggressive you want to be.

Now let's say you achieve 60% return in the second year.
This means that you would make $78,000 in trading profits, and your account grows to $208,000.

You keep trading your account until it reaches the threshold that you set in Step 4 (see above).

In our example, that was $400,000.

As you can see, in only 4 years you would achieve this goal:
In the beginning of 2027, you start with $332,800 and you achieve $199,680 in trading profits.

That's a total of $532,480, so you are exceeding the account size of $400,000 by $132,480

So what do you do with this "excess money"?
Well, that's where the magic begins:

You use this money to start building your INVESTING account, i.e. you transfer the money from your TRADING into your INVESTING account where you invest this money very conservatively to generate passive income.

As you can see, NOW we start building your INVESTING account to generate passive income.

Phase 2: Building Your Financial Fortress

Beginning of Year	Excess Profits	Dividend Account*	Goal per Year	Passive Income	Cost of Living	RPIC Index (TM)
2024	0	$250,000	10%	$25,000	$111,600	22
2025	0	$275,000	10%	$27,500	$111,600	25
2026	0	$302,500	10%	$30,250	$111,600	27
2027	$132,480	$465,230	10%	$46,523	$111,600	42
2028	$240,000	$751,753	10%	$75,175	$111,600	67
2029	$240,000	$1,066,928	10%	$106,693	$111,600	96
2030	$240,000	$1,413,621	10%	$141,362	$111,600	127
2031	$240,000	$1,794,983	10%	$179,498	$111,600	161
2032	$240,000	$2,214,482	10%	$221,448	$111,600	198
2033	$240,000	$2,675,930	10%	$267,593	$111,600	240
2034	$240,000	$3,183,523	10%	$318,352	$111,600	285

For me, a "good" goal per year for passive income is 10%.

So now you have both engines firing:

— Your TRADING ENGINE that builds your account more aggressively so that you can feed…

— Your INVESTMENT ENGINE that now generates passive income for you.

And as you can see, if everything goes according to plan, your RPIC Index will be above 120 within only 6 years from now!

The key is to use a mix of trading and investing to build your income machine.

If you start INVESTING too soon, your account will grow too slowly.

And if you keep TRADING all of your money and don't start feeding your investing account, you're taking on too much risk.

The key is to use BOTH to achieve your goal of an RPIC Index of 120 or higher as quickly as possible.
And if you are a more visual type, here's a graph that illustrates this principle:
First, you start building your TRADING account.
Once you reach a certain level, you start building your INVESTING account so that you can start generating passive income.

And soon your passive income will cover all of your living expenses … and more.

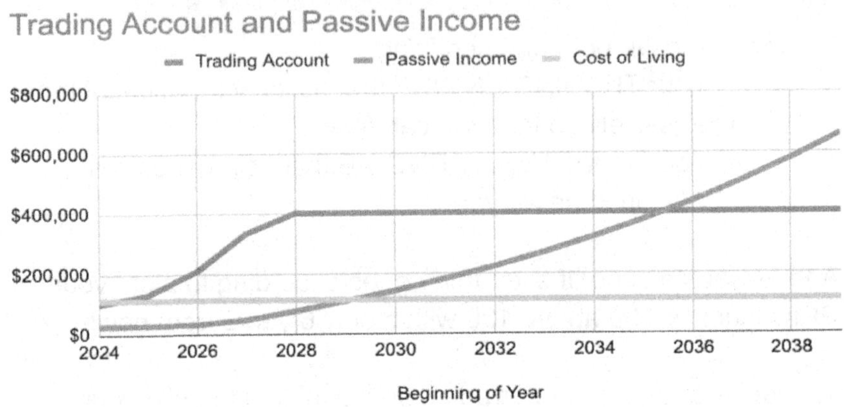

And there you have it.
A crystal clear roadmap guiding you step-by-step to constructing your financial fortress and achieving true passive income freedom.

Using the Income Calculator, you now understand exactly how to blend trading and investing to systematically build the levels of your fortress over time. No more haphazard decisions or analysis paralysis!

This tailored blueprint provides the strong foundation needed before we start laying bricks in the next chapter.

Remember one of the biggest struggles we discussed in Chapter 3 was Muddled Investment Strategy Syndrome? This data-driven **Infinite Income Roadmap** that we developed here is the cure!

No more weekend "research" sessions picking random assets out of confusion.
No more getting derailed by conflicting opinions.
No more good intentions that never materialize into action.

You now have your North Star — a guiding light based on hard numbers, not guesses. And you understand precisely why following this calculated path is essential.

With your roadmap in hand, you can start constructing your financial fortress with clarity of purpose and confidence in your direction.

And now that your blueprint is set, the next chapter will uncover the specific trading strategies and techniques required to start actively building up the walls of your fortress.

The planning is complete.

Let's get to work.

Chapter 8: Step 2: Winning Strategy Selector

Let me tell you about a painful lesson I learned in my early days of trading.

It was back in 2002, shortly after I quit my job and moved from Germany to America with big dreams of becoming a successful trader. I was confident I had made the right decision. This was my chance to finally take control of my financial future!

In the beginning, my account was growing steadily. I was making sensible trades based on research and profiting from small, consistent gains.

But then I got impatient.

I started looking around at others flashing their wins and lifestyles. Big houses, nice cars, fancy vacations, all thanks to their windfall trading profits, or so they claimed.

The "fear of missing out (FOMO)" set in. I wanted my slice of the pie too!

So I abandoned my measured approach and started swinging for the fences. I wasn't satisfied with 5-10% returns anymore. I wanted 100% ... 500% ... 1000% gains, and I wanted them NOW!

I started chasing hype, trading on emotions, and taking reckless risks trying to hit homeruns on long shots. I was trying to double my money within a few days on some "surefire trades."

But of course, this was a recipe for disaster. More often than not, I ended up losing on these gambles rather than gaining.

As the saying goes: *The quickest way to lose your money is trying to double it.*

And that's exactly what happened. My account dwindled rapidly as I lost big on one speculative bet after another.

All because I didn't have a proven, disciplined trading approach, just greed and impulsiveness.

This painful period taught me an invaluable lesson though: seeking windfall profits is a fool's game.

The real path to trading success is having a rule-based system optimized for repeatable, sustainable gains.

It finally clicked that I needed to shift my focus to systematically grow my account through moderate but consistent profits. Slow and steady wins the race!
Once I made this mindset shift, my results dramatically improved. It felt like I had finally cracked the code and came out on the other side a better trader.

I share this story because making consistent profits in the market requires following a defined, calculated strategy — not just taking shots in the dark.

In the previous chapter, we designed the high-level blueprint for our financial fortress. Now it's time to determine exactly HOW we will build it.

Let me equip you with the strategies and techniques to actively build wealth through smart trading.

You will discover my favorite trading methodology and I will show you a tool to identify the optimal strategy for YOUR goals.

In short: you will get everything you need to build your financial fortress brick by brick.

But first things first.
You have to adopt the right mindset to execute trades rationally, not emotionally!

Action Step 1: Adopt a Winning Mindset

Let me tell you about one of the most brilliant minds when it comes to cultivating the optimal trading mentality: the legendary Warren Buffett.

Wa itional"
pa r
wo
rea
you're making somebody else rich!

So at just 31 years old, Warren took control and started his trading and investment career by buying Sanborn stock. In just two years, he made 50% returns on his investment!

This was just the beginning.

By 32 he was a millionaire.
By 60, a billionaire.

For years, Warren was the richest person alive, thanks to his mastery of "SRC Profits" — the ability to generate Systematic, Repeatable and Consistent profits regardless of market conditions.

Picture this … I'm sure you've heard the story of the tortoise and the hare, right?
But have you seen it play out in real life?

You should check it out here:
https://youtu.be/m7NuVjpi72c?si=PVLgO2WYePWX29yB

Back to trading:
Let's look at an example.

In January 2021, Bitcoin was $28k. By November, it hit an all-time high of $69k!
A massive 246% gain before crashing down below $18,000.

Tesla (TSLA) - everybody's darling - also exploded from $240 to $414, a 172% profit.

Same with Netflix (NFLX): It went from $100 to $675, a factor of 6x!

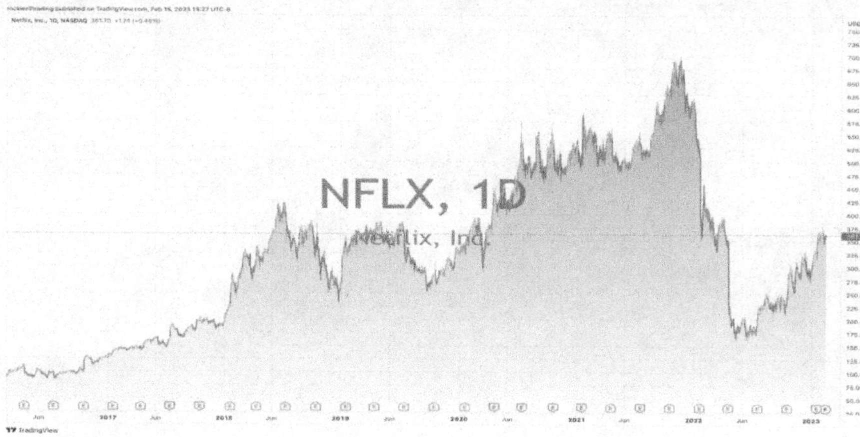

But then they crashed, hard.

In the beginning of 2023, Bitcoin, Tesla, and Netflix are WAY below their 2021 highs.

Now take a look at the orange line in these charts:

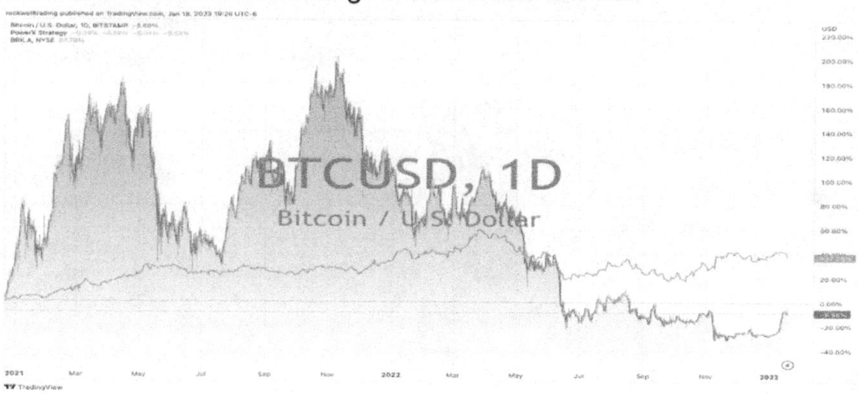

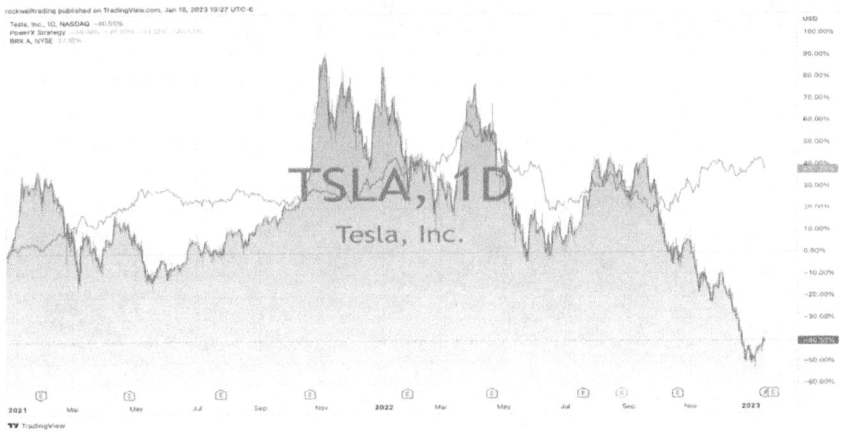

If you think: "*Oh that must be an index, e.g. S&P 500.*"

Nope! Here's the S&P 500 vs. the "mysterious orange line":

As you can see, the "orange line" outperformed all of these examples.

So what is it?

It's Warren Buffet's Berkshire Hathaway portfolio (BRK.A).

During the same period, when everybody's darlings crashed, Warren Buffet's company steadily climbed 38% during the same period and is now trading at $562,800!

Slow and steady won the race!

This is no short-term anomaly. Over decades, Warren Buffet's Berkshire Hathaway has absolutely crushed the market. Warren's strategy has generated over 5X the returns of the S&P 500!

The lesson? Ditch the short-term hunting for hype and windfalls.

Take a page from Warren's playbook and start focusing on long-term, sustained compound growth through discipline and consistency.

Don't fear taking reasonable risks for growth.
But act rationally, not out of greed or FOMO.

Embrace the progress from small but steady profits. This mentality shift is the foundation for executing trades systematically to construct yout financial fortress brick by brick.

Write this down:
Trading is a marathon — not a sprint.

The hare may win a race every now and then.
But the tortoise wins the marathon to financial freedom!

Now that you have the optimal mindset, let's move on to the specific trading techniques utilized by the pros, including Warren, to generate lasting wealth.

Action Step 2: Learn Techniques Used by Professional Traders

Warren Buffett is famous for buying and holding quality stocks for the long run.Here are some of his quotes that gives us a better understanding how Warren Buffett thinks:

1. *"If you aren't willing to own a stock for 10 years, don't even think about owning it for 10 minutes."*

2. *"It's far better to buy a wonderful company at a fair price, than a fair company at a wonderful price."*

3. *"Never invest in a business you cannot understand."*

In a nutshell: He is a VALUE investor. Warren Buffet doesn't look at technical indicators trying to make a few bucks in the next few minutes. He isn't concerned about the daily fluctuations of the markets. He uses a long-term investing approach which has made him billions and billions of dollars.

But here's a little known fact — he also uses options to generate systematic profits.

Specifically, Warren is a master of selling cash-secured puts. This strategy provides a clever way to get paid to buy stocks you want to own anyway. (Source: https://www.yahoo.com/now/really-want-rich-3-warren-134000222.html)

Here's a quick example to illustrate how it works:

One of Warren Buffet's investments is Coca Cola (KO). And years ago, when Coca-Cola was around $39 per share, Warren sold 50,000 put option contracts with a $35 strike price for $1.50 per share premium.(Source: https://www.thepennyhoarder.com/investing/naked-investment-strategy-helped-warren-buffett-make-millions/)

He pocketed $7.5 million upfront instantly from the premium! Now, there were two potential outcomes before expiration:

1. If Coke stayed above $35, the options expire worthless and Warren keeps the full $7.5 million.

2. If Coke drops below $35, Warren is obligated to buy at $35. But he was happy to buy more Coke stock at that discounted price anyway.

Either way — Warren wins! He gets paid to buy a great stock he wants to own.

This is the beauty of selling cash-secured puts.

You get paid to buy quality stocks at a discount!

Warren has used this strategy successfully for decades to systematically build wealth in his long-term portfolio.

And "The Wheel Strategy" is taking this core principle to the next level!

Because this trading strategy is a one-two punch combo that generates consistent income from options premiums. Here's how it works in a nutshell:

1.First, you sell cash-secured puts on a quality stock you want to own. You collect income from the premium upfront.

If the puts expire worthless, you keep the full premium.
If assigned, you buy the shares at a discounted price.

2. Once assigned on the shares, you then sell covered calls against them.
This generates additional income from the call premiums.
If the calls expire worthless, you keep collecting premiums.
If the calls are exercised, you sell your shares at the strike price.

And then you can sell more cash-secured puts and repeat the process!

The key is combining both strategies into a wheel — continuously collecting income from premiums as the wheel turns.

With the wheel, time becomes your ally. As the wheel continues turning day after day, week after week, the income snowballs.This steady stream of premiums compounds into a growing mountain of wealth over time.

The wheel isn't exciting but it is effective.
Like a well-oiled machine, it systematically grinds out "SRC Profits."

Now let's walk through a real example together so you can see exactly how it works.

Example 1: General Motors (GM)

Alright, enough theory. Let's look at how this played out with an actual trade I made on GM recently.Based on my criteria, that I will explain later, General Motors (GM) is a quality stock that I don't mind owning!

On September 11th, GM was trading around $33 per share. But as you know by now, we never buy stocks for the “retail price”, since we use Warren Buffett’s “secret trading strategy” to buy stocks at a discount.

In this case, I decided that I would be happy to buy GM for $32, which is a discount of 3%.

In order to do this, I decided to sell cash-secured puts with a $32 strike expiring that Friday on September 15th.

Each contract controlled 100 shares, so for every put option contract I sold I received $20 in premium. Nice!

Now, I like to trade in $200,000 positions. Based on the premium amount, I could sell 62 put contracts and collect $1,240 total premium.

Since it was a 4 day trade, that came out to $310 in income per day for selling those puts! Not bad for just a few minutes of "work."

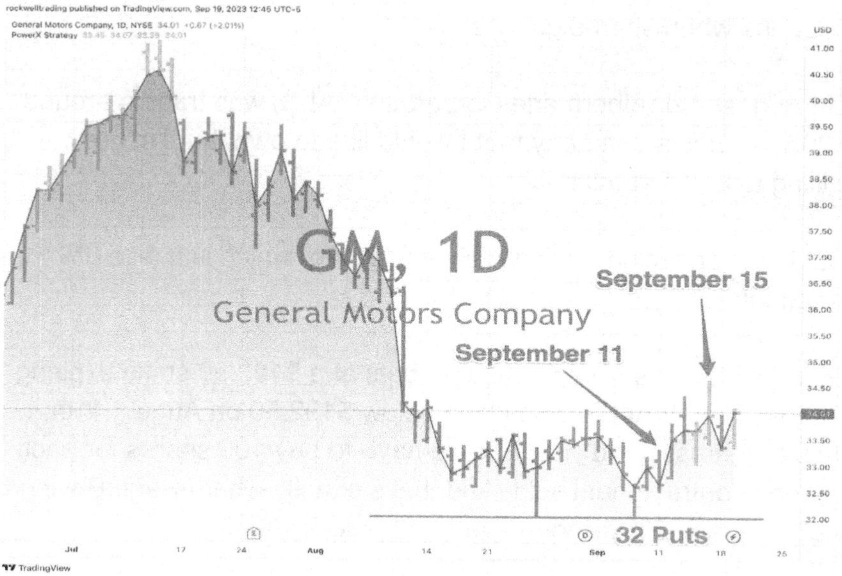

So Friday came around and GM closed at $33.95, above my $32 strike price.

The puts expired completely worthless. I pocketed the full $1,240 premium and could immediately sell more puts!

What's not to love? I collected a solid income stream just for obligating myself to buy a great American company like GM at a discounted price of $32 when it was trading at $33.

The power of the options wheel is generating this steady premium income week after week, month after month.

Example 2: Albermarle Corporation (ALB)

Let's walk through another real trade, this time showing what happens when shares get assigned.

On August 3rd, Albermarle Corporation (ALB) was trading around $205. ALB is a company that I would like to own, but I'm not willing to buy it at full price.

But I wouldn't mind buying ALB at $192.50, which is a nice 6% discount!

So I decided to sell cash-secured puts at a $192.50 strike expiring August 11th. If ALB would close below $192.50 on August 11th, I would "get assigned", i.e. I would have to buy 100 shares for each options contract that I sold. And that's exactly what I want: Buying ALB at a nice 6% discount - and get paid for it!

Based on a $200k position size, I could sell 10 put contracts and collect $165 premium per contract, adding up to $1,650 total.

August 11th came around and ALB closed at $187.49, below my strike.
So I was assigned 1,000 shares at $192.50.

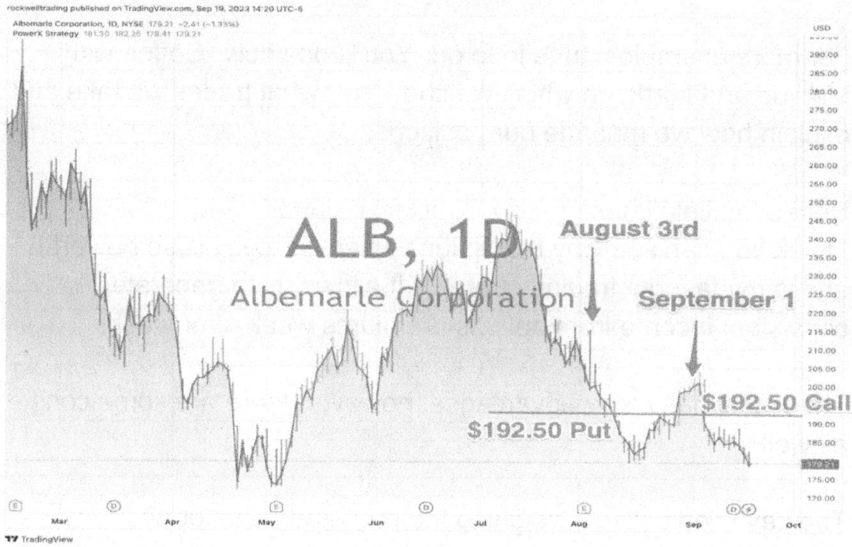

And that's good! Because based on my criteria, Albermarle is a quality stock that I like to have in my portfolio!

Now that I own it, it's time to sell calls against my new shares. On August 21st, I sold covered calls on those shares at a $192.50 strike for $180 premium each. That's another $1,800 in income.

A few days later on the 24th, I rolled the calls out a week for $260 more premium per contract. The total collected from rolling was $2,600.

Finally, on September 1st, the calls were exercised with ALB at $200.26, and I had to sell my 1,000 shares at the $192.50 strike.

All in all over 4 weeks, I brought in $6,050 income on a $200k position. And I'm ready to sell more puts to restart the wheel!

This example demonstrates the power of combining puts and calls. Even when assigned shares, you can generate more premiums from covered calls.

Rinse and repeat — that's the beauty of the options wheel!

For more examples, tune in to our YouTube show "Coffee with Markus and Mark", in which we show you what trades we take and explain how we manage our positions.

Here's the link: https://rockwell.rocks/youtube.
I think you can see why the options wheel strategy is so powerful and is my favorite trading strategy. It allows us to generate consistent income from options premiums week after week.

The wheel has many advantages; however, there are some cons as well.

The key is objectively weighing the pros and cons for your personal situation. The options wheel is a favorite strategy of mine but it's not necessarily right for everyone.

That's why in the next section, we'll introduce the **Winning Strategy Selector Tool** to help determine if the Wheel Strategy aligns with YOUR goals and risk tolerance.

Action Step 3: Choose the Best Trading Strategy for You

Now that you understand how powerful the options wheel strategy can be, let's take a step back and recognize there is no one-size-fits-all approach.

The Wheel Strategy may be a great fit for some traders but not the optimal choice for others based on their unique goals, preferences and risk appetite.

Every strategy brings a different blend of pros, cons and trade-offs.

Therefore, it's critical to objectively assess and select the techniques best aligned with your needs.

The ideal trading methodology maximizes returns within YOUR acceptable level of risk, effort and preferred market conditions.

With so many dynamics involved, finding this sweet spot can be challenging.

But that's where our unique **Winning Strategy Selector Tool** comes in.This proprietary tool allows you to evaluate trading strategies according to 11 key criteria:

1. **RIsk** — What is the potential risk for each trade for this strategy?
2. **Reward Potential** — The expected percentage returns are balanced against the risk.
3. **Time Commitment** — How much active management is required from monitoring to adjusting positions.
4. **Knowledge Level** — The baseline trading education and skills needed to successfully implement.
5. **Account Size** — The approximate minimum capital required to properly utilize the strategy.
6. **Market Conditions** — How the strategy performs in bull, bear, and range-bound market environments.
7. **Hold Time** — The typical duration that trade positions are open before closing out.

8. **Number Positions** — How concentrated or diversified the strategy is across multiple trades.
9. **Probability of Profit** — The historical percentage of winning trades when properly executed.
10. **Implementation Complexity** — The operational difficulty in actually executing the strategy's trades. As an example, an Iron Condor is more complex to implement than simply buying a stock.
11. **Account Permissions** — Whether advanced permissions like margin or options are needed from your broker.I also like to define the importance of each criteria since not all criteria have equal weight. As an example, for me, the "account size" and "account permissions" don't matter.

But it's critical for me that the strategy works in all market conditions and not just a few times a year. Of course, this might be different for you.But with this comprehensive criteria, the tool can identify your ideal strategy match based on your unique goals, preferences, and current situation.

Let's look at how it works…

Below you will find a filled out version of the Winning Strategy Selector for The Wheel Strategy.

	Strategy 1 Wheel Strategy	Average	4.42
Criteria	**Your Comments**	**Weight (optional)**	**Rating 1 - 5**
Risk What is the potential risk for each trade for this strategy?	After you get assigned a stock, the stock might drop and you might not be able to sell calls until the stock recovers.	1 - Normal	2 - Not Good
Reward Potential The expected percentage returns possible balanced against the risk.	Based on my experience, you can expect an ROI of 30-60% based on realized profits.	1 - Normal	4 - Pretty Good
Time Commitment How much active management is required for monitoring to adjusting positions?	I usually only trade 15-30 minutes per day, and I'm not even trading every day.	2 - Important	4 - Pretty Good
Knowledge Level The baseline trading education and skills needed to successfully implement.	Straightforward to learn but experience with options trading helps	1 - Normal	4 - Pretty Good
Account Size The approximate minimum capital required to properly utilize the strategy.	$10k minimum but ideally $25k+	0 - Doesn't m...	4 - Pretty Good
Market Conditions How the strategy performs in bull, bear, and range-bound market environments.	Works in bull markets, excels in range-bound markets and works even well in downward trending markets	3 - Critical	5 - Great!
Hold Time The typical duration that trade positions are open before closing out.	Put contracts held briefly until expiration. My own average trade length is 9 days	1 - Normal	5 - Great!
Number of Positions How concentrated or diversified the strategy is across multiple trades. As an example, a trading strategy that only trades Tesla (TSLA) is not very diversified	Diversified across multiple uncorrelated underlyings. I like to trade up to 5 positions in my account.	1 - Normal	5 - Great!
Probability of Profit The historical percentage of winning trades when properly executed.	My winning percentage based on closed trades is 98%	1 - Normal	5 - Great!
Implementation Complexity The operational difficulty in actually executing the strategy's trades. As an example, an Iron Condor is more complex to implement than simply buying a stock.	Easy to understand and execute	1 - Normal	5 - Great!
Account Permissions Whether advanced permissions like margin or options are needed from your broker. Another example would be the min requirement of $25,000 when day trading	Requires margin account and options approval	0 - Doesn't m...	4 - Pretty Good

Obviously, the "Rating" is subjective, and you might apply a different rating. And that's ok!

That's why you can download the "Winning Strategy Selector Tool" here and fill it out for yourself: https://rockwell.rocks/strategyselector

Now, you may be wondering … what's the big deal about this selector tool?

Well, first of all, it forces you to evaluate a strategy across 11 different criteria. I bet you never considered things like, "Account Permissions Needed" before, did you?

And even though the ratings are subjective, comparing a few strategies side by side makes the differences crystal clear. There are tons of strategies out there for you to choose from. This tool pushes you to do your homework.

Take three strategies that interest you and run them through the selector. See those pros and cons stacked up right in front of you!

This makes picking YOUR winning strategy simple. No more chasing flavor of the month methods or relying on what worked for your neighbor.

The selector tool helps you filter through noise and aligns your approach with your personal goals and individual situation.

So use this tool as your guiding light through the maze of strategies available today. It provides clarity on the best path FOR YOU.

Conclusion

Phew — we covered a lot of ground here! Now you understand how to choose the ideal trading strategy based on your personal goals and preferences.

This is extremely important because you will use this strategy to build your financial fortress.

I get this question all the time: “What is the best trading strategy?”

And here’s my answer:

The best trading strategy is the one that lets you sleep at night. The one that lets you wake up in the morning, looking at the markets and being RELAXED. On the other hand, the worst trading strategy is the one that lets you stare at the ceiling at night, worrying about your positions.

Keep in mind that you will use the strategy you select here for YEARS to build your financial fortress. So don't rush through this step.

Too many traders are starting to trade a strategy without making sure that it fits their needs.

And since they are uncomfortable with their strategy, they are quick to abandon it and bounce from one strategy to another.

But not you!
You now have your proven blueprint for generating systematic profits.
And you have selected a trading strategy that's perfect for YOU.

Next, it's time to start supplying our building site with trading materials.

We'll need to find the right brokerage for our selected strategies.

And that's what we will talk about in the next chapter.

Chapter 9: Step 3: Ultimate Broker Guide

This step will help you select the ideal broker for your needs and potentially save you thousands in commissions annually.

Here's the bad news: When trading stocks and options, and even futures and Forex, you need a broker. You can't buy and sell your stocks directly at the stock exchange.

And here's the good news: Fortunately, there are thousands of brokers out there and many of them will work for you for free!

Did you know that according to rentechdigital.com, there are a total of 19,668 Stock brokers in the United States as of August 12, 2023?

So there's plenty to choose from. But how do you find the "best" broker"?

Think about your broker as your supplier for the building materials for your financial fortress. The broker is your partner and provides you with everything you need ....

... BUT: you want to make sure that you're getting QUALITY for a FAIR price.

Having the wrong broker is like trying to build a fortress with poor quality materials or with a vendor constantly overcharging on each supply purchase.

Let me give you an example:

In the first 6 months of 2023 alone, I traded 1,859 options contracts. If I had paid the standard $0.65 per contract fee many brokers charge, that would have cost me a massive $1,208 in commissions. That's almost $2,500 per year!

But fortunately, my optimized broker offers unlimited commission-free trading.

So my total commissions paid? ZERO!

That's almost $2,500 per year that I can invest in additional wealth building *or* going on a nice vacation for a few days.

But don't make the mistake of just looking for "FREE."

There's more to it and you want to make sure that you find the best broker for YOUR needs.

So let's dive in.

Action Step 1: Select The "Best" Broker

In this step, the goal is to find the right broker with low fees, an easy to learn trading platform and great customer service.

Of course, commissions are important – as you have just seen above.

But there's more to it:

I like to evaluate a broker based on 4 criteria:

1. **Commissions:** What are the rates for stocks and options? Any minimums?
2. **Other fees**: What are the other fees that the broker charges, e.g. wire fees, platform fees, etc.
3. **Trading Platform:** What does the broker offer? Desktop app, web-based platform, or mobile app? And how easy is it to use these platforms?
4. **Customer service**: Phone, chat, email support, and availability

There are some other criteria that you could consider:

- Account minimums – Any minimum deposit required to open an account?
- Available asset classes – Stocks, options, futures, forex, crypto, what can you trade?
- Research and tools — Quality of fundamental data, charting, screeners, etc.
- Educational resources — Guides, videos, courses to build skills.
- Ease of use — Simple account opening, funding, withdrawals.
- Company reputation — Reviews, complaints, years in business.

For me, these criteria are not that important.

Oh, and if you are wondering if your funds are safe: Make sure your broker is a member of the Securities Investor Protection Corporation (SIPC).

The SIPC protects you against the loss of cash and securities - such as stocks and bonds - if your broker gets in trouble. But only if they are a SIPC-member. And there's also a limit: The SIPC protection is good for $500,000, which includes a $250,000 limit for cash.

So let's evaluate a few well-known brokerage firms according to my criteria.

Broker Comparison Calculator

		Broker 1		Broker 2		Broker 3		Broker 4		Broker 5	
Name	Importance	TD Ameritrade / Schwab		Fidelity		Interactive Brokers		tastytrade		Tradier	
Commission		0.65 per contract		0.65 per contract		0.65 per contract		$1 per contract		$10 per month	
Trading 5 contracts*	1 - Normal	$3.25	2	$3.25	2	$3.25	2	$5.00	1	$0.00	5
Trading 10 contracts*	1 - Normal	$6.50	2	$6.50	2	$6.50	2	$10.00	1	$0.00	5
Trading 50 contracts*	3 - Critical	$32.50	1	$32.50	1	$32.50	1	$10.00	4	$0.00	5
Broker assisted	1 - Normal	$25.00	4	$32.95	4	$95.00	1	unknown	2	$10.00	5
Other Fees											
Assignment Fee	1 - Normal	$0.00	5	$0.00	5	$0.00	5	$5.00	2	$9.00	1
Wire Fee	0 - Doesn't ...	$25.00	2	$30.00	1	$10.00	5	$25.00	2	$30.00	1
Data Feed	1 - Normal	$0.00	5	$0.00	5	$30.00	1	$0.00	5	$0.00	5
Margin Interest **	2 - Important	12%	1	12.00%	1	7.83%	5	9.50%	4	9.50%	4
Platform	1 - Normal	4 - Good	4	4 - Good	4	4 - Good	4	4 - Good	4	4 - Good	4
Customer Support	2 - Important	3 - Ok	3	3 - Ok	3	1 - Horri...	1	4 - Good	4	5 - Great	5
		2.31		2.31		2.23		3.00		4.08	

* Selling and exp. worthless
** for a $100,000 account
All data as of 12/28/2023

rockwelltrading.com/broker

I'm doing my best to keep this up to date for you but of course, all of these numbers are subject to change, so please make sure to double check them before making a final decision.

And if you would like a copy of this Broker Comparison Calculator, simply go to https://rockwell.rocks/brokercomparison

Here's how to use it:

First, you can see how much you would pay trading 5 contracts, 10 contracts and 50 contracts. This is important because based on your account size, one broker might be better for you than another.

You can also rate the importance of each criteria.

As you can see in the example above, I set the importance for "Trading 50 contracts" to critical since I'm trading a larger account and regularly place options trades for 30, 50 or even 60 contracts.

Of course, this might be different for you. If you are trading a smaller account, it would be more important to have a broker with low fees for trading 5 contracts. But that's the beauty of this tool: You can simply adjust the importance of a criteria based on your needs.

As an example, the cost of a wire doesn't matter for me since I'm typically using ACH for any account transactions. But if you live in Germany and need to regularly wire money to a broker in the US, this criteria might be more important to you.

After you decide on the importance of each criteria, the tool will automatically calculate a rating for each criteria between 1-5: 1 being the worst and 5 being the best.

After calculating the rating of each criteria, the tool will then use the importance that you assigned to each criteria and give you an overall rating.

In the example above, you will see that Tradier receives the highest rating of 4.08, and Interactive Brokers receives the lowest rating of 2.23.

Of course, this is based on MY criteria and the importance that I assigned.

But as you can see, the best broker for my needs is "Tradier," and here's why:

> – I pay a monthly flat fee of $10 and ZERO commissions, no matter how many stocks or options I trade.
>
> – I like to trade on margin and the margin interest is lower than most other brokers.
>
> – Their platform is easy to use: You can learn how to use the platform in a matter of minutes. On the other spectrum, TD Ameritrade's / Schwab's thinkorswim® platform will take weeks to master.

– Their customer support is the best I have ever seen: An English speaking HUMAN is answering the phone after three rings and will help you with everything you need. On the other spectrum, you have Interactive Brokers where you first have to battle through a touch tone system ("For support with .... press 1"), then you're on hold forever and finally the "representative" sends you an online article. The last time I needed some basic information from Interactive Brokers, it took me 26 minutes to finally get it!

If you would like to learn more about the broker that I use in my trading, simply go here: https://rockwelltrading.com/broker.

Action Step 2: Select the Right Account Type

The goal of this step is to understand the different account types and options trading levels and choose the best one based on your trading style and needs.

Now that you know how to evaluate and select the best broker for your needs, the next step is deciding which type of account to open. Brokers offer a variety of account types, each with their own pros and cons.

The three most common account types are:

Cash Account – This is the most basic account. You can only buy stocks and options with the cash you have in your account and must wait for trades to settle before reusing those funds.

Margin Account – This account allows you to borrow funds from the brokerage to purchase securities. This provides leverage but this also incurs interest costs and higher risk.

Retirement Account - These accounts like IRAs provide tax benefits for retirement savings. But withdrawals before retirement age can lead to penalties.

Account Type	Pros	Cons
Cash	Simple to open and manage.	Trade settlement delays.
Margin	Can trade with borrowed funds.	Interest costs and higher risk.
Retirement	Tax benefits for retirement.	Penalties for early withdrawal.

Here's a comparison of the key features:

In addition, you can also open these accounts as:

Personal Account: Only you can trade the account and access the funds

Joint Account: Both you and a partner, e.g. your spouse or your child, can trade and access the funds.

Company Account: You can open an account in the name of a company, which might have some tax benefits. We will talk more about this in Chapter 14: Step 8: Wealth Empire Architect.

So what's the best account?

Many active traders, like myself, utilize margin accounts. This is about having a line of credit: You don't need to use it but it's good to have it in case you need it. And in Chapter 13: Step 7: Turbo Growth Accelerator, you will learn how to use margin and leverage responsibly to grow your account even quicker.

If you are unsure about the best account type for you, just talk to your broker! They will be happy to assist you.

When you open an account, there's one more thing you need to know:
Because if you choose to trade options, you need to choose an "Option Level" so that you can trade the strategies you want.

Here are the typical tiers offered by most brokers like Tradier:

Level	Permissions
1	Covered Calls, Cash Secured Puts (Cash only)
2	Level 1 + Long Calls and Puts
3	Level 2 + Spreads
4	Level 3 + Naked Puts
5	Level 4 + Naked Calls

6	Level 5 + Naked Index Options

During the account opening process, the broker will ask you what options level you would like to have.

If you want to trade "The Wheel Strategy," here's the level you need:

– If you have a **Cash Account**, you only need Level 1.
– If you have a **Margin Account**, you need Level 4.

Here's a catch:
These higher levels allow you to trade some more sophisticated (in other words … risky) options strategies.

So don't expect your broker to hand Level 4 or 5 to you on a silver platter.

You have to let them know that you know your stuff!

The broker wants to see you have plenty of experience and training under your belt before you start selling options. They just want to make sure you don't blow up your account.

So when the broker asks for your trading experience and you say "none," they probably won't grant you a higher level.

Also, getting approved for a higher tier once your account is already funded and running can be a headache.

That's why it's key to open your account and apply for the appropriate options level from the get-go.

So save yourself the hassle by starting at the right level on day one. Then you can focus on executing those trades to build your financial fortress!

Here are some tips for getting approved for higher options trading levels and avoiding pitfalls:

- Highlight your trading experience and education. Brokers want to see you have the knowledge to use advanced strategies responsibly. Share any training, mentors, books that prepared you.

- Answer all questions thoroughly and accurately. Any inconsistencies or dubious claims will work against you.

- If you don't know how to answer a question, call your broker and ask for help. They will be happy to help you.

- Your answers are not set in stone! If you get denied for whatever reason, you can fill out another application right away and correct anything you need.

Most brokers will approve you within a few hours.

If you don't get an answer after 48 hours, call the broker and ask for the status.

While you are waiting, there is one more important step to take before you can start trading:

Action Step 3: Mastering the Trading Platform

The goal of this step is to learn how to use the trading platform and place trades like a pro.

Let me ask you something. Have you ever struggled trying to build IKEA furniture with vague instructions? I sure have!

Trying to trade without knowing your platform is kinda like that – totally frustrating and not effective.

I learned this lesson the hard way:

Back when I first started actively trading, I was eager to make my first big trade. I'd done all the due diligence and felt ready to pull the trigger. But then disaster struck!

There I was, frantically clicking around on my trading platform trying to figure out how to place the trade before the price jumped away. But everything just felt so confusing!

Long story short – by the time I finally placed the trade, I'd missed most of the profit opportunity because I didn't take the time to properly learn my trading "cockpit"!

The good news is: you can easily avoid my painful mistake. You have to master your broker's trading platform before investing real capital.

Become an absolute expert at placing trades quickly and efficiently.
Navigating your platform should feel like second nature.

Trust me, the time spent upfront will give you the confidence to act fast and with confidence when opportunity comes knocking. No more fumbling around when the market is moving!

So in this section, I'll share my proven tips to rapidly get up to speed on your broker's platform.

I know: staring at your broker's platform screen can be intimidating at first. All those boxes, buttons, menus – yikes!

But here's the good news: Placing a trade only requires five key bits of info:

1. What you want to trade — the symbol, like AAPL or SPY.
2. If you want to buy or sell it.
3. How many shares or contracts you're trading.
4. At what price you want to trade.
5. How long your order remains active before expiration.

That's it! Let me walk you through an example so you can see just how straightforward it is.

Imagine we want to buy 10 shares of Tesla at $180 and we want the order to be valid for the day.

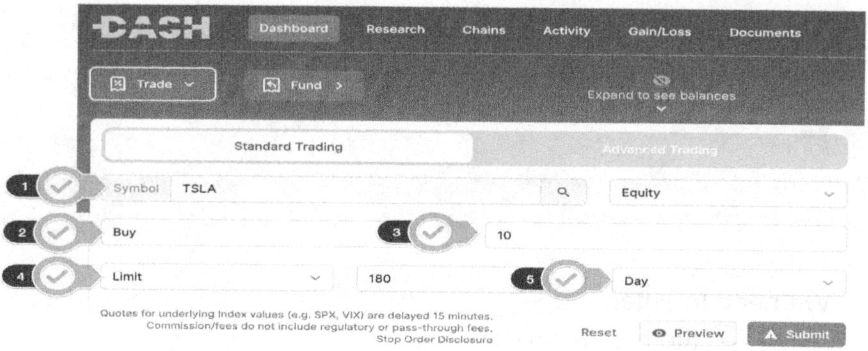

1. First, we'd enter TSLA as the symbol.
2. Then choose "Buy."
3. Enter 10 shares.
4. Next, we include the limit price of $180 per share.
5. Finally, we set the order to expire at the end of the trading session.

Boom – just like that, our TSLA buy order is entered and waiting for execution!

Now let's talk about option trades, since I like to trade options.

When placing an option trade, you need to give your broker a little bit more info. Because there are "call and put options", and options also have "strike prices" and "expiration dates"

So here's how you would place an option trade:

Let's say you want to sell 10 Put options of GM with a strike price of $32 expiring September 29 for at least 0.25 in premium.

Now we need to enter some more information for "(1) - What To Trade":

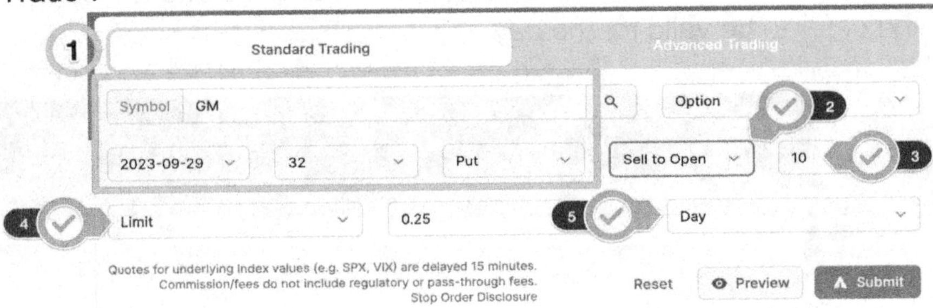

We need to enter

— the expiration date
— the strike price, and
— whether we want to trade a CALL or a PUT option

The rest is the same.

As you can see, it's not that difficult once you know the basics.

It's like driving a car:

You know that there's a lever somewhere that allows you to shift into gears.
Some cars have it in the middle console.
Some cars have it on the steering wheel.
And some cars might have it somewhere else.

It's the same with broker platforms.

They all allow you to enter these five key information bits that you need to place a trade. They just might be arranged differently. Take your time to get familiar with the platform.

The key is to practice trades on a simulator until placing orders becomes second nature.

Trading on a simulator has another huge advantage:
You can practice the trading strategy that you selected in Step 2 and get some performance numbers.
I always recommend placing at least 40 practice trades to get familiar with the platform and the strategy!

Alright, we made some serious progress here!

No more fumbling around trying to place orders during market moves. Soon you will be able to execute trades with confidence like a pro.

Now that we have laid the foundation, it's time to start building our financial fortress.

In the next chapter, we'll start creating the rock-solid trading plan needed to withstand any storm the markets brew up. Remember – a fortress built without a solid plan will crumble under pressure.

So let's get started!

Chapter 10: Step 4: Bulletproof 100k Trading Plan

Let me tell you about the time I learned the hard way just how crucial it is to have a proven trading system in place before putting real money on the line.

Early on in my journey, I was eager to start actively trading. I had some high level ideas of what I wanted to achieve and I knew a few basic tactics. But no defined, concrete plan.

So I just started buying and selling stocks arbitrarily based on tips and hunches with no rhyme or reason guiding my approach. Sometimes I'd get lucky and profit. But more often, I lost money on reckless, emotional trades.

The problem with that: I would never be able to create “SRC Profits”:

— Systematic
— Repeatable
— Consistent

Think about it:

Without a SYSTEM, you won’t be able to generate SYSTEMATIC profits. And based on my experience from my early days of trading, I can assure you that my random trades were not REPEATABLE.

It was like trying to build a fortress without blueprints, just grabbing materials and winging it.
Chaotic and ineffective.

Another challenge is the "Fear To Push The Button." Without a defined trading strategy, I second-guessed my choices and hesitated to push the "PLACE TRADE" button.

Without a solid foundation, my trades collapsed under pressure.

After months of frustration, I finally realized the problem — I was trading without a bulletproof trading plan optimized for repeatable success.

So let's recap:

In our previous steps, we laid the groundwork:

- In Step 1, we created a blueprint to define WHAT we want to do, how high and how big we want to build our financial fortress.
- In Step 2, we identified HOW we are going to build the fortress, i.e. what trading and investing strategy we are going to use.
- In Step 3, we got ready by selecting the best broker for our needs and getting familiar with the trading platform.

Now, in Step 4, it's time to define our "daily routine," i.e. what exactly do we do every time we fire up the computer and look for trades.

In this chapter, you'll learn how to create a bulletproof trading plan with these 3 elements:

1. **What to trade**: Stock selection rules.

2. **When to enter and exit**: Precise tactics for entering and exiting your trades without second-guessing yourself.
3. **Money management:** Controlling risk.

The right trading plan will allow you to make money in any market condition.

Let's start building a fortress that can weather any storm! The time for winging it has passed. Let's create a bulletproof trading plan engineered for profits.

Let's get started.

Action Step 1: Stock Selection Mastery

The first element of a bulletproof trading plan is defining WHAT you want to trade, i.e. objective rules for selecting the best stocks to trade.

Very few traders have a written trading plan. And I get it: In the beginning of my trading career, I just wanted to trade. When somebody told me to write out a trading plan, I rolled my eyes.

But over the years I realized that ALL of the top traders in the world have a written plan.

For me, there were two reasons NOT to write down my plan:

Reason 1: I would have to think about objective criteria for creating SRC Profits instead of just winging it.

Reason 2: I thought it would take me hours and even days to create a solid plan.

Boy, was I wrong!

A trading plan doesn't have to be a dissertation. In fact, my trading plan is just over one page long!

So how do you know how detailed it needs to be?

Well, the guidelines in your plan need to be clear and concrete enough for someone else to follow.

Let me give you an example ...

As you know, I frequently travel for weeks at a time to sailing regattas with my kids. And when I'm on the water without internet access, I can't look for potential trades.

But I can hand my written trading plan to my head coach, Mark Hodge, and he can execute it for me.

Mark is familiar with my general options trading strategy. So by following the defined stock selection criteria in my plan, he can identify trades that fit my system.

Example: My Trading Plan For The Wheel Strategy

Here's my current trading plan for selecting the best stocks for "The Wheel Strategy:"

1. **I like to trade Value Stocks and here are my criteria for defining them:**
    - The company needs to have been **profitable over the past five years**.

It's ok if they weren't profitable during the "Covid Years," 2020 and 2021, since even big companies like Walmart and Target were struggling during the pandemic.
You can easily find the financials of a company when you go to Google Finance. Here's an example for UPS:
https://www.google.com/finance/quote/UPS:NYSE

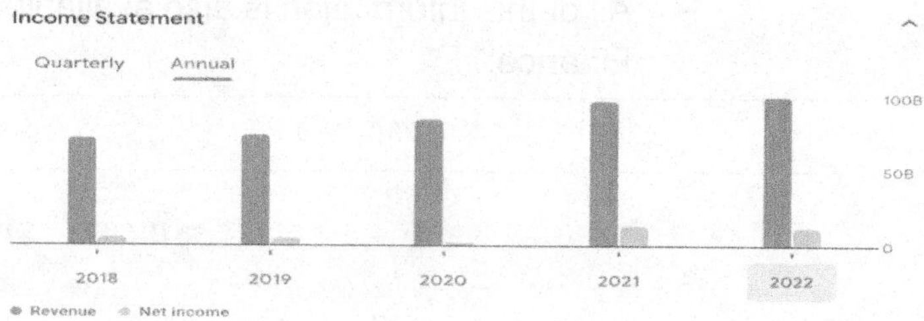

The blue bar is the revenue and the orange bar is the profits. As you can see, UPS is steadily growing while maintaining a healthy profit margin. That's one of the criteria for a value stock.

- I like to see a **P/E Ratio of less than 50**. The average P/E Ratio of S&P 500 stocks is between 22 - 26. I'm ok trading stocks that are a little bit higher than the average but I don't want to go too crazy. And when a stock has a P/E ratio of 100 or more, then it's usually a "growth stock," and I don't like trading those.

- Another criteria is the "market cap." I only trade stocks that have a **market cap of 2B or more.** This way, I'm avoiding penny stocks or smaller companies whose stock price can easily be manipulated.

- My final criteria for selecting the best stocks to trade are "Dividends." I prefer stocks that are **paying a dividend** because this means that they are financially stable and give back some of their profits to their shareholders, which is us. On the other hand, "growth stocks" usually keep all of their profits and reinvest it in their very aggressive growth goals.
-
- All of this information is also available on Google Finance:

PREVIOUS CLOSE	$159.27
DAY RANGE	$156.50 - $158.75
YEAR RANGE	$133.68 - $197.80
MARKET CAP	133.78B USD
AVG VOLUME	3.60M
P/E RATIO	15.89
DIVIDEND YIELD	4.13%
PRIMARY EXCHANGE	NYSE

2. **Other Criteria**
3. There are a few other criteria that I like to apply:

- **Only choose stocks with Weekly Options**. This way, I can collect "weekly paychecks" when trading options.

- **Earnings must be after the expiration date of the option** because the reaction to earnings can be unpredictable. And I don't want to gamble on whether a company beats earnings or misses earnings. So I just skip companies that are reporting earnings this week or next.

- **No leveraged ETFs.** I don't like to trade leveraged ETFs like TQQQ or SQQQ since they usually move two to three times as much as the underlying index or commodity.

- **No Biotech Stocks.** These are tricky because when a company announces that they "found a cure for Alzheimers," their stock might explode. And when clinical trials show that it's not as effective as they thought, their stock price could drop 30% - 80%. That's not for me.

- **No Chinese stocks, e.g. BABA, PDD.** Only in China can the CEO of a company disappear for weeks and nobody knows what happened to them. And do you remember 2021, when the Chinese government announced that all education companies should be non-profit companies? That's when super solid stocks like TAL tumbled from $90 to $5 in a matter of weeks, just because the Chinese government decided that they are no longer allowed to make profits. CRAZY!

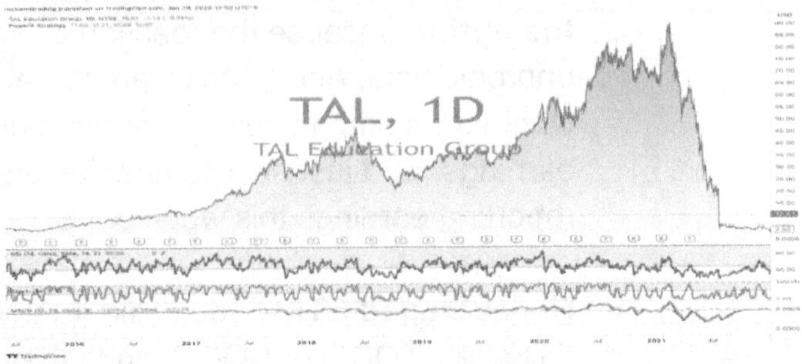

- Speaking of crazy… Here's another criteria: **No "Crazy Stocks,"** e.g. Meme Stocks that had a gain of more than 100% in a matter of a few weeks. I'm sure you remember Gamestop, AMC Theaters, and Bed Bath and Beyond?
  These companies went crazy during the "Meme Mania" in 2021 and many of these are now bankrupt.

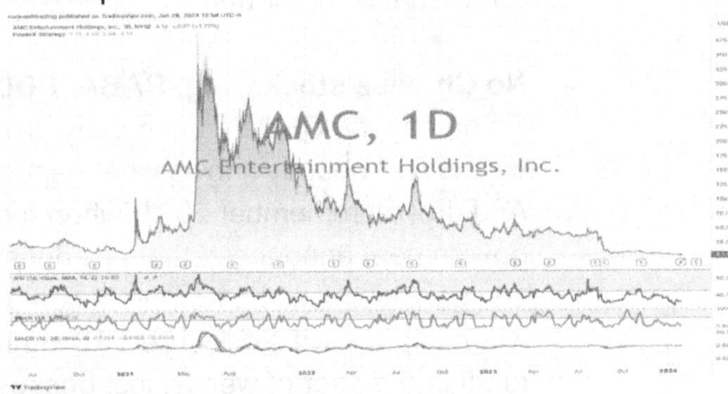

As you can see, a trading plan doesn't have to be super complicated. Without the explanations that I added for you, this part of the trading plan is less than one page.

And you might also notice that I used mainly fundamentals like the P/E ratio, profitability, and dividends, etc.

I don't use any technical indicators other than the "Lowest Low Indicator" which defines the lowest closing price of the past eight weeks.

But if it's important to you, you can incorporate technical indicators, e.g.

— Must be above 200-day moving average.
— Average daily volume above 500,000
— Relative Strength Index (RSI) above 50.

Here's another tip:
Don't think that you need to get it right the first time!

Just start jotting down some criteria and then place the next trades.

After each trade, check if it was according to your plan or if you used another criteria that you haven't defined yet. If so, just add it.

Your trading plan is a living document and not a "one and done" exercise.

Just start with a draft and keep refining it.
Within a few weeks, it will be 95% complete or more!

Action Step 2: Precision Entry and Exit Strategies for Profit Optimization

The next section in your trading plan are your exact entry and exit rules.

In the previous step we already identified value stocks that we don't mind owning.

Since we are trading the Wheel Strategy, the next step is selling put options.

So the question is: WHEN do we trade the option?
What criteria must be true to push the button and execute the trade?

Here are my rules:

Example: My Entry Rules

1. **Selling Puts**
    - **Get at least 30% annualized ROI.**

      Ok, I think I need to explain what this means. When trading options, you can drive yourself crazy with delta, gamma, theta and a bunch of complicated stuff.

      I like to keep it easy: I just identify a strike price at which I don't mind buying the stock, and then I'm looking at how much premium I can get.

      The premium for options varies based on the volatility of the stock as well as the expiration date and the price of the stock… and that's getting too complicated for me.

      So I was looking for an easy way to determine whether I'm getting paid well to sell the option or not.

For me, the most important metric is "how much money will I make per day?"

And that's why I look at the annualized ROI. Here's how to calculate it:

Let's say we identified Occidental Petroleum (OXY) as a stock that we don't mind owning. And looking at the chart, OXY has been trading between $56 and $68 for the past 2 years:

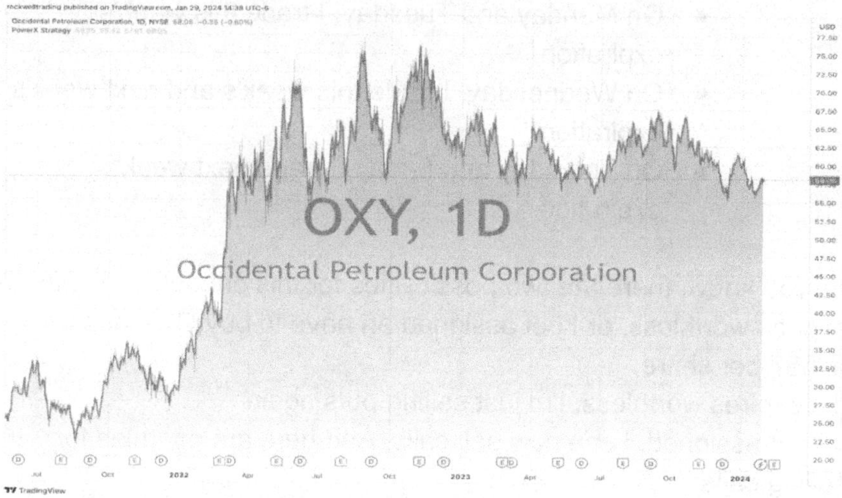

So I wouldn't mind buying OXY at $57. That's why I would sell a Put Option with a strike price of 57.

On Monday, January 19th, I could get $38 for the 57 Put Option expiring on Friday, in only 5 days.

So I would get 38 / 5 = 7.60 per day. And as you know, this strategy can be repeated over and over and over, so I could do this (almost) every day.

That's why I annualize the return: $7.60 * 360 days would give me $2,736 per year. However, if I need to buy OXY for $57, I would have to invest $5,700 since options are trading in "100 packs".

So I can make $2,736 based on the $5,700, i.e. 2,736 / 5,700 = 48% annualized.

This trade meets my criteria, so I took it.

Here are my criteria for choosing the right expiration. As you can see, I like to keep it simple:

- On Monday and Tuesday, I trade this week's expiration.
- On Wednesday, I trade this week's and next week's expiration.
- On Thursday and Friday, I trade next week's expiration.

As you know, there are two possibilities for this put option: It either expires worthless, or I get assigned an have to buy OXY at a price of $57 per share.
If it expires worthless, I'm just selling puts again.
If I get assigned, I can now sell calls. And here are my rules for selling calls:

2. **Selling Calls**

- Sell at the assigned price or above but make sure you get at least 30% annualized.
- Sell Calls AT the assigned price if I can get between 30 - 150% annualized ROI.
- Sell Calls ABOVE the assigned price when the annualized ROI at the assigned price is more than 150%.

Pretty simple, right?
Now let's talk about exits:

Example: My Exit Rules

When trading the Wheel Strategy, you could just wait until expiration day and then either let your options expire or get assigned.

However, when you buy back puts and calls strategically, you can enhance your trading profits.

Here are my very simply rules for closing both put and calls:

Closing Puts and Calls

- Close at 80% of max profits if possible within 24 hours or 1 trading day.
- Example: If I sold put options for $1.50 on Monday, and I can buy them back on Tuesday for 80% of the max profits, i.e. $0.30, I will do this. Because when the markets move quickly in your favor, they tell you: "Here's some fast money for you. Do you want it?"
- And you better say "Heck yes!" and take it, because markets can turn around on a dime and the profits can disappear quickly. So I take them while they are there.
- If I can't buy the options back at 90% of max profits after 1 day, then I will try to…
- Close at 90% of max profits until the day before expiration.
- And if I can't close them at 80% of max profits, then I will…

- Close on expiration day only if I need the buying power or don't want to get assigned.
- Otherwise, I just let them expire worthless or get assigned.

As you can see, it's not very complicated.
And that's my point: You can keep it easy.

Don't aim for perfection!

Just get something on paper and refine it as you go.
And Chapter 12: Step 6: Rapid Performance Analyzer will help you with that.

We will get to that shortly.

But for now, let's move on to the final step:

Action Step 3: Smart Money Management and Diversification to Minimize Risk

Alright, we've talked about crafting rules for selecting trades and how to enter and exit them. Now it's time to chat about the final piece of the trading plan puzzle: money and risk management.
Important: This has nothing to do with stop losses!
A stop loss is an EXIT criteria and should have been defined in the previous section.

I know it may seem boring but proper capital allocation and risk control is crucial for trading success!

When I was starting out, I stumbled into this painful trap ... I'd find a promising trade and put way too much money at risk without thinking it through.

Of course, Murphy's Law kicked in and I'd take a beating on those oversized positions.

Then I would get nervous and use very small positions on my next trades. Of course, they were winners!

I fell for the "Gambler's Fallacy."

The Ralph Vince Experiment

Ralph Vince is a well-respected and well-known financial investor and educator. He's published a number of books on trading and the trading industry, and he also performed a very famous experiment known as the "Ralph Vince Experiment."

Mr. Vince took 40 Ph.D.s and set them up to trade with a computer game.

Now, these 40 people all had doctorates but Mr. Vince made sure that none of their doctorates involved any sort of background in statistics or trading.

In the game, each of them were given $1,000 and 100 trades with a 60% winning percentage.

When they won, they won the amount of money they risked.
When they lost, they lost the amount of money they risked. Simple.

With a 60% winning percentage, they would have made 60 * 100 = $6,000.
And they would have lost 40 * 100 = $4,000
So after 100 trades, they would have made $2,000.

As you can see, ALL of them had a profitable trading strategy because they could have just bet $10 on each trade.

So, after all 40 had completed their 100 trades, how many do you think made money?

TWO!

Only 2 doctorates out of 40 were able to make money.
The other 38 lost money even though they had a winning trading strategy!

Why?

Poor Money Management and "Gambler's Fallacy."

Source: CSI News Journal, March 1992

As you can see, risk and money management is critical for your success.For me, the key is allocating my trading capital across multiple positions in a strategic way.
This way, I'm diversified and don't throw massive chunks of money on a single trade.

Proper position sizing balances risk and reward. Take on enough risk to generate solid returns but not so much it cripples you if things go south.
You also want to diversify across multiple uncorrelated trades. Don't put all your eggs in one basket. If one position takes a hit, others can balance it out.

Bottom line … ignoring money management is like building a fortress with sand instead of mortar.

Example: My Risk And Money Management

Here are my simple rules:

- Stocks must have a correlation of 0.65 or lower with other stocks / ETFs in the portfolio.

  This ensures that I'm not overexposed in one sector.

  I use the "Asset Correlation Tool" within my software PowerX Optimizer, but there are also free tools available that you can use. Just do a simple Google Search.

The other rules are:

- Distribute the buying power over 5 positions.

- Adjust the number of contracts to trade so that you would use 1/5 of the buying power if you had to buy the stock.
- Example: When trading a $500,000 account, I would allocate $100,000 in buying power to each position. So if I wanted to sell the 57 Put for OXY options, I would sell 100,000 / 5700 = 18 options contracts.

That's it.
Simple and easy.

Again. Don't overcomplicate it.
Keep it simple and stupid (KISS).
You can always refine it later.

Conclusion

Alright. We've made serious headway here. You now have the complete blueprint for your daily trading plan, from stock selection rules to precision entry and exit tactics, as well as money management.

With these detailed marching orders in hand, you can construct your financial fortress brick- by-brick, with confidence and discipline. No more just grabbing materials and winging it!

We've evolved from an abstract vision of the fortress we want to build, to outlining precisely HOW to build it through proven trading strategies.

And now in this chapter, we defined the DAY-TO-DAY PROCESS for actively assembling our wealth fortress.

Think of this trading plan as the step-by-step instructions that strengthen the fortress walls. They provide calculated guidance to maximize profits in all market conditions.

With the foundation set and materials secured, it's finally time to break ground on our wealth creation goals.

In the next chapter, we'll begin executing trades armed with our bulletproof trading plan — no more hesitation or fear of unknowns.

You have the blueprint, you have the strategies, and now you have the process. All the pieces are in place for trading mastery.

It's time to put our trading plan into consistent, profitable action.

Chapter 11: Step 5: Unshakeable Tech-Powered Trader

Let me tell you a story ...

Back in 1989 when I first started trading, real-time stock quotes didn't even exist! I had to rely on share prices from the daily newspaper and manually plot point-and-figure charts by hand.

Yes, that was before the internet!

By the way, if you want to blow your kids (or grandkids) mind, just tell them that you are older than the internet and take a picture of their facial expressions!

Fortunately, technology advanced quickly. By 1997, I used computers and "SuperCharts," which was later bought by TradeStation, if I remember correctly.

The change was night and day. Tasks that took hours could now be completed in seconds with just a few mouse clicks.

As the old saying goes: *The farmer with the tractor will always outperform the farmer with the plow, no matter how long and hard the farmer with the plow works.*

That's the power of technology. With the right tools, you can do the same task twenty times quicker!

Manually plotting trades from quotes in the newspaper felt like plowing fields by hand versus having powerful machines do the heavy lifting.

Now think back to our financial fortress metaphor. Would you rather construct a massive castle brick-by-brick by hand using basic tools? Or have a bunch of machines and sophisticated tools building your fortress 20 times quicker?

The difference is massive. Technology provides the competitive edge.

Using the right trading tools helps you overcome common struggles.

- **Don't worry about lacking skills and expertise:** As you will see in this chapter, the right tools can give you the data you need to make confident trading decisions.

- **Too busy and don't have time to analyze markets?** I'm using a tool that allows me to focus on the markets for only 15 minutes per day and some days I'm not even looking at charts at all!
- **Fear of missing opportunities (FOMO)?** The right tools can give you a shortlist of three to five of the best trading opportunities so that you don't have to sift through thousands of stocks and potentially miss out on great trades!

With sophisticated data analysis, you can identify high-probability trades more easily.

In short, technology transforms trading from a tedious manual task to an efficient wealth-building machine.

Let's explore how to unlock these benefits for your own trading.

With the proper technology toolkit, you will have the confidence and capacity to trade at the highest level.

The time of building sandcastles with basic tools is over. Let's upgrade to heavy machinery and start building your fortress!

Action Step 1: Identify High-Potential Trades Using Data Analysis

In the last chapter, we discussed the importance of having clear criteria for selecting the stocks you want to trade.

Over the years, I tried using many generic scanners offered by brokers or trading services. But none of them allowed me to define the specific filters I needed.

I'd spend hours trying to configure these tools or learning a programming language like ThinkScript from TD AmeriTrade or PineScript from TradingView or even Python to program a scanner in Interactive Brokers. It was incredibly tedious and inefficient.

Many times, I missed great setups simply because I lacked the right screening tools.

So several years back, I finally decided to take matters into my own hands and build a custom software solution .... the **PowerX Optimizer.** Of course, this is only one of many solutions but since I'm using it daily, I will use it as an example in this chapter.

With PowerX Optimizer, I can establish the exact filters, analytics, and visualizations I want to see based on my defined trading criteria.

Of course, you don't need to build your own software from scratch. The key is simply finding a scanner aligned to your personal needs.

However, you've heard the saying, *"If all you have is a hammer, everything looks like a nail."*

Well, you can't build an entire fortress using just a hammer alone. You need specialized tools for each task.

Make sure you choose scanning software that serves YOU, not the other way around. It should automate finding prospects based on your criteria, not limited by predefined filters.

Let me show you how I use PowerX Optimizer to quickly identify stocks matching my guidelines from Chapter 10: Step 4: Bulletproof 100k Trading Plan

If you remember, here are the criteria that I'm looking for:

- **P/E Ratio** of less than 50.
- **Market Cap** of 5B or more.
- **Paying a dividend is preferred**.

And here's what this looks like in the PowerX Optimizer software.

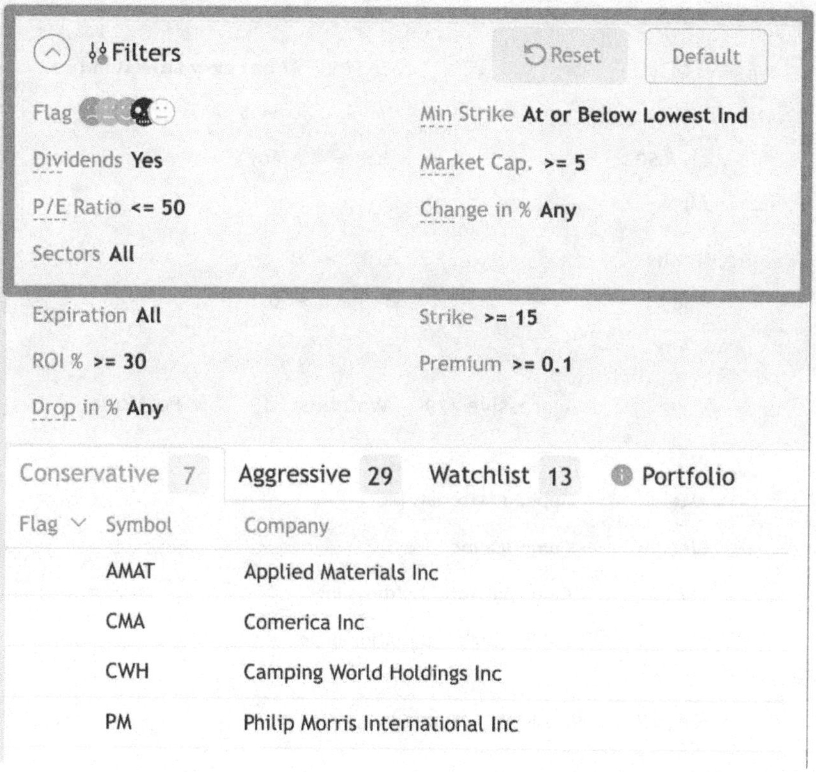

Plus, the following criteria from my trading plan are already built in:

- Only choose stocks with Weekly Options.
- Earnings must be after the expiration date of the option.

- If you remember, I also want to see that the companies have been **profitable over the past five years**.

So once a symbol appears in the scanner, I simply click on it and get all the information I need to make a decision:

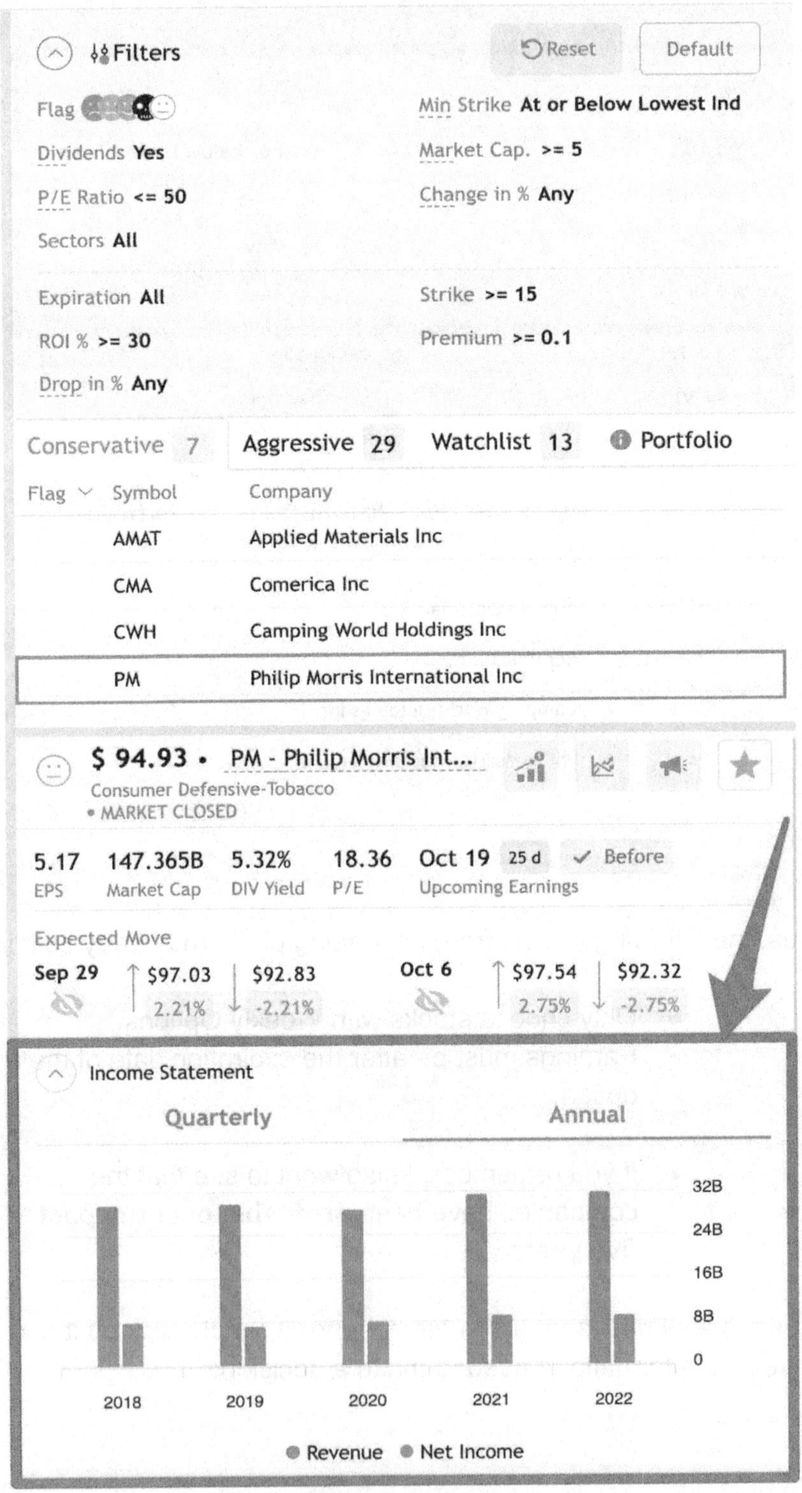
Filters
Reset
Default
Flag
Min Strike At or Below Lowest Ind
Dividends Yes
Market Cap. >= 5
P/E Ratio <= 50
Change in % Any
Sectors All
Expiration All
Strike >= 15
ROI % >= 30
Premium >= 0.1
Drop in % Any
Conservative 7
Aggressive 29
Watchlist 13
Portfolio
Flag
Symbol
Company
AMAT
Applied Materials Inc
CMA
Comerica Inc
CWH
Camping World Holdings Inc
PM
Philip Morris International Inc
$ 94.93 • PM - Philip Morris Int...
Consumer Defensive-Tobacco
• MARKET CLOSED
5.17
EPS
147.365B
Market Cap
5.32%
DIV Yield
18.36
P/E
Oct 19
25 d
Before
Upcoming Earnings
Expected Move
Sep 29
$97.03
2.21%
$92.83
-2.21%
Oct 6
$97.54
2.75%
$92.32
-2.75%
Income Statement
Quarterly
Annual
32B
24B
16B
8B
0
2018
2019
2020
2021
2022
Revenue
Net Income

As you can see, within seconds I can screen the entire market for companies fitting my specific parameters. Key info is instantly visible.

I can also tag stocks with custom labels like "Yes" (green emoji), "Maybe" (orange emoji), "No" (red emoji), or “Never” (black skull emoji) to easily categorize them for later review. Very handy!

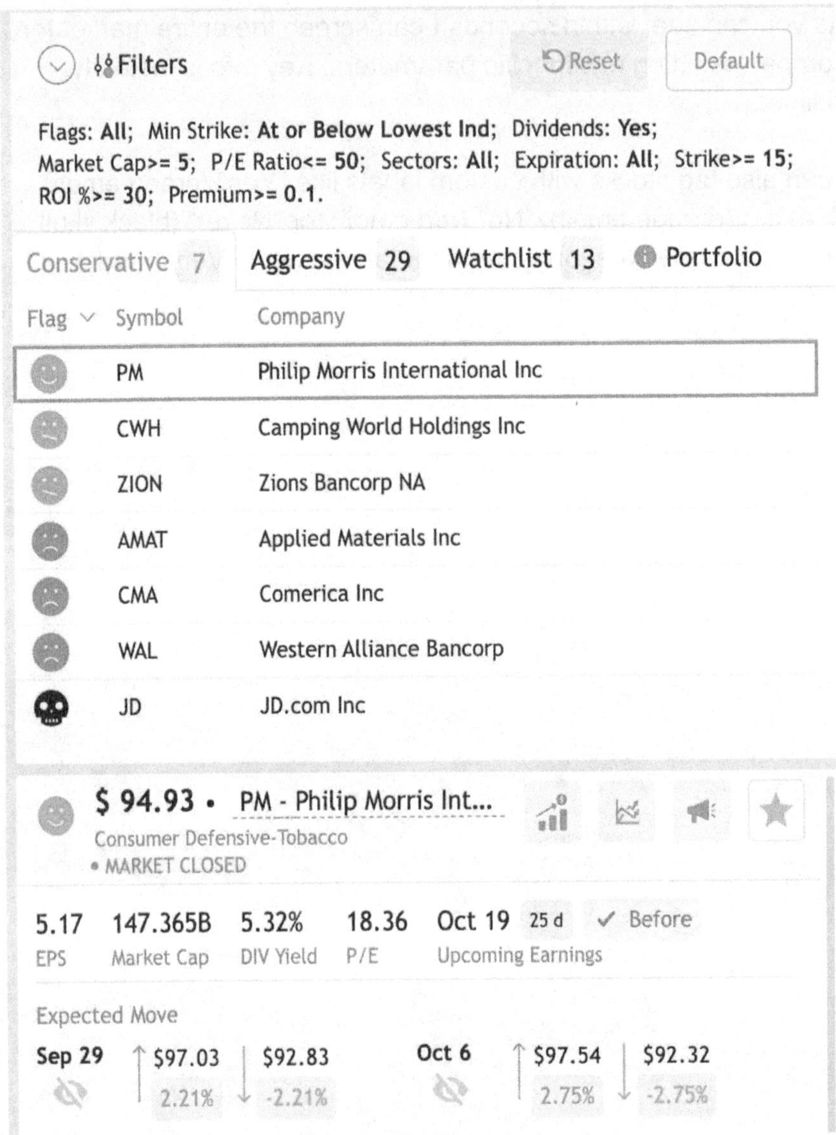

The tool does the heavy lifting so I can zero in on the best opportunities suited for my trading strategy. No more wasting hours sifting through thousands of irrelevant stocks.

Now I have a personalized shortlist of the most promising candidates aligned with my proven strategy. Extremely powerful!

And I can easily adjust the filters to scan for trades based on current market conditions and my evolving criteria. Having that flexibility is invaluable.

Okay, now you know how to find the best trades according to your criteria. The next step is learning to evaluate them and make informed decisions.

Action Step 2: Master Key Metrics for Informed Decisions

When it comes to trading, there are no absolute certainties or guarantees.

Many have tried to predict the market … and failed.

However, we can use data and key metrics to help tip the odds in our favor. Ultimately, it's all about making a decision with as much certainty as possible, knowing that we can never be 100% certain.

The difficulty lies in finding the right balance and getting enough data to make confident choices without falling victim to "analysis paralysis" from information overload.

I remember when I first started using advanced charting software back in 1996. I was fascinated by the ability to overlay endless technical indicators on the price charts. MACD, Bollinger Bands, RSI, Fibonacci Retracements — you name it, I plotted it!

Pretty soon my charts were cluttered with so many oscillating lines and shaded areas you could barely even see the underlying price action!.

Even worse ... often half the indicators were screaming "buy!" while the other half shouted "sell!" Talk about confusion.

So through trial and error, I learned there's a fine line between having enough useful metrics and going overboard into overcomplicated, decision-paralyzing analysis.

The key is determining the essential Key Performance Indicators (KPIs) that help you **intelligently** evaluate opportunities while ignoring the rest of the noise.

Of course, these KPIs can be different based on the trading strategy you trade.

Let me explain the KPIs that I like to look at when trading the *Wheel Strategy*:

As I mentioned in the previous chapter, for me, the most important metric is the **"Annualized Return on Investment."**

And here's how to calculate it:

1. We take the premium per option and multiply it by 100. In the example below, that would be 0.45 X 100 = $45.
2. Now we divide this amount by the remaining days to expiration (DTE). In our example, that's $45 ÷ 5 days = $9.
3. This gives us the **Premium Per Day**, so in this example, we would make $9 per day.
4. Now we take the Premium Per Day and multiply it by 360 days. In our example, that's $9 X 360 = $3,240. This number tells us how much we would make per year if we

could repeat this trade over and over. And of course, THAT is what we are doing: Generating "SRC Profits."

5. Finally, we take this number and divide it by the buying power that is required for trading one cash secured put. This is calculated by taking the strike price and multiplying it by 100. In our example: 91 × 100 = $9,100.
6. So the annual ROI would be 3,240 ÷ 9,100 = 36%.

Here's the formula in a nutshell:

$$\frac{(\text{Premium per Option } 100) \,/\, \text{DTE} \times 360}{\text{Strike Price} \times 100} = \text{Annualized ROI}$$

The good news is that I don't need to do this calculation for every option. The PowerX Optimizer does it for me.
Here's what it looks like:

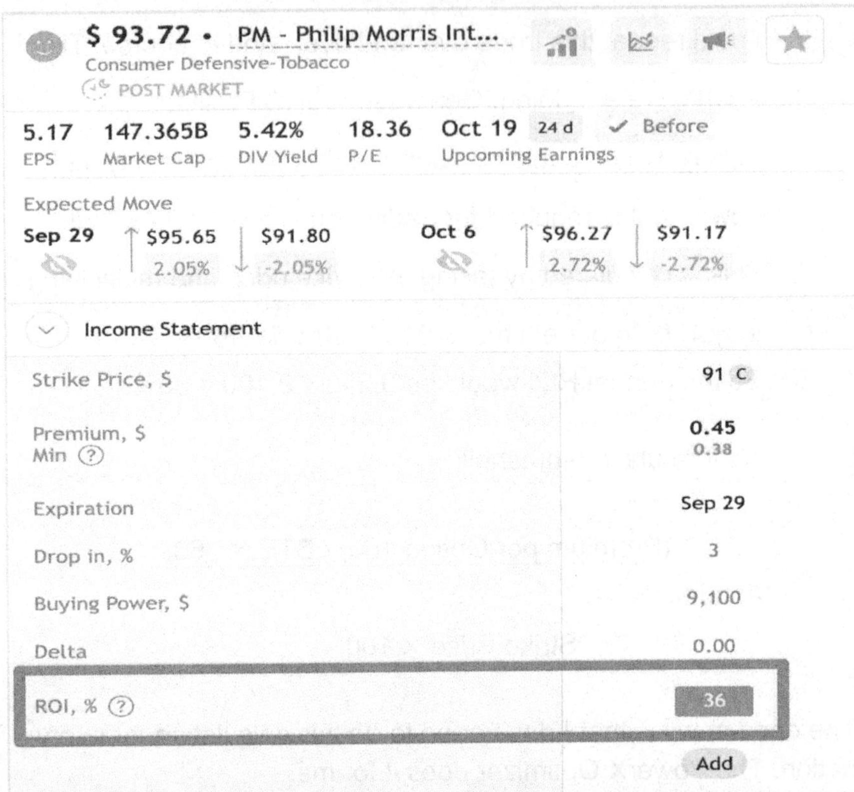

And as you know from the previous chapter, I only consider selling put and call options if I can get at least 30% annualized ROI.

So THIS option meets my criteria.

Now I click on “ADD” to add it to the calculator.

The calculator now gives me all the information I need to make a final decision:

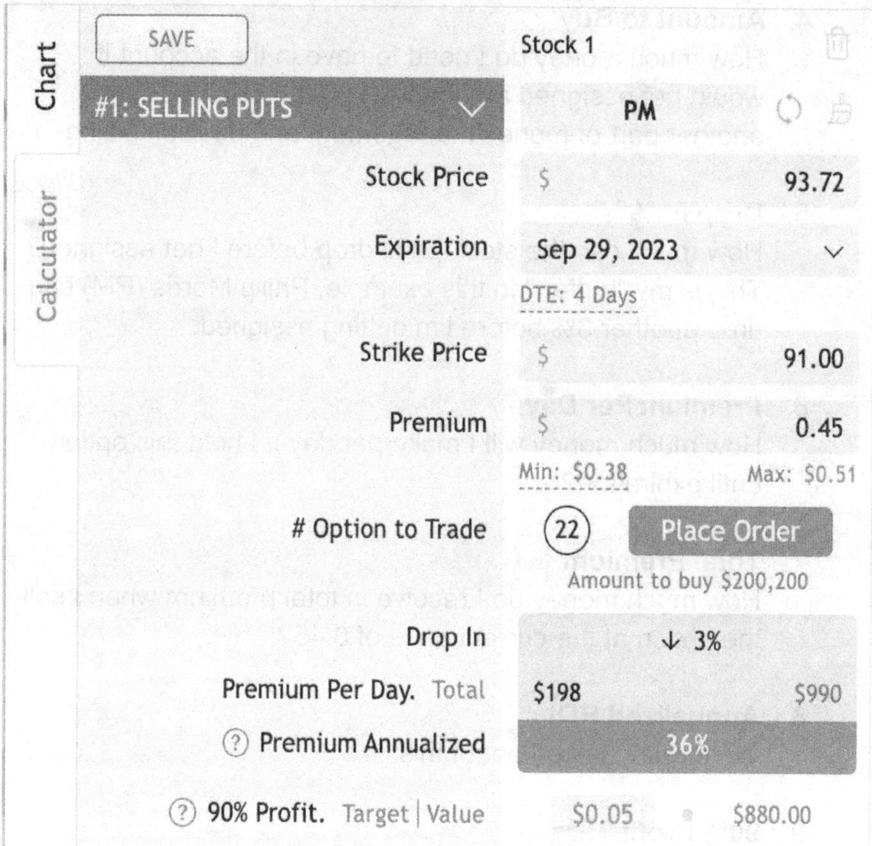

1. **Days To Expiration (DTE)**
   How many days are left before this option expires?

2. **Min Premium**
   That's the minimum premium I need to get 30% annualized ROI. In this example, that's 0.38.

3. **Options to Trade**
   How many options should I trade based on my money management approach? This is critical for position sizing, and as you have learned in the previous chapter, the wrong position sizing can lead to hefty losses.

4. **Amount to Buy**
   How much money do I need to have in the account if I would get assigned and had to buy the stock? That's another part of money management and position sizing.

5. **Drop in %**
   How much can the stock price drop before I get assigned? This is my "buffer." In this example, Philip Morris (PM) can drop another 3% before I'm getting assigned.

6. **Premium Per Day**
   How much money will I make per day if I hold this option until expiration?

7. **Total Premium**
   How much money do I receive in total premium when I sell the option at the current price of 0.45?

8. **Annualized ROI**
   We already talked about this.

9. **90% Profit Target**
   When should I buy back the option and how much money would I make if I close this option early? That's part of the trade management and as you saw in the previous chapter, it's part of my trading plan to close an option at 90% of max profits if I can do it before expiration day.

As you can see, it's only nine pieces of information but for me, these are the critical KPIs that I need to make a confident decision to pull the trigger.

You might be wondering:
Why this two-step approach?

Why do I need to add the option I want to trade to the calculator to see all this additional information?
Why don't I display everything on the *main screen*?

Well, remember when we talked about "analysis paralysis" in the beginning of this section? And how we need to walk a fine line between *enough information* and *too much information*?

That's the reason why I like the option to "dig deeper."
I get the most important information that I need on my main screen and then I can just push a button to dig deeper if I choose to.

For me, this is the best way to keep things simple and avoid "analysis paralysis."
Making sense?

The important thing is that you define the KPIs that YOU need before making a **confident** decision to take a trade. And that's where the "tech-powered trader" has a huge advantage!

Can you imagine calculating all of these numbers manually?
By the time you calculate everything, the trade is already gone.

Now that you have enough data to make a confident decision, let's talk about the next step:

Pulling the trigger!

Action Step 3: Confidently Execute Trades Even in Volatile Markets

This is probably the most challenging thing to do, especially as a beginner.

You did all the homework. ✓

You analyzed the data. ✓

You are ready to pull the trigger. ✓

... and doubt is creeping into your mind.

There's the little voice that says:

What if this trade will be a loser?
Is this really a good trade?
Maybe I overlooked something?
Will the stock fall a little bit further so that I can enter at a better price?
Or maybe I should run through the scanner just one more time to see if there's a better trade?

And just like that, all your confidence is gone and you are second-guessing yourself.

So what's the solution?

Here are three tips:

Tip 1: Make It as Easy as Possible to Place the Order

As you know from Chapter 9: Step 3: Ultimate Broker Guide, you need to specify at least 5 things when placing an order. This forces you to pause for a minute and enter all the necessary information.

While doing this, you allow doubt to creep in. As an example, when you enter the price of 0.45, your mind will wonder if THIS is the best price. And you might find yourself going back to the charts and hoping for a better price.

Right here and then, you have already paused for too long. You gave your brain a chance to seed doubt and second-guess yourself.

This is one of the reasons why I have the functionality in PowerX Optimizer to place a trade with two clicks:

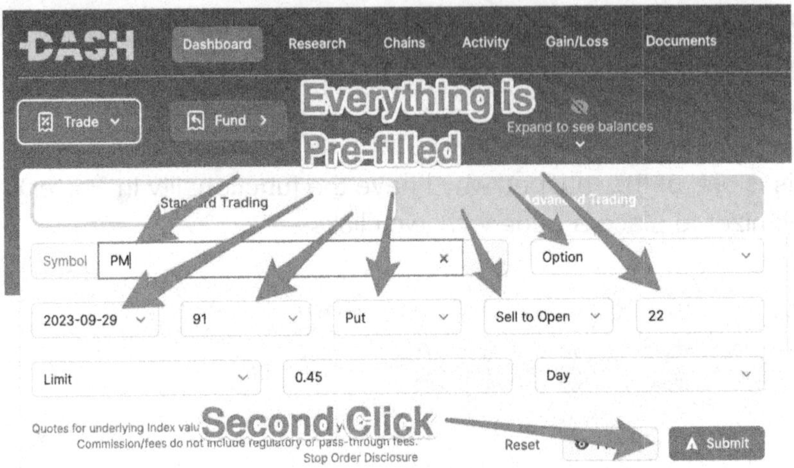

I linked my Tradier brokerage account and when I clicked on "PLACE TRADE," everything was pre-filled in my brokerage account and I simply clicked SUBMIT.
I don't give my brain time to second-guess myself.

Remember the Netflix Show, *Cobra Kai*?

The mantra of the Cobra Kai dojo was, **"Strike First, Strike Hard, No Mercy!"**

And that's how you should feel about your trades!
Place them quickly and confidently and remove as much friction as possible.

Here's another tip:

Tip 2: Get Used to Being Wrong

Here's a harsh truth:

There are only two ways to enter and exit a trade:

1. It's either too early.
2. Or it's too late.

Every now and then you might time it perfectly but that's rather luck.
No one can pick bottoms and tops consistently.

Think about it:
Was there somebody who bought a stock at its low today? Of course!
Was there somebody who sold that stock at its high today? Of course!
Was it the same person? Of course … NOT!

So get used to the fact that a few minutes later you would have gotten a better price.

The markets will taunt you by moving the price against you right after you enter. But don't second guess yourself.
Stick to the plan.

And once you are in a trade, follow THIS tip:

Tip 3: Don't Look back!

After you receive your fill, stop staring at the stock or option that you traded!

As you have just learned, most probably you entered too early … or too late.
So what happens if you keep watching the markets and see that you could have gotten a better price?

You're getting frustrated.
Maybe angry.

Or depressed.

Either way … whatever feeling you experience, it's not a good one.
No *normal* human being would say, "I'm so happy that I didn't get a better price."

So what good does it do if you get upset?

The trade is placed.
You got your fill.
That's done.

You can't change it.

And the worst thing you can do is change your plan because you didn't get the best price of the day.

So STOP IT!
Stop hypnotizing the markets!

Get used to being wrong and after you receive your fill, walk away from the computer.

Conclusion

Okay, we covered a lot of ground here.

Let's do a quick recap of the key lessons:

First, you learned how to use powerful trading technology to screen for high-probability setups tailored to your personal strategy and criteria. No more wasting precious time on thousands of irrelevant stocks or staring at the markets for hours!

Next, we discussed the importance of identifying your unique Key Performance Indicators for making informed, data-driven decisions. Remember, it's a balance between "enough information" and "too much information." Find that sweet spot!

Finally, we talked about the necessity of confident, decisive execution once you've done the upfront work. As they say at Cobra Kai, "Strike first, strike hard, no mercy!"

Don't let your mind play games with you.

When you leverage the right tech tools, focus on the metrics that matter and cultivate an unwavering mindset, you become an UNSHAKEABLE TRADER!
So, in this chapter, you acquired the heavy machinery needed to construct your financial fortress rapidly and efficiently. No more playing around with basic manual tools!

The time and energy you can save by using the right tools can now be invested into fortifying and expanding your structure even more.

Now here's what's next:

In the previous chapters, we laid the foundations and built the walls of our financial fortress brick-by-brick.

But a fortress isn't complete without assessing structural integrity from time to time and making adjustments if needed.

So in the next chapter, I'll show you how to use data-driven analytics to analyze the performance of your trading and make strategic adjustments.

Remember, excellence is not a destination but a never-ending journey of refinement.

Let's keep strengthening your skills and building on your success!

Chapter 12: Step 6: Rapid Performance Analyzer

This step will help you improve your trading performance through data-driven insights without feeling overwhelmed by data.

Think about this step as conducting routine maintenance and inspections on your financial fortress while you are building it. After all, you have the overall blueprint, you know what you want to build, and you need to evaluate your progress. Because you want to make sure that the walls are straight and strong so that your fortress will last forever, right?

And In order to identify and address any structural weaknesses, you need to rely on hard facts and metrics instead of hunches.

Let me tell you an important story about an "aha moment" I had regarding trade logging and performance analysis early in my trading career.

When I first started out, broker account statements confused and frustrated me to no end. And to be honest, they still do.

For most people, the easiest number to find is the “net liquidation value” of your account.

And that’s what I did in the beginning:

Every month, I only looked at the “net liquidation value.”

And for a while, I thought plotting my net liquidation value on a graph was useful.

But then I realized … This metric tells me nothing about my actual trading performance!

Think about it this way:

I believe that trading is a business and you should treat it as such.

And as you know when running a business, you have a Profit and Loss Statement and a Balance Sheet.

On your balance sheet, you list all of your business assets and liabilities that help you make a profit or a loss in the business.

And of course, these assets have a value and when you liquidate your assets you will get some money.

Back to trading:
The net liquidation value is the amount that you would get if you sold all of your assets right now.

But it would be pretty short sighted if you only looked at the value of your assets. Because if you sold all your assets, then you wouldn't have a business anymore.

So when you're running your business you need to look at your profit and loss statement. This P&L statement tells you whether you are profitable or not.

And it shows you exactly HOW you're making money:

- What products are profitable?
- What ads are leading to customers?
- Is your customer service department a profit center or costing you money?

Imagine running a business but not knowing which products are profitable and which are losing you money. Impossible to optimize.

In the beginning of my trading career, I fell for the “net liquidation value” illusion and thought that THIS was the most important metric.

But it was like looking at just the balance sheet of a business instead of also having the profit and loss statement. I didn't have the full picture.

The "aha moment" was realizing that to improve as a trader, I needed visibility into the profitability of specific trades and strategies. Actual P&L data, not vague aggregates like account value.

So I began diligently logging each trade with metrics like entry price, exit price, profit/loss, rationale, and notes. This finally gave me the trading insights I desperately needed.

With my detailed trade logs, I gained tremendous clarity. I could attribute performance to particular trades and make connections. This understanding enabled me to refine my trading plan based on real insights rather than guesses.

In this chapter, we will discuss the three steps to unlocking the gold in your trading:

1. Logging trades efficiently to extract the numbers you truly need.

2. Evaluating performance using key metrics to quantify your strengths and weaknesses.

3. Making strategic adjustments based on data-driven insights rather than emotions.

With the right analytics approach, you can conduct routine maintenance on your financial fortress and address vulnerabilities before they become structural risks. But you need actual data, not assumptions.

Let's begin optimizing your trading with proven performance tracking techniques!

Action Step 1: Log and Organize Trades Efficiently

Yes, I get it: Trading is exciting and logging trades is boring!

I know, I know, I don't like to do it either BUT I have found an easy and efficient way to do it.

So why is diligent trade logging so essential? Because it provides the raw data you need for meaningful performance analysis.

Garbage in, garbage out — if your trade history is disorganized or incomplete, you can't extract useful insights. So comprehensive logging is step one.

Let's start with the end in mind. What specific metrics would you like to evaluate?

Here's a snapshot of my trading log dashboard:

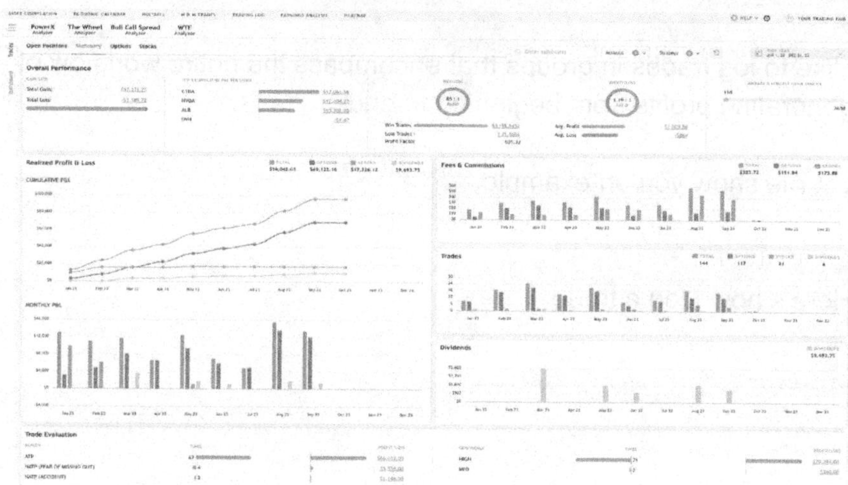

And yes, this might be difficult to read. But don't worry about it just yet. We will take a closer look at it in the next Action Step and I'll explain everything in detail.

The point is: If you take a few minutes to log your trades, you get very meaningful statistics — much better than the stuff your broker gives you.

Because your broker, and many "spreadsheet traders," are missing a key concept:

The key is organizing trades into logical "groups" that tell a story. This is especially important for multi-leg strategies like The Wheel or strategies like vertical spreads, iron condors, etc.

Again: think about your trading like a business. When you first purchase materials to manufacture a product, you're temporarily in a hole.

But ultimately the goal is to sell the final product for a profit. So you want to track the overall profitability of the production life cycle from start to finish.

I like to log trades in groups that encompass the entire workflow of generating profits from beginning to end.

Let me show you an example.

Here's how I log a trade:

ALB	AUG 3, 23 - SEP 1, 23	Tradier $2	The Wheel					
COST BASIS	BREAK EVEN	SHARES	CONTRACTS	FEES & COMM	PREMIUM	DIVIDENDS	BUYING POWER	REALIZED P&L
-	-	0	- / -	$22.44	$6,050	0	0	$6,027.56

	TYPE	DATE	TIME	EXPIRATION	STRIKE,$	SHARES/CONTR	PRICE/PREM,$	INITIAL BP,$	FEES,$	COMM,$
1	Sell Put	Aug 3, 23		Aug 11, 23	192.50	10	1.65	192,500	0.40	
2	Buy stock	Aug 11, 23				1,000	192.50	192,500		9.00
	Expired contracts			Partially						
3	Sell Call	Aug 21, 23		Aug 25, 23	192.50	10	1.80		0.79	
4	Buy Call	Aug 24, 23		Aug 25, 23	192.50	10	1.48		0.75	
5	Sell Call	Aug 24, 23		Sep 1, 23	192.50	10	4.08		0.81	
	Buy stock									
6	Sell stock	Sep 1, 23				1,000	192.50		1.69	9.00

+ Add

As you can see, this is a "full circle Wheel":

1. On Aug 3, I sold Puts.
2. On Aug 11, I got assigned the stock.
3. On Aug 21, I sold calls against my existing position.
4. On Aug 24, I rolled the calls into the next week.
5. On Sep 1, I got called away.

And I nicely put it in its own group.

In the broker statement, these trades would have been lumped in with other trades that I took between August 3rd, when I sold the put, and September 1, when I got called away.

It would have been very difficult to figure out how this trade performed.

But here, I have all the information in one place:

— I know I collected $6,050 in premium.

— I know I paid $22.44 in commissions and fees.

— I know that this trade made $6,027.56 net after commissions and fees.

Further, while I'm in this trade, I can see all the important information that I need for managing the trade.

Here's the trade before it got called away.

Take a look at the header row:

ALB | AUG 3, 23 - AUG 24, 23 | Tradier $2 | The Wheel

COST BASIS	BREAK EVEN	SHARES	CONTRACTS	FEES & COMM	PREMIUM	DIVIDENDS	BUYING POWER	REALIZED P&L
$192.5	$190.54	1,000	-10 / -	$11.75	$6,050	0	$192,500	$1,958.25

	TYPE	DATE	TIME	EXPIRATION	STRIKE,$	SHARES/CONTR	PRICE/PREM,$	INITIAL BP,$	FEES,$	COMM,$
1	Sell Put	Aug 3, 23		Aug 11, 23	192.50	10	1.65	192,500	0.40	
2	Buy stock	Aug 11, 23				1,000	192.50	192,500		9.00
	Expired contracts			Partially						
3	Sell Call	Aug 21, 23		Aug 25, 23	192.50	10	1.80		0.79	
4	Buy Call	Aug 24, 23		Aug 25, 23	192.50	10	1.48		0.75	
5	Sell Call	Aug 24, 23		Sep 1, 23	192.50	10	4.08		0.81	

+ Add

- My cost basis is $192.50.
- My break even is $190.54.
- I have 1,000 shares.
- I have sold 10 option contracts against these shares.
- I paid $11.75 in fees and commissions so far
- I collected $6,050 in premium.
- I'm tying up $192,500 in buying power in this trade.
- The realized P&L so far is $1,958.25 since I still have an open trade.

As far as I know, there's not a single broker in the world who gives you this information in a broker statement.

This tells the full story of the wheel strategy playing out from start to finish. I can clearly see the profitability of the overall trade sequence.

The grouped logging technique tames messy broker statements into a clear, coherent narrative that reveals the true trading performance.

Is this making sense?

Here are two more important things I like to track:

Reason: Why did I enter the trade?

Was it according to my plan from Chapter 10: Step 4: Bulletproof 100k Trading Plan, i.e. "ATP"?

Or did I take the trade not following my plan (NATP)?

If I didn't follow my plan, what was my reason for not doing so?

As you will see in the next section, this will help me evaluate whether not taking trades according to my plan is helping or hurting me.

Of course, you need a trading plan in the first place to evaluate your trades against it. But we already discussed this in Chapter 10: Step 4: Bulletproof 100k Trading Plan.

Confidence Level: How confident was I when entering the trade?

I remember dealing with emotional struggles early in my trading career: Whenever I had "high confidence" in a trade and felt that THIS is the trade that will turn into a winning trade, it often was a loser.

And when I second-guessed myself and placed a trade with very low confidence, the trade would be a winning trade.

I was able to overcome these emotional struggles but I still like to keep an eye on it. It's very easy for a trader to become overconfident. And it's also easy to lose confidence after a few losing trades.

For these reasons, I like to monitor the outcome of trades based on my confidence level to avoid emotional trading.

Reason

- Undefined
- According To Plan (ATP)
- Not According To Plan (NATP)

	Example
Accident	I meant to buy 100 shares of TSLA but bought 10,000 instead.
Following others	I placed a trade because M&M traded it.
Technical	I placed a trade because the-50 day moving average crossed below the 200-day.
Fundamental	I bought shares because of the companies low debt and year over year sales growth.
News	I placed a trade because Netflix subscribers are expected to increase next year.
Earnings	I placed a trade because I thought Google was going to report good earnings.
Research	I placed a trade because I was reading online and discovered 10 top analysts recommended the stock.
Fear of Loss	I closed my Bull Call Spread because I was afraid it was going to turn into a loss.
Fear of Missing Out	I placed a trade because I saw GameStop was going crazy.
Speculative	I bought GDX because gold should rally with higher interest rates.
Other	

Confidence

- Undefined
- High
- Medium
- Low

Now that you know how to log and organize trades efficiently, let me show you what you can do with all this data!

You are going to love this!

Action Step 2: Evaluate Performance Using Key Performance Indicators (KPIs)

When I first started trading, I'll admit I had no idea what key metrics I should be analyzing to evaluate my performance and improve.

I knew that I needed more than just my trading account statements for all the reasons we already discussed.
But what are the important key performance indicators (KPIs) that I should look for? Where should I even begin making sense of it all?

In the early days, the only thing I knew to look at was my equity curve, which simply shows your account value over time. This gave me a vague idea of whether I was making or losing money in aggregate.

I also started tracking basic monthly P&L breakdowns. Again, better than nothing but still not very insightful.

The problem was I lacked an understanding of leading indicators that could help me drill down into the specifics behind what was working and what wasn't. I was playing a guessing game.

Over many years and hundreds of trades, I eventually refined my approach to performance analysis. I identified the most insightful Key Performance Indicators (KPIs) that expose strengths, weaknesses, and opportunities.

Metrics like Profit Factor, Percent Profitable, Average Win/Loss Ratio, and many more unlock the keys to elevating your trading. But it takes time to discover which metrics are most meaningful.

In this Action Step, we'll start with the basics like equity curve analysis and monthly P&L, things I wish I had known about on day one!

These will provide the foundation. As you gain experience, we'll build up to more advanced KPIs that connect the dots on performance.

Here's my promise:

By mastering the financial metrics that matter most, you'll gain more clarity in six months than I did in six years early on. These proven indicators will shortcut your learning curve!

Let's begin translating the raw data from your trade logs into clear, actionable insights.

I will show you everything on my current trading log dashboard and in the next section you will discover how to use this data to make strategic adjustments to your trading plan.

So let's dive in.

Here's my trading log dashboard from January 1st thru September 30th, 2023:

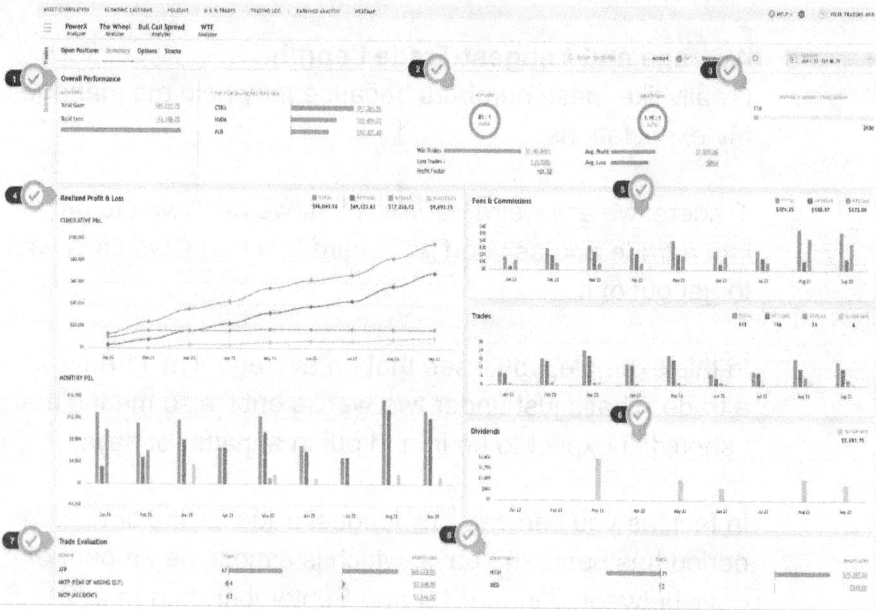

1. **Overall Performance**
   The Overall Performance shows me the Total Gain and the Total Loss. This is a high level overview to see the total amount of my profits and losses.

   Next to it, I see the three best trades during this time window. In this example, it's CTRA, NVDA and ALB.

2. **Basic Key Performance Indicators**
   In this section, I see my win/loss ratio, my profit factor, as well as my profit/loss ratio. For me, these numbers are "nice to know" but I don't make any decisions based on these numbers.

   For me, these are numbers like "YouTube viewers" and "likes per video." Everybody wants to know these numbers and you would look "dumb" if you didn't know these numbers but as you will see in a few moments, there are other numbers that are more meaningful for me.

3. **Average and Longest Trade Length**
I really like these numbers because they help me manage my expectations.

Traders, we are weird people. First, we can't wait to get into a trade and as soon as we are in a trade, we can't wait to get out of it.

In this example, you'll see that on average, I'm 11 days in a trade. That's just under two weeks but it also means that I shouldn't expect to be in and out in a matter of days.

In fact, as you can see, my longest trade for the time period has been 263 days, which is almost the amount of days between January 1st and September 30th (= 272 days).

This means that it's possible to be stuck in a trade for a while. And that's why it's important to know these things before you choose to trade this strategy. We discussed this in Chapter 8: Step 2: Winning Strategy Selector.

4. **Realized Profit And Loss**
This is a visual representation of the realized profit and loss, both cumulative and by month. This gives you a very good visual of how your trading business is doing.

As discussed earlier: This is NOT your "equity curve" since the equity curve is based on your net liquidation value, i.e. the assets of your business.

And I have never seen a business person plotting the value of their business on a monthly basis.

Or, if you prefer a real estate example, it's like plotting your house value every month instead of looking at the rental income.

Only in the trading world, you will find people who are obsessed with the "equity curve" and nothing else. As I said before ... traders are weird people.

Anyhow, let's move on to the next section:

5. **Fees and Commissions and Number of Trades**
I like to see how much I pay in commissions and fees per month

And I like to know how many trades I took since often there's correlation between the number of trades and realized profit.

In my example, I took 143 trades in nine months. That's approximately 16 trades on average per month.

As you can see, in June, I only took eight trades, which is way below my average. As a result, I also realized a fraction of the profits that I usually make in a month.

And that's no surprise to me since I had been on the road with my daughter, Vivian, in June and July. But we will get to the analysis in the next section.

6. **Dividends**
I like to see when I collected dividends and how much. Especially when we talk about the "Dividend Strategy" in the next chapters, you will see why this is important.

7. **Trade Evaluation - According To Plan Or Not?**

I would like to see if I made or lost money when I didn't follow my plan. That's why I like to capture the data in my trading log.

This helps tremendously with the discipline to follow your plan because in the beginning of my trading career, I noticed that whenever I didn't follow my plan, I lost money!

That's a huge motivation to stick to your plan.

As you can see, these days it's not that important for me anymore since most of my trades are according to my plan and the very few times I've deviated from my plan, I had a very good reason for it.

But in the beginning of my trading career, it was a huge help and motivator to see how much money I could have "saved" if I just followed my plan!

8. **Trade Evaluation - Confidence Level**
   This can be a huge help for a trader. As you know, being overly confident can hurt you. And sometimes the best trades happen when you have butterflies in your stomach.

   Here's a personal experience:

   To date, every single time I need to go on stage and talk to people, I'm so nervous that I throw up a few minutes before I have my talk. True story!
   But I believe that THIS keeps me on my toes. Because this "sick-to-my-stomach feeling" forces me to be super prepared versus just winging it.

   Recently, I gave a talk for the *MoneyShow* in Toronto. In the first ten minutes of my presentation, the projector went in and out and at some point, the lights in the room went out and it was pitch black. But that didn't rattle me. I was 100% prepared and knew exactly what I was going to say and the materials I would cover. I think if I was just "winging it," technical challenges like this would really throw me off.

And I believe the same is true in trading.
These are my "first level KPIs."

On page 2, I like to dive into my "second level KPIs."

I have second level KPIs for stocks and options.

Here are the ones that I'm looking at for options:

9. **Realized Profit and Loss**
   The first level KPIs show me the overall profit and loss for stocks, options and dividends. On this page, I like to see how much money I made specifically with options.

10. **Trade Performance**
    This is super interesting and worth zooming in:

Trades Performance

TRADES BY DAY | Table | Graph | CALL | PUT | ALL

	CALLS	PUTS	ALL
MON	24.32%	16.46%	18.97%
TUE	10.81%	22.78%	18.97%
WED	10.81%	21.52%	18.1%
THU	24.32%	22.78%	23.28%
FRI	29.73%	15.19%	19.83%
SAT	0%	1.27%	0.86%
SUN	0%	0%	0%

This table shows me when I traded calls and puts.
In this example, you see that overall my trades are fairly evenly distributed.

But when we look at Call Options, you will see that I trade calls more often on Mondays, Thursdays, and Fridays.

And I trade Put Options more often on Tuesdays, Wednesdays, and Thursdays.

Interesting, isn't it?

Here's why I like to see this data:

If I see that I rarely place trades on certain days, I might as well not fire up the charts at all and rather do something else.

11. **Days in Trade**

I really love this KPI and no broker in the world is giving you this information.

Here I see at a glance how long I am in a trade — both for the average and for the longest trade.

When trading the Wheel, this is invaluable information.

As an example, you see that this year I have been three days in a trade on average when I'm NOT getting assigned. And the longest trade without assignment has been nine days.

On the other hand, when I get assigned, the average trade duration is 101 days and the longest trade is 263 days.

So for all trades combined, assigned and not assigned, my average trade length is 52 days.

This information helps me tremendously to know what to expect when placing a trade.

As an example, if I trade UPS and get assigned, I can expect to be in this trade for approximately 3 months. Don't you think that THIS information is super helpful?

12. **Put & Call Performance**

THIS is probably the most powerful statistic. This alone has helped me to make some major improvement in my trading this year and I'll show you exactly what I did and how I did it in the next chapter.

So let's take a closer look at this statistic:

Put & Call Performance

		PREMIUM $69,274	FEES & COMM $150.37	PROFIT & LOSS $69,123.63	AVG. PROFIT & LOSS $595.89 | $253.2 / DAY	TRADES 116	ASSIGNED 13
PUT		$42,224	$80.18	$42,143.82	$533.47	79	13
SELL	EXPIRED	$11,474	$24.59	$11,449.41	$636.08	18	-
SELL	ASSIGNED	$18,059	$13.62	$18,045.38	$1,388.11	13	13
SELL	CLOSED	0	$21.33	-$21.33	-$0.89	24	-
BUY	-	$12,691	$20.64	$12,670.36	$527.93	24	-
CALL		$27,050	$70.19	$26,979.81	$729.18	37	-
SELL	-	0	$5.84	-$5.84	-$1.95	3	-
SELL	EXPIRED	$8,319	$19.17	$8,299.83	$1,659.97	5	-
SELL	CALLED AWAY	$10,690	$8.33	$10,681.67	$1,780.28	6	-
SELL	CLOSED	0	$15.06	-$15.06	-$1.51	10	-
BUY	-	$8,041	$21.79	$8,019.21	$616.86	13	-

In this example, you see that I made $69,274 in realized profits trading options.

$42,224 of these profits came from trading puts and $27,050 of these profits came from selling calls.

By the way: That's why I like getting assigned when trading the Wheel Strategy!
If I had avoided assignment, I wouldn't have been able to sell calls and I would have missed out on $27,050 in the first 9 months of the year.

Let's dig deeper:

79 Put Options sold
18 of these expired worthless = 23%
13 of these got assigned, i.e. I had to buy the stock = 16%

48 of these I closed early to take profits at 80% or 90% of max profits = 61%

Note: The 24 "buys" are actually "closes" but we introduced this feature in mid 2023, so some of the trades are shown as "buy" and after we implemented this feature, they are shown as "closed."
Isn't this super valuable information?

It tells me a lot about my trading style:

My assignment rate is rather low with 16% and I close the majority of options at 80% or 90% of max profits, which frees up buying power and allows me to take trades more frequently!

And I have the same information for trading call options.

I could go on and on about how super important all of this information is and you will see in the next section how I used that to become more profitable in the second half of 2023 vs. the first half.

13. **Symbols Performance**
This is actually a statistic that you can get from many brokers.
It simply shows you how much money you made on certain stocks or ETFs.

However, your broker usually just shows you the total amount.

I like to go one step further and see how much I made overall, how much of this came from trading call options and how much from put options.

Of course, there are many more KPIs that you consider but I like to focus on these first and second-level KPIs.

While digesting all of these analytics may seem daunting initially, stick with it!

Over time, you'll discover which metrics offer the most value based on your personalized trading style and strategy.

In the beginning, focus on the basics like monthly P&L and the other first-level KPIs you have learned in this chapter.

As you gain more experience, you can incorporate more advanced KPIs to uncover hidden opportunities.

The goal of performance tracking is clarity — not complexity. Prune away indicators that don't directly improve your trading.

With practice, you'll learn which metrics offer actionable insights to help refine your system.
Because I believe that trading is a never-ending optimization game.
Now that you understand how to extract meaning from data, we're ready for the final step — making strategic adjustments based on what the numbers tell you.

Action Step 3: Make Strategic Adjustments Based on Data Insights

Now you know how to log your trades.
And you know how to get some key performance indicators of your trading.

The question is:

WHAT do you do with all this?
And is it really WORTH it?

Well, let me walk you through a personal, real-world example that shows exactly how I used data from my trading logs just a couple months ago to significantly improve my own trading.

It all started in July 2023.

For 2023, my goal was to make $150,000 with trading.

And when I checked my performance after the first half of 2023, I saw THIS:

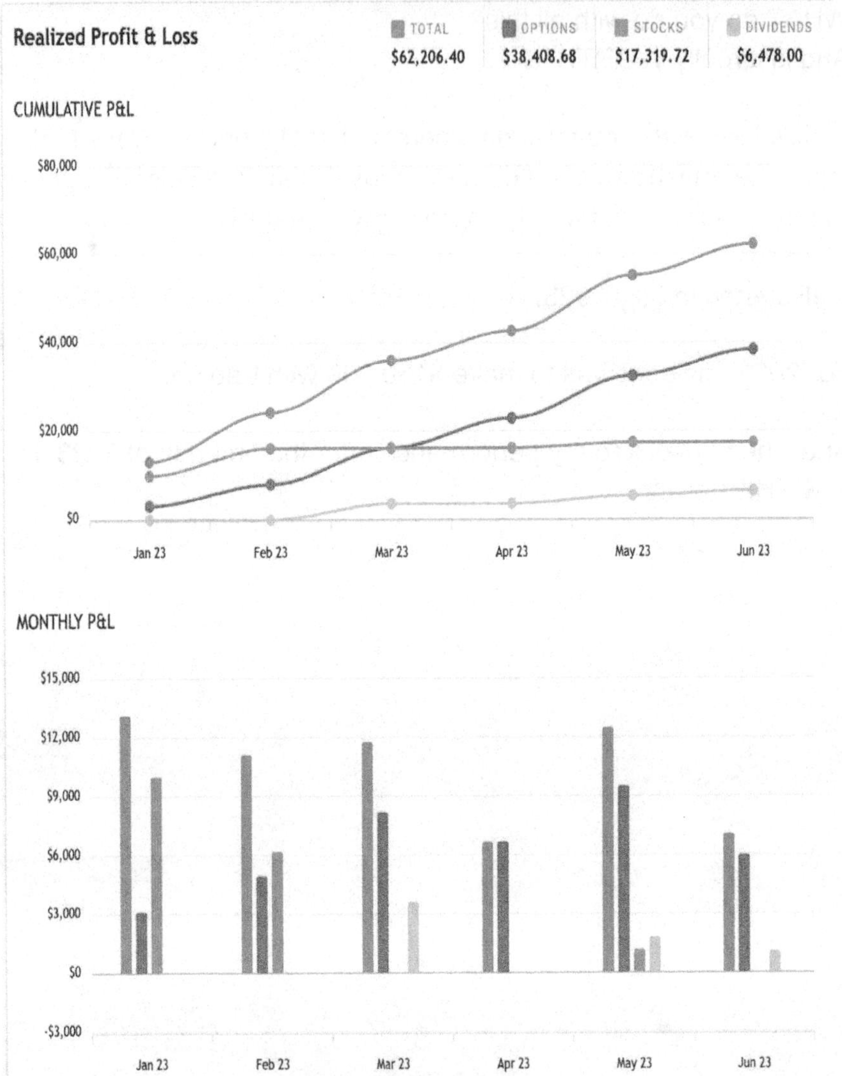

I "only" made $62,206.40 in the first half of 2023.

According to my goal, I wanted to make at least $75,000 in six months.
So I'm short of my goal.

Of course, I could blame "market conditions" or other external factors like many other traders like to do.

Instead, I decided to double-check if I was the one that caused the problem.

So let me walk you through my analysis step-by-step.

1. **Number of Trades**

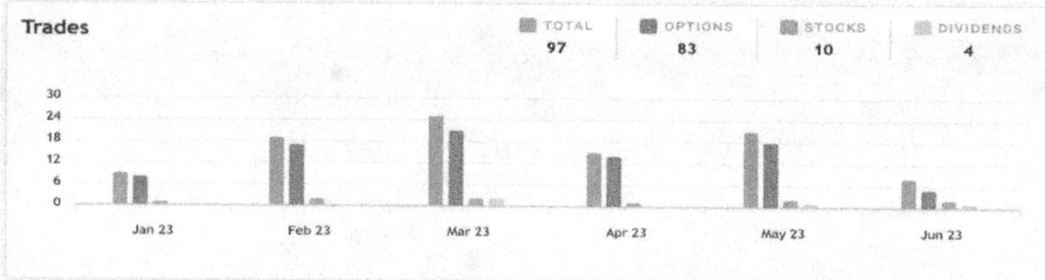

In the first 6 months of 2023, I did 97 trades.

In 2022, I did 250 trades.

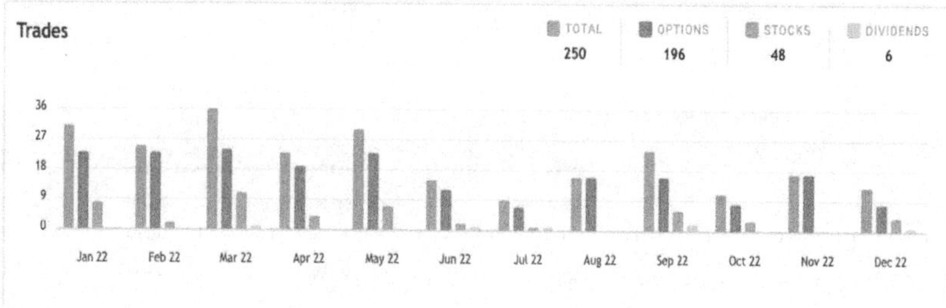

It was obvious: I was trading less.

The question is: WHY?

Was it external factors like "market conditions", or was it me?

As you know, I'm not a big fan of blaming others or external events for my trading performance, so I decided to dig deeper.

2. **Put/Call Analysis**
   Since I'm mainly trading options, I decided to look into the Put & Call Performance of 2023 compared to 2022:

First Half of 2023

Put & Call Performance

		PREMIUM $38,513	FEES & COMM $104.32	PROFIT & LOSS $38,408.68	AVG. PROFIT & LOSS $462.76 | $212.2 / DAY	TRADES 83	ASSIGNED 4
PUT		$18,998	$47.04	$18,950.96	$364.44	52	4
SELL	EXPIRED	$7,859	$13.29	$7,845.71	$653.81	12	-
SELL	ASSIGNED	$2,454	$2.46	$2,451.54	$612.89	4	4
SELL	CLOSED	0	$15.89	-$15.89	-$0.88	18	-
BUY	-	$8,685	$15.4	$8,669.6	$481.64	18	-
CALL		$19,515	$57.28	$19,457.72	$627.67	31	-
SELL	-	0	$5.84	-$5.84	-$1.95	3	-
SELL	EXPIRED	$6,804	$12.76	$6,791.24	$2,263.75	3	-
SELL	CALLED AWAY	$4,990	$3.37	$4,986.63	$1,246.66	4	-
SELL	CLOSED	0	$14.27	-$14.27	-$1.59	9	-
BUY	-	$7,721	$21.04	$7,699.96	$641.66	12	-

2022

Put & Call Performance

		PREMIUM $153,973	FEES & COMM $186.62	PROFIT & LOSS $153,786.38	AVG. PROFIT & LOSS $784.62 | $421.33 / DAY	TRADES 196	ASSIGNED 32
PUT		$90,072	$98.03	$89,973.97	$810.58	111	32
SELL	-	0	$16.1	-$16.1	-$0.73	22	-
SELL	EXPIRED	$20,039	$38.03	$20,000.97	$606.09	33	-
SELL	ASSIGNED	$57,653	$28.37	$57,624.63	$1,800.77	32	32
BUY	-	$12,380	$15.53	$12,364.47	$515.19	24	-
CALL		$63,901	$88.59	$63,812.41	$750.73	85	-
SELL	-	0	$27.37	-$27.37	-$1.05	26	-
SELL	EXPIRED	$20,633	$11.81	$20,621.19	$1,288.82	16	-
SELL	CALLED AWAY	$25,540	$24.2	$25,515.8	$1,594.74	16	-
BUY	-	$17,728	$25.21	$17,702.79	$655.66	27	-

In 2022, 33 out of the 111 Put Options that I sold were assigned.
This means that my assignment rate was 30%.

> In the first half of 2023, 4 out of the 52 Put Options that I sold were assigned.
> This means that my assignment rate was 8%.
>
> Wait a minute ….
> 30% assignment rate in 2022 and only 8% in 2023?
>
> That's a HUGE difference.

And when trading the Wheel, assignment is part of it.

Because after assignment, I can sell calls and collect more premium.

So now we already have identified two facts:

1. I was taking less trades.
2. On the trades that I took, I was assigned less.

As always, I decided not to blame it on "market conditions" and instead asked myself the question:

"If you saw these facts in a trading log of one of your Mastermind Members, what questions would you ask her?"

After a few minutes of thinking, one of the hardest things to do, the question became obvious:

Did I subconsciously take fewer trades and trade more conservatively to avoid assignment?

Well, the problem with the "subconscious" is that initially, we are not aware of it. But as soon as we ask somebody or ourselves a question, we can bring the thoughts and beliefs of the subconscious to the surface.

The trick is to wait for twenty seconds before giving an answer. Because if you don't wait, your conscious mind will jump in right away and say, "No!"

But that's not the real answer.

For me, the real answer was "YES!"

So I wanted to dig deeper and I asked myself:

"WHY did you trade less and more conservatively?"

Ready for some complete and brutal honesty?

The reason why I traded less and more conservatively was that I didn't want to be "stuck" in positions.

Because toward the end of 2022, I was stuck in NVidia (NVDA), Google (GOOGL), and Tapestry (TPR).

Look at the KPIs for just these three symbols:

Average trade duration with assignment: 186 days!

That's six months!

YES, of course, my subconscious said, *"Be more conservative and avoid assignment to avoid getting stuck in positions!"*

But instead of HELPING my overall performance, this was HURTING me.

The good news:
Once you are aware of a problem, it's quite easy to fix it.
And that's what I did.

Remember, in the first six months of 2023, I made $62,206 in realized profits.
That's on average $10,368 per month.

And I placed 97 trades which = 16 trades per month.

I did the analysis in July 2023.
And that's when I adjusted my trading.

Here's what happened in the next two months, August and September 2023:

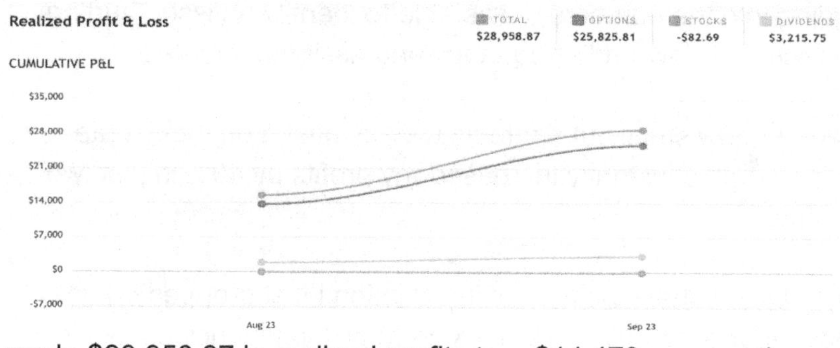

I made $28,958.87 in realized profits to = $14,479 per month.

That's a 40% increase.

Note: I'm writing this book in October 2023, so I don't have the numbers for the rest of the year yet.

Here's my Put & Call Performance for August and September:

Put & Call Performance

		PREMIUM $25,855	FEES & COMM $29.19	PROFIT & LOSS $25,825.81	AVG. PROFIT & LOSS $1,033.03 | $423.37 / DAY	TRADES 25	ASSIGNED 9
PUT		$21,020	$24.57	$20,995.43	$999.78	21	9
SELL	EXPIRED	$3,615	$11.3	$3,603.7	$600.62	6	-
SELL	ASSIGNED	$15,605	$8.93	$15,596.07	$1,732.9	9	9
SELL	CLOSED	0	$2.21	-$2.21	-$0.74	3	-
BUY	-	$1,800	$2.13	$1,797.87	$599.29	3	-
CALL		$4,835	$4.62	$4,830.38	$1,207.6	4	-
SELL	EXPIRED	$435	$2.27	$432.73	$432.73	1	-
SELL	CALLED AWAY	$4,080	$0.81	$4,079.19	$4,079.19	1	-
SELL	CLOSED	0	$0.79	-$0.79	-$0.79	1	-
BUY	-	$320	$0.75	$319.25	$319.25	1	-

As you can see, I sold 21 puts and got assigned 9 times. That's a 43% assignment rate.

Compare that to an 8% assignment rate in the first half for 2023! There you have it — a real-world example of how analyzing your trading data and metrics can lead to breakthrough improvements. By logging trades, tracking key performance indicators, and digging into the numbers, I was able to identify an issue hurting my results — low trade frequency and assignment rates.

Making a few small but strategic tweaks based on these data-driven insights instantly increased my profits by 40% in just two months!

Look, I know that was a lot of information I just dropped on you. And if your eyes glaze over looking at all those fancy analytics, I get it. I felt the same way for years until the lightbulb finally went on.

But let me be totally straight with you — even though trade tracking seems boring on the surface, it is absolutely critical to refine and fortify your financial fortress.

I don't know a single professional trader generating lasting success without having key performance numbers at their fingertips.

And it comes down to this: success leaves clues. By logging trades consistently, identifying key metrics, and then fine-tuning your plan based on data insights, over time the winning patterns reveal themselves.

So I totally understand if you are feeling a little bit overwhelmed.

But stick with it!

And you can always use tools like the PowerX Optimizer to make everything MUCH easier and almost effortless.

In the next chapter, we'll uncover advanced tactics to grow your account quicker and increase the strength of your financial fortress. Think upgraded cranes and heavy machinery over hand tools.

Let's keep laying bricks steadily … while turbo boosters now propel your wealth trajectory to new heights!

Let's unleash the full potential of your trading business!

Chapter 13: Step 7: Turbo Growth Accelerator

At this point in your trading journey, you've hopefully developed a solid foundation and core wealth-building skills.

In the same way as you would build sturdy fortress walls brick-by-brick, you diligently followed your trading plan and focused on generating systematic, repeatable, and consistent profits (SRC Profits).

Ideally, you now have six to twelve months of experience under your belt. No skipping steps or taking shortcuts along the way — just laying one row of bricks after another.

Through consistency and discipline, your account is growing nicely.

Now it's time to turbocharge your trading! Think of this as upgrading from hand tools to some heavy-duty machinery.

It is possible to grow your account quicker with advanced strategies and responsibly used leverage.

But please complete all of the previous steps before you consider implementing the advanced strategies outlined in this chapter.

Because using advanced tactics too early is like giving power tools to a toddler: it's super dangerous! You need to build a proper foundation first.
Many impatient traders try shortcuts before developing core skills. This is often why they fail and blow up accounts.

But YOU demonstrated patience and put in the time to lay a solid foundation. So now you're prepared to use these enhancements responsibly to take your account to the next level.

In this chapter, we'll uncover three advanced growth accelerators:

1. **Margin Trading**— Lean how to use margin and leverage responsibly to potentially double your returns without changing anything else.

2. **Strategy Adjustments** — Tiny tweaks to your winning system can improve your performance by 20-30% almost instantly.

3. **Repair Trades, a.k.a. "Rescue Missions"** — Potentially transform losers into winners. Use advanced techniques to rescue troubled positions rather than taking big losses.

Implementing these tactics is like going from hand tools to bulldozers and cranes. If you operate them carelessly, you could destroy your financial fortress.

So ease into these higher-octane tactics responsibly. Get ready for takeoff … but start nice and steady.

Action Step 1: Learn to use leverage responsibly

Trading on margin can skyrocket your returns when used correctly. But used irresponsibly, leverage could demolish your financial fortress. This power tool requires care and discipline.

In this section, I'll provide a comprehensive overview in margin trading — from mechanics to risks and rewards. My goal is to give you all the info you need to use leverage intelligently and accelerate your trading profits.

Let's start at the foundation and build up your margin mastery brick by brick!

1. What is Margin Trading?

In a nutshell: margin trading is borrowing money from your broker to buy more stocks and options.

The idea is to leverage your existing cash to increase buying power. You are essentially taking out a loan from your broker against the value of securities in your account.

This way, you get access to more capital to put to work, which means you can buy more stocks.

Now, to utilize margin you need a margin account approved by your broker. This is different from a standard cash account where you can only trade using your existing cash balances.

2. How Margin Trading Works

Opening a margin account is typically part of the standard account application process. The broker will ask what type of account you want — cash or margin.

By law, you must deposit a minimum of $2,000 to open a margin account. But some brokers require more: depending on the broker it can be $10,000 or even $25,000.

Once the account is funded, you can borrow up to 50% of the purchase price on securities. But just because you now have access to borrowed capital doesn't mean you have to use it!

Start slowly.

Let's walk through an example:

Imagine you deposit $10,000 cash into a new margin account. This deposit becomes your collateral. The broker will now lend you up to another $10,000 giving you $20,000 in total buying power.

You decide to use $10,000 of your cash and $10,000 margin to buy 200 shares of a stock trading at $10 per share for a total investment of $20,000.

The shares you purchase with the margin loan are now becoming collateral for that loan. If you later sold the shares for say $15, you first need to pay back the margin loan. Just like paying back a mortgage when selling a home.

Is this making sense so far? Then let's move on to discussing the advantages and risks of trading on margin.

3.The Pros of Using Margin

Trading on margin is very powerful. When used correctly, it can quickly double your return on investment without changing anything in your trading plan.

Here's a simplified example:

Imagine you have $10,000 cash in your account providing $10,000 buying power. Let's say you use it all to buy 1,000 shares of a stock at $10/share.

If the stock rises to $12/share, your position is now worth $12,000. That's a $2,000 profit on your $10,000 invested — a 20% return.

Now let's say you have $10,000 cash but also borrow $10,000 on margin. You can now buy 2,000 shares at $10 each using your full $20,000 buying power.

If the stock climbs to $12/share, your position is now worth $24,000. That's a $4,000 profit on your original $10,000 cash — **a 40% leveraged return vs just 20%!**

When used strategically, you could double your trading profits without changing anything else!

So if you have been making 30% trading cash, you could now make 60% by just using margin and adjusting your position size!

That's the easiest way to double your returns!

But we already talked about this previously: With greater returns often comes higher risk. So let's talk about the risks when using margin.

4. The Cons of Using Margin

Leverage goes both ways, Yes, it can boost your trading profits and in the same way, it amplifies your losses.

Let me explain.

We will use the same example as above:
You have $10,000 in your account and you borrow another $10,000 from your broker to get $20,000 in buying power.

You use this buying power to buy 2,000 shares at $10 per share.

But now imagine that the stock drops from your purchase price of $10 down to $8/share.

Without margin, your 1,000 share position would decline from $10,000 to $8,000, a $2,000 loss or 20%.

But with margin, your 2,000 shares are now worth just $16,000, down from $20,000 cost. That's a $4,000 total loss or 40% loss of your initial $10,000 cash!

So as you can see, margin amplifies both profits AND losses.

Other cons of margin trading include:

- Interest costs on borrowed funds — usually around 5-10% annually depending on your broker and the current interest rates set by the Federal Reserve. In 2023, when rates were at a 15-year high, margin interest rates were as high as 14%.

- Potential for margin calls if account equity falls below maintenance requirements. More on this shortly.

- Forced liquidations if unable to meet margin calls in a timely manner.

Clearly, utilizing margin isn't a decision to take lightly. But applied prudently, the reward CAN outweigh the risks. That's why this is "Step 7" and not "Step 2"!

5. What is a Margin Call?

Now let's discuss the dreaded margin call and how to avoid it. This catches many traders off guard if they don't fully grasp margin requirements.

I remember when I got my first margin call. It was in 2008 during the financial crises. I didn't know what it was but when I got an email, a text message, AND a call from my broker on the same day, I knew that it was something very serious.

So let's dive in.

First, understand there are initial and maintenance margin levels your broker monitors:

- **Initial Margin** is typically 50% of total account value. This is the max you can borrow to start. We talked about this in the previous section.
- After you initiate a position, your broker gives you some leeway to manage your position. Once you are in a trade, the broker requires a **maintenance Margin** which is usually only 25-30%.

I know, I know: This is super weird, isn't it?

Anyhow, when the value of your positions falls below the maintenance margin requirement, you get a margin call.

Let's use our example to explain this in more detail:

Same as before: you have $10,000 cash and borrow $10,000 margin — $20,000 total buying power used to buy 2,000 shares at $10 = $20,000 total market value.

If the shares decline to $7, your position is now worth 2,000 shares × $7 = $14,000.

But your equity is $14,000 less the $10,000 loan = only $4,000k.

If your broker sets the maintenance margin to 25%, you calculate the margin requirement as following $14,000 × 25% = $3,500.

Your $4,000 in equity is above that, so you're "safe". No margin call yet.

But if the stock drops further to $6 per share, now your position is worth 2,000 shares × $6 = $12,000. So your equity is only $2,000 since you still owe the broker $10,000.

And the margin requirement is 25% of the position value, i.e. $12,000 × 0.25 = $3,000.

So you have $2,000 in equity and need $3,000 to meet the maintenance margin requirement.

This means: Margin call!

Now you must promptly take action by either depositing $1,000 or more in cash or by selling shares to increase your equity.

If you fail to act in time, your broker will start force-liquidating positions potentially at the worst prices until the requirement is met.

Never let this happen!

As you can see, trading on margin is definitely an advanced concept and that's why we saved this for Step 7 of our 9-Step Wealth Building Blueprint.

If you are still building your account or you just started trading, don't worry about trading on margin and all of this stuff just yet. I just wanted to include it in this book because eventually, you will get here and you might consider trading on margin.

But now you know why I don't recommend doing this in the first few months of your trading career.

Ok, let's continue our margin discussion ...

6. How to Avoid Margin Calls

Dealing with margin calls can be a headache.

So here are five tips on how to avoid them:

1. Start with Low Leverage
When first utilizing margin, don't max out your buying power. Add conservatively over time as you gain experience. It's the same principle as using a credit card: Don't max it out immediately!

2. Use Stop Losses
Manage the downside risk in volatile markets by implementing stop loss orders on your positions if possible.

3. Monitor Your Portfolio At Least Weekly
As a trader, you probably watch your portfolio every day. But if you don't watch it daily, check it at least once a week and monitor your equity to make sure that you're not getting close to a margin call.

4. Maintain Excess Margin
Keep equity well above just the minimum maintenance requirement for an added safety buffer.
Make sure that you know at any time how much "buffer" you have.

5. Plan Ahead
Have additional cash available or credit lines open to meet any potential margin calls quickly.

Following these guidelines will help you reap the benefits from trading on margin without nasty surprises. Always respect the risks and use margin carefully!

Now you understand exactly what triggers a margin call and how to proactively avoid them.

But you still might get a margin call.
So what do you do if this happens?

7. Responding to Margin Calls

First, you will typically receive notice by email that you must meet the call within a specific time-frame, usually one to three days. Read the email carefully since the broker WILL specify how much time you have to respond.

No matter how much time you have, start thinking about one of the following three options to satisfy the margin call:

Solution 1. Deposit Additional Cash
Transfer funds into your margin account to increase equity. Beware, transfers can take one to three days to clear — so act fast!

Solution 2. Sell Current Positions

If you sell enough of your current positions, it will increase the cash in your account and your equity will move above the maintenance margin level. This will cancel the margin call. However, this solution means that you might be selling a stock at its low. After you sell it, the stock might recover, but you are locked in a loss.

Solution 3. A Combination Of Both

In my opinion, the best solution is a strategic mix of depositing some more cash and maybe selling select positions to meet the margin call. They key: Plan ahead!

For example, at tastytrade, you usually have three days to meet a margin call.

But if you are with Interactive Brokers, no formal warning is issued — they liquidate immediately once you hit the threshold!

So know your broker's rules and have a plan to act quickly.

Never ignore or delay responding to margin calls — that's asking for disaster!

Okay, so now you have a solid understanding of how to trade margin responsibly. Let's finish up with a brief overview of portfolio margin, available for larger accounts.

8. Portfolio Margin

Portfolio margin is "margin on steroids." It provides even greater leverage — like going from a 2X buying power with standard margins to 5X or even 6X. It's like racing a Formula 1 car!

And the maintenance margin calculation is much more complex and uses a calculation involving volatility.

In a nutshell: Portfolio Margin is really for very experienced traders only, and that's why your broker requires a minimum of $125,000 - $200,000 in your account before you can even apply for it.
But I wanted to mention it here so that you know what's available once you get to this level.

Conclusion

I know ... trading on margin is an advanced concept and can make your head spin.

But here's the *CliffsNotes* version:

Used correctly, trading on margin can dramatically increase your profits without changing your trading strategy one bit. It's like a magic multiplier once you understand how to use it!

But used incorrectly, it can destroy your account faster than you think. Margin calls are no joke, and if you don't have more money to put into the account when you get one, you could be in deep trouble.

So respect the power of leverage and ease into it slowly.

Take things one step at a time and then revisit this section of the book after a few months of trading experience.

Ready for the next advanced concept?

Action Step 2: Discover Strategy Tweaks to Increase Profits By 20-30%

As you have seen, using margin the right way can double your profits. The tactic that I'm showing you now won't double your profits but it can easily increase your profits by 20-30%.

Let me walk you through an advanced tactic using intraday charts to fine tune your entry points. As you will see, with this concept you can squeeze more premium profit out of every trade.

Recently, the PowerX Optimizer flagged Devon Energy (DVN) as a promising candidate to sell cash secured puts on. Fundamentals looked solid — a profitable energy company paying dividends.

Now typically, I would just sell the puts right away after confirming it meets my criteria.

But when I see the stock falling like a rock, I use a more tactical entry using the 5-minute chart.

Here's what I did:

Rather than entering immediately, I would watch the price action to try catching it at or near the low of the current move.

Why? Because then I can collect even more premium for the obligation of buying DVN at that lower price, if assigned.

So I waited patiently for the 5-minute chart to show an intraday reversal signaling a potential bottom in DVN.

Here is how it played out:

On the daily chart, DVN had dropped from around $54 down to $46 — a key support level that it bounced off several times.

And on October 2, 2023, PowerX Optimizer identified the 45 Strike as a possibility to sell put options and gather some good premium.

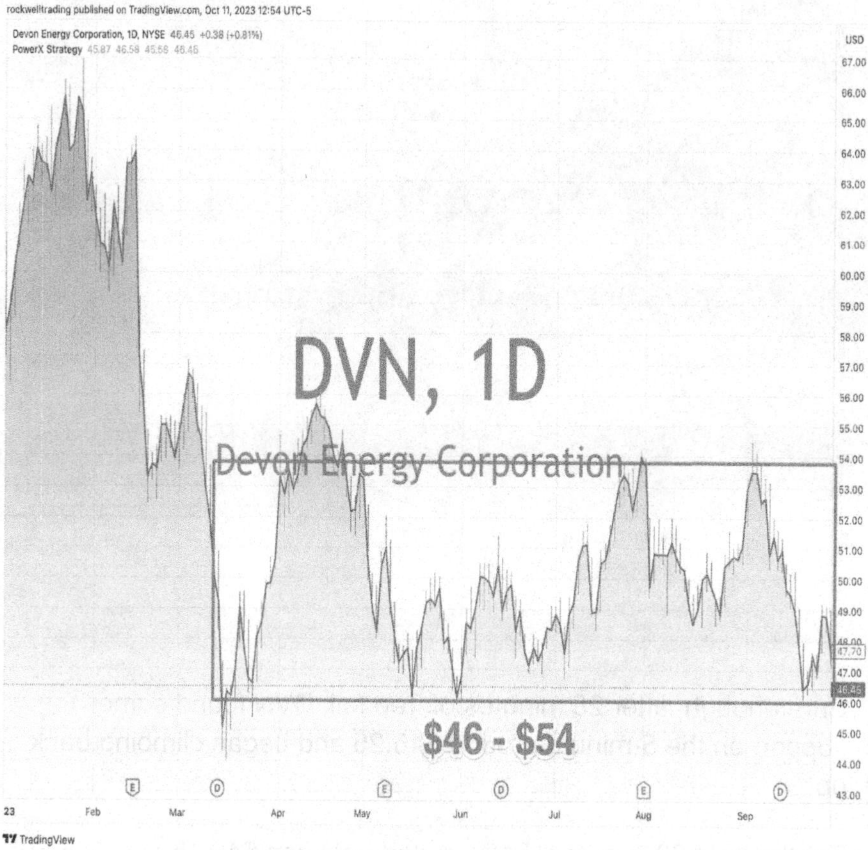

But I didn't want to sell my puts at $45 and then watch it immediately drop lower. So I monitored the 5-minute chart waiting for confirmation that it stopped falling and found a bottom.

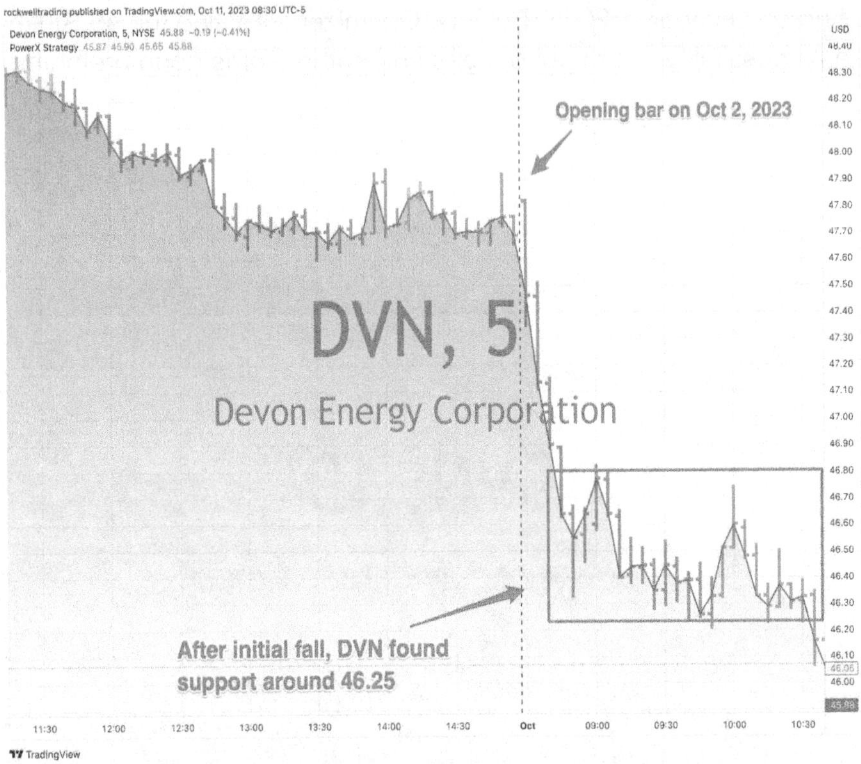

Sure enough, after 25 minutes of free fall, DVN found some support on the 5-minute around $46.25 and began climbing back up.

For the next 90 minutes, DVN traded between $46.25 and $46.60.

And that's when I decided to pull the trigger and enter the trade.

As you can see, when timing your entry on a 5-minute chart, chances are that you will get a higher premium than just entering the trade at the open.

Now, this tactical timing does have some trade-offs that are important to consider:

Pros:

- Capturing an extra 20-30% premium per trade adds up quickly.

Cons:

- Requires greater focus and time commitment per trade.
- Forces you to watch a stock fall and manage emotions.
- Overthinking can lead to missing opportunities.

In summary, using intraday charts allows you to pinpoint ideal entry points and get more premium.

However, don't get greedy chasing every last penny of premium. Remember, there are only two ways to enter a trade: too early or too late. Don't let "perfect" be the enemy of "great."

So ease into this advanced technique slowly. Stay disciplined and follow your strategy. And then use the shorter time frame charts for fine tuning entries, not making impulsive decisions.

With practice, you can use this tactic to easily get an extra 20-30% in premium, and these profits can add up nicely.

But you MUST walk before you run, so don't attempt this with an unproven trading plan. Only optimize a working system after months of results, and never before establishing a successful foundation.

Trust me: THIS tweak will not make or break you as a trader.

Only attempt this if you're already making SRC profits with your "bread and butter strategy." In my case: The Wheel Strategy.

But once you master your strategy, minor strategy adjustments like this one can fine tune your financial fortress, strengthening the walls to reach even greater heights.

Action Step 3: Repair Losing Trades to Avoid Major Losses

When trading the wheel strategy, it can happen that you get assigned a stock and the stock keeps falling.

It's normal for a stock to fall 5-10% after assignment before recovering. I don't worry about minor dips like this.

But what do you do when the stock falls further, e.g. 20% or 30% below your assigned price?

In this case, you might not be able to sell calls at your assigned strike to collect premium. And if you sell calls below your assigned price, you might get called away at a lower price than your stock purchase price and lock in a loss. Not good!

So this is where a rescue mission can be a powerful technique to turn a losing trade into a winning one. Executed properly, repair trades transform positions gone bad into profitable winners.

Let's dive in and uncover exactly how to implement them.

1. When to Attempt to Fly A Rescue Mission

First, when should you consider executing a repair trade on an assigned stock that's falling?

Here are a few key guidelines:

— Wait until the position drops at approximately 30% below your assigned price.

— Don't rush into repairs too early, be patient and keep some "dry powder" ready.

— Wait until the stock has found a bottom and stops falling.

Caution: Don't even think about attempting repairs without sufficient experience first. You need a solid foundation of core trading skills plus an understanding of leverage and its risks.

With the right approach, repair trades can transform losers into winners. Now let's examine how to execute them.

2. How to Fly A Rescue Mission

The mechanics of a repair trade are straightforward:

— Sell additional cash secured puts after a stock drops approximately 30% and has found a bottom.

— This lowers your cost basis if you get assigned the shares again at the lower price.

— You also collect more premium income from the extra puts to help offset losses.

One of the major questions is: How much money should you allocate to a rescue mission?

I personally like to commit 30% - 50% of my initial position size, i.e. if my original position required $100,000 in buying power, I will commit another $30,000 - $50,000 to a rescue mission.

Here's a simple example:

Imagine you sold puts at a $100 strike and got assigned 200 shares. This means your cost basis is $100.

Let's say the stock then plummets to $70 per share.

To repair this trade, you'd sell 1 put contract with a $70 strike price. This obligates you to buy another 100 shares at $70 if assigned.

If the $70 put expires worthless, you simply pocket the premium. If it gets assigned, your new cost basis for 300 shares would be (200 X $100) + (100 X $70) = $27,000 ÷ 300 shares = $90 per share.

So if the stock rebounds, you can start selling calls at $90 instead of $100.

And the extra premium income further reduces your breakeven.

Of course, real trades are more dynamic. But this demonstrates the power of repair trades when applied strategically.

The idea of buying more shares at a lower price when the stock drops is nothing new. It's called "Dollar Cost Averaging," and has been used by professional traders forever.

In fact, Warren Buffett is a big fan of dollar-cost averaging and uses it for most of his investments.

Example: Repair Trade On NVDA

Now let's walk through an actual example together …

On April 20, 2022, I sold a $190 Put on NVDA.

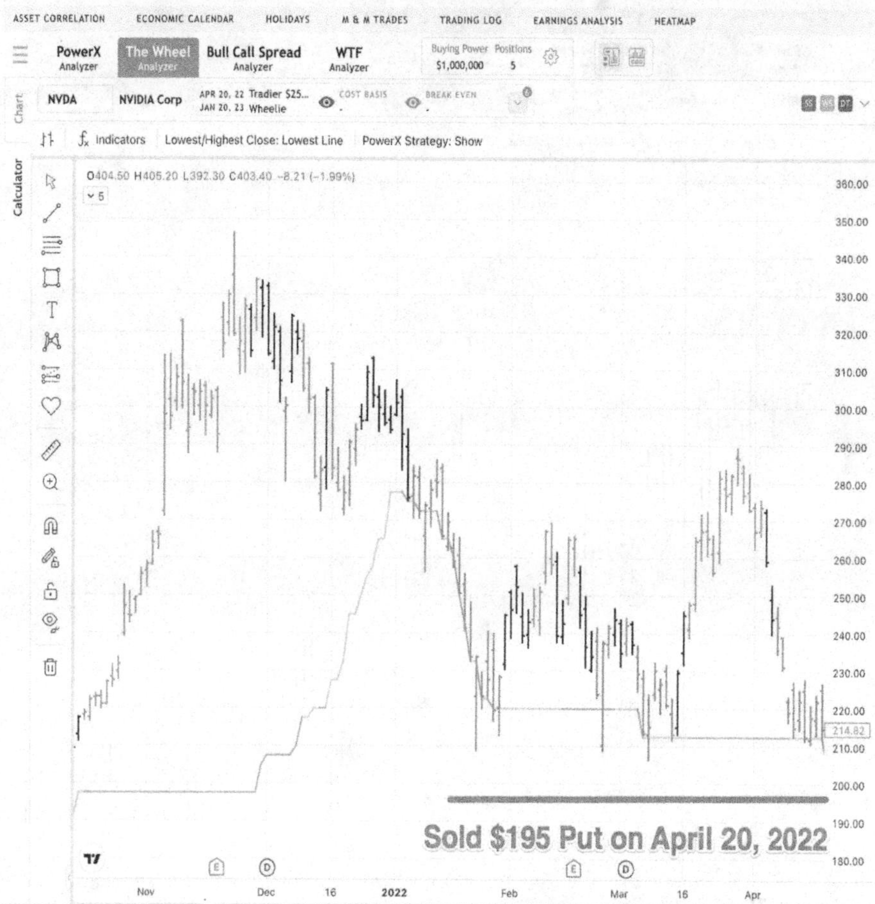

On May 2, 2022, NVDA closed below $195 and I got assigned, i.e. I had to buy 600 shares of NVDA at $195. The total investment was 600 shares X $195 = $117,000.

Over the next few weeks, NVDA was trading between $160 and $200 and I was able to sell covered calls against my existing position several times, lowering my break-even every time I received more premium.

But then NVDA started moving lower and by October 2022, NVDA was trading at $120. This means that NVDA is down more than 38% from my assigned price at $195.

Time to fly a rescue mission!

On October 10, 2022, I decided to sell 5 Puts with a strike price of $120.

NVDA kept moving lower, and on October 14, 2022, I got assigned and had to buy an additional 500 shares of NVDA at $120 for a total of $60,000.

Therefore, my new cost basis was (600 X $195 + 500 X $120) = $177,000 ÷ 1,100 shares = $160.90

As you can see, flying a rescue mission lowered my cost basis from $195 to $160.90.

Over the next few weeks, NVDA recovered and I was able to sell calls against my new cost basis of $160.90 several times.

On January 20, 2023, after 275 days of being in this trade, I finally got called away.

To date, this is one of my most profitable trades with a total of $38,467.78 in profits.

Nice trade!

3. Stock Selection Critical For Success

Attempting repair trades on the wrong stocks often ends poorly. You cannot rescue a sinking ship ignoring gaping holes in the hull.

However, high-quality stocks experiencing temporary weakness frequently rebound. Repairs work best under those circumstances.

Consider our example with NVDA:

I sold NVDA puts because the company is a dominant, innovative market leader in a key growth industry — GPUs and AI computing.

When shares were assigned, I felt confident because NVDA has solid long-term fundamentals. Therefore a rescue mission made sense to me: I wanted to lower my cost basis to be able to sell calls quicker when the stock recovered.

And that's exactly what happened — NVDA turned around and I profited handsomely.

But reckless Reddit meme stocks detached from reality like GameStop (GME), Bed Bath & Beyond (BBBY) and others lack that bedrock quality. Their holes go all the way through!

Repair attempts often fail with:

- Unproven or failing businesses.
- Unprofitable companies that just burn through money.
- Companies under SEC investigation.

Stick with stocks aligned to your proven selection methodology.

Trust me, I learned my lesson with Lordstown Motors (RIDE)!

Ensure prospects have strong fundamentals and a high probability of rebounding.

Repairs work best when high-quality stocks get temporarily pushed down by broader market forces, not when the business itself is cracking.

For example, I might sell puts on Apple (AAPL) without hesitation. It has exceptional brand loyalty and massive free cash flow.

If AAPL shares get assigned and fall from say $150 to $100, I am happy to sell more puts at $100 to lower my cost basis. Odds are in my favor for recovery.

But if a hyped clunker like Nikola dropped 50%, repairs would be foolish. That's not a temporary dip, it's a failing business.

Remember, time is your ally as a trader. Temporary dips in quality names frequently present opportunities.

With experience, you'll be able to discern when repairs offer high probability success versus low-chance "Hail Mary" plays.

Trade with your head, not your heart. Let logic guide your repairs, not hope or attachment to names.

Now that you understand the critical importance of stock selection, let's examine the key benefits and drawbacks of repair trades so you enter them with eyes wide open.

4. Pros and Cons of Rescue Missions

Repair trades can potentially help turn around losing positions when applied correctly. However, they also have limitations to consider.

Let's examine the key pros and cons so you can weigh them objectively:

Pros:

- Transform otherwise losing trades into winners - snatch victory from jaws of defeat!
- Generate additional premium income from extra puts sold to lower your break even.
- Lower your overall cost basis if assigned shares at the lower repair strike.
- Sell calls sooner when the stock rebounds.
- Get out of the position quicker when the stock rebounds since your cost basis is lower.

Those benefits are enticing. But repairs also have their downsides:

Cons:

- Require experience and comfort with leverage — beginners should avoid.
- Reduce available buying power for other potential trades.
- Not guaranteed to succeed if the underlying keeps dropping.
- Emotions and anxiety may tempt repairing too early.
- Can backfire and worsen losses if stock keeps plunging.
- Ineffective on low quality companies or sectors facing structural decline.

The bottom line is repair trades are a specialized and advanced technique requiring experience and strict adherence to rules. Don't attempt to do it if you don't have enough experience!

But when the situation aligns perfectly, a temporary setback in a high-quality stock, repairs can be extremely rewarding.

With practice, you will discover ideal repair candidates and situations. Patience and discipline are key.

In the right circumstances, repair trades transform troubled positions from pain to profit. But tread carefully and deliberately.

Summary and Recap

In this chapter, we discussed advanced tactics to turbocharge your trading once you've developed a solid foundation.

Think of it as upgrading from hand tools to heavy machinery in order to rapidly construct higher fortress walls.

First, we covered using margin responsibly to prudently apply leverage and amplify returns. Handled carelessly though, margin can demolish accounts faster than anything.

Next, we looked at strategy optimization — minor adjustments to improve performance 20-30%. But changes must align to proven, backtested systems.

Finally, we uncovered repair trades — transforming losing positions into winners. Executed properly, repairs snatch victory from the jaws of defeat.

Each of these enhancements provides specialized power tools. But just like operating bulldozers and cranes, they require preparation and care.

Used judiciously under the right conditions, these tactics allow you to build your financial fortress bigger and stronger than ever imaginable with basic techniques. But attempted prematurely, they invite disaster.

With the proper foundation, turbo-charged trading unlocks your full potential. With this heavy machinery, you construct rapidly with speed and efficiency.

Now that we have acquired the tools and materials to build an impenetrable financial fortress rapidly, it's time for the finishing touches.

In the next chapter, we will build a moat around your fortress using tax savings and entity structuring. This keeps more profits in your pocket. Let’s dive in.

Chapter 14: Step 8: Wealth Empire Architect

Taxes — the one certainty in life beside death.

And yes, I know … it's that topic everyone loves to hate. But stick with me here.

Because we're all in the business of making money, right? And part of making money is, well, not giving too much of it away to the IRS or whatever tax authorities are called in your country.

Navigating the tax maze as a trader can feel like trying to sail through a storm without a compass. It's tricky, often frustrating, and if you're not careful, you could end up paying more than you need to.

In this chapter, we're diving into the nuts and bolts of optimizing your "trader tax status" and structuring your trading business to keep more of your profits where they belong — with you.

Think of this as fortifying your financial fortress. It's not just about building wealth, it's about protecting it from those who want a piece of it, like the IRS, eyeing your trading gains. By aligning yourself with the right advisors — the seasoned knights in the realm of taxes, such as CPAs and tax attorneys — you're setting up a robust defense line. It's like having experienced "Fortress Defenders" on your side.

I've seen plenty of traders overpaying their taxes. But if you don't do it right, you can get tangled in tax troubles or sweat bullets over potential IRS audits. It doesn't have to be this way. With a savvy tax strategy, you'll keep more of your hard-won income and who doesn't want that?

Let me be 100% clear upfront — I am NOT a licensed tax professional. You should consult a qualified CPA or tax attorney for personalized advice. In a few moments, I will give you a great resource who can help you set up everything correctly.

My goal for this chapter is to give you a head start, a primer if you will, so when you do sit down with your tax guru, at least you have a basic understanding of what you will talk about.

Now let's start exploring how you may legally reduce your trading tax bill!

Action Step 1: Form the Ideal Trading Entity to Minimize Taxes

There's a lot of confusing tax myths floating around trading circles.

In this step, I'll debunk some common misconceptions so you can make informed decisions.

One big myth is that you need some special "trader tax status" from the IRS to benefit. But here's the reality — no such status exists! So don't fall for the myths and hype around a "trader tax status"
But here's the deal, we've got three players in the tax game:

1. **The Investor:** This person is all about the long game, collecting dividends like vintage wines. These are "buy-and-hold" investors and not active traders. Their tax story is pretty straightforward: The broker issues a statement at the end of the year and there are very few expenses that they can deduct.

2. **Trader in Securities (TIS):** These are traders who actively buy and sell stocks and options. This group is getting a little bit of a tax break because you can deduct a lot more, but you still need to watch out for those pesky wash sale rules and a cap on capital losses.

3. **Mark-to-Market (MTM) Trader:** THIS is the best classification when it comes to the US tax code. Electing for MTM means playing by a different set of rules — you can decide a lot of expenses. And the handcuffs of wash sale rules and loss limits? Gone.

So how do you qualify as a "Mark-to-Market Trader"?

Well, this is very muddy: The IRS doesn't hand out "rules". They just say that you "must direct his or her activities primarily to a short-term trading strategy designed to capture profits from the volatility of the market" and that your trading activity needs to be "substantial."

However, there are no specific guidelines of what "substantial means." So traders have been scratching their heads for years trying to figure out the exact number of trades per year, the length of the holding period, or the total activity during the year that's needed to qualify.

And here's the real kicker: You can decide at any time that you are now a "Mark-to-Market Trader." All you need to do is fill out a super simple form and submit it with your tax return.

BUT… the IRS can challenge this, and since there are no hard rules, you MUST be sure that you will qualify.

So PLEASE consult with a tax professional before you tell the IRS that you're now "Mark-to-Market."

Now, the million-dollar question:
Do you need to form an LLC?

Not exactly. An LLC doesn't automatically enroll you in the TIS or MTM club. Sure, LLCs do provide some benefits, like liability protection and simplified reporting. But they also have costs for formation, compliance, and tax filings.

My two cents: If you meet TIS or MTM thresholds, an LLC adds legitimacy to your trading business. But don't form one just hoping for tax perks — you must prove you qualify as an eligible type of trader first based on your own trading activities.

Finally, are there any deadlines you need to know about as a trader?

For TIS, there are no specific deadlines or time limitations. You can simply trade actively and document the expenses you want to deduct.

But for MTM, the clock's ticking. You need to file by April 15 to make the MTM magic happen for the next year. If you miss the deadlines, there's no MTM for that year!

So in summary, avoid falling for the "trader tax myths."
And having an LLC does not equal special status.

So make sure you have a trustworthy guide in this journey.
Check out https://rockwell.rocks/cpa for a CPA who gets it.

Action Step 2: Identify Deductible Business Expenses

Here's the good news:

As an active trader, you essentially operate a business managing your portfolio. Therefore, many common business expenses become deductible. But you must document and prove these are ordinary and necessary costs of your trading.

Remember, I am not a CPA!

But let's explore some of the most common write-offs available to properly substantiate:

- Computers.
- Multiple monitors for trading.
- Specific software for your trading, e.g. Power Optimizer.
- Mobile information device, cell phone or hot-spot (percentage use).
- Trading research services but not robo-trading, trade following automated trading or self created trading systems (your time is not deductible).
- Office supplies.
- Coaching and mentoring services.
- Subscriptions to investment advisers, websites, periodicals.
- Reference materials.
- Seminars/webinars.
- Travel to seminar, where the primary purpose is business not personal including meals where the travel is ordinary and necessary for trading purposes.

- Continuing education, but not education that would qualify you for another trade business.
- Interest, credit cards used to purchase trading items.
- Interest and margin interest charged by a brokerage.
- Office furniture conducive to trading.
- Home office, if used regularly and exclusively for your trading business this
  represents a pro-rata share of your home costs or a flat rate of $5 per square foot up to 300 sf. If qualified business use for a month is less than 15 days then that month is excluded. There are typically 22 trading days in a month.
- Entity formation fees, from your secretary of state and the third-party fees for filing the formation documents with your state.
- Brokerage data fees, typically for "professional" designated entities.
- Accounting/legal fees, tax compliance and planning.
- Franchise/business tax associated with the trading business, some states have a minimum tax just for having an entity.
- Vehicle expense for business use, all trading business mileage must be substantiated with a mileage log or other method (not percentage estimates).

Be careful with this one! Taxpayers lose on vehicle expense audits most of the time and it is because they do not have adequate substantiation (proof) for that mileage or a valid business purpose.

Advanced Expenses

- Health insurance benefits for employees or self-employed (no entity and filing on Schedule C).
- Retirement benefits.

Keep in mind that deductions must be ordinary and necessary for your trading business. Keep receipts and usage logs. And don't get greedy claiming a dinner with your spouse on Valentine's Day as a "business dinner."

But as you can see, you can maximize a lot of write-offs legally to keep more of your hard earned profits!

After all, trading is a business!

And with the right approach, you can substantially reduce your tax bill and build wealth faster. But always consult tax professionals to ensure you stay compliant.

Action Step 3: Build Your Team of Tax and Legal Professionals

As you can see, there's A LOT to consider. If you try to do this all by yourself, you can end up making big mistakes and get in trouble with tax audits.

That's why you should surround yourself with specialized professionals to navigate this complex topic and protect your hard-earned profits.

Think of it as building a team of **"Fortress Defenders"** — CPAs, tax strategists,and attorneys who deeply understand the nuances of trader tax code.

They will sit down with you and come up with a personalized plan to optimize your entity structure, filings, deductions, and overall tax strategy. But finding the right advisors is critical.

Here are key considerations when selecting your financial inner circle:

- **Experience**
  Ask about years of trader tax experience specifically, not just general accounting background. Find specialists.

- **Expertise**
  Align advisors to your needs — tax planning, compliance, entities, retirement plans,
  deductions. Build a well-rounded team.

- **Communication**
  Ensure you connect well and understand what they suggest. Meet in person if possible before committing.

- **Availability**
  Will they be there when time-sensitive issues pop up? Check response times and
  service guarantees.

- **Cost**
  Balance expertise with affordability long-term. Get free estimates upfront and understand billing structure.

- **Focus**
  Some experts spread themselves too thin by servicing too many clients. Make sure you get dedicated focus.

- **Mindset**

Find advisors who think creatively but abide strictly by the tax code. Avoid "yes men" looking for shortcuts.

• **Results**

Ask for referrals from other traders. Proven experience with clients like you is a must.

A few things to remember:

— Don't hand your trader tax obligations to just anyone.
— Don't try to do it yourself. TurboTax won't cut it
— If your sister-in-law has been doing your taxes, give her some flowers, a big hug,
and then find somebody who has the experience you need.
— If you talk to your current CPA about these things and he's trying to talk you out of it,
he's probably not the right person for the job. Get a second opinion!
— If your CPA tells you: "You are my biggest client!" it's time to look for a new one. You want a CPA who deals with high-net worth clients and knows the tax benefits for "the rich."

With the right team behind you, your tax bill gets smaller as your accounts get bigger. But only if you lean on true specialists to optimize your filings, entities, deductions and more.

Invest the time to find ideal advisors. Allow them to protect your hard-earned trading profits from being plundered unnecessarily by the IRS!

Conclusion

In this chapter, we explored how you can legally optimize your trader tax filings, entities, deductions, and more to substantially reduce your IRS bill.

With the right specialists advising you, it's possible to save thousands in unnecessary taxes being paid out prematurely or incorrectly.

Think of it as building a strategic moat around your financial fortress to defend against plundering by the IRS. Knowledgeable CPAs, attorneys and tax pros act as your "Fortress Defenders" against unnecessary taxation.

The key is approaching trader taxes proactively, not reacting hastily. Take time to fully understand the implications of your trader type, entity structure, elections, write-offs and retirement accounts.

Now that your tax fortress defenses are fortified, let's shift focus to establishing stability and prosperity for life.
In the next chapter, we'll unlock the power of building passive income streams that can provide lasting financial freedom for you and your family, year after year.

Chapter 15: Step 9: Passive Income Machine

Here's something very important before we start assembling the final pieces of our financial fortress ...

I know you're eager to dive into generating passive income streams. Most people are when they first learn about the fascinating power of cash flow on autopilot!

But here's the catch — this step is "Step 9" for a reason. You must have mastered the previous active wealth-building phases first or else it simply won't work!

Remember when we talked about the "ideal mix" between active trading and investing in Chapter 7: Step 1: Infinite Income Roadmap?

	Trading	Investing
Time needed	Active: 10-30 min per day	Passive: No actions needed
Return	30-60% per year	8 - 12% per year
Risk	30-60% drawdown	8 - 12% drawdown
Goal	Trading for Growth	Investing for Income
Account Size	25k - 50k	500k and more

If you start "investing" too early, your account will grow too slowly, and you might get frustrated.

The key to growing your account quickly and SAFELY is to find the ideal mix of "trading" and "investing".

I compare it to constructing a mighty castle. You wouldn't try hanging banners and flags before the main walls are built, would you? The entire thing would collapse!

Same goes for starting to build passive income engines too early.

So no skipping ahead or you'll undermine all our hard work so far! Patience and discipline are key.

Now, assuming you've laid the proper foundations and fortified the active income trading machine ... you're ready for the final enhancements that will cement your prosperity for generations to come.
I'm talking about establishing self-sustaining PASSIVE revenue streams that keep paying while you sleep!

This is the capstone to your financial fortress ... constructing an impenetrable wall of passive income. Once built, you can kick back as the automated cash flow compounds. Your future generations will reap the rewards as your legacy continues.

Let me show you exactly how to put the finishing touches on true financial freedom.

In this chapter, you will learn:

— What is "real" passive income versus active or portfolio income? Vital you understand the difference!

— The bulletproof assets that generate substantial passive revenue.

— How to engineer the perfect passive income mix for YOU.

— The genius yet overlooked concept of "infinite banking" to multiply gains forever.

When you combine trading and passive income, you cement complete financial freedom. As you sleep soundly, revenue streams steadily build, compound, and grow into an unlimited legacy for your family.

Let's dive in and create true generational wealth!

Action Step 1: Understand Passive Income Sources

What images come to mind when you hear "passive income?" For many, sitting somewhere on a tropical beach with an umbrella drink next to you.

But let's set this aside for a moment, we'll come back to it, I promise!

At its core, passive income means you make money through ASSETS instead of working for money. As Warren Buffett says: *"If you don't find a way to make money while you sleep, you will work until you die."*

Let's revisit Robert Kiyosaki's famous Cash Flow Quadrant for a moment to dive into this concept:

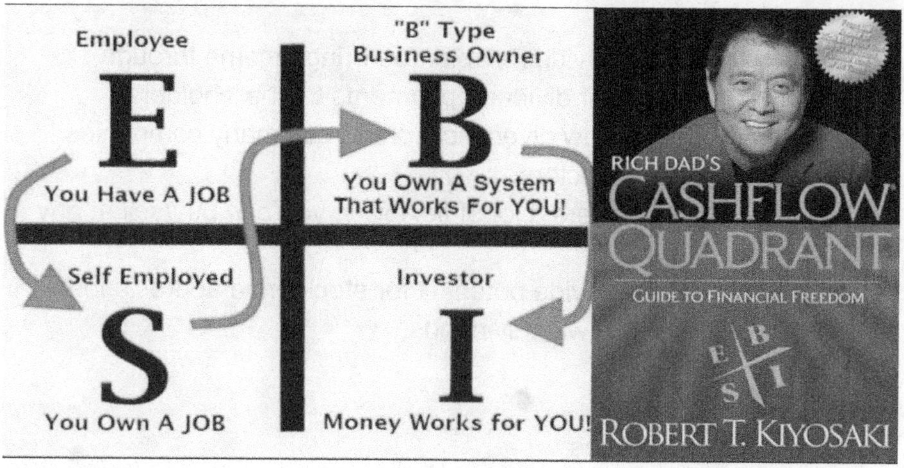

With active income, you trade time for money, whether as an employee or business owner. You work long hours and get burned out since there never seems to be enough hours in a day. It seems that your todo list is getting longer and longer? Does this sound familiar?

On the other hand, passive income is generated from assets like real estate, stocks, royalties, and maybe even businesses that make money without your direct involvement, i.e. making money while you sleep!

Now within the passive income universe, there are a lot of asset classes and investment types that you could invest in. And each passive stream has advantages and disadvantages.

Let's take a look at all the different possibilities to create passive income:

Asset Class: Dividend Stocks and ETFs

These provide passive income through regular dividend payments to shareholders.

Advantages:

— Provide reliable, recurring income through regular dividend payments to shareholders.
— Allow diversification across many companies and sectors.
— Offers a lot of flexibility, you can buy/sell at any time.
— Provide potential for stock price appreciation along with dividends.

Disadvantages:

— Exposed to stock market volatility and risk of dividend cuts.
— Income payments can fluctuate month to month.

Asset Class: Bonds and Fixed Income

Bonds generate interest income from governments, municipal bonds, and corporations who issue the debt.

Advantages:

— Provide predictable fixed interest payments.
— Offer low risk compared to stocks.
— Allow diversification across issuers and maturities.
— Appeal for conservative investors looking for stable income.
— Might have some tax advantages, especially if you invest in government or municipal bonds.

Disadvantages:

— Typically low yields.
— Typically no potential for capital appreciation.

Asset Class: Real Estate Investment Trusts (REITs)

A real estate investment trust is a company that owns, and in most cases operates, income-producing real estate. REITs own many types of commercial real estate, e.g. office and apartment buildings, warehouses, hospitals, shopping centers and hotels.

You can buy and sell these REITs like regular stocks, so investing in them is easy.

Advantages:

— Allows easy diversification into real estate without direct property ownership.
— Requires less capital than physical rental properties.
— Provides fairly steady dividend payments.
— Offers potential for appreciation along with dividends.

Disadvantages:

— Subject to stock market volatility like regular stocks and ETFs.
— No control over or insight into the underlying properties.
— Dividend payments are tied to REIT's rental income stream. Lower rents means lower dividends.
— Lower overall returns than direct property ownership.

Asset Class: Rental Properties, a.ka. Real Estate Investing

Real estate investing involves the purchase, management and sale or rental of real estate for profit. In a nutshell: Rental properties generate profits from rental income.

Advantages:

— Can provide higher returns compared to stocks and bonds.
— Generates steady cash flow from tenant rents.
— Allows control over property and tenant selection.
— Offers tax advantages, depreciation and expense deductions.

Disadvantages:

— Requires significant capital to purchase properties.
— Involves hands-on management responsibilities or hiring a property manager.
— Exposed to vacancies and maintenance costs.
— Offers low liquidity compared to securities: you can't easily buy and sell.
— Tenants can be a nightmare, and in many states, it's not easy to evict them.
— Unplanned repairs can cause stress for you and your hard-earned cash.

Asset Class: Royalties

You can get royalties from intellectual property like books, music, and patents. These royalties generate income without ongoing work.

Advantages:

— Allows creators to earn income perpetually from a single work.
— Requires no additional effort after initial creation.
— Provides potentially exponential income if work gains mass popularity.

— Offers easy diversification, because you can hold many royalty rights.

Disadvantages:

— Lots of work to create the song, book, etc. that creates the royalty.

— Difficult to predict royalty income reliability and amounts.

— Dependent on ongoing popularity and use of the work.

— Typically only lucrative for those with a following of hundreds of thousands of people.

Asset Class: Peer to Peer Lending

Peer-to-peer (P2P) lending is a way for people to lend and borrow money directly from each other online, bypassing traditional financial institutions like banks. Borrowers get access to funds they might not qualify for elsewhere, and lenders can earn higher interest on the money they lend out.

Advantages:

— Allows earning interest by investing in loans to individuals and businesses.

— Enables spreading capital across many small loans to mitigate risk.

— Often automated investing and underwriting through platforms.

Disadvantages:

— Exposed to defaults if borrowers stop repaying loans.

— Relies on a platform for borrower vetting and loan servicing.

Asset Class: High Yield Savings Accounts

These are bank accounts that offer higher interest rates compared to traditional savings accounts. They allow you to earn more money on your savings over time without taking on much risk.

Advantages:

— Provides security as cash deposits are FDIC insured.
— Offers daily liquidity, you can withdraw cash anytime.
— Gives peace of mind for risk averse investors.
— Requires low minimum deposits to open and start earning.

Disadvantages:

— Typically very low interest yields compared to other assets.

Asset Class: Certificates of Deposit (CDs)

This is a specific type of savings account offered by banks and credit unions. You generally agree to keep your money in the CD without taking a withdrawal for a specified length of time. Withdrawing money early means paying a penalty fee to the bank.

Advantages:

— Provides fixed interest rates and terms on cash deposits.
— Offers FDIC insurance up to $250,000 per depositor.
— Gives peace of mind for risk averse investors.
— Allows ladder strategies aligning maturities of the CD with future cash needs.

Disadvantages:

— Ties up funds for defined periods with penalties for early withdrawal.
— Typically very low interest yields compared to other assets.

Asset Class: Business Ownership

Owning a profitable business can provide passive income but only if the business truly runs without you. If you are involved in the business in any shape or form, you're generating active income and not passive income.

Advantages:

— Allows earning money from selling company products and services.
— Provides equity that could appreciate substantially over time.
— Enables scaling up income by growing the customer base.
— Offer tax benefits like deductions and strategic income distribution.

Disadvantages:

— Often requires major upfront capital and ongoing operating expenses.
— Involves significant time and effort to start and manage.
— Exposed to risk of declining sales and falling profits.
— Typically less predictability than bonds, REITs, and royalties.
— SUPER difficult to build a business that runs without you.

So which of all these asset classes is the best for earning passive income?

Well, let's dive in and create a passive income strategy tailored to YOUR goals.

Action Step 2: Create a Passive Income Strategy Tailored to Your Goals

Let's take a step back: When creating a plan for building a fortress, you need to keep the end in mind. Because a two-person cottage requires a vastly different blueprint than a majestic castle for an entire kingdom!

In the same way, your passive income fortress must be aligned to the lifestyle and expenses you want it to support. Therefore, the first step is determining your "enough" number — how much monthly or annual income do you need to cover costs and live abundantly?

Remember those earlier calculations we did with the RPIC Index — your **Reliable Passive Income Coverage** ratio? We did this in Chapter 7 where we discussed your "Infinite Income Roadmap." We use the Income Calculator to determine the income target that would give you complete financial freedom.

Now with that number in mind, we can reverse engineer a passive income strategy to reach it.

With the end defined, we can plot the journey. Here's how to do it:

Step 1: Start by determining how much you have available to invest. This would be money in a savings account, cash reserves, retirement accounts, etc. This is seed capital. Enter the number in the SETTINGS section of the "Income Calculator Tool."

Settings		
	--> Fill out all fields that are highlighted in yellow	
Step #1	How would you like to determine your "cost of living"?	
	Rough Estimate ▼ <<= Select a method first!	
Step #2	Cost of Living (see "Budget Tab)	$111,600
Step #3	**How much do you have currently in your retirement account?**	$100,000
Step #4	**What account size are you comfortable trading?**	$400,000
	i.e. at what level will you stop growing your account and start building your income machine?	
	Suggested:	$390,600

And don't worry if it is small or non-existent right now.

Keep in mind that we're on Step 9! Before we get here, you will have found a way to generate SRC Profits through trading, and as you remember from Chapter 7: Step 1: Infinite Income Roadmap, after a few years of trading, you should have grown your account to a level where you can start "feeding" your investment account.

Don't start the investment account too early! Make sure to follow the steps outlined in this roadmap in sequence and not jump around like a drunken goat.

Step 2: Choose 2-3 core passive asset classes that I explained earlier that are aligned to your risk tolerance and knowledge.

I have tried most of the asset classes above. In fact, at some point I owned eleven single family homes and then I invested in apartment complexes.

And as you know, I do own a business, Rockwell Trading Services, and I'm very involved in it.

Also, this is my fifth book. All previous books have been bestsellers at some point and I can assure you that royalties from these books sales only buy me a nice steak dinner or two. It's not a major money maker.

Anyhow, after trying most if not all of these asset classes, I decided that investing in Dividend Stocks and ETFs to generate passive income is best for me.

But everybody is different so do your research and pick the asset class that YOU are most comfortable with.

Step 3: Track progress closely using KPIs like portfolio value, dividend income per month, and projected RPIC. And fine tune the capital allocation periodically as needed.

As an example, right now, I'm considering turning my previous house into an AirBnb, even though previously I said that I don't want to invest in real estate anymore.

The point is: Be flexible in your approach and take advantage of opportunities when they arise. If the real estate market crashes and I can buy investment properties for 50 cents on the dollar, I will definitely do that.

With this simple 3-step approach, you take a data-driven approach to constructing your passive income fortress brick-by-brick. Patience and discipline are required but the rewards are immense.

Now let's discuss "Infinite Banking." This is a fascinating concept, and you are going to love it.

Action Step 3: Utilize "Infinite Banking" to Multiply Your Income

This is one of my favorite strategies to build wealth even faster! It's often called "The Rockefeller Strategy."

The main idea: You are becoming your own bank.

Here's a simplified overview of the mechanics:

1. You build a diversified dividend stock portfolio that appreciates over time.

2. Your broker allows you to borrow money against these equities at low interest. This is called a "Portfolio Loan."

3. You can then access these portfolio credit lines to acquire rental properties, which generate monthly cash flow.

4. The profits from your real estate portfolio and the dividends from your stocks and ETFs compound and your investment portfolio will grow over time. So you can continually re-borrow against your growing portfolio to buy even more real estate.

The key is utilizing your own banking system, the portfolio, rather than relying on external lenders.

And the best part? Since YOU are your own bank, you will never need to fill out a "loan application" ever again!

In a nutshell:
You turn your stock portfolio into a bank that allows you to buy more properties to earn rental profits, which you can use to buy more stocks. This creates a bigger portfolio and you can borrow more money from your "bank."

As you can see, it compounds infinitely, hence the name ,"Infinite Banking."

Plus, real estate provides a major benefit: tax deductions. So you increase your net worth while decreasing your tax liabilities!

Told you that you will love this!

As you can see, your financial fortress transforms into an impenetrable income machine that never runs out of money. And just like that, you are building generational wealth.

Conclusion

Through this final step, your financial fortress is now complete. You are now generating abundant active trading income while also feeding your self-renewing passive income machine.

Congratulations!

You have now built a financial fortress for yourself and your family that will last for generations.

We've covered immense ground in this wealth creation journey. But remember, success is not a destination but a lifelong process of continuous growth and mastery. Build on what you've learned and keep strengthening your skills and knowledge.

You now hold the blueprint for engineering complete financial independence and creating generational wealth.

The fortress you once envisioned is now a thriving reality. Congratulations on taking control of your financial destiny!

But never rest on your laurels, this is only the beginning …

Chapter 16: Avoiding Pitfalls

Listen. I get it. Constructing your financial fortress requires serious effort and patience.

Believe me, I know!

You're out there day after day, laying those bricks, working on growing your account.

But let me ask you something and I want you to be honest with yourself here ...

Do you ever feel like your own habits and behaviors are sabotaging all that hard work? Like you're taking two steps forward and one step back?

I'm the first to admit it. I've been there!

In the early days I fell for every shiny object and "surefire" shortcut that crossed my path. I let impatience get the best of me.

I tried to cut corners and I battled those same self-defeating patterns over and over again. It was like groundhog day and not the funny Bill Murray kind!

Here's a story of me trying to cut corners:

Picture this: It's 1997 and I get a call from this broker. He's telling me Gold has hit rock bottom at $340 and he's got the inside scoop that it's about to skyrocket. Me, being the trusting, naive soul I was, jumped in head first. I invested $20,000 in Gold futures, thinking I was about to make it big. After all, the broker said that it would only take a few weeks and I would "easily make $15,000 - $20,000."

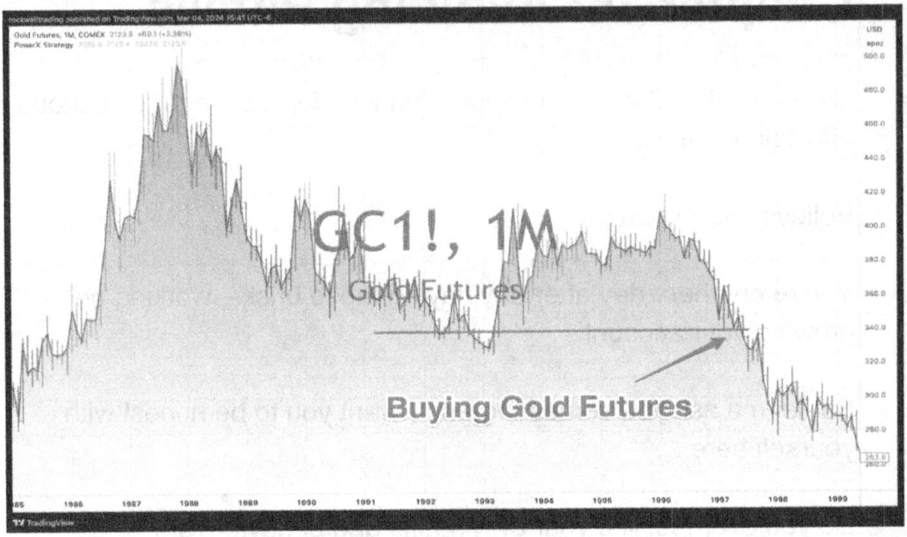

Well, fast forward a few months … Gold drops from $340 to $300, and my futures contracts? Worthless!

My account? Wiped out. Poof. Gone.

Talk about a harsh lesson in the dangers of "hot tips"!

So in this chapter, I'm pulling back the curtain on three types of "account killers."

1. Bad Habits (the silent killers).
2. "Helpful Advisors" (more like hinderers, am I right?).
3. Tempting Shortcuts (that lead you straight off a cliff).

Alright, here's some more straight talk:

How do I know this toxic trio? I know because they set up shop in my own mind for far too long! If only someone had told me about these "account killers" sooner, I could've saved myself a whole lot of headaches … and MONEY.

As the legendary trader, Jesse Livermore, put it: "There is nothing new on Wall Street. Most of the time when voices begin to say, *this time is different*, it's right before investors lose a lot of money." Truer words, my friend, truer words.

So, if you ever catch yourself feeling impatient, overwhelmed, or tempted to stray off the path on your wealth-building journey, you just come right back to this chapter, ok?

Think of it as your personal roadmap for sidestepping all the landmines that yours truly (and countless others) have already triggered.

How Bad Habits Sabotage Your Financial Fortress

Bad Habit #1: Procrastination

Here's a secret. I'm naturally a world-class procrastinator. Always have been.

You should see the mail piled up on my kitchen island for weeks on end before I finally start tackling it. And don't get me started on getting my accountant documents for taxes. Let's just say he has to file an extension for me every single year!

So when I first started investing, of course the same patterns emerged. I'd delay taking action, making excuses like I was too busy, the markets seemed too dicey, or that pesky thing called "life" always got in the way. Sound familiar?

But the real issue was plain old fear and uncertainty. I didn't know where to start and I was afraid that I might lose money!

Here's the harsh truth though — every day we procrastinate is another 24 hours our cash sits idle instead of growing. Compound interest waits for no one! You don't need to move mountains on day one but you do need to START.

Solution: *Commit to taking one small step daily. Read a chapter in a trading book, journal your goals. Heck, log into a charting software and stare at the screen for 5 minutes! Because tiny actions still beat ZERO action every time. And that micro-momentum quickly snowballs into massive progress.*

Bad Habit #2: Impulsiveness

Pretty much every trader I know had this problem at some point:

Being way too impulsive and changing strategies every other week!

And yes, I've been there too. Especially when first starting out and a few trades moved against me. Panic would take over and I'd make rash, emotional decisions. The classic "shiny object syndrome," chasing one method after the next.
It's so easy to fall for the emails or invitations to webinars that you receive, promising you that "THIS time, it will be different."

Keep this in mind: The grass is always greener on the other side because it's fertilized with bullsh*t!

In hindsight, the real problem was the lack of a clear trading plan. Without that north star, I was drifting like a ship without a rudder, desperately moving from one strategy to another.

But constantly hopping from one approach to another meant mastery of none. And it often led to overtrading, recklessly playing "Trading Roulette" with no real edge. A recipe for disaster.

Solution: *Institute a mandatory waiting period of at least 40 trades before judging any strategy. Every trading strategy has winning streaks and losing streaks. Make sure that you experience BOTH before deciding whether the trading strategy works or not.*

If you jump ship after just a few trades with a strategy you never give your account a chance to recover.

I know it's tempting to bail at the first signs of turbulence. But you need a decent sample size to assess true potential. Knee-jerk changes just lead to spinning your wheels.

The same applies to any changes in your trading plan: take the time to TEST the change you want to make instead of changing a criteria after one or two losses.

Bad Habit #3: Terrible Time Management Skills

Okay, it's painful to admit but I used to completely waste my most precious resource,TIME, especially when it came to prioritizing wealth building.

Sure, I thought about trading constantly. But when it came to carving out dedicated practice hours or really focusing on trading meaningfully ... I'd always find ways to put it off. Emails, busy work, you name it.

And of course that lack of focused skill development meant my account went essentially nowhere for way too long. Frustrating!

The lesson finally sunk in that building a financial fortress doesn't happen by accident. It requires concentrated effort and diligent time management.

You don’t need a lot of time to make progress but you need to work on it regularly!

Think about it this way: 10 push-ups for 100 days are better than 100 push-ups in 1 day!
Solution: *Block off non-negotiable "money hours" in your calendar for education, deliberate practice, testing, and journaling. Treat this time as sacred as an appointment with your biggest client or board of directors.*

Because the reality is, nobody will protect this time but you! So guard it fiercely and shut your door and silence phone notifications.

Bad Habit #4: Analysis Paralysis

Oh boy, do I remember the days of analysis paralysis!

When I first started trading, I was like a kid in a candy store, except replace the candy with technical indicators, fundamental data, and economic reports. I wanted it all!

After all, I’m German AND I am the son of an engineer! So I thought I always needed more data, more indicators, more opinions, before I could place a trade.

I thought, "Hey, the more data I crunch, the better my trades will be, right?"

Wrong!

All that information overload just left me more confused than a chameleon in a bag of Skittles. I was so busy analyzing every little detail that I missed the bigger picture.

It's like that old saying, "Can't see the forest for the trees." Well, I plotted so many indicators on my charts that I couldn't see the stock price anymore!

The turning point came when I realized that I needed to simplify my trading. I'm talking bare-bones, back-to-basics simplicity.

So I sat down and really thought about the few key pieces of information I needed to make a solid trading decision. Everything else? Throw it out the window like yesterday's stale bagel.

Because keep in mind that we will never KNOW if a stock goes up or down or if a trade will work out. All we do is use the data we have to put the odds in our favor and make an informed decision.

So what's the solution: Keep it simple, silly! (KISS).

Identify the 4-5 essential data points you need and dump the rest. As you have seen in Chapter 10 when we talked about my trading plan, there's only a few bullet points.
Your trading plan should fit on one page, not rival War and Peace in length. Focus on quality, not quantity.
And start with ONE strategy, like, "The Wheel Strategy."

Keep it simple!

Bad Habit #5: Short-Term Thinking

I'll admit, I used to be a sucker for the idea of quick riches. I became obsessed with windfall profits and lottery ticket trades rather than steady, systematic gains.

I knew deep down that real wealth was built slowly and steadily, but man, those stories of traders turning $2,000 into 2 million within a year were just too tempting!

So what did I do? I started chasing those elusive "unicorn" trades. You know, the ones that are supposed to bring you 200% ... 300% ... even 1000% returns in a matter of days!

I was swinging for the fences every single time, hoping to hit that one "big trade" that would set me up for life.

But here's the thing about unicorns: they're not real. And chasing them in the markets is a surefire way to watch your account go up in flames.

More often than not, I'd end up striking out and those "10-bagger" trades would never happen. Yes, my losses were rather small but steady and I was bleeding through 1,000 cuts. My account went down, week after week and month after month.

Solution: *Focus on consistent base hits, not occasional home runs. Aim for 5-10% returns per month, not 500% in a week. Longevity beats lottery tickets every time.*

Bad Habit #6: Impatience

I know I've already touched on this but it's worth repeating because it's just that important.

When I started trading, I so badly wanted to believe that I could shortcut my way to millions. I thought, *Hey, if I just find that one magic strategy or that one perfect trade, I can skip all the hard work and start living the life I always wanted!*

Well, all I can say is I was young and naive. The truth is, there are no shortcuts to lasting success in the markets. Believe me, I've tried them all and all they got me was a one-way ticket to Brokeville, population: me.

I learned the hard way that get-rich-quick schemes are just that … schemes. They might work for a lucky few, but for most of us, they're just a fast track to blowing up our accounts.

The real path to trading success is paved with patience, discipline, and consistency. It's about showing up day after day, putting in the work, and trusting the process.

Solution: *Commit to your education and your strategy and let time and compound growth work their magic. There's no elevator to trading success, you just take the stairs, one step at a time.*

How Enemies Undermine Your Progress

Let me tell you something … building a financial fortress is TOUGH.

The markets are trying to prove you wrong, all the time!

Self-doubt wears down your discipline.

It's just you versus an army of enemies conspiring to deter you from building your financial fortress. And perhaps the most dangerous adversaries are the ones promising shortcuts and quick relief for your struggles.

If only you would have listened to them.

Just stopped what you were doing and did what THEY told you to do.

Their siren songs tempt even the savviest traders sometimes.

In this section, I'll show you the true face of these enemies, plotting to undermine your wealth plans by exploiting those all-too-human vulnerabilities.

I've fallen for their wily tricks countless times over the decades.

By illuminating their tactics, you can spot manipulation disguised as opportunity.

Their ultimate goal is to distract you from building your financial fortress while lining their own pockets.

Forewarned is forearmed — let's keep your walls intact!

Enemy #1: Expensive Advisors

Now don't get me wrong:

Tax pros, accountants, even lawyers can provide tremendous value strategizing your financial fortress construction and defense. But the key is finding specialists, not salespeople masquerading as advisors, a.k.a "financial advisors."

You know who I'm talking about, right? It's Sean, a family friend who is working at one of the "big firms."

And Sean's pitch is enticing: "Let us handle your investing using our proven secret strategies and seasoned pros. We have a whole team that takes care of your investments."

BS!

Just look at the fine print and you will see that "Sean" makes a lot of money in commissions by selling you the investments the company wants him to push on you.

And all the fancy titles and certifications are just there to hide a simple fact: Sean is a salesman!

Don't believe me? Well, I have proof:

According to Glassdoor, financial advisors make between $95,000 - $177,000 per year.
However, their "base pay" is only $58,000 - $109,000 per year.

The estimated additional pay is $48,650 per year. And "additional pay" could include cash bonuses (probably for achieving their sales goals), commission, and tips!

Tips?!? Who is "tipping" their financial advisor?
"Here's an extra 20, buy yourself something nice." Give me a break!

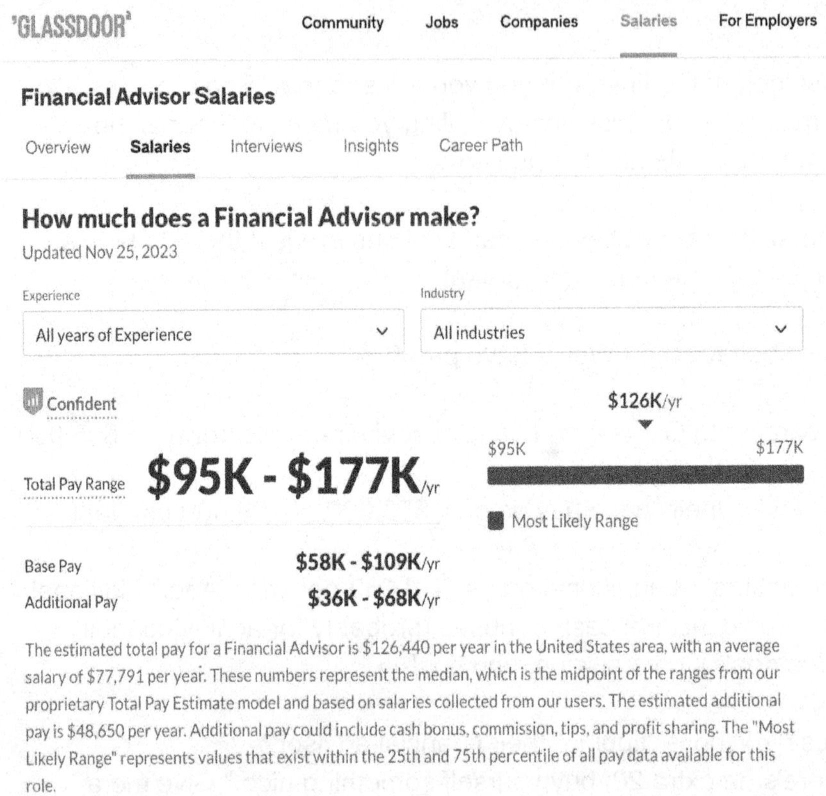

GLASSDOOR

Community Jobs Companies Salaries For Employers

Financial Advisor Salaries

Overview **Salaries** Interviews Insights Career Path

How much does a Financial Advisor make?

Updated Nov 25, 2023

Experience: All years of Experience

Industry: All industries

Confident

Total Pay Range **$95K - $177K**/yr

$126K/yr

$95K $177K

Most Likely Range

Base Pay **$58K - $109K**/yr

Additional Pay **$36K - $68K**/yr

The estimated total pay for a Financial Advisor is $126,440 per year in the United States area, with an average salary of $77,791 per year. These numbers represent the median, which is the midpoint of the ranges from our proprietary Total Pay Estimate model and based on salaries collected from our users. The estimated additional pay is $48,650 per year. Additional pay could include cash bonus, commission, tips, and profit sharing. The "Most Likely Range" represents values that exist within the 25th and 75th percentile of all pay data available for this role.

Source: https://www.glassdoor.com/Salaries/financial-advisor-salary-SRCH_KO0,17.htm

So here's the deal: These advisors? They're not in it to make YOU rich. They're in it to make themselves rich off of YOU.

Think about it for a moment: Why would you hire somebody who is making less than you to manage your finances?

Do you think they would be cold calling for new clients if they knew how to build wealth? Of course not!

They make money by upselling you on expensive funds and products to maximize their bonuses.

And the worst part? When the markets take a tumble, they've got a million fancy explanations for why it's not their fault. Meanwhile, your portfolio is bleeding out but they're still cashing those commission checks.

Bottom line: be wary of anyone promising the world and trying to get their hands on your hard-earned cash. Do your own research, trust your gut, and remember ... if it sounds too good to be true, it probably is!

And if you follow the steps in this book, you can run circles around "Sean" and his gang!

Here's another enemy:

Enemy #2: Online Forums

Ah, online forums. The virtual wild west of the trading and investing world.

It's like a big ol' saloon where everyone's got an opinion and they're not afraid to share it, no matter how misguided or downright dangerous it might be.

Sure, these forums might seem like a friendly place at first. *"We're all in this together!"* they'll say. *"We're here to help each other succeed!"*

But let me tell you, for every one nugget of wisdom you might uncover, you'll have to sift through a hundred piles of ... well, you know.

It's like panning for gold, except instead of gold, you're looking for good advice and instead of water, you're wading through a river of bad hot takes and armchair experts.

And don't even get me started on the "keyboard cowboys." You know the type. They talk a big game, throwing around technical jargon like they're the *Wolf of Wall Street* himself.

But you know what they say about an empty can ... it makes the most noise. Most of these keyboard cowboys have never even placed a real trade in their lives!

And that's the real danger of these forums. It's just a breeding ground for misinformation and confusion. You'll find yourself drowning in a sea of conflicting opinions, rumors, and speculation.

And before you know it, you've wasted months chasing your tail, trying to make sense of it all, when you could have been actually learning and growing as a trader.

Here's the hard truth: reading about trading on a forum isn't going to make you a successful trader any more than watching Grey's Anatomy is going to make you a surgeon.

The only thing that's going to get you there is rolling up your sleeves, getting a proper education, and putting in the hard work to hone your skills. There's no substitute for that.

So by all means, enjoy the forums for the entertainment value. But when it comes to your trading education and strategy? Stick to reputable sources and your own hard-won experience. Your future self (and your account balance) will thank you.

Enemy #3: TV Personalities

Don't even get me started on these TV "gurus"!

They're like the weathermen of the trading world. They'll tell you there's a 50% chance of markets moving higher with a chance of it moving lower or sideways but at the end of the day, they're just guessing like the rest of us.

Except they get paid the big bucks to do it on national television!

It never ceases to amaze me how many people hang on every word that comes out of these talking heads' mouths. It's like they think just because someone has a camera pointed at them, they must have all the answers.

If I had a dollar for every broadcast "guru" claiming he knows what the Fed, the markets, or a stock is doing, I'd have enough money to buy a Caribbean island!

But many people fall for their scripted authority and convincing narratives.

So let's be real. If these so-called experts really had the secret to untold riches, do you think they'd be waking up at the crack of dawn to sit under hot studio lights and ramble on about market trends?

No way! They'd be on a beach somewhere, sipping umbrella drinks and enjoying the good life.

But instead, they're stuck in a never-ending cycle of filling airtime and boosting ratings. They'll say whatever it takes to keep viewers tuned in through the commercial breaks.

And don't forget, they're getting paid whether your portfolio goes up, down, or sideways. Their loyalty is to their paycheck, not your success.

Now, I'm not saying these folks are intentionally trying to lead you astray. But at the end of the day, their job is to entertain, not to educate.

They're not in the trenches, putting their own money on the line and learning from the wins and losses. They're just armchair quarterbacks, playing Monday morning market analyst.

So the next time you find yourself getting sucked into the hype of some TV guru's latest "can't miss" prediction, just remember ... they're getting paid to talk, not to trade.
Your time and energy are better spent focusing on your own education and strategy, not hanging on the every word of some smooth-talking "expert" who's more interested in their ratings than your returns.

Enemy #4: Friends And Family

You know what they say, opinions are like belly buttons. Everybody's got one.

And when it comes to trading, it seems like everyone and their mother (literally) has some "surefire" tip or piece of advice they just can't wait to share with you.

It never fails. The moment you mention that you're an active investor, suddenly every distant cousin and high school acquaintance comes out of the woodwork with a "hot tip" or an "insider secret."

But here's the thing. Most of the time, these so-called tips are just regurgitated nonsense they heard from a friend of a friend or read in some obscure corner of the internet.

It's like playing a game of telephone, except instead of a silly phrase, it's your hard-earned money on the line.

And don't even get me started on the ones who try to rope you into their own crazy investment schemes.

They'll come to you with some "can't miss" opportunity, swearing up and down that it's a sure thing.

And if you ask them, “How much money did you invest in this tip?” they usually say, “Oh, that’s not for me but I think it will be perfect for YOU!” Yeah, right ...

Or they say, “Well, I invested XXX dollars but right now the stock is down. But that’s a GREAT opportunity for you to get in at a lower price than I did.”

Often, they already know that this was a bad investment but now they need a “partner in crime” so that they are not alone with their “not-so-smart idea.”

Listen, I know these people usually mean well. They're not trying to sabotage your success (at least, not intentionally).

But the road to financial ruin is paved with good intentions and bad advice from unqualified sources.

So the next time cousin Jimmy comes to you with a "foolproof" penny stock pick or your college roommate swears they've got the inside scoop on the next big thing, just smile, nod, and change the subject.

Your financial future is too important to risk on the half-baked theories of armchair traders and wannabe gurus.

Stick to your guns, trust your own research and instincts and politely tune out the noise from the peanut gallery. Your bank account will thank you.

Enemy #5: Trading "Gurus"

Ah, the "trading gurus."

I'll admit it. I've fallen for their schtick more times than I care to count, especially in my early days of trading.

They just make it all sound so easy, you know? *"Sign up for my foolproof system and watch the profits roll in while you sip piña coladas on the beach!"*

It's like they've cracked some secret code to the markets that us, mere mortals, just can't access without their help.

But here's what they don't tell you in their flashy sales pitches:

Trading is hard. It takes time, discipline and a whole lot of trial and error to get it right. There's no magic bullet or secret sauce that's going to turn you into an overnight millionaire.

But these gurus? They're not in the business of teaching you how to trade. They're in the business of selling you a dream.

And the way they keep you hooked is by always having a new "revolutionary" product or "game-changing" indicator to push on you.

Special indicator!
Crazy AI bots!
New system guaranteed to 10X your money!

It's a constant cycle of upsells and upgrades, each one promising to be the missing piece to your trading success.

But the truth is, the only ones getting rich off these schemes are the gurus themselves. They're laughing all the way to the bank while you're left holding the bag, wondering why their "foolproof" system didn't quite pan out the way they promised.

Now, I'm not saying there's no value in education and mentorship. Far from it. Learning from those who have come before you is an essential part of any trader's journey.

But there's a big difference between a legitimate educator who's invested in your success and a smooth-talking charlatan who's only interested in lining their own pockets.

So how do you tell the difference? It's simple. Look for the ones who are more interested in teaching you how to fish than selling you a fancy new rod and reel.

The real mentors, the ones worth learning from, they'll give you the tools and the knowledge you need to navigate the markets on your own. They won't try to keep you dependent on their "exclusive" indicators or "secret" strategies.

Because at the end of the day, the only foolproof trading plan is the one you develop yourself through hard work, persistence, and a healthy dose of trial and error.

So don't be afraid to invest in your education. But be discerning about who you learn from.

Tune out the noise of the "gurus" and their empty promises and focus on building your skills and financial fortress, brick by brick.

It might not be as flashy or exciting as the dream they're selling, but I promise you, it's the only real path to lasting success in this game.

Look, I know you may be asking yourself:

"Is Markus a guru? He sells software, he's a personality on YouTube, and he has books for sale on Amazon.

Absolutely not! I'm just a guy who has tried a bunch of different things and failed ... a lot. I am just sharing what works for me and I encourage everybody to try it out for themselves. My hope is that you can avoid some of the mistakes I've already made for you.

So keep your head down, stay the course, and remember ... Slow and steady wins the race. Those get-rich-quick schemes? They're just a detour on the road to disappointment.

Why Shortcuts And Quick Fixes Backfire

Now, before you shake your head thinking, "I'd never fall for crazy get-rich-quick claims," believe me: it's more tempting than you realize when your wealth building efforts start to feel like an uphill battle.

And trust me, I've been there. I've fallen for those shiny promises of overnight riches more times than I care to admit.

It's like everywhere you turn, there's another story popping up about some average Joe who turned a couple grand into a couple million in just under a year!

And let's be honest, who wouldn't want a piece of that action?

Especially when you've had a taste of success and you're hungry for more but suddenly you hit a plateau and your account growth stalls out, no matter how hard you hustle.

That's when the siren song of the shortcut starts to sound pretty darn appealing. We've all been there, seduced by the promise of an easier path, even when our gut tells us it's too good to be true.

Here are the 4 most common shortcuts that wealth builders fall for:

Shortcut #1: Relying on Hot Tips

In my early days, when I was struggling to gain traction, I was convinced that the key to unlocking overnight success was hidden in the chatter of online forums or the bombastic claims of self-proclaimed gurus.

I mean, come on, those “insiders” had to know something we didn't, right? There had to be a secret system or a loophole in the markets that would lead me to the promised land of surefire wins and easy money.

But you know what? Those "hot tips" and "insider secrets"? They were about as useful as a screen door on a submarine.

Here's the hard truth: Consistent, repeatable success in trading doesn't come from chasing the next big thing or betting the farm on some half-baked tip.

It comes from putting in the work to educate yourself, understanding the fundamentals of risk management, and developing a strategy based on solid probabilities, not just hunches and hearsay.

So do yourself a favor and tune out the noise of the rumor mill. Stop chasing unicorns — they don’t exist!

Shortcut #2: Expensive Courses

Okay, so when the hot tips turned out to be more "miss" than "hit," I turned to expensive "guru" courses. And I thought the more expensive the course the better.

In fact, in the beginning of my trading career, I bought books for $175 to $195.
And over time I bought 12 of them. They are still standing on a shelf in my library.

Not only did I fall for the “expensive must be better” trick but I also fell for the “more is better” fallacy. I thought the more I learned the better my trading!

I bought books like, “Options as a Strategic Investment,” which is 1001 pages and, “The Big Book of Technical Indicators,” which is 648 pages.

I bought trading courses that took me months to complete!

Because I thought, the more I know, the better my trading decisions will be.

Oh boy, was I wrong!

First of all, it requires tremendous discipline to read 1,001 pages or go through 87 lessons in a trading course, each two hours long.

And all it did was lead to *"analysis paralysis."*
Now, don't get me wrong, I'm not saying there's no value in investing in your learning. A good mentor or a solid course can absolutely accelerate your growth.

But the key word here is "good."

So before you go dropping your life savings on the latest and greatest guru course, ask yourself: *"Do I really need to know 56 options trading strategies that all traders should know?"*

Or would my time and money be better spent focusing on a few core principles and putting them into practice consistently?

I think you know the answer. Keep it simple, focus on the fundamentals and don't let the temptation of the "expensive equals better" myth lead you astray.

Shortcut #3: Chasing One Big Trade

After failing to crack success through hot tips or expensive courses, I became convinced my big break must be one monumental winner around the corner. If I hit it big, I could quit trading and live happily ever after!

So I started hunting unicorn "10-baggers" or even "100x trades" throwing a lot of money at long shots, hoping to strike it rich fast. No more grinding out small consistent winners if going huge could shortcut years of minor gains, right?

And let's be real: Who wouldn't want to skip straight to the champagne and caviar lifestyle with one well-timed trade?

But as it turns out, those "unicorn" trades are called that for a reason. They're about as rare and elusive as, well, a unicorn.

Chasing them was like playing the lottery with my trading account. Sure, every once in a blue moon, someone hits the jackpot. But the odds of it being me? About as slim as winning the Powerball with a single ticket.

Over the years, I have learned that slow and steady truly wins the trading race.

Greed might be good but it is a heck of a drug and it can make us do some crazy things like throw risk management out the window in pursuit of that one big score.
But trust me, the tortoise had it right. Or … to use a baseball analogy: Take singles and doubles consistently, not reckless moonshot gambles.

That's the path to fortune.

Shortcut #4: Predicting Rather Than Adapting

Okay, last one, I promise. But this one might be the most insidious of all the trading shortcuts, because it's just so darn tempting to believe.

After watching my account get absolutely destroyed chasing hot tips, expensive courses, and long shot trades, I thought I'd finally found the answer: **Predicting the future**.

I mean, think about it: If I could just figure out exactly where the markets were headed next, I could place the perfect trades and watch the profits roll in, right?

No more guesswork, no more uncertainty, just pure, unadulterated trading prophecy.

So I set out on a quest to find the holy grail of indicators, the one that would give me an unbeatable edge and let me see the future of every chart with perfect clarity.

I was convinced that if I just looked hard enough, I could find that magic combination of lines and squiggles that would unlock the secrets of price movement.

And man, did I look. I tested out every oscillator, every moving average crossover, every obscure pattern and wave count I could get my hands on.

But here's the thing about the markets: They don't care about your indicators or your predictions.

They're going to do whatever the heck they want, whenever the heck they want, and no amount of lines on a chart is going to change that.

Trying to predict the future of something as complex and chaotic as the financial markets is like trying to predict the weather on a specific day three years from now. It's a fool's errand, plain and simple.

The cold, hard truth is this: The only thing predictable about the markets is their unpredictability.

So what should you do? Simple. Stop trying to predict and start learning to adapt.

I always say, “Trade what you SEE and not what youTHINK!” Focus on developing a robust, adaptable strategy that can handle whatever the markets throw at you.

Learn to think in probabilities, not certainties. And above all, stay humble and keep learning.
Because in the end, the only thing standing between you and trading success is your own ability to stay disciplined, stay focused, and stay in the game for the long haul.

There's no crystal ball, no magic indicator, no guru or system that can do that for you. All we can do is put the odds in our favor by placing high-probability trades.

Conclusion

Well, there you have it.

I know it's not always easy to resist the siren song of the quick fix, especially when times are getting tough and your account is not growing as fast as you want.

But trust me when I say that nothing will derail your progress faster than falling for shortcuts.

I've watched too many traders, myself included, sabotage their own success by trying to skip steps and cheat the process.

And every single time, it ends in frustration, disappointment and a whole lot of lost capital.

So if there's one thing I want you to take away from this chapter, it's this:

There are no shortcuts to trading success.

It's a marathon, not a sprint, and the only way to win is to stay in the race and keep putting one foot in front of the other, even when it feels like you're not making any progress.

Every setback, every obstacle, every challenge along the way? That's just an opportunity to strengthen your discipline and your resolve.

Because in the end, the traders who succeed aren't the ones who got lucky or found some magic formula. They're the ones who had the grit and the determination to keep going, even when the odds seemed stacked against them.

So embrace it, welcome the challenges, and keep your eye on the prize. Your financial fortress isn't going to build itself but with the right tools and the right mindset, you've got everything you need to make it happen.

And speaking of tools, that's exactly what we're going to dive into in the next chapter.
I'm going to share with you some of my favorite resources and strategies for staying on track and keeping your wealth-building journey moving forward, no matter what the markets throw at you. Think of it like your own personal trading toolkit, packed with everything you need to stay focused, stay disciplined, and keep making progress, one brick at a time.

So if you're ready to ditch the shortcuts and start building your financial future the right way, keep reading. The best is yet to come.

Chapter 17: Wealth Building Toolbox

Let me ask you something … When you're building your dream house, what do you need?

That's right, you need the right tools! You wouldn't show up to a construction site with just a hammer and a prayer, would you?

Of course not!

Well, the same goes for building your financial fortress.

You need the right wealth building tools to make the process systematic, efficient, and dare I say, even enjoyable!

Because let's face it, who wants to spend countless hours crunching numbers and pulling their hair out trying to make sense of it all?

That's why I've put together this chapter — to give you a peek inside my personal wealth building toolbox. These are the tools that have helped me (and countless others) streamline the process and make building wealth a whole lot easier.

Tools for Phase 1: Wealth Foundation

Remember the three phases of the wealth building blueprint we talked about earlier? Well, in Phase 1,you're laying the foundation. You're creating your roadmap to financial freedom.

And these tools are going to be your best friends:

Income Calculator

We covered this in Chapter 7, remember? This handy tool helps you determine the perfect mix of trading and investing based on your current situation and your big, audacious goals. It's like having a personal financial architect in your pocket!

You can download it here: https://rockwell.rocks/incomecalculator

Winning Strategy Selector

As you know, there are a million different trading strategies out there. It's enough to make your head spin!

But fear not, because in Chapter 8, we introduced the Winning Strategy Selector. This tool helps you cut through the noise and find the strategy that's just right for you, based on your goals, risk tolerance, and lifestyle.

You can download this tool here:
https://rockwell.rocks/strategyselector

Broker Comparison Calculator

Not all brokers are created equal! And in Chapter 9, we dove into how to choose the best one for you.

The *Broker Comparison Calculator* makes it a breeze to compare different brokers based on factors like commissions, fees, trading platform, and customer service.

Because life's too short to deal with a broker that doesn't have your back!

You want the best broker on your wealth building team.

So download the Broker Comparison Calculator and fill it out: https://rockwell.rocks/brokercomparison

Tools for Phase 2: Trading Mastery

Alright, so you've laid the foundation. Now it's time to start building those walls! In Phase 2 - Trading Mastery, you're focusing on developing your trading skills and creating a daily process that works for you. And there's one tool that I absolutely swear by:

The PowerX Optimizer

This is the Swiss Army Knife of trading tools. It has everything you need for Phase 2.

It's designed to help you with every aspect of your trading journey, from finding the best trades to analyzing your performance and making adjustments on the fly.

Remember Step 4 - Bulletproof Trading Plan from Chapter 10?

This is where you create your daily action plan — your trading roadmap.

PowerX Optimizer is like your GPS for this journey. It helps you:

— Scan for stocks that meet your specific criteria, so you're always trading what's right for you.

— Identify optimal entry and exit points, so you're not left guessing when to pull the trigger.

— Manage your risk like a pro, with built-in position sizing and risk management tools.

With **PowerX Optimizer**, creating and executing your 100k trading plan becomes a systematic,
streamlined process. No more second-guessing yourself or getting lost in the weeds of analysis paralysis.

And we talked about how technology is your secret weapon for building wealth faster and smarter.

Well, I might be biased … but I believe that **PowerX Optimizer** is the epitome of trading technology. It's like having a NASA supercomputer crunch the numbers for you, so you can focus on what really matters — making smart trading decisions.

With **PowerX Optimizer**, you're not just trading — you're trading like a pro, with the best technology in the business backing you up.

And do you remember when we discussed how regular performance analysis is crucial for continuously improving your trading results in Step 6 - The Rapid Performance Analyzer?

Well, **PowerX Optimizer** makes this process a breeze:

— It logs and organizes all your trades, so you always have a clear record of your trading history.

— It calculates key performance metrics like win rate, profit factor, and average win/loss, so you can see exactly how you're doing.

— It provides visual charts and graphs of your performance over time, so you can spot trends and make adjustments as needed.

As you can see, **PowerX Optimizer** is the ultimate tool for building your trading skills in Phase 2.

It's like having a trading coach, analyst, and assistant all rolled into one powerful package.

But don't just take my word for it. Try it out for yourself and see the difference it makes in your trading. I promise you won't be disappointed

You can learn more about it at rockwell.rocks/pxo.

Tools for Phase 3: Wealth Mastery

When you enter Phase 3 of the Wealth Building Blueprint, you've built your fortress and now it's time to put the finishing touches on it.

Now it's all about protecting your wealth and making sure it lasts for generations to come. And when it comes to Step 8 - the Wealth Empire Architect, there's one resource I always recommend:

Traders Accounting:

These guys are the tax and accounting wizards for traders. When you're ready to take your wealth protection to the next level, book a call with them. They'll help you structure your trading business for maximum tax efficiency and make sure you're keeping Uncle Sam happy.

And you can get a professional consultation, valued at $300, right here for free: https://rockwell.rocks/cpa.

Recommended Reading and Education Sources

I know you're probably thinking, "Markus, I'm already reading your book! What more do I need?"

First of all: THANKS! I'm flattered.

But the truth is, the learning never stops.

The markets are always changing and there's always more to discover. That's why I recommend checking out these resources:

Our YouTube Channel

Subscribe to our channel for tons of videos packed with trading tips, strategies, and “What’s happening in the markets right now.”

You can subscribe right here: https://rockwell.rocks/youtube

Morning Brew:

This daily newsletter is like the espresso shot of business news. It's a quick, entertaining read that will keep you up to date on the markets and the economy.

And the best: It’s free.

You can get it here: rockwell.rocks/morningbrew

Wall Street Breakfast:

If you want to start your day with a comprehensive overview of what's happening in the financial world, look no further than Wall Street Breakfast.

It's like having a personal analyst deliver the news straight to your inbox every morning - for free!

You can get it here: rockwell.rocks/breakfast

Conclusion

So there you have it, folks — your very own wealth building toolbox! With these tools and resources at your fingertips, you'll be well on your way to constructing that financial fortress of your dreams.

But remember, tools are only as good as the person using them. It's still up to you to put in the work, stay disciplined, and keep pushing forward, even when the market throws you a curveball.

But hey, that's what makes this journey so exciting, right? It's all about the thrill of the challenge, the satisfaction of seeing your hard work pay off, and the joy of knowing that you're building a legacy that will last for generations.

So grab your tools, roll up your sleeves, and let's get to work!

In the next chapter, I have an action plan for you that shows you exactly what to do next.

Chapter 18: Your Next Steps

Congratulations! You've made it to the end of the book.

You now have a comprehensive blueprint for building your financial fortress and creating generational wealth.

But here's the thing — knowledge alone isn't enough.

As the legendary Tony Robbins says, "Knowledge isn't power, it's potential power. Action is power."

So in this final chapter, I'm going to give you a clear action plan to get started, maximize your chances of success, and keep the momentum going.

The Action Plan for Getting Started

First things first, let's recap the 9-step Wealth Building Blueprint we've covered throughout this book:

Step 1 - Infinite Income Roadmap
This is where you define your wealth-building goals and create a personalized plan to achieve them. It's about knowing where you are now and where you want to be.

Step 2 - Winning Strategy Selector
Choosing the right trading and investing strategy is crucial. This step helps you identify the approach that aligns with your goals, risk tolerance, and lifestyle.

Step 3 - Ultimate Broker Guide

Your broker is your partner in wealth building. This guide helps you select the best broker for your needs based on factors like commissions, fees, and trading platform.

Step 4 - Bulletproof 100k Trading Plan
This is your daily action plan for trading success. It covers everything from stock selection to entry and exit rules, and risk management.

Step 5 - Unshakeable Tech-Powered Trader
Technology is your secret weapon for building wealth faster. This step shows you how to leverage powerful tools like PowerX Optimizer to maximize your trading potential.

Step 6 - Rapid Performance Analyzer
Regular performance analysis is key to continuous improvement. This step teaches you how to track your progress, identify your strengths and weaknesses, and make data-driven adjustments.

Step 7 - Turbo Growth Accelerator
This is where you apply advanced strategies to accelerate your account growth, such as using margin and repairing losing trades. It's about taking your trading to the next level.

Step 8 - Wealth Empire Architect
Protecting your wealth is just as important as building it. This step covers tax optimization strategies and entity structuring to maximize your wealth preservation.

Step 9 - Passive Income Machine
The ultimate goal is to create a self-sustaining passive income stream. This step shows you how to invest your trading profits wisely to generate reliable, hands-off income.

Now, I know that might seem like a lot. But remember, Rome wasn't built in a day and neither is your financial fortress. The key is to start small and build momentum over time.

Don't try to tackle everything at once. Set realistic goals for yourself and focus on taking consistent action, day after day. Even if it's just 30 minutes a day, that's still progress!

Next Steps Checklist

Alright, so you're fired up and ready to take action.
Here's your next steps checklist:

- Create your Infinite Income Roadmap so that you know exactly where you are right now and where you need to be.
- Fill out the Winning Strategy Selector and determine the best trading and investing strategy for you.
- Start practicing your trading strategy on a paper trading account.
- Make adjustments as needed.
- And if you want to get a powerful tool to help you on this journey, get the PowerX Optimizer.

That's it!

Just follow these simple steps and you'll be well on your way to building your financial fortress.

Don't overthink it and don't make it too complicated.

Take small steps toward your goal and get started TODAY!

Final Tips

Before I let you go, I want to leave you with a few final tips:

Be patient and persistent.
Building wealth takes time. Don't expect overnight results. Just keep showing up and putting in the work, day after day.

Embrace the journey.
Yes, the end goal is financial freedom. But don't forget to enjoy the process along the way. Every challenge you overcome, every lesson you learn — that's all part of the journey.

Remember your "why".
When things get tough (and they will), remember why you started on this path in the first place. What does financial freedom mean to you? What kind of life do you want to create for yourself and your loved ones? Keep that vision front and center.

And finally, I want to leave you with this:

You have what it takes to succeed.
You have the knowledge.
You have the tools and most importantly, you have the power to take action.

So go out there and make it happen. Build that financial fortress, brick by brick. And when you look back on this journey years from now, you'll be amazed at how far you've come.

I believe in you. Now it's time for you to believe in yourself.
And now it's time for me to let you go. My Harley is waiting …

Build your financial fortress through passive income while you sleep!

Picture yourself experiencing ...

True financial independence with reliable sources of passive income that never run out of money and build financial security for yourself and your family that don't require you to work anymore, simply by leveraging the concepts and strategies in this book!

Imagine Your Life Without Struggles ...

Have more time for yourself, your family, and your friends.

Make money while you sleep through multiple income streams so you can be secure in your finances, no matter what life throws at you, and break the vicious cycle of working hard and long hours for someone else.

This Is More Crucial Than You Believe!

By leveraging the strategies in this book, you can start generating the assets and investment income millionaires use to grow their wealth. You can achieve these results like so many of my clients do after they implement what I have to share with you in this book. You can do it, no special knowledge needed, no matter how much or how little money you have in your account right now.

Build your financial fortress today!

The Study and Use of Covalent Bonds In Chemistry:
New Insights and Old Knowledge

THE STUDY AND USE OF COVALENT BONDS IN CHEMISTRY: NEW INSIGHTS AND OLD KNOWLEDGE

Prof Ramesh Chandra and Dr. Snigdha Singh

ARCLER PRESS

www.arclerpress.com

The Study and use of Covalent Bonds in Chemistry: New Insights and Old Knowledge

Prof Ramesh Chandra and Dr. Snigdha Singh

Arcler Press

224 Shoreacres Road

Burlington, ON L7L 2H2

Canada

www.arclerpress.com

Email: orders@arclereducation.com

ISBN: 978-1-77469-841-9 (Hardcover)

ABOUT THE AUTHOR

Prof. Ramesh Chandra, Fellow of the Royal Society of Chemistry, London is a distinguished scientist and a pioneer leader in the field of Biomedical Sciences. He is known for his appetite for academic progress and vision for establishing state-of-the-art Institutions. He has received global recognition for his work in academia and research in Biomedical Sciences and Medicinal Chemistry. Apart from academia, he has been actively involved in other areas of development too. He is official resource person to the Minister and Department of Science and Technology in the kingdom of Lesotho, South Africa as well as President of the Indian Chemical Society (2004-2006), Member, Planning Commission, Government of U.P. India; Secretary - Zaheer Science Foundation, New Delhi and Non-Official Director, Rashtriya Ispat Nigam Ltd (RINL), Government of India. On 08th March, 2022, Prof. Ramesh Chandra assumed the Vice-Chancellorship of Maharaja Surajmal Brij University, Bharatpur, Rajasthan. Evidently, under his charge the University witnessed inception of new administrative structures and research facilities to the introduction of innovative management concepts, interdisciplinary courses, and global academic initiatives. Prof. Chandra has been Vice-Chancellor, Bundelkhand University, Jhansi for six years (1999-2005). He established 36 institutes and that, too, with minimal financial support of the State Government. These institutes are in the fields Pure and Applied Radiation Biology, Pharmacy, Criminology and Forensic Sciences, Mass Communication & Journalism, Law, Ayurveda and Alternate Medicine, Planning and Architecture, Computer Science, Engineering, Biotechnology, Hotel Management and others. In 1991, Prof. Chandra, established Dr. B. R. Ambedkar Center for Biomedical Research (ACBR) – pioneering Biomedical Education and Research Institute at Delhi University, which has acquired an international status in the field of Biomedical Research through its original and creative research. As an advisor, he has been instrumental in various academic developments of Indian Institute of Information Technology (IIIT - Allahabad). Prof. Chandra started his research career at the University of Delhi; thereafter he went to pursue his research at The New York Hospital-Cornell University Medical College, New York jointly at The Rockefeller University, New York; State University of New York at Stonybrook as Assistant Research Professor. He conducted advanced research at the Harvard University Medical School-Massachusetts General Hospital (MGH) jointly at MIT, Cambridge, USA. Prof. Chandra was awarded Capital Foundation Dr A.P.J. Abdul Kalam Award for outstanding Scientific Research and Administrative Qualities (2023) in recognition of his duties for more than three decades. An outstanding Scientist and revered teacher, Prof. Chandra has been the recipient of several professional national/international recognitions too: J. William Fulbright Scholarship (1993); The Rockefeller Foundation USA-Biotechnology Career Award (1993); Award of the Highest Honor of Soka University, Tokyo, Japan (2000); Millennium Plaques of Honor (Life Time Achievement Award for contribution in Science & Technology) by the Indian Science Congress Association (ISCA) {2017-2018}, Lifetime Achievement Award of the Indian Chemical Society (ICS) (2003); UGC Research Scientist Award (1988); UGC Career Award (1993); Rajib Goyal Award for Young Scientists (2002); Fellowship of: Indian Academy of Biomedical Sciences (IABS); International Academy of Physical Sciences; Institution of Chemists, India; Indian Chemical Society and others.

Dr. Snigdha Singh is a medicinal chemist, currently working as an Assistant Professor, Department of Chemistry, University of Delhi. She completed her doctoral studies from University of Delhi in the year 2021. Her research efforts are directed towards the synthesis of biologically active heterocyclic molecules. She went to Rensselaer Polytechnic Institute as Postdoctoral Research Associate to work on Design and Synthesis of Neuropathic Inhibitors. She also went to Humboldt University of Berlin to work as a guest scientist after her doctoral studies to work on Synthesis of potential analogs for ACER3 activity. She is recipient of Indo-Italy PhD Exchange Scholarship awarded by the MHRD, Govt. of India to carry out research at the University of Siena, Italy. She was one of the few students who were awarded Indo-UK Newton Bhabha Scholarship by the British Council (U.K.) to carry out research at the University of Oxford, U.K. She received various young scientist travel awards to attend International Conferences. Dr. Snigdha shows deep commitment to research and higher education. To illustrate, she has to her credit one international patent, 2 Books; and more than 29 original Scientific Research Papers in International journals of repute.

TABLE OF CONTENTS

LIST OF FIGURES

LIST OF TABLES

PREFACE

The exploration of covalent bonds has been a cornerstone of modern chemistry, shaping our understanding of the fundamental interactions that govern the behavior and properties of matter. The remarkable nature of covalent bonds lies in their ability to form strong connections between atoms, resulting in the formation of diverse and complex molecular structures. These bonds play a pivotal role in numerous chemical processes and are central to the functioning of biological systems, materials science, and the development of new technologies.

"The Study and Use of Covalent Bonds in Chemistry: New Insights and Old Knowledge" is a comprehensive volume that delves into the intricacies of covalent bonding, combining both cutting-edge research and fundamental concepts to provide a deep understanding of this vital area of chemistry. Throughout this book, we aim to unravel the mysteries of covalent bonding, shedding light on its underlying principles, exploring its wide-ranging applications, and presenting the latest advancements in the field. The book is structured into eight chapters, each addressing a crucial aspect of covalent bonds, from their basic principles to advanced characterization techniques. It is designed to cater to a diverse audience, including students, researchers, and professionals seeking to expand their knowledge and gain new perspectives on covalent bonding.

Chapter one serves as an introduction to covalent bonds, providing a comprehensive overview of the field. It elucidates the fundamental concepts, historical context, and key properties associated with covalent bonding, establishing a solid foundation for the subsequent chapters. By exploring the foundational principles of covalent bonds, this chapter paves the way for a deeper exploration of the subject matter. Chapter two delves into molecular structure and bonding theories, offering an in-depth examination of various models and theories that have been developed to explain the nature of covalent bonding. From Lewis structures to molecular orbital theory (MOT), this chapter unravels the intricacies of molecular structure, providing readers with a comprehensive understanding of the underlying principles that govern the formation and stability of covalent bonds.

The third chapter explores the critical aspects of bond length, bond energy, and bond polarity, shedding light on the factors that influence the strength and properties of covalent bonds. It delves into the activation of covalent bonds, presenting both classical and contemporary perspectives on bond activation processes and their significance in chemical reactions. Chapter four is dedicated to understanding molecular shapes and bond angles. It encompasses the concept of the viral theorem, which provides valuable insights into the geometric arrangement of atoms in molecules. By examining the relationship between molecular structure and bond angles, this chapter enables readers to grasp the profound impact of covalent bonds on the three-dimensional architecture of molecules.

The fifth chapter delves into the intricate interplay between intermolecular forces and covalent bonding. It explores the diverse forces that arise from covalent bonds, such as hydrogen bonding, van der Waals forces, and dipole-dipole interactions. Through an in-depth exploration of these forces, readers will gain a comprehensive understanding of how covalent bonds shape the properties and behavior of substances.

Chapter six introduces an exciting frontier in covalent bond research: the direct imaging of covalent bond structure in single-molecule chemical reactions. This chapter presents cutting-edge techniques that allow scientists to visualize and manipulate individual covalent bonds, offering unprecedented insights into the dynamics of chemical reactions at the molecular level. The seventh chapter examines chemical reactions involving covalent bonds, providing a comprehensive overview of the various types of reactions and their mechanisms. From substitution reactions to addition reactions, this chapter explores the fundamental principles underlying chemical transformations mediated by covalent bonds. In the final chapter, we delve into the various techniques used in covalent bond characterization, offering readers a glimpse into the sophisticated tools and methods employed to probe the intricacies of covalent bonds. From spectroscopy to microscopy, this chapter explores the latest advancements in characterization techniques, opening new avenues for further exploration and discovery.

"The Study and Use of Covalent Bonds in Chemistry: New Insights and Old Knowledge" brings together a diverse group of experts in the field of covalent bonding. Their collective knowledge, research findings, and practical insights enrich each chapter, providing readers with a comprehensive understanding of the chemistry, properties, and applications of covalent bonds. By combining new insights with established knowledge, this book aims to inspire the next generation of scientists to push the boundaries of covalent bond research and harness its potential in various scientific disciplines.

—Author

CHAPTER

1 Introduction to Covalent Bonding

Contents

1.1. INTRODUCTION

Covalent bonds are an elementary type of chemical bonding that plays a pivotal role in creating and maintaining molecules (Cao & Wang, 2022). In chemical bonding, a covalent bond refers to the sharing of electrons between two or more atoms, which serves to attain a more stable arrangement of electrons. The phenomenon of electron sharing facilitates the saturation of the outermost electron shells of atoms, thereby leading to a more desirable energy state. In contrast to ionic bonds, which entail the complete transfer of electrons from one atom to a different one, covalent bonds are characterized by the reciprocal sharing of electrons among atoms. The covalent bond is formed due to the localization of shared electrons among the bonded atoms, generating a potent electrostatic attraction responsible for holding the atoms close (Li et al., 2021) (Figure 1.1).

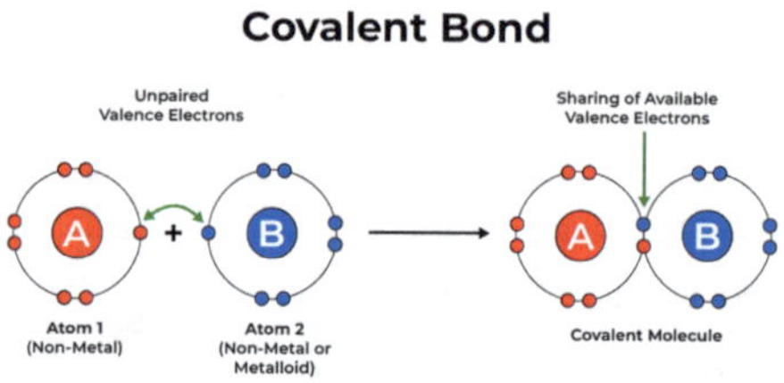

Figure 1.1. Illustration of covalent bond.

Source: Geeks for geeks, Creative Commons License.

The significance of covalent bonds in chemistry is substantial due to various factors. Primarily, they are indispensable for creating molecules, constituting matter's fundamental units. Covalent bonding enables the amalgamation of atoms, leading to the formation of stable molecular structures (Wang & Chen, 1999). This phenomenon is responsible for the vast array of chemical compounds present in nature and can be artificially synthesized in laboratory settings. Comprehending covalent bonds is imperative in forecasting and elucidating the reactivity of compounds. The chemical reactivity of molecules, including bond breaking and formation, is directly impacted by the makeup and strength of covalent bonds. By examining covalent bonding, researchers acquire significant knowledge regarding the actions of substances in chemical reactions, which facilitates the development and regulation of chemical conversions (Wilson et al., 2014). Covalent bonds facilitate compounds' stability, which enables atoms to attain a more suitable electron configuration. Using electron sharing, atoms can achieve enhanced stability and reduce their overall energy by filling their outermost electron shells (Huang et al., 2020). Maintaining stability is of utmost importance for the survival and operation of diverse chemical compounds. The impact of covalent bonds on the chemical and physical properties of substances is noteworthy. The physical characteristics of a substance, such as its boiling and melting points, the ability to dissolve, and electrical conductivity, are subject to the influence of the strength and configuration of covalent bonds present in its molecular or material structure. The comprehension of covalent bonding enables researchers to elucidate and control these characteristics for a diverse array of practical implementations. Covalent bonds play a crucial role in biological and life sciences, alongside their effects on non-living matter (Owen, 1955). Covalent bonds govern the form and function of biological molecules, such as nucleic acids, carbohydrates, proteins, and lipids. The bonds in question determine biomolecules' stability, three-dimensional structures, and interactions. They play a crucial role in various life processes, including but not limited to enzyme catalysis, cellular signaling, and DNA replication (Xiang et al., 2013) (Figure 1.2).

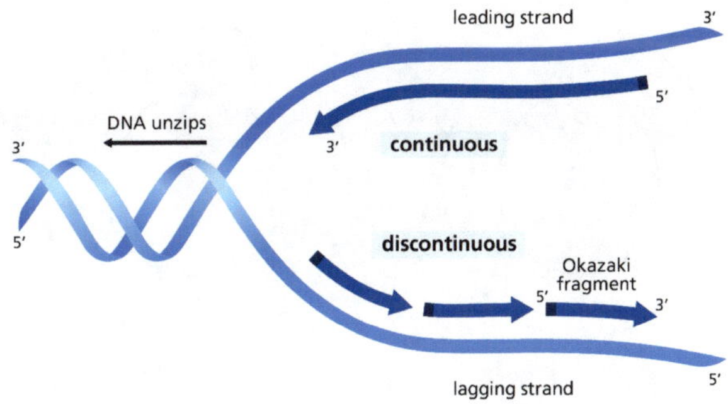

Figure 1.2. Schematic of DNA replication.

Source: Your genome, Creative Commons License.

Covalent bonding is a fundamental aspect of organic chemistry, the scientific discipline investigating carbon-based compounds. Covalent bonds are the primary means by which organic compounds, which serve as the fundamental building blocks of life on our planet, are bound together (Chen et al., 2014). A thorough comprehension of covalent bonding is crucial for gaining insight into organic compounds' synthesizing, characteristics, and chemical reactions. Additionally, this knowledge has many practical applications in medication, materials science, and energy. Covalent bonds play a crucial role in chemistry owing to their involvement in the molecular buildup, chemical responsiveness, substance stability, chemical and physical characteristics, biomolecular systems, and the expansive domain of organic chemistry. The investigation of covalent bonding is a fundamental basis for comprehending chemical systems, fostering novel materials, and propelling knowledge in diverse scientific and technological fields (Berdan et al., 2021).

1.2. TYPES OF CHEMICAL BONDS

1.2.1. Ionic Bonds

Ionic bonding occurs when a significant disparity in electronegativity values exists between atoms. Electronegativity is a fundamental concept in chemistry that quantifies an atom's capacity to draw electrons toward its nucleus in a chemical bond. The development of ions can occur when there is a notable disparity in electronegativity between two atoms, leading to the removal of any number of electrons from one atom by the other (Bader & Henneker, 1965) (Figure 1.3).

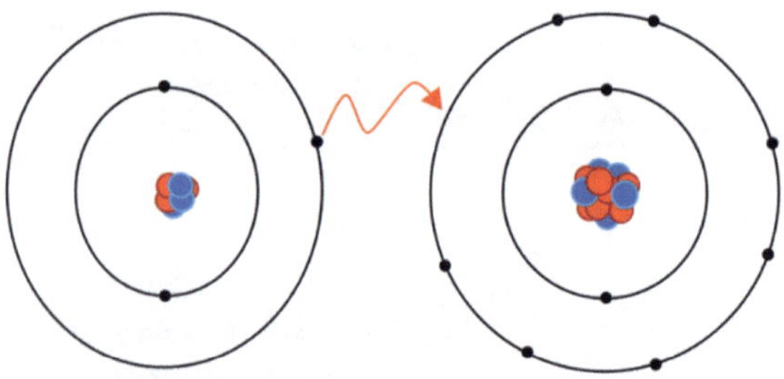

Figure 1.3. Schematic of ionic bond.

Source: Anne Marie Helmenstine, Creative Commons License.

Electron transfer generates cations, which are positively charged ions, and anions, which are negatively charged ions. The process of losing electrons by an atom results in the formation of a cation, whereas the acquisition of electrons by an atom leads to the formation of an anion. Electron transfer transpires due to the superior electronegativity of an atom, which exerts a greater attraction on the electrons, thereby inducing their relocation towards it (Spruijt et al., 2012).

The ions produced due to electron transfer exhibit a significant electrostatic attraction due to their opposite charges. The electrostatic attraction between the positively charged cation and the negatively charged anion results in the formation of an ionic bond. The phenomenon under consideration is attributed to the electrical force, which denotes the force that electrically charged particles exert on each other, either attracting or repelling (Schäfer et al., 1973). The electrostatic force's magnitude is directly correlated to the charges' magnitude and inversely correlated to the distance between the ions.

Ionic compounds typically demonstrate elevated melting as well as boiling points. The cohesive forces resulting from the electrostatic interactions among the constituent ions in the crystalline structure necessitate a considerable input of energy to overcome the bond strength and effectuate the transformation from a solid state to a liquid or gaseous state (Wang et al., 2020). Hence, it can be observed that ionic compounds exhibit elevated boiling and melting points in comparison to covalent compounds due to the stronger intermolecular forces present in the former.

Moreover, aqueous solubility is a common characteristic of ionic compounds. The polarity of water molecules is attributed to a partially positive charge on each hydrogen atom and an equal amount of negative charge on the oxygen atom. Water's polar characteristic facilitates its interaction with the ions of the ionic substance via ion-dipole interactions (Coll & Treagust, 2003). The dissolution of the compound is facilitated by the action of water molecules, which envelop and disperse the ions, thereby disrupting the ionic lattice.

Sodium chloride, commonly called NaCl, is a prototypical illustration of an ionic substance. Sodium exhibits a comparatively low electronegativity, whereas chlorine demonstrates a relatively high electronegativity (Hutskalov et al., 2023). The process of sodium donating an electron to chlorine leads to the creation of both sodium and chlorine ions. The ionic bond that forms the crystal structure of sodium chloride results from the potent electrostatic attraction between the sodium ion, which is positively charged, and the negatively charged chlorine ion.

Calcium carbonate, called $CaCO_3$, is a chemical compound exhibiting ionic bonding. Calcium exhibits a lower electronegativity as compared to oxygen and carbon. Calcium donating two electrons to every oxygen atom and one electron to every carbonate group leads to the creation of CO_3^{2-} and Ca^{2+} ions. The rigidity and form of calcium carbonate are attributed to the ionic bonds between the carbonate and the calcium ions (Reed & Schleyer, 1990).

1.2.2. Covalent Bonds

The formation of covalent bonds is attributed to the sharing of electrons between atoms, which aims to attain a stable electron arrangement. Covalent bonding involves the sharing of either one or more pairs of electrons between atoms, creating a covalent bond. Sharing electrons between atoms enables them to achieve greater electronic stability by completing their outermost energy level, also known as the valence shell (Picchioni & Muljana, 2018). Through electron sharing, atoms can attain a state of enhanced stability and reduced energy compared to their existence.

Did You Know?

Covalent bonds are formed when atoms share electrons in order to achieve a more stable electron configuration.

Covalent bonding is commonly observed among nonmetallic elements or between nonmetallic elements and hydrogen. Elements that lack metallic properties, including but not limited to nitrogen, oxygen, carbon, and halogens such as chlorine and fluorine, exhibit comparatively elevated electronegativities (Chakma & Konkolewicz, 2019). Electronegativity refers to the propensity of an atom to draw electrons toward its nucleus while bonding to other atoms. In the context of covalent bonding involving nonmetallic elements, electron sharing occurs due to the high electron affinity of both atoms involved. Similarly, despite being categorized as a nonmetal, hydrogen exhibits analogous behavior and can establish covalent bonds with different nonmetallic elements (Wilson et al., 2014).

The covalent bonding between atoms is facilitated by the sharing of electrons, forming a stable molecular structure. The formation of a covalent bond occurs when multiple atoms share electrons. The formation of this chemical bond is facilitated by the overlap of the atomic orbitals, which enables the electrons to be jointly used across the nuclei of the atoms participating in the bond (Grandbois et al., 1999). The movement of electrons within the spatial vicinity of two atoms establishes an attractive force that binds the atoms together. The resultant configuration is denoted as a molecule, which embodies the most diminutive constituent of the substance that sustains its chemical characteristics.

The electron sharing in covalent compounds can vary, categorizing covalent bonds as either polar or nonpolar. In certain instances, if the atoms participating in the covalent linkage exhibit distinct electronegativities, the distribution of electrons may not be symmetrical (Shieh et al., 2021). The outcome of this uneven distribution of electrons between atoms leads to the formation of a polar covalent bond. A polar covalent bond is characterized by the unequal sharing of electrons between two atoms, where one atom exhibits a greater electronegativity and consequently exerts a stronger pull on the shared electrons, resulting in a partially negative charge. The second atom, possessing a comparatively lesser electronegativity, exhibits a partially positive charge. The dipole moment is a consequence of the charge separation within the bond (Green & Parkin, 2014).

Conversely, in cases where the electronegativities of atoms are comparable, sharing of the electrons is equitable, resulting in the formation of a covalent bond that is not polar. In the context of chemical bonding, a covalent bond that is not polar refers to a situation where two atoms share electrons, resulting in equal electron density distribution between them. A lack of substantial variation in electronegativity between the atoms involved characterizes this type of bond (Held et al., 2017).

Illustrations of substances featuring covalent bonding are exemplified by water and methane. The chemical compound known as water comprises two hydrogen atoms covalently bonded to a single oxygen atom. Due to the higher electronegativity of the oxygen atom compared to hydrogen, the shared electrons tend to be located in closer proximity to the oxygen atom, resulting in the formation of a polar covalent bond (Wang et al., 2009). Consequently, the oxygen atom exhibits a partial negative charge (δ-), whereas the hydrogen atoms exhibit partial positive charges (δ+). The presence of polarity in water is responsible for its distinctive characteristics, including its capacity to establish hydrogen bonds and demonstrate elevated surface tension. In contrast, methane comprises a central carbon atom covalently bonded to four hydrogen atoms. The nonpolar covalent bonds in methane are attributed to the absence of a substantial electronegativity disparity between hydrogen and carbon.

The instances above underscore the adaptability of covalent bonds and their ubiquity in diverse chemical compounds (Kamaras et al., 2003). The presence of covalent bonds is a crucial aspect of forming and sustaining organic molecules. These molecules primarily comprise hydrogen and carbon atoms linked together through covalent bonds. Furthermore, covalent bonding plays a pivotal role in numerous inorganic compounds, including but not limited to carbon dioxide, ammonia, and sulfuric acid. Comprehending the characteristics of covalent bonds is a fundamental aspect of anticipating and elucidating substances' physical and chemical attributes (Santi et al., 1984). This knowledge is crucial in various domains, including organic chemistry and materials science.

1.2.3. Metallic Bonds

Metallic bonding is a type of chemical bonding that takes place between metal atoms. Elements classified as metals, positioned towards the left-hand side of the periodic table, exhibit a comparatively low electronegativity (Bay, 1983). This characteristic implies that they are more inclined to relinquish electrons than acquire them. Metallic bonding is a chemical bonding in which the electrons in the valence region of metallic atoms undergo delocalization and acquire the ability to move freely through the entire metal lattices (Figure 1.4).

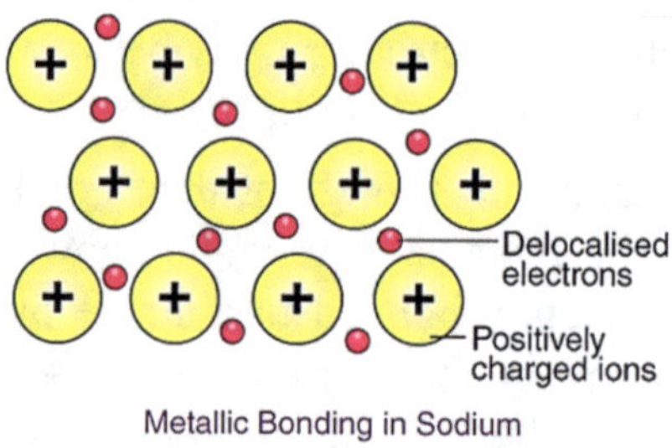

Figure 1.4. Diagram of metallic bond in sodium.

Source: Byju's, Creative Commons License.

Metallic bonding involves the cohesive force that arises from the electrostatic attraction between positively charged metal ions and the delocalized electrons that form a sea-like structure around them. Metallic atoms undergo cation formation upon electron loss, producing positively charged ions known as cations (Gade, 2000). The cations are enveloped by a collective of detached electrons, which exhibit an affinity towards the positively charged cations. The phenomenon of delocalized electrons entails the unrestricted movement of electrons amidst the metal cations, thereby generating a potent electrostatic force that binds the metal lattice.

The distinctive characteristics of metals can be attributed to metallic bonding (Lindahl, 2012). The characteristics above encompass:

- The efficient electrical conductivity of metals is attributed to delocalized electrons. The electrons can move unrestrictedly upon applying a voltage, thereby facilitating the conduction of electric current throughout the metallic lattice (Powers & Uyeda, 2017).

- The high thermal conductivity observed in metals can be attributed to the involvement of delocalized electrons. Metals exhibit efficient thermal conductivity due to the rapid transfer of heat energy facilitated by the movement of electrons throughout the lattice.
- The property of malleability allows metals to undergo deformation through hammering, rolling, or shaping without experiencing fracture or failure (Fleet, 1977). The characteristic above results from the capacity of delocalized electrons to reorganize themselves in response to external stimuli, thereby enabling the metallic lattice to maintain its integrity.
- Ductility is a property of metals that allows them to be attracted to tiny wires without undergoing fracture. The phenomenon of plastic deformation in metal lattices is facilitated by delocalized electrons, which permit the metal's elongation into slender wires (Collman & Boulatov, 2002).
- Metals exhibit a distinct visual property known as luster, which is attributed to the reflection of photons by the electrons that have been delocalized. The metallic luster is a consequence of the absorption and reemission of light by free electrons.

Iron, or Fe, and copper, or Cu, are among the metals that exhibit metallic bonding. The metals above demonstrate characteristics that are commonly linked with metallic bonding, including but not limited to electrical conductivity, the ability to be shaped without breaking, and the capacity to be drawn into thin wires (Brookhart & Green, 1983). Comprehending metallic bonding is crucial in comprehending the conduct and practical uses of metals in diverse sectors such as electronics, construction, and manufacturing.

1.3. CHARACTERISTICS OF COVALENT BONDS

1.3.1. Sharing of Electrons

Electron sharing is an essential principle in covalent bonding, whereby atoms share any pair of pairs of electrons to establish stable compounds. In contrast to ionic bonds, which entail the transfer of electrons from one atom to another, covalent bonds are characterized by a relatively equitable sharing of electrons between atoms (Ruedenberg & Schmidt, 2009). In the context of chemical bonding, the attainment of a more stable electronic arrangement is facilitated by sharing valence electrons between atoms.

The formation of covalent bonds occurs via the mutual sharing of pairs of electrons. Covalent bonds generally form between nonmetallic atoms with comparable electronegativities. Electronegativity refers to the quantifiable property of an atom that determines its capacity to draw electrons toward its nucleus in the context of a chemical bond. Covalent bonds form when two atoms with comparable electronegativities exhibit a strong attraction for electrons (Fulton & Mixon, 1993).

In chemical bonding, a covalent bond is formed when two atoms share any number of electrons to establish a pair or several pairs of electrons. The electrons shared between the bonding atoms are situated in the region of overlap between their respective atomic orbitals. The covalent bond between atoms is often depicted in Lewis dot structures using one or more lines, symbolizing the shared pairs of electrons (Figure 1.5).

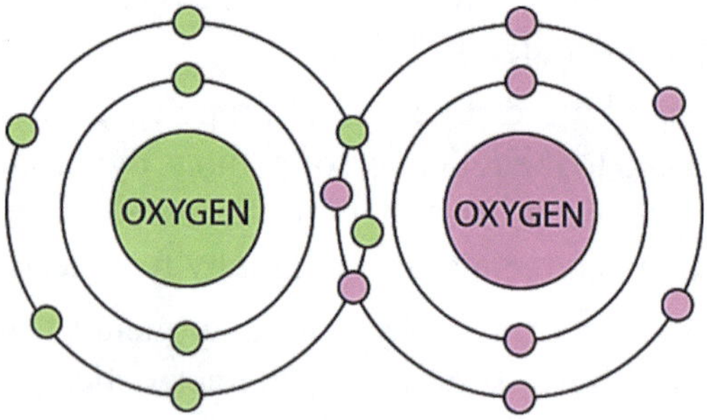

Figure 1.5. Image of sharing of electrons.

Source: Libretexts, Creative Commons License.

There are many instances where covalent compounds are generated by sharing electrons. An illustrative instance is that of water (H_2O), wherein each hydrogen atom shares an electron with the oxygen atom using a pair of electrons (Ruedenberg & Schmidt, 2007). The sharing enables the hydrogen atoms to attain a state of valence shell completion by acquiring two electrons. In contrast, the oxygen atom attains a state of stability by obtaining 8 electrons inside its valence shell. An additional illustration can be observed in the case of methane (CH_4), wherein the carbon atom forms four covalent bonds by sharing a pair of electrons with each of the four hydrogen atoms. Electron sharing enables carbon to attain octet configuration by acquiring eight electrons in its valence shell. In contrast, every hydrogen atom attains stability by obtaining a pair of electrons in its valence shells (Suat et al., 2010).

An additional illustration pertains to nitrogen gas (N_2), wherein a pair of nitrogen atoms partake in the sharing of 3 pairs of electrons, thereby resulting in the formation of a triple bond. In this instance, electron sharing facilitates a stable configuration of eight valence electrons for both nitrogen entities. Moreover, organic molecules such as ethanol (C_2H_5OH) exemplify the phenomenon of electron sharing among the atoms of carbon, hydrogen, and oxygen (Peterson et al., 1989). The compound can exist due to the attainment of stable electron configurations by forming covalent bonds between the constituent atoms.

1.3.2. Electronegativity and Polarity

Electronegativity is a fundamental concept in chemistry that quantifies an atom's capacity to draw shared electrons toward itself in a covalent bonding situation. The phenomenon of chemical bonds is explicable through an essential idea in chemistry. Elements are assigned values for electronegativity on different scales, and the Pauling scale has become the prevailing choice. The electronegativity associated with an atom is contingent upon various factors, including its nuclear charge, the radius of the atom, and the arrangement of electrons (Smyth, 1938) (Figure 1.6).

Remember

Electronegativity is a measure of an atom's ability to attract electrons towards itself in a chemical bond.

The polarity of a covalent bond is determined by the disparity in electronegativity exhibited by the two atoms involved in the bond. When the difference in electronegativity is relatively low, usually below 0.5, the bond is categorized as nonpolar. Nonpolar covalent bonds involve the equal sharing of electrons between the bonded atoms. This phenomenon occurs when the electronegativity values of the two atoms forming the bond are identical or closely matched. Methane and Ethane are instances of compounds that possess nonpolar covalent bonds. A polar bond is characterized by a moderate electronegativity difference, typically ranging from 0.5 to 1.7. Polar covalent bonds are characterized by an unequal sharing of electrons between the bonded atoms. The atom possessing greater electronegativity exhibits a heightened ability to attract the shared electrons, thereby developing a partially negative charge (δ-) upon that particular atom (Sanderson, 1983). On the other hand, the atom possessing lesser electronegativity exhibits a partially positive charge (δ+), owing to the displacement of electron density towards the comparatively more electronegative atom. Compounds that exhibit polar covalent bonds comprise hydrogen chloride and water.

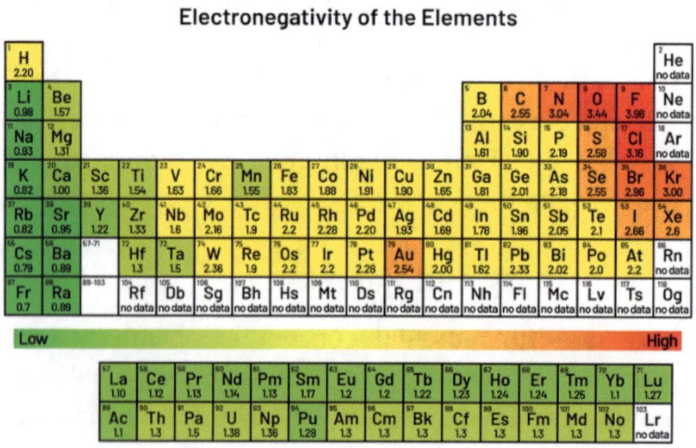

Figure 1.6. Picture of periodic table with electronegativity.

Source: Jensen, Creative Commons License.

The phenomenon of dipole moment arises from the presence of polar covalent bonds within a molecule, which results in charge separation. A dipole moment is a metric used to quantify a molecule's net polarity, symbolized by a vector pointing towards the atom with higher electronegativity. The dipole moment's magnitude and direction depend on the electronegativity and molecular geometry disparity (Burrows & Mooring, 2015). Compounds that exhibit nonpolar covalent bonding are characterized by a uniform spread of electronic density, which leads to the nullification of dipole moments. Carbon dioxide (CO_2) is an instance of a non-polar covalent molecule. The nonpolarity of the molecule can be attributed to its linear geometry, which leads to the nullification of dipole moments that are equal and opposite, despite the polar nature of the carbon-oxygen bonds (Li et al., 2018).

Comprehending the concepts of electronegativity and polarity holds significant importance in anticipation of the conduct of molecules, encompassing their boiling points, solubility, and intermolecular interactions. Polar molecules can engage in a range of intermolecular forces, such as dipole-dipole forces and hydrogen bonding, that substantially impact their chemical and physical properties. In contrast to polar molecules, nonpolar molecules typically demonstrate diminished intermolecular forces, resulting in decreased solubility in polar solvents and lower boiling points (Prodjosantoso & Hertina, 2019).

1.3.3. Bond Length and Bond Strength

The term "bond length" pertains to the spatial separation between the atomic nuclei of chemically bonded atoms. A crucial characteristic significantly influences a covalent bond's overall stability and strength. Typically, a negative correlation exists between the length of a bond and its strength. The relationship between bond length and bond strength is such that a decrease in bond length results in an increase in bond strength. The phenomenon above can be comprehended by considering the electrostatic interactions between the nuclei that bear a positive charge and the electrons that are shared and bear a negative charge (Gavezzotti, 2016). When the distance between nuclei decreases, the magnitude of the attractive forces increases, leading to the formation of a more robust chemical bond.

Multiple variables can influence the magnitude of the bond length within a covalent bond. The dimension of the atoms engaged is a crucial determinant (Bullett, 1975). The bond length of smaller atoms is typically shorter due to the proximity of their electron clouds to the nucleus, resulting in heightened attraction between the shared electrons and nuclei. On the contrary, atoms of greater size exhibit elongated bond lengths due to the augmented separation between their nuclei and the shared electrons.

Tip

In general, shorter bond lengths correspond to stronger bonds.

The existence of multiple bonds is a crucial aspect that impacts the length of a bond (Schomaker & Stevenson, 1941). Double and triple bonds are characterized by multiple pairs of shared electrons, which reduces bond length compared to a single bond involving the same atoms. The rationale behind this phenomenon is that the presence of supplementary electron pairs results in heightened electron density, thereby engendering more potent attraction forces between nuclei and shared electrons.

Bond energy, also called bond dissociation energy, denotes the quantum of energy necessary to disintegrate a covalent bond and disengage the associated atoms (Dolg et al., 2014). The strength of a bond is directly proportional to its bond energy. Bonds possessing greater strength exhibit elevated bond energies, signifying that a greater amount of energy is required to disrupt them. In contrast, bonds with lower bond energies exhibit weaker strengths and necessitate less energy for dissociation.

The correlation between bond strength and energy can be elucidated by utilizing the theoretical construct of potential energy (Tersoff, 1988). The process of bond formation results in a decrease in potential energy due to the release of energy. The reduction in potential energy indicates a heightened stability level and increased bond strength. Conversely, the act of bond dissociation necessitates an infusion of energy, leading to a rise in the potential energy and the debilitation of the bond. To demonstrate the correlation between bond length and its strength, we shall examine the diatomic molecules of the halogens.

In comparison to chlorine (Cl_2), fluorine (F_2) exhibits a higher bond energy and a shorter bond length (Phillips, 1967). This phenomenon is attributed to the comparatively smaller size of fluorine atoms than chlorine atoms, which results in heightened forces of attraction and a reduced bond length. Consequently, greater energy is necessary to dissociate the fluorine bond, suggesting a higher bond strength than chlorine.

The term "bond length" in covalent bonding pertains to the interatomic separation in the nuclei of the constituent atoms engaged in the bonding interaction. Determining the bond's stability and strength heavily relies on its crucial role (Hummel & Kern, 2004). Typically, a negative correlation exists between the length of a bond and its strength. The relationship between bond length and bond strength is inverse, whereby an increase in bond length results in a decrease in bond strength, and conversely, a decrease in bond length leads to an increase in bond strength.

There exist multiple variables that exert an influence on the length of a covalent bond. The size of the atoms engaged is considered a fundamental factor. The atomic radius of an atom increases with the number of electron shells it possesses (Brown, 1981). Hence larger atoms exhibit a greater atomic radius. Consequently, in the event of the amalgamation of two relatively larger atoms to create a covalent bond, the length of the bond is inclined to be greater compared to a bond established between smaller atoms.

Moreover, the bond length is influenced by multiple bonds among atoms. The sharing of numerous pairs of electrons between atoms forms double and triple bonds. The bonds in question exhibit reduced length and heightened strength relative to single bonds, owing to the heightened density of electrons (Simoes & Beauchamp, 1990).

Bond energy, also called bond dissociation energy, denotes the quantum of energy necessary to cleave a covalent bond and disengage the constituent atoms. The phenomenon in question directly correlates with the strength of chemical bonds. Bonds possessing greater strength exhibit elevated bond energies, necessitating greater energy for their dissociation. In contrast, bonds with lower bond energies are comparatively feeble and thus more susceptible to rupture (Blake et al., 1961).

The correlation between the length of the bond and its strength can be illustrated through diverse instances. This concept can be illustrated in the diatomic molecules of the halogens, namely chlorine, fluorine, bromine, and iodine. As one descends the group, the size of the atoms increases, leading to an increase in bond length. Concurrently, the intensity of the connections diminishes, as denoted by the reduction in bond energies. Among the halogens, fluorine exhibits the shortest and most powerful bond, whereas iodine displays the longest and least powerful bond (Schwaderer et al., 2008).

1.4. LEWIS DOT STRUCTURES

Lewis dot symbols, also called Lewis structures, are a highly effective instrument in chemistry that is utilized to depict the valence electrons of atoms and anticipate the bonding arrangements in molecules. The Lewis dot symbols, conceived by Gilbert N. Lewis, a chemist from the United States, offer a straightforward and intuitive approach to comprehending the electron allocation in chemical entities (Shultz & Gere, 2015). Lewis dot structures facilitate the visualization of covalent bond formation and the prediction of molecular geometry by depicting the valence electrons as crosses or dots surrounding the chemical symbol (Figure 1.7).

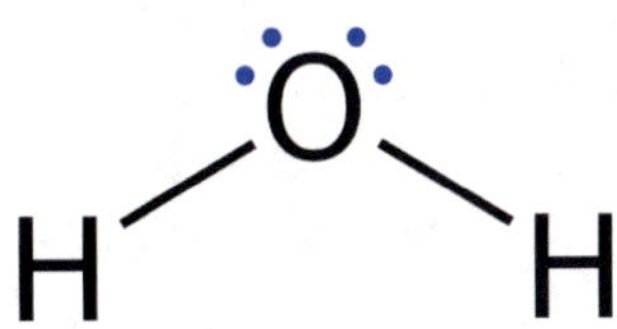

Figure 1.7. Depiction of Lewis dot structure.

Source: Fabian Z, Creative Commons License.

Valence electrons refer to the electrons located in the outermost shell of an atom and are involved in chemical bonding. An element's reactivity and capacity to form bonds are determined by its number of valence electrons. The utilization of Lewis dot symbols facilitates the comprehension of electron configurations by directing attention toward the valence electrons, which play a pivotal role in chemical bonding. Chemists may evaluate the chemical reactions between atoms by visualizing electrons through dots or crosses (Nassiff & Czerwinski, 2015).

1.4.1. Rules for Drawing Lewis Dot Structures

To precisely depict Lewis dot structures, established guidelines adhere to illustrate the arrangement of valence electrons.

- The process of ascertaining the number of valence electrons in an atom is commonly based on its group number placement within the periodic table. Elements belonging to Group 1, such as hydrogen and lithium, exhibit a single valence electron, whereas elements classified under Group 16, such as sulfur and oxygen, demonstrate six valence electrons (Curnow, 2021).
- The process of allocating electrons about the chemical symbol involves the utilization of dots or crosses to symbolize each valence electron. Electrons are arranged around a chemical's symbol in a dot configuration, wherein a pairing of electrons occurs only after a maximum of two electrons have been placed on each side (Nassiff & Czerwinski, 2015). If an atom possesses three valence electrons, it will allocate two electrons to one side and the remaining to the opposite.
- The distribution of electrons takes into consideration Hund's rule about electron pairing. According to Hund's rule, electrons tend to occupy distinct orbitals that possess identical energy levels before forming pairs. This principle maintains the stability of the electron configuration and indicates the inherent inclination of electrons to refrain from orbital sharing until it becomes imperative (Swartz & Schladetzky, 1996).
- In constructing Lewis dot arrangements for molecules, it is necessary to account for multiple atoms linked by covalent bonds represented by lines. In chemical bonding, a pair of shared electrons is represented by each bond. Lone pairs of electrons are positioned on atoms when they are not bonding. The adherence to

the octet rule is a crucial aspect of electron distribution, whereby atoms tend to attain an electron arrangement that is stable with 8 valence electrons through electron gain, loss, or sharing (Salame & Nikolic, 2021).

1.4.2. Examples of Lewis Dot Structures

Several examples can be examined to demonstrate the procedure of constructing Lewis dot structures.

- Hydrogen, with a chemical symbol of H_2, possesses a single valence electron. The sharing of electrons between two hydrogen atoms forms a solitary covalent bond. The Lewis dot structure H: H represents the molecular formula for hydrogen gas, where each dot signifies a valence electron (Shultz & Gere, 2015).
- Water (H_2O) is a compound consisting of two hydrogen atoms and one oxygen atom. The oxygen atom has six valence electrons, while each hydrogen atom has one valence electron. The element oxygen exhibits a valence of two, allowing it to form two covalent bonds with hydrogen. The remaining two electrons of the oxygen atom are utilized to form two distinct lone pairs on the oxygen molecule. The molecular structure of water can be represented by a Lewis dot diagram, which depicts two dots on the atom of oxygen and one on each of the hydrogen atoms (Nassiff & Czerwinski, 2015). The chemical formula for water is H:O: H.
- Carbon dioxide (CO_2) is a compound consisting of one carbon atom and two oxygen atoms. The carbon atom has four valence, while each oxygen atom has a valence of six. Carbon tends to establish double bonds with two oxygen atoms, thereby sharing a pair of electrons with each of them. The Lewis dot diagram of carbon dioxide is represented as O=C=O, wherein two lines depict the double bonds, and each oxygen atom is represented by two dots.

The instances above illustrate the utility of Lewis dot structures to visually depict the distribution of electrons within molecules visually, thereby enhancing comprehension of chemical bonds and molecular structure. Through adherence to the guidelines for constructing Lewis dot diagrams, scientists can effectively illustrate the distribution of electrons and anticipate the bonding behaviors present in various molecules. Lewis dot structures are a highly valuable instrument in chemistry, facilitating the prediction of molecular behavior, identification of bonding arrangements, and determination of compound polarity (Shaffer, 2006). Covalent compounds are characterized by intricate interatomic interactions, which can be comprehended through the fundamental principles of these compounds. These principles serve as a stepping stone for delving deeper into studying chemical processes and substance properties.

1.5. OCTET RULE

The octet rule is a fundamental principle in chemistry that governs our comprehension of chemical bonds and the stability of molecules and atoms. According to the statement, atoms tend to undergo electron gain, loss, or sharing to attain a stable configuration of electrons akin to noble gases. Noble gases possess a full valence shell of eight electrons (Gillespie & Silvi, 2002). The principle above is derived from the empirical evidence that atoms possessing a full octet exhibit greater stability and diminished reactivity (Figure 1.8).

Figure 1.8. Image of octet rule.

Source: Ben Mills, Creative Commons License.

The octet rule is based on the arrangement of electrons of atoms. The electrons of an atom are distributed in discrete energy levels or orbitals surrounding the nucleus. The electronic configuration of an atom is such that the first energy level can carry a maximum of two electrons (Noury et al., 2022). In contrast, the 2nd and 3rd energy levels have the potential to hold up to eight electrons each. The attainment of a complete valence shell allows atoms to reduce their energy level and enhance their stability.

Atoms endeavor to achieve a stable electron configuration using electron gain, loss, or sharing, ultimately resulting in a complete octet. In the context of chemical bonding, the process of forming ionic compounds involves the transfer of electrons between atoms, with the ultimate goal of attaining an electronic configuration that closely resembles that of the closest noble gas. Sodium (Na), possessing a single valence electron, exhibits a high propensity to donate a said electron to chlorine, which in turn possesses seven valence electrons. This exchange of electrons culminates in the creation of Sodium Chloride (NaCl). Sodium and chlorine attain the electronic configuration of noble gases neon (Ne) and argon (Ar), respectively, by achieving a complete octet. The phenomenon of covalent bonding takes place when atoms engage in the sharing of electrons to attain a state of electron configuration that is stable. In chemical bonding, a covalent bond refers to sharing one or more pairs of electrons between two atoms. Oxygen, an element with the atomic symbol O and six valence electrons, can engage in covalent bonding with another oxygen atom (Quayle et al., 2015). This involves the sharing of two pairs of electrons, ultimately forming a diatomic molecule known as oxygen gas (O_2). Each oxygen atom's attainment of a complete octet is accomplished through electron sharing.

1.5.1. Exceptions to the Octet Rule

Although the octet rule serves as a valuable principle for anticipating the electron arrangements of numerous molecules, certain atoms exhibit deviations from the anticipated octet, constituting exceptions. The anomalies above are predominantly detected in elements of the third period or later in the periodic table, as they can utilize the d orbitals (Gillespie & Robinson, 1995).

- Certain elements, namely boron (B) and aluminum (Al) have been observed to create compounds in which they possess fewer than 8 electrons within their valence shells, a phenomenon referred to as an incomplete octet. Elements can attain stability by possessing a complete or nearly full subshell, even if it entails possessing fewer than eight electrons. Boron frequently bonds with other elements, forming compounds that manifest a hexavalent state characterized by 6 electrons in its outermost shell.
- Elements of period 3 and beyond, such as sulfur, Phosphorus, and chlorine, can meet more than 8 electrons within their valence shells, commonly called an expanded octet. The feasibility of this phenomenon can be attributed to the presence of d orbitals alongside the orbitals s and p in these atoms. Elements that exhibit expanded octets can surpass the octet rule by leveraging their d orbitals to hold supplementary electrons, generally to a maximum of twelve or eighteen electrons (Gillespie & Robinson, 2007). Phosphorus pentachloride (PCl_5) is a frequently cited instance of expanded octets in chemical compounds. Phosphorus

possesses a total of five valence electrons and necessitates the acquisition of three additional electrons to attain a fully occupied octet. The covalent bonding in PCl_5 involves the contribution of one electron from each chlorine atom to form a shared pair of electrons with Phosphorus. This results in the formation of 5 shared pairs of electrons. The configuration above results in 10 electrons surrounding Phosphorus, exceeding the octet rule.

- Certain molecules possess an uneven count of valence electrons, known as odd-electron molecules. Such molecules include nitric oxide (NO) and nitrogen dioxide (NO_2). In certain scenarios, all atoms' attainment of an octet configuration is unattainable; however, stable molecules can still be formed using electron sharing. The molecules in question are called odd-electron molecules or free radicals (Straub, 1995). They possess distinctive chemical characteristics as a result of the existence of an unpaired electron.

1.5.2. Expanded Octets

The phenomenon of expanded octets is observed when atoms belonging to the third period or beyond participate in bonding and can accommodate over 8 electrons within their valence shells. The capability above results from d orbitals, which can engage in chemical bonding. Sulfur, Phosphorus, and chlorine are frequently linked with expanded octets.

Octet expansion occurs when an atom forms covalent bonds, leading to the mutual sharing of electron pairs (Malerich, 1987). In chemical compounds exhibiting expanded octets, multiple bonded atoms and unshared electron pairs commonly encompass the center atom. By utilizing d orbitals, the central atom can accommodate more electrons beyond the established limit of eight electrons.

The sulfur hexafluoride (SF_6) molecule is characterized by the formation of covalent bonds between sulfur and six fluorine atoms. Sulfur possesses 6 valence electrons and necessitates the acquisition of two additional electrons to attain an octet. Sulfur surpasses the octet rule by achieving 12 electrons surrounding it by sharing them with each fluorine atom. The d orbitals of sulfur accommodate the excess electrons (Klebe, 1968).

Notably, the ability to form expanded octets is not a universal characteristic among all chemical elements. Carbon and nitrogen usually adhere to the octet rule as they have restricted access to d orbitals. Elements capable of forming expanded octets typically possess a greater atomic number and principal quantum number, thereby enabling the participation of d orbitals. Expanded octets hold noteworthy consequences in chemical bonds and molecular geometry analysis (Sommer & Rodewald, 1963). This phenomenon facilitates the creation of intricate molecular configurations and can rationalize the stability of specific compounds that deviate from the rigorous adherence to the octet rule.

1.6. BONDING AND MOLECULAR GEOMETRY

1.6.1. Relationship between Bonding and Molecular Shape

The bonding pattern of a molecule is closely linked to its molecular shape since the positioning of its constituent atoms dictates the spatial configuration of a molecule. The bonding pattern pertains to the precise manner in which atoms are interconnected via ionic, covalent, or metallic bonding. For the sake of this discourse, our attention will be directed toward covalent bonding (Jackson et al., 2020).

Covalent bonding involves the mutual sharing of electron pairs among atoms. In covalent bonding, the sharing of electrons between atoms is a means of attaining a more stable arrangement of electrons, which often mimics that of noble gases. The phenomenon of electron sharing facilitates the attainment of electron requirements by atoms, thereby forming a stable molecule.

Molecular geometry is influenced by how atoms are interconnected through chemical bonding. The underlying cause of this phenomenon can be attributed to the electrostatic repulsion between pairs of electrons, which motivates the system to adopt a configuration that minimizes this repulsion and maximizes stability (Krygowski et al., 2005). Molecular geometry is largely influenced by the spatial configuration of atoms and the interatomic bond angles. The correlation between bonding and the shape of molecules is investigated within the realm of molecular geometry.

1.6.2. VSEPR Theory and Its Application

The Valence Shell Electron Pair Repulsion (VSEPR) theory is a theoretical framework that facilitates the anticipation of molecular geometries by considering the repulsive forces between electron pairs present in the valence shell of the central atom. Per the postulated theory, electron pairs exhibit mutual repulsion and endeavor to maintain maximum possible distance between themselves regardless of their bonding or non-bonding nature. This repulsion determines the relative position of bonds and atoms in the molecule (Gillespie, 1963).

The application of the VSEPR theory involves a series of procedural steps. The molecular Lewis structure is initially ascertained, furnishing insights into the atoms' disposition and the number of electron pairs engaged. The identification of the atom in the center is based on its role as the nucleus to which all other atoms are attached through chemical bonds. Subsequently, the tally of bonding and non-bonding electron pairs surrounding the center atom is conducted.

A molecule's geometry can be anticipated based on the number of electron pairs present. The VSEPR theory offers a prescribed set of principles and directives for ascertaining molecular geometry. The principles governing the arrangement of electrons in a molecule consider the repulsive forces between electron pairs and prioritize the minimization of such repulsion to attain a state of stability (Fujiwara et al., 2020).

1.6.3. Examples of Molecular Geometries

According to the VSEPR theory, diverse molecular geometries can be anticipated by considering the number of electron pairs surrounding the central atom. Linear, tetrahedral, trigonal planar, trigonal bipyramidal, and octahedral are among the most frequently occurring molecular geometries.

In a linear molecular geometry, the central atom is surrounded by two bonding electron pairs, and no non-bonding or lone pairs are present. Consequently, a linear molecular geometry is obtained, featuring a bond angle measuring 180°. CO_2 is an instance of a molecule that exhibits a linear geometry (Gillespie & Robinson, 2005). The molecule exhibits a linear configuration, whereby the carbon atom is covalently bonded to two oxygen atoms.

The trigonal planar geometry is observed when the central atom is surrounded by three pairs of bonding electrons and no unshared pairs. The molecular configuration under consideration exhibits bond angles roughly equivalent to 120°. Boron trifluoride (BF_3) is an exemplar of a molecule that exhibits a trigonal planar geometry (Bruno et al., 2004). The molecular geometry of the compound entails a planar, triangular configuration whereby the boron atom is covalently bonded to 3 fluorine atoms. The tetrahedral molecular geometry is manifested in instances where the central atom is surrounded by four pairs of bonding electrons and no non-bonding electron pairs. The bond angles in this particular geometry exhibit an approximate value of 109.5°. CH_4 is an exemplar of a molecule that exhibits tetrahedral geometry. The molecule exhibits a symmetrical, 3-D tetrahedral shape due to the carbon atom being covalently bonded to 4 hydrogen atoms. The trigonal bipyramidal molecular geometry is observed in cases where 5 pairs of electrons are bonded and the absence of non-bonding electron pairs. The molecular geometry under consideration exhibits variation in bond angles, whereby the axial positions demonstrate a bond angle of 180°, while the equatorial positions exhibit a bond angle of 120°. Phosphorus pentachloride (PCl_5) is an instance of a molecule exhibiting trigonal bipyramidal geometry (Fogarasi et al., 1992). The molecular structure in question comprises a phosphorus atom covalently bonded to 5 chlorine atoms. The resulting geometry of the molecule can be described as two triangular pyramids interconnected at their bases.

The octahedral geometry manifests in situations where 6 pairs of bonding electrons exist and an absence of lone pairs. The bond angles in this geometric configuration exhibit an approximate value of 90°. Sulfur hexafluoride (SF_6) is an instance of a molecule exhibiting octahedral geometry. The molecular configuration of the compound involves the covalent bonding of a single sulfur atom with six fluorine atoms, resulting in a symmetrical and three-dimensional octahedral shape. The instances above merely constitute a portion of the conceivable molecular configurations (Tang & Yip, 1995). The VSEPR theory enables the anticipation of molecular geometries by considering the quantity of bonding and non-bonding electron pairs. The methodology above offers a systematic framework for comprehending the spatial configurations of atoms within molecules.

1.7. TYPES OF COVALENT COMPOUNDS

1.7.1. Binary Covalent Compounds

Binary covalent compounds are compounds that consist of a pair of distinct elements bonded together through covalent bonding. Within these chemical compounds, the constituent atoms engage in electron sharing to attain a stable state of electron configuration. The formation of a molecule is facilitated by establishing a bond between atoms through electron sharing. Binary covalent compounds are generally composed of two nonmetallic elements (Guo et al., 2008; Bagno & Saielli, 2003).

- The process of assigning names to binary covalent compounds. The nomenclature of binary covalent compounds follows a systematic approach that employs prefixes to denote the quantity of each constituent element present in the compound. The prefixes above are utilized: mono, di, tri, etc. In cases where a single atom represents the first element, the prefix "mono-" is typically excluded. The suffix "-ide" is appended to denote the second element. The molecular composition of carbon dioxide (CO_2) comprises a singular carbon atom and 2 oxygen atoms, whereas dinitrogen tetroxide (N_2O_4) is composed of 2 nitrogen atoms and 4 oxygen atoms.
- The characteristics of binary covalent compounds typically include relatively lower melting and boiling points than their ionic counterparts (Gutowsky & Hoffman, 1951). The rationale is that the intermolecular forces present among molecules in covalent substances are comparatively feeble compared to the electrostatic forces between ions in ionic compounds. Furthermore, binary covalent compounds frequently manifest as gaseous, liquid, or malleable solid states at ambient temperature, contingent upon the potency of the intermolecular interactions that are prevalent.

Binary covalent compounds display diverse chemical characteristics based on constituent elements. Hydrogen chloride (HCl) is classified as a potent acid, whereas carbon dioxide is a non-polar molecule that exhibits a relatively low level of reactivity. The characteristics of binary covalent compounds hold considerable importance in their utilization across diverse domains, including electronics, pharmaceuticals, and materials science (Blank, 1974; Morris, 2011).

1.7.2. Polyatomic Covalent Compounds

Polyatomic covalent substances are chemical compounds that consist of a minimum of two elements and are bound together using covalent bonding. The chemical above entities comprises at least three atoms, encompassing nonmetallic elements and occasionally polyatomic ions. Polyatomic covalent compounds display intricate atomic arrangements, giving rise to various chemical characteristics and configurations (Colton et al., 2010; Newman & Reynolds, 2004).

- The process of assigning names to polyatomic covalent compounds. The nomenclature of polyatomic covalent compounds adheres to analogous principles as those of binary covalent compounds. In the context of polyatomic compounds, the vocabulary of the polyatomic ions remains unaltered and is utilized as is. Sulfuric acid (H_2SO_4) is a covalently bonded compound composed of 2 hydrogen atoms, a single sulfur atom, and 4 oxygen atoms.

- Polyatomic covalent compounds display various properties contingent upon the specific combination of atoms and the bonding configuration within the molecule. These chemical compounds can potentially exist at ambient conditions in gaseous, liquid, or solid states. Certain polyatomic covalent compounds, such as H_2O and NH_3, exhibit distinctive characteristics due to hydrogen bonding, which impacts their solubilities and boiling points (Champagne et al., 2015).

Polyatomic covalent compounds play a pivotal role in numerous biological and chemical processes. They participate in synthesizing biomolecules such as nucleic acids, proteins, and carbohydrates. The compounds above are crucial in regulating biological entities' constitution, operation, and control.

1.7.3. Organic Compounds

Covalent compounds composed mainly of carbon atoms bonded to hydrogen atoms are called organic compounds. The compounds above serve as the fundamental building blocks of organic chemistry, an academic discipline investigating carbon-containing compounds and their corresponding chemical reactions. Organic compounds are of paramount importance in comprehending the processes of biology, the science of materials, and medicinal chemistry due to their diverse range of structures and properties (Caira, 1998; Rohling et al., 2019).

The process of assigning names to organic compounds. The nomenclature system utilized for the nomenclature of organic compounds is recognized as the International Union of Pure and Applied Chemistry (IUPAC) nomenclature. The IUPAC nomenclature system offers a systematic methodology for designating organic compounds by considering their structural and functional group characteristics. The process entails the identification of the primary hydrocarbon chain, assigning numerical values to the carbon atoms, and denoting the existence of substitutes or functional groups. The physical and chemical properties of organic compounds are varied owing to the varied nature of carbon bonding. Substances can exist in different physical states, namely gas, liquid, or solid, and exhibit diverse melting and boiling points (Benson, 1965). Furthermore, isomerism is a common phenomenon observed in organic compounds, whereby distinct compounds possess identical molecular formulas but vary in structural configurations. Isomerism is a significant factor in the extensive range of organic substances and their distinct characteristics.

Comprehending organic compounds holds paramount importance in diverse scientific and industrial contexts. Organic compounds are fundamental for synthesizing fibers, plastics, and pharmaceuticals. Hydrocarbons, the primary components of fossil fuels, are also implicated in energy generation.

1.8. BOND ENERGIES AND CHEMICAL REACTIONS

1.8.1. Bond Energy and Bond Dissociation Energy

The concepts of bond energy and bond dissociation energy are basic in chemistry as they offer valuable insights into the stability and strength of chemical bonds (Li et al., 2022; Gázquez, 1998).

The term "bond energy" pertains to the quantum of energy necessary to dissociate a particular chemical bond. The measure of the bond's strength is conventionally expressed in units of kilojoules per mole (kJ/mol). Experimental techniques, such as spectroscopy and computational methods, are utilized to measure bond energies. By examining atom-to-atom connections within molecular structures, researchers can ascertain the energy necessary to sever a chemical bond.

The magnitude of bond energy is subject to variability contingent upon the identities of the atoms participating in the bond and their respective electronic configurations. Diverse categories of chemical bonds, including singular, dual, or tripartite bonds, exhibit distinct bond energies. Typically, bonds with greater strength exhibit elevated bond energies, indicating a greater amount of energy is necessary to disrupt them (Blanksby & Ellison, 2003; Griller et al., 1998). The rationale behind this phenomenon is that enhanced bonding entails heightened electron density amidst the bonding atoms, thereby leading to intensified attractive forces.

Bond dissociation energy, also referred to as bond enthalpy, is a distinct form of bond energy that denotes the alteration in energy that occurs when a bond is disrupted. The bond dissociation energy refers to the quantity of energy necessary to cleave one mole of a particular bond within a gaseous molecule, producing two distinct atoms or radicals. Determining bond dissociation energies is crucial in assessing the stability of molecules and the potency of their component bonds.

Greater bond dissociation energies signify more robust bonds that necessitate more energy to be broken. The bond dissociation energy of the C-C bond in Ethane is comparatively greater than that of the C-H bond in methane (Clark & Wayner, 1991). This suggests that the C-C bond exhibits greater strength and cleavage resistance than the C-H bond. The magnitude of bond dissociation energies is subject to significant variation based on the identities of the constituent atoms and the surrounding molecular context.

Reduced values of bond dissociation energies indicate the presence of bonds that possess lower strength and are comparatively more susceptible to breakage. The N-N bond in N_2, known as nitrogen gas, exhibits a comparatively low bond dissociation energy, signifying its feeble nature. The observation above aligns with the inherent reactivity of nitrogen gas, which exhibits a propensity to engage in chemical reactions that form comparatively more stable compounds (Frenette et al., 2004; Beyer & Clausen-Schaumann, 2005).

Comprehending the concepts of bond energies and bond dissociation energies holds paramount importance in diverse domains of the field of chemistry. The application of molecular orbital theory (MOT) facilitates the anticipation and elucidation of the stability and reactivity of molecules, in addition to the energetics of chemical reactions. Furthermore, these values above are employed within computational Chemistry and molecular simulation to simulate and analyze intricate chemical systems.

1.8.2. Role of Covalent Bonds in Chemical Reactions

The significance of covalent bonds is paramount in chemical reactions, especially those that involve nonmetallic elements. The phenomenon of atoms sharing electrons to attain a relatively stable electron configuration is called a covalent bond. The phenomenon of electron sharing facilitates the creation of molecules that exhibit stability. Chemical reactions involve the breaking and forming of covalent bonds, resulting in the reorganization of atoms and the production of novel compounds.

Breaking covalent bonds necessitates an infusion of energy to surmount the cohesive forces that bind the constituent atoms (Shieh et al., 2021). Bond breaking involves energy absorption and is classified as an endothermic process. The magnitude of energy necessary to disrupt chemical bonds is contingent upon the potency of the bonds in question. Diverse chemical bonds exhibit varying bond energies, and the energy demand for their dissociation may differ. Bonds with lower bond energies are comparatively feeble. They can be disrupted with less energy, whereas bonds with higher bond energies are robust and require greater energy for their separation.

Conversely, the formation of fresh covalent bonds results in the liberation of energy, thereby rendering the process exothermic (Kariyawasam et al., 2021). The process of bond formation entails the electrostatic attraction between the negatively charged electrons of one atom and the positively charged nuclei of other atoms. When two atoms approach each other and form a bond, the conversion of potential energy into kinetic energy occurs, resulting in the emission of energy in either heat or light, the energy that is liberated during the process of bond formation plays a significant role in the overall energy alterations that occur in chemical reactions.

The idea of chemical equilibrium fundamentally relies on destroying and creating covalent bonds during chemical reactions. The state of equilibrium is attained when the pace of the forward reaction, which involves bond formation, is equivalent to the rate of the reverse reaction, which involves bond breaking, leading to a dynamic balance. At a state of equilibrium, the concentrations of both reactants and products remain stable and unchanging throughout the reaction process. A reaction's equilibrium position and thermodynamic nature are influenced by the energy changes that occur during bond breaking and formation (Kroll et al., 2003). These energy changes ultimately dictate whether a reaction is classified as exothermic or endothermic. Exothermic reactions are characterized by releasing more energy during the bond formation process than the energy necessary for bond breaking. The surplus energy is dissipated into the environment through thermal or radiant energy. Exothermic reactions are exemplified by the combustion of fuels, such as the combustion of hydrocarbons. In this process, forming new covalent bonds releases a substantial amount of energy.

On the contrary, in endothermic reactions, the energy required for bond breaking exceeds the energy released during bond formation. These reactions are endothermic, meaning they require energy to be supplied from the surrounding environment. An instance can be observed in photosynthesis, wherein plants assimilate energy from sunlight to transform water and carbon dioxide into glucose and oxygen. The energy consumed during the bond cleavage process facilitates the creation of fresh covalent bonds, thereby leading to the amalgamation of glucose molecules (Samanta et al.,

2004). The energy alterations linked with the rupture and establishment of chemical bonds bear significant consequences for the natural tendency of chemical reactions. Spontaneous reactions are characterized by a negative overall energy change, signifying that the reaction proceeds without requiring external energy input. This phenomenon is commonly associated with exothermic reactions, wherein the energy liberated during bond formation propels the reaction in a forward direction. In contrast to spontaneous reactions, non-spontaneous reactions exhibit a positive net energy alteration and necessitate an exogenous energy input to advance. Typically, such reactions exhibit endothermicity because the energy necessary for bond cleavage surpasses the energy liberated during bond creation.

1.8.3. Energy Changes in Bond Formation and Bond Breaking

The thermodynamics of chemical reactions necessitates including energy changes during bond formation and breaking. These alterations can be quantified by utilizing the principles of enthalpy and Hess's law (Hu & Chen 2015).

Enthalpy (H) is a thermodynamic property that quantifies the internal energy of a system in terms of the heat it contains. The symbol ΔH denotes the alteration in enthalpy that occurs during a chemical reaction, and it measures the total energy of a given chemical entity. The alteration in enthalpy is a significant parameter that offers valuable insights into the energy transfer linked with the formation and rupture of chemical bonds.

Breaking a bond requires an input of energy to overcome the cohesive forces that bind the constituent atoms. The introduction of energy increases enthalpy ($\Delta H > 0$), an endothermic process. The bond dissociation energy is indicative of the strength of a bond, which in turn determines the energy necessary for bond cleavage (Tielens & Santos, 2010). Various categories of chemical bonds exhibit distinct bond dissociation energies, denoting their relative potency levels. The energy required to break bonds increases proportionally with the strength of the bonds. In contrast, forming a bond leads to the liberation of energy, which causes a reduction in enthalpy ($\Delta H < 0$). The exothermic process is characterized by the liberation of energy during the formation of chemical bonds (Strieth-Kalthoff et al., 2018). The bond energy determines the correlation between the energy released during bond formation and the strength of the bond being formed. Chemical reactions exhibit energy changes that are influenced by the bonds' strength. Specifically, the energy released during the formation of stronger bonds significantly contributes to the overall energy changes observed in such reactions.

The principle of Hess's law is a fundamental concept in the field of thermodynamics that facilitates comprehension of alterations in energy that occur during chemical reactions (Strieth-Kalthoff & Glorius, 2020). As per the law in question, the total alteration in energy during a chemical reaction remains unaffected by the specific route undertaken. Stated differently, the aggregate alteration in enthalpy is equivalent to the summation of the alterations in enthalpy about the discrete stages or intervening reactions implicated in the process above. Applying Hess's law enables the determination of the net energy variations in intricate chemical reactions by evaluating the energy changes linked to the dissociation and formation of discrete chemical bonds. Using Hess's law enables the computation of the overall energy variation in a chemical reaction by evaluating the enthalpy modifications linked to the dissociation of bonds in the reactants and the establishment of bonds in the products (Costentin et al., 2006). The determination of specific bonds' energy contributions within a reaction relies on the individual bond energies and bond dissociation energies, which hold significant importance in such calculations.

Comprehending the alterations in energy during the formation and breaking of chemical bonds is advantageous in forecasting the course of a reaction and evaluating its overall plausibility. Exothermic reactions, which involve the release of energy, are typically more favorable and spontaneous. Conversely, endothermic reactions necessitate an influx of energy and may necessitate extrinsic factors such as heightened temperature or the existence of catalysts to advance (Saveant, 1993).

Activity 1.1

Imagine you are a chemist working in a research lab, and you are tasked with designing a new material with specific properties. You know that covalent bonding plays a crucial role in determining the properties of substances. Describe how you would utilize covalent bonding principles to create a material with high thermal conductivity and electrical insulating properties. Discuss the types of atoms or elements you would select for the covalent bonds, the arrangement of the atoms in ?the material, and how the covalent bonds would contribute to the desired properties

1.9. SUMMARY

In this chapter, we delve into the fundamental concepts and principles surrounding covalent bonds. The chapter starts by providing an overview of the different types of chemical bonds, including ionic bonds, covalent bonds, and metallic bonds.

We begin by exploring covalent bonds, where a fascinating "Did you know?" fact emerges: covalent bonds are formed through the sharing of electrons between atoms, a process that leads to a more stable electron configuration. This knowledge sets the stage for understanding the characteristics of covalent bonds. Electronegativity and polarity are discussed as key characteristics of covalent bonds. As a "Remember" point, we learn that electronegativity measures an atom's ability to attract electrons towards itself in a chemical bond. This concept is essential in determining the polarity of covalent bonds.

Next, we explore the relationship between bond length and bond strength. As a helpful "Tip," it is worth noting that shorter bond lengths typically indicate stronger bonds. This insight provides a useful framework for comprehending the structural properties and stability of covalent compounds.

The chapter then shifts focus to Lewis Dot Structures, which are invaluable tools for representing the valence electrons of atoms in a molecule. We discuss the rules for drawing Lewis Dot Structures and examine examples to solidify our understanding. The octet rule, a foundational principle in covalent bonding, is introduced. We explore how atoms strive to achieve a stable electron configuration by either gaining, losing, or sharing electrons, and we also discuss exceptions to the octet rule, such as elements that can expand their valence shells.

The impact of bonding on molecular geometry is thoroughly explored. We learn about the relationship between bonding and molecular shape and delve into the VSEPR theory, which helps predict molecular geometries based on the repulsion of electron pairs. Various examples of molecular geometries are provided to enhance our comprehension. The chapter further delves into different types of covalent compounds, including binary covalent compounds, polyatomic covalent compounds, and organic compounds. By understanding the characteristics and naming conventions of these compounds, we gain a comprehensive view of the diverse world of covalent bonding. Finally, the chapter touches upon bond energies and their influence on chemical reactions. We explore how the strength of covalent bonds affects the energy changes in chemical reactions, providing insights into the dynamics of molecular transformations.

REVIEW QUESTIONS

1. What is the main difference between ionic bonds and covalent bonds?
2. What is electronegativity and how does it influence the polarity of a covalent bond?
3. How do bond length and bond strength relate to each other?
4. Explain the rules for drawing Lewis Dot Structures.
5. Give examples of Lewis Dot Structures for different molecules.
6. What is the octet rule and are there any exceptions to it?
7. Describe the concept of expanded octets in covalent compounds.
8. How does molecular geometry relate to the bonding between atoms?
9. Explain the VSEPR theory and its application in determining molecular shapes.
10. What are the three types of covalent compounds mentioned in the chapter?

REFERENCE

1. Bader, R. F. W., & Henneker, W. H., (1965). The ionic bond. *Journal of the American Chemical Society*, *87*(14), 3063–3068.
2. Bagno, A., & Saielli, G., (2003). DFT study of the NMR properties of xenon in covalent compounds and van der Waals complexes—Implications for using 129Xe as a molecular probe. *Chemistry–A European Journal*, *9*(7), 1486–1495.
3. Bay, N., (1983). Mechanisms producing metallic bonds in cold welding. *Welding J.*, *62*(5), 137.
4. Benson, S. W., (1965). III-bond energies. *Journal of Chemical Education*, *42*(9), 502.
5. Berdan, V. Y., Klauser, P. C., & Wang, L., (2021). Covalent peptides and proteins for therapeutics. *Bioorganic & Medicinal Chemistry*, *29*, 115896.
6. Beyer, M. K., & Clausen-Schaumann, H., (2005). Mechanochemistry: The mechanical activation of covalent bonds. *Chemical Reviews*, *105*(8), 2921–2948.
7. Blake, E. S., Hammann, W. C., Edwards, J. W., Reichard, T. E., & Ort, M. R., (1961). Thermal stability as a function of chemical structure. *Journal of Chemical and Engineering Data*, *6*(1), 87–98.
8. Blank, H., (1974). Covalent and ionic crystal radii and Phillips ionicity. *Solid State Communications*, *15*(5), 907–910.
9. Blanksby, S. J., & Ellison, G. B., (2003). Bond dissociation energies of organic molecules. *Accounts of Chemical Research*, *36*(4), 255–263.
10. Brookhart, M., & Green, M. L., (1983). Carbon hydrogen-transition metal bonds. *Journal of Organometallic Chemistry*, *250*(1), 395–408.
11. Brown, I. D., (1981). The bond-valence method: an empirical approach to chemical structure and bonding. *Structure and Bonding in Crystals*, *2*(1–30), 84.
12. Bruno, I. J., Cole, J. C., Kessler, M., Luo, J., Motherwell, W. S., Purkis, L. H., & Orpen, A. G., (2004). Retrieval of crystallographically-derived molecular geometry information. *Journal of Chemical Information and Computer Sciences*, *44*(6), 2133–2144.
13. Bullett, D. W., (1975). Chemical pseudopotential approach to covalent bonding. II. Bond lengths and bond energies in diamond, silicon, and graphite. *Journal of Physics C: Solid State Physics*, *8*(17), 2707.
14. Burrows, N. L., & Mooring, S. R., (2015). Using concept mapping to uncover students' knowledge structures of chemical bonding concepts. *Chemistry Education Research and Practice*, *16*(1), 53–66.

15. Caira, M. R., (1998). Crystalline polymorphism of organic compounds. *Design of Organic Solids*, 163–208.
16. Cao, L., & Wang, L., (2022). New covalent bonding ability for proteins. *Protein Science*, *31*(2), 312–322.
17. Chakma, P., & Konkolewicz, D., (2019). Dynamic covalent bonds in polymeric materials. *Angewandte Chemie International Edition*, *58*(29), 9682–9695.
18. Champagne, P. A., Desroches, J., Hamel, J. D., Vandamme, M., & Paquin, J. F., (2015). Monofluorination of organic compounds: 10 years of innovation. *Chemical Reviews*, *115*(17), 9073–9174.
19. Chen, X. H., Xiang, Z., Hu, Y. S., Lacey, V. K., Cang, H., & Wang, L., (2014). Genetically encoding an electrophilic amino acid for protein stapling and covalent binding to native receptors. *ACS Chemical Biology*, *9*(9), 1956–1961.
20. Clark, K. B., & Wayner, D. D., (1991). Are relative bond energies a measure of radical stabilization energies? *Journal of the American Chemical Society*, *113*(24), 9363–9365.
21. Coll, R. K., & Treagust, D. F., (2003). Investigation of secondary school, undergraduate, and graduate learners' mental models of ionic bonding. *Journal of Research in Science Teaching: The Official Journal of the National Association for Research in Science Teaching*, *40*(5), 464–486.
22. Collman, J. P., & Boulatov, R., (2002). Heterodinuclear transition-metal complexes with multiple metal–metal bonds. *Angewandte Chemie International Edition*, *41*(21), 3948–3961.
23. Colton, R. J., Ross, M. M., & Kidwell, D. A., (1986). Secondary ion mass spectrometry: Polyatomic and molecular ion emission. *Nuclear Instruments and Methods in Physics Research Section B: Beam Interactions with Materials and Atoms*, *13*(1–3), 259–277.
24. Costentin, C., Robert, M., & Savéant, J. M., (2006). Electron transfer and bond breaking: Recent advances. *Chemical Physics*, *324*(1), 40–56.
25. Curnow, O. J., (2021). Facile method for constructing Lewis (electron dot) structures. *Journal of Chemical Education*, *98*(4), 1454–1457.
26. Dolg, M., Cao, X., & Ciupka, J., (2014). Misleading evidence for covalent bonding from EuIIIX and AmIIIX density functional theory bond lengths. *Journal of Electron Spectroscopy and Related Phenomena*, *194*, 8–13.
27. Fleet, M. E., (1977). The crystal structure of heazlewoodite, and metallic bonds in sulfide minerals. *American Mineralogist*, *62*(3, 4), 341–345.
28. Fogarasi, G., Zhou, X., Taylor, P. W., & Pulay, P., (1992). The calculation

of ab initio molecular geometries: efficient optimization by natural internal coordinates and empirical correction by offset forces. *Journal of the American Chemical Society*, *114*(21), 8191–8201.

29. Frenette, M., Aliaga, C., Font-Sanchis, E., & Scaiano, J. C., (2004). Bond dissociation energies for radical dimers derived from highly stabilized carbon-centered radicals. *Organic Letters*, *6*(15), 2579–2582.
30. Fujiwara, D., Kellar, K., Humer, I., Pietroszek, K., & Eckhardt, C., (2020). VSEPR theory, an interactive and immersive virtual reality. In *2020 6th International Conference of the Immersive Learning Research Network (iLRN)* (pp. 140–146). IEEE.
31. Fulton, R. L., & Mixon, S. T., (1993). Comparison of covalent bond indexes and sharing indexes. *The Journal of Physical Chemistry*, *97*(29), 7530–7534.
32. Gade, L. H., (2000). Highly polar metal–metal bonds in "early–late" heterodimetallic complexes. *Angewandte Chemie International Edition*, *39*(15), 2658–2678.
33. Gavezzotti, A., (2016). Comparing the strength of covalent bonds, intermolecular hydrogen bonds and other intermolecular interactions for organic molecules: X-ray diffraction data and quantum chemical calculations. *New Journal of Chemistry*, *40*(8), 6848–6853.
34. Gázquez, J. L., (1998). A hardness and softness theory of bond energies and chemical reactivity. In: *Theoretical and Computational Chemistry* (Vol. 5, pp. 135–152).
35. Gillespie, R. J., & Robinson, E. A., (1995). Hypervalence and the octet rule. *Inorganic Chemistry*, *34*(4), 978, 979.
36. Gillespie, R. J., & Robinson, E. A., (1996). Electron domains and the VSEPR model of molecular geometry. *Angewandte Chemie International Edition in English*, *35*(5), 495–514.
37. Gillespie, R. J., & Robinson, E. A., (2005). Models of molecular geometry. *Chemical Society Reviews*, *34*(5), 396–407.
38. Gillespie, R. J., & Robinson, E. A., (2007). Gilbert N. Lewis and the chemical bond: The electron pair and the octet rule from 1916 to the present day. *Journal of Computational Chemistry*, *28*(1), 87–97.
39. Gillespie, R. J., & Silvi, B., (2002). The octet rule and hypervalence: two misunderstood concepts. *Coordination Chemistry Reviews*, *233*, 53–62.
40. Gillespie, R. J., (1963). The valence-shell electron-pair repulsion (VSEPR) theory of directed valency. *Journal of Chemical Education*, *40*(6), 295.
41. Gillespie, R. J., Spencer, J. N., & Moog, R. S., (1996). Bonding and

molecular geometry without orbitals-the electron domain model. *Journal of Chemical Education*, *73*(7), 622.

42. Grandbois, M., Beyer, M., Rief, M., Clausen-Schaumann, H., & Gaub, H. E., (1999). How strong is a covalent bond? *Science*, *283*(5408), 1727–1730.
43. Green, M. L., & Parkin, G., (2014). Application of the covalent bond classification method for the teaching of inorganic chemistry. *Journal of Chemical Education*, *91*(6), 807–816.
44. Griller, D., Kanabus-Kaminska, J. M., & Maccoll, A., (1988). Bond dissociation energies for common organic compounds. *Journal of Molecular Structure: Theochem*, *163*, 125–131.
45. Guo, X., Li, L., Liu, Z., Yu, D., He, J., Liu, R., & Wang, H. T., (2008). Hardness of covalent compounds: Roles of metallic component and d valence electrons. *Journal of Applied Physics*, *104*(2), 023503.
46. Gutowsky, H. S., & Hoffman, C. J., (1951). Nuclear magnetic shielding in fluorine and hydrogen compounds. *The Journal of Chemical Physics*, *19*(10), 1259–1267.
47. Held, P. A., Fuchs, H., & Studer, A., (2017). Covalent-bond formation via on-surface chemistry. *Chemistry–A European Journal*, *23*(25), 5874–5892.
48. Hu, C., & Chen, Y., (2015). Biomolecule-compatible chemical bond-formation and bond-cleavage reactions induced by visible light. *Tetrahedron Letters*, *56*(7), 884–888.
49. Huang, S., Kong, X., Xiong, Y., Zhang, X., Chen, H., Jiang, W., & Ren, C., (2020). An overview of dynamic covalent bonds in polymer material and their applications. *European Polymer Journal*, *141*, 110094.
50. Hummel, M., & Kern, M., (2004). Durability of the resin bond strength to the alumina ceramic Procera. *Dental Materials*, *20*(5), 498–508.
51. Hutskalov, I., Linden, A., & Čorić, I., (2023). Directional ionic bonds. *Journal of the American Chemical Society*, *145*(15), 8291–8298.
52. Jackson, B. A., Harshman, J., & Miliordos, E., (2020). Addressing the hypervalent model: A straightforward explanation of traditionally hypervalent molecules. *Journal of Chemical Education*, *97*(10), 3638–3646.
53. Kamaras, K., Itkis, M. E., Hu, H., Zhao, B., & Haddon, R. C., (2003). Covalent bond formation to a carbon nanotube metal. *Science*, *301*(5639), 1501.
54. Kariyawasam, L. S., Hossain, M. M., & Hartley, C. S., (2021). The

transient covalent bond in abiotic nonequilibrium systems. *Angewandte Chemie International Edition*, *60*(23), 12648–12658.

55. Klebe, J. F., (1968). Disilaoxadiazines. Silyl tautomerism in cyclic silylamides involving expanded-octet silicon. *Journal of the American Chemical Society*, *90*(19), 5246–5251.
56. Kroll, J., RAWEL, H. M., & Rohn, S., (2003). Reactions of plant phenolics with food proteins and enzymes under special consideration of covalent bonds. *Food Science and Technology Research*, *9*(3), 205–218.
57. Krygowski, T. M., Szatyłowicz, H., & Zachara, J. E., (2005). How H-bonding modifies molecular structure and π-electron delocalization in the ring of pyridine/pyridinium derivatives involved in H-bond complexation. *The Journal of Organic Chemistry*, *70*(22), 8859–8865.
58. Li, C., Ju, B., & Zhang, S., (2021). Construction of a new green vitrimer material: introducing dynamic covalent bond into carboxymethyl cellulose. *Cellulose*, *28*, 2879–2888.
59. Li, K., Wang, X., & Xue, D., (2008). Electronegativities of elements in covalent crystals. *The Journal of Physical Chemistry A*, *112*(34), 7894–7897.
60. Li, Y., Zhang, L., & Luo, S., (2022). Bond energies of enamines. *ACS Omega*, *7*(7), 6354–6374.
61. Lindahl, P. A., (2012). Metal–metal bonds in biology. *Journal of Inorganic Biochemistry*, *106*(1), 172–178.
62. Malerich, C. J., (1987). Lewis structures for compounds with expanded octets. *Journal of Chemical Education*, *64*(5), 403.
63. Morris, T. A., (2011). Go chemistry: A card game to help students learn chemical formulas. *Journal of Chemical Education*, *88*(10), 1397–1399.
64. Nassiff, P., & Czerwinski, W. A., (2015). Teaching beginning chemistry students simple Lewis dot structures. *Journal of Chemical Education*, *92*(8), 1409–1411.
65. Newman, L. A., & Reynolds, C. M., (2004). Phytodegradation of organic compounds. *Current Opinion in Biotechnology*, *15*(3), 225–230.
66. Noury, S., Silvi, B., & Gillespie, R. J., (2002). Chemical bonding in hypervalent molecules: is the octet rule relevant? *Inorganic Chemistry*, *41*(8), 2164–2172.
67. Owen, J., (1955). The colors and magnetic properties of hydrated iron group salts, and evidence for covalent bonding. *Proceedings of the Royal Society of London: Series A Mathematical and Physical Sciences*, *227*(1169), 183–200.

68. Peterson, R. F., Treagust, D. F., & Garnett, P., (1989). Development and application of a diagnostic instrument to evaluate grade-11 and-12 students' concepts of covalent bonding and structure following a course of instruction. *Journal of Research in Science Teaching*, *26*(4), 301–314.
69. Phillips, J. C., (1967). A posteriori theory of covalent bonding. *Physical Review Letters*, *19*(8), 415.
70. Picchioni, F., & Muljana, H., (2018). Hydrogels based on dynamic covalent and non covalent bonds: a chemistry perspective. *Gels*, *4*(1), 21.
71. Powers, I. G., & Uyeda, C., (2017). Metal–metal bonds in catalysis. *ACS Catalysis*, *7*(2), 936–958.
72. Prodjosantoso, A. K., & Hertina, A. M., (2019). The misconception diagnosis on ionic and covalent bonds concepts with three tier diagnostic test. *International Journal of Instruction*, *12*(1), 1477–1488.
73. Quayle, P. C., Blanton, E. W., Punya, A., Junno, G. T., He, K., Han, L., & Kash, K., (2015). Charge-neutral disorder and polytypes in heterovalent wurtzite-based ternary semiconductors: The importance of the octet rule. *Physical Review B*, *91*(20), 205207.
74. Reed, A. E., & Schleyer, P. V. R., (1990). Chemical bonding in hypervalent molecules. The dominance of ionic bonding and negative hyperconjugation over d-orbital participation. *Journal of the American Chemical Society*, *112*(4), 1434–1445.
75. Rohling, R. Y., Tranca, I. C., Hensen, E. J., & Pidko, E. A., (2019). Correlations between density-based bond orders and orbital-based bond energies for chemical bonding analysis. *The Journal of Physical Chemistry C*, *123*(5), 2843–2854.
76. Ruedenberg, K., & Schmidt, M. W., (2007). Why does electron sharing lead to covalent bonding? A variational analysis. *Journal of Computational Chemistry*, *28*(1), 391–410.
77. Ruedenberg, K., & Schmidt, M. W., (2009). Physical understanding through variational reasoning: Electron sharing and covalent bonding. *The Journal of Physical Chemistry A*, *113*(10), 1954–1968.
78. Salame, I. I., & Nikolic, D., (2021). Examining some of the challenges students face in learning about solubility and the dissolution process. *Interdisciplinary Journal of Environmental and Science Education*, *17*(3), e2237.
79. Samanta, A. K., Czakó, G., Wang, Y., Mancini, J. S., Bowman, J. M., & Reisler, H., (2014). Experimental and theoretical investigations of energy transfer and hydrogen-bond breaking in small water and HCl clusters. *Accounts of Chemical Research*, *47*(8), 2700–2709.

80. Sanderson, R. T., (1983). Electronegativity and bond energy. *Journal of the American Chemical Society*, *105*(8), 2259–2261.

81. Santi, D. V., Norment, A., & Garrett, C. E., (1984). Covalent bond formation between a DNA-cytosine methyltransferase and DNA containing 5-azacytosine. *Proceedings of the National Academy of Sciences*, *81*(22), 6993–6997.

82. Saveant, J. M., (1993). Electron transfer, bond breaking, and bond formation. *Accounts of Chemical Research*, *26*(9), 455–461.

83. Schäfer, H., Eisenmann, B., & Müller, W., (1973). Zintl phases: transitions between metallic and ionic bonding. *Angewandte Chemie International Edition in English*, *12*(9), 694–712.

84. Schomaker, V., & Stevenson, D. P., (1941). Some revisions of the covalent radii and the additivity rule for the lengths of partially ionic single covalent bonds. *Journal of the American Chemical Society*, *63*(1), 37–40.

85. Schwaderer, P., Funk, E., Achenbach, F., Weis, J., Bräuchle, C., & Michaelis, J., (2008). Single-molecule measurement of the strength of a siloxane bond. *Langmuir*, *24*(4), 1343–1349.

86. Shaffer, A. A., (2006). Let us give Lewis acid-base theory the priority it deserves. *Journal of Chemical Education*, *83*(12), 1746.

87. Shieh, P., Hill, M. R., Zhang, W., Kristufek, S. L., & Johnson, J. A., (2021). Clip chemistry: diverse (bio)(macro) molecular and material function through breaking covalent bonds. *Chemical Reviews*, *121*(12), 7059–7121.

88. Shultz, G. V., & Gere, A. R., (2015). Writing-to-learn the nature of science in the context of the Lewis dot structure model. *Journal of Chemical Education*, *92*(8), 1325–1329.

89. Simoes, J. M., & Beauchamp, J. L., (1990). Transition metal-hydrogen and metal-carbon bond strengths: the keys to catalysis. *Chemical Reviews*, *90*(4), 629–688.

90. Smyth, C. P., (1938). The polarities of covalent bonds. *Journal of the American Chemical Society*, *60*(1), 183–189.

91. Sommer, L. H., & Rodewald, P. G., (1963). Racemization of an optically active fluorosilane without displacement of fluoride ion: evidence for an expanded-octet mechanism. *Journal of the American Chemical Society*, *85*(23), 3898–3899.

92. Spruijt, E., Van, D. B. S. A., Cohen, S. M. A., & Van, D. G. J., (2012). Direct measurement of the strength of single ionic bonds between hydrated charges. *ACS Nano*, *6*(6), 5297–5303.

93. Straub, D. K., (1995). Lewis structures of boron compounds involving multiple bonding. *Journal of Chemical Education*, *72*(6), 494.
94. Strieth-Kalthoff, F., & Glorius, F., (2020). Triplet energy transfer photocatalysis: unlocking the next level. *Chem.*, *6*(8), 1888–1903.
95. Strieth-Kalthoff, F., James, M. J., Teders, M., Pitzer, L., & Glorius, F., (2018). Energy transfer catalysis mediated by visible light: Principles, applications, directions. *Chemical Society Reviews*, *47*(19), 7190–7202.
96. Suat, Ü. N. A. L., Coştu, B., & Alipaşa, A. Y. A. S., (2010). Secondary school students' misconceptions of covalent bonding. *Journal of Turkish Science Education*, *7*(2), 3–29.
97. Swartz, J. E., & Schladetzky, K., (1996). Experimental illustration of the utility of Lewis structures. *Journal of Chemical Education*, *73*(2), 188.
98. Tang, M., & Yip, S., (1995). Atomic size effects in pressure-induced amorphization of a binary covalent lattice. *Physical Review Letters*, *75*(14), 2738.
99. Tersoff, J., (1988). New empirical approach for the structure and energy of covalent systems. *Physical Review B*, *37*(12), 6991.
100. Tielens, F., & Santos, E., (2010). AuS and SH bond formation/breaking during the formation of alkanethiol SAMs on Au (111): A theoretical study. *The Journal of Physical Chemistry C*, *114*(20), 9444–9452.
101. Wang, T. Z., & Chen, K. N., (1999). Introduction of covalently bonded phosphorus into aqueous-based polyurethane system via postcuring reaction. *Journal of Applied Polymer Science*, *74*(10), 2499–2509.
102. Wang, X. B., Wang, Y. L., Yang, J., Xing, X. P., Li, J., & Wang, L. S., (2009). Evidence of significant covalent bonding in Au $(CN)_2^-$. *Journal of the American Chemical Society*, *131*(45), 16368–16370.
103. Wang, Z., Wang, Y., Zhang, Z., Chen, X., Lie, W., He, Y. B., & Guo, Z., (2020). Building artificial solid-electrolyte interphase with uniform intermolecular ionic bonds toward dendrite-free lithium metal anodes. *Advanced Functional Materials*, *30*(30), 2002414.
104. Wilson, A., Gasparini, G., & Matile, S., (2014). Functional systems with orthogonal dynamic covalent bonds. *Chemical Society Reviews*, *43*(6), 1948–1962.
105. Xiang, Z., Ren, H., Hu, Y. S., Coin, I., Wei, J., Cang, H., & Wang, L., (2013). Adding an unnatural covalent bond to proteins through proximity-enhanced bioreactivity. *Nature Methods*, *10*(9), 885–888.

CHAPTER 2

Molecular Structure and Bonding Theories

Contents

2.1. INTRODUCTION

The Molecular Orbital Theory (MOT) is more effective in predicting electronic spectra and Para magnetism than the VSEPR and V-B Theories. The molecular orbital (MO) theory obviates the necessity of incorporating resonance structures in the depiction of molecular species while enabling the prognostication of bond lengths and energy. A significant limitation is that the discourse is confined to diatomic molecules composed of only two bonded atoms to avoid excessive complexity in theory (Streitwieser, 2013; Ballhausen & Gray, 1965).

The MOT postulates that the bonding between atoms in a molecule arises from the overlap and sharing of electrons between their respective atomic nuclei. In contrast to the V-B theory's treatment of electrons to localized balloons of electron mass, the MO theory posits that electrons are delocalized. This implies that the atoms are distributed throughout the entirety of the molecule (Roothaan, 1951; Hehre, 1976).

2.1.1. Forming Molecular Orbitals

The MO theory posits that the formation of molecular bonds can be explained by the mutual exchange of electrons among the nuclei of atoms. In contrast to the V-B theory's treatment of electrons as localized balloons of electron abundance, the MO theory posits that electrons are delocalized (Wolters & Bickelhaupt, 2015). This implies that the constituent elements are distributed uniformly throughout the molecular structure (Figure 2.1).

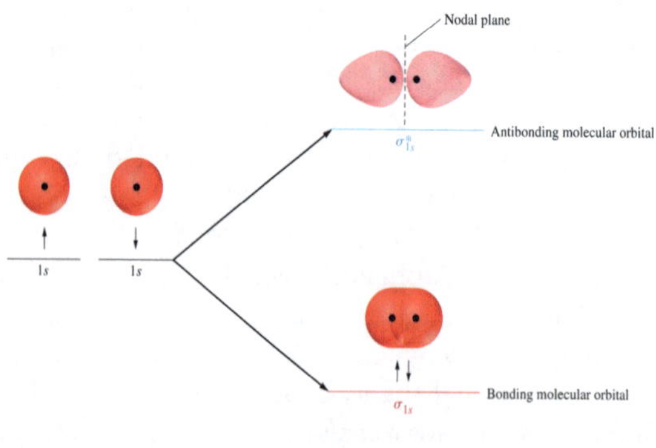

Figure 2.1. Illustration of forming of molecular orbital theory.

Source: Libre texts, Creative Commons License.

A molecular orbital is designated as a bonding molecule orbital due to the predominant localization of electrons within the inter-nuclear region.

The molecular orbital denoted by the symbol sigma σ is so named due to its resemblance to the s orbital when observed from the perspective of the H-H bond. Electrons in the alternate orbital tend to spend most of their temporal existence distanced from the inter-nuclear region (Fernández & Bickelhaupt, 2014). Consequently, this particular orbital can be classified as a molecular orbital of the sigma star (σ*) type, which exhibits antibonding properties.

The σ molecular orbital responsible for bonding is characterized by the localization of electrons in the inter-nuclear region. The stabilization of the H_2 molecule is achieved through the placement of an electron in the respective orbital. The placement of an electron in the σ antibonding molecular orbital results in reduced stability of the molecule due to the electron being forced to spend a significant amount of time away from the inter-nuclear region (Hehre, et al., 1970).

The MO theory comprises five fundamental principles:

- The quantity of molecular orbitals is equivalent to the quantity of atomic orbitals that have been merged.
- Two MOs are present, one bonding orbital with lower energy, while the other consists of an anti-bonding orbital with greater energy. Electrons enter the lowest orbital available.
- According to the Pauli Exclusion Principle, an orbital can accommodate a maximum of two electrons (Hariharan & Pople, 1974).
- According to Hund's Rule, electrons distribute themselves before pairing up.

2.1.2. Calculating Bond Order

Determining bond orders in molecular orbital science involves postulating that a pair of electrons housed within a bonding molecule orbital accounts for a single net bond. In contrast, a pair of electrons situated within an antibonding molecule orbital nullifies the effect of one bond (Foresman et al., 1992).

$$\textit{Bond order} = \frac{\textit{bonding electrons} - \textit{antibonding electrons}}{2}$$

Figure 2.2. Image of bond angle formula.

Source: Byju's, Creative Commons License.

The bond order of the O_2 molecule can be determined by considering the electron configuration for the molecule, which reveals the presence of eight electrons with valence in connecting molecular orbitals along with four valence electrons within antibonding molecular orbitals. Hence, the bond order has been determined to be two (Figure 2.2).

While the bond order obtained from the Lewis structure and molecular orbital examples of oxygen is identical, there is a significant distinction between these models. While the electrons to the Lewis structure have paired, a molecule can possess unpaired electrons in its molecular orbital depiction. Consequently, the veracity of these theories can be examined by analyzing the impact of magnetic fields on specific molecules (People et al., 1965; Fukui et al., 1952).

2.2. HOMO NUCLEAR DIATOMIC MOLECULES

2.2.1. Molecular Orbitals for Period 1 Diatomic Molecules

Adding electrons to molecules' orbitals occurs sequentially, incorporating electrons individually, commencing from the molecular orbital with the least energy. The molecular orbital diagram below illustrates the allocation of the two electrons about the pair of hydrogen molecules within the bonding molecular orbital of the lowest energy (Bernstein et al., 1963). The diagram presented indicates that the energy level of an H_2 molecule is comparatively lower compared to that of two separate and unconnected atoms. Consequently, the H_2 molecule exhibits greater stability than a duo of unconnected atoms (Figure 2.3).

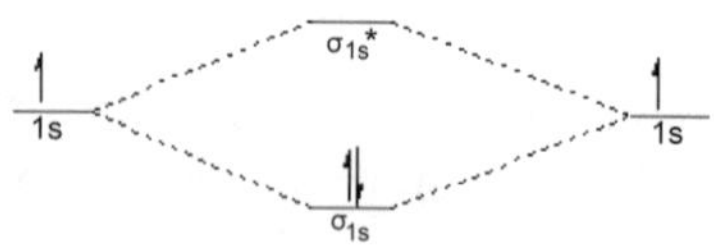

Figure 2.3. Illustration of diatomic molecule.

Source: Byju's, Creative Commons License.

According to the stability criteria, lithium is the preferred option as it possesses an ordered bond for 1, which is considered stable. Conversely, beryllium possesses a bond sequence of 0, which is unsteady and thus incapable of forming (Kotani et al., 1957). The unavailability of the He_2 molecule can be elucidated through the utilization of the molecular orbital model. Utilizing the molecular orbital model facilitates an explanation for the nonexistence of He_2 molecules. The fusion of two helium atoms, each with 1s2 electron configurations, would form a molecule with a pair of electrons in both the bonding and the antibonding molecular orbitals. The aggregate energy of a He_2 molecule will be nearly identical to the energy of two separate helium atoms, and no cohesive force would exist to facilitate the formation of a molecular structure from the helium atoms (Parr & Borkman, 1968; Toulouse & Umrigar, 2008).

The principle that the stability of a single He_2 molecule is equivalent to that of two separate helium atoms highlights a significant concept: The core orbits of an atom do not play a role in the stability of molecules that incorporate said atom. In the context of molecular orbitals, the pertinent ones arise from the amalgamation of valence shell orbitals (Lie & Clementi, 1974; Odžak & Milošević, 2009).

2.2.2. Molecular Orbitals for Period 2 Diatomic Molecules and Li_2 and Be_2 (Figure 2.4)

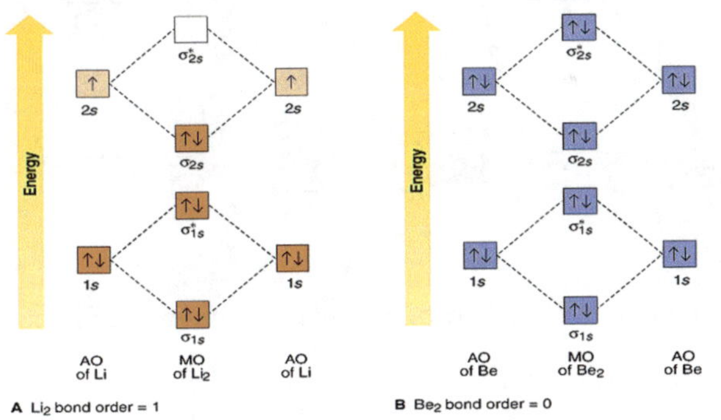

Figure 2.4. Schematic of molecular orbitals for period 2 diatomic molecules and Li_2 and Be_2.

Source: Bartleby, Creative Commons License.

2.3. MOLECULAR ORBITALS OF THE SECOND ENERGY LEVEL (2S AND 2P TOGETHER)

The molecular orbits for the next energy level can be described as the combination of the 2s orbitals of two atoms, resulting in the formation of a σ_{2s} bonding along with a σ^*_{2s} antibonding molecular orbital. This process is analogous to forming σ_{1s} and σ^*_{1s} orbitals from the 1s atomic orbitals. By defining the Z axis of the spatial coordinate system over the O_2 molecule just like the direction along which the bond between molecules forms, the $2p_z$ orbits upon atoms next to it will intersect directly to generate a σ_{2p} bonding along with a σ^*_{2p} antibonding molecules orbital. The term "sigma orbitals" is employed due to their resemblance to s orbitals when observed along the bond between oxygen atoms (Wahl, 1964; Peterson et al., 1997) (Figure 2.5).

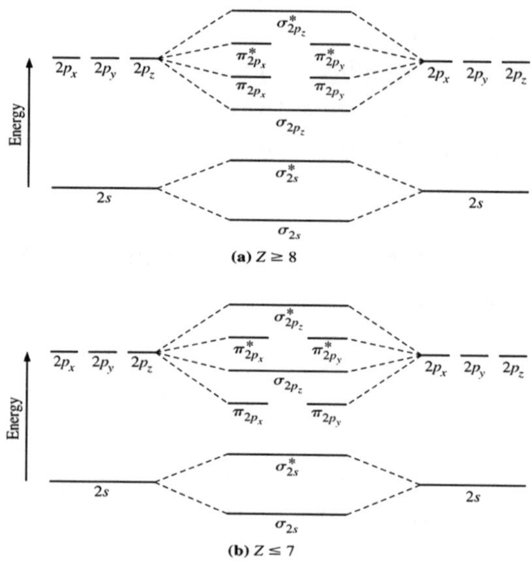

Figure 2.5. Schematic of MO's for 2nd row diatomic molecules.

Source: Chemistry 301, Creative Commons License.

The molecular orbits for the next energy level can be described as the combination of the 2s orbitals of two atoms, resulting in the formation of a 2s bonding along with a 2s* antibonding molecular orbital. This process is analogous to forming 1s and 1s* orbitals from the 1s atomic orbitals. By defining the Z axis of the spatial coordinate system over the O_2 molecule just like the direction along which the bond between molecules forms, the 2pz orbits upon atoms next to it will intersect directly to generate a 2p bonding along with a 2p* antibonding molecules orbital. The term "sigma orbitals" is employed due to their resemblance to s orbitals when observed along the bond between oxygen atoms (Broyer et al., 1978; Krishnan et al., 1980).

The two 2px atomic orbitals combine to generate π_x bonding molecular orbital denoted as ${}_x\pi^*$ and an antibonding molecular orbital denoted as x*.

Similar to the previous scenario, the interaction between the 2py orbitals forms a pair of molecular orbitals: aπ_y and a π_y* antibonding orbital. The energy levels of the 2px and 2py atomic orbitals are equivalent, resulting in the energies of the π_x and π_y and the π_x* and π_y* molecular orbitals (People et al., 1964; Vreven et al., 2000). The amalgamation of four valency orbitals of atoms (2s, 2px, 2py, and 2pz) on one atom with a group of four atomic orbitals upon another element results in the generation of a combined eight-molecule orbital:

σ_{2s}, σ_{2s}* ,σ_{2p} , σ_{2p}* , π_x , π_y , π_x* , and π_y*.

A notable disparity exists in the energy levels of the 2s along with 2p orbitals within atom. Consequently, it can be observed that the energy levels of the 2s and *2s orbitals are comparatively lower than those of $_{2p}$, $_{2p}$*, $_x$, y, $_x$*, and σ_y* orbitals. To determine the corresponding energies of each of the six orbitals of molecules resulting from the combination of 2p atomic orbitals upon a pair of atoms, it is necessary to comprehend the correlation between the intensity of the interaction among a pair of orbitals along with the relative energy levels for the orbitals of molecules that ensue (People & Segal, 1965; Hehre et al., 1969).

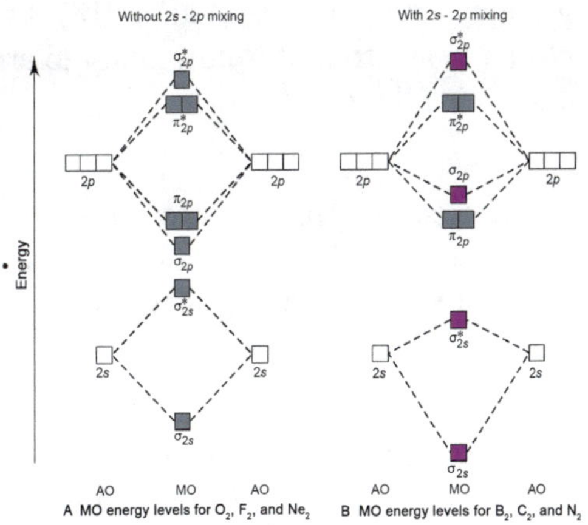

Figure 2.6. Schematic of energy level for O_2, F_2 and Ne_2.

Source: Byju's, Creative Commons License.

The strength of the interaction between both 2pz orbitals is greater than that of the interaction among the 2px or 2py orbitals due to their head-on meeting, while the latter meet edge-on. Consequently, it can be observed from the diagram below that the 2p orbital is situated at a lower energy level compared to the π_x and π_y orbitals. The σ_{2p}* orbital is positioned at a higher energy level than the σ_{x*} and σy* orbitals. Regrettably, this model lacks interaction. The interaction between the 2s orbital of one atom and the 2pz orbital of another is plausible. The present interaction incorporates the concept of s-p mixing, also known as hybridization, within the framework of the orbital theory. The outcome is a minor alteration in the comparative energies for the molecular orbitals (Fischer, 1971; Cradock et al., 1973). Conversely, the molecular structures of B_2, C_2, and N_2 are most accurately represented by a representation that incorporates hybridization (Figure 2.6).

2.3.1. Construct a Molecular Orbital Diagram for the O_2 Molecule

A neutral oxygen atom possesses six valence electrons, while an O_2 molecule has 12 valence electrons. The electrons are commencing with the molecule's orbital of the least energy (Del Bene & Pople, 1970; Gordy, 1947).

According to Hund's rules, which govern the occupation of molecular orbitals, it is predicted by the MOT that the molecule in question will possess a pair of unpaired electrons, with one electron occupying the πx* orbital and the other occupying the πy* orbital (Oda et al., 2018). In documenting the arrangement of electrons of an atom, it is customary to arrange the orbitals within the sequence of their filling.

Pb: [Xe] $6s^2\ 4f^{14}\ 5d^{10}\ 6p^2$

The arrangement of electrons for a molecule can be determined by employing a similar methodology. Focusing solely on its valence orbits, the electron's configuration for O_2 is expressed as follows.

$$O_2 : S_{2s}^{2} S_{2s}^{*2} S_{2p}^{2} \cdot p_{\cdot x}^{2} \cdot p_{\cdot y}^{2} \cdot p_{\cdot x}^{*1} \cdot p_{\cdot y}^{*1}$$

The molecular orbital diagram of N_2 represents the energy levels and electron occupancy of the molecular orbitals formed by combining the atomic orbitals of two nitrogen atoms (Horsfield et al., 1996; Mayer, 2007) (Figure 2.7).

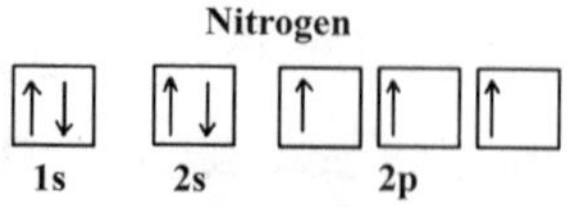

Figure 2.7. Image of example of Hund's rule.

Source: Libratext chemistry, Creative Commons License.

2.4. BOND ORDER

The quantification of the total number of chemical bonds existing among a pair of molecules is referred to as the bond order. The determination of bond orders can be accomplished by utilizing Lewis structures, which serve as the fundamental basis of the valence-bond system. Oxygen exhibits a bond arrangement of two (Mayer, 1983; Sun, 2007).

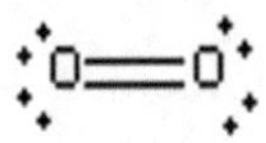

In cases where a molecule possesses multiple Lewis structures, the bond order is determined as the mean value of these structures. The bond rank for sulfur dioxide is 1.5, which is determined by taking the average of the bond orders of an S-O single bond within one Lewis structure and a S=O double bond within the other (Lendvay, 1989; Pettifor, 1989).

The determination of bond orders in the theory of molecular orbitals involves the postulation that a pair of electrons in a bonding molecule's orbital accounts for one effective bond. In comparison, a pair of electrons situated in an anti-bonding molecular orbital nullifies the influence of one bond. The bond structure of the O_2 molecule can be determined by observing that the electron configuration within this molecule contains eight valence electrons within the bonding orbitals of molecules and four valence electrons within antibonding molecular orbitals, respectively (Sun et al., 2002). Hence, the bond order has been determined to be two.

$$Bond\ order = \frac{bonding\ electrons - antibonding\ electrons}{2} = \frac{8-4}{2} = 2$$

While the bond order obtained from both the Lewis structure and cellular orbital oxygen models is identical, a significant distinction exists between these models. Although the electrons within the structure of Lewis are paired together, the molecular orbiting description for the molecule reveals the presence of two unpaired electrons. Consequently, the veracity of these theories can be examined by analyzing the impact of magnetic fields on oxygen (Gross et al., 2012; Lechner & Dellago, 2008).

Diamagnetic atoms or molecules possess paired electrons and tend to be repelled from both poles of a field of magnetic attraction. Paramagnetic materials possess several unpaired electrons, which causes them to exhibit attraction toward a magnetic field. The phenomenon of liquid oxygen being drawn towards a field of magnetic attraction and exhibiting the ability to connect the poles for a horseshoe magnet has been observed. The superiority of the molecular orbital models over the valence-bond model is evidenced by their ability to account for the property as mentioned above of oxygen (Klemenz et al., 2020; Velasquez et al., 2020).

Examine the subsequent molecular orbital diagrams depicting the electronic structure of select period two elements. Could one identify the molecules that exhibit Para magnetism? What are the molecules with the highest and lowest bond energy, respectively? In terms of bond energy and bond length, the ranking of the three types of bonds is as follows: triple bonds have the highest bond energy and shortest bond length, followed by double bonds, and then single bonds with the lowest bond energy and longest bond length. A bond order of 1 represents a single bond, while a bond order of 2 represents a double bond (Savin et al., 1996; Szczepanik et al., 2017).

2.5. DELOCALIZED BONDING

It was previously noted that the MO Theory does not require using resonance structures for explanatory purposes. The MOT posits that the electrons do not belong to a single location. Conversely, the distribution of these entities is observed to be dispersed throughout the entirety of the molecular structure. The following image depicts the molecular structures of Benzene along with Ozone. It can be observed that instead of possessing a pair of resonance structures, a singular structure can be envisioned wherein the electrons are distributed throughout the entirety of the molecule (Dimroth, 2006) (Figure 2.8).

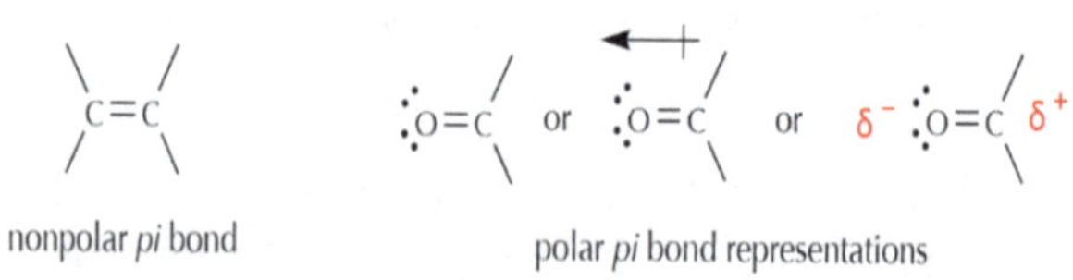

Figure 2.8. Illustration of delocalization of electron.

Source: Libertext chemistry, Creative Commons License.

2.6. MOLECULAR ORBITALS FOR HETERONUCLEAR DIATOMIC MOLECULES

One notable dissimilarity in the molecular orbitals of heteronuclear diatomic, including HF, compared to homonuclear diatomic, is the uneven distribution of electron density across the atoms (Hoffmann & Fässler, 2003). It should be noted that the orbitals of the molecules for Hydrogen Fluoride, denoted as "1-sigma" along with "2-sigma," are predominantly derived from the atomic orbitals of Fluorine 2s and 2p, respectively. The orbitals in question exhibit a high level of fluorine due to the comparative electronegativity of fluorine and hydrogen. This is a qualitative observation. The molecular orbitals exhibit significant coefficients on Fluorine and relatively minor coefficients on Hydrogen from a mathematical standpoint. The 1 pi orbits exhibit non-bonding behavior and possess a significant Fluorine 2p character. The anti-bonding "3sigma" orbiting is predominantly composed of H 1s character (Nalewajski, 2009; Szczepanik & Sola, 2021) (Figure 2.1).

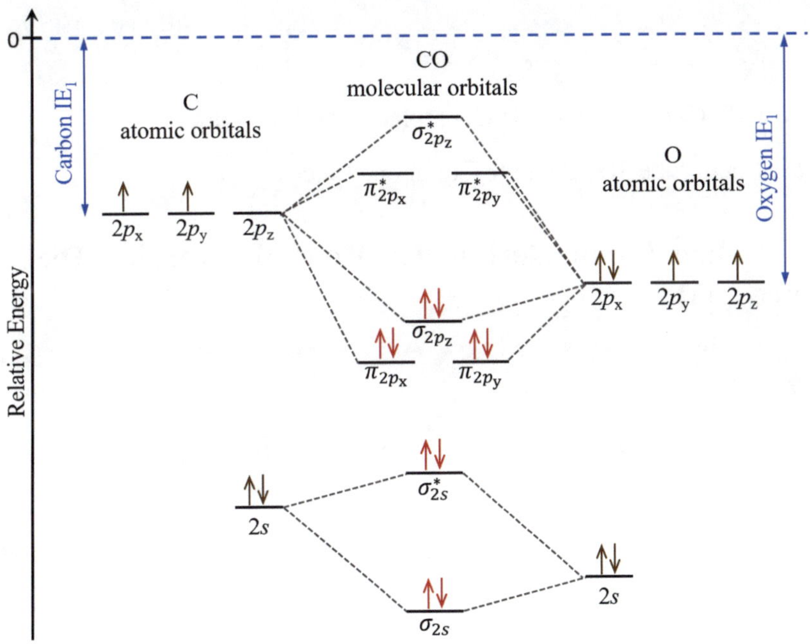

Figure 2.9. Schematic of heteronuclear diatomic molecules.

Source: Pressbooks, Creative Commons License.

Employing nodes to convey a broad understanding of the hierarchy of energy levels remains effective. The molecular orbitals denoted as "1-sigma" exhibit a nodeless configuration, whereas "2-sigma" and "1-pi" orbitals possess a single node. The "3-sigma" molecular orbital, on the other hand, displays a two-node configuration (Liu et al., 2018; Gross et al., 1981).

2.6.1. Carbon Monoxide CO Molecular Orbital Diagram (Figure 2.10)

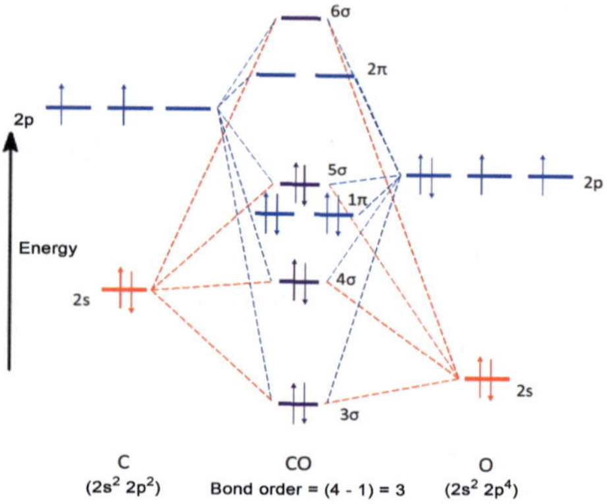

Figure 2.10. Carbon monoxide CO molecular orbital diagram.

Source: Chem tube 3D, Creative Commons License.

2.6.2. Iodine Monochloride ICl Molecular Orbital Diagram (Figure 2.11)

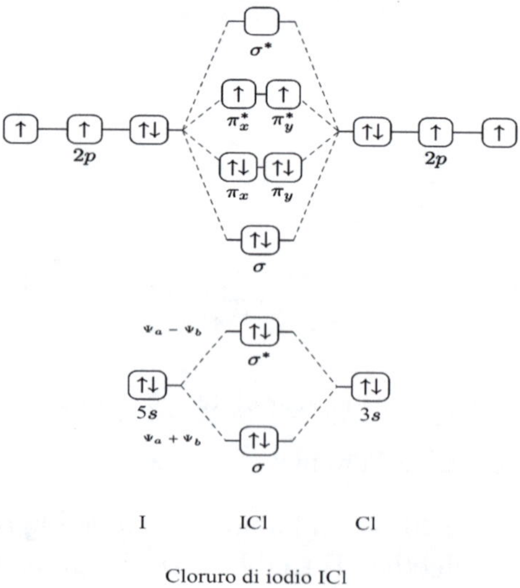

Figure 2.11. Iodine monochloride ICl molecular orbital diagram.

Source: Tex, Creative Commons License.

2.7. THE ISOLABLE ANALOGY

2.7.1. Extension of Valence Bond and Molecular Orbital Theory to Complex Molecules

Diverse assemblages of atoms have the potential to generate analogous configurations of fragments. As an illustration, both the C-H group and the P atom possess 5 electrons, which can potentially contribute 3 electrons towards forming a cluster. Specifically, the C-H group comprises 4+1 electrons and utilizes 2 electrons to form the C-H bond. The element P possesses 5 electrons, of which 2 electrons are utilized over a lone pair. Both fragments exhibit a deficit of three electrons within their 4 valency orbitals (s and 3*p), thereby preventing them from achieving an octet (King & Zhao, 2006; Calzaferri et al., 1989). The clusters C_4H_4 also referred to as tetrahedrane $(CH)_4$, and P4 exhibit identical shapes due to their equivalent number of cluster electrons:

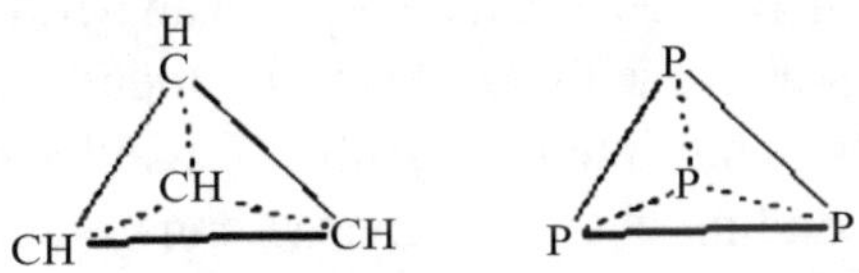

The organometallic moiety $Co(CO)_3$ is comprised of a total of 15 electrons. Carbon monoxide possesses nine valence electrons, and each molecule of CO contributes two electrons to the metal. The fragment is deficient by three electrons in achieving the stable electron count required to produce an organometallic breakdown of eighteen electrons. Utilizing all nine valence orbitals for the transition metal(s + 3× p and 5× d) corresponds to eighteen electrons being present. By forming three covalent bonds, it is possible to attain 18 electrons through electron sharing. The $Co(CO)_3$ moiety exhibits analogous prerequisites to the C-H group and the P element (Dobbs & Hehre, 1987). The cluster $[Co(CO)_3]_4$ thus also has the same tetrahedral shape as that shown by C_4H_4 and P_4. It is also possible to swap the three fragments around. Rearranging the three fragments additionally presents a viable option:

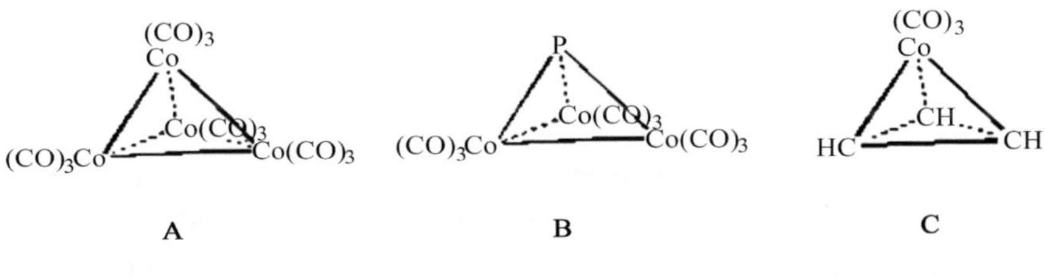

Clusters B and C commonly represent distinct entities $(\mu^3\text{-P})[CoCO)_3]_3$ and $(\eta^3\text{-}C_3H_3)Co(CO)_3$, yet this conventional understanding obscures these clusters' underlying structural and electronic connections.

Roald Hoffmann thoroughly investigated the similarities between these fragments and other fragments. Fragments can be classified as isolable if their frontier orbitals exhibit comparable characteristics in terms of their number, symmetry characteristics, approximate power, and shape, as well as the number of electrons they contain (Parr, 1960; Bartell et al., 1970).

The isolable relationship can be symbolized by a double-headed arrow featuring a tear-drop shape;

$$CH \underset{0}{\longleftrightarrow} P \underset{0}{\longleftrightarrow} Co(CO)_3$$

The isolobal analogy establishes a correlation between the bonding along with orbitals in inorganic and organometallic, alongside cluster chemistry, with those in organic and main group chemistry. The isolable analogies are a useful tool in chemical synthesis as they replace an MLn fragment, typically found in transition metals, with an AHn fragment, commonly found in main group elements. This interchangeability results in novel molecules that exhibit similar bonding characteristics (Lennard-Jones & Pople, 1951; Tubert-Brohman, 2005).

2.8. GENERATING ISOLOBAL FRAGMENTS

Main group fragments may be produced by initiating the process with methane or any other molecule that adheres to the octet rule (Yannello & Fredrickson, 2015). The hemolytic cutting of a C-H bond results in the formation of the methyl radical, 1a. This radical possesses a single frontier orbital oriented towards the absent hydrogen, containing a solitary electron. Hemolytic cutting of a second C-H bond results in the formation of methylene, denoted as 1b.

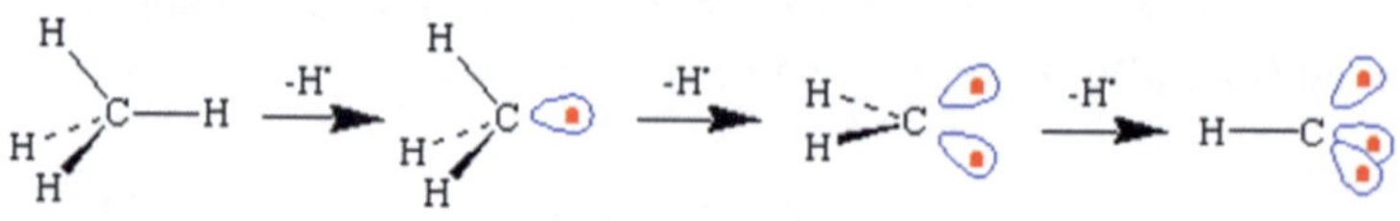

1 1a 1b 1c

This species possesses two singly occupied hybrid orbitals oriented toward the two unoccupied hydrogen positions (Stone, 1984; Kiremire, 2015). The elimination of third atomic hydrogen results in the formation of methane, denoted as 1c, which possesses three hybrid orbitals that are singly occupied.

The fragments of transition metals are produced similarly. Starting from the initial position of CrL6, 2, where L represents a two-electron donor that includes CO (or any molecule that adheres to the eighteen electron rule, with the value to be 3), the fragments 2a, 2b, and 2c are produced through a series of hemolytic cleavages of M-L bonds on a single octahedral plane. Upon hemolytic splitting of CrL6, the resulting products are CrL5– and L^+, where L serves as a two-electron donor (Byers & Hall, 1987; Evans et al., 1982). To neutralize the charge, the material is subsequently substituted with Mn, the element located to the right of the original metal in the 3d series.:

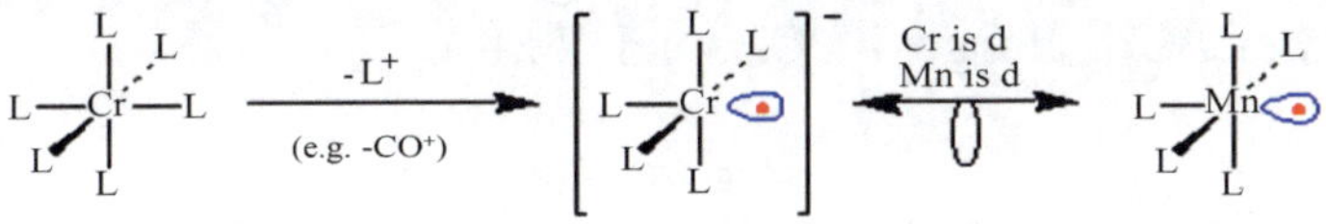

2 2a

2.9. ISOLOBAL SCHEME

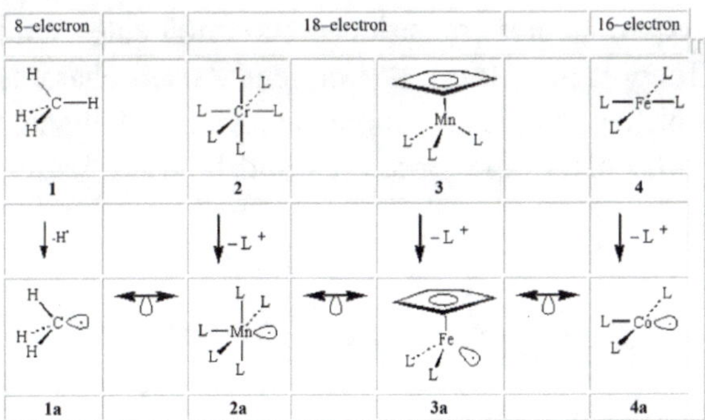

The metal or main group element can be substituted if the electron count is maintained or consistent changes are made (Williams & Whitehead, 1997). Thus,

$CH_3 \leftrightarrow Me_3Sn \leftrightarrow Mn(CO)_5 \leftrightarrow Fe(PPh_3)_5^+ \leftrightarrow Mo(CO)_5^-$

$CH_3^+ \leftrightarrow BH_3 \leftrightarrow Mn(CO)_5^+ \leftrightarrow Cr(CO)_5 \leftrightarrow Rh(PPh_3)_3^+$

$CH_3^- \leftrightarrow NH_3 \leftrightarrow Mn(CO)_5^- \leftrightarrow Fe(CO)_5 \leftrightarrow Rh(CO)_5^+$

Notably, the primary application for the isolobal analogy lies in producing alternative fragments within molecules (Miyazaki et al., 2017). When it is not considered an independent entity, the significance of the geometry of a molecular fragment holds academic relevance. According to scientific classification, CH_3, along with BH_3, are categorized as pyramidal species rather than planar (Robilotto et al., 2012; Kamp & Fredrickson, 2021). Similarly, $Cr(CO)_5$ is classified as a pyramid with a square base instead of a trigonal bipyramid.

2.10. APPLICATIONS OF ISOLOBILITY

The compounds in question exhibit analogous bonding due to the isolobal analogy among CH_3 along with CH_3 and d^7 $MnL_{5.}$

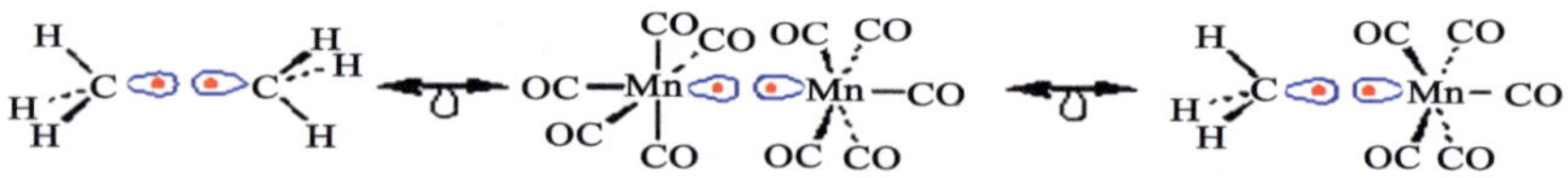

The compounds depicted below are generated through the isolobal relationship between CH_2 and $Fe(CO)_4$. The metallocyclopropane structure has been utilized to depict transition-metal molecules (Sundermeyer & Runge, 1994; Tang et al., 1993). A frequently used characterization is to regard it as complexes of ethene, denoted as. An isolobal analog of ethylene due to their similar electronic structures and bonding patterns ($\eta2–C_2H_4$) CH_2.

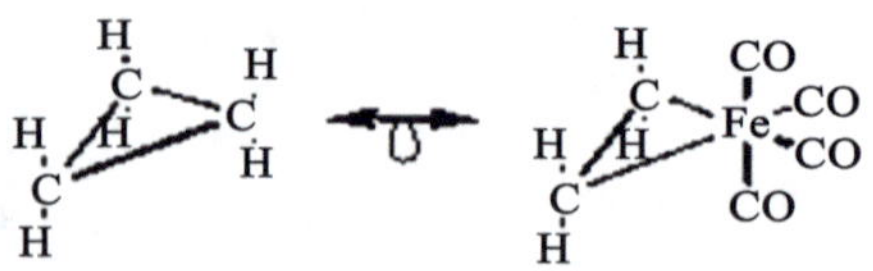

Additional compounds that have been produced through this correlation are also documented as ($\eta2–C_2H_4$)CH_2:

The following are frequently encountered isolobal fragments.

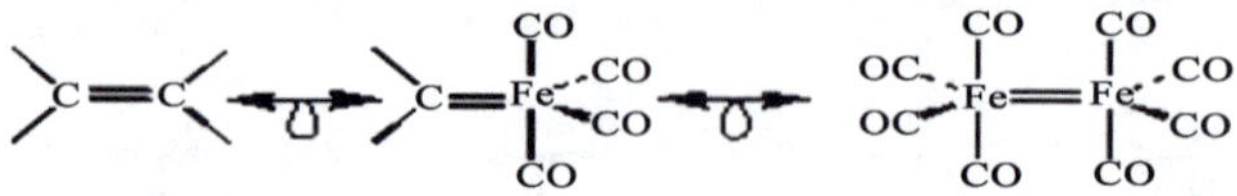

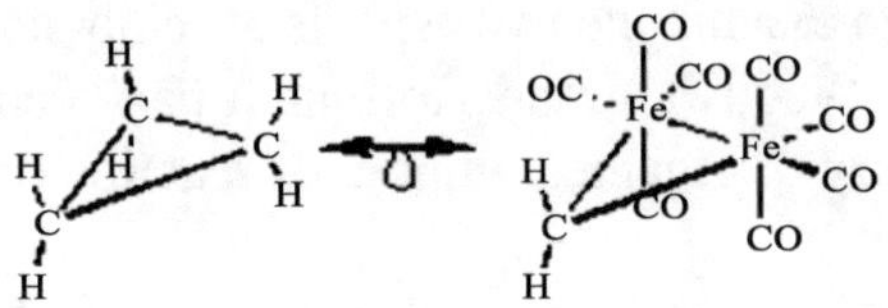

2.11. LEWIS THEORY

The advancement of chemistry in contemporary times has relied on the utilization of progressively intricate models. The depiction of atoms as interconnected spheres via cylinders or sticks is common. Lewis's Theory, formulated by Robinson and Ingold, has proven to be a successful approach in elucidating the mechanisms of numerous chemical reactions (Latimer & Rodebush, 1920).

The Lewis Theory employs curly arrows to represent the movement of electrons during a chemical reaction, thereby enhancing comprehension of the determinants that govern chemical reactions. Pauling and his colleagues formulated the Resonance Theory, the basis for a comprehensive orbital theory. Using "canonical forms" along with "resonance hybrids" in conjunction with the extensive implementation of curvilinear arrows, has established the foundational framework for contemporary organic theory. However, in the case of Diels-Alder, along with pericyclic reactions, the curvilinear arrow configuration may not be entirely lucid.

Figure 2.12. Illustration of lowest and highest unoccupied molecular orbital.

Source: Nadia Salami, Creative Commons License.

In certain scenarios, the reactions are denoted as non-mechanistic reactions. Woodward and Hoffmann demonstrated that the analysis of the interplay between the frontier molecular orbitals, specifically the Highest Occupied Molecular Orbital (HOMO) and the Lowest Unoccupied Molecular

Orbital (LUMO), can explain the two aspects of regio- and stereospecificity. The contribution of Woodward and Hoffmann has been incorporated into the overarching theory of organic compounds reaction (Figure 2.12).

2.11.1. Theory of Linear Combination of Atomic Orbitals (LCOA)

The proposed theory involves the concept of bonding through the overlapping of ligand orbitals alongside those of the central atom. The generation of "hybrid" molecular orbitals for a compound can be achieved by adding the wavefunctions of the bonding orbitals in the constituent species. If present, the newly formed orbitals exhibit an intermediate nature between the pre-existing s, p, and d orbitals in the outermost energy level. These orbitals facilitate the formation of supplementary bonding sites (Weatherson, 2013; Paik, 2015). The nomenclature of hybridization is predicated upon the implicated orbitals, along with the hybrid wavefunction representing the summation of each wavefunction that has been renormalized. The addition of each wave function may be performed with any arbitrary sign. The orthogonality of composite wavefunctions using differing signs can be established per the principles of quantum mechanics.

$$\int(\psi_1+\psi_2)(\psi_1-\psi_2)^* dV = \int\left(|\psi_1|^2+\psi_1\psi_2^*-\psi_1^*\psi_2-|\psi_2|^2\right) dV. \qquad (1)$$

But

$$\int\psi_1\psi_2^* dV = \delta_{1,2}, \qquad (2)$$

So

$$\int(\psi_1+\psi_2)(\psi_1-\psi_2)^* dV = (1 + 0 + 0 - 1) = 0. \qquad (3)$$

The most elementary illustration is the phenomenon of s2-hybridization. There exist two potential combinations;

$$\psi_1 = \frac{1}{\sqrt{2}}(\psi_{s,1}+\psi_{s,2}) \qquad \sigma_{1s}^{b} \qquad (4)$$

$$\psi_2 = \frac{1}{\sqrt{2}}(\psi_{s,1}-\psi_{s,2}) \qquad \sigma_{1s}^{*}, \qquad (5)$$

the wavefunctions on the right are the solutions to Schrödinger's equation, and the normalization constants are needed so that the hybrid wavefunction is normalized. Ψ_1 The electron density is greatest between the two nuclei. It binds the nuclei together and is called a bonding molecular orbital. Ψ_2 Has the electron density greatest on the sides of the nuclei (Fernández-Seivane et al., 2006). Therefore, it pulls the nuclei apart and is called an antibonding molecular orbital. In some instances, a nonbonding molecular orbital may be generated for which the electron density is uniformly distributed between and on the sides of the nuclei. A measure of the stability of a compound based on the occupancy of its molecular orbitals is given by the body order.

$$[bond\ order] \equiv \frac{1}{2}\left([\#BMO\ electrons] - [\#ABMO\ electrons]\right).$$

Bonding interactions of a more intricate nature involve orbitals such as s, p, and d. The orbitals of molecules of a homonuclear diatomic in-nature compound alongside orbitals that are hybridized and constructed via 1s, 2s, and 2p atomic orbitals can be expressed in the following manner.

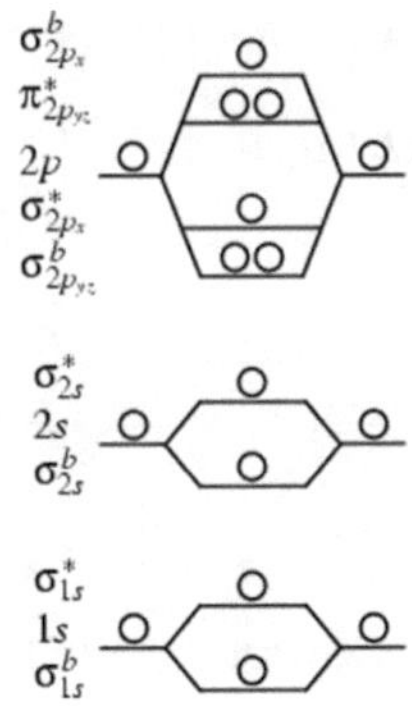

In the case of heteropolar molecules or intricate systems, the energy diagram of molecular orbitals can exhibit significant complexity. The orbital molecules for CO_2 (O_1=C=O_2) can be arranged in ascending energy sequence (Zicovich-Wilson et al., 2016; Barklem, 2021; Autschbach, 2012).

The valence shell contains 12 electrons, filled via the nonbonding orbitals. Consequently, the compound above exhibits stability, which can be attributed to its bond number 4. For a more intricate illustration, let us contemplate benzene. In some compounds, there exists a phenomenon of electron delocalization. Compounds of this nature possess a significantly high quantity of molecular orbitals (Usachenko & Chu, 2005). As the total amount of levels approaches infinity, the outcome is a collection of bonding and antibonding orbitals, forming a conduction band where free electrons may exist. This conduction band may either overlap or be separated through a gap. The energy levels in metallic compounds exhibit overlapping characteristics, leading to the complete filling of bonding orbitals. Semiconductors exhibit discrete energy levels be separated through a narrow bandgap, also known as a "forbidden zone." Consequently, introducing a minute quantity of energy results in the ejection of an electron from the occupied bonding orbital, traversing the forbidden region and transitioning into the conduction band (Valdés et al., 2005; Kullie et al., 2006).

$$\begin{cases} S_s & C(2s)+O_1(p_z)-O_2(p_z) \\ S_p & C(2p_z)-O_1(p_z)-O_2(p_z) \end{cases}$$

$$\begin{cases} \Pi_x & C(2p_x)+O_1(p_x)+O_2(p_x) & \Pi_x=\Pi_y \\ \Pi_y & C(2p_y)+O_1(p_y)+O_2(p_y) & \Pi_x=\Pi_y \end{cases}$$

$$\begin{cases} n_1 & C(2p_x)+O_1(p_y)+O_2(p_y) & n_1=n_2 \\ n_2 & C(2p_y)+O_1(p_x)+O_2(p_x) & n_1=n_2 \end{cases}$$

$$\begin{cases} \Pi_x^* & C(2p_x)-O_1(p_x)-O_2(p_x) & \Pi_x^*=\Pi_y^* \\ \Pi_y^* & C(2p_y)-O_1(p_y)-O_2(p_y) & \Pi_x^*=\Pi_y^* \end{cases}$$

$$S_p^* \quad C(2p_z)+O_1(p_z)+O_2(p_z)$$
$$S_s^* \quad C(2s)-O_1(p_z)+O_2(p_z)$$

2.12. ATOMIC AND MOLECULAR ORBITALS

Molecules can establish chemical bonds by sharing electrons, whereby the sharing of two electrons between two atoms can be considered a chemical bond. Atoms can share any number of electrons, forming single, double, or triple bonds respectively (Edmiston & Ruedenberg, 1963).

The fundamental structure of a hydrogen atom comprises a solitary proton located in the nucleus and a lone electron. The precise localization of an electron is not feasible. However, it is feasible to compute the likelihood of detecting the electron during any given point surrounding the nucleus. In the case of a hydrogen atom, the electron's probability distribution is spherically symmetrical concerning the nucleus (Magnasco & Perico, 1967). A spherical boundary surface can be delineated, within which the likelihood of locating the electron is 95%. The electron is characterized by a definite energy and a specific spatial arrangement called an orbital. The helium atom comprises a pair of electrons linked with helium's nucleus. The distribution of space and energy of electrons are identical, as they encompass the same orbital. However, their spin distinguishes them from one another by the Pauli exclusion principle. Electrons within atomic nuclei typically occupy orbitals with a predetermined energy level and spatial configuration. Furthermore, each orbital can accommodate a maximum of two exhibiting anti-parallel spins (Tsaparlis, 1997; Edmiston et al., 1965).

The wave equation is commonly linked to periodic phenomena in physics, while the Schrödinger Equation is the relevant equation within the atomic theory. The wave equation yields discrete solutions for a single dimension over a particle restricted to a box alongside the infinite wall. The solutions may be illustrated as depicted in the accompanying figure:

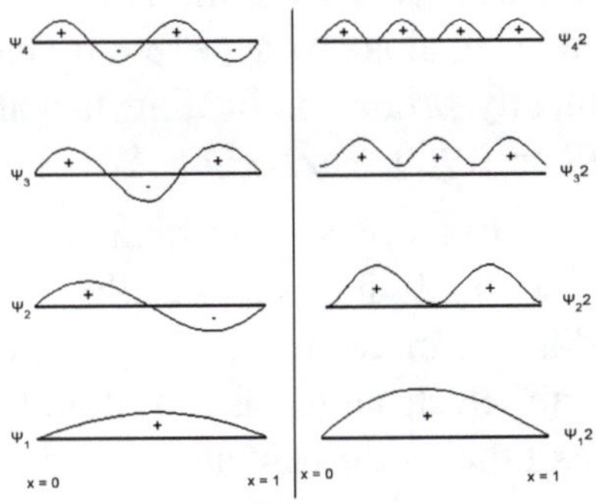

$\psi_1 - \psi_4$ represent solutions for increasing energy. The equation in three dimensions is utilized to ascertain the energy and establish the location in the space of individual electrons. Determining the "shape" for every orbital can be achieved by computing the solutions for the wave equations with three dimensions (Roothaan, 1951; Von Niessen, 1972). The initial quintuplet of solutions to the wave equation governing the behavior of an electron about a proton is visually depicted in the accompanying diagram:

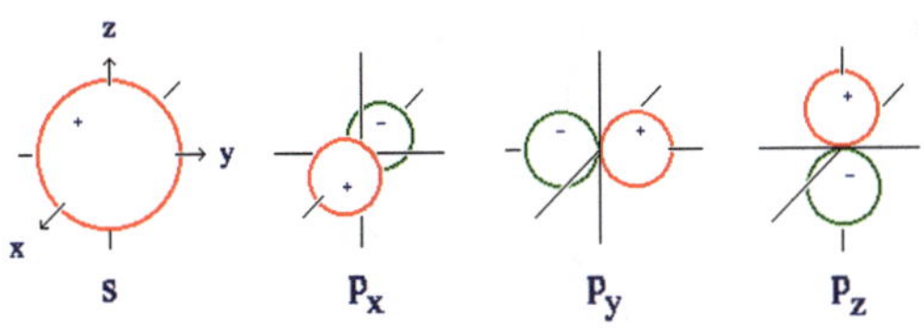

The energy levels of atomic orbitals within the hydrogen atom are such that the 1s orbital possesses the minimum energy, whereas the remaining orbitals (2s, 2px, 2py, and 2pz) are degenerate. However, in every other atom, the second atomic orbital exhibits lower energy levels than the degenerate 2px, 2py, and 2pz orbitals (Lykos et al., 1962; Magnasco & Perico, 1968). Electrons in atoms are found to be in atomic orbitals, whereas, in molecules, they are observed to occupy analogous molecular orbitals that encompass the molecule. The most elementary chemical compound is hydrogen, which comprises two distinct entities of protons and electrons. Hydrogen exhibits two distinct molecular orbitals, with the less energetic orbital characterized by a higher electron density positioned between each nucleus. The molecular circular in question pertains to bonding and is characterized by lower energy levels than the two 1s orbitals that are part of hydrogen atoms. This property renders the orbital more durable than two distinct atomic hydrogen orbitals. The electronic waveform of the upper molecule orbital exhibits a node, resulting in low electron density among the two strongly charged nuclei. An antibonding molecule orbital is characterized by having a higher energy level than the 1s atomically orbital, indicating that the energy in the top orbital is greater (Mulliken, 1960; Vozzi et al., 2011).

Typically, the two electrons present in hydrogen take up the bonding molecules' orbital while exhibiting anti-parallel spins. Upon exposure to ultraviolet (UV) radiation, molecular hydrogen can undergo electronic excitation, promoting an electron to its anti-bonding orbital (σ*) and subsequent dissociation of the constituent atoms. A diagram may be utilized to depict the energy levels of a hydrogen molecule, which showcases the amalgamation of both of the 1s orbitals in an atomic structure to generate two molecule orbitals, namely the bonding (σ) and the antibonding (σ*) orbitals. The graphical representation of the σ or σ* atomic orbital can be displayed by selecting either option in the diagram. This can be achieved by clicking on the respective option.

2.13. HOMONUCLEAR DIATOMIC MOLECULES

The diatomic hydrogen molecular structure occupies the orbital, indicating a bond order 1 and exhibiting stability.

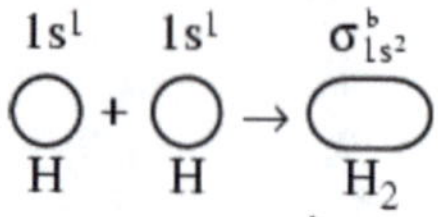

The diatomic helium molecules occupy both orbitals, resulting in a bond with an order of zero, rendering it unstable (Bernstein et al., 1963; Kotani et al., 1957).

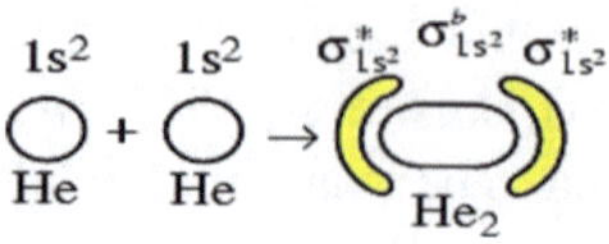

2.13.1. Diatomic Molecules H_2 and He_2

A more comprehensive understanding of the HA and HB bonding mechanism can be attained by examining the electron energies within the interacting atoms in contrast to their energies within the non-interacting atoms. The process involves inserting the LCAO wave equations of the molecule into the corresponding Scrödinger equation, which is analogous to the procedure employed for the atom's wave operations of individual atoms. The molecular orbitals ψ_1 and ψ_2 are occasionally denoted as σ (1s) or σ*(1s) to signify their molecular orbital type and lineage (Parr & Borkman, 1968; Toulouse & Umrigar, 2008).

The employment of molecular orbitals comprising solely of 1s orbits for bonding purposes applies to any molecule or molecule-ion. Several potential molecular species exist, namely He_2^+, H_2^{2-}, H_2^+, H_2^-, and H_2, along with He_2. The cationic species with a positive charge are inherently unstable. However, they have been observed in the gaseous state under circumstances of elevated energy. The observation of negatively charged molecule-ions and He_2 has yet to be documented (Lie et al., 1974; Odžak et al., 2009).

- **Nitrogen:** The chemical, as mentioned above entity is composed of a total of ten electrons. The cellular orbital diagram is a result of the combination of the orbitals of an atom:

  The 2πg orbiting is filled with a pair of electrons, resulting in a bond with an order of three. The statement aligns with the structure of Lewis representation (N≡N), even though the orbital methodology indicates the presence of a single σ and two π orbitals (Wahl, 1964; Peterson et al., 1997).

- **Oxygen:** The molecule in question possesses a total of twelve electrons, which is two more than the element nitrogen. These additional electrons are distributed within a pair of degraded π_g orbitals. The molecular orbital diagram is a result of the combination of atomic orbitals:

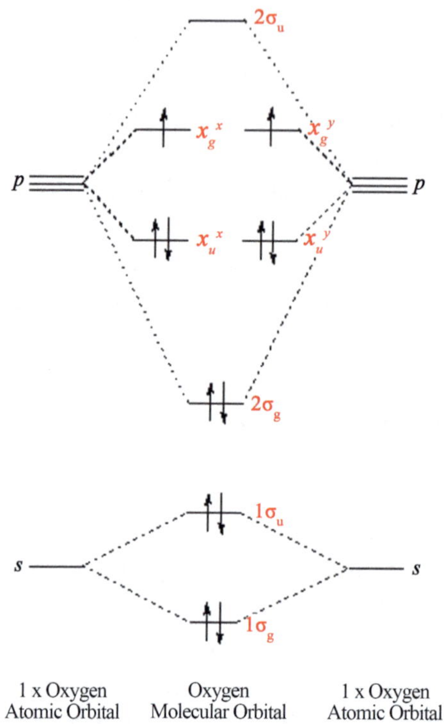

Upon comparing the diagram of energy levels presented above with that of nitrogen, it can be observed that the $2\sigma_g$ levels are situated at a lower energy level than that of π_u. At this juncture, the anti-bonding orbitals arising from the orbital p relationships are populated, reducing bond order from three to two (Broyer et al., 1978; Politzer, 1969).

According to Hund's rule, the arrangement with the lowest energy involves the presence of a single electron in each of π_g^x and π_g^y the orbitals, with parallel spins. The resulting outcome is a molecule that exhibits Para magnetism, featuring two bonds and possessing a pair of unpaired electrons.

2.13.2. Heteronuclear Diatomic Molecules

If the molecule exhibits heteronuclear characteristics, it follows that the energy levels of the parent orbitals of atoms will be dissimilar. In the illustrated arrangement, it can be observed that the circular atomic level closest to E = zero corresponds to the atom with lower electronegativity or higher ionization potential (Figure 2.13):

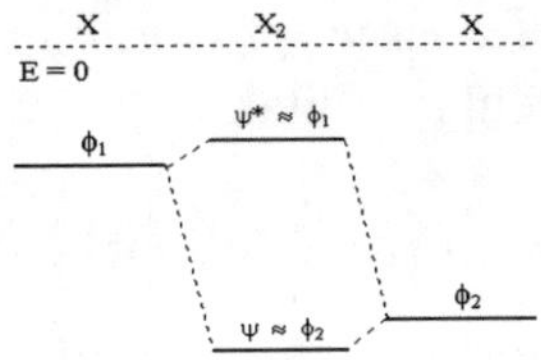

Figure 2.13. Illustration of heteronuclear diatomic molecules.

Source: A. Braun, Creative Commons License.

The molecular orbital involved in bonding exhibits both an energy and a wave function that closely approximates the atom's higher electronegativity (Foley, 1947). The energy and wavefunction of the antibonding molecules' orbital will bear similarity to those of the atom with lower electronegativity. To illustrate, let us contemplate the chemical compound known as hydrogen chloride. The 1s orbital of hydrogen, which contains a single electron ϕ_1, is expected to be paired with the 3p orbital of chlorine ϕ_2, which also contains a single electron ψ^* and forms a chemical bond with it. The resultant molecular orbital ψ is anticipated to bear a strong resemblance to the 3p orbital of chlorine and is expected to accommodate both electrons (Bytautas et al., 2005).

Conversely, the resultant orbital is expected to resemble the initial 1s orbital of hydrogen and remain unoccupied. The theory of molecular orbitals accurately depicts the situation (. However, it is important to remember that the above treatment is incomplete as it fails to consider the potential contribution of the third orbital of chlorine $H^{\delta+}Cl^{\delta-}$.

2.13.3. A_2 Molecules

- **Hydrogen Fluoride:** Hydrogen fluoride is a diatomic molecule in nature. Eight valence electrons occupy four molecular orbitals. The two MOs with the highest energy exhibit degeneracy and lack electron density linked to the hydrogen atom. These MOs are classified as Non-Bonding Orbitals (NBOs) and are symbolized as two "Lone Pairs" in Lewis Theory. An additional noteworthy distinction between Hydrogen Fluoride and antecedent molecules is the uneven allocation of electron density across the molecule. The fluorine atom exhibits a significantly higher electron density (Kleier et al., 1974). The rationale behind this phenomenon is rooted in the high electronegativity of fluorine, which results in the acquisition of a larger proportion of electron density in each connecting molecular orbital.

2.13.4. Bond Properties in the Molecular Orbital Formalism

- **Bond Lengths and Covalent Radii:** There are multiple aspects to consider in this context:

The determination of bond lengths is based on the summation of covalent radii. The determination of the covalent radius can be initially achieved by dividing the length of the homonuclear link by two:

$d_{Cl\text{-}Cl}$ (in Cl_2) = 1.988 Å therefore r_{Cl} = 0.99 Å

$d_{C\text{-}C}$ (in diamond) = 1.54 Å therefore r_C(single bond) = 0.77 Å

Predicted $d_{C\text{-}Cl}$ = r_C(single bond) + r_{Cl} = 0.99 + 0.77 = 1.76 vs actual 1.77 Å

The bond lengths observed in compounds may exhibit slight variations according to the remaining atoms bonded for the two atoms involved in the bond being examined. The bond length observed can be influenced by the bond order, for instance:

$d_{N\&o\rho\delta\mu;N}$ = 1.10 Å $d_{N=N}$ = 1.25 Å $d_{N\text{-}N}$ = 1.45 Å

The radii of double and triple bonds are estimated to be around 0.87 and 0.78 times the radius of a single bond, respectively. Utilizing an atom's hybridization impacts its covalent radius in the context of single bonds (Hurley et al., 1953; Mulliken, 1935). As the number of p-characters in the hybrid increases, there will be a corresponding increase in the radius:

$r_C(sp^3)$ = 0.77 Å $r_C(sp^2)$ = 0.73 Å $r_C(sp)$ = 0.70 Å

When there is a significant difference in electronegativity between the atoms that are bonded, resulting in substantial ionic nature, the bonds' length will be shorter than what is predicted according to covalent radii. The bond length between carbon and fluorine in CF_4 is measured to be 1.32 Å, lower than the predicted value of 1.44 Å.

The Si-F bond's length to SiF_4 is observed to be 1.54 Å, which is lower than the predicted value of 1.81 Å. According to sources, the reduction in the size of SiF_4 is attributed to the occurrence of pi-bonding between unoccupied silicon d-orbitals and occupied fluorine p-orbitals (Mulliken, 1932; Kleier et al., 1975).

2.13.5. Overlap of Orbitals

- **Bonding Overlap**: The atomic orbitals that exhibit overlapping possess identical signs (i.e., color). The electron density experiences an increase in regions of overlap $2\psi_1 \cdot \psi_2$, resulting in a rise relative to the mere summation $\psi_1^2 + \psi_2^2$. This phenomenon gives rise to an attractive element in the interaction between the two atoms (Cusachs, 1965).
- **Antibonding Overlap**: The areas of atomic orbitals that intersect exhibit contrasting polarities. A node is generated within regions where the electron density reaches zero. The presence of electrons in these particular molecular orbitals produces a repulsive factor contributing to the relationship among both atoms (Boys, 1960; Hall Jr, 1975).
- **Non-Bonding Overlap**: If certain regions display congruence in sign while others exhibit opposition, the resultant effect of said molecular orbital on the interplay among the two atoms will be null. Due to this rationale, such combinations of molecular orbitals have yet to be formulated (Torres et al., 2007).
- **The σ, π and δ Notation:** In summary, it can be stated that a σ-molecular orbiting lacks a node that traverses all the nuclei implicated; a π-molecular orbital possesses a single such node. A δ-molecular orbiting possesses two such nodes (Dixon et al., 1978; Wallace et al., 1977).

Tip

A helpful tip to understand the concept of overlap of orbitals is to visualize it as the merging or interaction of atomic orbitals to form molecular orbitals, which determines the bonding and properties of the molecule.

2.14. MOLECULAR ORBITALS OF POLYATOMIC MOLECULES

- **Construction of molecular orbitals:** This section presents visual representations of molecular orbitals about various organic and inorganic compounds. The energy level illustration is provided, and selecting the corresponding level will produce the associated molecular orbital within the frame on the right (Kuenzer, U., & Hofer, 2019). Please select from the available options:

2.15. POLYATOMIC MOLECULES IN GENERAL: SATURATED MOLECULES

As mentioned above, those are molecular entities in which all valence electrons participate in individual covalent bonds. The lack of non-covalently bonded unshared electron pairs is noted. Typically, these molecules demonstrate reduced reactivity compared to species possessing electron-rich or electron-deficient characteristics. This phenomenon can be attributed to the relatively lower energies of the orbitals employed (Tully, 1973; McDowell, 2003).

- **Water:** The water molecule exhibits a non-bonding highest-used orbital in nature, specifically the (1b1) orbital, which is highly localized upon the oxygen atom. This characteristic is comparable to the non-bonding orbits observed in hydrogen fluoride. The subsequent sub-shell (2a1) may be conceptualized as a non-bonding orbital in nature, given that it exhibits a lobe that extends away from both hydrogen atoms. The analysis of fewer energy-bonding orbitals reveals that oxygen tends to acquire more of the overall electron density than expected (Trinquier & Malrieu, 1991; Tian et al., 2008).
- **Ammonia:** Ammonia possesses two sets of orbitals that are degenerate, comprising one bonding along with a single antibonding orbital. Like water and hydrogen fluoride, ammonia also possesses a non-bonding orbital, specifically the 2a1 orbital. The orbital with the highest occupancy exhibits a lobe extending beyond the three hydrogen atoms, indicating a localized lone pair orbiting the nitrogen atom. Conversely, the three smallest-energy molecular orbitals describe all three N-H bonds in the Lewis structure (Eastham, 1967; Davis et al., 1968). The ammonia molecule exhibits Lewis base properties due to its lone pair's relatively high energy level.

The subsequent molecule in the sequence comprising HF, H_2O, and H_3N is H_4C (methane), which has been previously discussed. In contrast to the three molecules above, H_4C lacks any NBOs (Longuet-Higgins, 1957; Williams, 1992).

- **Methane:** The valence orbitals of the molecules of methane exhibit delocalization across the complete nuclear framework, thereby rendering it arduous to attribute any specific orbital to a distinct C-H bond. The augmentation of energy levels can lead to an escalation in the intricacy of the orbital configuration. Methane exhibits four valence orbitals of molecules that are bonding in nature. Among these orbitals, one orbital is characterized by a single nodal plane and is the lowest-used orbital. The remaining three orbitals are degenerate, meaning they possess equal energy and are characterized by the presence of a nodal plane (Powell et al., 1940).
- **Ethane:** The ethane's molecular structure consists of fourteen valence electrons distributed across seven bonding orbitals in the molecular structure. The energy diagram reveals that four different molecular orbitals exist as degenerate pairs. Like methane, the orbitals of ethane molecules exhibit a heightened degree of nodal structure as the energy level of the orbital increases (Fridland et al., 1978).

2.15.1. A Linear Triatomic – BeH_2

Beryllium is the central atom in this molecular complex, while the ligands consist of hydrogen atoms. Notably, the hydrogen orbits' energy levels are comparatively lower than those of beryllium orbitals. This can be attributed to the higher electronegativity of hydrogen, a non-metal, compared to beryllium, a metal, making it relatively more difficult to ionize (Becke-Goehring et al., 1962).

Two linear arrangements can be formed from each of the hydrogen 1s orbits:

$\psi_1 = 1/\sqrt{2}(\psi_{1sHa} + \psi_{1sHb})$ and $\psi_2 = 1/\sqrt{2}(\psi_{1sHa} - \psi_{1sHb})$

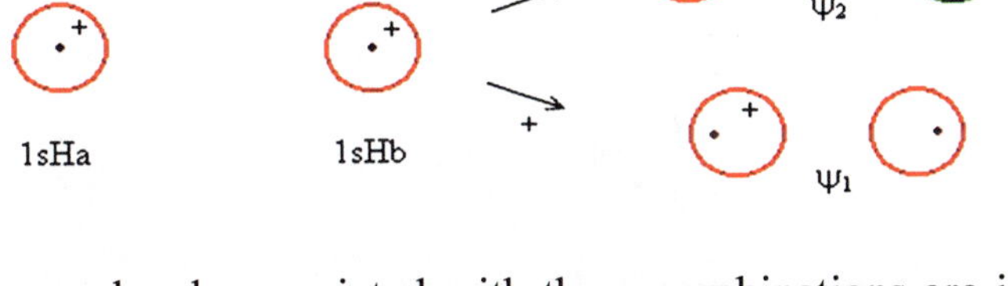

The energy levels associated with these combinations are indicated in the following expression: 2H(combos).

The beryllium 2s orbiting exhibits appropriate symmetry for generating combinations alongside orbital ψ_1, while the Be 2p orbital, oriented towards the internuclear axis (z), displays suitable symmetry for forming combinations with ψ_2:

$$\sigma_1 = 1/\sqrt{2}(\psi_1 + \psi_{2sBe}) \quad \text{and} \quad \sigma^*_3 = 1/\sqrt{2}(\psi_1 - \psi_{2sBe})$$

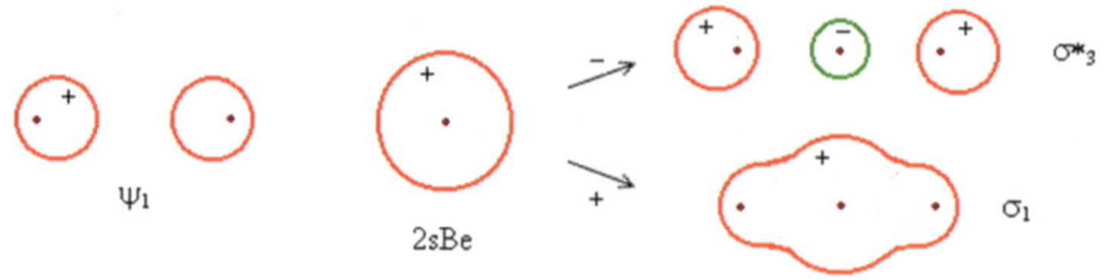

$$\sigma_2 = 1/\sqrt{2}(\psi_2 + \psi_{2pzBe}) \quad \text{and} \quad \sigma^*_4 = 1/\sqrt{2}(\psi_2 - \psi_{2pzBe})$$

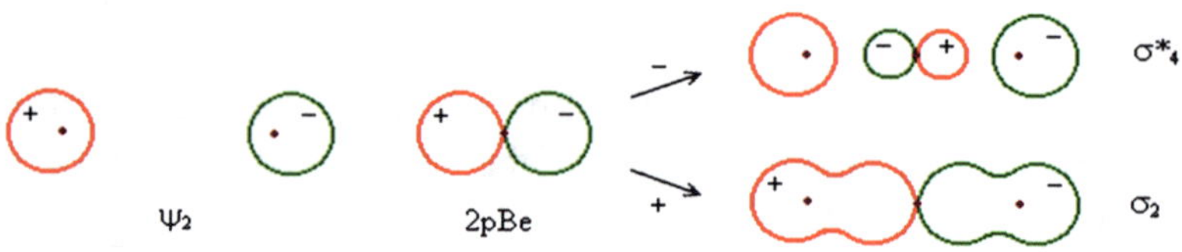

The orbitals 2px and 2py of beryllium exhibit dissimilar symmetry ligand combos.

- The energy levels diagram displays the molecular orbitals, which encompass the localized 2px along with 2py orbitals situated beneath BeH_2.
- As energy level diagrams illustrate, the four valence electrons are situated in the σ1 and σ2 molecular orbitals and bond to three-center orbitals. The bond order of a single Be-H relation shall be determined (Sharghi et al., 2003).

B.O = ((# bonding electrons)/2)/(# of 2-center bonds) = (4/2)/(2) = 1

2.15.2. An Electron Deficient Molecule with Bridging Hydrogen – Diborane, B_2H_6

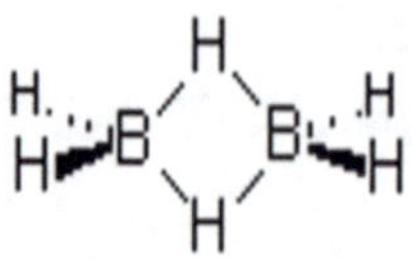

The structure of the diborane is depicted on the right. Upon initial observation, the molecule appears to possess eight bonds. However, upon closer examination, it is revealed that there are only twelve electrons among the two boron atoms and the six hydrogen atoms. This is sufficient to form only "conventional" six 2-center – 2-electron bonds (Poater et al., 2005).

The subjoined diagram depicts how this scenario is addressed through the utilization of MOT:

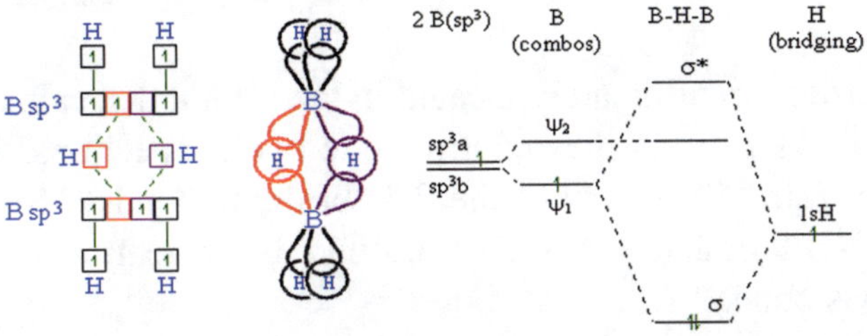

- The diagram on the left side depicts a valence bond model altered to represent the entire molecule. Notably, the sp^3 hybridization of boron atoms is attributed to their (anticipated) nearly tetrahedral configuration. While the MOT has the potential to describe bonding within the entire molecule lacking the need for a separate step involving hybridization, in this context, it is solely applied to hydrogen bridges (Nalewajski, 2009).
- The molecular orbital level of energy diagram depicted on the far right of the illustration solely considers one of the two gas hydrogen bridges, either the red or the purple. The employed orbitals consist of a single sp^3 hybrid on every boron atom and the 1s orbital of the bridging hydrogen. This system has been assigned two electrons (Ferrer-Correia et al., 1976).
- The hydrogen-ligating property of boron atoms results in the formation of two linear arrangements by combining their orbitals:

$$\psi_1 = 1/\sqrt{2}(\psi_{sp^3 Ba} + \psi_{sp^3 Bb}) \quad \text{and} \quad \psi_2 = 1/\sqrt{2}(\psi_{sp^3 Ba} - \psi_{sp^3 Bb})$$

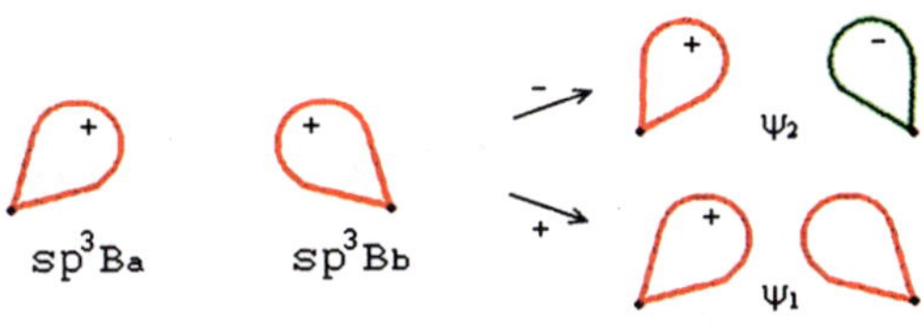

The 1s orbital of hydrogen can undergo a combination with ψ_1, resulting in the formation of both bonding and antibonding molecular orbitals. The alternative ligand mixture ψ_2 is not utilized (Ichikawa et al., 1985).

$\sigma = 1/\sqrt{2}(\psi_1 + \psi_{1sH})$ and $\sigma* = 1/\sqrt{2}(\psi_1 - \psi_{1sH})$

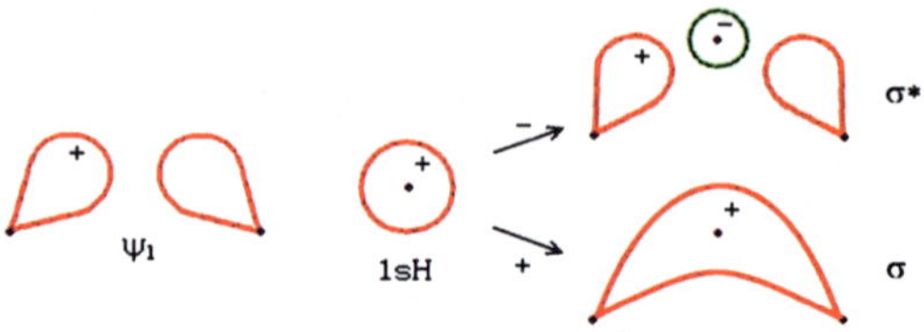

The two electrons are ultimately located in the orbital delocalized throughout the bridge. As a result, they contribute to two connections, leading to a bond order of ½ in any of the B-H bridging bonds (Morisaki et al., 2002). The B-H terminal bonds are classified as conventional 2-electron – 2-center Lewis bonds.)

2.15.3. Phosphorus Pentachloride

According to the principles of natural valence connect theory, the method of bonding in PF_5 necessitates the utilization of the 3d orbits of phosphorus to facilitate the formation of five conventional 2-center – 2-electron obligations. Utilizing the MOT's three-center bonding can serve as an alternative approach to circumvent the employment of the strategy, which has been criticized for its impracticality (Uce, 2015; Baldauf et al., 2005). The bonding of fluorenes within equatorial sites is explained by Valence Bond Theory (VBT), which utilizes sp^2 hybrids upon phosphorus. MOT exclusively describes the axial system. The following diagram depicts the given scenario:

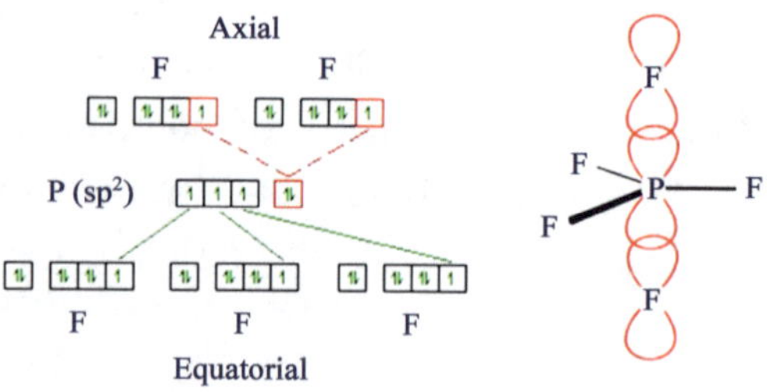

The 2p orbitals that are aligned with the molecules axis on both fluorine atoms are initially merged:

$\psi_1 = 1/\sqrt{2}(\psi_{2pFa} + \psi_{2pFb})$ and $\psi_2 = 1/\sqrt{2}(\psi_{2pFa} - \psi_{2pFb})$

The graphical representation depicted below illustrates the various combinations.

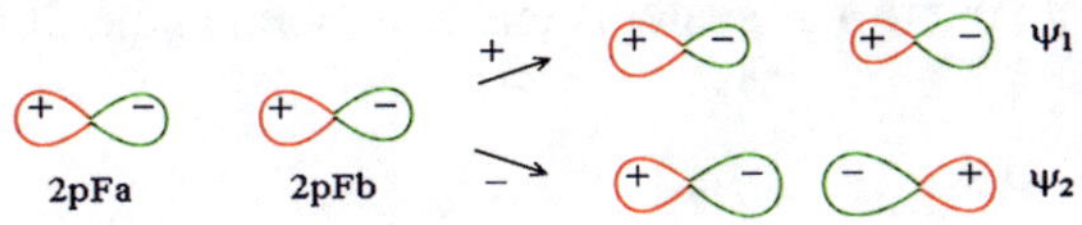

The unhybridized 3p orbital of phosphate has the potential to form a bonding along with an antibonding mixture using the ligand arrangement. The simplified treatment does not utilize the ligand ψ_2 combination denoted as.

$$\sigma = 1/\sqrt{2}(\psi_1 + \psi_{3pP}) \quad \text{and} \quad \sigma* = 1/\sqrt{2}(\psi_1 - \psi_{3pP})$$

The graphical representation of the combinations above is depicted in the diagram presented below.

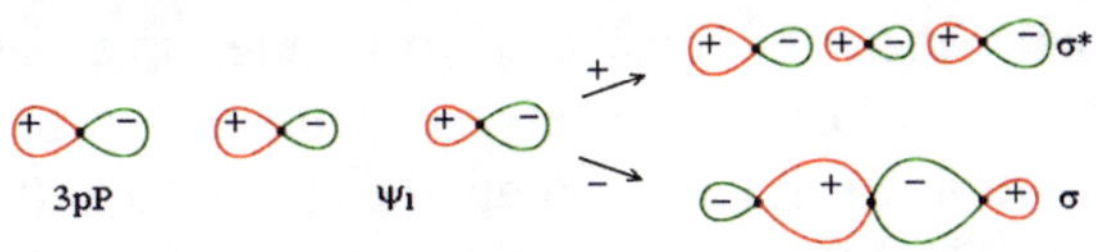

The provided illustration depicts solely the energy levels within the axial orbital system. The connecting orbital (σ) accommodates a pair of electrons, resulting in a bond order for each phosphorus-fluorine linkage. The non-bonding electrons in order (in ψ_2) do not participate in bonding (Weiss, 1946). Consequently, it is anticipated that the axial bonds will exhibit lower strength than the equatorial bonds. The empirical data corroborate this assertion.

2.16. DELOCALIZED APPROACH TO BONDING

The construction of molecular orbital wavefunctions within MOT involves the formation of linear mixtures of atomic orbitals. In cases where only two atoms are present, the resultant wavefunction can be obtained by adding and subtracting the two atomic orbiting wavefunctions. In cases where the number of atoms exceeds two, forming combinations becomes more intricate. Typically, the problem is simplified by leveraging the symmetry characteristics of the molecular and molecular ion (Zeng et al., 2015). It is important to note that simplification can only be achieved significantly if the mathematical theory that encompasses symmetry, namely group theory, has been comprehensively addressed. The initial segment pertains to entities composed of two atoms, commonly called diatomic species. Subsequently, a series of intricate exemplar systems ensue (Cohen et al., 2007; El Bakouri et al., 2022).

2.17. MOLECULES AND IONS WITH DOUBLE BONDS

In cases where the number of electron pairs that bond surpasses the number of unions among atoms within a molecule, the additional electrons take up molecular orbital spaces of higher energy compared to the orbitals present in molecules in which the total amount of bonding electron pairs is equivalent to the number of unions among atoms (Coulson, 1952; Fukui et al., 1954). The molecular system under consideration exhibits double bonds, whereby the orbitals involved in the bonding process possess a nodal plane encompassing the atoms engaged in sharing these orbitals of the π-type.

- **Ethene:** Ethene is considered to be the most basic alkene. As mentioned earlier, the substance's chemistry is primarily governed by two frontier orbitals, namely the HOMO and the LUMO. The ethene orbital power diagram displays π_{CC} the HOMO and π^*_{CC} the LUMO (Slagle et al., 1981).

  The ethene molecule and alkenes, in general, possess a significant characteristic of a formidable barrier to rotation around the C=C bond, which results in the molecule's planar conformation. Please refer to the energy illustration and visual representation of the orbitals provided below:
- **Molecules with Triple Bonds:** Please refer to the provided energy diagram along with a pictorial representation of the orbitals:

Trigonal-Planar Molecule/Ion – CO_3^{2-}

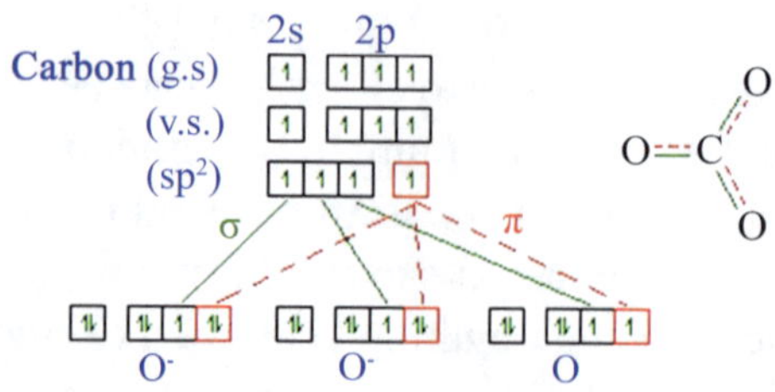

In this instance, the σ-bonding is typically addressed utilizing VBT. When regarding the molecule/ion's three-fold axis as the z-axis, a σ-bond structure entails the hybridization of the carbon 2s, 2px, along with 2py orbitals (sp^2) to facilitate the attachment of the oxygens via a 2p orbital situated in the molecular plane. This corresponds to six valence electrons (Blush et al., 1992; Korth et al., 1981).

The molecular orbitals involved in -bonding arise from combining the 2pz orbitals of carbon and three oxygen atoms, with six additional electrons to be accommodated. Therefore:

- The carbon atom is the central atom, while the ligands comprise oxygen.
- The atomic orbitals used for the π-bonding system *only* are shown under C and O in the energy level diagram below (f). The relative positioning of the p-orbitals of oxygen and carbon can be attributed to the difference in electronegativity between the two elements, with oxygen exhibiting a higher electronegativity and thus occupying a lower energy state than carbon (Bryce et al., 1960; Quapp et al., 2011). The three 2pz orbitals of oxygen must combine linearly into three distinct orbitals:

  $\psi_1 = 1/\sqrt{3}\psi_{2pzOa} + 1/\sqrt{3}\psi_{2pzOb} + 1/\sqrt{3}\psi_{2pzOc}$
  $\psi_2 = 1/\sqrt{2}\psi_{2pzOb} - 1/\sqrt{2}\psi_{2pzOc}$ (no contribution from O_A)
  $\psi_3 = \sqrt{(2/3)}\psi_{2pzOa} - 1/\sqrt{6}\psi_{2pzOb} - 1/\sqrt{6}\psi_{2pzOc}$

- The 2pz orbital of carbon exhibits appropriate symmetry for ψ_1 amalgamation.

  $\pi_1 = 1/\sqrt{2}(\psi_1 + \psi_{2pzC})$ and $\pi^*_4 = 1/\sqrt{2}(\psi_1 - \psi_{2pzC})$

This combination solely involves carbon ψ_2 and ψ_3, which is identified as non-bonding and relabeled accordingly π_2 and π_3.

The energy level illustration below displays the molecular orbitals that arise from CO_3^{2-}.

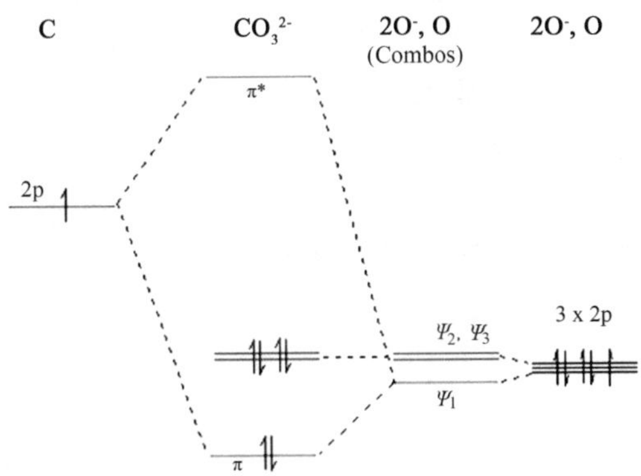

The energy levels diagram depicts the arrangement of the 6 electrons π_1, ψ_2 and ψ_3. The sole bonding π-orbital comprises two electrons distributed across four centers, all involved in three distinct C-O connections. The nonbonding ψ_2 and ψ_3 orbitals do not make any contribution. Thus, the bond order attributed to every carbon-oxygen linkage is 1/3. It is imperative to consider σ-bonds who were excluded from this program.

2.18. CONJUGATED AND AROMATIC MOLECULES

π Bonds that are nearby tend to interact with one another. Certain delocalized molecular orbitals will experience stabilization, whereas others will undergo destabilization. The unique permutations may exhibit polarization, amplifying the wave function amplitude at certain centers while simultaneously reducing the amplitude at others. This phenomenon presents the potential for a wider range of reactive patterns than those typically observed for uncomplicated alkenes (Kovács et al., 2002; Pribble et.al 1994).

Aromatic compounds display diverse reactivity patterns towards species possessing both electron-rich and electron-deficient characteristics. The factors above are primarily contingent upon the configurations and potential energies that comprise the frontier π-molecular orbitals, namely the HOMO and the LUMO. Except for non-bonded single pairs, the σ framework's contribution to the overall reactivity is negligible.

- **Trans-1,3-Butadiene**: Conjugated molecules such as butadiene exhibit pairs of π-molecular orbitals alongside energies that are equivalent to $(\alpha \pm x\beta)$ a constant multiplied by the sum of the indices of the orbitals. A related antibonding orbital exists for power for every bonding orbital with energy. The molecular orbitals exhibit spatial extension across the entirety of the molecule.

The electronic configuration of butadiene is determined by the presence of four electrons $\pi_1^2\pi_2^2$ in its manifold.

Please refer to the following over-energy illustration and visual representation of the π-molecular orbitals:

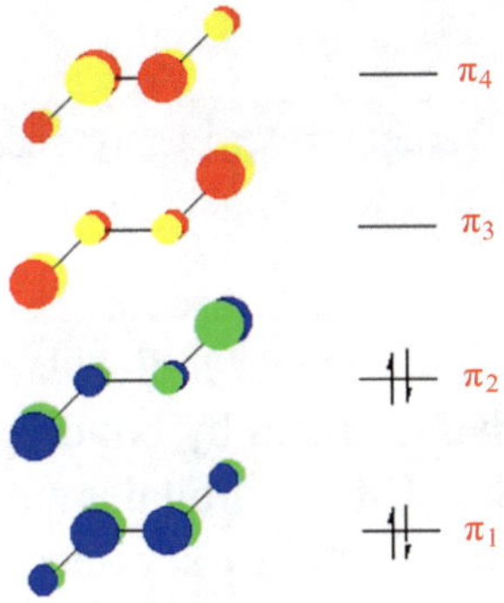

2.19. ALLYL RADICAL

The radicals allyl:

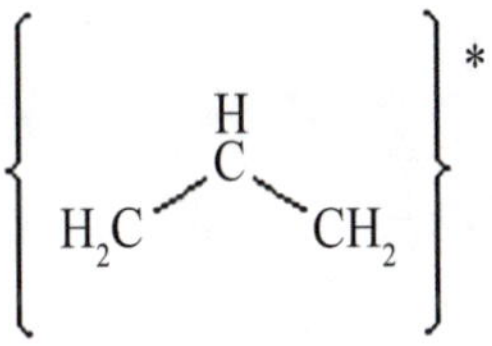

And pentadactyl:

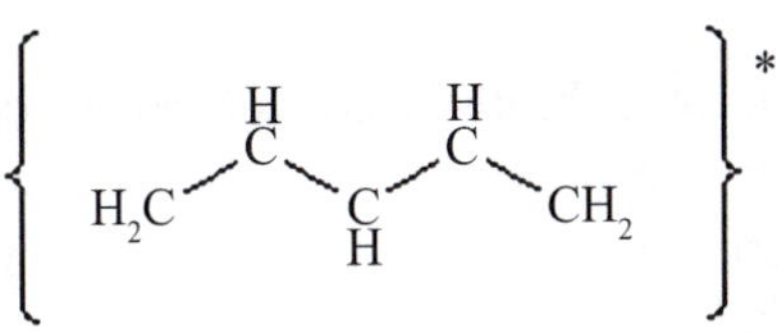

Have the conjugate chain exhibit a symmetrical distribution of π-orbitals, occurring in pairs of equivalent energy levels $\alpha \pm x\beta$. However, due to an odd amount of carbon atoms in the chain, a non-bonding **π** orbital exists alongside an energy level of $x=0$. Furthermore, owing to the pairing characteristics found in the π -molecular orbits of conjugated chains, a node will manifest at every other carbon atom within the NBO. The occupation of the NBO by the unpaired electrons of allyl holds significant importance. Upon the addition of an electron into the allyl radical, which forms the anion, the negative charge will manifest at the tip of the carbon atoms. Upon removal of the unpaired electron to form the cation, the resultant extra charge is also delocalized over the terminal carbon atoms (Anderson et al., 1994; Gilman, 1999).

Remember

Remember that the allyl radical is a highly reactive molecule with an unpaired electron, making it a radical species.

The allyl molecule exhibits three π-molecular orbitals, namely $\boldsymbol{\pi}_1$, $\boldsymbol{\pi}_2$, and $\boldsymbol{\pi}_3$. The π_1 orbital is characterized by bonding, while the π_2 circular is non-bonding. On the other hand, the π_3 orbital is anti-bonding in nature. Each neutral allyl species contains a total of seventeen electrons with valence, with three of them occupying the π-orbital manifold (Sherman, 1987). The energy illustration depicting the neutral, cationic, and anionic allyl species is presented in a pictorial format below. The orbitals are exclusively depicted for the cationic species):

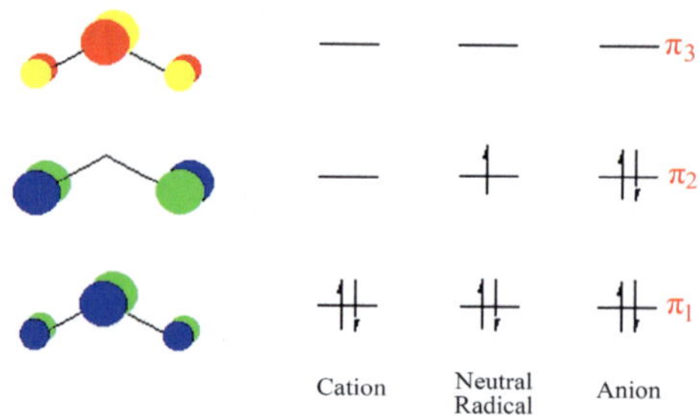

The pentadactyl anion exhibits a concentration of negative charge at the carbon atoms located in positions 1, 3, and 5. Analogously, the cation displays a concentration of positive charge at these same positions.

The resonance theory depicts these ions as up to three canonical structures:

Resonance structures for the allyl cation

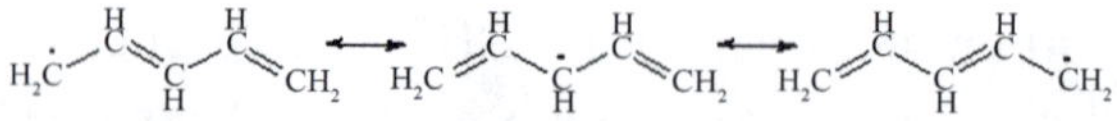

Resonance structures for the pentadienyl radical

The reduction in orbital energy is linked to the dispersion of π-electrons. Consequently, the aggregate energy that comprises the occupied π-orbitals in butadiene is comparatively lower than that of two separate double-bonded bonds of ethene-type (Abell, 1985; Wang et al., 1989).

2.20. BONDING IN BENZENE

The diagram above illustrates that the circular coefficients associated with the orbital, π one, are uniform, which means the bonding character between adjacent carbon atoms. In the context of π 2 bonding, it can be observed that bonding occurs solely between atoms C2 and C3 and between C5 and C6. This is because the coefficients upon C1 and C4 are determined to be zero. Within the π 3 molecular orbitals, C1 forms bonds with C2 and C6, while C4 forms bonds with C3 and C5. Notably, anti-bonding interactions occur between C2 and C3, as well as between C5 and C6. Hence, considering the π 2 and π 3 orbitals pair, it can be inferred that the C-C π interacting contribution is equivalent for both bonds. The π bond sequence can be determined to be 1/2 based on three occupied interacting orbitals and six CC linkages. As mentioned above, the depiction aligns with the two resonant mesomeric structures (or Kekulé constructions in a) depicted below, wherein the ring exhibits alternating single along with double bond characters (Rodriguez et al., 1992).

Traditionally, the diagram depicted in b) illustrates the delocalization of the six electrons surrounding the ring:

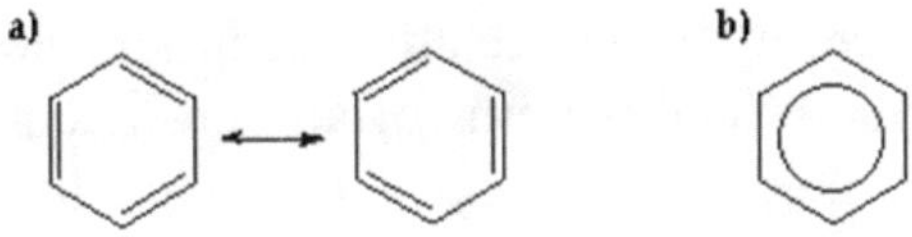

2.21. MOLECULAR ORBITAL THEORY OF SOLIDS' METALLIC BONDING

The third primary category of chemical bonding pertains to the interatomic bond that occurs among two metal atoms. Metals tend to undergo oxidation by losing electrons, and they typically cannot undergo reduction by accepting electrons. In the context of metallic bonding, it can be inferred that the absence of electron acceptor atoms is a characteristic feature. Rather than retaining their identities, the electrons are relinquished to a collective pool of electrons enveloping the metallic atoms. This phenomenon resembles ionic bonding, albeit with the distinction that the "ions" in question are electrons. The cohesive force that binds the metal is attributed to the electrostatic attraction between the negatively charged electrons and the positively charged metal ions. Metals constitute the largest group of chemical elements in the periodic table. Approximately 80% of the approximately 100 known elements are classified as metals. Based on personal experience, one possesses knowledge regarding the bonding of metallic atoms (Inerrante et al., 1971). It is a well-established fact that metals possess substantiality and exhibit high resistance to deformation. The material in question exhibits ductility and malleability. This implies that they can be manipulated into various forms, similar to the wire utilized in the production of this paper clip, and their physical configuration can be altered. They exhibit thermal and electrical conductivity. Alloys can be formed by mixing them. Metals, along with metallic atoms, are characterized by the presence of valence electrons that exhibit relatively low binding energy, rendering them susceptible to facile removal. Utilizing this notion, we can construct a metallic bonding model to elucidate these characteristics. Potassium will be utilized as an illustrative instance. A dot can denote the valence electron of the atom. When arranged in a cluster, the configuration would appear as such. The valence electron exhibits relatively weak binding energy and can readily undergo interatomic migration. Each atom possesses a valence electron nearby. However, it is uncertain which specific electron corresponds to each respective atom. The proximity of a nearby option is the determining factor, regardless of other considerations.

The cohesive forces in metals are attributed to the delocalized bonding that arises through the orbital patterns of all constituent atoms within the crystal lattice. The molecular orbitals are formed by blending orbitals that are distributed over multiple atoms, resulting in a band-like structure. The energy levels of these orbitals exhibit a narrow spacing. The musical ensemble comprises several tiers equivalent to the quantity of participating atomic orbitals, with each tier able to accommodate electrons exhibiting opposing spin. The phenomenon of bonding within metallic solids can be attributed to the delocalization or spreading of the molecular orbitals across the atoms of the metal piece, which form a band of energy levels. The scientific concept that describes the bonding of metals is referred to as the band theory. The material's band structure is divided into two distinct regions: the upper portion of the vacant levels or the anti-bonding orbitals, and the lower portion of the filled levels and the bonding orbitals. In metallic materials, the energy level band is incompletely occupied. The energy level occupied by the last electron at absolute zero temperature is called the Fermi level. The electronic configuration of the metal determines the melting points of transition metals.

2.22. BONDING MODELS FOR METALS

2.22.1. Band Theory of Bonding in Solids

The comprehension of bonding in solids, including metals, insulators, and semiconductors, can be enhanced by extending the basic MO theory to encompass large groups of atoms. In the context of MOT, it was postulated that the combination of orbitals found on two distinct atoms could give rise to the formation of bonding along with antibonding orbitals (Frenking & Froehlich, 2000).

Combining three atoms makes it possible to generate a chain of atoms that are bonded together, linking all three. A set of orbitals is presented here consisting of a bonding orbital, an antibonding orbital, and a nonbonding orbital. In essence, a nonbonding orbital refers to an orbital that does not contribute to the overall bonding of the molecule. The salient aspect to consider is that the resultant molecular system must exhibit three molecular orbitals derived from the combination of three atomic orbitals. The conservation of the overall number of orbitals is a fundamental principle that must be upheld. Now, we broaden these concepts by contemplating amalgamations of four and ten particles. As illustrated below, the combination of four atoms (i.e., four atomic orbitals) forms four molecular orbitals comprising two bonding orbits and two anti-bonding orbits (Kubas, 2001; Howe, 1993).

It should be noted that the energies of the two bonding orbitals and two antibonding orbitals are not identical. The lower connecting orbital exhibits a marginally higher degree of bonding than the other, while one antibonding orbital displays a slightly greater degree of antibonding. A set of five bonding along with five antibonding orbitals would be obtained for the ten atoms, each exhibiting slight energy variation.

Considering a large number of atoms, denoted by the variable n, which may approach the magnitude of Avogadro's constant, it becomes apparent that a significant quantity of bonding along with antibonding orbitals will be present. The proximity of these orbitals in energy is such that they become indistinct, resulting in the formation of bonding and antibonding orbital bands. The presence of these orbitals' bands constitutes the fundamental basis for comprehending the characteristics of solids. Notably, there is a certain threshold at which the characteristics of a collection of atoms transform distinct, individual orbitals (and, consequently, quantum properties akin to atoms) to groups of orbitals. Utilizing nanodots, which are minute clusters of approximately twenty atoms that exhibit quantum behavior, is the foundation for developing advanced technology. Once a cluster of atoms, even of small size, such as the power source submicron objects present in a chip for a computer, is formed, band theory is the most appropriate way to describe its properties (Li, 1992; Bagus et al., 1984; Guo et al., 1987).

The MOT is applied to solids. We shall contemplate a linear arrangement of n indistinguishable atoms, where each atom contributes its valence s orbital towards forming molecular orbitals. When the value of n equals 2, two molecular orbitals are generated, comprising a bonding molecular orbital and an antibonding molecular orbital. When the value of n is equal to 3, it forms three molecular orbitals, namely bonding, nonbonding, and antibonding. As the value of n approaches Avogadro's number, it is anticipated that a total of No MOs will be generated. These MOs will span the spectrum from complete bonding (+++++.) to complete anti-bonding (+-+-+-.) alongside numerous other MOs occupying intermediate positions along this continuum The energy difference between the lowest and highest molecular orbitals is predominantly governed by the degree of overlap between adjacent atoms.

Consequently, this energy difference will remain finite despite an increase in the number of atoms comprising the chain, even as it approaches infinity. Consequently, many molecular orbitals are densely packed within a limited energy range. The energy levels will be so close that they will amalgamate to form a band of electrical energy levels that is effectively continuous. Due to this rationale, the nomenclature "Band Theory" frequently refers to the MO theory about solids. A significant outcome of this treatment is the delocalization of every molecular orbital within the band across all atoms in the chain (Föhlisch et al., 2000; Eberhart et al., 2012).

The concepts above are equally applicable to a three-dimensional, densely packed conglomeration of atoms. Every valence atomic orbital on the atoms will give rise to a band of molecular orbitals. The MOs exhibit delocalization across the entire aggregate of atoms, thereby conferring the property of electron ubiquity upon them. The nomenclature employed in molecular orbitals designates the highest occupied band as the valence band, while the lowest unoccupied band is called the conduction band. The energy difference between the band of valence's apex and the band's nadir used for conduction is commonly known as the band gap. When a band is incompletely occupied, it can function as both the valence and conduction band. Consequently, the band gap in such a scenario is effectively negligible (Ramani & Zhao, 1997; Spanjaard & Desjonquères, 1984).

Let us utilize this image to comprehend the electronic properties of the previously-mentioned diverse categories of materials.

A solid material, typically composed of a metallic element, is classified as a conductor due to its partially occupied band structure, as illustrated in the accompanying diagram. The facile movement of electrons in a solid lattice, according to the effect of an electric field that is applied, enables the conduction of electricity. Specifically, an electron that is in the molecular orbital with the greatest occupancy can be readily promoted into the next higher devoid delocalized molecular orbital, allowing it to roam freely throughout the lattice (Frenking, 2001; DeBeer George et al., 2005). The elevated reflectivity of metals can be attributed to the abundance of unoccupied MOs positioned above the highest occupied MO (HOMO). The absorption and reemission of light of various wavelengths can occur when electrons within the occupied molecular orbitals of a partially-filled band undergo transitions to unoccupied molecular orbitals within the same band. This imparts a lustrous and reflective aspect to the metallic surface. An instance of a substance that can conduct electricity is sodium (Na) metal. The crystal possesses an s band comprising N MOs, with N denoting the quantity of sodium (Na) atoms in the crystal. The ensemble of electrons in the band is comprised of N particles, each originating from a distinct Na atom and arranged in N/2 pairs. Half of the N electron pairs are accommodated within the N/2 bonding molecular orbitals, while the remaining N/2 antibonding molecular orbitals remain unoccupied but easily accessible. Sodium displays typical metallic properties and functions as an electrical conductor (Frenking et.al 2021).

An insulator has become a solid material with a complete band structure and a substantial band gap. The conduction band's MOs exhibit significant energy, rendering them unpopulated by the Boltzmann distribution under typical thermal conditions. Consequently, ordinary temperatures do not facilitate conductivity. Solid carbon that has undergone diamond modification is an instance of an insulator (Sangiorgi et al., 1988; Cheng et al., 2014). The structure of a diamond is composed of a network of carbon molecules that are covalently bonded. This network is arranged in a face-centered cubic (fcc) array, with additional carbon atoms occupying half of the tetrahedral holes. The bonding in diamond is achieved through the use of sp^3 hybrid orbitals. The presence of N carbon atoms results in forming of 4N sp^3 hybrids that exhibit significant overlap and consequently yield 2N bonding MOs along with 2N antibonding Mos. The energy difference between the bonding MOs and the antibonding MOs is 5.47 eV. The 4N electrons precisely occupy this band of bonding molecular orbitals. Due to the thermal inaccessibility of the antibonding band, diamond exhibits non-conductive properties (Scherer et al., 2003; Mingos et al., 1990; Lee, 1994).

2.22.2. Semi Conduction

At standard temperature, a minor thermal populace within the conduction band exists, resulting in a limited level of conductivity. Silicon exhibits a diamond-like crystal structure akin to carbon, albeit with a narrower band gap of 1.12 eV. This is attributed to the inferior overlap between the sp^3 hybrids about the comparatively larger Si atoms. Due to the occupation of the antibonding band through the Boltzmann distribution, silicon displays limited conductivity at standard room temperature (Josephson. 1974).

The elements of the 4A group exhibit a distinctive arrangement that renders them capable of demonstrating semi-conductivity because their valence electrons are equivalent to twice the number of molecular orbitals present in the bonding band. The chemical elements ranging from carbon (C) to tin (Sn) demonstrate a crystal structure similar to diamond's. However, the magnitude of their band gap reduces as the size of the atoms increases, owing to the weakening of orbital overlap. The present study illustrates the trend of band gap reduction within the 14th group of elements: Si and Ge exhibit semiconductor properties at room temperature, while Sn demonstrates conductive behavior. Semiconductors include pure compounds that exhibit electronic properties analogous to group 14 elements. The entities above encompass the chemical compounds boron nitride (BN) and gallium arsenide (GaAs) (Van Delft & Kes, 2010; Mo et al., 2012).

It should be noted that the aforementioned compounds comprise a single element sourced from group 13 and another element sourced from group 15, with a stoichiometric ratio of 1:1. Consequently, the number of valence electrons in these elements is identical to that of the group 14 component. They will organize the electrons in a band structure resembling group 14. The compounds in question are called 3–5 compounds, denoting their composition of elements sourced from groups thirteen and fifteen. Likewise, binary compounds comprising 2–6 elements, such as Zinc Sulfide (ZnS) and Cadmium Sulfide (CdS), exhibit semiconductor properties due to their zincblende crystal structure, comparable to the diamond structure. In general, the band gaps exhibit variation across the periodic table based on position but tend to decrease as the molecular weight of the semiconductor increases.

Element	Band Gap
C	5.47
Si	1.12
Ge	0.66
Sn	0

The relationship between conductivity and temperature can be comprehended through the principles of band theory. At any given temperature, it is easy for a conductor to promote electrons within a band. As temperature (T) increases, the vibrational motions of metal atoms within the lattice become more pronounced, leading to interference with the motion of conducting electrons. As temperature increases, there is a reduction in conductivity. The number of members for the band of conduction within a semiconductor experiences an exponential rise due to an increase in temperature, which can be attributed to the Boltzmann distribution. Hence, the electrical conductivity of semiconductors exhibits a significant increase with temperature. Insulators can be classified as semiconductors with a wide band gap. Consequently, elevating the temperature within an insulator can result in a significant increase in its conductivity.

The amounts of energy in solid materials are closely spaced due to the extensive atom interactions, resulting in the formation of bands. The valence band has the highest energy level comparable to a molecule's HOMO. The conduction band is the subsequent higher energy level, which resembles the LUMO found in a molecule. The energy differential amidst these bands is denoted as the energy gap, Eg.

2.22.3. Idealized Representation of Energy Bands and Gaps

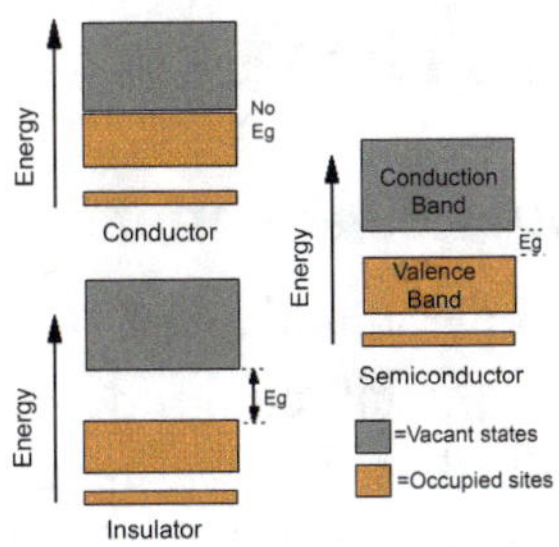

The occupation of energy bands and the magnitude of the band gap are the key factors that dictate the electrical conductivity of a material, classifying it as either a semiconductor, a metal (conductor), or an insulator. Metals are characterized by the absence of an energy gap between their filled and empty energy levels. Many electrons undergo thermal excitation and transition to unoccupied energy levels, generating vacancies in the occupied band. The facile conduction of electricity in a material is facilitated by the mobility of electrons within conduction bands and holes within a valence band, which enables them to traverse the material. Semiconductor materials possess a relatively small value of Eg, sufficient to limit the number of electrons in the band that conducts electrons due to thermal energy (Xiang et al., 1995).

Consequently, these materials exhibit poor conductivity. Insulators possess a large band gap energy (E_g), which prevents electrons from being excited to the conduction spectrum by thermal energy. Consequently, these materials exhibit negligible electrical conductivity.

The categorization of materials can be facilitated by comprehending the energy differential between the bonding and antibonding bands, which can be classified into three distinct groups. In a substantial energy gap, the substance is classified as an insulator. The substance can be classified as a semiconductor if the gap is limited. Conversely, the substances are called conductors if there is a negligible gap between the two bands. The properties above manifest due to the mobility of electrons within the crystal lattice upon their entry into the antibonding band. This behavior is correlated with the phenomenon of electrical conduction. To illustrate the magnitudes of energies, it is noteworthy that the band gap value in diamond remains 502 kJ/mol. In contrast, the corresponding value with Si is 100 kilograms, while that of Ge remains at 67 kJ/mol. The material known as diamond exhibits insulating properties, whereas the remaining two materials are classified as semiconductors.

2.23. SUPER CONDUCTION

2.23.1. Discovery of Super Conduction

Before the discovery of superconductivity, it was established that the electrical conductivity of a metal could be enhanced by reducing its temperature, which was attributed to a reduction in electron-phonon interactions. Following the discovery of liquefied helium, which enabled the cooling of objects to temperatures within 4K of zero degrees Celsius, it was observed by Onnes in 1911 that the electrical resistance of mercury abruptly and surprisingly decreased to zero upon being cooled to 4.15K, indicating the onset of superconductivity (Bardeen, 1955).

1913 marked the discovery that lead exhibits superconductivity at 7.2 Kelvin. Subsequently, it took 17 years to discover that niobium exhibits superconductivity at a comparatively elevated temperature of 9.2K. Onnes observed that a powerful magnetic field might reestablish normal conduction traits (Geim et al., 1998).

2.23.2. Meissner Effect

The phenomenon of perfect diamagnetism in superconductors was brought to the attention of physicists in the year 1933. Meissner and Oschenfeld discovered that a superconducting substance would exclude the magnetic energy flux upon being cooled beneath the critical temperature while in a magnetic field. The phenomenon is commonly referred to as the Meissner effect (Furusaki et al., 1991).

The critical growing strength, denoted as B_c, refers to the maximum magnitude of a magnetic field from the outside that a superconducting material can repel.

Type II superconductors exhibit two distinct critical field strengths, namely B_{c1} and B_{c2}. The former marks the threshold above which the magnetic field begins to penetrate the superconductor. At the same time, the latter denotes the critical point beyond which superconductivity is lost, analogous to the B_c value observed in Type I superconductors (Lichtenstein et al., 2000; Barker, 1973).

2.23.3. Theory of Super Conduction

The Meissner influence and the extent of magnetic field penetration into a superconductor were initially expounded by Fritz along with Heinz London through their proposed equations. However, significant theoretical advancement in this area was not achieved until 1950, when the Ginzburg-Landau theory was introduced. This theory not only explained superconductivity but also derived the London equations (Davtyan et al., 2005; Amitay et al., 1994).

The BCS theory has largely replaced the Ginzburg-Landau concept, which provides a more microscopic approach to studying superconductivity.

The Theory section discusses the BCS theory, introduced in 1957 by J. Bardeen, L. Cooper, and J. R. Schrieffer. The BCS theory posits the emergence of Cooper pairs and effectively aligns with the predictions of Ginzburg-Landau along with London.

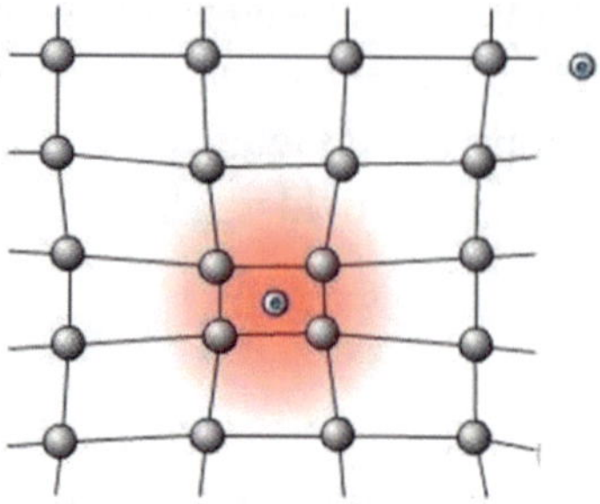

The process of Cooper pair formation through electron-phonon interaction involves the attraction of an electron to the higher charge density, indicated by a red glow generated by the first electron's distortion of the lattice surrounding it. Despite its usefulness in explaining superconductivity at low temperatures, the BCS theory falls short of adequately explaining high-temperature superconductivity, which remains incomplete (Das et al., 2019).

2.23.4. High-Temperature Super Conduction

The uppermost recorded temperature when a substance exhibited superconductivity demonstrated a gradual increase as researchers discovered novel materials with elevated values of T_c. However, in 1986, a Ba-La-Cu-O structure was discovered to manifest superconductivity at 35K, notably the most elevated value. The observation is intriguing as per the BCS theory, the anticipated threshold for T_c, owing to thermal vibrations, was approximately 30–40K. Subsequently, materials exhibited superconductivity at temperatures exceeding 77K, the boiling point of liquid nitrogen. This is a significant development as liquid nitrogen is a more cost-effective and safer refrigerant than liquid helium (Kotani et al., 1960). While the term "high-temperature superconductors" generally denotes materials that exhibit superconductivity above 30–40K, it is worth noting that their practical utility is more pronounced when their superconducting properties are observed above 77K.

Did You Know?

High-temperature superconductors are materials that can exhibit superconductivity at temperatures above the boiling point of liquid nitrogen (77 Kelvin or -196 degrees Celsius).

2.24. NEW INSIGHTS INTO MOLECULAR STRUCTURE AND BONDING THEORIES

2.24.1. Quantum Mechanical Calculations for Molecular Orbitals

Quantum mechanical computations are of utmost importance in elucidating the complex intricacies of molecular orbitals, thereby furnishing valuable perspectives into the essence of chemical bonding along with electronic configuration. The computations mentioned above employ basic tenets of quantum mechanics to resolve the Schrödinger equation, which delineates the conduct of electrons within a molecular framework.

The significance of quantum mechanical computations in the context of molecular orbitals is of utmost importance. Such techniques enable researchers to ascertain the electron's energy levels and spatial distribution within a molecule, thereby providing insights into its spectroscopic properties, stability, and chemical reactivity. By comprehending molecular orbitals, researchers can anticipate and elucidate diverse phenomena, including establishing chemical bonds, electron dispersion, and bonding and antibonding relations (Usachenko et al., 2005).

Various techniques are utilized in quantum mechanical motion computations, each presenting a distinct trade-off between computational expense and precision. The techniques encompassing post-Hartree-Fock methods, Hartree-Fock theory, and density functional theory (DFT), such as MP2 and CCSD, are among the methods utilized. These methodologies employ mathematical estimates and algorithms to address the Schrödinger equation, facilitating the computation of orbitals of molecules and their corresponding properties.

In recent times, there have been notable advancements in computational methodologies and software, which have enabled the execution of quantum mechanical calculations with greater precision and efficiency. The increased availability of high-performance computing resources has facilitated the ability of researchers to conduct intricate computations on larger molecules and explore a broader spectrum of chemical systems. In addition, advanced algorithms and software implementations have notably enhanced the precision and velocity of these computations, thereby empowering researchers to address progressively complex issues. Several case studies have been conducted to demonstrate the efficacy of quantum mechanical motion calculations in different domains of chemistry, highlighting their potency. These investigations have yielded significant knowledge regarding molecular makeup, reaction, and spectroscopy ranging from the elucidation of organic reaction mechanisms to the prediction of electronic characteristics of transition metal complexes. Quantum mechanical calculations have demonstrated their potential to advance the understanding of science and technological innovation by aiding in the design of novel substances, catalysts, and drugs. This contribution has been instrumental in showcasing the transformative power of such calculations (Habibović et al., 2020).

In contemporary scientific research, quantum mechanical computations have become essential for exploring molecular orbitals, facilitating researchers to gain a more profound understanding of the fundamental principles underlying chemical bonding and reactivity. These techniques' persistent advancement and utilization exhibit significant potential for augmenting our comprehension of the molecular realm.

2.24.2. Advancements in Bond Order Determination Techniques

Bond order has become a fundamental aspect of chemical bonding that offers valuable insights into the stability and strength of chemical bonds. The VBT posits that the bond order, which denotes the number of pairs of electrons shared among two atoms, is a fundamental parameter that is pivotal in predicting diverse molecular properties. Over time, notable progress has been achieved in determining bond order, resulting in enhanced accuracy and precision in computations.

Conventional techniques for ascertaining bond order, like the Lewis structure and VBT, yielded a non-quantitative comprehension of bond potency. The techniques above were predicated on quantifying both the communal and individual electron pairs to approximate the degree of bonding. Although these approaches have utility, they frequently oversimplify the intricacy of actual molecules and possess limitations in their ability to make predictions (Vega et al., 2016).

Contemporary methodologies have transformed the determination of bond order by integrating more rigorous computational methodologies. Quantum mechanical computations, including ab initio techniques and DFT, were developed as potent instruments for precise bond order estimations. The methodologies mentioned above take into account the quantum mechanical properties of electrons and offer a more all-encompassing portrayal of molecular bonding.

By utilizing computational methodologies, scholars can now ascertain bond order with greater accuracy through the computation of electrical wavefunctions along with energy levels. This facilitates a more comprehensive examination of the strength, length, and polarity of chemical bonds. Moreover, contemporary methodologies incorporate the impact of the correlation between electrons and electron delocalization, which are pivotal in comprehending the conduct of intricate molecules.

The significance of bond order in prognosticating bond strength and characteristics is paramount. In general, bonds with higher orders are associated with greater bond strength and reduced bond length. Furthermore, the bond order exerts an impact on various aspects that, include bond strength, bond dissociation, along with reactivity. The precise identification of the bond order facilitates informed prognostications regarding chemistry, stability, and the conduct of molecules in diverse surroundings. Sophisticated methodologies for determining bond order have been widely utilized across various domains of chemistry. As an illustration, they play a crucial role in developing and enhancing catalysts, forecasting molecular reactivity, and comprehending the characteristics of intricate materials. By integrating empirical data and utilizing computational advancements, scholars can now investigate complex molecular connecting scenarios and attain a more profound understanding of the complexities of chemical bonding (Hummer et al., 2000).

2.24.3. Emerging Trends in Delocalized Bonding Studies

The concept of delocalized bonding, which refers to the dispersion of electrons across multiple atoms rather than being restricted to just one pair of atoms, has garnered considerable interest in contemporary times. The comprehension of strength, reactivity, and electronic properties of diverse compounds is contingent upon this type of bonding. The decentralized bonding field has witnessed several novel trends that have significantly transformed our comprehension of chemical bonding.

New insights into the characteristics and actions of delocalized bonds have been revealed through recent findings and hypotheses. Using computational techniques and theoretical frameworks has facilitated the investigation of intricate systems and enabled the anticipation of the existence and importance of delocalized connections in molecules and materials. The studies above have contributed to the advancement of our comprehension regarding the concepts of aromaticity, resonance, and conjugation in organic compounds. Furthermore, they have provided insights into extended systems' decentralized bonding systems, including polymers and supplies (Biswal, 2015).

New methods are being developed for investigating photoelectron spectroscopy and delocalized bonding. Advanced spectroscopic techniques, including scanning tunneling microscopy (STM), offer valuable insights through delocalized systems' electronic makeup and bonding configurations. The emergence of the ultrafast spectrum has facilitated the contemporaneous monitoring of charge transfer mechanisms and electron delocalization kinetics, elucidating the complexities of delocalized bonding in situ.

The utilization of delocalized bonding has been observed in diverse domains of chemistry. The comprehension of the aromaticity of compounds, the durability of radical types, and the responsiveness of conjugated structures are crucial in organic chemistry. The comprehension for as well and graphene-based materials' characteristics in materials science is reliant on the significance of delocalized bonding. The presence of delocalized bonding networks can have significant implications in the field of catalysis since they can impact both reaction mechanisms and selectivity (Khan et al., 2022; Yao et al., 2023).

2.24.4. Experimental Techniques for Probing Isolobal Analogies

The concept of isolobal analogy, which Roald Hoffmann first proposed along with Kenneth B. Wiberg during the 1960s, has significantly transformed our comprehension of both chemical connection and the development of novel molecules. The notion above is grounded on the premise that fragments possessing comparable valence electron arrangements may demonstrate analogous chemical responsiveness. Researchers have devised multiple experimental techniques to investigate and characterize molecular connections about isolobal analogies.

Spectroscopic techniques are a prevalent method for investigating isolobal analogies. The field of spectroscopy is instrumental in providing significant insights into the electronic configuration, vibrational characteristics, and various other attributes of molecules. Various analytical methods have examined isolobal analogies, including infrared (IR) spectroscopy, X-ray crystallography, and nuclear magnetic resonance (NMR) spectroscopy. The utilization of IR spectroscopy allows for detecting distinctive vibrational frequencies linked to particular functional groups, thereby facilitating researchers' recognition of shared attributes among isolobal molecules. The utilization of NMR spectroscopy enables the ascertainment of the interconnectivity and surroundings of atoms within a given molecule, thereby facilitating the process of identifying and comparing isolobal fragments. The technique of X-ray crystallography offers accurate and precise data on the structural characteristics of molecules, thereby enabling a comprehensive examination of isolobal relationships (Mittermaier & Kay, 2006).

Various case studies have evidenced the efficacy of experimental methods in investigating isolobal analogies. The investigation of reactivity patterns among isolobal fragments within complexes of transition metals has been a subject of research by scholars. Through synthesizing and characterizing a range of complexes that possess distinct isolobal ligands, researchers can investigate the impact of modifications in ligand structure on various chemical properties, including but not limited to reactivity, stability, and catalytic activity. The application of spectroscopic techniques has played a crucial role in the clarification of the electronic structures along with bonding interactions within these complexes, thereby confirming the validity of the isolobal comparison concept.

The progressions in experimental methodologies persist in augmenting our comprehension of isolobal comparisons. Advanced spectroscopic techniques, including time-resolved and two-dimensional connection spectroscopy, offer valuable insights into intricate interactions between molecules and dynamic processes. The utilization of these methodologies enables researchers to examine isolobal analogies dynamically, facilitating the exploration of nuanced modifications in molecular configuration and reactivity (Heifetz et al., 2016).

The outlook for research in the field of isolobal analogy is auspicious. The utilization of advanced analytical equipment and computational tools has enabled researchers to investigate isolobal connections in larger and more intricate molecules. Furthermore, incorporating empirical and conceptual methodologies provides a holistic comprehension of isolobal analogies, facilitating the anticipatory development and composition of innovative substances possessing targeted characteristics.

2.24.5. Applications of Isolobal Concept in Modern Chemistry

The isolobal concept, initially introduced through Roald Hoffmann, is now extensively utilized in diverse domains of contemporary chemistry. Utilizing this potent concept allows chemists to establish meaningful correlations between diverse chemical entities, thereby expediting the development and production of innovative compounds possessing specific characteristics. This chapter delves into the different uses of the isolobal idea in fields such as chemistry, catalyst design, discovering drugs, and materials science. Additionally, the potential repercussions of this concept are also highlighted.

The isolobal idea has significantly transformed the methodology employed by chemists in constructing intricate molecules during chemical synthesis. Chemists can strategically synthesize new compounds with customized structures and functionalities by discovering isolobal fragments and combining them. This methodology facilitates effective and precise synthesis, optimizing the exploration of novel chemical reactions and methodologies (Kai et al., 2021).

The concept of isolobal relationship has been instrumental in developing catalyst design. Identifying isolobal comparisons between enzymes and reactants is a crucial step in developing highly effective catalysts for various transformations, as per the researchers. The application of this methodology has yielded significant achievements in the realm of homogeneous catalysis, as catalysts originating from isolobal parts have exhibited exceptional efficacy and specificity in diverse chemical processes.

The isolobal idea is a valuable tool in drug discovery as it provides insights that can aid in designing novel pharmaceutical agents. Researchers can enhance drug development and optimization by predicting the behavior and properties of potential drug candidates by identifying isolobal interactions between existing medications and these candidates. Applying the isolobal principle has enabled the creation of novel pharmaceutical compounds that exhibit heightened potency, diminished adverse reactions, and superior pharmacokinetic characteristics.

The isolobal concept has proven to be highly advantageous in materials science. Researchers can create novel materials with customized functionalities by identifying isolobal analogies between established materials and the desired properties. The methodology above is being utilized to fabricate substances exhibiting heightened electrical conductivity, superior catalytic efficacy, and innovative optical characteristics, among other attributes (Atanasov et al., 2003).

Various instances exemplify the effective application of the isolobal idea. Identifying isolobal analogies among metal complexes or olefin monomers facilitated the discovery and the synthesis of novel transition catalysts made from metals for olefin polymerization. Identifying isolobal connections among various organic building blocks has aided in designing naturally occurring semiconductors possessing the desired electronic characteristics.

Prospectively, the isolobal concept exhibits potential for further progressions in diverse research domains. Prospective applications may encompass creating operative materials for energy storage and conversion, establishing novel synthetic approaches, and investigating isolobal correlations within intricate biological systems.

2.24.6. Recent Developments in Lewis Theory and LCOA

The Lewis theory, formulated by Gilbert's N. Lewis, has become a fundamental principle in chemistry that elucidates chemical bonding through the lens of electron pairs. The framework offered is uncomplicated and robust, facilitating comprehension of chemical bond formation and anticipating molecular characteristics. In the contemporary era, there have been noteworthy progressions in Lewis's theory and its corresponding methodologies, specifically in the Linear combination of Atomic Orbitals (LCOA) domain.

The Lewis theory is a fundamental concept in elucidating the mechanism of covalent bond formation, wherein atoms share electron pairs to attain a stable electron configuration. Lewis's theory facilitates the anticipation of bond types, including single, double, or triple-bonded bonds, and the general connection of atoms in molecules by considering the outermost electrons, known as the valence electrons of atoms. Comprehending chemical bonding is a crucial aspect of explicating the configuration and responsiveness of diverse compounds (Goedhart, 2007).

A noteworthy advancement in Lewis's theory pertains to the enhanced comprehension of electron pairs along with their influence on the formation of chemical bonds. Scholars have investigated the notion of non-bonding electron pairs and their impact on molecular structure and polarity. The conducted investigations have demonstrated that lone pairs can substantially impact the shape of molecules, resulting in deviations from the anticipated bond angles and exerting an influence on molecular characteristics such as reactivity and dipole moments.

Furthermore, the progressions in computational methodologies have facilitated enhanced and effective prognostications of molecular characteristics grounded on Lewis's theory. The utilization of quantum chemical computations and molecular modeling techniques has broadened the range of Lewis theory, facilitating the examination of larger and more intricate molecules. Computational tools provide significant insights through molecules' electronic makeup, energetics, and spectroscopic properties. This, in turn, facilitates the design and optimization of novel compounds for diverse applications.

Within the domain of LCOA, scholars have implemented novel methodologies to enhance the precision and adaptability of this technique. The LCOA is a theoretical framework that combines atomic orbitals to generate molecular orbitals. This approach enables a precise and quantitative analysis of the bonding or distribution of electrons within molecules. Recent advancements in the field have involved the integration of higher-level basis sets, more advanced algorithms, and progress in parallel computing. These developments have led to more accurate calculations and expedited simulations (Saykally & Blake, 1993).

The efficacy of Lewis's theory, along with LCOA, in diverse chemical systems has been evidenced by several case studies. The application of this theory of Lewis within the investigation of transition metal complexes yields valuable information regarding their coordination chemistry and stability. Through utilizing LCOA, scholars have effectively elucidated and foretold the spectral characteristics, magnetic conduct, and reaction of metallic transition complexes, thereby expediting the advancement of catalysts and materials with customized attributes.

2.24.7. Cutting-edge Research on Atomic and Molecular Orbitals

In the past few years, notable advancements in nuclear and molecular orbitals have allowed researchers to gain new insights into the complex realm of electrons. Investigating atomic and molecular orbitals has demonstrated significant importance in comprehending the fundamental characteristics of chemical reactions, bonding, and reactivity. Through a comprehensive exploration of orbital configurations, energies, and intermolecular interactions, scholars have made significant breakthroughs that have revolutionized our comprehension of chemical systems.

An area of contemporary research is centered on acquiring a more comprehensive comprehension of the shapes of orbits. Conventional models have presented a rudimentary depiction of orbitals. However, contemporary investigations have divulged a plethora of novel insights. With the advent of sophisticated experimental methods, including scanning tunneling microscopes and nuclear force microscopy, researchers can now observe atomic and molecular orbitals with unparalleled precision. As mentioned, the advancements have furnished empirical validation of hypothetical conjectures and exposed the complex configurations of electrons in molecules. As an illustration, scholars have employed visualization techniques to observe the p-orbitals for carbon atoms in graphene, thereby elucidating its exceptional electronic characteristics (Bursten, 2014).

The field of orbital characterization has undergone a significant transformation due to the progress made in theoretical methodologies. In recent years, quantum chemistry techniques, including DFT and wavefunction-based methodologies, have notably advanced complexity and precision. Computational tools enable researchers to compute properties such as orbital energies and electron densities, thereby facilitating a comprehensive comprehension of electronic structure. In addition, theoretical investigations have examined the interplay among orbitals and the impact of exogenous variables, including electric fields and solvation, upon orbital dynamics. The ability to anticipate and elucidate the conduct of molecules in diverse settings has empowered researchers to advance novel materials and reactions of chemicals.

The significance of atomic and molecular orbitals in comprehending bonding and reactivity is paramount. By examining orbital interactions in chemical reactions, scholars can obtain valuable insights into how reactions work and predict the probability of creating bonds or cleavage. Studies have provided clarification on the function of frontier orbitals of molecules within organic reactions, which has aided chemists in creating catalysts with greater efficiency and devising methods for targeted bond activation. Furthermore, scholars have investigated the notion of orbital steering, whereby extrinsic disturbances can manipulate the trajectory of a chemical reaction by preferentially enhancing particular orbital interactions (Pareek et al., 2019).

Recent research on atomic and molecular orbital shapes has yielded remarkable examples of pioneering discoveries. Scholars have discovered unforeseen electronic phenomena, including topological states, which challenge conventional notions of bonding along with reactivity. The findings of this study hold significant ramifications for the field of materials science, as they can be utilized in various domains such as electronics, storage of energy, and quantum computing. Moreover, research on photoexcitation dynamics has revealed the complex mechanisms of energy transfer and electron mobility, facilitating progress in solar energy converting and light-emitting devices.

2.24.8. Latest Studies on Bond Properties in the Molecular Orbital Formalism

This formality has witnessed noteworthy progress in the investigation of bond properties in recent times. The theory of molecular orbitals offers a robust conceptual framework for comprehending the electronic configuration and bonding within molecules, thereby facilitating a more profound exploration of the complexities of chemical bonding. This section elucidates recent research endeavors that have provided insights into the characteristics of chemical bonds, encompassing bond lengths, assets, and polarities, as well as the mechanisms of building bonds and cleavage.

An area of present-day interest pertains to examining bond lengths across diverse molecules. Using molecular orbital calculations, researchers can precisely forecast and elucidate the observed bond lengths present in diverse compounds. According to recent research, various factors significantly influence bond lengths, including electron density dispersion, bond order, and the hybridization of orbitals in atoms. The discoveries above enhance comprehension of chemical bonds and provide valuable perspectives on the reactivity and characteristics of molecules.

The progress made in the field of MOT has facilitated a more exhaustive examination of the potency of chemical bonds. Researchers have devised quantitative metrics to evaluate the potency of chemical bonds, incorporating factors that include bond separation energies along with bond enthalpies. The studies above have demonstrated associations among bond strengths and additional characteristics, including bond lengths and disparities in electronegativity among atoms. By examining bond strengths, researchers can acquire significant knowledge regarding the reactivity and stability of molecules, which can facilitate the development of novel materials along with catalysts (Kusoglu & Weber, 2017).

Recent advancements in the molecule's orbital formalism have significantly contributed to comprehending bond polarities. By means of molecular orbital calculations, scientists can evaluate the polarity of a molecule and figure out how much electron density is distributed along a bond. Acquiring this knowledge is of paramount importance in comprehending intermolecular associations, solubilization phenomena, and molecular interplays within biological frameworks. Through the analysis of bond polarities, scholars can acquire knowledge regarding the chemical and physical features of molecules, as well as their capacity for interacting with other substances.

The molecular orbital formality has enabled the quantitative evaluation of bond properties, including bond lengths, strengths, and polarities. Researchers have devised computational methods and instruments to extract useful data from circular molecular calculations. The tools mentioned above offer a mechanism for assessing diverse bond parameters, encompassing bond orders, electron concentrations, and electron localization functions. The utilization of quantitative analyzes facilitates an improved assessment of bond properties, thereby enabling investigators to make precise forecasts and connections between connect properties and overall molecular behavior. Several case studies are being conducted to demonstrate the usefulness of molecule orbital formalization in investigating bond properties. The investigations cover a broad spectrum of molecules, from elementary diatomic entities to intricate organic substances. The bond characteristics of complexes of transition metals have been investigated by researchers, revealing the correlation between metal-ligand bonding along with the catalytic activity. Moreover, inquiries about the bonding within aromatic systems have yielded significant revelations regarding the stability and reactivity of attached molecules. The case above studies demonstrate the efficacy of the theory of molecular orbits in elucidating the complex characteristics of chemical bonds and their consequential effects on molecular properties (Lee, 1993).

2.24.9. Novel Approaches for Constructing Molecular Orbitals in Polyatomic Molecules

Generating molecular orbitals over polyatomic molecules presents considerable difficulties owing to their intricate nature and the substantial quantity of constituent atoms. Integrating experimental data and computational techniques has provided new opportunities to analyze the electronic configuration of such systems precisely. This section delves into some innovative methodologies that have surfaced in polyatomic molecular orbitals.

The computationally demanding task of building molecular orbitals over complex molecules is a significant challenge. Conventional techniques frequently depend on estimations and reductions, potentially resulting in imprecise depictions of the electronic configuration. To tackle this matter, advancements in computational techniques have facilitated the development of more intricate methodologies. Quantum mechanical computations, including DFT along with coupled group theory, have emerged as potent techniques for forecasting the molecular orbital patterns of polyatomic systems. Utilizing these techniques yields enhanced precision and the ability to process extensive computations, allowing scholars to investigate intricate molecular systems with heightened accuracy (Li et al., 2017).

Integrating experiment data has become crucial in developing molecule orbitals for polyatomic molecules alongside computational techniques. Empirical methodologies such as X-ray crystallography, spectroscopy, & microscopy with electrons offer significant insights into molecular architecture and intermolecular interactions. Through the integration of empirical observations and computational simulations, scholars can enhance the development of orbitals for molecules and attain a more exhaustive comprehension of the electronic characteristics of polyatomic compounds. The amalgamation of theoretical principles and empirical observations augments the precision of orbital development and establishes a robust groundwork for subsequent scrutiny.

The utilization of sophisticated orbital construction methodologies has extensive implications. Polyatomic molecules are subject to investigation to understand their electronic properties and reactivity better. This research is essential in providing valuable insights through chemical bonding, material properties, and reaction mechanisms. Through precise characterization of molecular orbitals, scientists can make predictions regarding the behavior of intricate systems, create innovative functional materials, and provide direction for advancing effective catalysts.

Prospective developments and emerging trends in studying polyatomic orbitals for molecules are generating considerable excitement. An emerging area of interest is investigating non-local and long-range interactions within polyatomic systems. Conventional methodologies frequently prioritize proximal bonding interactions while disregarding the importance of distal impacts. Including non-local interactions in the orbital construction process enables researchers to comprehend polyatomic molecules' electronic makeup and characteristics more profoundly (Ninham et al., 2011).

Another emerging phenomenon pertains to advancing hybrid methodologies that amalgamate diverse computational methods and approaches. Hybrid methodologies utilize the advantageous features of various techniques to surmount constraints and augment precision. Integrating post-Hartree-Fock techniques with the DFT or artificial intelligence algorithms within orbital construction procedures can enhance accuracy and expedite computational processes (Olszta et al., 2007).

Activity 2.1

In a research project focused on developing new materials for energy storage, you synthesized a novel compound containing conjugated π-systems. Using molecular orbital theory, how would you analyze the delocalized bonding and electronic properties of this compound to understand its potential for efficient charge transport and energy storage applications?

2.25. SUMMARY

This chapter of the book focuses on molecular structure and bonding theories. It begins with an introduction to the formation of molecular orbitals and the calculation of bond order. The chapter then discusses homo nuclear diatomic molecules and molecular orbitals of the second energy level (2s and 2p orbitals). A molecular orbital diagram for the O_2 molecule is constructed, and bond order is explained. The concept of delocalized bonding is introduced, followed by an exploration of molecular orbitals for heteronuclear diatomic molecules. The isolable analogy is discussed, along with its extension to valence bond and MOT in complex molecules. The generation of isolobal fragments and the isolobal scheme are explained, highlighting their applications. Lewis theory is introduced, along with the theory of LCOA. The chapter further explores atomic and molecular orbitals, with a focus on homonuclear and heteronuclear diatomic molecules. The bonding properties in the molecular orbital formalism and the overlap of orbitals are discussed. The molecular orbitals of polyatomic molecules are explained, particularly focusing on saturated molecules. Examples such as BeH_2, diborane (B_2H_6), and phosphorus pentachloride are provided. The delocalized approach to bonding is explored, along with the discussion of molecules and ions with double bonds. The concepts of conjugated and aromatic molecules are introduced, with a specific focus on the bonding in the allyl radical and benzene. The chapter then transitions to the MOT of solids and bonding models for metals. The band theory of bonding in solids, semiconduction, and idealized representations of energy bands and gaps are discussed. The discovery of superconductivity, the Meissner effect, and the theory of superconductivity are explained. The chapter concludes with a discussion of high-temperature superconductivity and provides insights into recent advancements and developments in molecular structure and bonding theories. Quantum mechanical calculations for molecular orbitals, advancements in bond order determination techniques, emerging trends in delocalized bonding studies, and experimental techniques for probing isolobal analogies are highlighted.

REVIEW QUESTIONS

1. What are the steps involved in forming molecular orbitals?
2. How is bond order calculated?
3. Explain the concept of delocalized bonding.
4. How do molecular orbitals differ for homo nuclear and heteronuclear diatomic molecules?
5. What is the isolable analogy and how is it used in valence bond and molecular orbital theory?
6. How are isolobal fragments generated and what is the isolobal scheme?
7. Provide examples of the applications of isolobility.
8. Explain the Lewis theory of bonding.
9. What is the theory of linear combination of atomic orbitals (LCOA)?
10. Describe the bonding properties in the molecular orbital formalism.
11. What is the significance of overlap of orbitals in bonding?
12. Discuss the molecular orbitals of polyatomic molecules and provide examples of saturated molecules.

REFERENCES

1. Abell, G. C., (1985). Empirical chemical pseudopotential theory of molecular and metallic bonding. *Physical Review B, 31*(10), 6184.
2. Amitay, Z., Zajfman, D., & Forck, P., (1994). Rotational and vibrational lifetime of isotopically asymmetrized homonuclear diatomic molecular ions. *Physical Review A, 50*(3), 2304.
3. Anderson, W. P., Burdett, J. K., & Czech, P. T., (1994). What is the metallic bond? *Journal of the American Chemical Society, 116*(19), 8808, 8809.
4. Atanasov, M., Daul, C. A., & Rauzy, C., (2003). New insights into the effects of covalency on the ligand field parameters: A DFT study. *Chemical Physics Letters, 367*(5, 6), 737–746.
5. Autschbach, J., (2012). Orbitals: some fiction and some facts. *Journal of Chemical Education, 89*(8), 1032–1040.
6. Bagus, P. S., Hermann, K., & Bauschlicher, Jr. C. W., (1984). A new analysis of charge transfer and polarization for ligand–metal bonding: Model studies of Al_4CO and Al_4NH_3. *The Journal of Chemical Physics, 80*(9), 4378–4386.
7. Baldauf, C., Günther, R., & Hofmann, H. J., (2005). Control of helix formation in vinylogous γ-peptides by (E)-and (Z)-double bonds: A way to ion channels and monomolecular nanotubes. *The Journal of Organic Chemistry, 70*(14), 5351–5361.
8. Ballhausen, C. A., & Gray, H. B., (1965). *Molecular Orbital Theory: An Introductory Lecture Note and Reprint Volume.* WA Benjamin, Inc.
9. Bardeen, J., (1955). Theory of the Meissner effect in superconductors. *Physical Review, 97*(6), 1724.
10. Barker, J. R., (1973). Quantum transport theory of high-field conduction in semiconductors. *Journal of Physics C: Solid State Physics, 6*(17), 2663.
11. Barklem, P. S., (2021). Correspondence between the surface integral and linear combination of atomic orbitals methods for ionic-covalent interactions in mutual neutralization processes involving H−/D−. *Physical Review A, 104*(6), 062806.
12. Bartell, L. S., Su, L. S., & Yow, H., (1970). Lengths of phosphorus-oxygen and sulfur-oxygen bonds. extended Hueckel molecular orbital examination of Cruickshank's d. pi.-p. pi. picture. *Inorganic Chemistry, 9*(8), 1903–1912.
13. Becke-Goehring, M., & Fluck, E., (1962). Phosphonitrilic chlorides from phosphorus pentachloride. *Angewandte Chemie International Edition in English, 1*(6), 281–285.

14. Bernstein, R. B., Dalgarno, A., Massey, H. S. W., & Percival, I. C., (1963). Thermal scattering of atoms by homonuclear diatomic molecules. *Proceedings of the Royal Society of London. Series A. Mathematical and Physical Sciences, 274*(1359), 427–442.
15. Biswal, H. S., (2015). Hydrogen bonds involving sulfur: New insights from ab initio calculations and gas phase laser spectroscopy. *Noncovalent Forces*, 15–45.
16. Blush, J. A., Minsek, D. W., & Chen, P., (1992). Electronic spectrum of allyl and allyl-d5 radicals: the B [12A1]. rarw. X [12A2], C [22B1]. rarw. X [12A2], and D [12B2]. rarw. X [12A2] band systems. *The Journal of Physical Chemistry, 96*(25), 10150–10154.
17. Boys, S. F., (1960). Construction of some molecular orbitals to be approximately invariant for changes from one molecule to another. *Reviews of Modern Physics, 32*(2), 296.
18. Broyer, M., Vigué, J., & Lehmann, J. C., (1978). Effective hyperfine Hamiltonian in homonuclear diatomic molecules. Application to the B state of molecular iodine. *Journal de Physique, 39*(6), 591–609.
19. Bryce, W. A., & Ruzicka, D. J., (1960). Reactions of allyl radicals with olefins. *Canadian Journal of Chemistry, 38*(6), 835–844.
20. Bursten, J. R., (2014). Microstructure without essentialism: A new perspective on chemical classification. *Philosophy of Science, 81*(4), 633–653.
21. Byers, B. P., & Hall, M. B., (1987). Comparison of isolobal fragments: photoelectron spectra and molecular orbital calculations of (arene) tricarbonylchromium,-molybdenum, and-tungsten complexes. *Organometallics, 6*(11), 2319–2325.
22. Bytautas, L., & Ruedenberg, K., (2005). Correlation energy extrapolation by intrinsic scaling. IV. Accurate binding energies of the homonuclear diatomic molecules carbon, nitrogen, oxygen, and fluorine. *The Journal of Chemical Physics, 122*(15), 154110.
23. Calzaferri, G., Forss, L., & Kamber, I., (1989). Molecular geometries by the extended Hueckel molecular orbital (EHMO) method. *The Journal of Physical Chemistry, 93*(14), 5366–5371.
24. Cheng, M. M., & Gilbert, J. K., (2014). Students' visualization of metallic bonding and the malleability of metals. *International Journal of Science Education, 36*(8), 1373–1407.
25. Cohen, R., Stokbro, K., Martin, J. M., & Ratner, M. A., (2007). Charge transport in conjugated aromatic molecular junctions: Molecular conjugation and molecule– electrode coupling. *The Journal of Physical*

Chemistry C, 111(40), 14893–14902.

26. Coulson, C. A., (1952). Factors affecting the bond lengths in conjugated and aromatic molecules. *The Journal of Physical Chemistry, 56*(3), 311–316.
27. Cradock, S., Findlay, R. H., & Palmer, M. H., (1973). The molecular energy levels of the azoles: A study by photoelectron spectroscopy and ab initio molecular orbital calculations. *Tetrahedron, 29*(14), 2173–2181.
28. Cusachs, L. C., (1965). Semiempirical molecular orbitals for general polyatomic molecules. II. One-electron model prediction of the H–O–H angle. *The Journal of Chemical Physics, 43*(10), S157–S159.
29. Das, A., & Arunan, E., (2019). Chemical bonding in period 2 homonuclear diatomic molecules: A comprehensive relook. *Journal of Chemical Sciences, 131*, 1–17.
30. Davis, R. E., & Murthy, A. S. N., (1968). Diborane as a model system for carbonium ions. *Tetrahedron, 24*(12), 4595–4603.
31. Davtyan, S. P., Tonoyan, A. O., Hayrapetyan, S. M., & Manukyan, L. S., (2005). A note on the peculiarities of producing of high-temperature super-conducting polymer–ceramic composites. *Journal of Materials Processing Technology, 160*(3), 306–312.
32. DeBeer, G. S., Brant, P., & Solomon, E. I., (2005). Metal and ligand K-edge XAS of organotitanium complexes: Metal 4p and 3d contributions to pre-edge intensity and their contributions to bonding. *Journal of the American Chemical Society, 127*(2), 667–674.
33. Del Bene, J., & Pople, J. A., (1970). Theory of molecular interactions. I. Molecular orbital studies of water polymers using a minimal slater-type basis. *The Journal of Chemical Physics, 52*(9), 4858–4866.
34. Dimroth, K., (2006). Delocalized posphorus-carbon double bonds: Phosphamethin-cyanines, λ3-phosphorins and λ5-phosphorins. In: *Phosphorus-Carbon Double Bonds* (pp. 1–147). Berlin, Heidelberg: Springer Berlin Heidelberg.
35. Ditchfield, R. H. W. J., Hehre, W. J., & Pople, J. A., (1971). Self-consistent molecular-orbital methods. IX. An extended gaussian-type basis for molecular-orbital studies of organic molecules. *The Journal of Chemical Physics, 54*(2), 724–728.
36. Dixon, D. A., Kleier, D. A., & Lipscomb, W. N., (1978). Localized molecular orbitals for polyatomic molecules. 6. Condensed aromatic ring systems. *Journal of the American Chemical Society, 100*(18), 5681–5694.
37. Dobbs, K. D., & Hehre, W. J., (1987). Molecular orbital theory of the

properties of inorganic and organometallic compounds. 6. Extended basis sets for second-row transition metals. *Journal of Computational Chemistry, 8*(6), 880–893.

38. Eastham, J. F., (1967). The structure of B_2H_6-base complexes. Molecular electron deficiency and acidity. *Journal of the American Chemical Society, 89*(9), 2237–2238.
39. Eberhart, M. E., & Jones, T. E., (2012). Cauchy pressure and the generalized bonding model for nonmagnetic bcc transition metals. *Physical Review B, 86*(13), 134106.
40. Edmiston, C., & Ruedenberg, K., (1963). Localized atomic and molecular orbitals. *Reviews of Modern Physics, 35*(3), 457.
41. Edmiston, C., & Ruedenberg, K., (1965). Localized atomic and molecular orbitals. II. *The Journal of Chemical Physics, 43*(10), S97–S116.
42. El Bakouri, O., Szczepanik, D. W., Jorner, K., Ayub, R., Bultinck, P., Solà, M., & Ottosson, H., (2022). Three-dimensional fully π-conjugated macrocycles: When 3D-aromatic and when 2D-aromatic-in-3D? *Journal of the American Chemical Society, 144*(19), 8560–8575.
43. Evans, D. G., Michael, D., & Mingos, P., (1982). Molecular orbital analysis of the bonding in low nuclearity gold and platinum tertiary phosphine complexes and the development of isolobal analogies for the M (PR3) fragment. *Journal of Organometallic Chemistry, 232*(1), 171–191.
44. Fernández, I., & Bickelhaupt, F. M., (2014). The activation strain model and molecular orbital theory: Understanding and designing chemical reactions. *Chemical Society Reviews, 43*(14), 4953–4967.
45. Fernández-Seivane, L., Oliveira, M. A., Sanvito, S., & Ferrer, J., (2006). On-site approximation for spin–orbit coupling in linear combination of atomic orbitals density functional methods. *Journal of Physics: Condensed Matter, 18*(34), 7999.
46. Ferrer-Correia, A. J. V., Jennings, K. R., & Sharma, D. S., (1976). The use of ion-molecule reactions in the mass spectrometric location of double bonds. *Organic Mass Spectrometry, 11*(8), 867–872.
47. Fischer, D. W., (1971). Soft x-ray band spectra and molecular orbital structure of Cr_2O_3, CrO_3, CrO_4^{-2} and $Cr_2O_7^{-2}$. *Journal of Physics and Chemistry of Solids, 32*(11), 2455–2480.
48. Föhlisch, A., Nyberg, M., Bennich, P., Triguero, L., Hasselström, J., Karis, O., & Nilsson, A., (2000). The bonding of CO to metal surfaces. *The Journal of Chemical Physics, 112*(4), 1946–1958.
49. Foley, H. M., (1947). Note on the nuclear electric quadrupole spectrum of

a homonuclear diatomic molecule in a magnetic field. *Physical Review, 71*(11), 747.

50. Foresman, J. B., Head-Gordon, M., Pople, J. A., & Frisch, M. J., (1992). Toward a systematic molecular orbital theory for excited states. *The Journal of Physical Chemistry, 96*(1), 135–149.
51. Frenking, G., & Froehlich, N., (2000). The nature of the bonding in transition-metal compounds. *Chemical Reviews, 100*(2), 717–774.
52. Frenking, G., (2001). Understanding the nature of the bonding in transition metal complexes: from Dewar's molecular orbital model to an energy partitioning analysis of the metal–ligand bond. *Journal of Organometallic Chemistry, 635*(1, 2), 9–23.
53. Frenking, G., Fernández, I., Holzmann, N., Pan, S., Krossing, I., & Zhou, M., (2021). Metal–CO bonding in mononuclear transition metal carbonyl complexes. *JACS Au, 1*(5), 623–645.
54. Fridland, S. V., & Chernokal'skii, B. D., (1978). The structure and reactivity of phosphorus pentachloride. *Russian Chemical Reviews, 47*(8), 742.
55. Fukui, K., Yonezawa, T., & Shingu, H., (1952). A molecular orbital theory of reactivity in aromatic hydrocarbons. *The Journal of Chemical Physics, 20*(4), 722–725.
56. Fukui, K., Yonezawa, T., Nagata, C., & Shingu, H., (1954). Molecular orbital theory of orientation in aromatic, heteroaromatic, and other conjugated molecules. *The Journal of Chemical Physics, 22*(8), 1433–1442.
57. Furusaki, A., Takayanagi, H., & Tsukada, M., (1991). Theory of quantum conduction of supercurrent through a constriction. *Physical Review Letters, 67*(1), 132.
58. Geim, A. K., Dubonos, S. V., Lok, J. G. S., Henini, M., & Maan, J. C., (1998). Paramagnetic Meissner effect in small superconductors. *Nature, 396*(6707), 144–146.
59. Gilman, J. J., (1999). In defense of the metallic bond. *Journal of Chemical Education, 76*(10), 1330.
60. Gimarc, B. M., (1970). Shapes of simple polyatomic molecules and ions. I. Series HAAH and BAAB. *Journal of the American Chemical Society, 92*(2), 266–275.
61. Gimarc, B. M., (1971). Shapes of simple polyatomic molecules and ions. II. Series AH2, AH3, and AH4. *Journal of the American Chemical Society, 93*(3), 593–599.

62. Goedhart, M. J., (2007). A new perspective on the structure of chemistry as a basis for the undergraduate curriculum. *Journal of Chemical Education, 84*(6), 971.

63. Gordy, W., (1947). Dependence of bond order and of bond energy upon bond length. *The Journal of Chemical Physics, 15*(5), 305–310.

64. Gross, L., Mohn, F., Moll, N., Schuler, B., Criado, A., Guitián, E., & Meyer, G., (2012). Bond-order discrimination by atomic force microscopy. *Science, 337*(6100), 1326–1329.

65. Gross, M. E., Trogler, W. C., & Ibers, J. A., (1981). Delocalized. pi. bonding in tetraazadiene metallocycles. *Journal of the American Chemical Society, 103*(1), 192–193.

66. Guo, Z. X., & Ridley, N., (1987). Modeling of diffusion bonding of metals. *Materials Science and Technology, 3*(11), 945–953.

67. Habibović, D., & Milošević, D. B., (2020). Ellipticity of high-order harmonics generated by aligned homonuclear diatomic molecules exposed to an orthogonal two-color laser field. In: *Photonics* (Vol. 7, No. 4, p. 110). MDPI.

68. Hall, Jr. J. H., Dixon, D. A., Kleier, D. A., Halgren, T. A., Brown, L. D., & Lipscomb, W. N., (1975). Localized molecular orbitals for polyatomic molecules. II. Structural relations and charge distributions for open boron hydrides and ions. *Journal of the American Chemical Society, 97*(15), 4202–4213.

69. Hariharan, P. C., & Pople, J. A., (1974). Accuracy of AH n equilibrium geometries by single determinant molecular orbital theory. *Molecular Physics, 27*(1), 209–214.

70. Hehre, W. J., (1976). Ab initio molecular orbital theory. *Accounts of Chemical Research, 9*(11), 399–406.

71. Hehre, W. J., Ditchfield, R., Radom, L., & Pople, J. A., (1970). Molecular orbital theory of the electronic structure of organic compounds. V. Molecular theory of bond separation. *Journal of the American Chemical Society, 92*(16), 4796–4801.

72. Hehre, W. J., Stewart, R. F., & Pople, J. A., (1969). Self-consistent molecular-orbital methods. I. Use of gaussian expansions of slater-type atomic orbitals. *The Journal of Chemical Physics, 51*(6), 2657–2664.

73. Heifetz, A., Chudyk, E. I., Gleave, L., Aldeghi, M., Cherezov, V., Fedorov, D. G., & Bodkin, M. J., (2016). The fragment molecular orbital method reveals new insight into the chemical nature of GPCR–ligand interactions. *Journal of Chemical Information and Modeling, 56*(1), 159–172.

74. Hertwig, R. H., & Koch, W., (1995). On the accuracy of density functionals and their basis set dependence: An extensive study on the main group homonuclear diatomic molecules Li_2 to Br_2. *Journal of Computational Chemistry, 16*(5), 576–585.

75. Hoffmann, S., & Fässler, T. F., (2003). $SrSn_4$: A superconducting stannide with localized and delocalized bond character. *Inorganic Chemistry, 42*(26), 8748–8754.

76. Horsfield, A. P., Bratkovsky, A. M., Fearn, M., Pettifor, D. G., & Aoki, M., (1996). Bond-order potentials: Theory and implementation. *Physical Review B, 53*(19), 12694.

77. Howe, J. M., (1993). Bonding, structure, and properties of metal/ceramic interfaces: Part 1 Chemical bonding, chemical reaction, and interfacial structure. *International Materials Reviews, 38*(5), 233–256.

78. Hummer, G., Garde, S., Garcıa, A. E., & Pratt, L. R., (2000). New perspectives on hydrophobic effects. *Chemical Physics, 258*(2, 3), 349–370.

79. Hurley, A. C., Lennard-Jones, J. E., & Pople, J. A., (1953). The molecular orbital theory of chemical valency XVI. A theory of paired-electrons in polyatomic molecules. *Proceedings of the Royal Society of London; Series A: Mathematical and Physical Sciences, 220*(1143), 446–455.

80. Ichikawa, H., Ebisawa, Y., & Shigihara, A., (1985). Potential energies of rotation of double bond in ethylene molecule and ion. *Bulletin of the Chemical Society of Japan, 58*(12), 3619–3620.

81. Inerrante, L. V., & Messmer, R. P., (1971). Intermolecular interactions in square-planar d8 metal complexes. II. Molecular orbital study of Magnus' green salt. *Inorganic Chemistry, 10*(6), 1174–1180.

82. Josephson, B. D., (1974). The discovery of tunnelling supercurrents. *Reviews of Modern Physics, 46*(2), 251.

83. Kai, M. F., Zhang, L. W., & Liew, K. M., (2021). New insights into creep characteristics of calcium silicate hydrates at molecular level. *Cement and Concrete Research, 142*, 106366.

84. Kamp, K. R., & Fredrickson, D. C., (2021). Frustrated packing in simple structures: Chemical pressure hindrance to isolobal bonds in the $TiAl_3$ type and $ZrAl_{2 \cdot 6}Sn_{0.4}$. *Inorganic Chemistry, 60*(7), 4779–4791.

85. Khan, S. N., Griffith, A., De Proft, F., Miliordos, E., Havenith, R. W., Bykov, D., & Cunha, A. V., (2022). $[Fe_4S_4]$ cubane in sulfite reductases: New insights into bonding properties and reactivity. *Physical Chemistry Chemical Physics, 24*(31), 18543–18551.

86. King, R. B., & Zhao, J., (2006). The isolable matryoshka nesting doll icosahedral cluster [As@ Ni_{12}@As_{20}]$^{3-}$ as a "superatom": analogy with the jellium cluster Al_{13}^{-} generated in the gas phase by laser vaporization. *Chemical Communications,* (40), 4204, 4205.
87. Kiremire, E. M., (2015). Isolobal series of chemical fragments. *Orient. J. Chem, 31*(3), 2015.
88. Kleier, D. A., Dixon, D. A., & Lipscomb, W. N., (1975). Localized molecular orbitals for polyatomic molecules: III. Monocyclic aromatic rings. *Theoretica Chimica Acta, 40*, 33–45.
89. Kleier, D. A., Halgren, T. A., Hall, Jr. J. H., & Lipscomb, W. N., (1974). Localized molecular orbitals for polyatomic molecules. I. A comparison of the Edmiston-Ruedenberg and boys localization methods. *The Journal of Chemical Physics, 61*(10), 3905–3919.
90. Klemenz, S., Hay, A. K., Teicher, S. M., Topp, A., Cano, J., & Schoop, L. M., (2020). The role of delocalized chemical bonding in square-net-based topological semimetals. *Journal of the American Chemical Society, 142*(13), 6350–6359.
91. Korth, H. G., Trill, H., & Sustmann, R., (1981). [1-2H]-allyl radical: Barrier to rotation and allyl delocalization energy. *Journal of the American Chemical Society, 103*(15), 4483–4489.
92. Kotani, M., Mizuno, Y., Kayama, K., & Ishiguro, E., (1957). Electronic structure of simple homonuclear diatomic molecules I. Oxygen molecule. *Journal of the Physical Society of Japan, 12*(6), 707–736.
93. Kotani, M., Mizuno, Y., Kayama, K., & Ishiguro, E., (1960). Some problems in the theory of homonuclear diatomic molecules. *Reviews of Modern Physics, 32*(2), 266.
94. Kovács, A., Szabó, A., & Hargittai, I., (2002). Structural characteristics of intramolecular hydrogen bonding in benzene derivatives. *Accounts of Chemical Research, 35*(10), 887–894.
95. Krishnan, R. B. J. S., Binkley, J. S., Seeger, R., & Pople, J. A., (1980). Self-consistent molecular orbital methods. XX. A basis set for correlated wave functions. *The Journal of Chemical Physics, 72*(1), 650–654.
96. Kubas, G. J., (2001). Metal–dihydrogen and σ-bond coordination: The consummate extension of the Dewar–Chatt–Duncanson model for metal–olefin π bonding. *Journal of Organometallic Chemistry, 635*(1–2), 37–68.
97. Kuenzer, U., & Hofer, T. S., (2019). A four-dimensional Numerov approach and its application to the vibrational eigenstates of linear triatomic molecules–The interplay between anharmonicity and inter-mode coupling. *Chemical Physics, 520*, 88–99.

98. Kullie, O., Zhang, H., Kolb, J., & Kolb, D., (2006). Relativistic density functional calculations using two-spinor minimax finite-element method and linear combination of atomic orbitals for ZnO, CdO, HgO, UubO and Cu_2, Ag_2, Au_2, Rg_2. *The Journal of Chemical Physics, 125*(24), 244303.
99. Kusoglu, A., & Weber, A. Z., (2017). New insights into perfluorinated sulfonic-acid ionomers. *Chemical Reviews, 117*(3), 987–1104.
100. Latimer, W. M., & Rodebush, W. H., (1920). Polarity and ionization from the standpoint of the Lewis theory of valence. *Journal of the American Chemical Society, 42*(7), 1419–1433.
101. Lechner, W., & Dellago, C., (2008). Accurate determination of crystal structures based on averaged local bond order parameters. *The Journal of Chemical Physics, 129*(11), 114707.
102. Lee, L. H., (1993). New perspectives in polymer adhesion mechanisms--importance of diffusion and molecular bonding in adhesion. *Adhesives Engineering, 1999*, 6–21.
103. Lee, L. H., (1994). Molecular bonding and adhesion at polymer-metal interphases. *The Journal of Adhesion, 46*(1–4), 15–38.
104. Lendvay, G., (1989). Bond orders from ab initio calculations and a test of the principle of bond order conservation. *The Journal of Physical Chemistry, 93*(11), 4422–4429.
105. Lennard-Jones, J. E., & Pople, J. A., (1951). The molecular orbital theory of chemical valency IX. The interaction of paired electrons in chemical bonds. *Proceedings of the Royal Society of London; Series A: Mathematical and Physical Sciences, 210*(1101), 190–206.
106. Li, J. G., (1992). Wetting and interfacial bonding of metals with ionocovalent oxides. *Journal of the American Ceramic Society, 75*(11), 3118–3126.
107. Li, L., Nagai, K., & Yin, F., (2008). Progress in cold roll bonding of metals. *Science and Technology of Advanced Materials, 9*(2), 023001.
108. Li, P., Niu, W., & Gao, T., (2017). Systematic analysis of structural and topological properties: New insights into $PuO_2(H_2O)_n^{2+}$(n= 1–6) complexes in the gas phase. *RSC Advances, 7*(8), 4291–4296.
109. Lichtenstein, A. I., & Katsnelson, M. I., (2000). Antiferromagnetism and d-wave superconductivity in cuprates: A cluster dynamical mean-field theory. *Physical Review B, 62*(14), R9283.
110. Lie, G. C., & Clementi, E., (1974). Study of the electronic structure of molecules. XXII. Correlation energy corrections as a functional of the Hartree-Fock type density and its application to the homonuclear diatomic

molecules of the second-row atoms. *The Journal of Chemical Physics, 60*(4), 1288–1296.

111. Liu, C., Popov, I. A., Li, L. J., Li, N., Boldyrev, A. I., & Sun, Z. M., (2018). $[Co_2@ Ge_{16}]^{4-}$: Localized versus delocalized bonding in two isomeric intermetalloid clusters. *Chemistry–A European Journal, 24*(3), 699–705.

112. Longuet-Higgins, H. C., & Murrell, J. N., (1955). The electronic spectra of aromatic molecules V: the interaction of two conjugated systems. *Proceedings of the Physical Society. Section A, 68*(7), 601.

113. Longuet-Higgins, H. C., (1957). The structures of electron-deficient molecules. *Quarterly Reviews, Chemical Society, 11*(2), 121–133.

114. Lykos, P. G., & Schmeising, H. N., (1961). Maximum overlap atomic and molecular orbitals. *The Journal of Chemical Physics, 35*(1), 288–293.

115. Magnasco, V., & Perico, A., (1967). Uniform localization of atomic and molecular orbitals. I. *The Journal of Chemical Physics, 47*(3), 971–981.

116. Magnasco, V., & Perico, A., (1968). Uniform localization of atomic and molecular orbitals. II. *The Journal of Chemical Physics, 48*(2), 800–808.

117. Mayer, I., (1983). Charge, bond order and valence in the AB initio SCF theory. *Chemical Physics Letters, 97*(3), 270–274.

118. Mayer, I., (2007). Bond order and valence indices: A personal account. *Journal of Computational Chemistry, 28*(1), 204–221.

119. McDowell, S. A., & Forde, T. S., (2003). Isotope effects in $BeH_2\cdots$ HCN. *Journal of Molecular Structure: THEOCHEM, 624*(1–3), 109–114.

120. Mingos, D. M. P., Slee, T., & Zhenyang, L., (1990). Bonding models for ligated and bare clusters. *Chemical Reviews, 90*(2), 383–402.

121. Mitchell, T. W., Pham, H., Thomas, M. C., & Blanksby, S. J., (2009). Identification of double bond position in lipids: From GC to OzID. *Journal of Chromatography B, 877*(26), 2722–2735.

122. Mittermaier, A., & Kay, L. E., (2006). New tools provide new insights in NMR studies of protein dynamics. *Science, 312*(5771), 224–228.

123. Miyazaki, K., Yannello, V. J., & Fredrickson, D. C., (2017). Electron-counting in intermetallics made easy: the 18-n rule and isolobal bonds across the Os–Al system. *Zeitschrift für Kristallographie-Crystalline Materials, 232*(7–9), 487–496.

124. Mo, Y., Ong, S. P., & Ceder, G., (2012). First principles study of the $Li_{10}GeP_2S_{12}$ lithium super ionic conductor material. *Chemistry of Materials, 24*(1), 15–17.

125. Morisaki, N., Kobayashi, H., Yamamura, Y., Morisaki, M., Nagasawa, K., & Hashimoto, Y., (2002). Coordination of sodium cation to an oxygen

function and olefinic double bond to form molecular adduct ion in fast atom bombardment mass spectrometry. *Chemical and Pharmaceutical Bulletin, 50*(7), 935–940.

126. Mulliken, R. S., (1932). Electronic structures of polyatomic molecules and valence. II. General considerations. *Physical Review, 41*(1), 49.

127. Mulliken, R. S., (1933). Electronic structures of polyatomic molecules and valence. V. Molecules RX_n. *The Journal of Chemical Physics, 1*(7), 492–503.

128. Mulliken, R. S., (1935). Electronic structures of polyatomic molecules and valence VI. On the method of molecular orbitals. *The Journal of Chemical Physics, 3*(7), 375–378.

129. Mulliken, R. S., (1939). Intensities of electronic transitions in molecular spectra III. Organic molecules with double bonds. Conjugated dienes. *The Journal of Chemical Physics, 7*(2), 121–135.

130. Mulliken, R. S., (1960). Self-consistent field atomic and molecular orbitals and their approximations as linear combinations of slater-type orbitals. *Reviews of Modern Physics, 32*(2), 232.

131. Nalewajski, R. F., (2009). Multiple, localized, and delocalized/conjugated bonds in the orbital communication theory of molecular systems. *Advances in Quantum Chemistry, 56*, 217–250.

132. Nelson, J. H., Wheelock, K. S., Cusachs, L. C., & Jonassen, H. B., (1969). New bonding model for olefinic and acetylenic complexes of transition metals. *Journal of the American Chemical Society, 91*(25), 7005–7008.

133. Niemann, T., Neumann, J., Stange, P., Gärtner, S., Youngs, T. G., Paschek, D., & Ludwig, R., (2019). The double-faced nature of hydrogen bonding in hydroxy-functionalized ionic liquids shown by neutron diffraction and molecular dynamics simulations. *Angewandte Chemie International Edition, 58*(37), 12887–12892.

134. Ninham, B. W., Duignan, T. T., & Parsons, D. F., (2011). Approaches to hydration, old and new: Insights through Hofmeister effects. *Current Opinion in Colloid & Interface Science, 16*(6), 612–617.

135. Oda, A., Ohkubo, T., Yumura, T., Kobayashi, H., & Kuroda, Y., (2018). Room-temperature activation of the C–H bond in methane over terminal ZnII–oxyl species in an MFI zeolite: A combined spectroscopic and computational study of the reactive frontier molecular orbitals and their origins. *Inorganic Chemistry, 58*(1), 327–338.

136. Odžak, S., & Milošević, D. B., (2009). Interference effects in high-order harmonic generation by homonuclear diatomic molecules. *Physical Review A, 79*(2), 023414.

137. Olszta, M. J., Cheng, X., Jee, S. S., Kumar, R., Kim, Y. Y., Kaufman, M. J., & Gower, L. B., (2007). Bone structure and formation: A new perspective. *Materials Science and Engineering: R: Reports, 58*(3–5), 77–116.

138. Paik, S. H., (2015). Understanding the relationship among Arrhenius, Brønsted–Lowry, and Lewis theories. *Journal of Chemical Education, 92*(9), 1484–1489.

139. Pareek, S., Jain, D., Hussain, S., Biswas, A., Shrivastava, R., Parida, S. K., & Behera, D., (2019). A new insight into corrosion inhibition mechanism of copper in aerated 3.5 wt.% NaCl solution by eco-friendly imidazopyrimidine dye: experimental and theoretical approach. *Chemical Engineering Journal, 358*, 725–742.

140. Parr, R. G., & Borkman, R. F., (1968). Simple bond-charge model for potential-energy curves of homonuclear diatomic molecules. *The Journal of Chemical Physics, 49*(3), 1055–1058.

141. Parr, R. G., (1960). Three remarks on molecular orbital theory of complex molecules. *The Journal of Chemical Physics, 33*(4), 1184–1199.

142. Peterson, K. A., Wilson, A. K., Woon, D. E., & Dunning, Jr. T. H., (1997). Benchmark calculations with correlated molecular wave functions XII. Core correlation effects on the homonuclear diatomic molecules B2-F2: XII. Core correlation effects on the homonuclear diatomic molecules B2-F2. *Theoretical Chemistry Accounts, 97*, 251–259.

143. Pettifor, D. G., (1989). New many-body potential for the bond order. *Physical Review Letters, 63*(22), 2480.

144. Pique, J. P., Hartmann, F., Churassy, S., & Bacis, R., (1986). Hyperfine interactions in homonuclear diatomic molecules and ug perturbations. I. *Theory. Journal de Physique, 47*(11), 1909–1916.

145. Poater, J., Duran, M., Sola, M., & Silvi, B., (2005). Theoretical evaluation of electron delocalization in aromatic molecules by means of atoms in molecules (AIM) and electron localization function (ELF) topological approaches. *Chemical Reviews, 105*(10), 3911–3947.

146. Politzer, P., (1969). Bond orders of homonuclear diatomic molecules. *The Journal of Chemical Physics, 50*(6), 2780, 2781.

147. Pople, J. A., & Santry, D. P., (1964). Molecular orbital theory of nuclear spin coupling constants. *Molecular Physics, 8*(1), 1–18.

148. Pople, J. A., & Segal, G. A., (1965). Approximate self-consistent molecular orbital theory. II. Calculations with complete neglect of differential overlap. *The Journal of Chemical Physics, 43*(10), S136–S151.

149. Pople, J. A., Santry, D. P., & Segal, G. A., (1965). Approximate self-

consistent molecular orbital theory. I. Invariant procedures. *The Journal of Chemical Physics, 43*(10), S129–S135.

150. Powell, H. M., Clark, D., & Wells, A. F., (1940). Crystal structure of phosphorus pentachloride. *Nature, 145*(3665), 149.

151. Pribble, R. N., & Zwier, T. S., (1994). Probing hydrogen bonding in benzene–(water) n clusters using resonant ion–dip IR spectroscopy. *Faraday Discussions, 97*, 229–241.

152. Quapp, W., Bofill, J. M., & Aguilar-Mogas, A., (2011). Exploration of cyclopropyl radical ring opening to allyl radical by Newton trajectories: importance of valley-ridge inflection points to understand the topography. *Theoretical Chemistry Accounts, 129*, 803–821.

153. Ramani, K., & Zhao, W., (1997). The evolution of residual stresses in thermoplastic bonding to metals. *International Journal of Adhesion and Adhesives, 17*(4), 353–357.

154. Robilotto, T. J., Bacsa, J., Gray, T. G., & Sadighi, J. P., (2012). Synthesis of a trigold monocation: an isolobal analogue of $[H_3]^+$. *Angewandte Chemie International Edition, 51*(48), 12077–12080.

155. Rodriguez, J. A., & Goodman, D. W., (1992). The nature of the metal-metal bond in bimetallic surfaces. *Science, 257*(5072), 897–903.

156. Roothaan, C. C. J., (1951). New developments in molecular orbital theory. *Reviews of Modern Physics, 23*(2), 69.

157. Sangiorgi, R., Muolo, M. L., Chatain, D., & Eustathopoulos, N., (1988). Wettability and work of adhesion of nonreactive liquid metals on silica. *Journal of the American Ceramic Society, 71*(9), 742–748.

158. Savin, A., Silvi, B., & Colonna, F., (1996). Topological analysis of the electron localization function applied to delocalized bonds. *Canadian Journal of Chemistry, 74*(6), 1088–1096.

159. Saykally, R. J., & Blake, G. A., (1993). Molecular interactions and hydrogen bond tunneling dynamics: Some new perspectives. *Science, 259*(5101), 1570–1575.

160. Scherer, W., Sirsch, P., Shorokhov, D., Tafipolsky, M., McGrady, G. S., & Gullo, E., (2003). Valence charge concentrations, electron delocalization and β-agostic bonding in d0 metal alkyl complexes. *Chemistry–A European Journal, 9*(24), 6057–6070.

161. Sharghi, H., & Nejad, A. H., (2003). Phosphorus pentachloride (PCl_5) mediated synthesis of tetraarylporphyrins. *Helvetica Chimica Acta, 86*(2), 408–414.

162. Sherman, D. M., (1987). Molecular orbital (SCF-Xα-SW) theory of metal-

metal charge transfer processes in minerals: I. application to $Fe^{2+} \rightarrow Fe^{3+}$ charge transfer and "electron delocalization" in mixed-valence iron oxides and silicates. *Physics and Chemistry of Minerals, 14*(4), 355–363.

163. Shoji, Y., Tanaka, N., Hashizume, D., & Fukushima, T., (2015). The molecular and electronic structures of a thioaroyl cation formed by borinium ion-mediated C [double bond, length as m-dash] S double bond cleavage of CS_2. *Chemical Communications, 51*(69), 13342–13345.
164. Slagle, I. R., Yamada, F., & Gutman, D., (1981). Kinetics of free radicals produced by infrared multiphoton-induced decompositions. 1. Reactions of allyl radicals with nitrogen dioxide and bromine. *Journal of the American Chemical Society, 103*(1), 149–153.
165. Spanjaard, D., & Desjonquères, M. C., (1984). Comment on universal features of bonding in metals. *Physical Review B, 30*(8), 4822.
166. Stone, F. G. A., (1984). Metal-carbon and metal-metal multiple bonds as ligands in transition-metal chemistry: The isolobal connection. *Angewandte Chemie International Edition in English, 23*(2), 89–99.
167. Streitwieser, A., (2013). Molecular orbital theory for organic chemists. In: *Pioneers of Quantum Chemistry* (pp. 275–300). American Chemical Society.
168. Sun, C. Q., (2007). Size dependence of nanostructures: Impact of bond order deficiency. *Progress in Solid State Chemistry, 35*(1), 1–159.
169. Sun, C. Q., Tay, B. K., Zeng, X. T., Li, S., Chen, T. P., Zhou, J. I., & Jiang, E. Y., (2002). Bond-order–bond-length–bond-strength (bond-OLS) correlation mechanism for the shape-and-size dependence of a nanosolid. *Journal of Physics: Condensed Matter, 14*(34), 7781.
170. Sundermeyer, J., & Runge, D., (1994). The bonding capability of imido complex fragments of groups 5–7 with regard to the isolobal relationship. *Angewandte Chemie International Edition in English, 33*(12), 1255–1257.
171. Szczepanik, D. W., & Solà, M., (2021). The electron density of delocalized bonds (EDDBs) as a measure of local and global aromaticity. In: *Aromaticity* (pp. 259–284). Elsevier.
172. Szczepanik, D. W., Andrzejak, M., Dominikowska, J., Pawełek, B., Krygowski, T. M., Szatylowicz, H., & Sola, M., (2017). The electron density of delocalized bonds (EDDB) applied for quantifying aromaticity. *Physical Chemistry Chemical Physics, 19*(42), 28970–28981.
173. Tang, H., Hoffman, D. M., Albright, T. A., Deng, H., & Hoffmann, R., (1993). $[Ni(PtBu)_6]$ and $[Ni(SiH_2)_6]$ are isolobal, related to $[In\{Mn(CO)_4\}_5]^{2-}$, and have 16-electron counts. *Angewandte Chemie International Edition in English, 32*(11), 1616–1618.

174. Tian, S. X., Li, H. B., Bai, Y., & Yang, J., (2008). Unique interactions between diborane and π orbitals: Blue-or red-shifted hydrogen bonding? *The Journal of Physical Chemistry A, 112*(35), 8121–8128.
175. Torres, R., Kajumba, N., Underwood, J. G., Robinson, J. S., Baker, S., Tisch, J. W. G., & Marangos, J. P., (2007). Probing orbital structure of polyatomic molecules by high-order harmonic generation. *Physical Review Letters, 98*(20), 203007.
176. Toulouse, J., & Umrigar, C. J., (2008). Full optimization of Jastrow–Slater wave functions with application to the first-row atoms and homonuclear diatomic molecules. *The Journal of Chemical Physics, 128*(17), 174101.
177. Trinquier, G., & Malrieu, J. P., (1991). Trends in electron-deficient bridges. *Journal of the American Chemical Society, 113*(23), 8634–8647.
178. Tsaparlis, G., (1997). Atomic orbitals, molecular orbitals, and related concepts: Conceptual difficulties among chemistry students. *Research in Science Education, 27*, 271–287.
179. Tubert-Brohman, I., Guimarães, C. R. W., & Jorgensen, W. L., (2005). Extension of the PDDG/PM3 semiempirical molecular orbital method to sulfur, silicon, and phosphorus. *Journal of Chemical Theory and Computation, 1*(5), 817–823.
180. Tully, J. C., (1973). Diatomics-in-molecules potential energy surfaces. I. First-row triatomic hydrides. *The Journal of Chemical Physics, 58*(4), 1396–1410.
181. Uce, M., (2015). Constructing models in teaching of chemical bonds: Ionic bond, covalent bond, double and triple bonds, hydrogen bond and molecular geometry. *Educational Research and Reviews, 10*(4), 491.
182. Usachenko, V. I., & Chu, S. I., (2005). Strong-field ionization of laser-irradiated light homonuclear diatomic molecules: A generalized strong-field approximation–linear combination of atomic orbitals model. *Physical Review A, 71*(6), 063410.
183. Valdés, D., Goldberg, E. C., Blanco, J. M., & Monreal, R. C., (2005). Linear combination of atomic orbitals calculation of the Auger neutralization rate of He^+ on Al (111),(100), and (110) surfaces. *Physical Review B, 71*(24), 245417.
184. Van, D. D., & Kes, P., (2010). The discovery of superconductivity. *Physics Today, 63*(9), 38–43.
185. Vega, L. F., & Llovell, F., (2016). Review and new insights into the application of molecular-based equations of state to water and aqueous solutions. *Fluid Phase Equilibria, 416*, 150–173.

186. Velasquez, J. D., Echeverria, J., & Alvarez, S., (2020). Delocalized bonding in Li_2X_2 rings: Probing the limits of the covalent and ionic bonding models. *Inorganic Chemistry, 60*(1), 345–356.

187. Von, N. W., (1972). Density localization of atomic and molecular orbitals. I. *The Journal of Chemical Physics, 56*(9), 4290–4297.

188. Vozzi, C., Negro, M., Calegari, F., Sansone, G., Nisoli, M., De Silvestri, S., & Stagira, S., (2011). Generalized molecular orbital tomography. *Nature Physics, 7*(10), 822–826.

189. Vreven, T., & Morokuma, K., (2000). On the application of the IMOMO (integrated molecular orbital+ molecular orbital) method. *Journal of Computational Chemistry, 21*(16), 1419–1432.

190. Wahl, A. C., (1964). Analytic self-consistent field wavefunctions and computed properties for homonuclear diatomic molecules. *The Journal of Chemical Physics, 41*(9), 2600–2611.

191. Wallace, W. E., Sankar, S. G., Rao, V. U. S., Hoffman, D. K., Ruedenberg, R., Verkade, J. G., & Verkade, J. G., (1977). Molecular orbital bonding concepts in polyatomic molecules: A novel picorial approach. In: *New Concepts* (pp. 57–96). Springer Berlin Heidelberg.

192. Wang, S., Garzon, G., King, C., Wang, J. C., & Fackler, Jr. J. P., (1989). Luminescent extended one-dimensional heterobimetallic chain compounds with relativistic metal-metal bonds. Synthesis, crystal structures, and spectroscopic studies of $AuTl(MTP)_2$ and $Au_2Pb(MTP)_4$ (MTP=[CH_2P (S) $Ph_2]^-$. *Inorganic Chemistry, 28*(26), 4623–4629.

193. Weatherson, B., (2013). The role of naturalness in Lewis's theory of meaning. *Journal for the History of Analytical Philosophy, 1*(10).

194. Weiss, J., (1946). Simple electron transfer processes in systems of conjugated double bonds. *Transactions of the Faraday Society, 42,* 116–121.

195. Williams, C. I., & Whitehead, M. A., (1997). Aromatic nitrogen heterocyclic heats of formation: A comparison of semiempirical and ab initio treatments. *Journal of Molecular Structure: THEOCHEM, 393*(1–3), 9–24.

196. Williams, R. E., (1992). The polyborane, carborane, carbocation continuum: Architectural patterns. *Chemical Reviews, 92*(2), 177–207.

197. Wolters, L. P., & Bickelhaupt, F. M., (2015). The activation strain model and molecular orbital theory. *Wiley Interdisciplinary Reviews: Computational Molecular Science, 5*(4), 324–343.

198. Xiang, X. D., Sun, X., Briceno, G., Lou, Y., Wang, K. A., Chang, H., &

Schultz, P. G., (1995). A combinatorial approach to materials discovery. *Science, 268*(5218), 1738–1740.

199. Yannello, V. J., & Fredrickson, D. C., (2015). Generality of the 18-n rule: intermetallic structural chemistry explained through isolobal analogies to transition metal complexes. *Inorganic Chemistry, 54*(23), 11385–11398.
200. Yao, C. X., Zhong, Y., & Guo, Y. R., (2023). New insights into the excited state of an ADA quadrupolar molecule strongly hydrogen bonded to molecules of methanol and hexafluoro isopropanol. *Journal of Molecular Structure, 1273*, 134294.
201. Zeng, Z., Shi, X., Chi, C., Navarrete, J. T. L., Casado, J., & Wu, J., (2015). Pro-aromatic and anti-aromatic π-conjugated molecules: an irresistible wish to be diradicals. *Chemical Society Reviews, 44*(18), 6578–6596.
202. Zicovich-Wilson, C. M., Hô, M., Navarrete-López, A. M., & Casassa, S., (2016). Hirshfeld-I charges in linear combination of atomic orbitals periodic calculations. *Theoretical Chemistry Accounts, 135*, 1–13.

CHAPTER

3 Activation of Covalent Bonds through Non-Covalent Interactions

Contents

3.1. INTRODUCTION

Numerous essential chemical processes entail the breaking down and/or alteration of robust covalent bonds, necessitating a considerable amount of energy to satisfy the thermodynamic as well as kinetic requirements of the reaction. The identification of routes that involve the creation of intermediates with reduced energy expenditure is a prevalent technique for promoting a reaction, and the formation and reinforcement of intermediates can be significantly influenced by non-covalent interactions. Non-covalent interactions, such as hydrogen as well as halogen bonds, van der Waals pulls, and π-effects, typically possess lower energy compared to common covalent bonds (Figure 3.1).

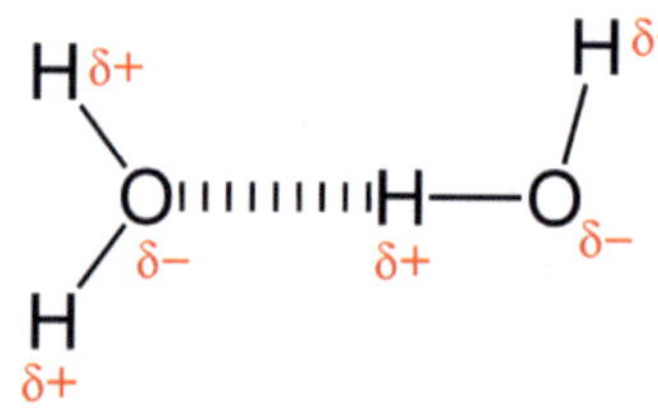

Figure 3.1. Illustration of hydrogen bond.

Source: Chemistry talk, creative common license.

However, due to their multiplicity and ease of transformation, these interactions can significantly impact the outcome of a reaction. The activation regarding covalent bonds may be influenced by the "soft force" of numerous low-energy as well as low-level connections, which can guide the "brute action" of more pronounced powers like heat, current, as well as light. The efficient simulation of covalent bonds may be attributed to the collaboration between "strong" external forces and "weak" non-covalent interactions (Maharramov et al., 2016).

When examining hydrogen bonds, it can be inferred that they have a variety of effects on substrate reactivity, as depicted in Figure 3.2. The electrophilic nature of the carbon atoms within a carbonyl group or just a thioketone is enhanced towards nucleophilic attack while a robust bifurcated hydrogen bonding occurs, wherein the oxygen or just sulfur atom participates. This phenomenon is in contrast to a simple hydrogen bonding, as demonstrated by a comparison of II with I and IV with III. Furthermore, it is typically more favorable for a nucleophilic assault to occur at the carbon atom within a carbonyl as opposed to a thioketone, as evidenced by the comparison of I with III as well as II with IV. Therefore, these factors can be utilized to achieve regiospecific stimulation of an identifiable moiety (Breugst et al., 2017) (Figure 3.2).

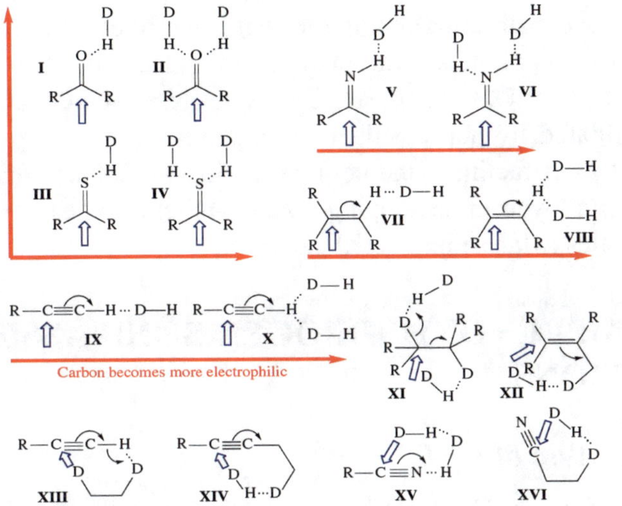

Figure 3.2. Some modes of covalent bond activation by hydrogen bonds.

Source: ACS Publications, Creative Commons License.

Comparable methodologies may be employed for the activating process of a carbon atom within imines (V as well as VI), alkenes (VII as well as VIII), along with alkynes (IX as well as X). An alternative strategy entails the development of adaptable or periodic hydrogen bonding networks in close proximity to the intended covalent bond to facilitate the intended nucleophilic assault (XI–XVI). The proper positioning in space regarding electron-poor atomic carbon is facilitated, thereby enabling a smooth attack through an electron-rich nucleophilic category. The formation of supportive non-covalent bonds can be explained in numerous instances, however, forecasting the impact of activation is frequently challenging. Therefore, it is imperative to allocate additional resources towards the examination and organization of this particular area (Murai, 2003).

The utilization of non-covalent interactions within the method of synthesis is currently a burgeoning field of study that holds promise for various applications, including but not limited to separation methods, catalysis, medicine, as well as biomolecular systems. The majority of the established possibilities for synthesis are associated with the extensively prevalent hydrogen bonds, as evidenced by sources. Various forms of interactions, including O···B, O···Si, O···S, N···B, N···N, N···P, N···S, along with halogen bonding, have evolved from being a mere scientific curiosity to a practical tool for facilitating numerous inorganics as well as organic changes and for constructing supramolecular assemblies. The present chapter furnishes instances of the activation of diverse categories of covalent bonds (namely C—C, C = C, C≡C, C—N, C = N, C≡N, C—O, C = O, C—S, and C = S) facilitated by non-covalent connections. It is anticipated that the present work will facilitate the comprehension of fundamental principles that can be employed in developing novel synthetic routes toward specific target molecules (Maharramov et al., 2016).

3.2. EXAMPLES OF HYDROGEN BOND-ASSISTED ACTIVATIONS

3.2.1. Activation of C—C Bond

The breaking down of C—C bonds via oxidative or hydrolytic means, which involves the integration of oxygen or just water, respectively, is a pivotal process in various biochemical pathways utilized by microorganisms for assimilating xenobiotics and hazardous environmental substances. The reactions in question are of significant interest owing to their diverse range of potential applications, like the generation of fuel via biomass, elimination of organic pollutants, or treatment of medical conditions. In numerous instances, the initiation of a C—C link proximal to a carbonyl functional group is a crucial process in achieving the objective. The catalysis of hydrolase enzymes involved with the hydrolytic breakdown of C—C bonds seem to be a significant process in the microbial breakdown of aromatic substances (Gossage & Van, 2001). The Ser-His-Arg system catalyzes the C-C cleavage in 2-hydroxy-6-keto-6-phenyl-hexa-2,4-dienoic acid through a proposed mechanism (Figure 3.3). The reaction begins with the substrate's keto-enol tautomerization, resulting in the formation of a type of keto intermediate (I). This has been confirmed through stopped-flow kinetics as well as deuterium isotope exchange studies. The process involves the nucleophilic assault for H_2O onto the C6 carbonyl, facilitated by hydrogen bonding. This is subsequently subsequent to a stereotypical C—C fragmentation resulting in the formation of (E/Z)-2-hydroxypenta-2, 4- dienoic as well as benzoic acids (Bohm et al., 2001). Elaborate synthetic structures have been developed to facilitate hydrogen bond-assisted C-C link stimulation in β-diketones, which are crucial precursors for various heterocyclic substances such as pyrazoles and triazoles. The retro-Claisen response, which involves the cleavage for C-C bonds within β-diketones, has garnered attention in various fields such as bioremediation, metabolism for aromatics along with terpenes, as well as preparative biocatalysis. The enzyme known as Acetylacetone dioxygenase (Dke1) carries out the process of oxidative fission that results in the C–C bond through a series of coordinated steps involving the βdiketone molecule as well as an iron (II) center (Xia & Dong, 2020).

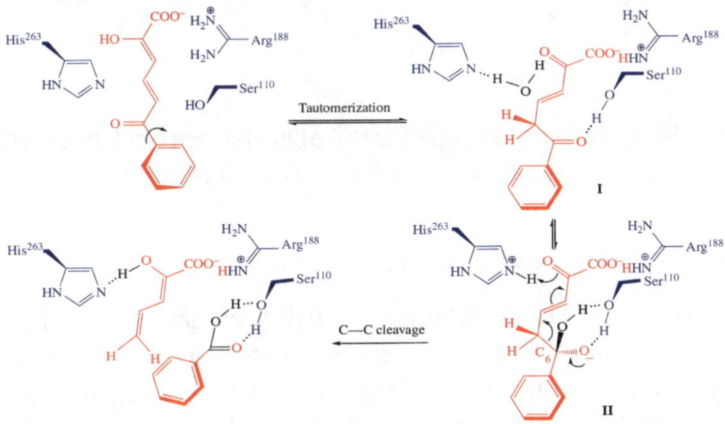

Figure 3.3. C–C cleavage in 2-hydroxy-6-keto-6-phenyl-hexa-2,4-dienoic acid.

Source: Bugg, Creative Commons License.

This process also involves the incorporation of dioxygen with creating a C–O bond, followed by a nucleophilic assault for the peroxidation component upon a carbonyl group, as illustrated in Figure 3.4 a. This information has been documented in previous research. Various retro-Claisen catalytic reactions have been documented, utilizing catalysts including indium, iron, platinum, and copper salts, as well as complexes. The implementation of hydrogen binding as an assisting factor in the cleavage of C–C bonds in β-diketones, devoid of any metallic element, can considerably enhance the environmental viability of the reaction. In order to facilitate targeted nucleophilic assaults on carbonyl groups, a triazine moiety was incorporated into β-diketones, thereby establishing an intramolecular hydrogen-bonding system (as depicted in Figure 3.4b) (Colby et al., 2010).

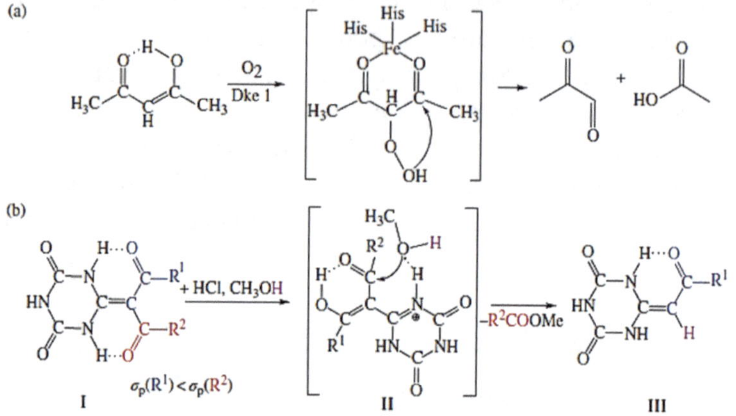

Figure 3.4. Acetylacetone dioxygenase (Dke1)-catalyzed oxidative C—C cleavage in acetylacetone (retro-Claisen reaction) (a); regioselective H-bond-assisted C—C cleavage in β-diketones (b).

Source: C. J. Allpress, Creative Commons License.

The enolic form (II) is obtained through protonation with the triazine derivatives regarding β-diketone (I). The enolic form undergoes a nucleophilic assault by MeOH, facilitated by hydrogen bonding, resulting in the liberation within the R2COOMe ester and the creation of the unsymmetrical ketones product III. The electron donor/acceptor properties of substituents inside the β-diketone component exhibit a narrow range of values, as indicated by Hammett's σp unaltered (-0.13 for C_3H_7, -0.17 for CH3, -0.24 for OC_2H_5, -0.27 for OCH_3, as well as -0.83 for $N(CH_3)_2$). Despite this, the C-C bond selectively cleaves on the side that contains the weakened electron-releasing substitute in every instance studied. This regioselectivity may be enhanced by the development of a hydrogen-bonded system (Wang & Bower, 2018).

In a previous study, an analogous method was employed to achieve regioselective activation through the C—C bond within 4,4,4-trifluoro-1-(thiophen-2-yl)butane-1,3-dione. This involved the incorporation of an arylhydrazone component to facilitate the formation of an intramolecular hydrogen link at a specific location. The C—C cleavage in Figure 3.5 is attributed to the stability for intramolecular hydrogen bonding, resulting in the cleavage occurring at the most electron-accepting portion of the replaced 1,3-dione. The C—C bond cleavages facilitated by hydrogen bonding and resulting in the omission of a group called acetyl are devoid of any catalyst and exhibit favorable progress under standard conditions, thereby diverging from other established reactions of similar nature (Xu et al., 2019).

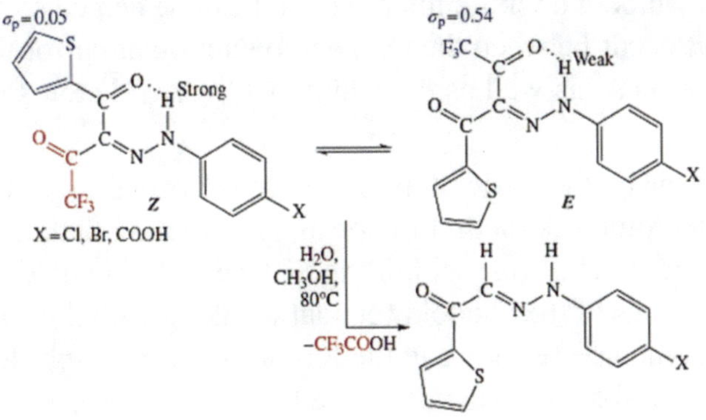

Figure 3.5. Regioselective C—C cleavage in (E, Z)-2-(2-(4-substitutedphenyl) hydrazono)-4,4,4-trifluoro-1-(thiophen-2-yl) butane-1,3-dione.

Source: N. J. Cooper, Creative Commons License.

3.2.2. Activation of C=C Bond

Alkenes are widely used as bases in numerous reactions. The stimulation for the C=C dual bond cost-effectively, particularly with the aid of hydrogen bonding, received significant attention in recent times. The between-molecular Cope-type hydroamination about alkenes, directed by hydrogen bonding provides a means of accessing a range of vicinal diamines that are highly functionalized while maintaining atom economy. The formation of between-molecular hydrogen bonding within this instance results in the accumulation of charged particles at the nitrogen atoms of intermediate I. The synthesis of vicinal diamines II, as observed, is believed to stem from the synergistic interplay between the H-bonding influence and the inclination of Cope-type hydroamination to prefer Markovnikov addition items (Shaw & Bower, 2016).

The Michael addition, a well-established method in organic synthesis, involves the addition of a nucleophile into an electron-deficient olefin, resulting in the formation of C-C or C-heteroatom bonds. The catalysis of a Michael addition reaction between diethyl malonate and chalcones alongside a high degree of enantioselectivity is achieved through bifunctional tertiary amine-thioureas for cinchona origin (Jun, 2004). The introduction of a hydroxyl group to the catalyst results in the formation of several hydrogen bonds, which greatly improves the catalytic performance as well as the stability of the anticipated transition state. This, in turn, leads to elevated levels of enantioselectivity along with activity. The activation of the carbonyl compound within intermediate I can be helped by the bonds of hydrogen that occur between the oxygen-containing atom for the carbonyl, the thiamine moiety, as well as the additional hydroxyl atoms in A (Segura et al., 2007).

Simultaneously, the basic atomic nitrogen that makes up the cinchona component deprotonates diethyl malonate. The diethyl malonate is able to target the triggered chalcone within the Si-face (intermediate I) due to the chiral surroundings of the alkaloid foundation along with the corresponding amino alcohol moiety, resulting in the formation of the R-product. When B acts as a catalyst for the chalcone as well as diethyl malonate connection, it results in the formation of intermediate II as well as a preference for a Re-face approach (Li et al., 2007). This ultimately leads to the production of the S-configured item. Cyclopropanes exhibit favorable characteristics as substrates over synthetic purposes, owing to the electrical effects of substitutes that facilitate their selective activation. This property enables the generation of a diverse range of products that have several stereocenters, rendering them highly versatile in synthetic applications (Hu et al., 2022) (Figure 3.6).

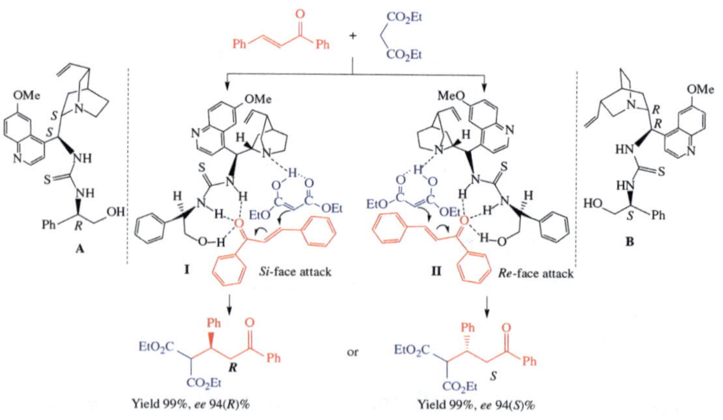

Figure 3.6. Asymmetric Michael reaction between chalcone and diethyl malonate.

Source: X. Wang, Creative Commons License.

Various synthetic techniques have been devised to produce unsymmetrical vinyl cyclopropanes. One such method involves the activating of C=C in methyl cinnamate through hydrogen bonding. The initial ylide exhibits two distinct conformations, wherein the vinyl group is either in a syn orientation (as observed in I as well as IV, as well as V and VIII) or just an anti-orientation (as seen in II and III, as well as VI and VII) with respect toward the sulfur isolated pair. Therefore, it is theoretically possible to form eight intermediaries assisted by hydrogen bonds for each ylide (Baratta et al., 2007). The model that has been proposed, which involves the creation of a hydrogen-bonded ring consisting of 10 members, offers a rationale for the divergent enantioselectivities observed during the cyclopropanetrione responses of exo as well as endo sulfur ylides. Intermediaries II, IV, V, along with VII undergo distortion as a result of the ring limitation as well as steric hindrances posed by the norbornyl group's CH–O and CH–S (Seiser & Cramer, 2008). The hydroxyl group is of utmost importance in regulating enantioselectivity (98 or just 99%) as well as diastereoselective (99/1) because of the oriented nature of hydrogen bonds. The involvement of the solvents in non-covalent associations with intermediates may contribute to the improvement of both diastereo- as well as enantioselectivity, thereby underscoring the significance of the solvents in this context (Winter & Krause, 2009).

3.2.3. Activation of C≡C Bond

Alkynes exhibit both nucleophilic and electrophilic characteristics, thereby enabling their participation in a broad spectrum of chemical reactions. As an illustration, the direct formation of diverse carbocyclic compounds through intermolecular cycloadditions with alkynes typically requires the use of catalysts containing metals. Conversely, a plethora of substrates engaged in responses with alkynes are able to be activated through the utilization of amines or just ammonium salts when combined with inorganic bases, wherein non-covalent bonds assume a significant role. The stimulation for the C≡C triple bonds within acetylenic β-diketones through hydrogen bonding can result in enantioselective carbocyclization, specifically the Conia-ene response. (Ravelli et al., 2016).

This chemical reaction is considered to be among the most straightforward methods for synthesizing carbocycles, while particularly appealing for the production of cyclopentane derivatives. The catalyst 3,5-bis(pentafluorosulfanyl)phenylboronic acids, which acts as a hydrogen-bond acceptor, exhibits greater efficacy in nonpolar solutions, like toluene as well as 1,1,1,3,3-pentafluorobutane, when compared to 3-nitro phenylboronic acids. This suggests that the SF_5 moiety can serve as a lipophilic and sterically demanding substitute for the NO_2 collection within the design of catalysts. The possible mechanism of this reaction involves

H-bond-assisted enolization of starting 2-alkynic β-diketones; a subsequent concerted ene reaction of the enol form affords the product (Titov et al., 2019).

The enantioselective isomeric formation of 3-alkynoates to harmonic allenoates facilitated by benzothiadiazine-1,1-dioxide-type enzymes through H-bond assistance, holds significant significance in the formation of numerous biologically active substances. The isomeric formation of alkynoates into allenoates alongside an elevated enantioselectivity can be facilitated through the utilization for the Brønsted base-catalyzed 1,3-proton shifts, as reported in reference. The reaction's enantioselectivity is capable of being rationalized through the Hbond-assisted decay that releases the alkynoate agonists present in intermediaries A and B, thereby facilitating their interconversion (Tobisu & Chatani, 2008).

The intermediary C, which is the E-enol derivative of A, exhibits no isomeric formation into (R)-allenoate D due to the inaccessibility of the γ-sp-carbon for the alkynoate to the ammonium proton. On the other hand, the isomeric transformation of B into (S)-allenoate F proceeds effortlessly through the aid of a hydrogen bond-assisted intermediary Z-enol E, leading to the formation of intermediary F as well as ultimately the desired allene. (Jun et al., 2001).

3.2.4. Activation of C—N Bond

Various catalysts have been employed to initiate the C—N bond within amines as well as associated compounds. In numerous instances, the activation mechanisms involve an intermediary using hydrogen bonding. The hydrolysis of polypeptides catalyzed through aspartic proteases, which is most likely to occur through a mechanism that involves hydrogen bonding assistance. As per the proposed mechanism, the enzyme experiences protonation for a single aspartate residue, whereas the other residue undergoes ionization. Experimental evidence exists to support the notion that both aspartates possess a single proton under physiological pH conditions (Nakao, 2014). The activation of the water molecule is facilitated by the abstraction of a proton by a single aspartate. This activation allows for the water molecule to initiate an attack upon the carbonyl carbon that forms the substrate scissile bond, resulting in the formation of a tetrahedral zwitterionic intermediate. The rearranging within this intermediate ultimately leads towards the protonation process of the scissile amide. The protein's scissile peptide bonds are believed to be twisted out of planarity, making it easier to cleave, by an extra water molecule that links the substrate along with the primary chain of amides segments of the enzyme through hydrogen bonding (Nakao, 2020).

Did You Know?

The activation of C—N bonds through non-covalent interactions has shown promising results in catalytic processes.

The hydrolysis for carboxamides towards the formation of carboxylic acids has become an additional illustration of the stimulation of a C—N link through hydrogen bonding. Typically, the conversion of a nitrile into a carboxylic acid via one-step hydrolysis involves the creation of an amide that acts as an intermediary and necessitates the use of severe acidic or basic reactions (Watson & Jacobsen, 2008). Nonetheless, a catalytic triad composed of Glu, Lys, as well as Cys can serve as an organic catalyst over the hydrolysis of the C≡N link as well as resulting cleavage about the C—N bond within nitriles. According to the suggested mechanism, the catalyst's retained cysteine residue initiates a nucleophilic assault upon the nitrile carbon atom. This results in the formation of a thioimidate, which subsequently leads to the formation of a tetrahedral intermediary through the inclusion of water via the assistance of an H-bond. The intermediaries involved in this process are denoted as I, II, and III. Within the context of the third stage, it has been observed that glutamate functions as a base, whereas the lysine residue plays a crucial role in stabilizing a tetrahedral change state. The formation of H-bonding intermediate IV is facilitated by the inclusion of a water molecule. The removal of NH_3 from the aforementioned intermediate results in the formation of thioester V. Subsequently, the thioester V interacts with an additional molecule made up of water to yield carboxylic acid (Ping et al., 2016).

3.2.5. Activation of C=N Bond

Numerous chemical compounds, including cucurbituril, ox aziridines, visually active amines having a stereo genic core, etc., can be made easily and by a variety of different pathways by activating the C-N dual bonds with imines. The creation of novel techniques to enable the stereoselective synthesis of nitrogen-bonded center molecules has received a lot of interest recently, with reactions involving additions to C-N functionalities receiving the most in-depth study (Padwa, 1977). For example, in enantio- as well as diastereoselective Manniche responses involving chiral Ni(II) complexes of glycine as well as amino sulfones like tert-butyl(phenyl(phenylsulfonyl) methyl)carbamate, the formation of a carbon-carbon bond as well as two stereo genic centers are promoted by the H-bond within just one run. This approach is appealing for the manufacturing of pharmaceutical & peptide/ peptidomimetic chemical science, as well as adaptable chiral auxiliaries along with ligands for asymmetrical synthesis. Three phases make up the suggested mechanism (Zhang et al., 2018).

Ni(II) enolate reacts with tert-butyl(phenyl(phenylsulfonyl) methyl) carbamate to produce the syn as well as anti-Di stereoisomers regarding compound B, along with (iii) releases diamino acids as a HCL adduct as well as $NiCl_2$ following the intramolecular hydrogen bond-aided recovery to generate the agonist precursor (Enders & Reinhold, 1997).

Among the quickest and easiest methods to make chiral amines, as well as their derivatives, is through the enantioselective hydrolysis of imines. Therefore, the hydrogen bond-directed diastereoselective elimination of enantiopure N-tert-butanesulfinylketimines required for the asymmetrical formation of nonracemic 1,3-diamines requires solvent-dependent E/Z isomeric formation of N-tert-butanesulfinylketimines. The association of a cyclical transition phase stabilized by a hydrogen bond is suggested by the association between the face selectivity of reduced and E / Z geometries of the initial ketoimines. In order to regulate the geometries of N-tert-butanesulfinylketimines, an ortho-substituent engages in bonding with hydrogen. E-imines are decreased to produce the R arrangement at the newly generated chiral center, while the Z-isomer provides the S arrangement (Padwa et al., 1973).

Another practical method for activating C-N bonds is the aza-Henry response, which involves the nucleophilic incorporation of nitroalkanes into amines to produce nitroimine derivatives. To achieve better din stereo- & enantioselectivities—which are frequently primarily controlled by H-bonding—many organ catalysts are used (Belzner et al., 1996). Thus, during the asymmetrical azaHenry response of ketoimines produced by I satins alongside nitroalkanes utilizing cinchona alkaline substances to be organic catalysts, the third amine grouping of the catalyst decays the α-proton about nitroethane, triggering it for a nucleophilic assault onto the Re-face for ketoimines, that, in their consequences, become active via hydrogen bonds by the —OH grouping of the catalyst, offering the (R)-enantiomer regarding the outcome. A dual-functional alkaloid organ catalyst was used in this reaction to activate nitroalkanes as well as ketoimines in a synergistic manner, yielding high diastereomer- as well as enantioselectivities (Jutzi et al., 1996).

3.2.6. Activation of C≡N Bond

Among the most important reactions within organic compound synthesis involves electrophilic or nucleophilic reactions involving organ nitriles. The C-N bond can be activated via a variety of techniques, such as the employment of an electron-withdrawing R group within R-C-N nitrile molecules, protonation, or the alkylation process for the nitrile N atoms, or coordinating to an inner metal (Tamaru & Kimura, 1997). For instance, the costly nature of the catalysts, challenges separating the catalyst from the product, managing air-sensitive metallic catalysts within an inert environment, etc. As a result, there is increased interest in triggering the C-N bonds with the help of non-covalent relationships. An arylhydrazone component was inserted into malononitrile to produce a supportive hydrogen bond system to facilitate regioselective stimulation of C-N bonds (Takaya et al., 1998). The resulting compound possesses six-membered cycles with hydrogen bonds (A); the inclusion of a nucleotide (Nu1) results in the stabilization of the compound's output by a second hydrogen linking system (B), effectively "freezing" the result of a single attack. The inclusion of acid causes the amino group's nitrogenous atom to protonate, encouraging the creation of an additional hydrogen bond that facilitates the nucleophilic assault by the additional nucleophile (Nu2). This product can only be acidified before the nucleophilic assault on the extra C-N group is conceivable. Two further six- & five-membered H-bond rounds (C and D) help to stabilize this product. As a result, it is possible to execute practical regioselective metal-free synthesis of many different compounds (Oinuma et al., 2003).

Tetrazoles, which are frequently used as catalysts, firearms, and ligands within coordination chemistry, also nonclassical isosteres for carboxylic acids within medical science, is another instance of a C-N bond that has been activated by a hydrogen bond. The traditional cycloaddition in azides plus nitriles is a highly direct approach for synthesizing tetrazoles because of its wide range of applications. As a result, under specific circumstances, the reaction of azide-based salts together with nitrile provides large yields for the matching tetrazoles (Lausarot et al., 1984). Mechanistic investigations back the production of an intermediary that is helped form by an H-bond. When R = Me, the intermediary is 3.3 kcal/mol less resilient than the free-reacting substances HN_3 plus MeCN; however, where R = $CH_3S(O)_2$, it exhibits 11.4

kcal/mol lesser energy over the free-reacting substances. This indicates that the stability associated with the intermediates improves by enhancing the electron-withdrawing capacity of the alternative compared to nitrile. Nitrile is activated via a proton within the phase of transition, enabling azide to penetrate the carbon for nitrile and subsequently undergo a 1,5-cyclization to produce tetrazole (Singh et al., 2021).

Nitrile oxide reacts with aliphatic or electron-rich aromatic nitriles to form 3,4-functionalized 1,2,4-oxadiazoles, which occurs under mild circumstances regardless of lacking Lewis's acids. The 1,2,4-oxadiazoles that have been functionalized have drawn a lot of interest due to their biological functions and potential for treating diabetes. The carbamoyl compound can also introduce additional functional groups by acting as a precursor. The carbamoyl collection of nitrile oxides is thought to stimulate the diplographic nitrile via hydrogen bonding, according to scientific investigations that support the opposite hypothesis of electron-demanding 1,3-dipolar cyclic addition (Nomura et al., 2013). As a result, the carbamoyl ring of nitrile oxides is crucial in forming a hydrogen bond when combined with dipolarophilic nitrile as well as acting as a group that withdraws electrons and an H donor. Two intermediary molecules, where only the carbamoyl collective's orientation varies, were taken into consideration so as to examine the impact of the bond formed by hydrogen Since the intermediate produced by a hydrogen connection that links the carbamoyl arrangement of nitrile oxide appears more stable compared to its unaided one in 4.4 kcal/mol, an alternative electron-demanding cyclic addition is made possible (Konishi et al., 2014).

3.3. ACTIVATION OF C—O BOND

The equimolar blend of α-hydroxy amides I as well as II was obtained through an interaction between rac-(1-naphthyl) (trifluoromethyl) O-carboxy-anhydride as well as (R)-α-methyl benzylamine, which was driven by hydrogen bonding. The identified compounds exhibited high ΔδRS data in their 1H NMR spectrum, attributed to resilient intramolecular hydrogen bonds. This phenomenon has been linked to a significant inclination of the related α-hydroxyamide towards the eclipsed conformation. The aforementioned phenomenon can be elucidated by optimizing the anisotropic impact of the naphthyl moiety. The present study demonstrates that the staggered configurations found in O-methylated amides can be seen for comparison, thereby providing evidence for the significant contribution of intramolecular hydrogen bonds in optimizing the anisotropic impact. The O-carboxy-anhydride exhibits potential as a chiral deriving agent. At the same time, it is likely that modifications to the replacement pattern will lead to enhanced reactivity as well as resolution efficiency (Lou et al., 2021).

Thehydrolysisforesterstoacidsalongwithalcoholscanbecatalyzedthrough the ionic fluid choline hexanoate, $[(CH_3)_3NCH_2CH_2OH]+[C_5H_{11}COO]^-$, through the assistance of hydrogen bond-mediated C—O bond stimulation, as demonstrated in a previous study (Yamamoto, 1992).

The reaction system comprises two distinct steps.

- The nucleophilic assault of water for the carbon (intermediate I) is facilitated by the hydrogen link between the hydroxyl moiety within the choline cation and the oxygen-containing atom for the carbonyl section of the lipid ester. Consequently, the water molecule undergoes protonation, leading to the transfer of a proton into the $C_5H_{11}COO^-$ anion, which forms an intermediate species denoted as II.
- The formation of a six-membered hydrogen bond system through intramolecular proton transfer results in the weakening of the C-O bond within intermediate III. Ultimately, the acid, along with alcohol-based compounds, are generated, alongside the regeneration of the ionic liquid, thereby completing the catalytic cycle facilitated by hydrogen bonding (Zhao et al., 2018).

3.3.1. Activation of C=O Bond (Figure 3.7)

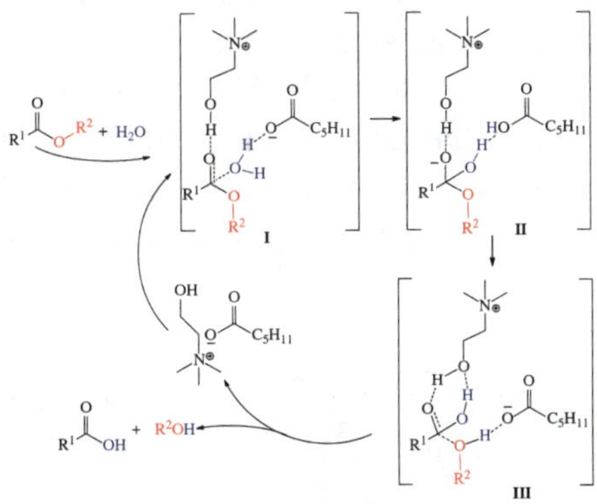

Figure 3.7. Hydrogen bonding in hydrolysis of ethers.

Source: R. Chinchilla, Creative Commons License.

The stimulation of the C=O dual bonds present in carbonyl substances is a crucial strategy employed in the production of numerous building blocks, including but not limited to β-hydroxy carbonyl substances (via Aldol reaction), β-nitro alcohols (via Henry or just nitro-aldol response), thioacetals, hemiacetals, hemiketals, cyanohydrins, among others. Several methodologies, such as metal-mediated methods, were established to facilitate the stimulation of C=O bonds. Additionally, the feasibility of non-covalent relationships in aldol as well as associated reactions was demonstrated. In such instances, the C=O link of a carbonyl substance is weakened by non-covalent interactions, specifically through hydrogen bonds alongside the oxygen atom's isolated pair, rendering it more vulnerable to nucleophilic damage. The utilization of a potent protic acid (a proton donor) in conjunction with a carbonyl substance along with a nucleophile may promote a diverse range of carbonyl chemistry reactions. This phenomenon is not unexpected. An instance can be observed in the creation of β-nitro alcohols through the reaction between carbonyl substances along with nitroalkanes (Lu & Shi, 2008). The uneven aldol reaction pertains to the stimulation of the C=O bond alongside facilitates the synthesis of diverse pharmacologically significant compounds, particularly those containing polyoxygenated substructures. The enamine intermediary is believed to be involved in the proline-catalyzed uneven aldol response. The nucleophilic reaction for the amino groups of pyro line upon the C=O carbon can be assisted by intermolecular hydrogen bonding, leading to the creation of pyrrolidine carboxylate as well as concomitant removal of a water-based molecule. Consequently, proline exhibits a bifunctional behavior by serving as an additional amine to create a crucial nucleophilic enamine intermediary for the synthesis of acetone, along with a carboxylic acid group that stimulates the aldehyde over the nucleophilic assault against the enamine. The relationship between the enantioselectivity for the reaction and the durability of H-bond-assisted intermediary substances, which ultimately result in the predominant product, is able to be established (Li et al., 2019).

Remember

Understanding the factors that influence the activation of C=O bonds is crucial for developing efficient synthetic methodologies.

Despite being weaker than conventional hydrogen bonds, C–H···O/N connections offer sufficient stabilization to exert selectivity control. The significance of C–H···O relationships in regulating the stereo selection associated with Hajos–Parrish-type aldol as well as Mannich responses, was also observed. The study demonstrated that the intramolecular Hajos-Parrish change in 2-methyl-2-(3-oxo butyl) cyclopentane-1,3-dione could be helped by C–H···O relationships. This reaction was catalyzed through proline (Wismeijer et al., 1985).

The high stereoselectivity observed in the experiment can be attributed to two factors. Firstly, the (R, R) syn-enamine experiences bigger iminium straightness distortion contrasted to the (S, S) anti-enamines due to the presence of only one hydrogen bond. Secondly, the prolinyl C(sp^3)-H group is capable of stabilizing the negative charge within the carbonyl oxygen, resulting in the significant (S, S) item showing a shorter C-H···O interacting and less energy (3.4 kcal/mol) versus the minor (R, R) item, when this relationship appears more detached as well as presumably weaker.

The compound known as quinone mono acetals has become notable for containing both α, and β-unsaturated carbonyl as well as allyl acetal functionalities within a single molecular structure. This feature renders it a versatile compound with numerous applications in organic changes, serving to be both an intermediary and a crucial building block within the production of various natural products. Various nucleophilic attacking reactions can occur on quinone monoacetate carbons, such as addition from the carbonyl element (known as 1,2-additions), linked addition to the enone component (referred to as 1,4-additions), and cyclizations that involve these processes. In the context of chemo- as well as regioselective responses, a multitude of inorganic as well as organic catalysts have been employed that rely on cooperative mechanisms such as non-covalent interactions as well as coordination, as reported in the literature.

The [3+2] connection of quinone acetal with various alkene nucleophiles is executed through a technique that involves the activation of a Brønsted acid onto a hydrogen link to the donor solution, hexafluoroisopropanol. The aforementioned polar solvent exhibits a notable capacity for donating hydrogen bonds while not demonstrating a propensity for accepting such bonds. The formation of a hydrogen-bonded intermediate facilitates the cyclic transformation for the carbonyl group within the keto tautomer. This process is followed by aromatization, which serves as an extra operating force, resulting in the production of the official [3+2] coupling item (Wismeijer et al., 1985).

3.3.2. Activation of C—S Bond

The modifications of thiol (R—SH) or just thioether (R—S—R′) moieties as well as their derivatives have been pivotal stages in numerous enzyme reactions along with metabolic pathways. Coenzyme A (HSCoA) serves as a co-catalyst over the enzymatic activation of various substrates within organisms. One such example seems the transformation of (S)-citryl-SCoA into citrate within the Krebs process. The aforementioned reaction is initiated through the process of H-bond-assisted nucleophilic approach, whereby either an enolate or just thioester molecule reacts with the α-carbon for citrylate.

The process of hydrolyzing the thioester, specifically citryl-SCoA, that is produced during aldol condensation, results in a noteworthy decrease in free energy ($\Delta G^{\circ\prime} = -31.5$ kJ/mol or just -7.5 kcal/mol). This decrease in free energy serves as the driving force for the overall reaction to proceed (Manriquez et al., 1978).

3.3.3. Activation of C=S Bond

The stereotypical nucleophilic assault upon the carbon atom for C=S is a straightforward and adaptable method for generating stereocenters adjacent to heteroatoms, resulting in a complete inversion for stereochemistry. The stereochemistry for thioketones or just thioaldehydes is often governed by intermolecular as well as intramolecular bonding of hydrogen, which also exert an impact on their reactivity as well as other characteristics. Thioketones exhibit a comparatively elongated C=S bond in comparison to the C=O bond within ketones, with the length of the former being contingent upon the nature of the substituents. In accordance with, the sulfur atom exhibits a lower affinity for accepting hydrogen bonds from oxygen compared to hydrogen, resulting in a preference for between molecules O—H···S hydrogen bonds over S—H···O connection. The responsiveness of 4-thioxopentan-2-one can be seen through a particular response, whereby solely the regioselective thicket change is observed in its condensing with phenylhydrazine (Murahashi et al., 2008).

3.4. HALOGEN BOND-ASSISTED ACTIVATIONS

Halogen bonding pertains to the non-covalent relationships between the final halogen atoms present in substances of the R—X type, where X represents Cl, Br, or I, as well as Lewis bases. This has been extensively studied and documented in literature sources. The polyfluorinated alkyl or just phenyl substituents result in the formation of stronger halogen connections due to the high electronegativity of R. . Several primary differences between halogen and hydrogen bondings can be mentioned [54]:

- Halogen bonds tend to be more directional than (single) hydrogen bonds;
- The strength of a halogen bonding can be easily tuned, while in the case of a hydrogen bond, considerable changes are required into the residue the donor site is bound to.
- Halogen bonds exhibit hydrophobic characteristics, while hydrogen bonds display hydrophilic properties.
- The atomic size of the halogen link donor is considerably greater than that of hydrogen. Halogen bonding has been applied in various fields, including crystal construction and engineering, recognition of molecules, synthesizing, catalysis, molecules conductors, fluid crystals, as well as bioorganic chemistry, as reported in literature sources. The prominence of halogen connection in the creation of organic compounds is increasingly recognized (Ranu & Samanta, 2003).

The utilization of the fluoronium cation F^+ obtained from an N-fluoroheterocyclic salt serves as a practical and efficient catalyst in facilitating the interaction between N-substituted imines as well as ethyl diazoacetate, ultimately resulting in the production of N-substituted aziridines. The pronounced electrophilicity exhibited by the fluoride cation facilitates the facile activation of imines, thereby enabling the ensuing nucleophilic assault by ethyl diazoacetate. The utilization of N···X halogen connection, where X represents either Br or I, has the potential to activate C=N bonds via haloalkanes, thereby facilitating electrophilic hydride improvements. The reduction of 2-phenyl quinoline was carried out utilizing a Hantzsch ester (diethyl 2,6-dimethyl-1,4-dihydropyridine-3,5-dicarboxylate) as a reducing agent. In the lack of a haloalkane, no discernible reaction was observed. However, when 10 mol% of perfluoroiodooctane, $CF_3(CF_2)7I$, was present, yields as high as 98% were attained. The 1H NMR spectrum did not exhibit any signal shifts, whereas the 13C NMR spectra displayed a different behavior, with the quinoline commands being marginally shifted towards the lower field by a range of 0.01–0.06 ppm. The observed phenomenon suggests a feeble connection between the nitrogen within quinoline as well as the iodide within the perfluoro substance. This is corroborated by the

19F NMR spectra, where the resonance signal associated with the CF_2I moiety was detected at a less powerful field strength ($\Delta\delta = 0.1$ ppm). It is noteworthy that all chemical changes are highly contingent on concentration (Zugic et al., 2014).

The results acquired can be attributed to the resilient halogen bonds formed between sp^2-type nitrogenous atoms and fluorinated iodoalkanes, including $CF_3(CF_2)7I$ or $CF_3(CF_2)7Br$. The electrophilic nature of halogen atoms within halogen attachment is typically noteworthy when they are attached to a potent electron-withdrawing moiety, including fluorocarbon chains, as exemplified by $CF_3(CF_2)_7I$. The exceptional halogen-bonding capacity exhibited by perfluoroalkyl halides may as a substitute for interconnected perfluorinated ponytails in the transportation of hydrocarbon-reacting substances from an organic stage, as reported in reference. The halogen-bonded expansion formed by the combination of 1,4-diazabicyclo[2.2.2]octane (DABCO) along with 2 molecules for perfluorooctyl iodide ($DABCO{\cdot}(C_8F_{17}I)_2$) has been used as a supramolecular fluorous organocatalyst that can be recycled for the incorporation of aromatic solvents to methyl acrylate, specifically in the Morita-Baylis-Hillman response. The formation of the additive $DABCO{\cdot}(C_8F_{17}I)_2$ was achieved via halogen bonding. Following the catalytic reaction, the adduct $DABCO{\cdot}(C_8F_{17}I)_2$ can be readily retrieved through filtration (Islam et al., 2015).

The C—Br link of benzhydryl bromide can be activated during its interaction with deuterated acetonitrile by a catalyst that includes halogen, as demonstrated in Diagram 1.29. N-benzhydryl acetamide was obtained in a satisfactory yield through the hydrolysis involving the nitrilium intermediary, facilitated by small amounts of water. Within the absence of the catalysts or despite the inclusion of its hydrogen analog, the resultant yield decreases to below 5%. Therefore, it can be concluded that the halogen-bonding booster effectively enhances the rate of this chemical reaction, alongside the highest level of stimulation being observed when the BF_4^- anion is present (yielding a 97% product yield). In contrast, the use of CF_3SO_3H resulted in a significantly lower product yield of only 25% (Feng et al., 2020).

3.5. OTHER TYPES OF NON-COVALENT INTERACTIONS AND PERSPECTIVES

In addition to covalent interactions, various non-covalent relationships, including S···O, S···N, P···P, P···N, B···N, as well as B···O, play a crucial role within molecular recognition, the biology of certain compounds, along with supervision for contributing functions. It has been proposed that S···O interactions have a significant impact on the production of chiral sulfoxides through the Pummerer reaction. The generation of an intermediate I is hypothesized to occur through the interactions of acetic anhydride into trimethylsilyl triflate within amide (or lactam). Simultaneously, a chiral sulfoxide interacts with an amide (or lactam), resulting in the formation of intermediaries II as well as III, which exhibit inter- as well as intramolecular S···O relationships. The comparative stability of structure II over III can be attributed to the steric repellent that arises from the interaction between aryl groups as well as the carbonyl group within III. Following this, the sulfonyl oxygen atoms of compound II undergo acetylation through acetic anhydride within the presence of the reactant species I, resulting in the formation of a chiral sulfurane-type intermediary IV. The removal of the methylene α-hydrogen atoms by $CF_3S(=O)_2O-$ via IV results in the formation of a firm ylide intermediary V, which is stabilized by both inter- as well as between molecules S···O relationships. The process of stereoselective 1,2-acetoxy transmission within V is believed to occur through three possible modes: familiar ion pair, sliding, as well as cyclic. The end result of this process is the production of the envisioned chiral Pummerer substance (De Sousa et al., 2016).

Numerous organic sulfur compounds, including acetazolamide, thiadiazolines, leinamycin, cyclic sulfilimine, as well as 1,3-dithiole, exhibit intramolecular nonconventional S···X (X = O or S) relationships that play a significant role in regulating their structural characteristics and chemical behavior. The study conducted by researchers demonstrated the involvement of intramolecular S···O interactions in regulating the regiochemistry associated with the 4-oxothiazolidine → 1,2-dithiole- 3-ylidene thione modification, as evidenced by previous findings. The utilization of Lawesson's substance during the ring-opening/ring-closing process of specific 4-oxo thiazolidine aminoketone results in the generation of modified 1,2-dithiole-3-ylidene thiones. The process is instigated by the oriented non-covalent interaction of the 1,5-type S···O within the 4-oxothiazolidines. The S···S distances observed in 1,2-dithiole-3-ylidene thiones are 2.3374 and 2.3408Å (Matsuzawa et al., 2016).

These distances have been smaller than the aggregate of van der Waals radius but longer than typical S—S covalent bonds (2.08 Å). Furthermore, the two integrated rings exhibit a difference in length, as evidenced by the isomeric formation of 1,2-dithiole-3-ylidene thiones. The pnicogen bond, which involves Lewis base as well as group 15 components (N, P, or As), has garnered significant attention as a type of non-covalent connection. In contrast to the hydrogen relationship, yet bearing a resemblance to halogen as well as chalcogen links, a pnicogen link is established through the movement of electrons carried by Lewis base D into the pnicogen atom A. The latter serves as a Lewis acid alongside exhibits a marked degree of the phenomenon. A is attached to H atoms that do not interact directly with D, while X represents substitution group(s). As per the literature, interactions such as B···N, P···N, As···N, S···N, as well as P···P have been acknowledged; however, their potential applications in formation are yet to be explored (Fourmigue & Batail, 2004).

3.6. NEW INSIGHTS INTO THE ACTIVATION OF COVALENT BONDS THROUGH NON-COVALENT INTERACTIONS

The latest developments in covalent bond stimulation have revealed the significant function of non-covalent relationships in promoting and intensifying bond cleavage mechanisms. The nascent field of inquiry has revealed novel perspectives on the interrelationship between non-covalent relationships, including hydrogen bonding along with halogen connection and the stimulation of covalent connections. By utilizing both experimental as well as computational methodologies, researchers have achieved notable advancements and revelations in their understanding of the fundamental mechanisms and motivating factors governing such relationships. The previously mentioned results have facilitated the emergence of innovative techniques, systems, and tactics for the activation of bonds, resulting in promising opportunities in the fields of catalysis, chemical engineering, as well as materials science. Additionally, the investigation of present obstacles, unresolved inquiries, and prospective utilities has broadened our comprehension of the consequences and forthcoming pathways of covalent bond stimulation via non-covalent relationships (Chen et al., 2009).

3.6.1. Recent Breakthroughs and Discoveries in the Field

The domain of non-covalent relationships within covalent bond stimulation has experienced noteworthy advancements and intriguing revelations in recent times. Scholars from diverse fields, such as organic synthesis, catalysis, as well as materials science, have achieved significant progress in comprehending the complexities of these relationships and their possible practical uses. This section elucidates significant recent progressions that have redefined our comprehension of covalent bond stimulation and have paved the way for novel avenues of investigation (Pastorczak & Corminboeuf, 2017).

A significant advancement pertains to the creation of novel approaches that utilize hydrogen bonds as a potent mechanism for bond stimulation. Hydrogen connection, which has long been acknowledged for its function in stabilizing molecules, has recently been identified as a multifaceted force in the disruption of covalent bonds. The ability to facilitate bond stimulation throughout different chemical changes has been effectively demonstrated by researchers. Research has indicated that the stimulation of C-H bonds can be facilitated through hydrogen bonding, leading to selective functioning and the ability to attain intricate molecular structures. In addition, progressions in the field of supramolecular science have facilitated the creation of customized host-guest systems that utilize hydrogen bonding to augment both reactivity as well as selectivity within bond activation mechanisms (Haque et al., 2023).

An additional noteworthy finding pertains to the utilization of halogen connection as a catalyst for the initiation of covalent bonding stimulation. Halogen bonding, a type of non-covalent interaction that involves halogen atoms acting as electron acceptors, has been observed to have a significant impact on bond breaking and activation. Through the strategic integration of halogen atoms toward molecular configurations, scholars have attained exceptional regulation over bond activation mechanisms. Halogen bonding is being utilized to aid in the activation of unreactive bonds, specifically C-F as well as C-Cl bonds, during complex synthetic reactions. The discovery above not only broadens the range of bond stimulation chemistry, but also presents novel opportunities for the development of practical materials as well as catalysts (DiLabio & Otero, 2016).

Apart from hydrogen along with halogen bonding, contemporary research has illuminated the participation of additional non-covalent connections, including π-π stacking as well as electrostatic forces, in the activating process of covalent bonds. The impact of these connections, which were once deemed subordinate to covalent bonds, upon the selectivity as well as the reactivity of bond stimulation processes has been discovered to be substantial. Through comprehension and utilization of the distinctive characteristics of these connections, scholars have devised innovative approaches for bond stimulation and attained unparalleled degrees of regulation in chemical conversions (Lohofener et al.,2015).

The discipline of covalent bond stimulation has undergone a significant transformation due to the progress made in computational science as well as machine learning. By utilizing advanced computational models as well as algorithms, scholars have acquired significant knowledge regarding the fundamental mechanisms for non-covalent connections and their influence on bond activation. The utilization of computational techniques has been implemented in order to forecast and enhance the results of bond stimulation reactions, thereby enabling the development of catalysts along with reaction conditions that are more effective. Machine learning methods have facilitated the investigation of extensive chemical spaces, expediting the identification of novel non-covalent interaction patterns and their prospective utilization in bond stimulation chemistry (Ahren, 2015).

The latest advancements and revelations in the domain of non-covalent connections over covalent bond stimulation have merely broadened our fundamental comprehension but also presented promising possibilities for pragmatic implementations. The advancement of bond activation techniques that are both selective as well as effective presents a significant potential for the production of intricate molecules, medications, as well as functional materials. In addition, the capacity to regulate bond activation via non-covalent connections presents prospects for devising catalysts with heightened activity and selectivity. Furthermore, the knowledge acquired through the examination of non-covalent connections is able to be utilized to fabricate intelligent materials, sensors, as well as apparatuses possessing customized characteristics (Mészáros et al., 2023).

3.6.2. Novel Approaches and Methodologies for Bond Activation

Scholars have been investigating innovative methods and techniques that utilize non-covalent relationships to activate covalent bonds. The implementation of novel tactics has demonstrated significant promise in disrupting and altering covalent bonds, thereby creating fresh opportunities for catalytic processes, synthesis, as well as the development of materials. The utilization of distinctive attributes of non-covalent relationships is transforming the comprehension of bond activation as well as broadening the range of techniques accessible for chemical conversions, as per the research conducted by scientists. This section explores the most auspicious and captivating developments in this domain (Tweedell & Kanneganti, 2020).

The incorporation of supramolecular chemical principles through bond stimulation processes represents a viable strategy. Supramolecular conversations are governed by non-covalent forces, including hydrogen bonds, π-π stacking, as well as metal-ligand coordination, which provide a flexible framework for regulating and guiding chemical reactions. Through the utilization of host-guest systems or self-assembled structures, researchers are able to accurately place reactants and catalysts in order to facilitate the activation of chemical bonds. The methodology above has been efficaciously implemented in a wide range of fields, encompassing the selective functionalization of intricate molecules, uneven catalysis, as well as changing covalent chemistry (Mack & Northcott, 2017).

An additional inventive approach entails the utilization of templating effects for the purpose of stimulating bond activation. The utilization of templating involves the exploitation of non-covalent relationships between an initial molecule as well as a reactant, which serves to pre-organize the sites that react as well as subsequently enhance the reactivity. Through the strategic design of designs that supplement the shift in the indicated or preferred reaction process, researchers may successfully decrease the activation energy required for bond stimulation. The methodology above methodology has exhibited noteworthy efficacy in activating of unreactive bonds, specifically C-H as well as C-C bonds. This bears considerable significance for the production of intricate organic compounds as well as the creation of organic substances (Sahlgren & Hall, 2023).

Metal-organic frameworks (MOFs) have gained significant attention as a potential strategy for bond activation in recent times. MOFs are a class of porous materials that consist of metallic nodes organized to organic links. The tunability of these materials is significant as it enables researchers to integrate diverse functionalities and customize the pore surroundings to facilitate specific non-covalent relationships. Through the utilization of these connections, MOFs have the ability to discriminate in the activation of covalent bonds and demonstrate outstanding catalytic efficacy. The catalytic capacity is further enhanced by the inclusion of metallic transitions in the structure, thus facilitating reactions that used to be considered difficult or unfeasible (Wegeberg & Wenger, 2021).

The potential collaboration between transitional metals as well as non-covalent associations has generated significant attention within the realm of dissatisfied Lewis pairs (FLPs). Fluorinated phosphonium ions (FLPs) are composed of a Lewis acid as well as a Lewis base that have been sterically impeded from developing a conventional Lewis acid-base adduct. Rather than forming covalent bonds, these pairs participate in non-covalent connections, like hydrogen bonding, in order to facilitate the activation and cleavage of difficult bonds, like those involving C-H, C-C, as well as C-X bonds (where X represents a heteroatom). The methodology above presents a distinctive approach to surmount the constraints of conventional transition metallic catalysis and facilitates entry to novel reaction pathways (Riant et al., 2004).

In addition, the emergence of computerized chemistry as well as machine learning approaches has significantly expedited the exploration and enhancement of innovative bond activation methods. Through the utilization of advanced algorithms as well as databases, scholars are able to forecast and develop catalysts with exceptional accuracy and efficacy. The utilization of computational techniques allows for the extensive examination of chemical space, providing significant elucidation on the characteristics of non-covalent bonds along with facilitating the methodical development of catalysts tailored to precise bond activation responses (Trouve & Gramage, 2021).

3.6.3. Current Challenges and Open Questions

Undoubtedly, the utilization of non-covalent connections to activate covalent bonds has exhibited significant potential and promise in diverse domains. Nevertheless, there exist various obstacles and unresolved inquiries, necessitating the continuation of scholarly investigation and examination. This section will address the present challenges and unresolved inquiries pertaining to this captivating field of research.

Selective stimulation of specific covalent connections poses a significant challenge. Although non-covalent relationships have the potential to facilitate the activation of chemical bonds, accomplishing selectivity between multiple bonds inside a single molecule is still a challenging endeavor. Scholars are currently engaged in the exploration of techniques for regulating and guiding the stimulation towards intended bonds, taking into account variables such as bond potency, electronic characteristics, and steric impacts. The development of effective and feasible techniques for activating selective bonds represents a crucial obstacle that necessitates additional exploration (Menon et al., 2015).

An additional obstacle pertains to comprehending the underlying mechanisms as well as patterns of non-covalent connections in the context of bond activation. Despite notable advancements, the exact correlation between non-covalent connections and the process of covalent bond cleavage and formation remains incompletely understood. Scholars are utilizing sophisticated computational techniques, such as molecular dynamics modeling as well as quantum mechanical computations, to decipher the complexities of these relationships on the atomically as well as molecular scales. Spectroscopy, crystallography using X-rays, as well as cryo-electron microscopy, are experimental techniques that provide important insights through the fluctuation of non-covalent relationships during link activation.

Tip

Exploring the role of non-covalent interactions in bond activation can lead to the development of new strategies for organic synthesis.

The investigation of novel categories of non-covalent interactions that extend beyond the conventional hydrogen bonding as well as halogen bonding phenomena poses an alluring obstacle. Although the efficacy of these interactions has been demonstrated, the exploration and utilization of further non-covalent interactions may lead to novel opportunities for bond activation. Scholars are currently exploring atypical interactions, including chalcogen connection, pnictogen connection, as well as π-π stacking, with the aim of broadening the range of non-covalent interactions available for bond activation. Comprehending the distinct attributes and constraints of such interactions is imperative for their efficacious implementation in the stimulation of covalent bonds (Colombo & Peretto, 2008).

In addition, scholars are currently investigating the potential for scalability as well as the synthetic relevance of non-covalent link activation methodologies. Several contemporary methodologies necessitate distinct catalysts or just reaction circumstances that might not be readily translatable to industrial processes on a large scale. The practical application of catalysts necessitates their robustness, cost-effectiveness, and compatibility with a diverse range of substrates. The continuous challenge in this area is to optimize the reaction circumstances, which involves the manipulation of solvent effects as well as temperature control, in order to attain high yields as well as selectivity (Liang & Jiao, 2017).

There are unresolved inquiries pertaining to the enduring stability as well as the reactivity of systems that are stimulated via non-covalent relationships.

The examination of stability along with the reactivity of resultant products is crucial despite the potential for bond activation through non-covalent interactions in certain circumstances. Comprehending the variables that impact the stability of products, including the impact of solvents, competing reactions, as well as catalyst efficacy, is of paramount importance for the efficacious implementation of non-covalent bond stimulation in diverse domains (Song et al., 2015).

3.6.4. Exploring Non-Covalent Interactions in Bond Activation

The activation of covalent bonds via non-covalent connections has recently gained attention as a promising area of research with a wide range of potential applications and significant implications. The utilization of non-covalent connections to expedite bond-breaking mechanisms presents novel opportunities for catalytic reactions, materials engineering, pharmaceutical exploration, and other related fields. Through the utilization of the distinctive attributes of non-covalent connections, researchers can attain discriminative and effective bond activation, resulting in heightened reaction velocities, upgraded product yields, along with augmented regulation over chemical conversions (Sharma & Sharma, 2018).

A prospective utilization can be observed within the domain of catalysis. The utilization of non-covalent connections is of utmost significance in the development of catalysts that facilitate the activation of bonds that are otherwise unreactive. Transition metal complexes that possess precisely placed hydrogen-bonding or just halogen-bonding amenities have the ability to facilitate the activation of difficult bonds within organic synthesis. The aforementioned methodology has exhibited significant potential in the discriminative functionalization of intricate molecules, enabling the fabrication of intricate chemical structures with exceptional accuracy (Wencel & Glorius, 2013).

The stimulation of bonds that are covalent via non-covalent reactions presents prospects for the advancement of materials science by enabling the creation of sophisticated materials with customized properties. Through the utilization of non-covalent connections, scientists can strategically weaken or break particular ties within a substance, thereby introducing advantageous properties like heightened durability, enhanced conductance, or adjustable reactivity. The utilization of non-covalent interactions to enable the reversible stimulation as well as the modification for covalent bonds, are being investigated in the development of self-healing substances. This method has resulted in the creation of substances that possess the ability to mend themselves upon sustaining damage (Campos, 2007).

In addition, the activation of covalent bonds via non-covalent connections presents considerable promise in the fields of drug discovery as well as medicinal chemistry. The significance of non-covalent connections in the binding affinity, along with the selectivity of ligands as well as proteins, cannot be overstated. The integration of non-covalent interaction patterns into drug compounds can be a strategic approach for researchers to augment their relationship with targeted proteins, ultimately resulting in heightened therapeutic efficacy as well as diminished off-target effects. The aforementioned methodology has been effectively utilized in the development of inhibitors for enzymes, as well as agonists/antagonists for receptors and disruptors for protein-protein interactions (Sosso et al., 2016).

The ramifications of activating covalent bonds via non-covalent interactions have broader implications that transcend particular use cases. The aforementioned of study has enhanced our comprehension of chemical responsiveness as well as reaction processes, furnishing significant perspectives into basic procedures within the realm of chemistry. This statement challenges conventional concepts regarding bond activation as well as highlights the efficacy of non-covalent connections in regulating and influencing chemical reactions. In addition, the advancement of new techniques and procedures for bond stimulation holds promise for stimulating inventive synthetic techniques and facilitating the production of intricate compounds and substances that were once unattainable (Karmali & Chaudhuri, 2007).

Nevertheless, there exist obstacles and unresolved inquiries that necessitate attention. The current research endeavors are focused on accomplishing selectivity in bond stimulation, regulating reaction pathways, as well as comprehending the fluctuation of non-covalent connections in intricate systems. Furthermore, the incorporation of non-covalent connections into pragmatic implementations necessitates the establishment of resilient and expandable synthetic techniques (Denoncin & Collet, 2013).

Activity 3.1

How can the activation of C—O bonds through non-covalent interactions be utilized in the design of novel drug molecules?

3.7. SUMMARY

In this chapter, the concept of utilizing non-covalent interactions to activate covalent bonds is thoroughly explored. The chapter starts by providing an introduction to the topic, setting the stage for the subsequent discussions. The examples of hydrogen bond-assisted activations are presented, showcasing how non-covalent interactions can play a crucial role in initiating bond activation. These examples cover various types of bonds, including C—C, C=C, C≡C, C—N, C=N, and C≡N bonds. The reader learns about the potential of non-covalent interactions in catalytic processes and their promising results.

A significant portion of the chapter is dedicated to understanding the activation of C—O bonds through non-covalent interactions, specifically focusing on the activation of C=O bonds. The factors influencing this type of bond activation are discussed in detail, emphasizing their importance in the development of efficient synthetic methodologies. The reader gains insights into the intricate interplay between non-covalent interactions and the activation of C=O bonds. Additionally, the chapter explores the activation of C—S bonds and C=S bonds through non-covalent interactions. The role of halogen bond-assisted activations is also highlighted, showcasing their significance in bond activation processes. Expanding further, the chapter delves into other types of non-covalent interactions and their perspectives in the field. The reader gains knowledge about the various types of non-covalent interactions beyond hydrogen bonding and halogen bonding. These interactions broaden the understanding of the possibilities for activating covalent bonds and expanding the synthetic toolbox.

Moreover, the chapter provides an overview of recent breakthroughs and discoveries in the field of bond activation through non-covalent interactions. It explores novel approaches and methodologies employed in this area, which contribute to advancing the understanding and application of non-covalent interactions for bond activation. The reader is encouraged to explore current challenges and open questions, as they provide opportunities for further research and development.

REVIEW QUESTIONS

1. What is the main focus of Chapter 3?
2. Provide an example of hydrogen bond-assisted activation.
3. How can non-covalent interactions influence the activation of C=O bonds?

4. Discuss the potential applications of activating C—N bonds through non-covalent interactions.
5. What is the significance of halogen bond-assisted activations?
6. Name one other type of non-covalent interaction mentioned in the chapter.
7. What are the recent breakthroughs and discoveries in the field of bond activation through non-covalent interactions?
8. Explain the importance of exploring non-covalent interactions in bond activation.
9. What are some current challenges and open questions in this area of research?
10. How can novel approaches and methodologies contribute to the activation of covalent bonds through non-covalent interactions?

REFERENCES

1. Ahrén, B., (2015). Glucagon–Early breakthroughs and recent discoveries. *Peptides*, *67*, 74–81.
2. Allen, C. L., & Williams, J. M., (2011). Metal-catalyzed approaches to amide bond formation. *Chemical Society Reviews*, *40*(7), 3405–3415.
3. Baratta, W., Ballico, M., Del Zotto, A., Zangrando, E., & Rigo, P., (2007). C-H activation and C=C double bond formation reactions in iridium ortho-methyl arylphosphane complexes. *Chemistry–A European Journal*, *13*(23), 6701–6709.
4. Belzner, J., Ihmels, H., Pauletto, L., & Noltemeyer, M., (1996). Reactions of a silanediyl with carbon− oxygen and carbon− nitrogen double bonds. *The Journal of Organic Chemistry*, *61*(10), 3315–3319.
5. Böhm, V. P., Gstöttmayr, C. W., Weskamp, T., & Herrmann, W. A., (2001). Catalytic C− C bond formation through selective activation of C− F bonds. *Angewandte Chemie International Edition*, *40*(18), 3387–3389.
6. Breugst, M., Von, D. H. D., & Schmauck, J., (2017). Novel noncovalent interactions in catalysis: a focus on halogen, chalcogen, and anion-π bonding. *Synthesis*, *49*(15), 3224–3236.
7. Campos, K. R., (2007). Direct sp^3 C–H bond activation adjacent to nitrogen in heterocycles. *Chemical Society Reviews*, *36*(7), 1069–1084.
8. Chen, S., Li, Y., Zhao, J., & Li, X., (2009). Chelation-assisted carbon-halogen bond activation by a rhodium (I) complex. *Inorganic Chemistry*, *48*(3), 1198–1206.
9. Colby, D. A., Bergman, R. G., & Ellman, J. A., (2010). Rhodium-catalyzed C− C bond formation via heteroatom-directed C− H bond activation. *Chemical Reviews*, *110*(2), 624–655.
10. Colombo, M., & Peretto, I., (2008). Chemistry strategies in early drug discovery: an overview of recent trends. *Drug Discovery Today*, *13*(15, 16), 677–684.
11. De Sousa, D. P., Wegeberg, C., Vad, M. S., Mørup, S., Frandsen, C., Donald, W. A., & McKenzie, C. J., (2016). Halogen-bonding-assisted iodosylbenzene activation by a homogenous iron catalyst. *Chemistry–A European Journal*, *22*(11), 3810–3820.
12. Denoncin, K., & Collet, J. F., (2013). Disulfide bond formation in the bacterial periplasm: major achievements and challenges ahead. *Antioxidants & Redox Signaling*, *19*(1), 63–71.
13. DiLabio, G. A., & Otero-De-La-Roza, A., (2016). Noncovalent interactions in density functional theory. *Reviews in Computational Chemistry*, *29*,

1–97.

14. Enders, D., & Reinhold, U., (1997). Asymmetric synthesis of amines by nucleophilic 1, 2-addition of organometallic reagents to the CN-double bond. *Tetrahedron: Asymmetry*, *8*(12), 1895–1946.
15. Feng, G., Hao, Y., Wu, L., & Chen, S., (2020). A visible-light activated [2 + 2] cycloaddition reaction enables pinpointing carbon–carbon double bonds in lipids. *Chemical Science*, *11*(27), 7244–7251.
16. Fourmigué, M., & Batail, P., (2004). Activation of hydrogen-and halogen-bonding interactions in tetrathiafulvalene-based crystalline molecular conductors. *Chemical Reviews*, *104*(11), 5379–5418.
17. Gossage, R. A., & Van, K. G., (2001). A general survey and recent advances in the activation of unreactive chemical bonds by metal complexes. *Activation of Unreactive Bonds and Organic Synthesis,1*(1), 1–8.
18. Haque, A., Alenezi, K. M., Khan, M. S., Wong, W. Y., & Raithby, P. R., (2023). Non-covalent interactions (NCIs) in π-conjugated functional materials: advances and perspectives. *Chemical Society Reviews*,*1*(1),1–20.
19. Hu, Z., Li, Y., Gan, C., Sheng, M., Sun, B., & Jiang, H., (2022). Photocatalytic C–H activation for C–C/C [double bond, length as m-dash] N/C–S bond formation over CdS: effect of morphological regulation and S vacancies. *Catalysis Science & Technology*, *12*(22), 6728–6739.
20. Islam, M. A., Tan, I. A. W., Benhouria, A., Asif, M., & Hameed, B. H., (2015). Mesoporous and adsorptive properties of palm date seed activated carbon prepared via sequential hydrothermal carbonization and sodium hydroxide activation. *Chemical Engineering Journal*, *270*, 187–195.
21. Jun, C. H., (2004). Transition metal-catalyzed carbon–carbon bond activation. *Chemical Society Reviews*, *33*(9), 610–618.
22. Jun, C. H., Lee, H., Moon, C. W., & Hong, H. S., (2001). Cleavage of carbon− carbon triple bond of alkyne via hydroiminoacylation by Rh (I) CATALYST. *Journal of the American Chemical Society*, *123*(35), 8600–8601.
23. Jutzi, P., Eikenberg, D., Neumann, B., & Stammler, H. G., (1996). Decamethylsilicocene chemistry: reaction with carbon− nitrogen triple-bond species. *Organometallics*, *15*(17), 3659–3663.
24. Karmali, P. P., & Chaudhuri, A., (2007). Cationic liposomes as non-viral carriers of gene medicines: Resolved issues, open questions, and future promises. *Medicinal Research Reviews*, *27*(5), 696–722.
25. Konishi, K., Ishida, K., Oinuma, K. I., Ohta, T., Hashimoto, Y., Higashibata, H., & Kobayashi, M., (2004). Identification of crucial histidines involved

in carbon-nitrogen triple bond synthesis by aldoxime dehydratase. *Journal of Biological Chemistry*, *279*(46), 47619–47625.

26. Lausarot, P. M., Turini, M., Vaglio, G. A., Valle, M., Tiripicchio, A., Camellini, M. T., & Gariboldi, P., (1984). Activation of a carbon—Nitrogen triple bond in the presence of $Ru_3(CO)_{12}$ and $H_4Ru_4(CO)_{12}$. *Journal of Organometallic Chemistry*, *273*(2), 239–246.
27. Li, Q., Wei, Y., Hao, J., Zhu, Y., & Wang, L., (2007). Unexpected CC bond formation via doubly dehydrogenative coupling of two saturated sp^3 C– H bonds activated with a polymolybdate. *Journal of the American Chemical Society*, *129*(18), 5810–5811.
28. Li, R., Huang, J., Li, W., Li, J., Cao, L., Xu, Z., & Lu, G., (2019). Controlling carbon-oxygen double bond and pseudographic structure in shaddock peel derived hard carbon for enhanced sodium storage properties. *Electrochimica Acta*, *313*, 109–115.
29. Liang, Y. F., & Jiao, N., (2017). Oxygenation via C–H/C–C bond activation with molecular oxygen. *Accounts of Chemical Research*, *50*(7), 1640–1653.
30. Lohöfener, J., Steinke, N., Kay-Fedorov, P., Baruch, P., Nikulin, A., Tishchenko, S., & Fedorov, R., (2015). The activation mechanism of 2′-5′-oligoadenylate synthetase gives new insights into OAS/cGAS triggers of innate immunity. *Structure*, *23*(5), 851–862.
31. Lou, Y., Zhao, Y., Liu, H., Gu, Q., Yang, B., Shi, Y., & Yang, B., (2021). Edge-confined Pt1/MoS_2 single-atom catalyst promoting the selective activation of carbon-oxygen bond. *ChemCatChem*, *13*(12), 2783–2793.
32. Lu, J. M., & Shi, M., (2008). Lewis acid catalyzed reactions of vinylidenecyclopropanes with activated carbon– oxygen double bond: A facile synthetic protocol for functionalized tetrahydrofuran and 3, 6-dihydropyran derivatives. *The Journal of Organic Chemistry*, *73*(6), 2206–2210.
33. Mack, S. C., & Northcott, P. A., (2017). Genomic analysis of childhood brain tumors: methods for genome-wide discovery and precision medicine become mainstream. *Journal of Clinical Oncology*, *35*(21), 2346–2354.
34. Maharramov, A. M., Mahmudov, K. T., Kopylovich, M. N., Aliyeva, R. A., & Pombeiro, A. J., (2016). Cooperation of non-covalent interactions and coordination in catalysis. *Non-covalent Interactions in the Synthesis and Design of New Compounds,1*(1), 327–344.
35. Maharramov, A. M., Mahmudov, K. T., Kopylovich, M. N., Da Silva, M. F. C. G., & Pombeiro, A. J., (2016). Activation of covalent bonds through non-covalent interactions. *Non-covalent Interactions in the Synthesis and*

Design of New Compounds, 1(1), 1–21.

36. Manriquez, J. M., Fagan, P. J., Marks, T. J., Day, C. S., & Day, V. W., (1978). Bis (pentamethylcyclopentadienyl) actinide alkyls: Facile activation of carbon monoxide, carbon-carbon double bond formation, and the production of unusual oxygen-bonded migratory insertion products. *Journal of the American Chemical Society*, *100*(22), 7112–7114.
37. Matsuzawa, A., Takeuchi, S., & Sugita, K., (2016). Iodoalkyne-based catalyst-mediated activation of thioamides through halogen bonding. *Chemistry–An Asian Journal*, *11*(20), 2863–2866.
38. Menon, R. S., Biju, A. T., & Nair, V., (2015). Recent advances in employing homoenolates generated by N-heterocyclic carbene (NHC) catalysis in carbon–carbon bond-forming reactions. *Chemical Society Reviews*, *44*(15), 5040–5052.
39. Mészáros, B., Park, E., Malinverni, D., Sejdiu, B. I., Immadisetty, K., Sandhu, M., & Babu, M. M., (2023). Recent breakthroughs in computational structural biology harnessing the power of sequences and structures. *Current Opinion in Structural Biology*, *80*, 102608.
40. Miyabe, H., Yamakawa, K., Yoshioka, N., & Naito, T., (1999). Alkylative amination of aldehydes via carbon-carbon bond formation based on radical addition to carbon-nitrogen double bond. *Tetrahedron*, *55*(37), 11209–11218.
41. Murahashi, S. I., Nakae, T., Terai, H., & Komiya, N., (2008). Ruthenium-catalyzed oxidative cyanation of tertiary amines with molecular oxygen or hydrogen peroxide and sodium cyanide: sp3 C− H bond activation and carbon− carbon bond formation. *Journal of the American Chemical Society*, *130*(33), 11005–11012.
42. Murai, S., (2003). The cleavage of "unreactive bonds" comes into reach for practicing synthetic chemists. *Advanced Synthesis & Catalysis*, *345*(9-10), 1033–1033.
43. Nakao, Y., (2014). Catalytic C–CN bond activation. *CC Bond Activation, 1*(1), 33–58.
44. Nakao, Y., (2020). Metal-mediated C–CN bond activation in organic synthesis. *Chemical Reviews*, *121*(1), 327–344.
45. Nomura, J., Hashimoto, H., Ohta, T., Hashimoto, Y., Wada, K., Naruta, Y., & Kobayashi, M., (2013). Crystal structure of aldoxime dehydratase and its catalytic mechanism involved in carbon-nitrogen triple-bond synthesis. *Proceedings of the National Academy of Sciences*, *110*(8), 2810–2815.
46. Oinuma, K. I., Hashimoto, Y., Konishi, K., Goda, M., Noguchi, T., Higashibata, H., & Kobayashi, M., (2003). Novel aldoxime dehydratase

involved in carbon-nitrogen triple bond synthesis of *Pseudomonas chlororaphis* B23: Sequencing, gene expression, purification, and characterization. *Journal of Biological Chemistry*, *278*(32), 29600–29608.

47. Padwa, A., (1977). Photochemistry of the carbon-nitrogen double bond. *Chemical Reviews*, *77*(1), 37–68.
48. Padwa, A., Dharan, M., Smolanoff, J., & Wetmore, S. I., (1973). Recent advances in the photochemistry of the carbon-nitrogen double bond. *Pure and Applied Chemistry*, *33*(2, 3), 269–284.
49. Pastorczak, E., & Corminboeuf, C., (2017). Perspective: Found in translation: Quantum chemical tools for grasping non-covalent interactions. *The Journal of Chemical Physics*, *146*(12), 120901.
50. Ping, Y., Ding, Q., & Peng, Y., (2016). Advances in C–CN bond formation via C–H bond activation. *ACS Catalysis*, *6*(9), 5989–6005.
51. Ranu, B. C., & Samanta, S., (2003). Remarkably selective reduction of the α, β-carbon– carbon double bond in highly activated α, β, γ, δ-unsaturated alkenes by the $InCl_3$– $NaBH_4$ reagent system. *The Journal of Organic Chemistry*, *68*(18), 7130–7132.
52. Ravelli, D., Protti, S., & Fagnoni, M., (2016). Carbon–carbon bond forming reactions via photogenerated intermediates. *Chemical Reviews*, *116*(17), 9850–9913.
53. Riant, O., Mostefai, N., & Courmarcel, J., (2004). Recent advances in the asymmetric hydrosilylation of ketones, imines, and electrophilic double bonds. *Synthesis*, *2004*(18), 2943–2958.
54. Sahlgren, B. K. M., & Hall, V. J., (2023). The breakthroughs and caveats of using human pluripotent stem cells in modeling Alzheimer's disease. *Cells*, *12*(3), 420.
55. Saveant, J. M., (1993). Electron transfer, bond breaking, and bond formation. *Accounts of Chemical Research*, *26*(9), 455–461.
56. Segura, Y., López, N., & Pérez-Ramírez, J., (2007). Origin of the superior hydrogenation selectivity of gold nanoparticles in alkyne+ alkene mixtures: Triple-versus double-bond activation. *Journal of Catalysis*, *247*(2), 383–386.
57. Seiser, T., & Cramer, N., (2008). Enantioselective C–C bond activation of allenyl cyclobutanes: access to cyclohexenones with quaternary stereogenic centers. *Angewandte Chemie International Edition*, *47*(48), 9294–9297.
58. Sharma, R., & Sharma, U., (2018). Remote CH bond activation/ transformations: A continuous growing synthetic tool; PART II. *Catalysis*

Reviews, *60*(4), 497–565.

59. Shaw, M. H., & Bower, J. F., (2016). Synthesis and applications of rhodacyclopentanones derived from C–C bond activation. *Chemical Communications*, *52*(72), 10817–10829.
60. Singh, S., Roy, V. J., Dagar, N., Sen, P. P., & Roy, S. R., (2021). Photocatalysis in dual catalysis systems for carbon-nitrogen bond formation. *Advanced Synthesis & Catalysis*, *363*(4), 937–979.
61. Song, R. J., Liu, Y., Xie, Y. X., & Li, J. H., (2015). Difunctionalization of acrylamides through C–H oxidative radical coupling: new approaches to oxindoles. *Synthesis*, *47*(09), 1195–1209.
62. Sosso, G. C., Chen, J., Cox, S. J., Fitzner, M., Pedevilla, P., Zen, A., & Michaelides, A., (2016). Crystal nucleation in liquids: Open questions and future challenges in molecular dynamics simulations. *Chemical Reviews*, *116*(12), 7078–7116.
63. Takaya, H., Naota, T., & Murahashi, S. I., (1998). Iridium hydride complex catalyzed addition of nitriles to carbon– nitrogen triple bonds of nitriles. *Journal of the American Chemical Society*, *120*(17), 4244, 4245.
64. Tamaru, Y., & Kimura, M., (1997). CN bond formation reactions via transition metal catalysis. *Synlett*, *1997*(7), 749–757.
65. Titov, A. A., Larionov, V. A., Smol'yakov, A. F., Godovikova, M. I., Titova, E. M., Maleev, V. I., & Shubina, E. S., (2019). Interaction of a trinuclear copper (i) pyrazolate with alkynes and carbon–carbon triple bond activation. *Chemical Communications*, *55*(3), 290–293.
66. Tobisu, M., & Chatani, N., (2008). Catalytic reactions involving the cleavage of carbon–cyano and carbon–carbon triple bonds. *Chemical Society Reviews*, *37*(2), 300–307.
67. Trouvé, J., & Gramage-Doria, R., (2021). Beyond hydrogen bonding: recent trends of outer sphere interactions in transition metal catalysis. *Chemical Society Reviews*, *50*(5), 3565–3584.
68. Tweedell, R. E., & Kanneganti, T. D., (2020). Advances in inflammasome research: recent breakthroughs and future hurdles. *Trends in Molecular Medicine*, *26*(11), 969–971.
69. Voit, B., (2005). Hyperbranched polymers—All problems solved after 15 years of research? *Journal of Polymer Science Part A: Polymer Chemistry*, *43*(13), 2679–2699.
70. Wang, G. W., & Bower, J. F., (2018). Modular access to azepines by directed carbonylative C–C bond activation of aminocyclopropanes. *Journal of the American Chemical Society*, *140*(8), 2743–2747.

71. Watson, M. P., & Jacobsen, E. N., (2008). Asymmetric intramolecular arylcyanation of unactivated olefins via C− CN bond activation. *Journal of the American Chemical Society, 130*(38), 12594–12595.
72. Wegeberg, C., & Wenger, O. S., (2021). Luminescent first-row transition metal complexes. *JACS Au, 1*(11), 1860–1876.
73. Wencel-Delord, J., & Glorius, F., (2013). C–H bond activation enables the rapid construction and late-stage diversification of functional molecules. *Nature Chemistry, 5*(5), 369–375.
74. Wencel-Delord, J., Dröge, T., Liu, F., & Glorius, F., (2011). Towards mild metal-catalyzed C–H bond activation. *Chemical Society Reviews, 40*(9), 4740–4761.
75. Winter, C., & Krause, N., (2009). Rhodium (I)-catalyzed enantioselective C–C bond activation. *Angewandte Chemie International Edition, 48*(14), 2460–2462.
76. Wismeijer, A. A., Kieboom, A. P. G., & Van, B. H., (1985). Improved activity and selectivity in carbon-oxygen double bond hydrogenation with Ru/TiO_2. *Reaction Kinetics and Catalysis Letters, 29*, 311–316.
77. Xia, Y., & Dong, G., (2020). Temporary or removable directing groups enable activation of unstrained C–C bonds. *Nature Reviews Chemistry, 4*(11), 600–614.
78. Xu, Y., Qi, X., Zheng, P., Berti, C. C., Liu, P., & Dong, G., (2019). Deacylative transformations of ketones via aromatization-promoted C–C bond activation. *Nature, 567*(7748), 373–378.
79. Yamamoto, A., (1992). Carbon-oxygen bond activation by transition metal complexes. In: *Advances in Organometallic Chemistry* (Vol. 34, pp. 111–147). Academic Press.
80. Zhang, Z., He, C., & Chen, X., (2018). Hydrogels based on pH-responsive reversible carbon–nitrogen double-bond linkages for biomedical applications. *Materials Chemistry Frontiers, 2*(10), 1765–1778.
81. Zhao, T., Song, W., Fan, C., Li, S., Glarborg, P., & Yao, X., (2018). Density functional theory study of the role of an carbon–oxygen single bond group in the NO–char reaction. *Energy & Fuels, 32*(7), 7734–7744.
82. Zugic, B., Bell, D. C., & Flytzani-Stephanopoulos, M., (2014). Activation of carbon-supported platinum catalysts by sodium for the low-temperature water-gas shift reaction. *Applied Catalysis B: Environmental, 144*, 243–251.

CHAPTER

4 The Virial Theorem and Covalent Bonding

Contents

4.1. INTRODUCTION

The comprehension of chemical structures as well as reactions is fundamentally reliant on the idea of covalent chemical bonding. The physical origin of bond formation, which is considered as the most basic chemical process, remains a topic of debate despite the availability of precise quantitative molecular calculations for electronic structures of increasing complexity in the present times (Rioux, 2003).

The concept that chemical bonding is primarily an electrostatic phenomenon has been a prevailing and enduring perspective in the field. The phenomenon of energy reduction leading to bond formation is commonly attributed to the electrostatic potential energy that attracts the nuclei and the quantum-mechanically accumulated electronic charge in the bond region. The aforementioned hypothesis is deduced by considering two pieces of information: firstly, the convenient interloping that occurs between atomic orbitals that combine to form molecular bonding results in an additional electronic charge being added in overlapped atomic charge densities within atomic bonds. Secondly, it is a well-established fact is the potential molecular energy is consistently less than individual constituent atoms, whereas the kinetic energy of the molecules is going to be consistently greater. The aforementioned inequalities can be derived straightforwardly from the virial theorem. This theorem asserts that the ratio of potential energy to kinetic energy, denoted as V/T, is always equal to -2 for both atoms and molecules at their respective equilibrium geometries. The depiction of interactions between charge distributions as essentially classical as well as static is attractive due to its simplicity. Additionally, the virial theorem's rigorous general validity seems to offer a solid basis for this depiction. The concept of bonding as presented in this perspective was initially proposed by Slater1 in 1933. Subsequently, Feynman2 in 1939 and Coulson, whose publication Valence3 in 1952 has had a significant impact on the chemical community, provided further support for this viewpoint. In more recent times, the model of covalent bonding proposed by Slater has been corroborated by Bader4,5 (Bacskay et al., 2018).

Hellmann (1933) presented an alternative perspective to the electrostatic viewpoint, suggesting that covalent bonding can be explained through quantum mechanics. Specifically, the delocalization of valence electrons among atoms in a molecule results in a reduction of its ground-state kinetic energy, leading to the formation of covalent bonds. For a considerable period, the kinetic rationale proposed by Hellmann was disregarded by the majority of chemists. This may have been due to the fact that Hellmann's argument relied on the statistical Thomas-Fermi model, which Teller demonstrated to produce no covalent bonding. Additionally, Hellmann was unable to reconcile his understanding with the virial theorem, which he was cognizant of, and his untimely demise may have also contributed to the lack of acceptance of his explanation. In 1955 and 1961, Peierls and Platt, physicists by profession, concurred with Hellmann's views on the matter (Gao & Weiner, 1989).

The discrepancy between the two distinct qualitative hypotheses regarding the covalent bonding system necessitated a meticulous and comprehensive analysis to achieve its resolution. Ruedenberg and colleagues conducted an analysis utilizing the quantum mechanical change principle. This analysis was performed beginning in 1962 and focused initially on H_2^+ and H_2, with subsequent investigation of other homonuclear diatomic molecules. The findings of these inquiries indicate that the essential contributions to covalent bonding arise from the reduction of kinetic energy via interatomic electron delocalization, which aligns with Hellmann's perspective. These findings were later supported by several theoretical chemists, including Fukui25 and Mulliken,26 who were both recipients of the Nobel Prize (Ruedenberg & Schmidt, 2009).

The investigations mentioned earlier have demonstrate the electrostatic potential relationships between the atomic nuclei as well as the mechanical waves shows that there is no bonding exist after the collected charge in the atomic bonds, but rather antibonding. This finding contradicts the first premise of the electrostatic model, as previously mentioned. The current investigation focuses on the second premise, specifically the significance of the virial theorem. Sections 3 and 4 demonstrate that bond formation can occur in systems where the virial theorem is not applicable. This phenomenon is primarily attributed to the reduction of kinetic energy resulting from delocalization. It can be inferred that the fundamental cause of bonding cannot be attributed to the virial theorem. The assertion that the virial theorem is a crucial factor in bonding, as posited by the electrostatic model, is deemed to be a diversion from the actual physical mechanisms that underlie the formation of covalent bonds (Clark et al., 2022).

The virial theorem establishes that the potential energy reduces and the kinetic energy improves upon the formation of a bond in a rigorous manner. How can this correspond with the observation that the formation of bonds is influenced by alterations in kinetic energy? This inquiry can also be expounded upon through an examination that relies on the principle of fundamental variation. Section 2 provides clarification on the intriguing and potentially advantageous function of the virial theorem in the context of variational examination of covalent bonding. Section 5 of the document discusses the covalent bonds that involve more than two electrons (Rutkowski et al., 1993).

4.2. VARIATION ANALYSIS, COVALENT BOND FORMATION, AND VIRIAL THEOREM

4.2.1. Important Basic Fact of Molecular Quantum Mechanics

[22] Comprehending the process of bond formation necessitates comprehension of the energy disparity between interconnected systems. It is crucial to note that, typically, analyzing the best possible values of the overall energy (E) and its constituent kinetic (T) or potential (V) components is insufficient in determining the underlying physical cause of the energy discrepancy. The restriction is demonstrated by the hydrogen atom equivalents which are characterized (in atomic units) by the Hamiltonian (Nordholm & Bacskay, 2012).

$$\hat{H} = -\frac{1}{2m}\nabla^2 - \frac{Z}{r} \tag{1}$$

The variable "m" represents the mass that has been reduced of a particle possessing an electronic charge of 1e, while "Z" denotes the nuclear charge. The system's lowest energy state is represented by $E = -mZ^2/2\ E_h$ so it satisfies the virial theorem. The present study involves a comparison between two systems, namely the first system characterized by (m = 1, Z = 1) and possessing an energy of $E_0 = -1/2$ Eh, and the second system whose values of m and Z are unknown, but has an energy of $E_1 = -2$ Eh. The virial theorem holds true for both of the aforementioned systems. The observed decrease in energy of the second system in comparison to the first system may be attributed to either an increase in particle mass ($m_1 = 4$, $Z_1 = 1$) or an increase in nuclear attraction ($m_1 = 1$, $Z_1 = 2$).19,21,22 The dissimilarity of the two cases cannot be discerned solely from the values of E_1, T_1, and V_1, as per the virial theorem, these values are equivalent for both cases (where $T_1 > T_0$ and $V_1 < V_0$). To discern the distinctions between the physical sources of the energies of the initial and subsequent systems, it is necessary to possess knowledge regarding the mechanism that produces the energies from the input variables m as well as Z (Feinberg & Ruedenberg, 1971).

4.2.2. Variational Analysis

A rigorous mathematical foundation is necessary for the conceptual recognition of the physical factors that drive bond formation. As per the fundamental variance principle, the wave functions Ψ that render the energy functional $\langle\Psi|\hat{H}|\Psi\rangle$ stationary are considered as the answers of the Schrödinger equation. In the ground state, the wave function assumes a spatial configuration that results in the minimum energy. The minimum referred to in the text represents the most favorable balance in the variational contest between two opposing factors. Firstly, the desire to decrease the kinetic energy by extending (i.e., delocalizing) the electronic wave function to the greatest extent possible. the drive to lower the potential energy by confining (localizing) the electronic wave function as closely around the nuclei as possible. The expansion of electron waves is limited by the restriction of nuclear attraction. Alternatively, the proximity of electron waves to nuclei is determined by their resistance to localization. General variational analyzes may be formulated based on this fundamental basis, which conceptually detect the components of physical synergisms responsible for driving changes in wave function and energy. These analyzes are deemed effective as they take into account not just the optimized solutions, but also appropriate comparison wave functions as well as their corresponding energies. In the systems examined in subsection 2.1, the variational evaluation indicates that the reduction in energy in the first scenario is due to the decrease in kinetic resistance to localization, as m is present in the denominator of $\hat{H}$. Conversely, in the second scenario, the decrease in energy is attributed to the enhancement of the localizing potential (Hurley, 1982).

The efficacy of the variation principle in elucidating bonding phenomena was acknowledged as early as the 1930s. To date, no other rigorous framework has been proposed for the identification of physical factors underlying covalent bonding. The conclusion that interatomic delocalization of electrons is the primary driving force behind covalent bond formation was reached through a meticulous variational analysis of the kinetic energy reduction. The analysis pertaining to the current investigation is expounded upon in Sections 2.3, 2.4, as well as 2.5. The rationale is founded upon the quantitative outcomes that were acquired and deliberated upon in prior publications in following molecules: H_2, B_2, H_2^+ C_2, O_2, F_2 and N_2 (Levine & Head-Gordon, 2020).

4.2.3. Covalent Bonding

One fundamental aspect of bonding analyzes entails the recognition that the bond energy is comprised of two components: the antibonding among the intra-atomic stretching energies of the constituent atoms within molecule, while more robust inter-atomic interacting energies that dominate that going to give rising power to the bonds. Interatomic interactions result in the formation of bonds as they reduce the overall energy of the molecule. The reduction of energy is of utmost importance and is contingent upon the decrease in interatomic kinetic energy resulting from delocalization. The phenomenon of delocalization arises as a result of the process commonly referred to as electron sharing. The aforementioned terminology connotes the phenomenon wherein electron waves, initially confined to individual atoms within incompletely occupied valence shells, possess the capability to extend their reach and encompass multiple atoms. The phenomenon of electron sharing leading to a reduction in kinetic energy is observed across all internuclear distances where there is significant overlap between the orbitals of distinct atoms (Owen & Thornley, 1966) (Figure 4.1).

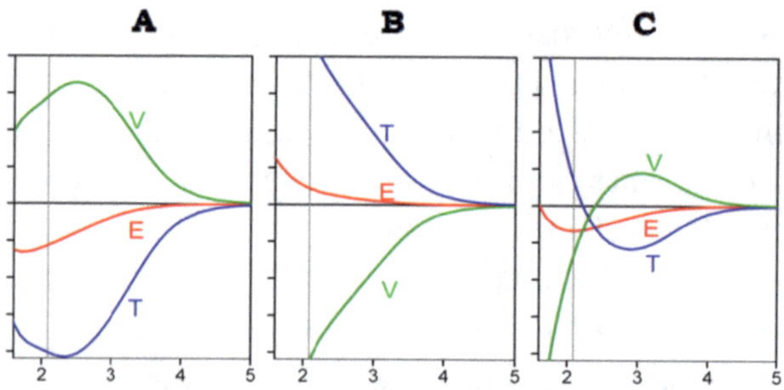

Figure 4.1. Variational binding energy analysis of the full valence space MC-SCF (multiconfigurational self-consistent field) calculation (with Dunning cc-pVQZ bases) of N_2 as a function of the internuclear distance. (A) Interatomic interactions using the molecule-optimized minimal basis set (MBS) orbitals. (B) Intra-atomic energy changes due to the change from the free-atom-optimized MBS orbitals to the molecule-optimized MBS orbitals. (C) Binding energy using the molecule-optimized MBS orbitals. Thus, (A) + (B) = (C).

Source: George B, Creative Commons License.

4.2.4. Covalent Bonding II

In the close proximity of the atomic orbitals, a further and intricate phenomenon is observed. In instances where the internuclear distance is reduced to less than two times are the equilibrium disjunction, intra-atomic retrenchments serve to amplify the interatomic delocalization, resulting to decrease the further interatomic kinetic energy. The previous publications have provided a comprehensive elucidation of the beginning of this extraordinary event, specifically with regards to its limitation to shorter internuclear distances 21,22. The penultimate section of the current paper provides a physical justification. It can be asserted that the contractions occurring within the atom lead to a simultaneous increase in the energies associated with antibonding intra-atomic deformations. However, the magnitude of this increment is comparatively reduced due to the application of the intra-atomic variance principle, which stipulates that intra-atomic energy variations from the atomic base state exhibit quadratic variation in any variation in the parameter. Consequently, the reduction in interatomic kinetic energy at these specific internuclear distances leads to a subsequent decrease in overall energy by inducing intra-atomic contractions (Hensel et al., 1965).

The contractions that occur within the atom, however, result in a significant side effect. The observed increase in intra-atomic energy can be attributed to the localization effect of the contraction, which causes a rise in intra-atomic kinetic energy and a corresponding reduction in intra-atomic potential energy, albeit to a slightly lesser extent. The potential and kinetic energy changes within an atom resulting from contraction act in opposition to the interatomic kinetic as well as potential changes responsible for binding. Secondly, it has been previously mentioned that the intra-atomic energy experiences a quadratic increase in the contraction parameters. However, the kinetic as well as potential components of the energy display a linear relationship with these parameters.21 Due to the significant magnitude of the intra-atomic nuclear Coulomb potentials, the sum of the two components is much smaller than each individual component. This results in a consequential effect. The two constituents are of significant magnitude such that they surpass the corresponding interatomic kinetic as well as potential components, in contrast to the overall contraction energy (Bullett, 1975).

Consequently, the combined kinetic energy of the molecules surpasses the mutual kinetic energies of fundamental atoms, while the overall potential energy of the molecule decreases below the collective potential energies of its individual atoms. Consequently, the indications of the kinetic and potential constituents in the binding energy are indicative of the corresponding kinetic energy along with potential energy which constituents the shrinkage energy of the antibonding intra-atomic molecules, that exhibit contrary indications to these interatomic overall energies of the kinetic and potential energy constituents. These interatomic total energies are responsible for the reduction of the overall energy that results in the formation of bonds. (Smith, 1970).

The variational analysis elucidates the reason behind the opposing signs of the energy components responsible for bond formation and the power elements that make up the binding energy in the vicinity of the equilibrium distance. It is noteworthy that the opposing distance dependencies of the energy alterations within atoms and between atoms offer a physical understanding of the familiar distortions observed in diatomic energy potential curves. On the other hand, it is possible to interpret these contortions as experimental proof of the existence of two distinct stages (namely, sections 2.3 and 2.4) in the process of covalent bond formation (Zhang et al., 2021).

4.2.5. The Virial Theorem

It has been determined that the formal minimization of a total atomic orbital scaling parameter, which may involve contractions, can be applied to wave functions of any nature.46,47 At the point of equilibrium, the minimization process results in the virial theorem, which asserts that V/T = -2. The aforementioned ratio pertaining to atoms indicates that $\Delta V = 2\Delta E < 0$ as well as $\Delta T = -\Delta E > 0$. It is noteworthy that the symbol "Δ" denotes the difference between the molecule at equilibrium and the sum of atoms. The signs obtained for ΔV as well as ΔT are consistent with those talked about earlier in section 2.4 (Tsai, 1979).

The virial theorem provides a systematic approach to quantify the qualitative outcomes of the contractive reduction of energy discussed in section 2.4. On the other hand, the examination presented in section 2.4 offers a theoretical explanation of the mathematical correlation in terms of physical concepts. Hence, the virial theorem presents a straightforward standard for determining whether the covalent bonding, as expounded by a particular wave function at the point of equilibrium, encompasses "part II" as elaborated in section 2.4. In a more precise manner, it can be observed that at the essential geometries, certain evaluations of an estimated wave function Ψ are possible. When 2T(Ψ) is less than the absolute value of V(Ψ), the optimal solution Ψo is comparatively more localized than Ψ. Conversely, when 2T(Ψ) is greater than the absolute value of V(Ψ), the optimized solution

Ψo is comparatively less localized than Ψ (Ballesteros-Paredes, 2006).

Thus, if a wave function has been formulated to embody only electron sharing, then its kinetic energy

If a wave function is designed to represent electron sharing exclusively, it follows that the kinetic energy of the wave function is usually reduced due to electron wave delocalization. This results in 2T(Ψ) being less than |V(Ψ)|. Therefore, the subsequent variational optimization process, which ensures the accurate determination of the virial ratio (V/T) = -2, involves a contraction towards the nuclei (Gourgoulhon & Bonazzola, 1994).

The discourse in section 2.1 indicates that the information derived from the virial theorem concerning ΔT and ΔV alone does not provide any insight into the underlying physical mechanisms responsible for the reduction in energy from individual atoms to a molecule. The virial theorem, which relies on the minimization of the scale parameter as outlined in section 2.4, accurately predicts the signs of ΔV and ΔT. These signs correspond to the antibonding intraatomic contributions and are in contrast to the interatomic contributions that facilitate bonding (Georgescu & Gérard, 1999).

The virial theory is a valuable tool in ensuring the precision of wave function calculations by establishing a necessary criterion for the accurate determination of the relationship between T as well as V. However, it should be noted that this criterion is not sufficient on its own. The virial theorem pertains to changes in the intra-atomic wave function, while covalent bonding arises from interatomic interactions. Nonetheless, molecular wave functions that do not account for the virial theorem, such as the Heitler-London wave equation or the Hückel model in organic chemistry, as well as Feynman's "two-state model" discussed in his renowned lectures, have yielded valuable theoretical insights into bonding.5Certain molecular properties exhibit a high degree of sensitivity to wave function characteristics that are dependent on the correct virial ratio, while others do not. Several molecular property calculations have been conducted, which do not involve the mention of virial ratios and have proven to be beneficial (Löwdin, 1959).

4.2.6. Covalent Bonding without the Virial Theorem

The principle of variation serves as the primary motivator in dictating the configurations and energy of electronic wave functions, and provides a rigorous foundation for discerning the cooperative interactions that give rise to covalent bonding. In the context of this theoretical framework, it can be asserted that the virial theorem provides assurance regarding the accurate scaling of atomic orbitals within a given molecule, as well as the appropriate correlation between the potential and kinetic energies. However, it does not induce delocalization via interatomic electron sharing, which is the fundamental principle underlying the formation of covalent bonds. This constrains the chemical knowledge it is capable of producing. The aforementioned observations raise the inquiry as to whether the veracity of the virial theory is indeed a fundamental component in the formation of covalent bonds. Is it possible for covalent bonds to occur between theoretical atoms that exhibit non-Coulombic interactions between their electrons and nuclei, characterized by enticing and repellent potentials when the virial ratio V/T can't be determined (Slater, 1933)?

The inquiry pertaining to sections 3 and 4 is addressed by investigating analogs of H_2^+ and H_2 molecules, wherein the Coulombic potential interactions are substituted with Gaussian forms that do not adhere to the virial theorem. Several potentials with varying strengths as well as ranges are taken into account, wherein a "electron" and a "nucleus" combine to form a "atom." It has been observed that bonds can form between atom analogs, despite variations in the virial ratios (V/T) in Gaussian-type systems. The specific values of these ratios are contingent upon the potential's range and strength, and the ratios for "atoms" consistently differ from those of their corresponding "molecules" (Nordholm, 1988).

The findings suggest that the concept of bonding is not restricted to systems that involve Coulombic interactions. Rather, it is observed across an array of circumstances in systems that comprise two distinct types of particles, where there are attractive forces between the different species and repulsive forces between the same species. The basic elucidation of bonding cannot encompass characteristics, like the virial theorem, which are distinctive to particular interaction potentials. While the virial theorem offers valuable insights in systems featuring Coulombic interactions, it lacks a causal role in the formation of chemical bonds (Shimizu et al., 2012).

Upon conducting variational analyzes on the "molecules" utilizing Gaussian potentials, it has been observed that the bonding mechanisms in these systems are identical to those previously identified for Coulombic connections in sections 2.3 as well as 2.4. The process of bonding can be explained through a wave mechanical phenomena that arises from a synergistic effect. This can be understood through an analysis that utilizes the variation principle (Takata, 2006).

4.3. THEORETICAL AND COMPUTATIONAL DETAILS

The present study conducts computations on H_2^+ and H_2 using a minimal atomic orbital (AO) foundation {ϕa(ζ), ϕb(ζ)} that is centered on nuclei a and b. The basis employs a variable orbital exponent ζ. The molecular orbital (MO) for the ground state of H_2^+ is the bonding wave function.

$$\Psi(\zeta, R) = C(\zeta, R)[\phi_a(\zeta) + \phi_b(\zeta)] \tag{2}$$

The variable R denotes the internuclear distance, while C(ζ, R) represents the normalization constant. In a conventional computation utilizing Coulombic interparticle potential, the adjusted atomic orbitals (AOs) correspond to 1s-type AOs (Beyer, 2000).

$$\phi_a = (\zeta^3/\pi)^{1/2}\exp(-\zeta r_a) \tag{3}$$

What is the distance of nucleus A? The two-electron wave function for H_2 can be represented by the twice occupied molecular orbital (2), which is the most basic form. The present study employs the valence-bond (VB) wave function, commonly referred to as the Heitler-London wave function, as the conventional H, 45 (spatial) wave function.48

$$\Psi_{VB}(\zeta, R) = N_{ab}(\zeta, R)[\phi_a(1)\,\phi_b(2) + \phi_b(1)\,\phi_a(2)] \tag{4}$$

The normalization constant is denoted as N_{ab}. The spatial locations of the two electrons are denoted by the numerical labels 1 and 2. The optimized orbital exponents ζ for the molecular hydrogen ions H_2^+ and H_2 exhibit variation across the range from the limit of separated hydrogen atoms, where R = ∞ and ζ = 1, to the limit of united helium ions and atoms, where R = 0 and ζ = 2.0 and 1.6875, respectively. At significant distances, there is a minor increase in the orbit, resulting in minima of approximately 0.995 as well as 0.990 for H_2^+ as well as H_2, respectively, in ζ. However, for distances below approximately 5.2 as well as 2.8 a0 in both systems, there are continuous contractions in the orbit (ζ > 1). Consequently, a "electron density reorganization" occurs in order to optimize the impact of covalent bonding through the expansion or contraction of atomic orbitals.

The present Gaussian models incorporate a Gaussian-shaped interparticle potential (Iozzi et al., 2009).

$$V(r) = q_1 q_2 A\exp(-\alpha r^2) \tag{5}$$

The distance among two particles carrying charges q1, q2, can be determined by utilizing the equation that involves the constants A and α. The electron's potential wells' depth and width can be adjusted by manipulating these two parameters, which leads to a spectrum of binding energies in atoms and molecules. The Gaussian potential exhibits significant dissimilarities from the Coulomb potential due to the absence of both the short-range singularity as well as the long-range, commonly known as infinite spectrum, of the Coulomb potential. The Coulomb potential, which sustains an infinite number of bound states, such as in the hydrogen atom, is characterized by these features. Despite the absence of the virial theorem, the Gaussian form offers both repulsion and attraction for particles with opposite or similar charges. It is noteworthy that a phenomenon similar to covalent bonding can be observed.

An optimized atomic orbital, specifically the 1s-like orbital ϕ, has been calculated for a particular potential using an even-tempered basis consisting of eight elements. This computation was performed with the aim of achieving optimization.

Gaussian orbitals

$$\phi = \sum_{p=1}^{8} c_p \chi_p \quad (6)$$

The variable χp denotes a Gaussian distribution that has been normalized, with an exponent of γp = 0.01(3p−1) where p is an integer ranging from 1 to 8. The 1s-type orbitals ϕ(ζ) are obtained through scaling (Yannacone et al., 2019).

$$\phi(\zeta) = \sum_{p=1}^{8} c_p \chi_p(\zeta) \quad (7)$$

The coefficients in equation 6 are identical to those found in the aforementioned text. Additionally, χp(ζ) denotes a Gaussian function that has been normalized and raised to the power of ζ2γp. Analogously to the case presented in equation 3 for the exponential orbital, it is noted that the term "orbital exponent" solely pertains to the factor of scale ζ in the subsequent discussions, and not to γp.

The molecular binding energies that were computed have been subjected to a decomposition process that separates them into contributions that are intra-atomic and inter-atomic in nature. Due to the detailed description of the procedure in previous literature,21,22 a concise overview will suffice in this instance. The wave function Ψ is initiated for a specific orbital exponent at a particular geometry. The molecular density ρ can be expressed as the sum of a quasi-classical contribution, denoted as ρqc, as well as an interference contribution, denoted as ρI.

$$\rho = \Psi^2 = \rho_{qc} + \rho_I \tag{8}$$

Where;

$$\rho_{qc} = \frac{n_{el}}{2}(\phi_a^{\,2} + \phi_b^{\,2}) \tag{9}$$

The variable "n_{el}" denotes the quantity of electrons present, specifically either 1 or 2 in the context of H_2^+ and H_2, respectively.

The summation of the quasi-atomic role T_A, as well as the interatomic contribution T_{inter}, defines the molecular kinetic energy (Plumley & Evanseck, 2008).

$$T_A = \frac{n_{el}}{2}[\langle\phi_a|\hat{T}|\phi_a\rangle + \langle\phi_b|\hat{T}|\phi_b\rangle] \tag{10}$$

And

$$T_{inter} = T_I = \langle\Psi|\hat{T}|\Psi\rangle - T_A \tag{11}$$

The symbol $\hat{T}$ represents the operator for kinetic energy. As stated in equation 11, the interatomic kinetic role is equivalent to the kinetic interference energy, denoted as T_I.

The summation of the quasi-atomic role V_A as well as the interatomic role V_{inter} defines the potential energy in a similar manner.

$$V_A = \frac{n_{el}}{2}[\langle\phi_a|\hat{V}_a|\phi_a\rangle + \langle\phi_b|\hat{V}_b|\phi_b\rangle] \tag{12}$$

And;

$$V_{inter} = [\langle\Psi|\hat{V}_a + \hat{V}_b + (n_{el} - 1)\hat{V}_{12}|\Psi\rangle + V_N] - V_A \tag{13}$$

The aforementioned equation involves the nuclear repelling energy (V_N), interelectron repelling operator in H_2 ($\hat{V}_{12}$), and potential energy operators ($\hat{V}_a$ and $\hat{V}_b$) which are responsible for nuclear attraction. Additionally, the potential energy of interatomic interaction, V_{qc}, is defined in a quasi-classical manner (Moncada et al., 2020).

$$V_{qc} = \frac{n_{el}}{2}[\langle\phi_a|\hat{V}_b|\phi_a\rangle + \langle\phi_b|\hat{V}_a|\phi_b\rangle] + (n_{el} - 1)[\phi_a\phi_a|\phi_b\phi_b] + V_N \tag{14}$$

Consequently, the contributions of both potential and kinetic energy to the intraatomic elements that make up binding energies can be expressed as follows:

$$T_{intra} = T_A - n_{el}T_H, \qquad V_{intra} = V_A - n_{el}V_H \tag{15}$$

The potential and kinetic energies of an atom of hydrogen, as calculated for various Gaussian potentials, are denoted by TH and VH, respectively.

The H_2^+ interatomic potential energy role is decomposed into the quasi-classical term V_{qc} and the interference term V_I, as per the analysis.

$$V_{inter}(H_2^+) = V_{qc} + V_I \tag{16}$$

The resolution pertaining to H_2 is comparatively intricate. Empirical evidence has demonstrated that it is indeed the case, as indicated by sources 21 and 22.

$$V_{inter}(H_2) = V_{qc} + V_{sc} + V_I + V_{II} \tag{17}$$

The expression comprises of three distinct components, namely the quasi-classical term Vqc, and two interference terms VI and VII. Additionally, there is a sharing role Vsc, which quantifies the rise in electron-electron repulsion energy due to electron sharing (Miller et al., 2022).

The overall molecular energy in relation to its separation products can be expressed as follows:

$$\Delta E = E_{intra} + E_{inter} = T_{intra} + V_{intra} + T_{inter} + V_{inter} \tag{18}$$

The interference density, denoted as ρ_I, is a measure of the charge redistribution that takes place during the formation of a chemical bond. It is calculated as the disparity among the molecular density as well as the combined densities of its constituent atoms. The Gaussian potential parameters $\alpha = 0.5$ as well as $A = 1.5$ in eq 5 were utilized to obtain a map of contours for the H_2 analog. Specifically, the map demonstrates the transfer of charge from each atom to the bonding region between them (Bersuker et al., 1993) (Figure 4.2).

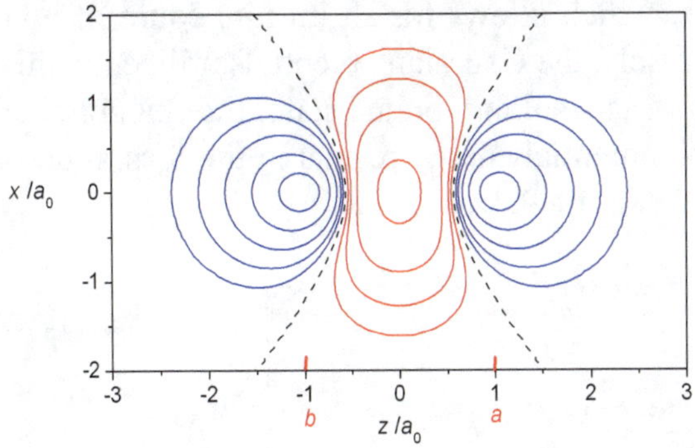

Figure 4.2. Contour map of interference density ρI in the xz-plane from the Gaussian potential representation of H_2^+ ***(α = 0.5, A = 1.5) at R = 2.47 a0 and ζ = 1.136. The positive contours (ρI+) in red are 0.02− 0.10 in steps of 0.02, while the negative contours (ρI−) in blue are −0.02 to −0.10 in steps of 0.02. The dashed lines represent zero contours. The nuclei (a, b) are at (0, ±1.235 a0).***

Source: Sture Nordholm, Creative Commons License.

The charge that is present in a bond, denoted as Q_I, can be precisely characterized as the overall density that is integrated among each sheet of zero density.21,22Although a mathematical formula for H_2^+ has been obtained in previous studies for the relevant integral under the Coulomb potential, this current research has utilized numerical integration to determine the QI values for different potentials for any provided internuclear distance.

The techniques of analysis employed in these computations have been comprehensively explicated in our prior publications21,22,42,43, which pertain to covalent bonds in H_2^+ and H_2 (Park et al., 2007).

4.4. COVALENT BINDING IN NON-COULOMBIC ANALOGS OF H_2^+ AND H_2

4.4.1. Gaussian Potentials and "Atoms"

The Gaussian interparticle potential, as expressed in equation 5, exhibits notable distinctions from the 1/r Coulomb potential. Specifically, the latter displays a single point at the origin and decays gradually as r approaches infinity, whereas the Gaussian potential is characterized by a short range and harmonic behavior at the origin. The Coulomb potential possesses an infinite range, which allows for an infinite count of bound states to be sustained. Conversely, the Gaussian potentials utilized in this study are only capable of supporting a solitary bound state. From a bonding perspective, it is crucial that the potential energy results in the formation of a stable atom (Wei et al., 2020) (Figure 4.3).

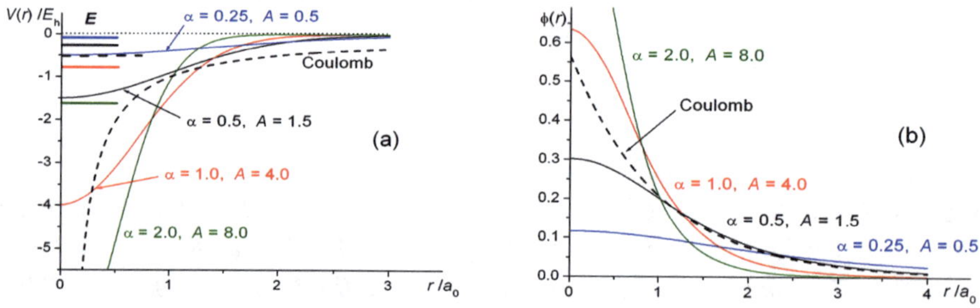

Figure 4.3. H atom Gaussian potentials and total ground state atomic energies and (b) corresponding AOs. Comparisons with Coulomb potential and H 1s AO.

Source: George B, Creative Commons License.

In this study, four distinct Gaussian potentials were chosen, with varying strengths ranging from α = 0.25, A = 0.5 (weak) to α = 2.0, A = 8.0 (strong). These potentials resulted in atoms with bound electrons and ground state energies that ranged from -0.019 to -1.568 Eh. The energy value, taking into account the Coulomb potential, is precisely -0.5 Hartree energy units (E_h) (Bianco et al., 2016).

Did You Know?

Gaussian potentials are mathematical functions commonly used to approximate the behavior of electrons around atoms in molecular quantum mechanics.

Table 4.1. Tabular Representation of total Ground State Atomic Energies (e) and Their Kinetic (t) and potential (v) Components Corresponding to the Four Gaussian Potentials and the Resulting Virial Ratios; Comparison with Coulombic Potential

		α, A			
parameter	0.25, 0.50	0.50, 1.5	1.0, 4.0	2.0, 8.0	Coulomb
E/E_h	−0.019	−0.185	−0.783	−1.568	−0.5

T/E_h	0.085	0.363	1.038	2.079	0.5
V/E_h	−0.103	−0.548	−1.821	−3.647	−1.0
−V/T	1.22	1.51	1.75	1.75	2.0

Source: Klaus Ruedenberg, Creative Commons License.

The Gaussian potentials exhibit virial ratios ranging from 1.22 to 1.75. The Coulombic wave function is characterized by an exponential function that exhibits a nuclear cusp. It demonstrates a slower decay rate at larger values of r compared to the wave functions of Gaussian potentials, with the exception of the most diffuse Gaussian potential that corresponds to $\alpha = 0.25$ and $A = 0.5$ (Scheurer et al., 2020).

It is noteworthy that when the potential $\alpha = 0.25$ and $A = 0.5$ is weakened further by decreasing A to 0.3, no bound states are supported in an atom. However, upon implementation within the molecule, it can be observed that the resultant double well potential possesses a bounded status with an energy of -0.0039 Eh at a neutral division of 4.6 a0. The aforementioned statement represents a noteworthy extension of the covalent bonding mechanism (Das et al., 2002).

Modifying the orbital exponent of a chosen Gaussian potential's ground state eigenfunction, among the four potentials chosen for this study, results in a similar impact on its radial behavior and energies as that of a typical hydrogenic 1s orbital, which is the eigenfunction of the Coulomb potential 1/r. The present study involves a comparison between the energy dependence on the orbital exponent of the 1s wave as a function of the $\alpha = 0.5$, $A = 1.5$ Gaussian potential and that of the conventional (Coulombic) 1s orbital. The congruence in quality between the two result sets is apparent, particularly in the significant correlation of the potential and kinetic energies with ζ in both instances. Conversely, the total energy exhibits a feeble dependence on ζ in comparison (Kantor et al., 1986).

4.4.2. Energies of H_2^+ and H_2 Molecules with Gaussian Potentials

The bimodal characteristic of the Gaussian potential is evident, as well as the qualitative distinctions between the two potentials, specifically the limited profundity of VG at the atomic nuclei. The most notable disparity among the wave functions pertains to the lack of nuclear cusps in ΨG. Although both of the wave functions exhibit similar qualitative characteristics, the inquiry pertains to whether the energetic patterns that arise during covalent bonding are fundamentally identical. The energy constituents outlined in section 2 pertaining to H_2^+ and H_2 were calculated for all four Gaussian potentials (Gavezzotti, 2016) (Figure 4.4).

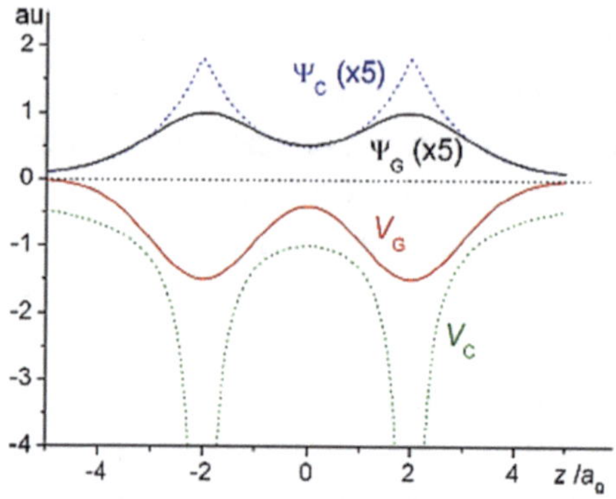

Figure 4.4. Gaussian (G) ($\alpha = 0.5$, $A = 1.5$) and Coulomb (C) potentials of H_2 + at R = 4 a0 and resulting ground state wave functions (with $\zeta = 1$ in both cases) as functions of internuclear coordinate z ($x = y = 0$).

Source: Sture Nordholm, Creative Commons License.

The bond lengths of H_2^+ were computed and found to range from 4.15 to 1.16 a0. The corresponding bond energies, represented by -ΔE, were determined to be between 0.025 and 0.658 Eh. These values were observed to be correlated with the potential strength and atomic energy, as presented in Table 4.1. The study reveals that the qualitative patterns observed in the potential, kinetic, as well as total energies remain consistent across all four Gaussian potentials, akin to those observed in the Coulomb potential (Shields et al., 2010). However, a slight yet perceptible variation is evident in the potential energy's behavior. In the context of fixed Gaussian potentials, it can be observed that fixed (Figure 4.5).

Table 4.2. Tabular Representation of H_2^+: Molecular Energies (e) and Their Kinetic (t) and Potential (v) Components (relative to H + H$^+$) at Computed Equilibrium Distances with Fixed ($\zeta = 1$) and Optimized Exponents for Gaussian Potentials; Comparison with Coulombic Potential

α, A										
Parameter	**0.25**	**0.50**	**0.5**	**1.5**	**1.0**	**4.0**	**2.0**	**8.0**	**coulomb**	**coulomb**
ζ	1.0	1.245	1.0	1.136	1.0	1.096	1.0	1.094	1.0	1.239
Re/a0	4.15	3.92	2.58	2.47	1.70	1.64	1.20	1.16	2.49	2.00
$\Delta E/E_h$	−0.025	−0.030	−0.110	−0.120	−0.312	−0.330	−0.624	−0.658	−0.065	−0.087
$\Delta T/E_h$	−0.020	0.013	−0.081	−0.002	−0.224	−0.062	−0.448	−0.125	−0.117	0.087
$\Delta V/E_h$	−0.005	−0.043	−0.029	−0.118	−0.089	−0.268	−0.175	−0.532	0.052	−0.174
−V/T	1.69	1.51	2.05	1.84	2.35	2.14	2.34	2.14	2.48	2.00

Source: Klaus Ruedenberg, Creative Commons License.

Table 4.3. Tabular Representation of H_2: Molecular Energies (E) and Their Kinetic (T) and Potential (V) Components (Relative to H + H) at Computed Equilibrium Distances Obtained by the VB Method with Fixed ($\zeta = 1$) and Optimized Exponents for Gaussian Potentials; Comparison with Coulombic Potential

α, A										
Param-eter	**0.25**	**0.50**	**0.5**	**1.5**	**1.0**	**4.0**	**2.0**	**8.0**	**coulomb**	**coulomb**
ζ	1.0	1.131	1.0	1.050	1.0	1.030	1.0	1.028	1.0	1.167
Re/a0	3.72	3.56	2.23	2.18	1.44	1.41	1.02	1.00	1.64	1.41
$\Delta E/E_h$	−0.036	−0.039	−0.121	−0.124	−0.296	−0.299	−0.593	−0.599	−0.116	−0.139
$\Delta T/E_h$	−0.031	0.007	−0.104	−0.039	−0.260	−0.150	−0.523	−0.313	−0.162	0.139
ΔV/E	-0.005	-0.046	-0.017	-0.085	-0.036	-0.150	-0.069	-0.285	0.046	-0.278
-V/T	1.53	1.44	1.79	1.72	2.03	1.97	2.03	1.97	2.33	2.00

Source: George B, Creative Commons License.

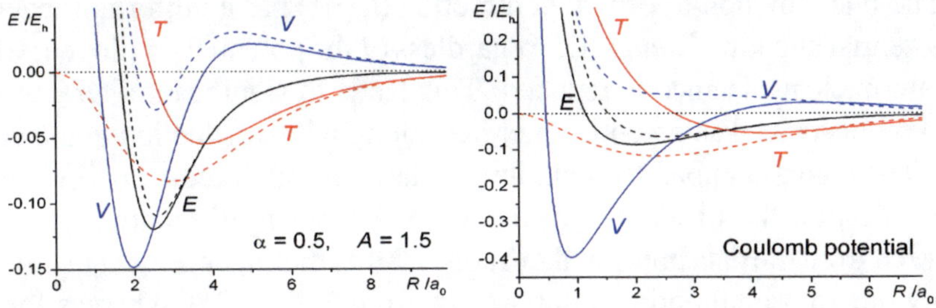

Figure 4.5. Energies of H_2^+ computed with a Gaussian (α = 0.5, A = 1.5) and the Coulomb potential. Results with optimized and fixed (atomic) exponents are shown with full and dashed lines, respectively. Total, kinetic, and potential energies are shown in black, red, and blue, respectively.

Source: Klaus Ruedenberg, Creative Commons License.

For orbital exponents, specifically when ζ = 1, the potential energy experiences an initial increase as the internuclear separation decreases (Table 4.3). However, it subsequently reaches a minimum value, which is actually lower than the atomic value, before transitioning into a highly repulsive state. The aforementioned conduct is notably amplified for orbital exponents that have been optimized. For the Coulomb potential, it can be observed that there exists no threshold in potential energy when ζ = 1 (Ruzsinszky et al., 2005). Regardless of the applied potential, molecular binding primarily arises from kinetic factors when ζ = 1 (Figure 4.6).

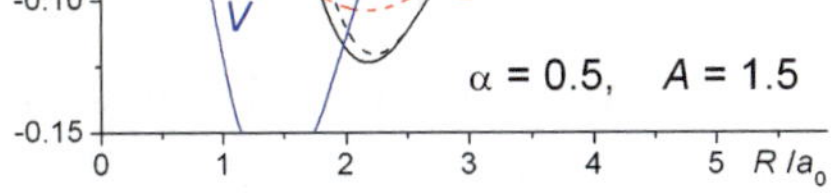

Figure 4.6. Energies of H_2 computed by the VB method with a Gaussian (α = 0.5, A = 1.5) potential. Results with optimized and fixed (atomic) exponents are shown with full and dashed lines, respectively. Total, kinetic, and potential energies are shown in black, red, and blue, respectively.

Source: George B, Creative Commons License.

The phenomenon of orbital contraction ($\zeta > 1$) has a uniform impact on the potential and kinetic energies, regardless of the potential employed, when the internuclear distance is reduced. This leads to significant alterations in both kinetic as well as potential energies, along with a reduction in the virial ratio. The Gaussian potentials exhibit a relatively small reduction in overall energy despite the observed net decrease. Regarding the latter, it can be observed from the data presented in Table 4.2 that the enhancement in binding energy due to orbital optimization ranges from 5% to 17%, whereas for the Coulomb potential, it is approximately 25%. The aforementioned outcomes are a direct result of the significant correlation between the potential and kinetic energy within a hydrogen atom, which is contingent upon minor fluctuations in the wave function, including contraction or expansion, regardless of the interparticle potential's characteristics. However, the Gaussian calculations suggest that H_2^+ and H_2 possess comparable stabilities concerning dissociation, in contrast to the Coulomb calculations which suggest that H_2 is notably more stable than H_2^+ (Peng et al., 2017).

As previously mentioned, the H_2 computations that were the subject of discussion in this study were predominantly conducted utilizing the VB theoretical framework. The scientific community has comprehensively documented and established the similarities and distinctions among the wave functions and energies of MO, setup communication (CI), as well as VB in the context of Coulomb interparticle potential. These calculations were performed using a minimal 1s AO basis.21,43 The Gaussian potentials exhibit a similar behavior in a qualitative manner. The initiation of orbital contraction is contingent upon the scope of the atomic potential. The onset of contraction for the greatest diffuse Gaussian potential (with $\alpha = 0.25$ and $A = 0.5$) occurs at approximately 18 atomic units, and the exponent reaches a united atom limit of 1.62. In contrast, for the tightest Gaussian potential (with $\alpha = 2.0$ and $A = 8.0$), contraction begins at approximately 2.2 atomic units, and the value of ζ is 1.36 at $R = 0$ (DiLabio et al., 2013).

The qualitative distinction among the Gaussian as well as Coulomb wells at and in proximity to the nuclei results in a dissimilar behavior of the exponents as R approaches 0 in the case of Gaussian potentials, in contrast to the Coulomb potential. Conversely, when R exceeds 1.6, the optimized exponents associated with the $\alpha = 0.5$, $A = 1.5$ potential are very similar to those of the Coulomb potential, suggesting that orbital contraction is realistically depicted with the Gaussian potential (Figure 4.7). The orbital coefficient in H_2, exhibits an analogous behavior. Evidently, despite the notable variations in the distance-dependent nature of the energy levels of the diverse potentials, they all demonstrate analogous traits at a fundamental level. Therefore, based on the energetics, the deductions made regarding the covalent bonding mechanism in H_2^+ and H_2 remain consistent, regardless of the characteristics of the potential responsible for binding electrons to the nuclei as well as accounting for both internuclear as well as interelectron repulsions (Schmidt et al., 2014).

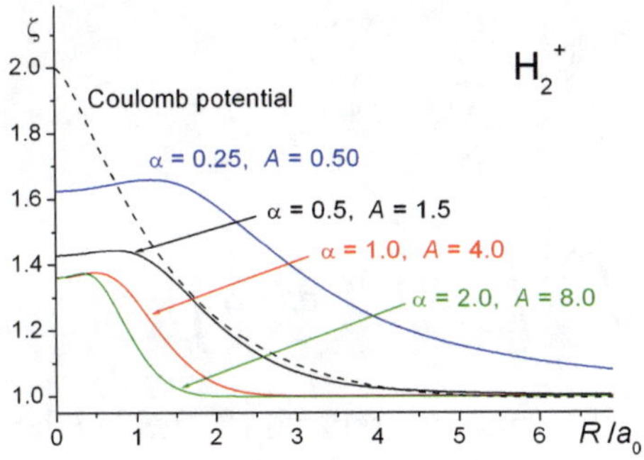

Figure 4.7. Internuclear distance (R) dependence of optimized orbital exponents (ζ) for the various Gaussian potentials (full lines) and the coulomb potential (dashed line) for H_2^+.

Source: Sture Nordholm, Creative Commons License.

4.4.3. Spatial Analysis of the Density and Energy Changes on Covalent Bonding in H_2^+ and H_2

This relationship has been a subject of debate and discord regarding the underlying mechanism of covalent bonding in H_2^+ as well as H_2. The matter at hand pertains to the underlying causes of the reduction in overall molecular energy as bond lengths decrease due to orbital optimization, which involves the utilization of an increased orbital exponent compared to that in the dissociation limit. Although the alterations in the orbital exponent are minor, the modifications in the binding energy's kinetic as well as potential components are substantial, regardless of the interparticle potential's characteristics. The present study employs spatial analysis techniques to investigate density and energy variations in H_2^+ and H_2. The aim is to pinpoint the specific regions where these changes are most pronounced (Gilli & Gilli, 2009).

This approach primarily involves the examination of density as well as density difference maps pertaining to both potential and kinetic energy integrals, alongside density integrals. Direct comparison of the fundamental spatial characteristics and outcomes of the electrostatic as well as kinetic interpretations is possible. The approach centers on the spatial correlation of density and energy integrals. Specifically, property P is represented as a sum of contributions, as outlined by the subsequent equations for one-electron properties (Soumya & Joe, 2021):

$$\langle P \rangle = \int \Psi * \hat{P} \Psi \, dx \, dy \, dz = \sum_n P_n \quad (19)$$

Where;

$$P_n = \int_{z_n}^{z_{n+1}} \left\{ \int_{-\infty}^{\infty} \int_{-\infty}^{\infty} \Psi * \hat{P} \Psi \, dx \, dy \right\} dz \quad (20)$$

Comprehensive information regarding the methodology employed, along with the outcomes achieved for H_2^+ as well as H_2 (with Coulomb potentials), can be found in our prior publications.42,43 The present study employs the aforementioned method to analyze molecules characterized by Gaussian potentials.

The discernible impacts of orbital optimizing are prominently observable in the disparity maps, where the alteration in characteristic P is delineated as.

$$\Delta P = P(\zeta_{\text{opt}}) - P(\zeta = 1) \quad (21)$$

This study aims to compare the effects of molecular and atomic contractions.

$$\Delta\Delta P = \Delta P_{\text{molecule}} - \Delta P_{\text{atoms}} \quad (22)$$

This statement pertains to the relative measurement of atomic as well as molecular contributions in terms of density and energy alterations during covalent bonding (Tarika et al., 2022). This increase leads to an elevation of electron density as well as kinetic energy contributions in the atomic regions, while simultaneously reducing the potential energy in that area. To clarify, the primary impact of orbital optimization, specifically contraction in this instance, is primarily localized within the atom. The analysis of the impact of orbital optimizing on the molecule as well as its noninteracting a component atoms provides significant insights into the bonding perspective. The transference of density towards the internuclear area is both conspicuous and significant, resulting in a homogeneous reduction in kinetic energy (Vincy et al., 2022). In contrast, it can be observed that although there is a reduction in the potential energy within the interatomic area, the rise in potential energy in the outer regions, where the negative interference part of the density is present, surpasses the decrease. This leads to a net rise in potential energy. The binding contributions resulting from orbital optimization lead to a reduction in the overall energy content of the molecule in relation to its constituent atoms. This phenomenon can be attributed to the decreased interatomic part of the molecule's kinetic energy. The phenomenon of electron repulsion leads to significant reduction of the attractive Coulomb energy between electrons and nuclei. The observed trends for H_2^+ are identical, thus the aforementioned observations and conclusions are equally applicable. In the case of molecules with Gaussian interparticle potentials, the impact of orbital optimization is relatively reduced compared to that of "real" molecules with Coulomb potentials. However, the energetic effects exhibit identical characteristics in both scenarios (Jain et al., 2010) (Figures 4.8 & 4.9).

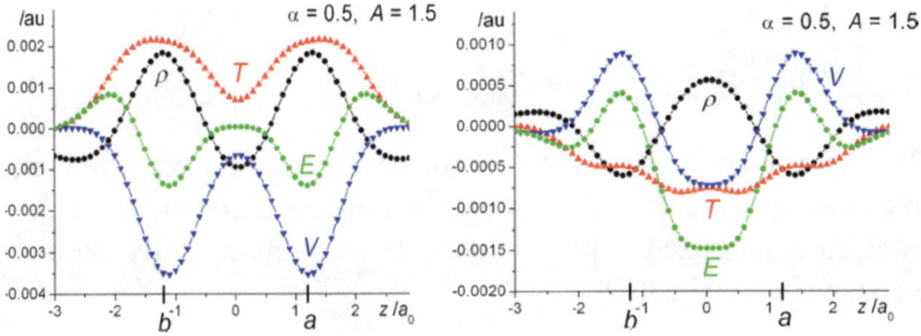

Figure 4.8. H_2^+. (left) Molecular contraction, i.e., difference map between spatial density and energy distributions with optimized exponent and fixed exponent of 1.0. Calculated with Gaussian potential at Re = 2.47 a0 with ζopt = 1.136. Total energy changes (in Eh): ΔT = 0.079, ΔV =–.089, and ΔE = −0.011. (right) Difference between molecular and atomic contractions. Total energy changes (in Eh), as defined in eq 22: ΔΔT = −0.027, ΔΔV = 0.005, and ΔΔE = −0.022.

Source: George B, Creative Commons License.

It should be noted that the outcomes specifically those defined in equation 22, have the potential to be expressed in the following manner.

$$\Delta\Delta P = P_{\text{inter}}(\zeta_{\text{opt}}) - P_{\text{inter}}(\zeta = 1) \tag{23}$$

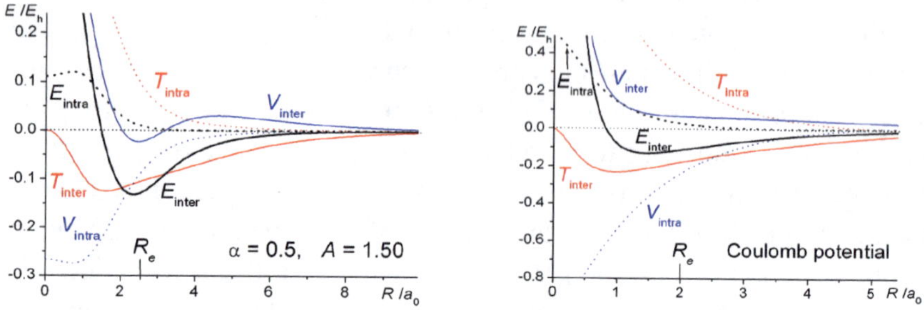

Figure 4.9. Intra- and interatomic components of kinetic, potential, and total energies of H^{2+} computed with a Gaussian ($\alpha = 0.5$, $A = 1.5$) and the Coulomb potentials, using optimized orbital exponents.

The interatomic parts of the element P with a variable ζ are formally defined as follows.

$$P_{\text{inter}}(\zeta) = P_{\text{molecule}}(\zeta) - P_{\text{atoms}}(\zeta) \tag{24}$$

The determination of interatomic contributions to a given property, such as kinetic energy, involves computing the molecular and atomic values via the molecule-optimized orbital exponent, and subsequently taking their difference (Zhu et al., 2019).

4.4.4. Intra- versus Interatomic Energies and Charge Transfer to Bond

The intra- and interatomic energies, including kinetic, potential, as well as total energies, were calculated for the optimized orbital exponents of the 4 Gaussian potentials for both H_2^+ and H_2, as presented in equations 8–18. To facilitate a direct comparison, the outcomes pertaining to the Gaussian ($\alpha = 0.5$, $A = 1.5$) are presented. Regardless of the chosen potential or molecule, similar trends are observed at a qualitative level. It is evident that in both H_2^+ as well as H_2, the bonding phenomenon is attributed to the interatomic part of the overall energy, denoted as Einter. The primary factor of significance is the interatomic kinetic energy, denoted as Tinter, which corresponds to the interference constituent of the kinetic energy, TI. Since covalent bonding is a wave physical quantity, it can be inferred that it is fundamentally a quantum phenomenon, regardless of the potential's characteristics. The total energy within an atom, known as Eintra, is consistently repulsive in nature. This is due to the fact that the intra-atomic kinetic energy, Tintra, which is repulsive, outweighs the attractive force generated by the intraatomic potential energy, or Vintra (Levina et al., 2021). The Vinter energies, which exist between atoms, are predominantly characterized by repulsion. However, in cases where Gaussian potentials are employed, they exhibit marginal minima that offer a degree of stabilization. This stabilization can be attributed to the presence of minimums in the quasi-classical potential energies. However, the impact of alterations in interatomic potential energy on bonding is not significant. The interatomic potential energy of H_2 is characterized by a higher degree of complexity compared to that of H_2^+ due to the presence of multiple components. Specifically, in alongside the quasi-classical Vqc term, the potential energy includes two types of interference (VI, VII) and Coulombic sharing (Vsc) contributions, each of which consist of both one- and two-electron components. An analysis of the outcomes derived from a Gaussian function with parameters α = 0.5 and A = 1.5. As previously mentioned, the Gaussian potential yields a Vinter term that exhibits a minor attractive minimum at a distance of approximately 2.3 a0 when examined quantitatively. The contributions of interatomic potential energy to bonding are relatively insignificant (Sun et al., 2020) (Figure 4.10).

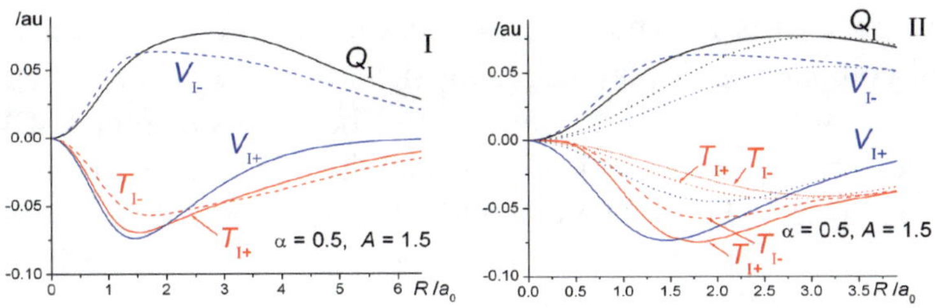

Figure 4.10. Interference terms for H_2^+ with a Gaussian potential as functions of the internuclear distance R. Black lines: Charge transfer QI into the bond. Red lines: Kinetic interference energies. Blue lines: Potential interferences energies. Full lines: Contributions (TI+, VI+) from the density accumulation region defined by ρI+. Dashed lines: Contributions TI− and VI− from the density depletion regions defined by ρI− (I) For wave function with ζ optimized. (II) Comparison of results for optimized ζ (full and dashed lines) with results for ζ = 1 (dotted lines) in the range near the equilibrium distance.

Source: Sture Nordholm, Creative Commons License.

The interatomic kinetic energy exhibits a high degree of sensitivity to the selection of orbital exponent, regardless of the potential employed, whereas the potential energy is minimally impacted. To clarify, the phenomenon of orbital contraction leading to decreased energy and heightened stability is primarily attributed to reduced interatomic kinetic energy. The phenomenon of electron delocalization is widely recognized to lead to charge transfer within the interatomic region, commonly referred to as the "bond" (Eskandari, 2016). The objective is to segregate the kinetic as well as potential constituents of the disruption energy by attributing them to both the positive and negative disruption density areas (ρi+ and ρi−). Thus,

$$T_I = T_{I+} + T_{I-} \quad \text{and} \quad V_I = V_{I+} + V_{I-} \tag{25}$$

The aforementioned terminologies, namely QI, TI+, TI−, VI+, as well as VI−, establish a correlation between the movement of charges and alterations in energy levels. Additionally, they serve to elucidate and measure the kinetic as well as potential components of the binding energy (Sakai et al., 2011).

Regardless of the characteristics of the potential, the accumulation of density in the bond (QI) is evident, exhibiting a peak value in the vicinity of the bond's equilibrium length. Clearly, there is a correlation between the charge buildup QI and the absolute values of the 4 terms TI+, TI−, VI+, and VI−, as they increase and decrease simultaneously. It is noteworthy that the kinetic parts TI+ and TI- exhibit negativity throughout, whereas the potential components display opposing signs throughout the system (VI+ < 0, VI- > 0, with the absolute value of VI+ being less than that of VI- for evident reasons). The resultant effect is that the overall interference part of the kinetic energy (TI+ + TI-) exhibits a highly negative value, while the total interference part of the potential energy is in close proximity to zero and displays a positive value (Giner et al., 1976) (Figure 4.11).

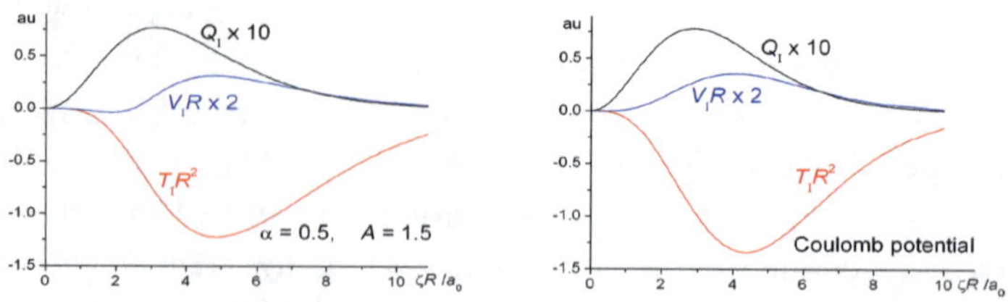

Figure 4.11. Kinetic (TI) and potential (VI) interference energies (plotted as TIR^2 and VIR) and total charge transferred into the bond (QI) computed with a Gaussian (α = 0.5, A = 1.5) and the Coulomb potential, using optimized orbital exponents.

Source: George B, Creative Commons License.

The aforementioned outcomes for H_2^+, pertains to the scaled internuclear separation σ (where σ = ζR). The figures above illustrate the kinetic as well as possible interference energy of H_2^+, TI(σ), as well as VI(σ), in addition to the total charge sent into the bonding area, QI(σ). The QI and TI curves exhibit a resemblance in their shape across a spectrum of potentials, albeit with varying ranges contingent upon the potential's intensity, akin to the equilibrium distances as well as binding energies. Nevertheless, the charge transfer maximum value (QI) to the bond remains relatively constant, with a range of 0.073 to 0.080, indicating minimal dependence on the applied potential. The maximum magnitude of the kinetic disruption energy (TI), which is the most negative value, exhibits a relatively stable behavior. The range of values observed is between negative 1.11 and negative 1.65 electron volts. The maximum of the aforementioned exhibits a higher degree of variation when measured concurrently (specifically at distances less than 4.0 a0). This concurrent measurement has the effect of augmenting the VI, thereby rendering it more antibonding. The maximum value of QI(σ) occurs at ζR ≈ 2.9 a0, or equivalently, R ≈ 2.5 a0. Consequently, any additional reduction in orbital distance leads to an increased overall charge accumulation within the bond. To summarize, when the equilibrium a separation is reached, the process of orbital contraction becomes more significant in bonding due to its ability to increase the extent of delocalization. The phenomenon is characterized by a rise in the quantity of charge that is conveyed into the bonding area, accompanied by a reduction in the interatomic part of the kinetic energy, which refers to the interference. Given the preceding discourse on the function of orbital contraction, it is reasonable to anticipate a significant correlation between the anticipated equilibrium bond length as well as the positions of the minimums and maximums of TI(σ)R^2, QI(σ), as well as VI(σ)R. The empirical evidence pertaining to the 4 Gaussian potentials does exhibit a substantial level of correlation. Although the Coulomb amounts do not precisely align with the curves, they exhibit a high degree of proximity. Thus, it can be inferred that the bonding functions of the interference parts of both kinetic and potential energies, as well as the overall charge sent to the bond, remain consistent regardless of the type of potential, whether it be weak or strong, Gaussian or Coulombic. Hence, it can be inferred that the selection of a potential does not exert a noteworthy impact on the factual process of covalent bonding. This process can be concisely described as the dispersion of electrons, whose fundamental energetic expressions are the actions of the interatomic kinetic energy, specifically interference (McDonagh et al., 2017).

4.4.5. Electron Densities and Orbital Contraction

The significance of orbital contraction in the quantitative depiction of covalent bonding, particularly those including hydrogen atoms, has been acknowledged for a considerable period. However, the consequences for the comprehension of covalent bonding remain a subject of debate. It is worth noting that the fulfillment of the virial theorem may be achieved through the optimization of orbital exponents for all atomic orbitals utilized in the construction of a molecular wave function. Reoptimization of the system often leads to a contraction that causes a reversal in the contributions of both potential and kinetic energy to the binding energy (Autschbach & Schwarz, 2000). The electrostatic perspective of bonding considers the reduction in potential energy as a direct consequence of the interaction between the nuclei and the heightened electron density within the bond. This assumption forms the fundamental principle of this viewpoint, which asserts that covalent bond formation is primarily driven by electrostatic factors, which supersede the repellent kinetic energy component. This interpretation is supported by existing literature. Ruedenberg and other scholars have presented an alternative perspective, contending that the principal mechanism governing covalent bonding between atoms is the sharing and delocalization of electrons, which is accompanied by a reduction in kinetic energy. According to this view, it is the increase in kinetic energy reduction that leads to the contraction of orbitals. The contractions involve alterations in the potential and kinetic energy within atoms, which collectively exhibit a slightly antibonding effect due to the principle of intra-atomic variation. The thorough discussion of these matters within the framework of the virial theorem's validity notwithstanding, it is pertinent and enlightening to investigate their general applicability, regardless of the specific characteristics of the interparticle possibility. Consequently, this topic is being discussed with greater specificity in this section compared to the previous ones (Krinsky et al., 2011).

The electron density contour map of H_2^+ has been computed using a Gaussian potential with parameters $\alpha = 0.5$ and $A = 1.5$, at its equilibrium geometry of Re = 2.47 a0 with an optimized orbital exponent of ζopt = 1.136. The structure exhibits a commonly recognized pattern, wherein the density is most concentrated in the vicinity of the nuclei. However, a significant accumulation of density in the interatomic area is readily apparent (Melin et al., 2007). The impact of orbital a contraction on the overall molecular density (ρ) and interference density (ρI) is to elevate both of these parameters within the internuclear region, as suggested by the QI behavior that has been previously examined. Regardless of the potential employed, a significant rise in the overall densities along the z-axis between nuclei is observed at equilibrium geometries, which is in line with the anticipated orbital contraction. The most significant augmentation, however, occurs in the proximity of the nuclei. The observed phenomenon can be attributed to the intra-atomic part, as evidenced by the decrease in interference density in the vicinity of atomic nuclei and its increase in the interstitial regions, particularly in the central region. The density plots associated with the 4 Gaussian potentials exhibit a similar qualitative nature to those derived from the Coulomb potential computations. Evident distinctions manifest in the vicinity of the nuclei, where the anomalies in the Coulomb potentials give rise to wave functions as well as densities that decay exponentially and conform to the nuclear cusp condition (Lehtola et al., 2013).

The plots of total and interference densities, computed at the bond midpoint across various internuclear distances, offer additional evidence and quantification of the impact of orbital contraction. Orbital contraction is observed to transpire at a distance approximately 1–3 a0 above the equilibrium distance, leading to an increase in both the total as well as interference densities, contingent on the potency of the atomic potential as well as the corresponding equilibrium distance. The distribution of the total density calculated using Coulomb potentials exhibits significant differences from those obtained with Gaussian potentials, particularly in the occurrence of orbital contraction, when examined at extremely short distances. This phenomenon can be attributed to the distinct nature of Coulomb as well as Gaussian potentials in the close proximity of the nuclei. The degree of molecular electron density restructuring varies based on the interaction potential and the flexibility or fullness of the basis set. Nonetheless, it does not have a noteworthy impact on the resultant covalent bond (Kubel et al., 1987).

4.5. COVALENT BONDS BETWEEN ATOMS WITH INNER SHELLS

The bonding characteristics between hydrogen molecules and molecule ions are anticipated to differ from those of other atoms due to the lack of closed inner shells. The pseudopotential method can yield valuable estimates for properties that are primarily reliant on valence electrons. The present methodology involves a wave function that is contingent solely upon the valence electrons, while the relationships with the fundamental electrons are assimilated into a powerful potential for the electrons with valence (Huhtala et al., 2004).

It is plausible that the outcomes of the preceding section retain their validity for suitable potentials that do not conform to the Gaussian structure. This suggests that they may also be applicable in cases where valence electrons are characterized by means of the pseudopotential technique.

Previous publications 21,22 have provided some insights into this matter through a review of the binding in B_2, C_2, N_2, O_2, and F_2 molecules, which were then compared to the binding in H_2^+ and H_2. It was discovered that the fundamental interaction between changes in intra-atomic as well as interatomic energy exhibits a striking similarity across molecules such as H_2^+, H_2, B_2, C_2, N_2, O_2, as well as F_2. The aforementioned deduction is derived from the fact that the fundamental attributes of the power curves exhibited by these molecules bear a striking resemblance to those of N_2, as reported in previous studies (Auvert, 2020).

An inquiry of noteworthy significance pertains to the potential influence of the completely filled inner shells on the orbital movements that constitute the binding mechanism. To provide further elucidation on the subject, supplementary individual computations were conducted at the equilibrium distance of every molecule for the two distinct components that collectively comprise the intra-atomic energy potential ΔVA on each atom. These components are the intra-atomic nuclear-electron attraction energy ⟨ΨA|−rA−1|ΨA⟩ as well as the intra-atomic electron-electron repulsion energy ⟨ΨA|r12−1|ΨA⟩, where ΨA pertains to the intra-atomic segment of the molecular wave function in relation to atom A (Auvert & Auvert, 2016).

For all molecules and both expectation numbers, the energy value in a molecule is greater in magnitude compared to the related energy in an empty atom. This increase in energy is attributed to the electron-electron repulsion, which accounts for approximately 45–50% of the total rise in the strength of the electron-nuclear attraction (Parthé, 1973). The presented inequalities provide evidence that the reduction in the intra-atomic potential energy experienced by individual atoms is indeed attributable to a general reduction in atomic size. Orbital contractions have been observed by Hiberty et al. (37) in bonds involving atoms apart from hydrogen (Miao, 2013).

Levine and Head-Gordon (52) conducted an investigation on several molecules that consist of atoms beyond hydrogen, utilizing an alternative form of energy decomposition analysis (EDA).54 The analyzes conducted revealed that orbital polarization played a significant role in reinstating the appropriate virial ratio, largely supplanting orbital contraction. The complexity of the present examines is compounded by the predetermined buildings of the nonbonded particles in the aforementioned approach (Wheatley & Gopal, 2012).

4.6. RECENT ADVANCES IN MOLECULAR QUANTUM MECHANICS

4.6.1. Application of Advanced Computational Methods

The application of sophisticated computational techniques has brought about a significant transformation in the domain of molecular quantum mechanics. This has facilitated the investigation of covalent bonding with an unparalleled level of precision and comprehensiveness. The aforementioned techniques employ advanced algorithms and numerical methods to resolve the Schrödinger equation and assess the electronic characteristics of molecules. Through the utilization of high-performance computing, researchers are able to investigate intricate molecular systems and decipher the complexities of chemical bonding (Diercksen et al., 2012).

The coupled cluster theory (CCT) is a precise method for electronic structure analysis that is extensively employed in the examination of covalent bonding. The approach presented provides a methodical and rigorous means of incorporating electron correlation effects that surpasses the constraints of conventional Hartree-Fock theory. Coupled cluster calculations offer accurate characterizations of molecular electronic energy levels as well as properties by integrating electron correlation via a set of mathematical equations. The employment of this technique has played a crucial role in comprehending the characteristics of covalent bonds, elucidating the energetic and spatial arrangement of electrons engaged in bonding interactions. Multireference configuration interaction (MRCI) techniques are essential in situations where covalent bonding occurs within intricate molecular systems. The MRCI method enables the incorporation of numerous electronic configurations that are unable to be sufficiently characterized by a solitary determinant. The capacity for adaptability allows for the investigation of molecular structures that exhibit significant electron correlation, which are commonly found in transitional metal structures, excited states, as well as highly correlated systems (Vogiatzis et al., 2018). The utilization of MRCI enables the capture of the intricate interplay among various electronic states, thereby providing helpful insights into complicated bonding scenarios. This approach facilitates an expanded comprehension of covalent interactions.

The utilization of advanced computational techniques presents a multitude of benefits in the examination of covalent bonding. Primarily, they furnish precise prognostications of molecular characteristics such as bond lengths, bond forces, as well as vibrational spectra, that are fundamental in comprehending the reactivity and stability of molecules. In addition, these methodologies exhibit the capability to manage extensive molecular systems, thereby facilitating inquiries into biological macromolecules, nanotechnology, and surface reactions. Moreover, sophisticated computational techniques provide the capability to investigate excited states, thereby facilitating a deeper understanding of photochemical mechanisms and electronic transitions (Schaefer, 2001).

Nevertheless, advanced computational techniques possess certain constraints. Initially, it is noteworthy that these tasks can pose a significant computational burden, necessitating substantial computational time and resources. The precision of these techniques is significantly reliant on the selected theoretical level and the caliber of basis sets utilized. In addition, certain molecular systems that exhibit pronounced static or dynamic correlations between electrons may pose challenges for certain electronic structure methods. Researchers must meticulously weigh the balance between computational expenses and the intended precision when opting for a suitable approach for a particular investigation (Christoffersen & Christoffersen, 1989).

In general, the utilization of sophisticated computational techniques has considerably enhanced our comprehension of covalent bonding. By employing advanced techniques such as coupled cluster principle, multireference configuration communication, and others, scientists are able to decipher the complexities of bonding interactions and offer significant understanding into chemical responsiveness, molecular security, and spectroscopic properties (Poater et al., 2010).

4.6.2. Incorporation of Electron Correlation Effects

The role of electron correlation is of paramount importance in the context of covalent bonding, as it transcends the constraints of the Hartree-Fock approach. The inclusion of repulsion as well as exchange interactions among electrons results in a more precise depiction of molecular characteristics and energetics. The phenomenon of covalent bonding is significantly influenced by electron correlation, which has an impact on bond dimensions, bond energies, as well as molecular spectra (Hernández & Sanz, 2000).

Remember

Remember that electron correlation effects play a crucial role in accurately describing the behavior of electrons in covalent bonding, going beyond the simple independent electron approximation.

Post-Hartree-Fock methodologies offer a systematic approach to precisely incorporate the effects of electron correlation. The Configuration Interaction (CI) method is a prevalent technique utilized to incorporate electron correlation effects. This approach involves the consideration of multiple electronic configurations as well as their corresponding mixing. The incorporation of excited states above the Hartree-Fock reference in computational chemistry enables the utilization of CI methods, which effectively account for electron correlation and enhance the precision of molecular properties. The exponential ansatz is utilized in CCT as a potent post-Hartree-Fock approach to incorporate electron correlation. Different degrees of approximation, like CCSD and CCSD(T), can be utilized depending on the level of precision required (Rice & Handy, 1992).

The utilization of perturbation theory presents a methodical strategy for addressing the correlation of electrons as a minor perturbation of the Hartree-Fock solution. The Møller-Plesset perturbation theory (MP2) is a widely used perturbative methodology that incorporates electron correlation effects by examining perturbative adjustments to the wavefunction. The MP2 method offers a computationally efficient as well as reasonably accurate account of electron correlation in numerous molecular systems. The utilization of higher-order perturbation theories, namely MP3 and MP4, has the potential to attain greater precision (Sommerfeld et al., 2008).

The accurate depiction of covalent bonding is hindered by dynamic electron correlation, which is a result of the swift movement of electrons. Current advancements have been directed towards the acquisition of dynamic correlation in order to enhance comprehension of covalent bonding phenomenon. Sophisticated techniques such as coupled cluster methods via perturbative triples (CCSD(T)) as well as multi-reference methods provide a thorough approach to electron correlation by addressing dynamic as well as static correlation effects. The aforementioned techniques exhibit the ability to depict the dissociation of bonds, excited states, and the processes of bond formation and breaking. The accuracy of Density Functional Theory (DFT) calculations has been improved through the creation of range-separated functionals as well as hybrid functionals, which have enabled the capture of dynamic correlation (Cremer, 2001).

4.6.3. Exploration of Higher Excited States

The concept of excited states as well as their significance in covalent bonding is a fundamental topic in chemistry. Excited states refer to the energy levels of an atom or molecule that are higher than the ground state, which is the lowest energy level. These higher energy levels are achieved when electrons in the atom or molecule absorb energy, typically in the form of light or heat. In covalent bonding, excited states (Wang et al., 2022).

The comprehension of the electronic structure as well as dynamics of molecules necessitates the consideration of excited states. Excited states play a crucial role in the process of covalent bonding, as the development of chemical bonds necessitates the advancement of electrons to greater energy levels, leading to the population of said excited states. The excited states have an impact on multiple facets of covalent bonding, such as bond strength, reactivity, as well as spectroscopic properties. The examination of excited states provides a more profound comprehension of the characteristics of covalent bonds as well as their response to varying circumstances (Baiardi et al., 2021).

The utilization of time-dependent quantum mechanical techniques presents a robust structure for the exploration of excited states within covalent bonding. The aforementioned methodologies facilitate the examination of the chronological progression of the electrical, thereby facilitating the computation of high state energies, change probabilities, and lifetimes. Time-dependent density functional theory (TDDFT) is a widely employed approach that applies the fundamental principles of DFT to temporal phenomena. The TDDFT methodology facilitates the computation of electronic excitation energies along with their properties, thereby serving as a useful instrument for investigating excited states in covalent bonding (Heller et al., 2021).

Calculations of excited states have numerous uses in photochemical reactions, wherein the absorption of light results in the creation of excited states, which subsequently initiate bond-breaking and bond-making processes. The aforementioned computations aid in the anticipation of the wavelengths of light that are absorbed by molecules, the recognition of routes for relaxation of excited states, and the comprehension of the mechanisms underlying photochemical reactions. The acquisition of such knowledge holds significant importance in the design of light-responsive materials, the advancement of photocatalytic processes, and the elucidation of the photochemical mechanisms underlying biological systems. Several case studies have illustrated the noteworthy function of states of excitement in the dynamics of covalent bonding. The efficacy of charge separation as well as transportation in organic photovoltaic devices is contingent upon the actions of excited states at the donor-acceptor interfaces (Mulliken & Roothaan, 1959). The photophysical characteristics of fluorescent dyes as well as phosphors, including emission spectra as well as quantum yields, are influenced by excited states. The catalytic performance of transition metal complexes is frequently influenced by the electronic configuration of excited states, which govern the initiation of reactant molecules and consequent bond-forming reactions. Through the analysis of these case studies, a more comprehensive comprehension of the influence of excited states on covalent bond dynamics can be attained, and approaches can be developed to regulate their behavior for specific purposes. The utilization of excited state computations, in conjunction with empirical inquiries, affords a comprehensive comprehension of the complicated interplay among excited states as well as covalent bonding. This acquired knowledge creates opportunities for the advancement of innovative materials, catalysts, as well as technologies (Shao et al., 2015).

4.7. INSIGHTS FROM THE VIRIAL THEOREM

The Virial Theorem offers important insights into the theoretical understanding of connecting energy within molecular systems. As per the theorem, there exists a direct correlation between the potential energy of a system and its time-averaged kinetic energy. Within the framework of covalent bonding, this correlation provides insight into the stability and potency of chemical bonds (Robitaille, 2018).

The energy necessary to dissociate a bond and isolate the individual atoms is denoted by the bonding energy. The Virial Theorem facilitates the comprehension of the energy nature by elucidating the interdependence between the potential and kinetic energies inside a molecule. The statement posits that the kinetic energy exhibited by electrons, which results from their movement within a molecule, is directly proportional to the negative value of the potential energy linked to interactions between electrons and nuclei, as well as between electrons themselves (Collins, 1978).

The Virial Theorem provides a comprehensive comprehension of the cohesive forces that bind atoms in a covalent bond. The equilibrium and stability of a bond are determined by the interplay between the attractive potential energy and the repulsive kinetic energy forces. The utilization of this conceptual framework enables an exploration of the various factors that exert an influence on the bonding energy, including but not limited to bond width, bond angle, as well as electron distribution.

Moreover, the Virial Theorem explicates the significance of the density of electrons in the energy of bonding. Through the examination of the distribution of electrons and their respective impacts on potential as well as kinetic energies, it is possible to assess the comparative potency of various covalent bonds. The Virial Theorem is a useful tool in comprehending the stability and resonance energy of systems with electrons that have been delocalized, like attached systems in organic chemistry (Nagy & Parr, 1990).

Relationship between Kinetic and Potential Energies

The Virial Theorem is a pivotal concept that elucidates the correlation between the potential and kinetic energies in molecular structures, thereby affording a precise comprehension of their interrelatedness. The aforementioned association enables us to deduce significant characteristics of covalent bonding, such as fluctuations in bond length and bond strength.

The kinetic energy within a molecular system is a result of the movement exhibited by both the electrons and nuclei. In contrast, potential energy is linked to the attractive and repulsive forces that exist between particles. According to the Virial Theorem, there exists a direct relationship between the time-averaged kinetic energy and the inverse value of the time-averaged energy potential, resulting in an equilibrium between the two energy components (Ryutov, 2008).

The interplay between both potential and kinetic energies provides insights into the stability and dynamics of covalent bonds. In instances where the potential energy is predominant, signifying robust forces of attraction, the system is deemed stable, as well as the connection energy is elevated. On the contrary, in cases where the kinetic energy surpasses the potential energy, the bond could potentially experience a reduction in strength or even fracture (Swenson, 1983).

Furthermore, alterations in the length of bonds can be comprehended by means of the Virial Theorem. Modifications to the bond length have an impact on the interactions between electrons and nuclei, as well as between electrons themselves, resulting in a change to the potential energy. The Virial

Theorem establishes a quantitative correlation between the potential energy and bond length by demonstrating their proportional relationship.

Furthermore, the Virial Theorem facilitates comprehension of the impact of molecular oscillations on the potential and kinetic energies. The vibrational motion has an impact on both the potential and kinetic energy components, leading to a modification of the overall equilibrium. The comprehension of this concept holds significant importance in the analysis of molecules at varying temperatures and their response to thermal stimulations (Weislinger & Olivier, 1974).

4.8. APPLICATION TO DIFFERENT MOLECULAR SYSTEMS

The Virial Theorem is a widely applicable concept in molecular systems that facilitates a comprehensive comprehension of covalent bonding in diverse contexts. Through the application of the theorem to various molecules, one can investigate the range of bonding scenarios as well as acquire knowledge regarding their distinctive characteristics (Abby et al., 2014).

The Virial Theorem is a useful tool in comprehending the equilibrium among the potential and kinetic energies in the covalent bond of uncomplicated diatomic molecules, like H_2 or N_2. The theorem offers a numerical assessment of the strength of a bond, enabling the evaluation of diverse molecules and deviations in bond distances (Rocchia et al., 2002).

The Virial Theorem exhibits a broader scope of relevance, encompassing intricate molecular systems. The aforementioned theorem can provide clarification regarding the interaction of various covalent bonds and the allocation of the potential and kinetic energies among distinct atoms and bonds in polyatomic molecules. The comprehension of this concept holds significant importance in the examination of the stability as well as reactivity of intricate organic compounds (Li et al., 2014).

Additionally, the Virial Theorem is utilized in the investigation of bonding within coordination compounds and transition metal complexes. The electronic structures as well as bonding patterns of these systems frequently display distinctive characteristics. The Virial Theorem provides insight into the characteristics of dative securities, metal-ligand interactions, as well as the long-term viability of these complexes through the examination of the potential and kinetic energy components. The theorem's adaptability is applicable to atypical molecular systems, including non-Coulombic counterparts and unorthodox bonding situations. The utilization of the Virial Theorem enables the examination of the function of non-conventional interactions, including hydrogen bonding or van der Waals forces, in the stabilization of molecular configurations. This methodology facilitates the broadening of our comprehension of bonding beyond the conventional covalent bonding paradigm (Paldus et al., 1972).

4.9. BEYOND THE VIRIAL THEOREM

4.9.1. Density Functional Theory (DFT) Perspectives

The utilization of DFT has been recognized as a potent instrument in the examination of covalent bonding, presenting a supplementary methodology beyond the Virial Theorem. The utilization of the DFT provides a pragmatic and effective structure for the computation of molecular electronic configurations and characteristics. The focus of this methodology centers around the electron density as the primary variable of significance, whereby the overall energy of the framework is represented as a functional expression of the electron density. The utilization of the Kohn-Sham equations in DFT enables the computation of the electronic structure in its ground state and facilitates the examination of covalent bonding. The comprehension of covalent bonding in DFT is achieved by means of the analysis of electron density. The analysis of the distribution of electron density offers valuable insights into the manner in which electrons are shared and localized within a covalent bond. Electron density analysis can provide bonding descriptors, including bond order, and bond length, as well as bond dissociation energies (Klimeš & Michaelides, 2012).

The utilization of calculations using DFT in covalent systems necessitates the meticulous selection of suitable basis sets and functionals, taking into account various factors like computational expenses, precision, and the particular characteristics of the chemical system being studied. The establishment of convergence criteria and the consideration of computational factors are crucial in guaranteeing the dependability of outcomes. The assessment of accuracy as well as the relevance of DFT in covalent bonding examines is crucially dependent on the validation as well as benchmarking of DFT leads to toward experimental data and higher-level theoretical methods (Becke, 2014).

The utilization of DFT studies yields enhanced comprehension of covalent bonding. The elucidation of electron density redistribution during the formation of chemical bonds can provide insight into the fundamental nature of such bonds. The employment of the DFT enables the examination of covalent bonding in diverse chemical surroundings, encompassing diminutive molecules and intricate materials. The investigation of the influence of molecular balance on the predictions of DFT can yield significant insights into the bonding characteristics and attributes of molecules (Matanovic et al., 2018).

4.9.2. Valence Bond Theory and its Interpretation

Valence Bond Theory (VBT) presents an alternative theoretical framework for comprehending covalent bonding. The fundamental concepts of atomic orbitals as well as resonance are emphasized for their overlap in this context. The concept of VBT elucidates the mechanism of covalent bonding by means of the sharing of localized electron pairs between two or more atoms. The process of hybridization, which entails the combination of atomic orbitals to generate novel hybrid orbitals, is a pivotal factor in the creation of chemical bonds. VBT offers a qualitative as well as intuitive understanding of covalent bonding through the use of Lewis structures as well as valence bond diagrams (McWeeny, 1954).

The VBT offers valuable insights into the description of bonding and the distribution of electrons in molecules. The assessment of bond strength can be accomplished by examining overlapping of atomic orbitals, which is reflected in the bond orders. Valence bond diagrams depict the electron distribution within covalent bonds, providing a graphical depiction of the bonding configurations. VBT offers explanations for aromaticity, conjugation, and various other covalent bonding phenomena. Acknowledging the constraints and difficulties of VBT is crucial, especially in chemical systems that are more intricate, wherein the effects of delocalization as well as electron correlation are significant (Chen et al., 2021).

4.9.3. Molecular Orbital Theory Revisited

The Molecular Orbital Theory (MOT) offers a quantum mechanical model for comprehending covalent bonding. This concept pertains to the generation of molecular orbitals via the process of linearly combining atomic orbitals. The stability as well as energy of a system can be determined by the bonding or antibonding nature of molecular orbitals. The utilization of molecular orbital diagrams as well as electron configurations in MOT provides a thorough comprehension of covalent bonding (Jhang et al., 2023).

Tip

A helpful tip when revisiting molecular orbital theory is to consider the linear combination of atomic orbitals (LCAO) approach, which allows the formation of molecular orbitals from atomic orbitals, enabling a comprehensive understanding of covalent bonding.

The utilization of MOT facilitates the prognostication of molecular characteristics such as bond lengths, bond angles, as well as other pertinent properties. The electronic structure as well as bonding in molecules can be elucidated by means of the MOT through the analysis of symmetry considerations. The utilization of molecular orbital coefficients in bonding analysis enables the identification of the distinct contributions of atomic orbitals in the creation of molecular orbitals as well as covalent bonds. The utilization of MOT extends to the examination of conjugated systems, wherein the critical involvement of electron delocalization is observed (Inokuti, 1971).

The scope and accuracy of MOT have been enhanced by recent advancements. The Extended Hückel theory as well as semiempirical methods provide computationally efficient and approximate techniques for analyzing large systems. The accuracy of MOT calculations has been enhanced by the inclusion of electron effects of correlation using post-Hartree-Fock methods as well as density functional methods. There have been developments in hybrid methodologies that integrate MOT with other theoretical frameworks. This integration has enabled a more comprehensive and precise depiction of covalent bonding in intricate systems (Suresh & Gadre, 1999).

4.10. FUTURE PERSPECTIVES AND CHALLENGES IN COVALENT BONDING STUDIES

The comprehension of covalent bonding is an essential idea in the realm of chemistry, and has been a longstanding pursuit in the area of molecular science due to its intricacies. As the study of covalent bonding progresses, novel perspectives and obstacles emerge, opening up avenues for future breakthroughs and revelations. In this discourse, we examine several prospective avenues and obstacles in the field of covalent bonding research (Altintas & Barner-Kowollik, 2012). The integration of machine learning techniques with quantum mechanics represents a promising avenue for future research. The efficacy of machine learning algorithms has been demonstrated in diverse domains, and their utilization in the investigation of covalent bonding exhibits significant promise. Through the integration of quantum mechanical computations and machine learning methodologies, scholars can effectively navigate the extensive chemical landscape, expedite the process of uncovering new materials, and obtain enhanced comprehension of the underlying principles that dictate the development of covalent bonds. The amalgamation of this approach has the potential to facilitate the anticipation of unprecedented bonding configurations and the formulation of customized compounds with distinct characteristics, thereby transforming the domain of materials science as well as pharmaceutical exploration (Kumalo et al., 2015).

An additional noteworthy obstacle encountered in the examination of covalent bonding pertains to the exploration of intricate systems that surpass conventional organic compounds. Transition metal complexes display a wide range of bonding patterns and are integral to catalysis, bioinorganic chemistry, as well as energy conversion. Advanced theoretical as well as computational approaches are necessary to comprehend the intricate interplay among metal centers as well as ligands in these systems. The challenge of reconciling experimental observations with theoretical predictions in complicated structures is a significant concern that researchers aspire to address in the coming years.

The utilization of multiscale modeling methodologies exhibits potential in addressing the intricacy of covalent bonding. The fundamental biological mechanisms, including enzyme reactions as well as DNA replication, rely heavily on covalent bonds. The examination of these phenomena necessitates the acquisition of data pertaining to the interplay among covalent bonds as well as their surroundings across various temporal and spatial dimensions. The amalgamation of quantum mechanics, molecular dynamics modeling, as well as coarse-grained models has the potential to facilitate the investigation of covalent bonding in biological systems. This approach can offer valuable perspectives on drug design, molecular recognition, and the operation of biological macromolecules (Bolina et al., 2021).

Although theoretical progress is imperative, the significance of experimental methods in investigating covalent bonds cannot be overstated. Recent developments in spectroscopic methodologies, including ultrafast spectroscopy as well as single-molecule imaging, have facilitated the in situ monitoring of bond formation and cleavage events in real-time. Furthermore, advanced imaging methodologies with high resolution, like scanning tunneling microscopy (STM), facilitate the observation of covalent bonds at the atomic level. The advancement of novel experimental techniques will augment our comprehension of covalent bonding as well as substantiate theoretical projections (Panda et al., 2022).

The investigation of inner shell effects presents additional difficulties in the examination of covalent bonding phenomena. The molecular properties and bond strength can be significantly affected by the inner shell electrons due to their close connection to the atomic nucleus. Accurate treatment of relativistic effects as well as electron correlation presents computational challenges in mathematical simulation of inner shell contributions. The resolution of these obstacles will yield more profound comprehension of the correlation among inner shell electrons as well as covalent bonding, thereby augmenting our knowledge of molecular structure as well as reactivity (Huang et al., 2022).

Activity 4.1

Suppose you are studying the covalent bonding in a complex organic molecule known for its unique electronic properties. How would you incorporate electron correlation effects into your computational calculations to gain a more accurate understanding of its bonding behavior and predict its reactivity with other molecules?

4.11. SUMMARY

Chapter 4 focuses on the Virial Theorem and covalent bonding. It begins with an introduction and discusses variation analysis, covalent bond formation, and the Virial Theorem. The theoretical and computational details related to covalent bonding are explored. The chapter examines covalent bonding in non-Coulombic analogs of H_2^+ and H_2 molecules using Gaussian potentials. It analyzes the spatial changes in density and energy during covalent bonding and discusses intra- versus interatomic energies and charge transfer. The contraction of electron densities and orbital contraction are also discussed. Advancements in molecular quantum mechanics, including the application of computational methods and the incorporation of electron correlation effects, are highlighted. The chapter provides insights from the Virial Theorem and its application to different molecular systems. It explores concepts beyond the Virial Theorem, such as DFT perspectives, VBT, and a revisited MOT.

The chapter concludes with future perspectives and challenges in covalent bonding studies.

REVIEW QUESTIONS

1. What is the significance of the Virial Theorem in molecular quantum mechanics?
2. How is variation analysis used to analyze covalent bond formation?
3. Explain the concept of covalent bonding and its characteristics.
4. How does the Virial Theorem contribute to the understanding of covalent bonding?
5. Describe the theoretical and computational details involved in studying covalent bonding.
6. What are Gaussian potentials and how are they used in studying covalent bonding?
7. Discuss the changes in density and energy during covalent bonding in H_2^+ and H_2 molecules.
8. What is the relationship between intra- and interatomic energies in covalent bonding?
9. How does charge transfer contribute to covalent bonding?
10. Explain the concept of orbital contraction and its role in covalent bonding.
11. What are the recent advances in molecular quantum mechanics related to covalent bonding studies?
12. Discuss the future perspectives and challenges in the field of covalent bonding research.

REFERENCES

1. Abby, S. S., Néron, B., Ménager, H., Touchon, M., & Rocha, E. P., (2014). MacSyFinder: a program to mine genomes for molecular systems with an application to CRISPR-Cas systems. *PloS One*, *9*(10), e110726.
2. Alkorta, I., Silva, A. F., & Popelier, P. L., (2020). An interacting quantum atoms (IQA) and relative energy gradient (REG) study of the halogen bond with explicit analysis of electron correlation. *Molecules*, *25*(11), 2674.
3. Altintas, O., & Barner-Kowollik, C., (2012). Single chain folding of synthetic polymers by covalent and non-covalent interactions: current status and future perspectives. *Macromolecular Rapid Communications*, *33*(11), 958–971.
4. Autschbach, J., & Schwarz, W. H. E., (2000). Relativistic electron densities in the four-component Dirac representation and in the two-component picture: Hydrogen-like systems. *Theoretical Chemistry Accounts*, *104*, 82–88.
5. Auvert, G., & Auvert, M., (2016). Introducing an extended covalent bond between oxygen atoms with an OXO-shape in ions and molecules: Compatibility with the even-odd and the isoelectronicity rules. *Open Journal of Physical Chemistry*, *6*(3), 67–77.
6. Auvert, G., (2020). Covalent bonds creation between gas and liquid phase change: Compatibility with covalent and even-odd rules based on a "specific periodic table for liquids." *Open Journal of Physical Chemistry*, *10*(1), 68.
7. Bacskay, G. B., Nordholm, S., & Ruedenberg, K., (2018). The virial theorem and covalent bonding. *The Journal of Physical Chemistry A*, *122*(39), 7880–7893.
8. Bagayoko, D., (1983). Contraction of gaussian basis sets and the total energy of fcc copper. *International Journal of Quantum Chemistry*, *24*(S17), 527–535.
9. Baiardi, A., Grimmel, S. A., Steiner, M., Türtscher, P. L., Unsleber, J. P., Weymuth, T., & Reiher, M., (2021). Expansive quantum mechanical exploration of chemical reaction paths. *Accounts of Chemical Research*, *55*(1), 35–43.
10. Ballesteros-Paredes, J., (2006). Six myths on the virial theorem for interstellar clouds. *Monthly Notices of the Royal Astronomical Society*, *372*(1), 443–449.
11. Becke, A. D., (2014). Perspective: Fifty years of density-functional theory in chemical physics. *The Journal of Chemical Physics*, *140*(18), 18A301.

12. Bersuker, G. I., Peng, C., & Boggs, J. E., (1993). The nature of the covalent bond: the existence and origin of nonnuclear attractors. *The Journal of Physical Chemistry*, *97*(37), 9323–9329.

13. Beyer, M. K., (2000). The mechanical strength of a covalent bond calculated by density functional theory. *The Journal of Chemical Physics*, *112*(17), 7307–7312.

14. Bianco, G., Forli, S., Goodsell, D. S., & Olson, A. J., (2016). Covalent docking using autodock: Two-point attractor and flexible side chain methods. *Protein Science*, *25*(1), 295–301.

15. Bolina, I. C., Gomes, R. A., & Mendes, A. A., (2021). Biolubricant production from several oleaginous feedstocks using lipases as catalysts: current scenario and future perspectives. *Bioenergy Research*, *4*(5), 1–19.

16. Bullett, D. W., (1975). Chemical pseudopotential approach to covalent bonding. II. Bond lengths and bond energies in diamond, silicon, and graphite. *Journal of Physics C: Solid State Physics*, *8*(17), 2707.

17. Chen, Z., Song, J., Chen, X., Zhou, C., & Wu, W., (2021). N-body reduced density matrix-based valence bond theory and its applications in diabatic electronic-structure computations. *Accounts of Chemical Research*, *54*(20), 3895–3905.

18. Christoffersen, R. E., & Christoffersen, R. E., (1989). Computational techniques for many-electron systems using single configuration wavefunctions. *Basic Principles and Techniques of Molecular Quantum Mechanics*, 481–575.

19. Clark, T., Politzer, P., & Murray, J. S., (2022). Interpreting the variations in the kinetic and potential energies in the formation of a covalent bond. *Physical Chemistry Chemical Physics*, *24*(20), 12116–12120.

20. Collins, G. W., (1978). *The Virial Theorem in Stellar Astrophysics (Astronomy and Astrophysics Series)* (pp. 148-198). Tucson, Ariz., Pachart Publishing House.

21. Cremer, D., (2001). Density functional theory: Coverage of dynamic and non-dynamic electron correlation effects. *Molecular Physics*, *99*(23), 1899–1940.

22. Das, D., Eurenius, K. P., Billings, E. M., Sherwood, P., Chatfield, D. C., Hodošček, M., & Brooks, B. R., (2002). Optimization of quantum mechanical molecular mechanical partitioning schemes: Gaussian delocalization of molecular mechanical charges and the double link atom method. *The Journal of Chemical Physics*, *117*(23), 10534–10547.

23. Diercksen, G. H., Sutcliffe, B. T., & Veillard, A., (2012). *Computational Techniques in Quantum Chemistry and Molecular Physics: Proceedings*

of the NATO Advanced Study Institute Held at Ramsau, Germany, 4–21 September, Springer Science & Business Media. *1974* (Vol. 15, pp. 56–60).

24. DiLabio, G. A., Johnson, E. R., & Otero-de-la-Roza, A., (2013). Performance of conventional and dispersion-corrected density-functional theory methods for hydrogen bonding interaction energies. *Physical Chemistry Chemical Physics*, *15*(31), 12821–12828.
25. Eskandari, K., (2016). Nature of beryllium bonds in view of interacting quantum atoms and natural energy decomposition analysis. *Computational and Theoretical Chemistry*, *1090*, 74–79.
26. Feinberg, M. J., & Ruedenberg, K., (1971). Paradoxical role of the kinetic-energy operator in the formation of the covalent bond. *The Journal of Chemical Physics*, *54*(4), 1495–1511.
27. Gao, J., & Weiner, J. H., (1989). Contribution of covalent bond force to pressure in polymer melts. *The Journal of Chemical Physics*, *91*(5), 3168–3173.
28. Gavezzotti, A., (2016). Comparing the strength of covalent bonds, intermolecular hydrogen bonds and other intermolecular interactions for organic molecules: X-ray diffraction data and quantum chemical calculations. *New Journal of Chemistry*, *40*(8), 6848–6853.
29. Georgescu, V., & Gérard, C., (1999). On the virial theorem in quantum mechanics. *Communications in Mathematical Physics*, *208*(2), 275–281.
30. Gilli, G., & Gilli, P., (2009). *The Nature of the Hydrogen Bond: Outline of a Comprehensive Hydrogen Bond Theory* (Vol. 23, pp. 457–460). Oxford University Press.
31. Giner, J., Van, D. R. J., Brouers, F., & Gautier, F., (1976). Charge transfer and ordering energy in a model binary alloy. *Journal of Physics F: Metal Physics*, *6*(7), 1281.
32. Gourgoulhon, E., & Bonazzola, S., (1994). A formulation of the virial theorem in general relativity. *Classical and Quantum Gravity*, *11*(2), 443.
33. Heisler, J., Tremaine, S., & Bahcall, J. N., (1985). Estimating the masses of galaxy groups-Alternatives to the virial theorem. *The Astrophysical Journal*, *298*, 8–17.
34. Heller, E. R., Joswig, J. O., & Seifert, G., (2021). Exploring the effects of quantum decoherence on the excited-state dynamics of molecular systems. *Theoretical Chemistry Accounts*, *140*(4), 42.
35. Hensel, J. C., Hasegawa, H., & Nakayama, M., (1965). Cyclotron resonance in uniaxially stressed silicon. II. Nature of the covalent bond.

Physical Review, *138*(1A), A225.

36. Hernández, N. C., & Sanz, J. F., (2000). Ab initio group model potentials including electron correlation effects. *The Journal of Chemical Physics*, *113*(15), 6082–6087.
37. Huang, W., Zhang, W., Gan, Y., Yang, J., & Zhang, S., (2022). Laccase immobilization with metal-organic frameworks: Current status, remaining challenges, and future perspectives. *Critical Reviews in Environmental Science and Technology*, *52*(8), 1282–1324.
38. Huhtala, M., Krasheninnikov, A. V., Aittoniemi, J., Stuart, S. J., Nordlund, K., & Kaski, K., (2004). Improved mechanical load transfer between shells of multiwalled carbon nanotubes. *Physical Review B*, *70*(4), 045404.
39. Hurley, A. C., (1982). Analysis of the covalent bond: One center floating functions for the hydrogen molecule ion. *International Journal of Quantum Chemistry*, *22*(2), 241–251.
40. Inokuti, M., (1971). Inelastic collisions of fast charged particles with atoms and molecules—The Bethe theory revisited. *Reviews of Modern Physics*, *43*(3), 297.
41. Iozzi, M. F., Helgaker, T., & Uggerud, E., (2009). Assessment of theoretical methods for the determination of the mechanochemical strength of covalent bonds. *Molecular Physics*, *107*(23, 24), 2537–2546.
42. Jain, I. P., Jain, P., & Jain, A., (2010). Novel hydrogen storage materials: A review of lightweight complex hydrides. *Journal of Alloys and Compounds*, *503*(2), 303–339.
43. Jhang, S. J., Pandidurai, J., Chu, C. P., Miyoshi, H., Takahara, Y., Miki, M., & Tobe, Y., (2023). s-indacene revisited: Modular synthesis and modulation of structures and molecular orbitals of hexaaryl derivatives. *Journal of the American Chemical Society*, *145*(8), 4716–4729.
44. Kantor, Y., Kardar, M., & Nelson, D. R., (1986). Statistical mechanics of tethered surfaces. *Physical Review Letters*, *57*(7), 791.
45. Klimeš, J., & Michaelides, A., (2012). Perspective: Advances and challenges in treating van der Waals dispersion forces in density functional theory. *The Journal of Chemical Physics*, *137*(12), 120901.
46. Krinsky, J. L., Minasian, S. G., & Arnold, J., (2011). Covalent lanthanide chemistry near the limit of weak bonding: Observation of $(CpSiMe_3)_3Ce$–ECp* and a comprehensive density functional theory analysis of Cp_3Ln–ECp (E= Al, Ga). *Inorganic Chemistry*, *50*(1), 345–357.
47. Kubel, F., Flack, H. D., & Yvon, K., (1987). Electron densities in VN. I. High-precision x-ray-diffraction determination of the valence-electron

density distribution and atomic displacement parameters. *Physical Review B*, *36*(3), 1415.

48. Kumalo, H. M., Bhakat, S., & Soliman, M. E., (2015). Theory and applications of covalent docking in drug discovery: Merits and pitfalls. *Molecules*, *20*(2), 1984–2000.
49. Lehtola, S., Manninen, P., Hakala, M., & Hämäläinen, K., (2013). Contraction of completeness-optimized basis sets: Application to ground-state electron momentum densities. *The Journal of Chemical Physics*, *138*(4), 044109.
50. Levina, E. O., Khrenova, M. G., & Tsirelson, V. G., (2021). The explicit role of electron exchange in the hydrogen bonded molecular complexes. *Journal of Computational Chemistry*, *42*(12), 870–882.
51. Levine, D. S., & Head-Gordon, M., (2020). Clarifying the quantum mechanical origin of the covalent chemical bond. *Nature Communications*, *11*(1), 4893.
52. Li, Y., Liu, T., Liu, H., Tian, M. Z., & Li, Y., (2014). Self-assembly of intramolecular charge-transfer compounds into functional molecular systems. *Accounts of Chemical Research*, *47*(4), 1186–1198.
53. Löwdin, P. O., (1959). Scaling problem, virial theorem, and connected relations in quantum mechanics. *Journal of Molecular Spectroscopy*, *3*(1–6), 46–66.
54. Matanovic, I., Artyushkova, K., & Atanassov, P., (2018). Understanding PGM-free catalysts by linking density functional theory calculations and structural analysis: Perspectives and challenges. *Current Opinion in Electrochemistry*, *9*, 137–144.
55. McDonagh, J. L., Silva, A. F., Vincent, M. A., & Popelier, P. L., (2017). Quantifying electron correlation of the chemical bond. *The Journal of Physical Chemistry Letters*, *8*(9), 1937–1942.
56. McWeeny, R., (1954). The valence bond theory of molecular structure-I. Orbital theories and the valence-bond method. *Proceedings of the Royal Society of London; Series A: Mathematical and Physical Sciences*, *223*(1152), 63–79.
57. Melin, J., Ayers, P. W., & Ortiz, J. V., (2007). Removing electrons can increase the electron density: a computational study of negative Fukui functions. *The Journal of Physical Chemistry A*, *111*(40), 10017–10019.
58. Miao, M. S., (2013). Caesium in high oxidation states and as ap-block element. *Nature Chemistry*, *5*(10), 846–852.
59. Miller, D. K., Chernyshov, I. Y., Torubaev, Y. V., & Rosokha, S. V., (2022).

From weak to strong interactions: Structural and electron topology analysis of the continuum from the supramolecular chalcogen bonding to covalent bonds. *Physical Chemistry Chemical Physics*, *24*(14), 8251–8259.

60. Moncada, F., Pedraza-González, L., Charry, J., Varella, M. T. D. N., & Reyes, A., (2020). Covalent bonds in positron dihalides. *Chemical Science*, *11*(1), 44–52.
61. Mulliken, R. S., & Roothaan, C. C., (1959). Broken bottlenecks and the future of molecular quantum mechanics. *Proceedings of the National Academy of Sciences*, *45*(3), 394–398.
62. Nagy, A., & Parr, R. G., (1990). Local virial theorem in density-functional theory. *Physical Review A*, *42*(1), 201.
63. Nordholm, S., & Bacskay, G. B., (2012). The role of quantum dynamics in covalent bonding—A comparison of Thomas–fermi and hückel models. *Advances in Quantum Theory*, *4*, 107–152.
64. Nordholm, S., (1988). Delocalization the key concept of covalent bonding. *Journal of Chemical Education*, *65*(7), 581.
65. Owen, J., & Thornley, J. H. M., (1966). Covalent bonding and magnetic properties of transition metal ions. *Reports on Progress in Physics*, *29*(2), 675.
66. Paldus, J., Čížek, J., & Shavitt, I., (1972). Correlation problems in atomic and molecular systems. IV. extended coupled-pair many-electron theory and its application to the BH_3 molecule. *Physical Review A*, *5*(1), 50.
67. Panda, S., Deshmukh, K., Pasha, S. K., Theerthagiri, J., Manickam, S., & Choi, M. Y., (2022). MXene based emerging materials for supercapacitor applications: recent advances, challenges, and future perspectives. *Coordination Chemistry Reviews*, *462*, 214518.
68. Park, N., Hong, S., Kim, G., & Jhi, S. H., (2007). Computational study of hydrogen storage characteristics of covalent-bonded graphenes. *Journal of the American Chemical Society*, *129*(29), 8999–9003.
69. Parthé, E., (1973). Valence-electron concentration rules and diagrams for diamagnetic, non-metallic iono-covalent compounds with tetrahedrally coordinated anions. *Acta Crystallographica Section B: Structural Crystallography and Crystal Chemistry*, *29*(12), 2808–2815.
70. Peng, F., Sun, Y., Pickard, C. J., Needs, R. J., Wu, Q., & Ma, Y., (2017). Hydrogen clathrate structures in rare earth hydrides at high pressures: possible route to room-temperature superconductivity. *Physical Review Letters*, *119*(10), 107001.
71. Plumley, J. A., & Evanseck, J. D., (2008). Hybrid meta-generalized

gradient functional modeling of boron– nitrogen coordinate covalent bonds. *Journal of Chemical Theory and Computation*, *4*(8), 1249–1253.

72. Poater, A., Saliner, A. G., Solà, M., Cavallo, L., & Worth, A. P., (2010). Computational methods to predict the reactivity of nanoparticles through structure–property relationships. *Expert Opinion on Drug Delivery*, *7*(3), 295–305.
73. Rice, J. E., & Handy, N. C., (1992). The calculation of frequency-dependent hyperpolarizabilities including electron correlation effects. *International Journal of Quantum Chemistry*, *43*(1), 91–118.
74. Rioux, F., (2003). The covalent bond examined using the virial theorem. *Chem. Educ*, *8*, 10–12.
75. Robitaille, P. M., (2018). Thermodynamics and the virial theorem, gravitational collapse, and the virial theorem: Insight from the laws of thermodynamics. *Progress in Physics*, *14*, 123–125.
76. Rocchia, W., Sridharan, S., Nicholls, A., Alexov, E., Chiabrera, A., & Honig, B., (2002). Rapid grid-based construction of the molecular surface and the use of induced surface charge to calculate reaction field energies: Applications to the molecular systems and geometric objects. *Journal of Computational Chemistry*, *23*(1), 128–137.
77. Ruedenberg, K., & Schmidt, M. W., (2009). Physical understanding through variational reasoning: Electron sharing and covalent bonding. *The Journal of Physical Chemistry A*, *113*(10), 1954–1968.
78. Rutkowski, A., Schwarz, W. H. E., & Kosłowski, R., (1993). Relativistic virial theorem for diatomic molecules. Application to H_2^+. *Theoretica Chimica Acta*, *87*, 75–87.
79. Ruzsinszky, A., Perdew, J. P., & Csonka, G. I., (2005). Binding energy curves from nonempirical density functionals. I. Covalent bonds in closed-shell and radical molecules. *The Journal of Physical Chemistry A*, *109*(48), 11006–11014.
80. Ryutov, D. D., (2008). On the virial theorem for interstellar medium. *The Astrophysical Journal*, *674*(2), 976.
81. Sakai, K., Stoychev, S., Ouchi, T., Higuchi, I., Schöffler, M., Mazza, T., & Ueda, K., (2011). Electron-transfer-mediated decay and interatomic coulombic decay from the triply ionized states in argon dimers. *Physical Review Letters*, *106*(3), 033401.
82. Schaefer, III. H. F., (2001). Computers and molecular quantum mechanics: 1965–2001, a personal perspective. *Journal of Molecular Structure: THEOCHEM*, *573*(1–3), 129–137.

83. Scheurer, M., Dreuw, A., Epifanovsky, E., Head-Gordon, M., & Stauch, T., (2020). Modeling molecules under pressure with Gaussian potentials. *Journal of Chemical Theory and Computation*, *17*(1), 583–597.

84. Schmidt, M. W., Ivanic, J., & Ruedenberg, K., (2014). Covalent bonds are created by the drive of electron waves to lower their kinetic energy through expansion. *The Journal of Chemical Physics*, *140*(20), 204104.

85. Shao, Y., Gan, Z., Epifanovsky, E., Gilbert, A. T., Wormit, M., Kussmann, J., & Rassolov, V. A., (2015). Advances in molecular quantum chemistry contained in the Q-Chem 4 program package. *Molecular Physics*, *113*(2), 184–215.

86. Shields, Z. P., Murray, J. S., & Politzer, P., (2010). Directional tendencies of halogen and hydrogen bonds. *International Journal of Quantum Chemistry*, *110*(15), 2823–2832.

87. Shimizu, A., Hirao, Y., Matsumoto, K., Kurata, H., Kubo, T., Uruichi, M., & Yakushi, K., (2012). Aromaticity and π-bond covalency: prominent intermolecular covalent bonding interaction of a Kekulé hydrocarbon with very significant singlet biradical character. *Chemical Communications*, *48*(45), 5629–5631.

88. Slater, J. C., (1933). The virial and molecular structure. *The Journal of Chemical Physics*, *1*(10), 687–691.

89. Smith, D. W., (1970). Relationship between electron spin resonance g-values and covalent bonding in tetragonal copper (II) compounds. *Journal of the Chemical Society A: Inorganic, Physical, Theoretical*, *23*(3), 3108–3120.

90. Sommerfeld, T., DeFusco, A., & Jordan, K. D., (2008). Model potential approaches for describing the interaction of excess electrons with water clusters: Incorporation of long-range correlation effects. *The Journal of Physical Chemistry A*, *112*(44), 11021–11035.

91. Soumya, S., & Joe, I. H., (2021). A combined experimental and quantum chemical study on molecular structure, spectroscopic properties, and biological activity of anti-inflammatory glucocorticosteroid drug, dexamethasone. *Journal of Molecular Structure*, *1245*, 130999.

92. Sun, Y., Sun, S., Yang, H., Xi, S., Gracia, J., & Xu, Z. J., (2020). Spin-related electron transfer and orbital interactions in oxygen electrocatalysis. *Advanced Materials*, *32*(39), 2003297.

93. Suresh, C. H., & Gadre, S. R., (1999). Clar's aromatic sextet theory revisited via molecular electrostatic potential topography. *The Journal of Organic Chemistry*, *64*(7), 2505–2512.

94. Swenson, R. J., (1983). Comments on virial theorems for bounded

systems. *American Journal of Physics*, *51*(10), 940–942.

95. Takata, T., (2006). Polyrotaxane and polyrotaxane network: supramolecular architectures based on the concept of dynamic covalent bond chemistry. *Polymer Journal*, *38*(1), 1–20.
96. Tarika, J. D., Rathika, A., Dexlin, X. D., Jayanthi, D. D., & Beaula, T. J., (2022). Consequence of proton transfer and hydrogen bonding interactions on the molecular, Vibrational, and biological properties of the novelly synthesized antibacterial compound bis-(4-dimethylaminopyridinium) bis-(3, 5-dinitrobenzoate) monohydrate using DFT study. *Journal of Molecular Structure*, *1261*, 132914.
97. Tsai, D. H., (1979). The virial theorem and stress calculation in molecular dynamics. *The Journal of Chemical Physics*, *70*(3), 1375–1382.
98. Vincy, C. D., Tarika, J. D., Dexlin, X. D., Rathika, A., & Beaula, T. J., (2022). Exploring the antibacterial activity of 1, 2 diaminoethane hexanedionic acid by spectroscopic, electronic, ELF, LOL, RDG analysis and molecular docking studies using DFT method. *Journal of Molecular Structure*, *1247*, 131388.
99. Vogiatzis, K. D., Polynski, M. V., Kirkland, J. K., Townsend, J., Hashemi, A., Liu, C., & Pidko, E. A., (2018). Computational approach to molecular catalysis by 3d transition metals: Challenges and opportunities. *Chemical Reviews*, *119*(4), 2453–2523.
100. Wang, Y., Seritan, S., Lahana, D., Ford, J. E., Valentini, A., Hohenstein, E. G., & Martínez, T. J., (2022). InteraChem: Exploring excited states in virtual reality with ab initio interactive molecular dynamics. *Journal of Chemical Theory and Computation*, *18*(6), 3308–3317.
101. Wei, H., Qi, R., Wang, J., Cieplak, P., Duan, Y., & Luo, R., (2020). Efficient formulation of polarizable gaussian multipole electrostatics for biomolecular simulations. *The Journal of Chemical Physics*, *153*(11), 114116.
102. Weislinger, E., & Olivier, G., (1974). The classical and quantum mechanical virial theorem. *International Journal of Quantum Chemistry*, *8*(S8), 389–401.
103. Wheatley, R. J., & Gopal, A. A., (2012). Covalent bond orders and atomic anisotropies from iterated stockholder atoms. *Physical Chemistry Chemical Physics*, *14*(6), 2087–2091.
104. Yannacone, S., Oliveira, V., Verma, N., & Kraka, E., (2019). A continuum from halogen bonds to covalent bonds: Where do λ 3 iodanes fit? *Inorganics*, *7*(4), 47.

105. Zhang, H., Ren, Q., Mohd, S., Yang, C., Li, J., Pei, Y., & Luo, X., (2021). Early-warning and semi-quantitative colorimetric detection of Hg (II) with lysine-bis-Schiff base cellulose membranes designed by simple interfacial covalent bonding. *Sensors and Actuators B: Chemical*, *346*, 130435.
106. Zhu, J., Hu, L., Zhao, P., Lee, L. Y. S., & Wong, K. Y., (2019). Recent advances in electrocatalytic hydrogen evolution using nanoparticles. *Chemical Reviews*, *120*(2), 851–918.

CHAPTER

5 Intermolecular Forces and Covalent Bonding

Contents

5.1. INTRODUCTION

The sharing of electrons between atoms leads to the formation of covalent bonds, which are a type of chemical bond. The formation of a stable molecule through the sharing of valence electrons occurs in a covalent bond, where two or more atoms are involved. The phenomenon of electron sharing facilitates the attainment of a comparatively stable electron configuration by each atom, which commonly leads to the creation of a molecular compound.

The robust bonding capability of covalent bonds can be attributed to the electrostatic attraction between the positively charged atomic nuclei and the shared electrons. Covalent bonds are commonly established among nonmetallic elements, owing to their greater inclination to acquire electrons and participate in covalent bonding (Dey et al., 2020).

Intermolecular forces refer to the attractive or repulsive forces that exist between molecules. The determination of physical and chemical properties of substances is heavily reliant on their pivotal role. Intermolecular forces, although weaker than covalent bonds, play a crucial role in the existence and behavior of molecular compounds. Intermolecular forces play a crucial role in a range of phenomena, including but not limited to the boiling and melting points of substances, their volatility, solubility, and the formation of condensed phases such as liquids and solids. Alterations to the physical characteristics of substances, such as their viscosity, surface tension, and solubility in various solvents, are induced by their influence (Gao & Weiner, 1993).

5.2. RELATIONSHIP BETWEEN INTERMOLECULAR FORCES AND COVALENT BONDS

Comprehending the behavior and characteristics of molecules and compounds necessitates a fundamental understanding of the correlation between intermolecular forces and covalent bonds. Intermolecular forces pertain to the attractive interactions that occur between distinct molecules, whereas covalent bonds are robust bonds that arise from the sharing of electrons between atoms within a given molecule. Despite variations in their intensity and characteristics, these forces and bonds are interrelated and hold significant importance in dictating the physical and chemical attributes of materials (Peterson & Treagust, 1989).

The formation of covalent bonds is attributed to the overlapping of atomic orbitals and the consequent sharing of electrons among atoms. The aforementioned entities exhibit distinctive features owing to the robust electrostatic force of attraction that exists between the nuclei that bear a positive charge and the shared electron pairs that bear a negative charge. The nature of covalent bonds is often characterized by a high degree of localization and specificity with respect to the constituent atoms participating in the bonding process. Chemical bonds confer stability to molecules and dictate their structural conformations (Fahmi & Irhasyuarna, 2017) (Figure 5.1).

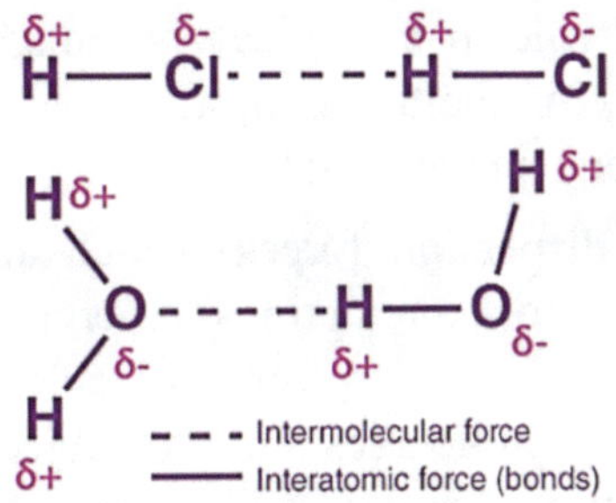

Figure 5.1. Illustration of intermolecular forces.

Source: Byju's, Creative Commons License.

In contrast, intermolecular forces refer to comparatively weaker interactions that transpire between molecules. The emergence of these phenomena is attributed to the variations in the distribution of electrons within molecules, leading to the formation of transient or enduring molecular dipoles. The categories of intermolecular forces encompass London dispersion forces, dipole-dipole interactions, and hydrogen bonding. The aforementioned forces exert considerable influence in dictating the physical characteristics of substances, including but not limited to their solubility, boiling points, and melting points (Coll & Treagust, 2002).

The correlation between intermolecular forces and covalent bonds can be comprehended by examining the molecular interactions implicated. The arrangement and behavior of molecules are influenced by intermolecular forces, whereas covalent bonds are confined to the interior of individual molecules. The impact of intermolecular forces can be influenced by the characteristics and potency of covalent bonds.

The existence of polar covalent bonds in a molecule generates a permanent dipole, which leads to dipole-dipole interactions among adjacent molecules. The strength of dipole-dipole interactions is contingent upon the polarity of the covalent bonds and the molecular configuration in space. Hence, molecules possessing robust covalent bonds and significant dipole moments tend to manifest more potent intermolecular forces. Furthermore, the phenomenon of hydrogen bonding, which is a distinct form of dipole-dipole interaction, is contingent upon the existence of strongly polar covalent bonds that involve hydrogen atoms that are bonded to highly electronegative atoms, such as oxygen, nitrogen, or fluorine. The intermolecular forces and the strength of hydrogen bonds are subject to the influence of the size and electronegativity of the atoms that participate in the bonding. Hydrogen bonding plays a crucial role in biological systems, as it confers stability upon the structure of DNA, facilitates protein folding, and influences the properties of water (Peterson et al., 1989).

Moreover, London dispersion forces, which are also referred to as induced dipole-induced dipole interactions, emerge as a result of transient variations in electron distribution within molecules. The aforementioned forces are ubiquitous in all molecules and are subject to direct modulation by the electron count and molecular configuration. As a result, molecules possessing larger electron clouds, which may be attributed to their higher molar mass or greater number of constituent atoms, demonstrate more robust London dispersion forces. Van der Waals forces are especially pertinent in nonpolar molecules or compounds, as they exert a substantial influence on the physical characteristics of such substances (Su & Li, 2009).

5.3. TYPES OF INTERMOLECULAR FORCES

5.3.1. Van der Waals Forces

Van der Waals forces constitute a comprehensive group of intermolecular forces that encompass both London dispersion forces and dipole-dipole interactions. The aforementioned forces exert a substantial influence on the physical characteristics and conduct of materials.

London dispersion forces, which belong to the category of Van der Waals forces, are considered to be the least potent intermolecular forces. They emerge as a result of transient variations in electron distribution among molecules. In molecules that lack polarity, there exists a perpetual motion of electrons, leading to the formation of momentary dipoles. The formation of temporary dipoles in molecules results in the induction of temporary dipoles in adjacent molecules, thereby generating an attractive force between them. The London dispersion forces, despite their inherent weakness, exhibit a growing significance in molecules that are larger and more polarizable. The rationale behind this phenomenon is that molecules with larger sizes possess a higher number of electrons, which facilitates greater oscillations and the consequent development of more robust and transient dipoles. The cohesive forces of nonpolar molecules are attributed to London dispersion forces, which play a crucial role in the determination of various properties, including but not limited to boiling points, melting points, and viscosity (Margenau, 1939).

Dipole-dipole interactions, which are a variant of Van der Waals forces, manifest between polar molecules. The phenomenon of electrostatic attraction occurs when polar molecules interact, whereby the positive pole of one molecule is drawn towards the negative pole of another molecule. The relative strength of intermolecular forces is influenced by the polarity of the molecules engaged, with dipole-dipole interactions being more potent than London dispersion forces. The strength of dipole-dipole interactions is positively correlated with the magnitude of the electronegativity disparity between atoms and the net dipole moment of the molecule. The intermolecular interactions between molecules are crucial factors in dictating the physical and chemical characteristics of polar substances, including their solubility, boiling points, and melting points (Hasse, 1931) (Figure 5.2).

Remember

Van der Waals forces play a crucial role in the interaction between nonpolar molecules.

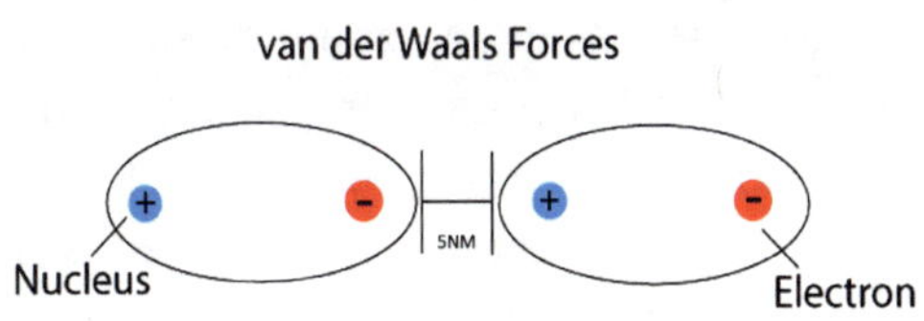

Figure 5.2. Illustration of Vander Waals forces.

Source: Revision Science, Creative Commons License.

5.3.1.1. London Dispersion Forces

The London dispersion forces, which are also referred to as London forces or induced dipole-induced dipole interactions, represent the least potent category of intermolecular forces. The aforementioned forces manifest in all molecules, irrespective of their polarity, and stem from transient perturbations in the electron distribution within the molecules.

The variations in electron allocation lead to momentary dipoles, wherein a molecule's one end experiences a transient negative charge while the other end undergoes a transient positive charge. The formation of temporary dipoles through electrostatic attraction induces neighboring molecules to also form their own temporary dipoles.

The electrostatic forces that arise between the temporary dipoles are commonly referred to as London dispersion forces. Although possessing a relatively low magnitude, their impact on the physical characteristics of materials is noteworthy. The magnitude of London dispersion forces is positively correlated with the dimensions and surface area of molecules, as larger molecules possess a greater number of electrons and a higher likelihood of exhibiting temporary dipoles (Liptrot & Power, 2017).

The aforementioned forces are crucial factors in a range of phenomena, including but not limited to the boiling and melting points, as well as the viscosity of substances. Additionally, they make a contribution to the molecular interactions in condensed phases and exert an influence on the behavior of molecules within solvents. In general, comprehending the intermolecular interactions and properties of substances necessitates a fundamental understanding of London dispersion forces (Kistyan & Pulay, 1994).

5.3.1.2. Dipole-Dipole Interactions

Dipole-dipole interactions represent a category of intermolecular forces that manifest between molecules possessing a net dipole moment due to their polar nature. In contrast to London dispersion forces, which manifest in all molecules, dipole-dipole interactions emerge exclusively from the allurement between the positively charged terminus of one polar molecule and the negatively charged terminus of another polar molecule (Stuhler et al., 2005). Several factors influence the magnitude of dipole-dipole interactions. The disparity in electronegativity among the constituent atoms of a molecule is a pivotal determinant, as a higher discrepancy in electronegativity results in an augmented dipole moment. Furthermore, the collective molecular polarity and spatial configuration are contributing factors in assessing the potency of dipole-dipole intermolecular forces (Gallagher & Pillet, 2008) (Figure 5.3).

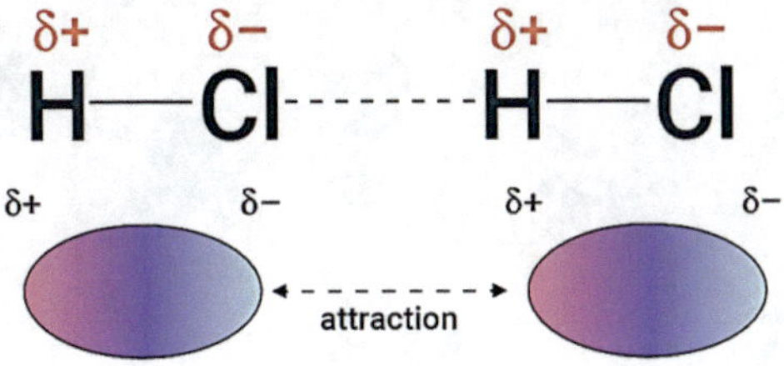

Figure 5.3. Schematic of dipole interaction.

Source: Breaking Atom, Creative Commons License.

The physical and chemical characteristics of polar substances are influenced by dipole-dipole interactions. The intermolecular forces have an impact on the physical properties of polar molecules, such as their boiling points, melting points, and solubility. This is because the strength of these forces directly affects these properties. The manifestation of dipole-dipole interactions can lead to the formation of highly organized and structured configurations of molecules in both solid and liquid phases (Persson & Ryberg, 1981).

Comprehending dipole-dipole interactions holds significant importance in various domains, including chemistry and materials science, as these interactions significantly impact the conduct and characteristics of polar compounds and solutions.

5.3.2. Hydrogen Bonding

The intermolecular force known as hydrogen bonding is a distinctive and potent phenomenon that holds significant importance in the characteristics and conduct of materials. This phenomenon takes place when a hydrogen atom, which is covalently bonded to an electronegative atom like oxygen, nitrogen, or fluorine, undergoes interaction with a lone pair of electrons present on another electronegative atom in a neighboring molecule. The robustness of hydrogen bonding emanates from the substantial contrast in electronegativity between the hydrogen atom and the electronegative atom with which it is bonded. The outcome of this phenomenon is the formation of a markedly polar covalent bond, wherein the hydrogen atom exhibits a partial positive charge and the electronegative atom manifests a partial negative charge. The electrostatic attraction between the positively charged hydrogen atom and the negatively charged neighboring electronegative atom is a significant force (Pimentel & McClellan, 1971) (Figure 5.4).

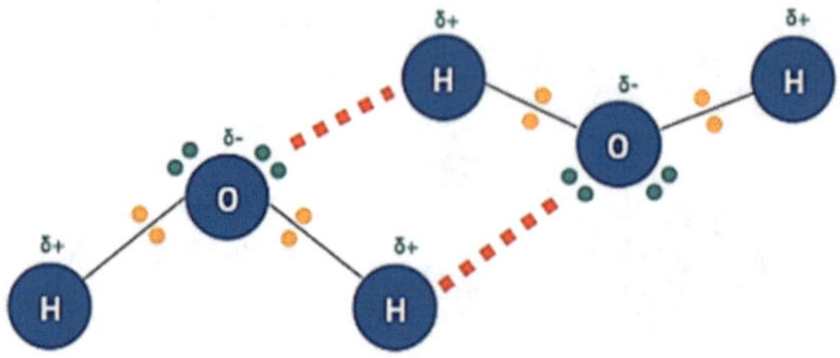

Figure 5.4. Image of hydrogen bonding in water.

Source: Study mind, Creative Commons License.

The phenomenon of hydrogen bonding is associated with a number of significant outcomes. Initially, it substantially elevates the boiling and melting points of substances. The existence of hydrogen bonds necessitates supplementary energy to disrupt the potent intermolecular attractions, thereby leading to elevated temperatures that are necessary for phase transitions. The presence of hydrogen bonding is apparent in the comparatively elevated boiling point of water in relation to analogous molecules lacking such bonding (Chen et al., 2003).

Additionally, the phenomenon of hydrogen bonding plays a significant role in the manifestation of high surface tension and capillary action in certain liquids, such as water. The intermolecular forces of hydrogen bonding among water molecules facilitate the development of a surface tension, resulting in a barrier to infiltration and the capacity to uphold objects with limited surface area. Hydrogen bonding is a pivotal factor in the configuration and operation of biomolecules within biological systems. DNA stabilization is facilitated by the molecule known as histone, which enables the maintenance of the double helix structure and promotes the occurrence of precise base pairing. Hydrogen bonding plays a crucial role in determining the three-dimensional conformation and stability of proteins, thereby exerting a significant influence on their functional properties (Emsley, 1980).

In general, the phenomenon of hydrogen bonding exerts a substantial impact on the characteristics and actions of materials. The distinctive attributes observed in diverse materials, biological systems, and chemical reactions are attributed to the potency and selectivity of their constituent components.

5.3.3. Ion-Dipole Interactions

Ion-dipole interactions are a type of intermolecular force that arises from the electrostatic attraction between an ion and a polar molecule. The aforementioned interactions hold significant importance in solutions where ions are present in a solvent. The electrostatic property of an ion elicits an attraction towards the polar end of a molecule with an opposite charge, thereby resulting in an interaction known as ion-dipole. The aforementioned interactions exhibit a relatively high degree of strength when compared to other types of intermolecular forces and are of paramount importance in a multitude of chemical processes. Ion-dipole interactions facilitate the dissolution of ionic compounds in polar solvents, leading to the separation of ions and their solvation. The aforementioned interactions hold considerable importance in the process of electrolysis, wherein the transportation of ions is expedited by the mutual attraction between said ions and polar molecules of the solvent (Grandbois et al., 1999).

5.4. COVALENT BONDS

Covalent bonds represent a fundamental type of chemical bond that arises from the sharing of electron pairs between atoms. A stable molecule is formed when two or more atoms participate in a covalent bond by sharing their outer shell electrons. The covalent bond formed by the sharing of electrons generates a robust Coulombic force of attraction between the positively charged atomic nuclei and the negatively charged electrons (Kamaras et al., 2003).

The fundamental principle underlying the concept of covalent bonding is the attainment of a stable electron configuration by atoms, which is typically akin to the configuration of noble gasses, through the filling of their outermost electron shells. Through the process of electron sharing, atoms can achieve a state of greater stability by obtaining a complete outer shell. The representation of shared electrons in a covalent bond is typically depicted by a line or a dash connecting the respective atoms. Each individual atom provides one or multiple electrons to the collective pair. The variability in the number of electrons shared between atoms is contingent upon their respective electron configurations and the imperative to attain a state of stability. Covalent bonds may entail the sharing of one, two, or three electron pairs, leading to the formation of single, double, or triple covalent bonds, correspondingly (Phillips, 1968).

The formation of covalent bonds is primarily observed between nonmetallic elements, although it is also possible for such bonds to manifest between a nonmetal and a metalloid. Covalent compounds such as H_2O,

CH_4, and CO_2 are commonly cited as examples. The molecular nature of these compounds is their defining characteristic, as they are comprised of discrete units consisting of a precise number of atoms that are bound together by covalent bonds. Covalent bonds possess various fundamental characteristics. In general, the strength of these entities is considerable, with bond energies typically falling within the range of several tens to a few hundred kilojoules per mole. The potency of a covalent bond is contingent upon various factors, including the nature of the constituent atoms, the quantity of electron pairs shared, and the inter-nuclear separation (Maeda et al., 2009).

In addition, it is common for covalent compounds to exhibit reduced melting and boiling points in comparison to their ionic counterparts. The reason for this is that the intermolecular forces present among covalent molecules, including London dispersion forces and dipole-dipole interactions, are typically less strong in comparison to the electrostatic forces that exist between ions in ionic compounds (Chakma & Konkolewicz, 2019).

5.4.1. Formation of Covalent Bonds

The formation of covalent bonds occurs through the sharing of electrons between atoms, with the ultimate goal of achieving a stable electron configuration. The process of covalent bond formation is a crucial mechanism for generating the diverse range of molecules and compounds that are present in the surrounding environment. The comprehension of the mechanism behind the formation of covalent bonds yields valuable knowledge regarding the characteristics, composition, and chemical behavior of covalent compounds (Heuts et al., 2009).

The initiation of covalent bonding is initiated by the interaction among atoms. The fundamental structure of atoms comprises a nucleus that bears a positive charge, which is encircled by electrons that bear a negative charge. Every atom endeavors to attain a stable electron configuration through the process of gaining, losing, or sharing electrons with other atoms. In the context of chemical bonding, atoms choose to participate in covalent bonding by sharing electrons with one another, with the aim of achieving a complete outer electron shell (Cope & Siekman, 1965).

Electron sharing is facilitated by the overlapping of atomic orbitals. An atomic orbital is a spatial domain encompassing the nucleus within which the probability of locating electrons is high. Upon the approach of two atoms, there exists a possibility for their respective atomic orbitals to undergo overlap, thereby facilitating the occupation of the overlapping region by electrons. The covalent bond is formed as a result of the shared electrons that are jointly possessed by both participating atoms (Held et al., 2009).

The characteristics of the covalent bond are impacted by the specific atomic orbitals that partake in the process of overlapping. The predominant form of covalent bonding arises from the overlapping of atomic orbitals, which are referred to as sigma (σ) bonds. The formation of sigma bonds occurs through the end-to-end overlap of either two s orbitals or a s orbital and a p orbital. The covalent bonds exhibit significant strength and facilitate unrestricted rotation along the bond axis. Apart from the formation of sigma bonds, it is possible for double and triple covalent bonds to arise through the sharing of multiple electron pairs between atoms. The formation of double bonds entails the overlapping of a sigma bond and a pi (π) bond, which arises from the adjacent overlap of two p orbitals. Triple bonds are formed through the overlapping of one sigma bond and two pi bonds, leading to the formation of bonds that are even more robust (Zhou et al., 2018).

The principle of electron pair repulsion governs the formation of covalent bonds, whereby electrons within a molecule exhibit repulsive behavior and strive to attain maximum separation from one another. Consequently, covalent bonds frequently exhibit distinct geometries or molecular configurations in order to reduce the repulsion between electron pairs. The prediction of these geometries can be accomplished through the utilization of the valence shell electron pair repulsion (VSEPR) theory. The process of covalent bonding is not restricted solely to the interaction between two individual atoms. In certain instances, it is possible for multiple atoms to engage in electron-sharing interactions, leading to the formation of intricate structures commonly referred to as molecules or polyatomic ions. The aforementioned structures may encompass numerous covalent bonds, thereby generating complex interlacing systems of mutually shared electrons (Yang et al., 2022).

In the field of chemistry, the process of forming covalent bonds holds significant importance as it facilitates the generation of a plethora of compounds possessing diverse properties and functionalities. Through comprehension of the fundamental principles governing the formation of covalent bonds, researchers are able to forecast and regulate the configuration and functionality of molecules, resulting in progressions in domains including materials science, pharmaceutical exploration, and nanotechnology (Owen & Thornley, 1966).

5.4.2. Properties of Covalent Compounds

Molecular compounds, commonly referred to as covalent compounds, arise from the sharing of electrons among atoms. The distinctive characteristics of these compounds stem from the properties of covalent bonding and the intermolecular interactions that occur between molecules. Comprehending the characteristics of covalent compounds holds significant importance in diverse domains, such as chemistry, materials science, and pharmaceutical investigation (Kumar et al., 2021). The present discourse aims to examine several fundamental characteristics of covalent compounds.

- **Physical State:** Covalent compounds are capable of existing in diverse physical states, such as solids, liquids, and gasses. The determination of the physical state of a substance is contingent upon various factors, including but not limited to the magnitude of intermolecular forces, the dimensions of the constituent molecules, and the configuration of the molecular structure. Small covalent molecules with relatively weak intermolecular forces, such as oxygen (O_2) and nitrogen (N_2) gasses, typically maintain a gaseous state at standard room temperature. In contrast, it is observed that larger covalent molecules possess stronger intermolecular forces, which consequently lead to their solid state at room temperature. This is particularly evident in the case of polymers.
- **Melting and Boiling Points:** In comparison to ionic compounds, covalent compounds typically exhibit lower boiling and melting points. The relative strength of intermolecular forces in covalent compounds, including London dispersion forces and dipole-dipole interactions, is comparatively lower than the electrostatic forces present in ionic compounds. As a result, a reduced amount of energy is necessary to disrupt the intermolecular forces, leading to a decrease in the melting and boiling points.
- **Solubility:** The solubility of covalent compounds is contingent upon their polarity. Compounds with polar covalent bonds exhibit an asymmetrical distribution of charge and can undergo dissolution in polar solvents such as water owing to the advantageous interactions between the solute and solvent molecules. In contrast, nonpolar covalent compounds exhibit limited solubility or insolubility in polar solvents, while they may exhibit solubility in nonpolar solvents (Leckband & Israelachvili, 2001.

- **Electrical Conductivity:** In general, covalent compounds exhibit low electrical conductivity. Covalent compounds, in their unadulterated state, do not undergo dissociation into ions and are devoid of freely mobile charged particles that are imperative for the conduction of electricity. Nevertheless, select covalent compounds have the ability to conduct electrical current upon undergoing ionization or engaging in particular chemical reactions.
- **Chemical Reactivity:** Covalent compounds display a diverse array of chemical reactivity. The stability and reactivity of covalent compounds are contingent upon various factors, including but not limited to bond strength, bond polarity, and the existence of functional groups. Covalent compounds are capable of engaging in diverse chemical reactions, such as oxidation-reduction reactions, acid-base reactions, and organic synthesis reactions (Qin et al., 2017).
- **Optical Properties:** Covalent compounds exhibit distinctive optical characteristics, including but not limited to chromaticity, luminescence, and phosphorescence. The aforementioned characteristics stem from the absorption and emission of distinct light wavelengths as a result of electronic transitions occurring within the molecular configuration.

5.5. COVALENT BONDS VS. INTERMOLECULAR FORCES

5.5.1. Comparison of Covalent Bonds and Intermolecular Forces

The fundamental principles of chemistry are governed by covalent bonds and intermolecular forces, which play a crucial role in determining the behavior and properties of molecules and compounds. Although atomic and molecular forces share the commonality of involving interactions between atoms and molecules, they diverge in their respective magnitudes, characteristics, and extents.

The formation of covalent bonds involves the sharing of electrons between atoms, leading to the establishment of strong chemical bonds that confer greater stability to the electron configuration of the participating atoms. The chemical bonds in question exhibit localization within discrete molecular entities and entail a robust electrostatic attraction between the mutually shared electron pairs and the nuclei that bear a positive charge. The strength of covalent bonds is comparatively high, necessitating a considerable input of energy to disrupt them. Molecules' overall structure, stability, and reactivity are determined by them (Reichhelm et al., 2017).

Did You Know?

The strength of covalent bonds is typically much greater than that of intermolecular forces.

Conversely, intermolecular forces refer to relatively feeble forces of attraction that occur among molecules. The intermolecular forces are accountable for maintaining the cohesion of molecules in their solid and liquid forms and exerting an impact on their physical characteristics. The category of intermolecular forces encompasses London dispersion forces, dipole-dipole interactions, and hydrogen bonding. In contrast to covalent bonds, intermolecular forces exhibit significantly lower strength and act over extended ranges. Covalent bonds are generally significantly stronger than intermolecular forces in terms of their strength, often by multiple orders of magnitude. The formation of a covalent bond is characterized by the sharing of electrons between atoms, which leads to the establishment of a robust bond within a given molecule. Intermolecular forces, conversely, originate from transient or enduring perturbations in electron allocation and exhibit comparably lower strength (Bonn & Hunger, 2021) (Figure 5.5).

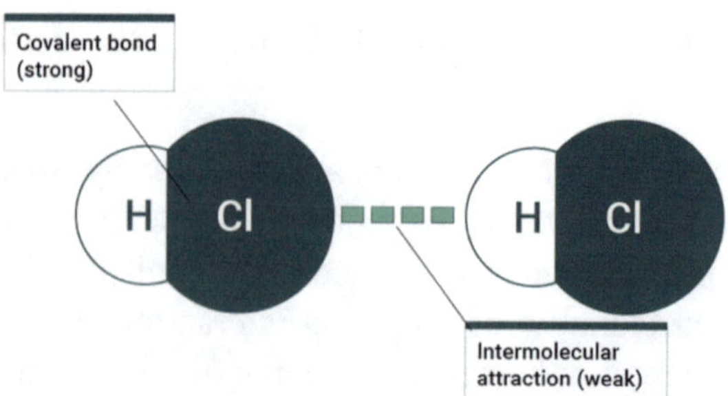

Figure 5.5. Image of intermolecular forces in covalent compound.

Source: Breaking Atom, Creative Commons License.

A significant disparity exists in the range of their respective scopes. The covalent bonds exhibit atom-specific characteristics and dictate the molecular connectivity and arrangement of atoms. In contrast, intermolecular forces are non-directional and exert their effects between molecules, thereby influencing the arrangement and behavior of molecules in bulk materials.

5.5.2. Interplay between Covalent Bonds and Intermolecular Forces

The complex and dynamic relationship between covalent bonding and intermolecular forces plays a significant role in determining the behavior and properties of molecules and compounds. Covalent bonds are responsible for providing robust intramolecular bonding within a molecule. However, intermolecular forces are significant in determining the overall structure, physical properties, and chemical reactivity of substances as they act between molecules (Jia et al., 2022).

Various categories of intermolecular forces, including London dispersion forces, dipole-dipole interactions, and hydrogen bonding, are significant in this domain. The aforementioned forces are subject to modification based on the existence and characteristics of covalent bonds present within the pertinent molecules. Polar covalent bonds within a molecule elicit a permanent dipole moment, thereby inducing dipole-dipole interactions among adjacent molecules. The determination of the strength and orientation of said interactions is contingent upon the spatial arrangement and overall polarity of the molecules involved. The phenomenon of hydrogen bonding, which is a distinct form of dipole-dipole interaction, is notably impacted by covalent bonding that involves hydrogen atoms that are bonded to atoms with high electronegativity. The probability of hydrogen bonding between adjacent molecules is increased by the existence of robust covalent bonds within the molecule, resulting in distinctive characteristics and actions. The interaction between covalent bonds and hydrogen bonding is particularly significant in biological systems, as it plays a crucial role in the stability and functionality of molecules such as DNA and proteins (Zheng et al., 2019).

Moreover, the potency and configuration of covalent bonds can have an indirect impact on intermolecular forces. Molecules that are larger and more complex, containing a greater number of covalent bonds, tend to display stronger London dispersion forces. This is attributed to the greater number of electrons that are available for temporary fluctuations in electron distribution. The interaction between covalent bonding and intermolecular forces plays a crucial role in determining the physical characteristics of substances, including their solubility, boiling points, and melting points (Zakeri et al., 2012).

In general, the intricate interplay between covalent bonding and intermolecular forces significantly impacts the behavior and properties of molecules and compounds. The nature and magnitude of intermolecular forces are contingent upon the existence and characteristics of covalent bonds. These intermolecular forces, in turn, exert a significant influence on the overall structure and properties of the substances. Comprehending the interplay between molecular interactions and their effects on the macroscopic properties of matter is crucial for gaining a comprehensive understanding of the complex nature of this phenomenon (Luxford & Bretz, 2014).

5.5.3. Influence of Intermolecular Forces on Covalent Bonding Strength and Properties

Comprehending the behavior and characteristics of molecules and compounds necessitates a significant consideration of the impact of intermolecular forces on covalent bonding strength and properties. The stability, physical properties, and reactivity of covalent compounds can be significantly influenced by intermolecular forces (Birk & Kurtz, 1999).

The impact of intermolecular forces on the strength of covalent bonding can be attributed to their capacity to attenuate or interrupt the cohesive forces that exist between molecules. Under certain circumstances, intermolecular forces may contend with or surpass the potency of covalent bonds, resulting in alterations in the physical characteristics of materials. In the event of a phase transition from solid to liquid or gas, the intermolecular forces need to be surmounted to disrupt the cohesive forces among molecules. The process of transitioning from one state of matter to another is characterized by specific temperatures referred to as melting and boiling points. These points are subject to the influence of intermolecular forces' strength. The solubility of covalent compounds in various solvents can be influenced by the potency of intermolecular forces. The dissolution of a solute in a solvent is dependent upon the intermolecular forces that exist between the solute and solvent molecules. When the intermolecular forces between the solute and solvent are of comparable strength, the solute's solubility is enhanced. In cases where there exists a substantial discrepancy between the intermolecular forces of the solute and solvent, the solute may exhibit limited or no solubility. The solubility characteristics are contingent upon the interplay of intermolecular forces and the potency of the covalent bonds present in the solute (Taber & Coll, 2003).

In addition, the physical characteristics of covalent compounds, such as surface tension, viscosity, and volatility, can be affected by intermolecular forces. Surface tension is a physical property that characterizes the degree of intermolecular attraction at the interface of a liquid. This phenomenon is determined by the cohesive forces between molecules, which are in turn influenced by the intermolecular forces that exist between them. The property of viscosity, which refers to the degree of resistance to flow, is influenced by the nature and potency of intermolecular forces that are operative. Materials possessing greater intermolecular forces generally exhibit elevated viscosity levels. The phenomenon of volatility, denoting the proclivity of a substance to undergo vaporization, can be modulated by the intermolecular forces that exist between the constituent molecules. In general, substances exhibiting weaker intermolecular forces tend to possess higher volatility (Burrows & Mooring, 2015).

Additionally, the chemical reactivity and behavior of covalent compounds can be influenced by intermolecular forces. The hindrance of reactant molecules' accessibility to each other can be attributed to the existence of robust intermolecular forces, which ultimately diminishes the probability of chemical reactions occurring. On the other hand, diminished intermolecular forces can facilitate heightened molecular movement and augment reactivity (Abramowitz et al., 1990).

5.6. EFFECTS OF INTERMOLECULAR FORCES ON PHYSICAL PROPERTIES

5.6.1. Melting and Boiling Points

The physical characteristics of substances, namely their melting and boiling points, are subject to the effects of intermolecular forces. The aforementioned characteristics offer significant perspectives on the potency and characteristics of the intermolecular forces present within a given substance. Comprehending the correlation between intermolecular forces and the phenomena of melting and boiling points holds significant importance in diverse domains such as chemistry, materials science, and pharmaceutical research (Mewes & Schwerdtfeger, 2021).

The melting point is defined as the temperature at which a solid undergoes a phase transition to transform into a liquid state. The degree of influence is contingent upon the magnitude of the intermolecular or intramolecular forces that are responsible for maintaining the structural integrity of the solid lattice. Compounds possessing robust intermolecular forces, such as those involving covalent bonds or hydrogen bonding, exhibit elevated melting points. This phenomenon can be attributed to the increased energy demand for overcoming intermolecular forces during the transition from a solid to a liquid phase. Conversely, materials possessing weaker intermolecular forces, such as those governed by van der Waals forces, exhibit a tendency to display reduced melting points. The boiling point of a substance refers to the temperature at which it undergoes a phase transition from a liquid to a gaseous state. Boiling points, akin to melting points, are subject to the influence of intermolecular forces. The boiling point of a substance is directly proportional to the strength of its intermolecular forces. This is due to the fact that a greater amount of energy is required to break these forces and transition the substance from a liquid to a gaseous state. On the other hand, substances that possess weaker intermolecular forces exhibit lower boiling points. The determination of melting and boiling points is contingent upon the intermolecular forces that are operative, which can be subject to variation contingent upon the nature of bonding that is present within the substance. Substances that exhibit covalent bonding, such as diamond or quartz, possess elevated melting and boiling points as a result of the robust covalent bonds that exist between constituent atoms. In contrast, materials that possess metallic bonding, such as copper or iron, demonstrate elevated melting points due to the robust attraction between metal cations and delocalized electrons (Barrall,1973).

The investigation of the melting and boiling points of substances yields significant insights into their physical characteristics and stability. The process facilitates the identification and characterization of chemical compounds, as well as the evaluation of their purity and potential performance in diverse applications. Furthermore, comprehending the correlation between intermolecular forces and the phenomena of melting and boiling points plays a significant role in the advancement of novel materials possessing distinct characteristics and practical uses (Stull, 1947).

5.6.2. Vapor Pressure

The physical property of vapor pressure is significantly impacted by intermolecular forces. This statement pertains to the vapor molecules' pressure in a state of equilibrium with their corresponding liquid or solid phase at a particular temperature. Comprehending the notion of vapor pressure yields valuable insights into the characteristics of substances in enclosed as well as unconfined environments. The vapor pressure of a substance is largely influenced by intermolecular forces. The propensity of molecules to transition from the liquid phase to the gas phase is influenced by the potency of intermolecular attractions. Molecules of non-polar compounds, which possess weaker intermolecular forces, exhibit higher kinetic energy resulting in an elevation of their vapor pressure. In contrast, materials possessing heightened intermolecular forces, such as polar substances or those with the ability to engage in hydrogen bonding, demonstrate diminished vapor pressures due to the increased energy necessary to disrupt these cohesive interactions (Thomson, 1946).

Tip

To increase surface tension, decrease the temperature or increase the intermolecular forces between the molecules.

The correlation between intermolecular forces and vapor pressure can be elucidated by contemplating the state of equilibrium between the gaseous and liquid phases. At elevated temperatures, the mean kinetic energy of molecules escalates, leading to a higher number of molecules that possess adequate energy to surmount intermolecular forces and undergo a phase transition into the gaseous state. Consequently, the vapor pressure exhibits a positive correlation with temperature (Yaws & Yang, 1989).

In addition, the boiling point of a substance can be influenced by intermolecular forces, which is defined as the temperature at which the vapor pressure of the substance is equivalent to the external pressure. The boiling point of substances is directly proportional to the strength of their intermolecular forces. This is due to the fact that a greater amount of energy is required to overcome the cohesive forces between molecules and transition them into the gaseous phase.

The comprehension of vapor pressure and its correlation with intermolecular forces has a plethora of pragmatic implementations. A comprehensive comprehension of phase transitions, including but not limited to evaporation, condensation, and boiling, is of utmost importance. Moreover, vapor pressure finds application in diverse industrial sectors such as chemical engineering, pharmaceuticals, and food processing, where it plays a crucial role in regulating the volatility of substances to enhance operational efficiency and maintain product standards (Lin et al., 1988).

5.6.3. Solubility and Miscibility

The properties of solubility and miscibility are significant and are subject to the influence of intermolecular forces. Solubility pertains to the capacity of a substance, referred to as the solute, to undergo dissolution in a solvent and generate a uniform solution. The term miscibility pertains to the capacity of two or more substances to blend and generate a uniform amalgamation.

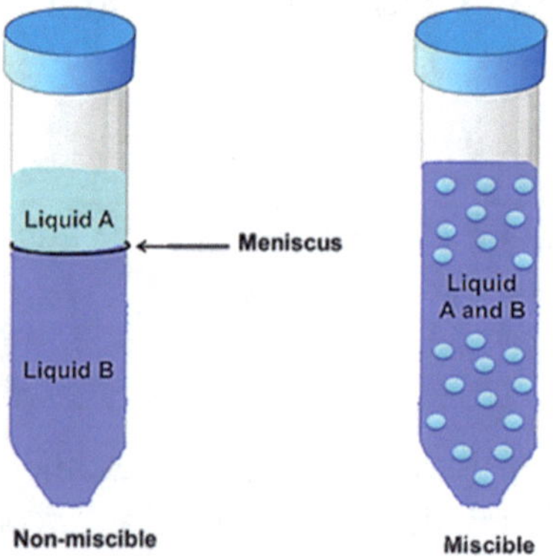

Figure 5.6. Schematic of miscible liquids.

Source: Study, Creative Commons License.

The solubility of a solute in a given solvent is contingent upon the quality and characteristics of the intermolecular forces that exist between the solute particles and the molecules of the solvent. The principle of "like dissolves like" is a fundamental concept that applies to solubility phenomena. Compounds possessing analogous intermolecular forces exhibit a propensity to dissolve in one another. Polar solvents, such as water, are capable of dissolving polar solutes, such as sugar or salt, as a result of the existence of dipole-dipole interactions. Likewise, nonpolar solutes such as oil can be dissolved by nonpolar solvents like hexane. The notion of miscibility is frequently employed in the context of liquid substances. In the event that two liquids exhibit miscibility, they have the capacity to blend uniformly in varying proportions, resulting in the formation of a homogeneous liquid phase. The phenomenon of miscibility is determined by the degree of agreement between the intermolecular forces exhibited by the molecules of distinct liquids. The high miscibility of ethanol and water can be attributed to the existence of hydrogen bonding in both compounds. In contrast, oil and water are immiscible due to the significant differences in their intermolecular forces (Qian et al., 2010) (Figure 5.6).

Comprehending the concepts of solubility and miscibility holds paramount significance in diverse domains such as chemistry, pharmaceuticals, and industrial operations. This facilitates the conceptualization and enhancement of procedures such as pharmacological composition, extraction methodologies, and the innovation of novel substances. Through the manipulation of intermolecular forces, researchers have the ability to augment solubility and miscibility, thereby facilitating the effective dissolution and amalgamation of various substances (Mondal et al., 2009).

5.6.4. Surface Tension and Capillary Action

The intermolecular forces give rise to surface tension and capillary action, which are intriguing phenomena that hold considerable importance in diverse natural and industrial processes. The phenomenon of surface tension pertains to the intermolecular cohesive force that is exhibited by molecules present at the surface of a liquid, resulting in the formation of a surface layer that reduces the surface area. Capillary action refers to the phenomenon whereby liquids are capable of flowing in opposition to the force of gravity within confined spaces, such as narrow tubes or porous materials. The phenomenon of surface tension is a result of the intermolecular cohesive forces that exist between molecules. The cohesive forces between liquid molecules, including hydrogen bonding and dipole-dipole interactions, result in the formation of a robust surface layer. The manifestation of this characteristic is observable through the formation of spherical shapes by water droplets or the ability of insects to glide on the surface of a pond without submerging. The phenomenon of capillary action takes place when the attractive forces between the liquid and the inner surface of a confined tube or permeable substance surpass the cohesive forces that exist within the liquid. This phenomenon leads to the ascent of the liquid within the tube in opposition to the gravitational force. Phenomena such as the ascent of water in a slender glass tube or the imbibition of water by a sponge can be observed (Morrow, 1970).

These phenomena possess various practical implications. Capillary action facilitates the movement of water and nutrients from the roots to the leaves in plants via minute channels present in the stem. Capillary action plays a critical role in medical disciplines, particularly in facilitating blood circulation and the uptake of fluids by cells. The phenomenon of surface tension is of significant importance in the creation of soap bubbles, the ascent of liquid in a pipette, and the characteristics of ink on paper.

Comprehending the concepts of surface tension and capillary action holds paramount significance in diverse domains such as inkjet printing, microfluidics, and the development of materials with tailored characteristics. Researchers in the scientific and engineering communities are currently investigating and utilizing these phenomena to make progress in various areas, including drug delivery systems, lab-on-a-chip devices, and nanotechnology (Hajduk & Greer, 2007).

5.7. APPLICATIONS OF INTERMOLECULAR FORCES IN COVALENT BONDING

5.7.1. Pharmaceutical Industry and Drug Design

The comprehension of intermolecular forces and their involvement in covalent bonding plays a crucial role in drug design and development within the pharmaceutical industry. The interactions between drugs and their target molecules, as well as the solubility, stability, and pharmacokinetic properties of drugs, are significantly influenced by intermolecular forces. The pharmaceutical industry utilizes intermolecular forces to develop drugs that possess the ability to selectively interact with target receptors or enzymes, which is a crucial application of these forces. The establishment of intermolecular bonds, such as hydrogen bonding or dipole-dipole interactions, between the drug molecule and its target is crucial for achieving selective binding and augmenting the therapeutic efficacy of the drug. Scholars conduct an analysis of the intermolecular forces implicated in the process of binding to enhance drug-receptor interactions and optimize drug efficacy (Selvaraj et al., 2021).

Furthermore, the solubility of drugs is influenced by intermolecular forces, a crucial aspect that impacts their absorption and distribution within the human body. Pharmaceutical scientists can improve drug dissolution and bioavailability by designing formulations and delivery systems that take into account the interplay between intermolecular forces and drug solubility. Moreover, the stability and solid-state characteristics of pharmaceuticals are impacted by intermolecular forces. The presence of covalent bonds within the drug molecule and intermolecular forces between drug molecules are influential factors that affect crystal packing, polymorphism, and amorphous state. The regulation of intermolecular forces facilitates the creation of drug formulations that are both stable and bioavailable.

In general, the comprehension of intermolecular forces within covalent bonding yields significant perspectives regarding the development, enhancement, and composition of pharmaceuticals within the pharmaceutical sector. The utilization of this approach facilitates the creation of pharmaceuticals that are characterized by enhanced safety, efficacy, and performance, thereby enabling them to selectively address particular ailments and optimize patient results (Shackelford & Clode, 2005).

5.7.2. Materials Science and Engineering

The field of Materials Science and Engineering is of paramount importance in leveraging the potential of intermolecular forces inherent in covalent bonding for diverse applications. The comprehension and control of intermolecular forces enable scientists to devise and produce materials possessing targeted characteristics and functionalities.

The discipline of Materials Science and Engineering leverages intermolecular forces to fabricate materials that exhibit improved strength, durability, conductivity, and other desirable properties. Through the manipulation of intermolecular interactions, scientists have the ability to engineer polymers that possess distinct mechanical characteristics, such as notable tensile strength or flexibility. These polymers are utilized in a variety of industries, including but not limited to automotive and aerospace. Moreover, the incorporation of intermolecular forces plays a significant role in the development of materials that exhibit enhanced electrical and thermal conductivity. Through the manipulation of atomic and molecular arrangements, it is possible to engineer materials, such as semiconductors and superconductors, for utilization in electronic devices and energy-related applications. Aside from their physical characteristics, intermolecular forces are crucial in the creation of functional materials. The development of self-healing materials is contingent upon the reversible character of intermolecular interactions, which permits the material to undergo self-repair upon sustaining damage. The process of creating biomaterials with customized properties necessitates a comprehensive comprehension and application of intermolecular forces to attain biocompatibility and encourage tissue integration (Verkhoturov et al., 2007).

The utilization of intermolecular forces in the field of Materials Science and Engineering has been extended to the realm of nanotechnology. The assembly and stabilization of nanomaterials are heavily dependent on intermolecular forces due to their distinct size-dependent properties. Through the manipulation of intermolecular interactions, researchers can systematically design the characteristics and conduct of nanomaterials, thereby creating novel opportunities for cutting-edge technologies (Karplus & McCammon, 2002).

5.7.3. Biological Systems and Biomolecules

The significance of Biological Systems and Biomolecules is paramount in diverse biological processes, and the comprehension of intermolecular forces is indispensable in elucidating their configuration, operation, and interplay. The stability, conformation, and binding of biomolecules are heavily influenced by intermolecular forces, which in turn have a notable impact on the behavior and functionality of biological systems (Monopoli et al., 2012).

The stability of essential biomolecules such as proteins, nucleic acids (DNA and RNA), and lipids is dependent on their complex structures and intermolecular forces. The maintenance of structural integrity in biomolecules is significantly influenced by hydrogen bonding. Hydrogen bonds play a crucial role in the development of secondary structures, such as alpha helices and beta sheets, in proteins. These structures are integral to the protein's overall conformation and stability. Moreover, the phenomenon of hydrogen bonding between the complementary base pairs present in DNA and RNA molecules facilitates the conveyance and retention of hereditary data (Gorenstein, 1987). Biomolecular interactions, such as those involved in enzyme-substrate binding, antigen-antibody recognition, and receptor-ligand interactions, are heavily dependent on intermolecular forces. The aforementioned interactions play a pivotal role in cellular signaling, metabolic pathways, immune responses, and drug-target interactions. The strength and specificity of molecular interactions, which have an impact on their efficiency and biological outcomes, are determined by intermolecular forces such as electrostatic interactions, van der Waals forces, and hydrophobic interactions (Beharry & Woolley, 2011).

Comprehending the intermolecular forces that are implicated in biological systems can facilitate the formulation of therapeutic approaches and the design of drugs. The process of rational drug design entails the identification and optimization of intermolecular interactions between small molecules and target biomolecules, with the aim of achieving desired therapeutic effects.

Through the analysis of intermolecular forces, researchers are able to create molecules that have the ability to specifically attach to certain proteins or enzymes, thereby regulating their function and impacting various biological mechanisms (Elstner et al., 2000).

Furthermore, the examination of intermolecular forces is of utmost importance in the field of membrane biology, as the interplay between lipids and proteins governs the architecture and operation of membranes. The formation of lipid bilayers, which constitute the fundamental structure of cell membranes, is driven by hydrophobic interactions among lipid tails. The interplay between proteins and lipids, which is regulated by intermolecular forces, plays a crucial role in a range of cellular mechanisms such as signal transduction and membrane transport (Weiss, 2000).

Activity 5.1

How do intermolecular forces affect the solubility of different substances in water?

5.8. SUMMARY

This chapter explores the relationship between intermolecular forces and covalent bonding. It discusses various types of intermolecular forces, such as Van der Waals forces, hydrogen bonding, and ion-dipole interactions. Covalent bonds are compared to intermolecular forces, highlighting their differences and interplay. The effects of intermolecular forces on physical properties like melting and boiling points, vapor pressure, solubility, and surface tension are examined. The chapter also touches upon the applications of intermolecular forces in fields like the pharmaceutical industry, materials science, and biological systems

REVIEW QUESTIONS

1. What are the three types of intermolecular forces discussed in this chapter?
2. Explain the difference between covalent bonds and intermolecular forces.
3. How do Van der Waals forces contribute to the properties of nonpolar molecules?

4. What factors influence surface tension and capillary action?
5. How do intermolecular forces affect the boiling and melting points of substances?
6. Describe the role of hydrogen bonding in intermolecular interactions.
7. How do ion-dipole interactions differ from other types of intermolecular forces?
8. What are the applications of intermolecular forces in the pharmaceutical industry?
9. Discuss the importance of intermolecular forces in materials science and engineering.
10. How do intermolecular forces influence biological systems and biomolecules?

REFERENCES

1. Abramowitz, R., & Yalkowsky, S. H., (1990). Melting point, boiling point, and symmetry. *Pharmaceutical Research*, *7*, 942–947.
2. Ahlrichs, R., Penco, R., & Scoles, G., (1977). Intermolecular forces in simple systems. *Chemical Physics*, *19*(2), 119–130.
3. Barker, V., & Millar, R., (2000). Students' reasoning about basic chemical thermodynamics and chemical bonding: what changes occur during a context-based post-16 chemistry course? *International Journal of Science Education*, *22*(11), 1171–1200.
4. Barrall, II. E. M., (1973). Precise determination of melting and boiling points by differential thermal analysis and differential scanning calorimetry. *Thermochimica Acta*, *5*(4), 377–389.
5. Beharry, A. A., & Woolley, G. A., (2011). Azobenzene photoswitches for biomolecules. *Chemical Society Reviews*, *40*(8), 4422–4437.
6. Birk, J. P., & Kurtz, M. J., (1999). Effect of experience on retention and elimination of misconceptions about molecular structure and bonding. *Journal of Chemical Education*, *76*(1), 124.
7. Bonn, M., & Hunger, J., (2021). Between a hydrogen and a covalent bond. *Science*, *371*(6525), 123, 124.
8. Boo, H. K., (1998). Students' understandings of chemical bonds and the energetics of chemical reactions. *Journal of Research in Science Teaching: The Official Journal of the National Association for Research in Science Teaching*, *35*(5), 569–581.
9. Buckingham, A. D., & Utting, B. D., (1970). Intermolecular forces. *Annual Review of Physical Chemistry*, *21*(1), 287–316.
10. Burrows, N. L., & Mooring, S. R., (2015). Using concept mapping to uncover students' knowledge structures of chemical bonding concepts. *Chemistry Education Research and Practice*, *16*(1), 53–66.
11. Campanario, J. M., Bronchalo, E., & Hidalgo, M. A., (1994). An effective approach for teaching intermolecular interactions. *Journal of Chemical Education*, *71*(9), 761.
12. Chakma, P., & Konkolewicz, D., (2019). Dynamic covalent bonds in polymeric materials. *Angewandte Chemie International Edition*, *58*(29), 9682–9695.
13. Chen, B., Ivanov, I., Klein, M. L., & Parrinello, M., (2003). Hydrogen bonding in water. *Physical Review Letters*, *91*(21), 215503.
14. Coll, R. K., & Taylor, N., (2001). Alternative conceptions of chemical bonding held by upper secondary and tertiary students. *Research in*

Science & Technological Education, *19*(2), 171–191.

15. Coll, R. K., & Treagust, D. F., (2002). Exploring tertiary students' understanding of covalent bonding. *Research in Science & Technological Education*, *20*(2), 241–267.
16. Cooper, M. M., Williams, L. C., & Underwood, S. M., (2015). Student understanding of intermolecular forces: A multimodal study. *Journal of Chemical Education*, *92*(8), 1288–1298.
17. Cope, A. C., & Siekman, R. W., (1965). Formation of covalent bonds from platinum or palladium to carbon by direct substitution. *Journal of the American Chemical Society*, *87*(14), 3272–3273.
18. Dey, J., Lee, S. J., Kim, J., Lim, S. H., Ha, J. M., Lee, M. J., & Choi, S. M., (2020). Spontaneous formation of highly stable nanoparticle supercrystals driven by a covalent bonding interaction. *Nano Letters*, *21*(1), 258–264.
19. Elstner, M., Frauenheim, T., Kaxiras, E., Seifert, G., & Suhai, S., (2000). A self-consistent charge density-functional based tight-binding scheme for large biomolecules. *Physica Status Solidi (b)*, *217*(1), 357–376.
20. Emsley, J., (1980). Very strong hydrogen bonding. *Chemical Society Reviews*, *9*(1), 91–124.
21. Fahmi, F., & Irhasyuarna, Y., (2017). The misconceptions of senior high school students in banjarmasin on chemical bonding. *Journal of Education and Practice*, *8*(17), 32–39.
22. Gallagher, T. F., & Pillet, P., (2008). Dipole–dipole interactions of Rydberg atoms. *Advances in Atomic, Molecular, and Optical Physics*, *56*, 161–218.
23. Gao, J., & Weiner, J. H., (1993). Screened intermolecular forces and covalent bond forces in polymer melts. *The Journal of Chemical Physics*, *98*(10), 8256–8261.
24. Glazier, S., Marano, N., & Eisen, L., (2010). A closer look at trends in boiling points of hydrides: Using an inquiry-based approach to teach intermolecular forces of attraction. *Journal of Chemical Education*, *87*(12), 1336–1341.
25. Gorenstein, D. G., (1987). Stereoelectronic effects in biomolecules. *Chemical Reviews*, *87*(5), 1047–1077.
26. Grandbois, M., Beyer, M., Rief, M., Clausen-Schaumann, H., & Gaub, H. E., (1999). How strong is a covalent bond? *Science*, *283*(5408), 1727–1730.
27. Hajduk, P. J., & Greer, J., (2007). A decade of fragment-based drug design: strategic advances and lessons learned. *Nature Reviews Drug Discovery*, *6*(3), 211–219.

28. Hassé, H. R., (1931). The calculation of the van der Waal forces for hydrogen and helium at large inter-atomic distances. In: *Mathematical Proceedings of the Cambridge Philosophical Society* (Vol. 27, No. 1, pp. 66–72). Cambridge University Press.
29. Held, P. A., Fuchs, H., & Studer, A., (2017). Covalent-bond formation via on-surface chemistry. *Chemistry–A European Journal*, *23*(25), 5874–5892.
30. Heuts, D. P., Scrutton, N. S., McIntire, W. S., & Fraaije, M. W., (2009). What's in a covalent bond? On the role and formation of covalently bound flavin cofactors. *The FEBS Journal*, *276*(13), 3405–3427.
31. Jia, S., Ye, H., & You, L., (2022). Interplay between chalcogen bonds and dynamic covalent bonds. *Organic Chemistry Frontiers*, *9*(15), 3966–3975.
32. Kamaras, K., Itkis, M. E., Hu, H., Zhao, B., & Haddon, R. C., (2003). Covalent bond formation to a carbon nanotube metal. *Science*, *301*(5639), 1501.
33. Karplus, M., & McCammon, J. A., (2002). Molecular dynamics simulations of biomolecules. *Nature Structural Biology*, *9*(9), 646–652.
34. Kristyán, S., & Pulay, P., (1994). Can (semi) local density functional theory account for the London dispersion forces? *Chemical Physics Letters*, *229*(3), 175–180.
35. Kumar, A., Nutan, B., & Jewrajka, S. K., (2021). Modulation of properties through covalent bond induced formation of strong ion pairing between polyelectrolytes in injectable Conetwork hydrogels. *ACS Applied Bio Materials*, *4*(4), 3374–3387.
36. Leckband, D., & Israelachvili, J., (2001). Intermolecular forces in biology. *Quarterly Reviews of Biophysics*, *34*(2), 105–267.
37. Lin, P., Clash, C., Pearce, E. M., Kwei, T. K., & Aponte, M. A., (1988). Solubility and miscibility of poly (ethyl oxazoline). *Journal of Polymer Science Part B: Polymer Physics*, *26*(3), 603–619.
38. Liptrot, D. J., & Power, P. P., (2017). London dispersion forces in sterically crowded inorganic and organometallic molecules. *Nature Reviews Chemistry*, *1*(1), 0004.
39. Luxford, C. J., & Bretz, S. L., (2014). Development of the bonding representations inventory to identify student misconceptions about covalent and ionic bonding representations. *Journal of Chemical Education*, *91*(3), 312–320.
40. Maeda, T., Otsuka, H., & Takahara, A., (2009). Dynamic covalent polymers: Reorganizable polymers with dynamic covalent bonds.

Progress in Polymer Science, *34*(7), 581–604.

41. Margenau, H., (1939). Van der Waals forces. *Reviews of Modern Physics*, *11*(1), 1.
42. Mewes, J. M., & Schwerdtfeger, P., (2021). Exclusively relativistic: periodic trends in the melting and boiling points of group 12. *Angewandte Chemie International Edition*, *60*(14), 7703–7709.
43. Mondal, S. K., Mitra, A., Singh, N., Sarkar, S. N., & Kapur, P., (2009). Optical fiber nanoprobe preparation for near-field optical microscopy by chemical etching under surface tension and capillary action. *Optics Express*, *17*(22), 19470–19475.
44. Monopoli, M. P., Åberg, C., Salvati, A., & Dawson, K. A., (2012). Biomolecular coronas provide the biological identity of nanosized materials. *Nature Nanotechnology*, *7*(12), 779–786.
45. Morrow, N. R., (1970). Physics and thermodynamics of capillary action in porous media. *Industrial & Engineering Chemistry*, *62*(6), 32–56.
46. Owen, J., & Thornley, J. H. M., (1966). Covalent bonding and magnetic properties of transition metal ions. *Reports on Progress in Physics*, *29*(2), 675.
47. Persson, B. N. J., & Ryberg, R., (1981). Vibrational interaction between molecules adsorbed on a metal surface: The dipole-dipole interaction. *Physical Review B*, *24*(12), 6954.
48. Peterson, R. F., & Treagust, D. F., (1989). Grade-12 students' misconceptions of covalent bonding and structure. *Journal of Chemical Education*, *66*(6), 459.
49. Peterson, R. F., Treagust, D. F., & Garnett, P., (1989). Development and application of a diagnostic instrument to evaluate grade-11 and-12 students' concepts of covalent bonding and structure following a course of instruction. *Journal of Research in Science Teaching*, *26*(4), 301–314.
50. Phillips, J. C., (1968). Covalent bond in crystals. I. Elements of a structural theory. *Physical Review*, *166*(3), 832.
51. Pimentel, G. C., & McClellan, A. L., (1971). Hydrogen bonding. *Annual Review of Physical Chemistry*, *22*(1), 347–385.
52. Qian, F., Huang, J., & Hussain, M. A., (2010). Drug–polymer solubility and miscibility: Stability consideration and practical challenges in amorphous solid dispersion development. *Journal of Pharmaceutical Sciences*, *99*(7), 2941–2947.
53. Qin, X., Wang, T., & Jiang, L., (2017). Surface engineering of nanoparticles for triggering collective properties of supercrystals. *National Science Review*, *4*(5), 672–677.

54. Reichhelm, A., Haubold, D., & Eychmüller, A., (2017). Ligand versatility in supercrystal formation. *Advanced Functional Materials*, *27*(39), 1700361.

55. Schlier, C., (1969). Intermolecular forces. *Annual Review of Physical Chemistry*, *20*(1), 191–218.

56. Selvaraj, C., Chandra, I., & Singh, S. K., (2021). Artificial intelligence and machine learning approaches for drug design: challenges and opportunities for the pharmaceutical industries. *Molecular Diversity*, 1–21.

57. Shackelford, J. F., & Clode, M. P., (2005). *Introduction to Materials Science for Engineers, 1*(1), 1–20.

58. Stuhler, J., Griesmaier, A., Koch, T., Fattori, M., Pfau, T., Giovanazzi, S., & Santos, L., (2005). Observation of dipole-dipole interaction in a degenerate quantum gas. *Physical Review Letters*, *95*(15), 150406.

59. Stull, D. R., (1947). Vapor pressure of pure substances. Organic and inorganic compounds. *Industrial & Engineering Chemistry*, *39*(4), 517–540.

60. Su, P., & Li, H., (2009). Energy decomposition analysis of covalent bonds and intermolecular interactions. *The Journal of Chemical Physics*, *131*(1), 014102.

61. Taber, K. S., & Coll, R. K., (2003). Bonding. *Chemical Education: Towards Research-Based Practice, 1*(1), 213–234.

62. Thomson, G. W., (1946). The Antoine equation for vapor-pressure data. *Chemical Reviews*, *38*(1), 1–39.

63. Verkhoturov, D., Ershova, T. B., & Konevtsov, L. A., (2007). Basic ideas, paradigms, and methodologies of materials science. *Theoretical Foundations of Chemical Engineering*, *41*(5), 623–627.

64. Weiss, S., (2000). Measuring conformational dynamics of biomolecules by single molecule fluorescence spectroscopy. *Nature Structural Biology*, *7*(9), 724–729.

65. Williams, L. C., Underwood, S. M., Klymkowsky, M. W., & Cooper, M. M., (2015). Are noncovalent interactions an Achilles heel in chemistry education? A comparison of instructional approaches. *Journal of Chemical Education*, *92*(12), 1979–1987.

66. Yang, D., Wei, Q., Yu, L., Zhao, C., & Zhang, L., (2022). Enhanced thermal conductivity and mechanical properties of polymeric composites through formation of covalent bonds between boron nitride and rubber chains. *Polymers for Advanced Technologies*, *33*(1), 212–220.

67. Yaws, C. L., & Yang, H. C., (1989). To estimate vapor pressure easily. *Hydrocarbon Processing;(USA)*, *68*(10).

68. Yayon, M., Mamlok-Naaman, R., & Fortus, D., (2012). Characterizing and representing student's conceptual knowledge of chemical bonding. *Chemistry Education Research and Practice*, *13*(3), 248–267.

69. Zakeri, B., Fierer, J. O., Celik, E., Chittock, E. C., Schwarz-Linek, U., Moy, V. T., & Howarth, M., (2012). Peptide tag forming a rapid covalent bond to a protein, through engineering a bacterial adhesin. *Proceedings of the National Academy of Sciences*, *109*(12), E690–E697.

70. Zheng, H., Ye, H., Yu, X., & You, L., (2019). Interplay between n→ π* interactions and dynamic covalent bonds: Quantification and modulation by solvent effects. *Journal of the American Chemical Society*, *141*(22), 8825–8833.

71. Zhou, G., Wu, M. F., Xing, Q. J., Li, F., Liu, H., Luo, X. B., & Zhang, A. Q., (2018). Synthesis and characterizations of metal-free semiconductor/MOFs with good stability and high photocatalytic activity for H_2 evolution: A novel Z-Scheme heterostructured photocatalyst formed by covalent bonds. *Applied Catalysis B: Environmental*, *220*, 607–614.

CHAPTER 6

Direct Imaging of Covalent Bond Structure in Single-Molecule Chemical Reactions

Contents

6.1. INTRODUCTION

Comprehending the minuscule alterations in the configuration of matter that transpire throughout chemical processes holds significant significance for catalytic systems. It has the potential to result in substantial enhancement of industrially pertinent procedures. Conventional techniques for characterizing chemical arrangements are generally restricted to ensemble methods, wherein distinct molecular structures, if any, are merged in every measurement (de Oteyza et al., 2003). The constraint above poses a challenge in ascertaining the ultimate chemical products and frequently renders recognizing these goods unfeasible, particularly when they exist in minute quantities. The utilization of scanning tunneling microscopy (STM) and other single-molecule measurement methods has the potential to overcome the limitations above. The utilization of STM for structural verification is constrained by the tiny contrast that emanates from the electrical local density of states (LDOS). This difference is occasionally not straightforwardly associated with chemical structure. Transmission electron microscopy (TEM) is a significant technique with sub-nanometer resolution. In this context, the electron beam with high energy is frequently deemed excessively detrimental to image organic molecules. The latest developments in noncontact atomic force microscopy (nc-AFM) that utilize tuning forks have resulted in a technique that can achieve sub-nanometer spatial clarity without causing damage to the sample (Dong et al., 2021). The images acquired through this methodology depict individual molecules and resemble skeletal chemical structures. Furthermore, they facilitate the identification of variations in chemical bond order. In this study, we demonstrate the feasibility of utilizing nc-AFM to elucidate the intramolecular alterations in structure and bond reconfigurations linked to intricate surface-assisted cyclization cascades. This approach enables the identification of the underlying microscopic mechanisms governing chemical response pathways.

6.2. EXPERIMENTAL DESIGN

The category of molecules that can undergo heat pericyclic reorganization is an appropriate platform for precisely observing chemical reorganizations via nc-AFM. Enediynes are a group of molecules that possess alternating triple as well as dual bonds. They demonstrate a range of radical cyclization mechanisms that can compete with conventional Bergman cyclizations. As a result, they often produce multiple products with complicated arrangements that are challenging to analyze using ensemble techniques (Song et al.,

2020). The Bergman cyclization represents a thoroughly investigated organic response that necessitates precise reactions to achieve the intended reaction item. For instance, the reaction mixture is usually inundated using a quenching intermediary to capture the product before it undergoes polymerization. As illustrated in Diagram 2.1, enediynes exhibit a variety of reaction pathways that are accessible to them (Endo & Sugiyama, 2014). Depending upon their substitution pattern, one can force a system to favor one.

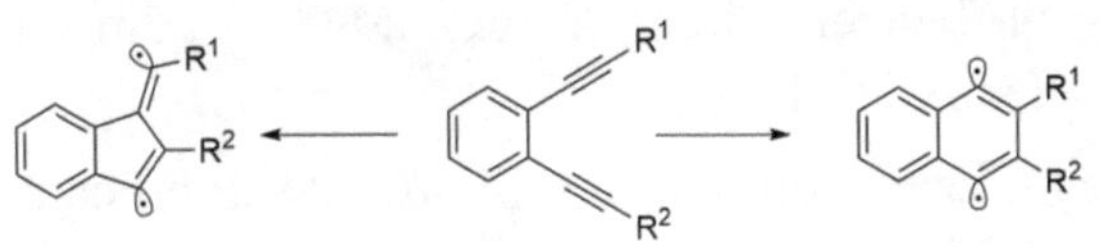

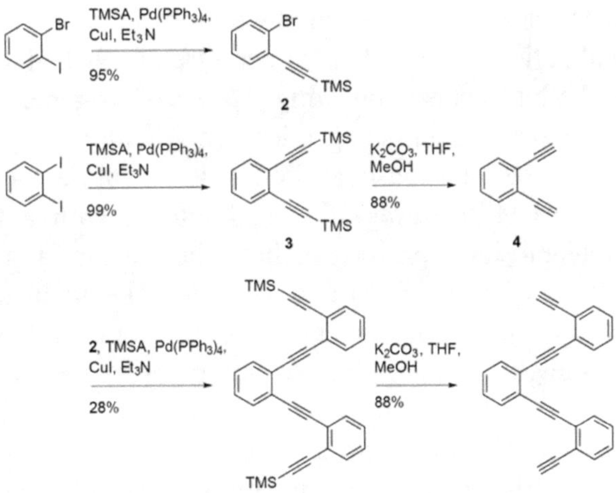

(Note: In figures, the product 1,2,3,4,5,6,7,8,9,10 will be named as 1,2,3,4,5,6,7,8,9,10 throughout the chapter)

By substituting the R group in the acetylene molecules from H to Ph, the energy needed to activate the C1-C6 bond is observed to increase from 24.6 kcal/mol to 32.9 kcal/mol, whereas the activation energy for the C1-C5 bond reduces via 37.2 kcal/mol for 35.1 kcal/mol (Fan et al., 2019).

To further investigate the intricacies of enediyne reactivity, a compound known as 1,2-bis((2-ethynyl phenyl) ethynyl)benzene was synthesized using converging recursive Sonogashira cross-coupling responses. The synthesis of Prerequisite Product 2 was achieved through Sonogashira cross-coupling, utilizing a single equivalent for trimethylsilyl acetylene (TMSA). Product 3 has been produced using the Sonogashira cross-coupling method with the addition of two equivalents of TMSA. Terminal di-acetylene was obtained by deprotecting Product 3 using a blend of THF and methanol alongside potassium carbonate. 4 (de Oteyza, 2016). The study employed a coupling reaction between the secured bromophenyl acetylene items 2 and 4, utilizing 2 equivalents of the former. The resulting product, trimethylsilyl-shielded oligo-1,2-diethynyl benzene item 5, degraded, leading to the desired phenylene ethynylene item 1.

The selected molecule, product 1, will provide significant understanding regarding the favored rearrangements of an intricate enediyne system. To achieve sub-nanometer spatial accuracy for imaging these products, we transferred product 1 using a Knudsen cell over an atomically tidy Ag (100) surface maintained at an ambient temperature according to ultrahigh vacuum (UHV). The specimens decorated with molecules have been sent to a cryogenic visualization stage with a temperature of less than or equal to 7 Kelvin before and after the heat annealing process. Cryogenic visualization was conducted in a scanner tunneling microscope with a temperature of 7 K, which was constructed in-house, as well as in a commercially available Omicron LT-STM/AFM featuring Plus technology, with a temperature of 5 K. Only molecule level probing of both the reactant as well as final products was conducted using STM and nc-AFM. The acquisition of NC-AFM visuals involved measuring the harmonic shift for the qPlus resonators within a constant-height manner while scanning across the surface for the sample. Prior to conducting nc-AFM observations, the highest point of the tip underwent functionalization with a solitary CO molecule (Held et al., 2017). The thermal intricate bond reorganization of item 1 has been analyzed through images, leading to the discovery of a range of unforeseen products. The obtained information has allowed for a comprehensive understanding of the underlying mechanisms. To evaluate the energetics of the response pathway, initial DFT calculations were conducted utilizing the Grid-based Projector Augmented Wavefunction (GPAW) approach code inside the regional density approximation (Figure 6.1).

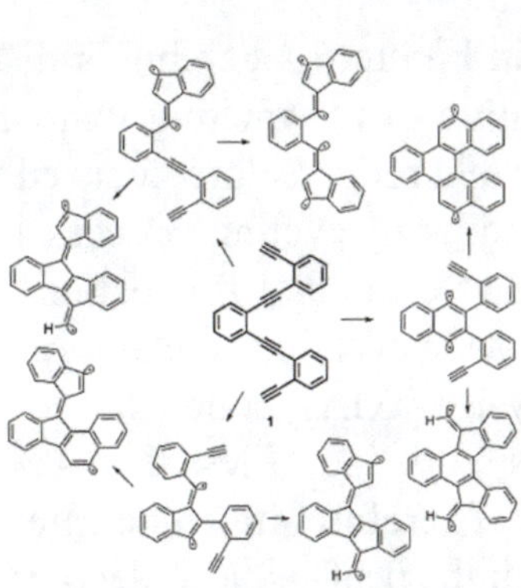

Figure 6.1. The intricate reorganization of oligo-phenylene ethynylene one is depicted in this illustration, showcasing six of the numerous feasible outcomes that could arise through a variety of reaction pathways.

Source: Gorman, Creative Commons License.

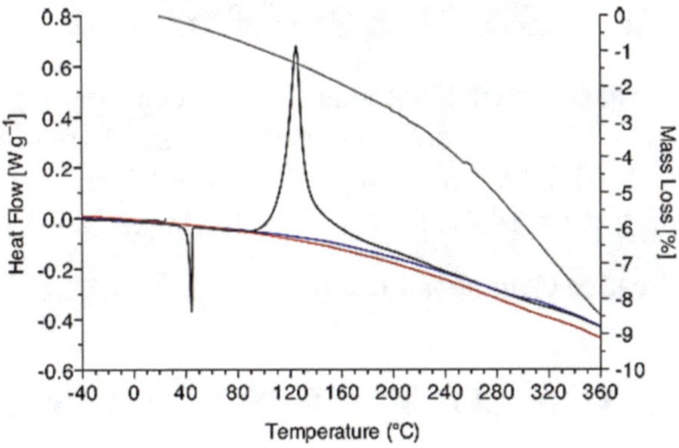

Figure 6.2. The thermal properties of product 1 were analyzed using differential scanning calorimetry (DSC) and thermogravimetric analysis (TGA). The DSC results were color-coded, with black indicating a temperature range of -40 to 360°C and blue indicating a range of 360 to -40°C. The TGA results were color-coded in gray and covered a temperature range of -40 to 360°C.

Source: Patrick, Creative Commons License.

Differential Scanning Calorimetry and Thermogravimetric Analysis

The thermal characteristics of product 1 were examined through differential scanning calorimetry (DSC) to assess the reactive nature of 1,2-diethynylbenzenes under elevated temperatures. The graphical representation depicted in Figure 6.2 exhibits a distinct endothermic peak at 44°C, which is indicative of the melting temperature of the specimen. Additionally, a broad exothermic feature focused at 120°C is observed, a hallmark of a heated-induced cycling process (Stenseng et al., 2001). The occurrence of successive thermal fluctuations suggests that the latter apex is correlated with an irreversible metamorphosis of product 1. The thermogravimetric analysis (TGA) conducted on the identical sample reveals a negligible mass reduction of less than 1% within the temperature interval of 100 to 150°C. Therefore, it can be inferred that the exothermic peak is not correlated with the heat-induced decomposition of item 1.

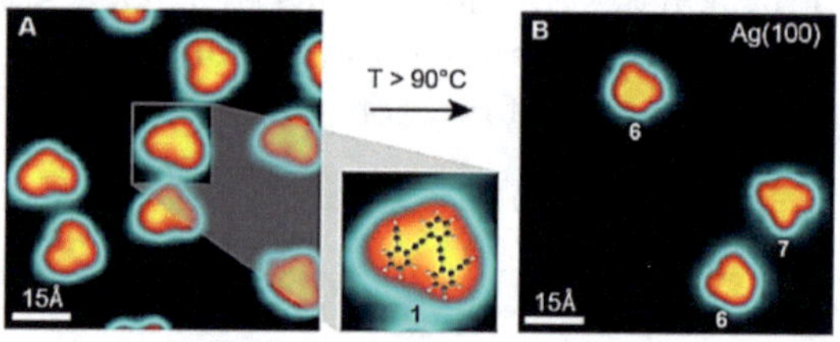

Figure 6.3. (A) Constant current STM image of 1 as deposited on Ag(100) (I = 25 pA, V = 0.1 V, T = 7 K). A model of the molecular structure is overlaid on a close-up STM image. (B) STM image of products 6 and 7 on the surface shown in (A) after annealing at T = 145°C for 1 minute (I = 45 pA, V = 0.1 V, T = 7 K).

Source: Patrick, Creative Commons License.

6.3. STM AND NON-CONTACT (NC)AFM IMAGING

The image in Figure 6.3A is a representative STM depicting item 1 on Ag(100) before undergoing thermal annealing. The adsorbed molecules displayed three maximum values in their LDOS at positions that indicated the presence of phenyl rings within product 1, as illustrated in Figure 6.2A. Heating the Ag surface embellished with molecules to a temperature of 80°C did not alter the molecular structure (Majzik et al., 2013). Subjecting the specimen to annealing at a temperature equal to or greater than 90°C resulted in the chemical conversion of item 1 into molecular items that were markedly dissimilar (with some instances of molecular adsorption being noted). The surface morphology after annealing at a temperature of 145°C, over a duration of 1 minute is depicted in Figure 6.2B using an STM visual. The present image displays two reaction products, denoted 6 as well as 7. The distinctiveness of the frameworks of the items is unequivocally discernible from each other and the initial material, namely product 1

(Guillermet et al., 2011). This is demonstrated by the high-resolution STM images of the prevalent items, including product 6, product 7, as well as product 8, as depicted in Figures 6.3B-D. The ratios for the products that have been identified are 6:7:8, which correspond to (51 ± 7)%, (28 ± 5)%, and (7 ± 3)%, respectively. The remainder of the goods comprises minority monomers and fused oligomers.

Did You Know?

Scanning Tunneling Microscopy (STM) and non-contact Atomic Force Microscopy (nc-AFM) are powerful imaging techniques that allow direct visualization of covalent bond structure at the single-molecule level.

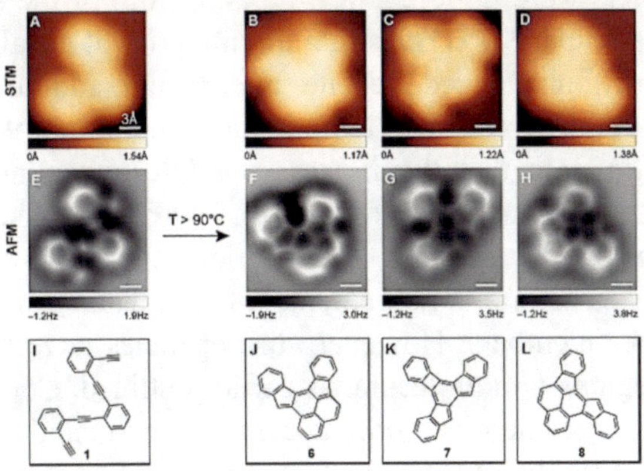

Figure 6.4. This study compares the images obtained from scanning tunneling microscopy (STM), non-contact atomic force microscopy (nc-AFM), and the structures of molecular reactants and products.

Source: Gorman, Creative Commons License.

The molecular reacting agent product 1, as well as products 6 to 8, were analyzed using nc-AFM measures of the molecule-decorated specimen. The structure, as well as bond configurations, were determined with sub-nanometer resolution (Garlant et al., 2020; Ko et al., 2019). The sample was analyzed before and after annealing at a temperature of 90°C or higher. The AFM image provides a highly settled internal bond framework of product 1, whereas the diffuse electrical LDOS within the molecule is reflected within the STM visual. The presence of a dark halo within the outer region within the molecule seems attributed to the influence of long-range electrostatic and van der Waals charges. The intricate intramolecular opposition is caused by short-range Pauli repelling, which attains its maximum value in the areas of greatest electron density (Calleja et al., 2004). The regions above encompass the locations of individual atoms as well as the covalent linkages between them. The number of electrons ascribed to distinct bond orders may be discerned, as demonstrated by the heightened contrast observed at the sites of the three bonds inside product 1. This indicates that even slight variations in electron density can be detected. The mentioned phenomenon should be discerned from the heightened contrast perceived at the molecule's periphery (Suderow et al., 2014). This area is susceptible to extraneous influences, such as a reduced van der Waals origin, amplified electron concentration at the borders of the decentralized π-electron arrangement, and molecular non-planarity, which can affect the contrast.

These products were noticed after the annealing of the specimen at a temperature greater than 90°CThe structural integrity of the aforementioned products remained unchanged despite undergoing additional annealing procedures within the investigated temperature spectrum of 90°C to 150°C. It is important to note that the highest possible annealing temperature examined in this study was 150°C (Mo et al., 1990; Hendriksen & Frenken, 2002). The non-contact atomic force microscopy (nc-AFM) images demonstrate the structural arrangements of annulated rings comprising six, five, and four members. However, discrepancies have been observed near the outer regions of a molecule, as earlier outlined. Consequently, the products' bonding geometries were successfully extracted, albeit without precisely determining their respective bond orders. The presence of delicate radial streaking emanating via carbon atoms located at the periphery implies that the valencies of said carbon atoms have been cut off by hydrogen. The observation above aligns with the principle of molecular mass preservation for all suggested product configurations, suggesting that the chemical responses that culminate in forming products 6 to 8 are solely isomerization processes. According to calculation using DFT, it has been determined that alternative structural isomers, specifically those featuring an 8-membered band adjacent to a 6-membered circle, exhibit a notably unfavorable energetic profile compared to the framework denoted as 7). Figure 6.4 incorporates depictions of additional minority commodities (9 and 10). The non-planar connecting structure of the entity with a numerical value of 9 results in a complicated contrast within the images obtained through non-contact atomic force microscopy (nc-AFM), which poses a challenge in determining its structure directly (Hendriksen et al., 2014). Product 10 is obtained through the concomitant C1-C5 cyclizations that occur in the outer enediynes, which are less sterically impeded, and a C1-C6 cyclization for the inside enediyne. The atomic force microscopy (AFM) contrast exhibited by the last carbon atom present within the bonds between the carbons in product 10 seems comparatively lower than the anticipated value. The observed phenomenon can be explained by a molecular deformation arising from the sustaining interaction among the Ag surface and the ends of sp2 carbon-concentrated radicals. According to DFT calculations, the proximity of the carbon atom within the exocyclic dual bond with the Ag surface is increased (Jensen et al., 1998; Butcher et al., 2011).

6.4. REACTIVITY AND REACTIVE PATHWAYS

The visual representation of the bonding geometry for the ensuing products offers valuable insights into the intricate thermal reaction processes involved in converting product 1 through the resulting products. The focus of our discourse is presently confined to the response pathways that originate via product 1 and culminate in the two most prevalent products, namely products 6 and 7 (Dragone et al., 2017). The rationalization of the responsiveness of product 1, which is oligo-1,2-diethynylbenzene, may be achieved by considering the independent yet overlapping enediyne structures that comprise the 1,2-diethynylbenzene components. These components are either replaced by 2 phenyl rings for the core enediyne or by using one phenyl ring along with a hydrogen atom within the terminal sections. The treatment proposes three probable cyclizations during the response pathway, leading to the formation of 6-membered, 5-membered, or just 4-membered rings. Furthermore, other feasible isomerization processes, including [1,2]-radical moves or just bond rotations, which have been previously observed in similar systems, may also take place (Gervay-Hague, 2016; Migdal et al., 2003). The present study involved an examination and analysis of the computations using DFT to investigate the various processes and their combinations that result in the production of the desired products within the most efficient manner possible.

6.4.1. Description of DFT Calculations

The DFT computations were executed utilizing the PAW method within the GPAW programs package. The exchange as well as correlation (xc)-functional is subjected to the specific density proximity (LDA) (Bucko et al., 2020). It should be noted that the disparities in energetics resulting from the application of the local density approximation (LDA), generalized gradient approximation (GGA), or range-separated blended xc-functionals are anticipated to be significantly less significant than the power of the least strongly bound transition phase compared to the reactant after the first cyclization for every reaction pathway (Körzdörfer & Bredas, 2014; Aksenov et al., 2020). Moreover, the LDA frequently yields more accurate estimations of bond length as well as geometry in comparison to mathematically more demanding techniques such as (GGAs as well as hybrid methods. This implies that the outcomes of LDA are precise enough to depict the chemical mechanisms being examined.

Remember

Remember that Density Functional Theory (DFT) calculations provide a theoretical framework for understanding the electronic structure and reactivity of covalent bonds, based on the principles of quantum mechanics.

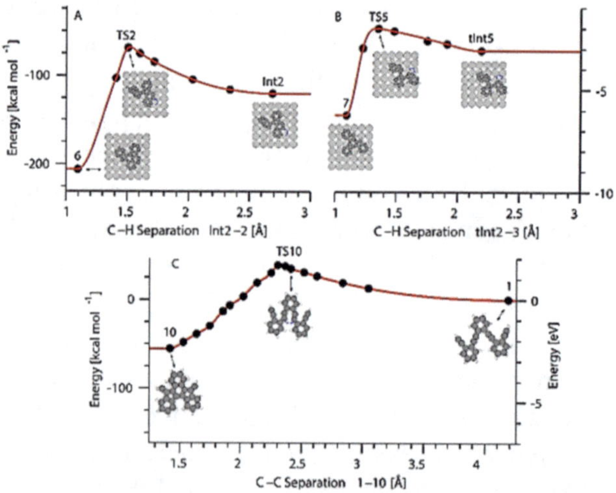

Figure 6.5. The comparison between schematics and energies concerning C-H separation in angstroms for the system is being discussed. A hydrogen shift has been observed from Int2 to product 6, as indicated by the notation. The hydrogen change from tInt2 to the final product 7 is being analyzed with the C-C separation in angstroms for the initial cyclization in order from the first product to product 10. The blue markings denote hydrogen shifts along with cyclizations.

Source: Gorman, Creative Commons License.

The calculations at the Γ point were carried out with a grid distance of h = 0.2 Å, an electrical temperature equal to kBT = 0.1 eV, as well as all energies were extrapolated to T = 0 K. Additionally, the molecular structures were relaxed until an upper limit force beneath 0.05 eV/Å was achieved. The process of adsorption within the Ag(100) surface has been simulated by utilizing a 6×6×3 slab affixed to the testing coordinates determined by lattice parameters of 4.09 Å over Ag. The simulation also incorporates a significant amount of vacuum space, measuring more than 12 Å, among the layer of molecules and the successive pictures of the Ag(100) slab (Forster et al., 2003; Dey et al., 2021). The slab with dimensions of 6×6×3 units ensures a minimum separation of 4 Å between the replicated molecular images in the surface plane. The values identified are deemed adequate for achieving convergence of both energy variations and densities of electrons for all systems being examined (Figure 6.5).

6.4.2. Results of DFT Modeling

The initial step involved the computation of the aggregate energy of an individual retained molecule for reactant 1 onto an Ag(100) substrate. The study involved the computation of activation obstacles and the energy regarding metastable intermediaries, considering molecule-surface connections (Boukhvalov, 2013; Nifant'ev & Ivchenko, 2019). This was done for a range of isomeric, building together the chain of reactions that ultimately leads to the formation of products 6 as well as 7. The findings suggest that the configuration of reacting substances on Ag(100) stays unaltered at temperatures below 90°C. The absence of reactive intermediates within the final products implies that the primary enediyne cyclization is linked to a significant activation obstacle that serves as the controlling factor within the pace of the reaction (Vlček Jr & Záliš, 2007). Consistent with empirical observations, density functional theory (DFT) computations anticipate an initial elevated energy barrier during the original cyclization reactions, succeeded by a sequence of diminished barriers linked to subsequent link rotations and hydrogen shifts.

Tip

A helpful tip when interpreting the results of DFT modeling is to pay attention to the energy profiles and reactive pathways predicted for single-molecule chemical reactions, as they provide valuable insights into the underlying bond-breaking and bond-forming processes.

The reactivation of the barrier that controls the rate of reaction is linked to the Bergman cyclization in order of a terminals enediyne with a C1-C5 cyclization within the internal enediyne section, resulting in the formation of an intermediary diradical Int1 (Bruska et al., 2011; Koposov et al., 2011). This process is exothermic with a value of -60.8 kcal mol-1. Int2 is formed by rotating the third enediyne component within a double bond, which is subsequently followed by the C1-C5 cyclization in order of the fulvene revolutionary with the remained triple bond. The hindrance of rotation around an exocyclic double-bonded structure is observed in the presence of the Ag surface, which necessitates the cleavage of the bond that links the unsaturated valency on the sp^2 atom of carbon along with the Ag. However, it should be noted that the activation barrier of this particular process does not surpass the energy level of the initial material utilized as a point of reference. The stabilization of Int2 by -123.9 kcal mol-1 in comparison to 1 is attributed to the creation of three additional bonds of carbon with carbon and the consequent expansion of the aromatic conjugation (Nifant'ev et al., 2011). Ultimately, a series of [1,2]- and [1,3]-hydrogen shifts, succeeded by a C1–C6 cyclization, results in the formation of dibenzofulvalene 6 from Int2. Based on our calculations, it has been observed that the significant activation barriers that are typically linked alongside radical hydrogen switches in the gaseous state (50–60 kcal mol-1) are reduced due to the stabilizing impact of surface Ag atoms. Consequently, these barriers do not act as a limiting factor for the reaction rate.

The initial step determining the rate includes the cyclization in order of two C1-C5 molecules, specifically the sterically less impeded terminal enediynes, resulting in the formation of benzofulvene diradicals (Berardo et al., 2004). The exocyclic dual bonds serve as the site of localization for the radicals, which then undergo recombination in a C1-C4 cyclization process to produce four-membered rings within the brief intermediate in nature tInt1. The procedure, as mentioned earlier, entails the creation of three novel carbon-carbon bonds, albeit without the presence of the aromatic stabilization that is typically observed during the generation of known naphthyl fragments within Int2 (Nifant'ev et al., 2020; Parfenova et al., 2020). As a result, the process is comparatively less exothermic, with a value of -60.7 kcal mol-1. The transformation of tInt1 to tInt2 is achieved through a series of bond rotations involving Int3. The optimal arrangement of the unaltered carbon valence electrons in the diradical tInt1 is achieved through alignment with the that underlie Ag atoms. This arrangement results in a significant interaction alongside the substrate's surface and induces a non-planar configuration, facilitating barrierless rotations (Meelua et al.,

2020). The formation of biphenylene product 7 is achieved through a formal C1-C6 cyclization and hydrogen shifts.

Transition contends have been acquired through the process of constraining the total length for a bond that is either being broken or formed, followed by the relaxation of the geometry. The bond is incrementally extended by 0.1 Å until the point of maximum energy is reached, which corresponds to the bond length that defines the transition state. To account for hydrogen shifts, those calculations must include them (Shimizu, 1974; Chidsey, 1991).

It is recommended to explicitly consider the Ag(100) surface in the analysis, as the transition could potentially be facilitated by the surface, such as in the case of the -hydrogen move on Int2 (Houk, 1971). In order to determine the transition state, our initial focus is on identifying the fixed length of the bond rather than its energy. To achieve this, a 6×6×1 slab model of the Ag(100) surface can be used for simplification. Conversely, in the process of C bond formation, the surface's influence on figuring out the bond's length that characterizes the transition state is comparatively diminished. Gas phase calculations were utilized to model the initial cyclization barrier, specifically for the chain reaction pathway leading from reacting agent product 1 to the final product 10. The techniques mentioned above enable the prompt acquisition of the necessary bond length to feed the state change. Subsequently, we utilize this information in a 6×6×3 slab model to derive precise transition state energies (Shao et al., 2018). It can be inferred from the analogous product distribution observed after annealing to varying temperatures that the initial cyclizations leading to the formation of products 6 or 7 are anticipated to possess comparable energetic characteristics (Tobita et al., 1992; Eriksson et al., 1992). The computed energy of the transition state for the primary cyclization process is consistent with the estimated value derived from the experimental observation of the threshold temperature of 90°C when combined using the Arrhenius function and standard attempts the frequencies upon the scale of 1013 Hz.

The barriers related to the bond rotational motions, together with the change routes from 1 to 6 and 7, are determined through estimations as described below. During the Int1-Int2 step, the rotation is impeded by the Ag surface (Schreiner et al., 2011). An upper limit over the barrier can be estimated based on the energy necessary to break the connection between the unaltered C-atom and the Ag while simultaneously tilting the molecular structure permits unobstructed bond rotation. An alternative scenario arises when considering the order for bond shifts that convert tInt2 into Int3 and then back into tInt2. In this instance, the molecule tInt1 is optimized to enhance its interaction alongside the substrate by orienting its unsaturated fats C radicals toward the Ag exterior in a non-planar configuration. This arrangement facilitates barrierless shifts (Pace et al., 2011).

The estimation of charge transfer among the Ag(100) surface along with molecules that are absorbed is conducted through the implementation of the Bader dividing scheme on the all-electron density derived from DFT (Gutten & Rulisek, 2013). The aforementioned theoretical framework has been demonstrated to provide a precise depiction of charge transfer in the context of sizable molecules on Ag (Sharp et al., 1991).

The pathways leading to the formation of product 6 and product 7 both entail cyclizations of C1-C5 enediynes (Sundararajan & Flory,1974). Benzofulvene diradicals resulting from C1-C5 cyclizations are not as energetically advantageous as the preferred C1-C6 Bergman cyclizations. However, various factors, including steric congestion caused by alkynes' substituents, metal catalysts, or single-electron decreases of enediynes, are being demonstrated to influence the balance towards C1-C5 cyclizations (Jiao et al., 2008). The current instance of thermally caused cyclization for 1 on Ag(100) is influenced by three factors, namely the presence of a bulky phenyl substituent upon C1 and C6, the presence of a metallic substrate, along with the transfer of charge of 0.5 electrons compared to the substrate to 1. These factors collectively contribute to the facilitation of C1-C5 cyclizations (Wong et al., 1991). It is impossible to determine the exact sequence of low-energy processes, including the Int3/tInt2 rotation and the tInt2/7 [1,2]-hydrogen shifts that occur after the initial cyclizations that limit the progress of the reaction through experimental means. Nevertheless, the sequence of events remains inconsequential to the overarching reaction kinetics and thermodynamics expounded upon earlier (Jedlovszky & Mezei, 2000). Using bond-resolved single-molecule imaging enables the extraction of a comprehensive depiction and unparalleled comprehension of the chemical processes implicated in intricate enediyne cyclization cascades upon Ag(100) surfaces. The comprehensive comprehension of mechanisms subsequently informs the development of precursor materials for producing surface-bound molecular structures with desired functionalities (Spicher & Grimme, 2020).

Activity 1.1

Imagine you are conducting an experiment to investigate a novel single-molecule chemical reaction. How would you design and perform STM and nc-AFM imaging experiments to directly visualize the covalent bond structure and observe any changes in the bond arrangement during the reaction? Additionally, how would you utilize DFT calculations to complement the experimental findings and gain a deeper understanding of the reactive pathways involved?

6.5. SUMMARY

Chapter six explores the topic of direct imaging of covalent bond structure in single-molecule chemical reactions. The chapter begins with an introduction, followed by a discussion on the experimental design for capturing such imaging. It then delves into the imaging techniques of Scanning Tunneling Microscopy (STM) and nc-AFM. The reactivity and reactive pathways of single-molecule chemical reactions are examined, along with the description and results of DFT calculations.

REVIEW QUESTIONS

1. What is the significance of direct imaging of covalent bond structure in single-molecule chemical reactions?
2. How is the experimental design formulated to capture the direct imaging of covalent bond structure?
3. Explain the principles and working mechanism of Scanning Tunneling Microscopy (STM).
4. Discuss the capabilities and advantages of non-contact Atomic Force Microscopy (nc-AFM) in imaging covalent bond structure.
5. What factors influence the reactivity and reactive pathways in single-molecule chemical reactions?
6. How are Density Functional Theory (DFT) calculations used to describe and model the reactivity of covalent bonds?
7. What are the key findings and results obtained from the application of DFT modeling in studying single-molecule chemical reactions?

REFERENCES

1. Aksenov, S. M., Kuznetsov, A. N., Antonov, A. A., Yamnova, N. A., Krivovichev, S. V., & Merlino, S., (2021). Polytypism of compounds with the general formula $Cs\{Al_2[TP_6O_{20}]\}$(T= B, Al): OD (order-disorder) description, topological features, and DFT-calculations. *Minerals*, *11*(7), 708.
2. Berardo, E., Hu, H. S., Shevlin, S. A., Woodley, S. M., Kowalski, K., & Zwijnenburg, M. A., (2014). Modeling excited states in TiO_2 nanoparticles: On the accuracy of a TD-DFT based description. *Journal of Chemical Theory and Computation*, *10*(3), 1189–1199.
3. Boukhvalov, D. W., (2013). DFT modeling of the covalent functionalization of graphene: from ideal to realistic models. *RSC Advances*, *3*(20), 7150–7159.
4. Bruska, M. K., Czekaj, I., Delley, B., Mantzaras, J., & Wokaun, A., (2011). Electronic structure and oxygen vacancies in PdO and ZnO: validation of DFT models. *Physical Chemistry Chemical Physics*, *13*(35), 15947–15954.
5. Bucko, T., Hafner, J., Lebegue, S., & Angyan, J. G., (2010). Improved description of the structure of molecular and layered crystals: Ab initio DFT calculations with van der Waals corrections. *The Journal of Physical Chemistry A*, *114*(43), 11814–11824.
6. Butcher, D. R., Grass, M. E., Zeng, Z., Aksoy, F., Bluhm, H., Li, W. X., & Liu, Z., (2011). In situ oxidation study of Pt (110) and its interaction with CO. *Journal of the American Chemical Society*, *133*(50), 20319–20325.
7. Calleja, F., Arnau, A., Hinarejos, J. J., De Parga, A. V., Hofer, W. A., Echenique, P. M., & Miranda, R., (2004). Contrast reversal and shape changes of atomic adsorbates measured with scanning tunneling microscopy. *Physical Review Letters*, *92*(20), 206101.
8. Chidsey, C. E., (1991). Free energy and temperature dependence of electron transfer at the metal-electrolyte interface. *Science*, *251*(4996), 919–922.
9. De Oteyza, D. G., (2016). Enediyne cyclization chemistry on surfaces under ultra-high vacuum. In: *On-Surface Synthesis: Proceedings of the International Workshop On-Surface Synthesis, École des Houches, Les Houches 25–30 May 2014* (pp. 85–99).
10. De Oteyza, D. G., Gorman, P., Chen, Y. C., Wickenburg, S., Riss, A., Mowbray, D. J., & Fischer, F. R., (2013). Direct imaging of covalent bond structure in single-molecule chemical reactions. *Science*, *340*(6139), 1434–1437.

11. Dey, K. K., Deshmukh, M. M., & Ghosh, M., (2021). A description of the local structure and dynamics of ketoconazole molecule by solid-state NMR measurements and DFT calculations: Proposition for NMR crystallography. *ChemistrySelect*, *6*(38), 10208–10220.

12. Dong, J., Lu, Y., Xu, Y., Chen, F., Yang, J., Chen, Y., & Feng, J., (2021). Direct imaging of single-molecule electrochemical reactions in solution. *Nature*, *596*(7871), 244–249.

13. Dragone, V., Sans, V., Henson, A. B., Granda, J. M., & Cronin, L., (2017). An autonomous organic reaction search engine for chemical reactivity. *Nature Communications*, *8*(1), 15733.

14. Endo, M., & Sugiyama, H., (2014). Single-molecule imaging of dynamic motions of biomolecules in DNA origami nanostructures using high-speed atomic force microscopy. *Accounts of Chemical Research*, *47*(6), 1645–1653.

15. Eriksson, A. E., Baase, W. A., Zhang, X. J., Heinz, D. W., Blaber, M. P. B. E., Baldwin, E. P., & Matthews, B. W., (1992). Response of a protein structure to cavity-creating mutations and its relation to the hydrophobic effect. *Science*, *255*(5041), 178–183.

16. Fan, D., Sakai, Y., & Chelikowsky, J. R., (2019). Discrimination of bond order in organic molecules using noncontact atomic force microscopy. *Nano Letters*, *19*(8), 5562–5567.

17. Forster, F., Nicolay, G., Reinert, F., Ehm, D., Schmidt, S., & Hüfner, S., (2003). Surface and interface states on adsorbate covered noble metal surfaces. *Surface Science*, *532*, 160–165.

18. Garlant, A., Maughan, B., Zahl, P., & Monti, O. L., (2020). H2Pc and pentacene on Cu (110)-(2×1) O: A combined STM and nc-AFM study. *Surface Science*, *696*, 121590.

19. Gervay-Hague, J., (2016). Taming the reactivity of glycosyl iodides to achieve stereoselective glycosidation. *Accounts of Chemical Research*, *49*(1), 35–47.

20. Guillermet, O., Gauthier, S., Joachim, C., De Mendoza, P., Lauterbach, T., & Echavarren, A., (2011). STM and AFM high resolution intramolecular imaging of a single decastarphene molecule. *Chemical Physics Letters*, *511*(4–6), 482–485.

21. Gutten, O., & Rulisek, L., (2013). Predicting the stability constants of metal-ion complexes from first principles. *Inorganic Chemistry*, *52*(18), 10347–10355.

22. Held, P. A., Fuchs, H., & Studer, A., (2017). Covalent-bond formation

via on-surface chemistry. *Chemistry–A European Journal*, *23*(25), 5874–5892.

23. Hendriksen, B. L. M., & Frenken, J. W. M., (2002). CO oxidation on Pt (110): Scanning tunneling microscopy inside a high-pressure flow reactor. *Physical Review Letters*, *89*(4), 046101.
24. Hendriksen, B. L. M., Bobaru, S. C., & Frenken, J. W. M., (2004). Oscillatory CO oxidation on Pd (100) studied with in situ scanning tunneling microscopy. *Surface Science*, *552*(1–3), 229–242.
25. Hendriksen, B. L. M., Bobaru, S. C., & Frenken, J. W. M., (2005). Bistability and oscillations in CO oxidation studied with scanning tunnelling microscopy inside a reactor. *Catalysis Today*, *105*(2), 234–243.
26. Houk, T. L., (1971). Neutron-proton scattering cross section at a few electron volts and charge independence. *Physical Review C*, *3*(5), 1886.
27. Jedlovszky, P., & Mezei, M., (2000). Calculation of the free energy profile of H_2O, O_2, CO, CO_2, NO, and $CHCl_3$ in a lipid bilayer with a cavity insertion variant of the Widom method. *Journal of the American Chemical Society*, *122*(21), 5125–5131.
28. Jensen, J. A., Rider, K. B., Salmeron, M., & Somorjai, G. A., (1998). High pressure adsorbate structures studied by scanning tunneling microscopy: CO on Pt (111) in equilibrium with the gas phase. *Physical Review Letters*, *80*(6), 1228.
29. Jiao, D., Golubkov, P. A., Darden, T. A., & Ren, P., (2008). Calculation of protein–ligand binding free energy by using a polarizable potential. *Proceedings of the National Academy of Sciences*, *105*(17), 6290–6295.
30. Ko, W., Ma, C., Nguyen, G. D., Kolmer, M., & Li, A. P., (2019). Atomic-scale manipulation and in situ characterization with scanning tunneling microscopy. *Advanced Functional Materials*, *29*(52), 1903770.
31. Koposov, A. Y., Cardolaccia, T., Albert, V., Badaeva, E., Kilina, S., Meyer, T. J., & Sykora, M., (2011). Formation of assemblies comprising Ru–polypyridine complexes and CdSe nanocrystals studied by ATR-FTIR spectroscopy and DFT modeling. *Langmuir*, *27*(13), 8377–8383.
32. Körzdörfer, T., & Bredas, J. L., (2014). Organic electronic materials: recent advances in the DFT description of the ground and excited states using tuned range-separated hybrid functionals. *Accounts of Chemical Research*, *47*(11), 3284–3291.
33. Majzik, Z., Tchalala, M. R., Švec, M., Hapala, P., Enriquez, H., Kara, A., & Oughaddou, H., (2013). Combined AFM and STM measurements of a silicene sheet grown on the Ag (111) surface. *Journal of Physics: Condensed Matter*, *25*(22), 225301.

34. Meelua, W., Keawkla, N., Oláh, J., & Jitonnom, J., (2020). DFT study of formation and properties of dinuclear zirconocene cations: Effects of ligand structure, solvent, and metal on the dimerization process. *Journal of Organometallic Chemistry*, *905*, 121024.

35. Migdal, C., Botton, J., El Ali, Z., Azoury, M. E., Guldemann, J., Giménez-Arnau, E., & Pallardy, M., (2013). Reactivity of chemical sensitizers toward amino acids in cellulo plays a role in the activation of the Nrf2-ARE pathway in human monocyte dendritic cells and the THP-1 cell line. *Toxicological Sciences*, *133*(2), 259–274.

36. Mistry, A., Moreton, B., Schuler, B., Mohn, F., Meyer, G., Gross, L., & Fox, D. J., (2015). The synthesis and STM/AFM imaging of 'olympicene' benzo [cd] pyrenes. *Chemistry–A European Journal*, *21*(5), 2011–2018.

37. Mo, Y. W., Kariotis, R., Swartzentruber, B. S., Webb, M. B., & Lagally, M. G., (1990). Scanning tunneling microscopy study of diffusion, growth, and coarsening of Si on Si (001). *Journal of Vacuum Science & Technology A: Vacuum, Surfaces, and Films*, *8*(1), 201–206.

38. Nifant'ev, I., & Ivchenko, P., (2019). Coordination ring-opening polymerization of cyclic esters: A critical overview of DFT modeling and visualization of the reaction mechanisms. *Molecules*, *24*(22), 4117.

39. Nifant'ev, I., Vinogradov, A., Vinogradov, A., Karchevsky, S., & Ivchenko, P., (2019). Zirconocene-catalyzed dimerization of α-olefins: DFT modeling of the Zr-Al binuclear reaction mechanism. *Molecules*, *24*(19), 3565.

40. Nifant'ev, I., Vinogradov, A., Vinogradov, A., Karchevsky, S., & Ivchenko, P., (2020). Experimental and theoretical study of zirconocene-catalyzed oligomerization of 1-octene. *Polymers*, *12*(7), 1590.

41. Pace, C. N., Fu, H., Fryar, K. L., Landua, J., Trevino, S. R., Shirley, B. A., & Grimsley, G. R., (2011). Contribution of hydrophobic interactions to protein stability. *Journal of Molecular Biology*, *408*(3), 514–528.

42. Parfenova, L. V., Kovyazin, P. V., & Bikmeeva, A. K., (2020). Bimetallic Zr, Zr-hydride complexes in zirconocene catalyzed alkene dimerization. *Molecules*, *25*(9), 2216.

43. Schreiner, P. R., Reisenauer, H. P., Ley, D., Gerbig, D., Wu, C. H., & Allen, W. D., (2011). Methylhydroxycarbene: Tunneling control of a chemical reaction. *Science*, *332*(6035), 1300–1303.

44. Shao, Y., Shao, M., Kawazoe, Y., Shi, X., & Pan, H., (2018). Exploring new two-dimensional monolayers: pentagonal transition metal borides/carbides (penta-TMB/Cs). *Journal of Materials Chemistry A*, *6*(22), 10226–10232.

45. Sharp, K. A., Nicholls, A., Fine, R. F., & Honig, B., (1991). Reconciling

the magnitude of the microscopic and macroscopic hydrophobic effects. *Science*, *252*(5002), 106–109.

46. Shimizu, R., (1974). Secondary electron yield with primary electron beam of kilo-electron-volts. *Journal of Applied Physics*, *45*(5), 2107–2111.
47. Song, S., Guo, N., Li, X., Li, G., Haketa, Y., Telychko, M., & Lu, J., (2020). Real-space imaging of a single-molecule monoradical reaction. *Journal of the American Chemical Society*, *142*(31), 13550–13557.
48. Spicher, S., & Grimme, S., (2020). Efficient computation of free energy contributions for association reactions of large molecules. *The Journal of Physical Chemistry Letters*, *11*(16), 6606–6611.
49. Stenseng, M., Jensen, A., & Dam-Johansen, K., (2001). Investigation of biomass pyrolysis by thermogravimetric analysis and differential scanning calorimetry. *Journal of Analytical and Applied Pyrolysis*, *58*, 765–780.
50. Such, B., Kolodziej, J. J., Czuba, P., Krok, F., Piatkowski, P., Struski, P., & Szymonski, M., (2003). STM/nc-AFM investigation of (n× 6) reconstructed GaAs (0 0 1) surface. *Surface Science*, *530*(3), 149–154.
51. Suderow, H., Guillamón, I., Rodrigo, J. G., & Vieira, S., (2014). Imaging superconducting vortex cores and lattices with a scanning tunneling microscope. *Superconductor Science and Technology*, *27*(6), 063001.
52. Sundararajan, P. R., & Flory, P. J., (1974). Configurational characteristics of poly (methyl methacrylate). *Journal of the American Chemical Society*, *96*(16), 5025–5031.
53. Tobita, S., Meinke, M., Illenberger, E., Christophorou, L. G., Baumgärtel, H., & Leach, S., (1992). Polycyclic aromatic hydrocarbons: Negative ion formation following low energy (0–15 eV) electron impact. *Chemical Physics*, *161*(3), 501–508.
54. Vlček, Jr. A., & Záliš, S., (2007). Modeling of charge-transfer transitions and excited states in d6 transition metal complexes by DFT techniques. *Coordination Chemistry Reviews*, *251*(3, 4), 258–287.
55. Wong, M. W., Frisch, M. J., & Wiberg, K. B., (1991). Solvent effects. 1. The mediation of electrostatic effects by solvents. *Journal of the American Chemical Society*, *113*(13), 4776–4782.

CHAPTER

7 Chemical Reactions of Covalent Compounds

Contents

7.1. INTRODUCTION

The comprehension of the behavior and characteristics of various substances is fundamentally reliant on chemical reactions. Molecular compounds, commonly referred to as covalent compounds, represent a noteworthy category of substances that display distinctive properties and experience particular forms of chemical transformations. The present chapter aims to investigate the definition and attributes of covalent compounds, and to scrutinize the significance of comprehending the chemical reactions they experience. The formation of covalent compounds occurs via the sharing of electrons between atoms, which is facilitated by the presence of covalent bonds. In contrast to ionic compounds, wherein electron transfer occurs between atoms, covalent compounds arise from a mutually equitable distribution of electrons among participating atoms. The process of electron sharing results in the formation of molecular structures that exhibit stability (Green, 1995; Kemp, 1972) (Figure 7.1).

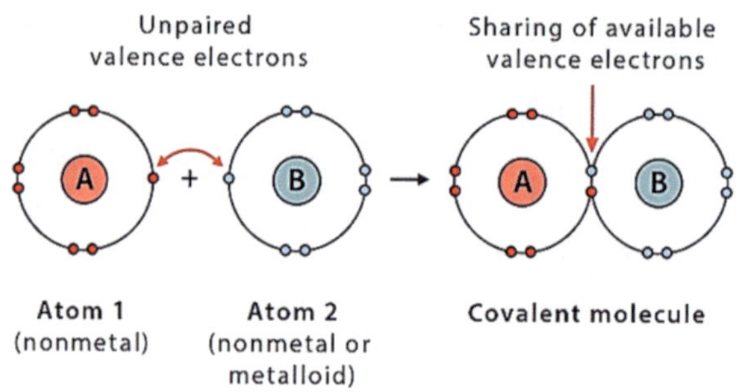

Figure 7.1. Schematic of covalent bond.

Source: Chemistry learner, Creative Commons License.

A salient feature of covalent compounds is their comparatively diminished melting and boiling points in relation to ionic compounds. This phenomenon can be attributed to the relatively diminished intermolecular forces of attraction among molecules. At ambient conditions, covalent compounds are frequently observed in either liquid or gaseous phases, with a few instances of solid-state existence. Furthermore, covalent compounds manifest a diverse array of physical characteristics, including scent, hue, and solubility, that are dictated by their molecular configurations and intermolecular associations. The aforementioned compounds have the ability to establish a range of covalent bonds, such as singles, doubles, and triples, which enables the creation of a broad spectrum of molecular configurations exhibiting distinct characteristics and reactivity. Comprehending the chemical responses of covalent compounds holds significant importance for multiple reasons. Initially, it offers perspectives on the conduct and alteration of materials that are frequently encountered in daily existence. Covalent compounds are widely present in various domains, such as pharmaceuticals, polymers, synthesis of organic compounds, as well as materials science. The comprehension of their responses empowers scholars and experts to formulate and create novel molecules possessing specific characteristics, enhance production procedures, and uncover fresh utilities (Gutmann, 1970; Baytekin et al., 2006).

Furthermore, the comprehension of chemical reactions involving covalent compounds plays a significant role in enhancing our understanding of biological systems. Covalent compounds, including proteins, nucleic acids, as well as carbohydrates, are among the significant biological molecules. Comprehending the chemical reactions and interactions between these compounds is crucial in the investigation of biochemical processes, pharmaceutical interactions, and the operation of biological entities. Moreover, the comprehension of reactions involving covalent compounds amplifies our capacity to tackle environmental predicaments. The chemical reactions undergone by covalent compounds, especially those that are released as pollutants, play a crucial role in determining their impact on ecosystems and ultimate fate. The examination of these reactions facilitates the formulation of efficacious approaches for the mitigation of pollution, remediation, and the adoption of sustainable practices (Zhang et al., 2005).

7.2. TYPES OF CHEMICAL REACTIONS

Chemical reactions are essential phenomena that entail the conversion of matter into distinct forms by means of the rupture and establishment of chemical linkages. The aforementioned reactions hold significant importance in diverse domains such as chemistry, biology, and industrial applications. Comprehending the fundamental principles and mechanisms underlying chemical reactions is a crucial aspect in the prediction and regulation of substance behavior, the creation of novel materials, and the elucidation of natural phenomena.

The fundamental components of any chemical process are the reactants as well as products. Reactants are the initial substances that undergo a chemical reaction, whereas products are the resultant compounds that are generated. Chemical equations conventionally depict the reactants on the left-hand side, demarcated by a plus sign (+), as well as the products on the right-hand side, additionally separated by a plus sign. The chemical reaction involving the combination of hydrogen (H_2) as well as oxygen (O_2) to produce water (H_2O) is characterized by the reactants hydrogen and oxygen reacting to generate the product H_2O (Bent, 1968).

The conservation of mass is a fundamental principle which governs chemical reactions. As per the principle of conservation of mass, the aggregate mass of the reactants ought to be equivalent to the aggregate mass of the products. Stated differently, the law of conservation of mass dictates that in the context of a chemical reaction, the total number of atoms remains constant as no new atoms are generated nor are any destroyed. Conversely, the constituent particles undergo reorganization, resulting in the formation of distinct amalgamations. The principle that matter undergoes transformation rather than creation or destruction during a chemical reaction is frequently encapsulated by the phrase "matter is neither created nor destroyed" (Baillie, 2021).

Chemical equations offer a succinct and symbolic depiction of chemical reactions. Chemical equations enable concise communication of the reactants, products, as well as their respective quantities. The course of the reaction is indicated by an arrow connecting the reactants and products. Furthermore, the coefficients that are positioned before the chemical formulas signify the relative ratios of each constituent present. The process of achieving equilibrium in a chemical equation entails modifying the coefficients to guarantee that the quantity of atoms for each element is identical on each side of the equation (Basi et al., 1971; Gómez-Aleixandre et al., 1995).

Chemical reactions exhibit diverse mechanisms that are contingent upon the characteristics of the reactants as well as the prevailing reaction conditions. The aforementioned mechanisms encompass the processes of chemical bond cleavage and formation, atomic rearrangement, and electron transfer. The trajectory of a reaction is subject to various factors, including but not limited to pressure, temperature, concentration, and the existence of catalysts.

7.3. CLASSIFICATION OF CHEMICAL REACTIONS INVOLVING COVALENT COMPOUNDS

The categorization of chemical reactions including covalent compounds is dependent on the characteristics of the reactants as well as the alterations that transpire during the reaction (Salzen et al., 1992). Comprehending these categorizations facilitates the recognition and anticipation of the conduct of covalent compounds in diverse chemical phenomena. The primary classifications of chemical reactions that involve covalent compounds are:

7.3.1. Combination Reactions

Combination reactions, which are also referred to as synthesis reactions, entail the amalgamation of multiple substances in order to generate a solitary product. In the context of covalent compounds, the process typically entails the exchange or transference of electrons, resulting in the formation of novel bonds. The aforementioned reactions exhibit the hallmark of synthesizing intricate molecules from relatively uncomplicated reactants (Bradley et al., 1973) (Figure 7.2).

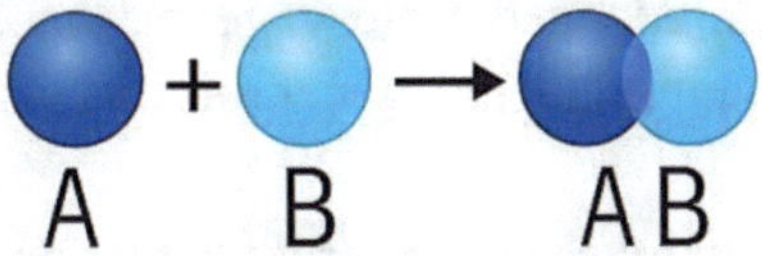

Figure 7.2. Illustration of combination reaction.

Source: Mettler Toledo, Creative Commons License.

An instance of a combination reaction is the chemical process in which hydrogen (H_2) as well as chlorine (Cl_2) react to produce hydrogen chloride (HCl).

$H_2 + Cl_2 \rightarrow 2HCl$

The present chemical reaction involves the amalgamation of hydrogen molecules (H_2) as well as chlorine molecules (Cl_2) to yield hydrogen chloride (HCl), wherein the hydrogen as well as chlorine atoms participate in electron sharing to establish covalent bonds. The phenomenon of combination reactions is frequently encountered in diverse natural and synthetic phenomena (Peng et al., 2018).

The aforementioned reactions hold significant importance in the production of organic compounds, including but not limited to the creation of hydrocarbons and the synthesis of intricate molecules in the pharmaceutical and chemical sectors. Combination reactions are of utmost importance in biological systems, as they are involved in the synthesis of biomolecules such as nucleic acids, proteins, and carbohydrates.

7.3.2. Decomposition Reactions

Decomposition reactions entail the disintegration of a solitary compound into a number of elementary substances. In the context of covalent compounds, fragmentation frequently arises from bond cleavage, leading to the generation of reduced-sized molecules or atoms (Alyea & Bradley, 1969; Purich, 1982). The aforementioned reactions can be regarded as the antithesis of combination reactions.

An instance of a decomposition reaction can be observed in the chemical process of hydrogen peroxide (H_2O_2) breaking down into water (H_2O) as well as oxygen (O_2).

$$2H_2O_2 \rightarrow 2H_2O + O_2$$

The given chemical process involves the decomposition of hydrogen peroxide into the formation of oxygen and water gas. The process of decomposition is triggered by the cleavage of the O-O bond present in hydrogen peroxide, leading to the generation of oxygen gas and water molecules.

Decomposition reactions are a frequently occurring phenomenon in the natural world, exemplified by the breakdown of organic matter through the activity of bacteria and fungi. These microorganisms hold significant importance in various industrial procedures such as the chemical manufacturing process where they aid in the decomposition of compounds and in composting where they assist in the decomposition of organic waste (Urone, 1959).

7.3.3. Displacement Reactions

Displacement reactions, which are also referred to as substitution reactions, transpire when an atom or a cluster of atoms within a compound is substituted by another atom or cluster of atoms. In the context of covalent compounds, the process of replacement generally entails the breaking and subsequent formation of chemical bonds. The chemical reactions in question entail the transfer of groups or atoms of atoms between the reactants, leading to the creation of novel compounds (Ossi & Pastorelli, 1998).

A paradigmatic illustration of a displacement reaction can be observed in the chemical reaction involving methane (CH_4) as well as chlorine (Cl_2), which results in the formation of chloromethane (CH_3Cl).

$$CH_4 + Cl_2 \rightarrow CH_3Cl + HCl$$

The aforementioned reaction involves the substitution of a chlorine atom within a chlorine molecule with a methyl group (CH_3) derived from methane. This substitution leads to the production of chloromethane as well as hydrogen chloride (Figure 7.3).

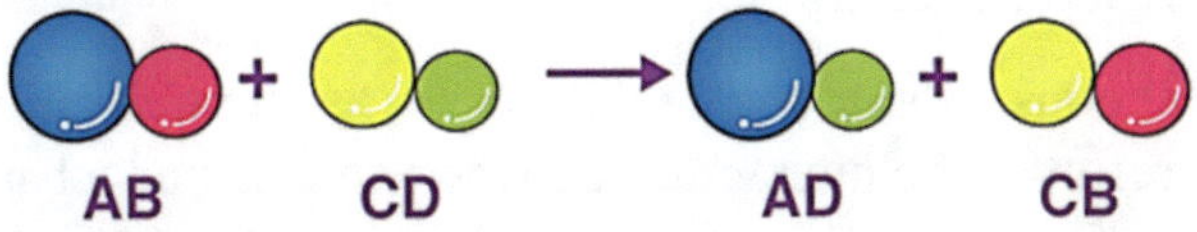

Figure 7.3. Diagram of displacement reaction.

Source: Byju's, Creative Commons License.

Displacement reactions are commonly observed in diverse chemical processes, encompassing organic synthesis, pharmaceutical fabrication, and industrial production. Their significance lies in the manufacturing of distinct chemicals, dyes, and medicinal compounds, wherein particular atoms or groups necessitate substitution to alter the characteristics of the molecules (Luxford & Bretz, 2013).

7.3.4. Redox Reactions

Reduction-oxidation (redox) reactions pertain to electron transfer between reactants. Reduction is defined as the process of acquiring electrons, whereas oxidation is defined as the process of losing electrons. The chemical reactions in question entail alterations in the oxidation states of the constituent atoms. Redox reactions frequently transpire in covalent compounds as a result of alterations in the electron distribution within the molecules (Zakeri et al., 2012; Chakma & Konkolewicz, 2019).

A redox reaction can be exemplified by the chemical reaction involving hydrogen sulfide (H_2S) as well as chlorine gas (Cl_2) which results in the formation of hydrogen chloride (HCl) as well as sulfur (S).

$$H_2S + Cl_2 \rightarrow 2HCl + S$$

The aforementioned chemical process involves the oxidation of hydrogen sulfide, resulting in the loss of hydrogen and the gain of oxygen. Simultaneously, chlorine undergoes reduction, leading to the gain of hydrogen and the loss of oxygen. Consequently, the chemical reaction yields the production of hydrogen chloride and sulfur.

Redox reactions are prevalent in various biological as well as chemical systems. They perform a pivotal function in energy generation, for instance, in the process of fuel combustion and cellular respiration. Redox reactions play a significant role in electrochemical phenomena, including but not limited to batteries and corrosion (Baltieri et al., 2021).

7.3.5. Acid-Base Reactions

Acid-base reactions, commonly referred to as neutralization reactions, transpire as a result of the interaction between an acid and a base, leading to the production of water and a salt. Covalent compounds generally comprise acids that are molecular compounds that liberate hydrogen ions (H+) upon dissolution in water. In contrast, bases are compounds that either receive hydrogen ions or discharge hydroxide ions (OH-) in water.

One instance of an acid-base reaction can be observed in the chemical reaction between hydrochloric acid (HCl) as well as sodium hydroxide (NaOH), which results in the formation of water and sodium chloride (NaCl) (H_2O).

$$HCl + NaOH \rightarrow NaCl + H_2O$$

The present reaction involves the combination of the hydrogen ion from hydrochloric acid with the hydroxide ion from sodium hydroxide, resulting in water formation. Additionally, the sodium and chloride ions react to form sodium chloride. Acid-base reactions are of great significance in numerous chemical and biological processes. They play a pivotal role in regulating the pH levels in biological systems and are crucial in metabolic processes and digestion. Furthermore, acid-base reactions have extensive applications in diverse industries, including pharmaceutical manufacturing, food production, and wastewater treatment (Zoltewicz & O'Halloran, 1975).

7.4. REACTION MECHANISMS

The comprehension of chemical reactions at the molecular level is facilitated by reaction mechanisms. The authors delineate the sequential progression of occurrences that transpire throughout a chemical reaction, encompassing the rupture and establishment of chemical bonds, the emergence of intermediate substances, and the comprehensive metamorphosis of reactants into resultant products. Comprehending reaction mechanisms is a crucial aspect in the prediction of reaction outcomes, development of efficient catalysts, and clarification of the fundamental principles of chemical reactivity.

- **Importance of Reaction Mechanisms:** The analysis of reaction mechanisms provides valuable understanding of the underlying principles that dictate chemical reactions. Chemists utilize these tools to comprehend the variables that impact the rates of reactions, the degree of selectivity, and the amount of product obtained. Through the elucidation of molecular modifications, reaction mechanisms facilitate the optimization of reaction conditions, the conception of innovative synthetic pathways, and the creation of novel chemical processes possessing desired properties (Lonsdale & Ward, 2018).

- **Steps in Reaction Mechanisms:** Reaction mechanisms generally comprise a sequence of elementary steps, that are discrete molecular occurrences that transpire throughout the entirety of the reaction. The fundamental processes that are frequently observed at the elementary level encompass the dissociation of bonds, establishment of bonds, transference of protons and electrons, and reorganization of atoms and groups. The aforementioned steps collectively govern the overall advancement of the reaction and the generation of intermediate species (Takeuchi et al., 1993).
- **Reaction Intermediates:** Transient species known as reaction intermediates are produced and utilized throughout the progression of a chemical reaction. Ephemeral molecular species transiently exist prior to undergoing transformation into their ultimate products. Reaction intermediates exhibit unique reactivity and are instrumental in dictating the selectivity and ultimate result of a chemical reaction. The identification and characterization of these intermediates offer significant insights into the reaction pathway and facilitate the clarification of the underlying mechanisms (Matyjaszewski et al., 1995).
- **Rate-Determining Step:** The rate-determining step, situated inside a reaction mechanism, is the step that exhibits the slowest rate and thereby restricts the general rate of the reaction. Frequently, it is distinguished by a substantial activation energy threshold. The step that determines the rate of a reaction, known as the rate-determining step, plays a crucial role in comprehending and regulating the kinetics of the overall reaction. Catalysts are frequently engineered to decrease the energy of activation of the rate-limiting step, consequently expediting the reaction (Aman, 2020).
- **Reaction Coordinates and Energy Diagrams:** Energy diagrams,

commonly referred to as reaction coordinate diagrams, are a useful tool for illustrating reaction mechanisms. The aforementioned diagrams depict the alterations in energy that transpire during the progression of the reaction pathway. The energy diagram depicts the energy levels of the reactants, intermediary molecules, states of transition, and goods involved in a chemical reaction. The graphical depiction illustrates the energy barriers as well as energetic alterations linked with every stage in the reaction mechanism (Martin et al., 2019).

- **Computational Methods and Experimental Techniques:** The process of clarifying reaction mechanisms frequently necessitates the utilization of a blend of experimental methodologies and computational approaches. Experimental methodologies, namely spectroscopy, kinetics measurements, as well as isotopic labeling, furnish significant information to corroborate and authenticate postulated mechanisms. Computational techniques, including quantum mechanics computations and molecular dynamic simulations, are employed to anticipate reaction energetics, investigate potential energy surfaces, as well as suggest mechanistic pathways (Palazzesi et al., 2019).

7.4.1. A Step-by-Step Explanation of Reaction Mechanisms Involving Covalent Compounds

- Bond cleavage in covalent compounds can occur through two distinct mechanisms, namely homolytic as well as heterolytic bond cleavage. Homolytic bond cleavage refers to a chemical process in which the electrons shared between two atoms in a bond are divided equally between them, leading to the creation of 2 highly reactive entities known as radicals. The presence of an unpaired electron in each radical confers high reactivity upon it, thereby enabling it to initiate subsequent reactions. The process of homolytic bond cleavage is commonly triggered by the absorption of energy, which may take the form of heat or light (Pienta et al., 1992).
- In contrast, heterolytic bond cleavage pertains to the asymmetric distribution of electrons within the bond. In the process of chemical bonding, one of the atoms involved gains electrons, leading to the formation of an anion with a negative charge, while the other

atom loses electrons, leading to in the creation of a cation with a positive charge. The phenomenon of bond cleavage is frequently observed in polar covalent compounds as well as in the presence of a polar solvent. The resultant ions have the potential to engage in diverse chemical reactions, including but not limited to ion-dipole interactions and ionic bonding with other entities (Fan et al., 2021).

- In the course of a chemical reaction, transient species known as intermediates are generated, which exist between the initial reactants and the ultimate products. The aforementioned intermediates are of paramount importance in the mechanism of the reaction. In the context of covalent compound reactions, the generation of intermediates frequently entails the rupture and establishment of numerous bonds. In the context of chemistry, it is possible for a covalent compound to experience a chemical reaction whereby a bond is cleaved, resulting in the formation of a highly reactive intermediate. This intermediate can subsequently engage in a reaction with another molecule, leading to the formation of a novel bond. The stability and reactivity of reaction intermediates may vary based on their electronic as well as structural characteristics. Certain intermediate species exhibit high reactivity and susceptibility to subsequent reactions, whereas others demonstrate greater stability and serve as catalysts and undergo further transformations. Comprehending the generation and conduct of intermediates is imperative in deciphering the complexities of reactions involving covalent compounds (Wu et al., 2022).
- Rearrangement and Bond Formation: The process of covalent compound reactions typically involves the occurrence of rearrangement as well as bond formation steps subsequent to the development of reaction intermediates. The process of rearrangement entails the displacement of groups or atoms inside a molecule, resulting in a modification of the molecular configuration. The process of rearrangement can occur either intramolecularly, within the confines of a single molecule, or intermolecularly, involving multiple distinct molecules. Upon undergoing rearrangement, atoms or groups have the potential to form novel bonds. The process of bond formation can take place through diverse mechanisms, including substitution of

nucleophilic molecules, electrophilic addition, and radical coupling. The rearrangement as well as bond formation steps are influenced by various factors such as the particular reaction circumstances, the nature of the reactants, as well as the inclusion of catalysts or reagents. The general mechanism of reactions involving covalent compounds typically involves a sequence of steps, such as bond cleavage, intermediate formation, rearrangement, as well as bond formation. Every individual step in the process plays a crucial role in the complete conversion of reactants into products, and entails a precise interaction between atoms and electrons (Palazzesi et al., 2020).

Remember

Understanding the step-by-step process of a reaction mechanism is crucial for predicting reaction outcomes accurately.

7.5. REACTION RATES AND FACTORS AFFECTING REACTIONS

Chemical reactions exhibit varying rates, which can be impacted by diverse factors. Comprehending the variables that impact the rate of chemical reactions is of paramount importance in various domains, including but not limited to chemistry, biology, and industrial applications. The present chapter delves into the fundamental determinants that impact the pace of chemical reactions, with a particular emphasis on reactions involving covalent compounds. The aforementioned factors encompassed in the discussion are the reactant concentration, temperature, as well as kinetic energy, catalysts, surface area as well as pressure, as applicable. Through an understanding of these variables, scientists and researchers possess the ability to manipulate the rates of reactions in order to enhance desired results and augment the efficiency of the reaction process (Yang et.la, 2015).

Did You Know?

Catalysts are substances that can speed up a chemical reaction without being consumed in the process, often by providing an alternative reaction pathway with lower activation energy

7.5.1. Concentration of Reactants

The concentration of the reactants significantly influences the speed of a chemical reaction. As per the collision theory, the occurrence of a reaction necessitates that the molecules of the reactants collide with the appropriate orientation and adequate energy. Elevated concentrations of reactants lead to a rise in collision frequency, thereby resulting in an augmentation of the reaction rate. At low concentrations of reactants, the probability of collisions reduces, leading to a deceleration of the reaction rates. In contrast, augmented concentrations of reactants result in an increased frequency of collisions, thereby accelerating the rate of the reaction. The mathematical expression of this relationship is represented by the rate equation, that establishes a correlation between the reaction rate and the amount of the reactants (Glendening et al., 1998).

7.5.2. Temperature and Kinetic Energy

The rates of reactions are significantly influenced by both temperature and kinetic energy. Elevating the temperature results in a rise in the kinetic energy of molecules, thereby inducing an increase in their velocity and frequency of collisions. The kinetic energy exhibited by molecules is a determining factor in the amount of energy needed for a collision to trigger a chemical reaction. An increase in temperature leads to a greater fraction of molecules having sufficient energy to surmount the activation energy threshold, thereby causing an acceleration in the rate of reaction. The Arrhenius equation is frequently utilized to quantify the correlation between temperature and reaction rate. This equation integrates the activation energy as well as temperature to compute the rate constant. The aforementioned equation illustrates that a minor elevation in temperature can result in a substantial augmentation in reaction rates (Scarpino et al., 2020; Trauner & Morstein, 2020; Zhou et al., 2018).

7.5.3. Catalysts

Catalysts are agents that expedite the pace of a chemical reaction by furnishing a different reaction pathway with a diminished activation energy. The entities in question retain their original state upon completion of the reaction as well as are capable of being employed again. Catalysts play a crucial role in promoting chemical reactions by increasing the frequency of reactant collisions and facilitating the development of the transition state. Catalysts function by diminishing the activation energy necessary for a chemical reaction to advance. This is accomplished through the provision of a different reaction mechanism that entails distinct intermediates or by the stabilization of the transition state. Catalysts can be classified into two distinct categories: homogeneous catalysts, that are present in the same stage as the reactants, as well as heterogeneous catalysts, which are found in a dissimilar phase (Hoffer et al., 2019; Hershko et al., 1980).

7.5.4. Surface Area and Pressure (if Applicable)

The reaction rates can be influenced by surface area and pressure, especially in reactions that involve gaseous reactants and solid-state reactions. In the context of gaseous reactions, elevating the pressure engenders a rise in the concentration of molecules, which in turn leads to a greater frequency of collisions and an augmented reaction rate. Likewise, diminishing the capacity of the reaction container can augment the pressure and, thus, the rate of the reaction. The reaction rate in solid-state reactions is notably influenced by the surface area of the reactants. Substances that are in a broken down or powdered state exhibit a greater surface area in comparison to materials in bulk form. This characteristic enables a higher number of contact points between particles of the reactants. The augmentation of surface area intensifies the frequency of collisions, thereby expediting the rate of reaction (Lonsdale et al., 2017).

7.6. REACTION STOICHIOMETRY

The concept of stoichiometry is an essential component of chemistry that pertains to the quantitative correlations among reactants and products within a chemical reaction. Quantitative analysis enables the determination of the quantity of each reactant and product involved in a chemical reaction, thereby facilitating the prediction of the final product of products. Stoichiometry is founded upon the fundamental principle of the law of conservation of mass, that posits that the total mass of the reactants and products in a chemical reaction remains constant, as matter cannot be generated or annihilated (Clair et al., 2019; Sekine et al., 2014).

Tip

The concept of mole ratios is vital in reaction stoichiometry, as it allows you to relate the amounts of reactants and products in a balanced chemical equation.

Stoichiometry is a crucial aspect of chemical reactions as it enables the provision of significant insights into the reaction. Through comprehension of the stoichiometry of a reaction, scientists as well as chemists are able to (Figure 7.4):

- The determination of optimal amounts of reactants required to yield a specific quantity of product is a critical aspect of industrial operations and manufacturing.
- Anticipate the quantity of the resulting product that can be acquired from a specified quantity of reactants, while taking into consideration the optimization of resource utilization.
- The identification of the limiting reactant is a crucial step in determining the maximum amount of product which may be formed, as it is the substance which is entirely consumed and restricts the quantity of product that may be generated.
- Compute the theoretical yield, whose value represents the upper limit of product that can be produced according to stoichiometric calculations.
- Calculate the theoretical yield, which denotes the maximum amount of product that may be produced based on stoichiometric computations.

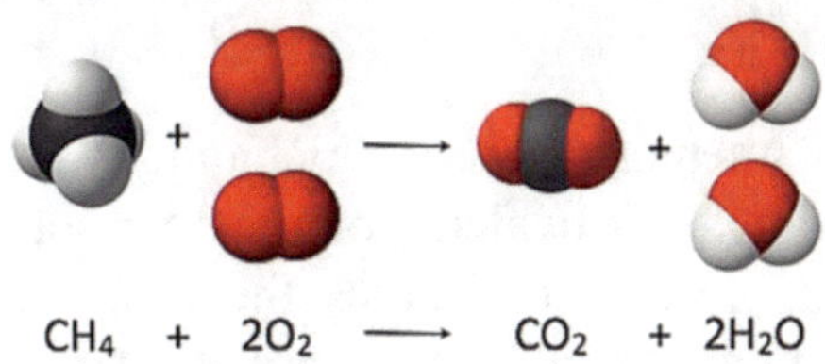

Figure 7.4. Illustration of stoichiometry reaction.

Source: Jynto, Creative Commons License.

7.6.1. Balancing Chemical Equations for Covalent Compounds

The process of balancing chemical equations is a fundamental aspect of stoichiometry, as it guarantees the preservation of the law of conservation of mass. The precise depiction of reactants and products in a reaction involving covalent compounds necessitates meticulous balancing due to the exchange of electrons between atoms. The process of achieving chemical equation balance for covalent compounds involves the following steps:

- Identify the reactants and products the task at hand is to ascertain the molecular formulas of all the reactants and products that are implicated in the given chemical reaction.
- **Count the Atoms:** Determine the stoichiometry of each element present on both reactant and product sides of the chemical equation. Commence the process by directing attention towards constituents that manifest in numerous chemical compounds.
- **Balance the Atoms:** The coefficients, which are integers positioned in front of chemical compounds, should be modified to achieve a balance in the number of atoms present on either side of the chemical equation. Maintaining the integrity of the subscripts inside a compound is of utmost importance, as any alteration to these values would result in a modification of the molecular formula (Djordjevic et al., 2001).
- **Check and Revise:** Following the process of balancing, it is recommended to verify the equation to ensure that the quantity of atoms has become equivalent on both sides. If the equation is not balanced, additional modifications should be made until balance is achieved.

7.6.2. Mole Ratios and Limiting Reactants in Covalent Compound Reactions

Mole ratios are a fundamental aspect of stoichiometry and are of significant importance in the context of covalent compound reactions. In a balanced chemical equation, a mole ratio denotes the proportion of moles of a particular compound to another. Chemists are able to perform conversions between the quantities of various substances that participate in a chemical reaction (Singh et al., 2011).

In order to establish mole ratios, it is necessary to initially balance the chemical equation. The balanced equation's coefficients serve as indicators of the mole ratios that exist among the products and the reactants. As an illustration, in the event that the equation representing a chemical reaction is balanced:

2A + 3B -> 4C

The stoichiometric ratio of A to B is 2:3, indicating that the reaction necessitates the presence of three moles of B for every two moles of A. The correlation between limiting reactants and mole ratios is a fundamental concept. The chemical species that is entirely consumed in a chemical reaction, thereby restricting the quantity of product that may be generated, is referred to as the limiting reactant. The process of determining the limiting reactant involves a comparison between the mole ratios of the reactants and the stoichiometry of the balanced equation.

Assuming a system containing four moles of A as well as five moles of B. Based on the mole ratio of 2:3, it can be inferred that a total of 3.33 moles of B would be sufficient to undergo complete reaction with 4 moles of A. Given the surplus of B (5 moles), it can be inferred that B is the reactant in excess, while A is the reactant that is limiting. Comprehending the concept of mole ratios and identifying the limiting reactant is imperative in ensuring precise calculations of yield. The quantity of product generated is ascertained by the reactant that is limited in quantity, and the stoichiometric proportions of the balanced chemical equation facilitate the computation of the theoretical yield, which represents the upper limit of the amount of product that may be produced under optimal circumstances (Rowan et al., 2002; Yan et al., 2020; Mah et al., 2014).

7.7. EXAMPLES OF COVALENT COMPOUND REACTIONS

- **Combination Reactions:** A chemical reaction known as combination reaction takes place if two or more covalent compounds undergo a reaction resulting in the formation of a solitary compound. An instance can be observed in the chemical reaction among hydrogen (H_2) as well as oxygen (O_2) resulting in the production of water (H_2O). The aforementioned chemical reaction can be expressed in the following manner: two molecules of hydrogen (H_2) combine with one molecule of oxygen (O_2) to produce two molecules of water (H_2O). The phenomenon of combination reactions is frequently encountered in the domain of organic chemistry, wherein several organic compounds amalgamate to yield more intricate molecules (Garber, 2013; Ashjari et al., 2020).
- **Decomposition Reactions:** A chemical process known as decomposition involves the breakdown of a solitary covalent compound into two or more less complex substances. One instance is the process of hydrogen peroxide (H_2O_2) decomposition, which results in the formation of water (H_2O) and oxygen

(O_2). The chemical equation presented is a representation of the decomposition reaction of hydrogen peroxide, where two molecules of hydrogen peroxide (H_2O_2) break down into two molecules of water (H_2O Decomposition reactions are commonly employed in laboratory settings for the purpose of synthesizing targeted compounds or conducting compositional analyzes of intricate substances (Mohammadi et al., 2016).

- **Displacement Reactions:** Displacement reactions entail the substitution of a particular element or group within a covalent compound with another element or group. One instance is the chemical reaction that occurs among hydrochloric acid (HCl) as well as sodium hydroxide (NaOH), resulting in the formation of NaCl (sodium chloride) and water (H_2O). The chemical equation representing the reaction between hydrochloric acid (HCl) and sodium hydroxide (NaOH) is NaCl + H_2O, where sodium chloride (NaCl) and water (H_2O) are the products formed. Displacement reactions play a pivotal role in a multitude of chemical processes, including but not limited to the manufacturing of salts, obtaining of metals, and creating pharmaceuticals (Osuka & Maruyama, 1986).
- **Redox Reactions:** Reduction-oxidation (redox) reactions entail the exchange of electrons between the participating chemical species. One instance is the chemical reaction of methane (CH_4) and oxygen (O_2) resulting in the formation of carbon dioxide (CO_2) as well as water (H_2O), commonly known as combustion. The chemical equation presented is the balanced formula for the combustion reaction of methane (CH_4) with oxygen (O_2), resulting in the production of carbon dioxide (CO_2) and water (H_2O). Redox reactions play a crucial role in the production of energy, as evidenced by their involvement in the combustion of fuels and the production of electricity in batteries (Miyabo et al., 1992).
- **Acid-Base Reactions**: Acid-base reactions transpire when an acidic substance reacts with a basic substance, leading to the production of a salt and water. One illustration can be observed in the chemical reaction of acetic acid (CH_3COOH) and sodium hydroxide (NaOH), which results in the production of water (H_2O) as well as sodium acetate (CH_3COONa): $CH_3COOH + NaOH \rightarrow H_2O + CH_3COONa$. Acid-base reactions play a fundamental role

in a variety of chemical processes, such as neutralizing reactions, the pH level regulation, and the synthesis of pharmaceuticals.

7.7.1. Discussion of Real-World Applications and Significance of These Reactions

Comprehending the reactions of covalent compounds holds paramount significance in numerous practical contexts. The amalgamation reactions that involve covalent compounds play a crucial role in organic synthesis, facilitating the formation of intricate molecules with distinct characteristics. The pharmaceutical sector extensively depends on combination reactions to produce novel drugs possessing the intended therapeutic properties (Backus et al., 2019; Fan et al., 2021; Zhu et al., 2023).

Decomposition reactions are of significant importance in diverse industrial sectors, such as chemical production and environmental assessment. Through comprehension of the process of decomposition, researchers can devise effective techniques for the extraction of high-value substances from raw materials or for the analysis of intricate mixtures for the purpose of quality control. Displacement reactions have practical implications in the field of metallurgy, as they are utilized for the extraction of metals from their respective ores by means of displacement reactions with elements that are more reactive. The aforementioned reactions hold significance in the domain of organic chemistry as they facilitate the creation of innovative compounds through the selective substitution of functional groups. Redox reactions play a crucial role in the generation of energy, particularly in the functioning of fuel cells as well as batteries. Redox processes play a critical role in environmental chemistry, as they govern the destiny and conversion of contaminants in ecological settings (Janes et al., 2018; Mohammadi et al., 2016).

Acid-base reactions play a fundamental role in a multitude of everyday activities, ranging from household sanitation to culinary practices. Acid-base reactions are employed in drug formulation within the pharmaceutical industry to optimize drug stability as well as enhance drug delivery.

Activity 7.1

Imagine you have a mixture of hydrogen gas (H2) and oxygen gas (O2) in a container. Describe step-by-step how you would carry out a chemical reaction between these two gases to produce water (H2O).

7.8. SUMMARY

This chapter explores the chemical reactions of covalent compounds, covering topics such as reaction mechanisms, factors affecting reaction rates, and reaction stoichiometry. Understanding the step-by-step process of reaction mechanisms and the factors influencing reaction rates is crucial for predicting and manipulating reactions accurately. Balancing chemical equations and utilizing mole ratios are essential in reaction stoichiometry to determine the quantities of reactants and products. The chapter also provides examples of covalent compound reactions to illustrate these concepts in practice.

REVIEW QUESTIONS

1. What are the different types of chemical reactions involving covalent compounds?
2. How can the step-by-step process of a reaction be described in a reaction mechanism?
3. What factors can affect the rate of a chemical reaction?
4. Explain the role of catalysts in chemical reactions.
5. How does temperature impact the rate of a chemical reaction?
6. What is the importance of balancing chemical equations for covalent compounds?
7. Define reaction stoichiometry and its significance in chemical reactions.
8. How can mole ratios be used to determine the amounts of reactants and products in a chemical reaction?

REFERENCES

1. Alyea, E. C., & Bradley, D. C., (1969). Covalent compounds of quadrivalent transition metals. Part I. Spectra and magnetic properties of vanadium (IV) alkoxides, dialkylamides, and NN-dimethyldithiocarbamate. *Journal of the Chemical Society A: Inorganic, Physical, Theoretical*, 2330–2333.
2. Aman, I. K., (2020). Changes occur from mixing chemical compounds: Electrovalent bonds and covalent bonds. *International Journal Papier Public Review, 1*(1), 8–13.
3. Ashjari, M., Garmroodi, M., Asl, F. A., Emampour, M., Yousefi, M., Lish, M. P., & Mohammadi, M., (2020). Application of multi-component reaction for covalent immobilization of two lipases on aldehyde-functionalized magnetic nanoparticles; production of biodiesel from waste cooking oil. *Process Biochemistry, 90*, 156–167.
4. Backus, K. M., Cao, J., & Maddox, S. M., (2019). Opportunities and challenges for the development of covalent chemical immunomodulators. *Bioorganic & Medicinal Chemistry, 27*(15), 3421–3439.
5. Baillie, T. A., (2021). Approaches to mitigate the risk of serious adverse reactions in covalent drug design. *Expert Opinion on Drug Discovery, 16*(3), 275–287.
6. Baltieri, R. S., Bego, A. M., & Cebim, M. A., (2021). Why the covalent bond is such a complex concept: a conceptual profile proposal. *International Journal of Science Education, 43*(12), 2007–2024.
7. Basi, J. S., Bradley, D. C., & Chisholm, M. H., (1971). Covalent compounds of quadrivalent transition metals. Part III. Chromium (IV) dialkylamides. *Journal of the Chemical Society A: Inorganic, Physical, Theoretical*, 1433–1436.
8. Baytekin, B., Baytekin, H. T., & Schalley, C. A., (2006). Mass spectrometric studies of non-covalent compounds: Why supramolecular chemistry in the gas phase? *Organic & Biomolecular Chemistry, 4*(15), 2825–2841.
9. Bent, H. A., (1968). Tangent-sphere models of molecules. VI. Ion-packing models of covalent compounds. *Journal of Chemical Education, 45*(12), 768.
10. Bradley, D. C., Rendall, I. F., & Sales, K. D., (1973). Covalent compounds of quadrivalent transition metals. Part VI. spectroscopic studies on titanium, vanadium, and zirconium diethyldithiocarbamates. *Journal of the Chemical Society, Dalton Transactions*, (21), 2228–2233.
11. Chakma, P., & Konkolewicz, D., (2019). Dynamic covalent bonds in polymeric materials. *Angewandte Chemie International Edition, 58*(29), 9682–9695.

12. Clair, S., & De Oteyza, D. G., (2019). Controlling a chemical coupling reaction on a surface: tools and strategies for on-surface synthesis. *Chemical Reviews, 119*(7), 4717–4776.
13. Djordjevic, A., Vojinovic-Miloradov, M. B., & Bogdanovic, G. M., (2001). Covalent and non-covalent derivatives of fullerene C60 and its biological activity. *Acta Period Technol (APTEFF), 32*, 91–112.
14. Fan, S., Yue, L., Wan, W., Zhang, Y., Zhang, B., Otomo, C., & Luo, C., (2021). Inhibition of autophagy by a small molecule through covalent modification of the LC3 protein. *Angewandte Chemie International Edition, 60*(50), 26105–26114.
15. Garber, K., (2013). Principia biopharma: A University of California, San Francisco, startup offers a reversible twist on covalent drugs. *Nature Biotechnology, 31*(5), 377–378.
16. Glendening, E. D., Badenhoop, J. K., & Weinhold, F., (1998). Natural resonance theory: III. Chemical applications. *Journal of Computational Chemistry, 19*(6), 628–646.
17. Gómez-Aleixandre, C., Sanchez, O., Albella, J. M., Santiso, J., & Figueras, A., (1995). CVD of covalent compounds and high-Tc superconductors. *Advanced Materials, 7*(2), 111–119.
18. Green, M. L. H., (1995). A new approach to the formal classification of covalent compounds of the elements. *Journal of Organometallic Chemistry, 500*(1, 2), 127–148.
19. Gutmann, V., (1970). The ionization (heterolysis) of covalent compounds as a coordination-chemical phenomenon. *Angewandte Chemie International Edition in English, 9*(11), 843–860.
20. Hershko, A., Ciechanover, A., Heller, H., Haas, A. L., & Rose, I. A., (1980). Proposed role of ATP in protein breakdown: Conjugation of protein with multiple chains of the polypeptide of ATP-dependent proteolysis. *Proceedings of the National Academy of Sciences, 77*(4), 1783–1786.
21. Hoffer, L., Saez-Ayala, M., Horvath, D., Varnek, A., Morelli, X., & Roche, P., (2019). CovaDOTS: in silico chemistry-driven tool to design covalent inhibitors using a linking strategy. *Journal of Chemical Information and Modeling, 59*(4), 1472–1485.
22. Janes, M. R., Zhang, J., Li, L. S., Hansen, R., Peters, U., Guo, X., & Liu, Y., (2018). Targeting KRAS mutant cancers with a covalent G12C-specific inhibitor. *Cell, 172*(3), 578–589.
23. Kemp, T. J., (1972). Oxidation-reduction reactions between covalent compounds and metal ions. *Comprehensive Chemical Kinetics, 7*, 274–509.

24. Lonsdale, R., & Ward, R. A., (2018). Structure-based design of targeted covalent inhibitors. *Chemical Society Reviews, 47*(11), 3816–3830.

25. Lonsdale, R., Burgess, J., Colclough, N., Davies, N. L., Lenz, E. M., Orton, A. L., & Ward, R. A., (2017). Expanding the armory: predicting and tuning covalent warhead reactivity. *Journal of Chemical Information and Modeling, 57*(12), 3124–3137.

26. Luxford, C. J., & Bretz, S. L., (2013). Moving beyond definitions: what student-generated models reveal about their understanding of covalent bonding and ionic bonding. *Chemistry Education Research and Practice, 14*(2), 214–222.

27. Mah, R., Thomas, J. R., & Shafer, C. M., (2014). Drug discovery considerations in the development of covalent inhibitors. *Bioorganic & Medicinal Chemistry Letters, 24*(1), 33–39.

28. Martin, J. S., MacKenzie, C. J., Fletcher, D., & Gilbert, I. H., (2019). Characterizing covalent warhead reactivity. *Bioorganic & Medicinal Chemistry, 27*(10), 2066–2074.

29. Matyjaszewski, K., Teodorescu, M., & Lin, C. H., (1995). Exchange reactions between covalent and carbocationic species in polymerization of vinyl ethers in the presence of Lewis acids: dynamic NMR studies. *Macromolecular Chemistry and Physics, 196*(7), 2149–2160.

30. Miyabo, A., Takeuchi, K. I., Komatsu, K., & Kitagawa, T., (1992). Small difference in cation stability in controlling the formation of hydrocarbon salt or covalent hydrocarbon. *Chemistry Letters, 21*(4), 683–686.

31. Mohammadi, M., Ashjari, M., Garmroodi, M., Yousefi, M., & Karkhane, A. A., (2016). The use of isocyanide-based multicomponent reaction for covalent immobilization of *Rhizomucor Miehei* lipase on multiwall carbon nanotubes and graphene nanosheets. *RSC Advances, 6*(76), 72275–72285.

32. Mohammadi, M., Gandomkar, S., Habibi, Z., & Yousefi, M., (2016). One pot three-component reaction for covalent immobilization of enzymes: Application of immobilized lipases for kinetic resolution of Rac-ibuprofen. *RSC Advances, 6*(58), 52838–52849.

33. Ossi, P. M., & Pastorelli, R., (1998). Modelling the structural stability of irradiated covalent compounds. *Surface and Coatings Technology, 103*, 9–15.

34. Osuka, A., & Maruyama, K., (1986). Laser induced CIDNP study of photochemical electron transfer reaction between covalently linked porphyrin–tryptophan compounds and 1, 4-benzoquinone. *Chemistry Letters, 15*(11), 1853–1856.

35. Palazzesi, F., Grundl, M. A., Pautsch, A., Weber, A., & Tautermann, C.

S., (2019). A fast ab initio predictor tool for covalent reactivity estimation of acrylamides. *Journal of Chemical Information and Modeling, 59*(8), 3565–3571.

36. Palazzesi, F., Hermann, M. R., Grundl, M. A., Pautsch, A., Seeliger, D., Tautermann, C. S., & Weber, A., (2020). BIreactive: A machine-learning model to estimate covalent warhead reactivity. *Journal of Chemical Information and Modeling, 60*(6), 2915–2923.
37. Peng, J., Huang, Q., Zhuge, W., Liu, Y., Zhang, C., Yang, W., & Xiang, G., (2018). Blue-light photoelectrochemical sensor based on nickel tetra-amined phthalocyanine-graphene oxide covalent compound for ultrasensitive detection of erythromycin. *Biosensors and Bioelectronics, 106*, 212–218.
38. Pienta, N. J., Kessler, R. J., Peters, K. S., O'Driscoll, E. D., Arnett, E. M., & Molter, K. E., (1992). Photolysis of covalent compounds composed of stable anions and cations. Transient absorption studies on coordination complexes formed from the triphenylcyclopropenyl cation and malononitrilo, acetonitrilo, and fluorenyl anions. [Erratum to document cited in CA114 (23): 228243q]. *Journal of the American Chemical Society, 114*(6), 2283–2283.
39. Purich, D. L., (1982). [1] Criteria for evaluating the catalytic competence of enzyme-substrate covalent compounds. In: *Methods in Enzymology* (Vol. 87, pp. 3–20). Academic Press.
40. Rowan, S. J., Cantrill, S. J., Cousins, G. R., Sanders, J. K., & Stoddart, J. F., (2002). Dynamic covalent chemistry. *Angewandte Chemie International Edition, 41*(6), 898–952.
41. Salzen, A. M. V., Meyer, H. U., & Du Mont, W. W., (1992). Diselenides and iodine: Influence of solution equilibria between covalent compounds and charge–transfer complexes. *Phosphorus, Sulfur, and Silicon and the Related Elements, 67*(1–4), 67–71.
42. Scarpino, A., Ferenczy, G. G., & Keserű, G. M., (2020). Covalent docking in drug discovery: Scope and limitations. *Current Pharmaceutical Design, 26*(44), 5684–5699.
43. Sekine, T., Kakuta, T., Nakamura, T., Kobayashi, Y., Takashima, Y., & Harada, A., (2014). A macroscopic reaction: Direct covalent bond formation between materials using a Suzuki-Miyaura cross-coupling reaction. *Scientific Reports, 4*(1), 1–6.
44. Singh, J., Petter, R. C., Baillie, T. A., & Whitty, A., (2011). The resurgence of covalent drugs. *Nature Reviews Drug Discovery, 10*(4), 307–317.
45. Takeuchi, K., Kitagawa, T., Miyabo, A., Hori, H., & Komatsu, K.,

(1993). Precise control of the formation of a covalent and an ionic bond in carbocation-carbanion combination reactions. *The Journal of Organic Chemistry, 58*(21), 5802–5810.

46. Trauner, D., & Morstein, J., (2020). Stereoselective covalent inhibitors of T-Cell activation. *Synfacts, 16*(12), 1484.
47. Urone, P., (1959). Spectrophotometric study of olefin-metal ion coordinate covalent compounds. *Analytical Chemistry, 31*(11), 1768–1770.
48. Wu, Y., & Brooks, III. C. L., (2022). Covalent docking in CDOCKER. *Journal of Computer-Aided Molecular Design, 36*(8), 563–574.
49. Xerxa, E., Miljković, F., & Bajorath, J., (2023). Data-driven global assessment of protein kinase inhibitors with emphasis on covalent compounds. *Journal of Medicinal Chemistry*.
50. Yan, Y., Chen, Z., Yang, J., Guan, L., Hu, H., Zhao, Q., & Wu, M., (2020). Controllable substitution of S radicals on triazine covalent framework to expedite degradation of polysulfides. *Small, 16*(51), 2004631.
51. Yang, H., Yu, K., Mu, X., Shi, X., Wei, Y., Guo, Y., & Qi, H. J., (2015). A molecular dynamics study of bond exchange reactions in covalent adaptable networks. *Soft Matter, 11*(31), 6305–6317.
52. Zakeri, B., Fierer, J. O., Celik, E., Chittock, E. C., Schwarz-Linek, U., Moy, V. T., & Howarth, M., (2012). Peptide tag forming a rapid covalent bond to a protein, through engineering a bacterial adhesin. *Proceedings of the National Academy of Sciences, 109*(12), E690–E697.
53. Zhang, C., Shu, Y., Wang, X., Zhao, X., Tan, B., & Peng, R., (2005). A new method to evaluate the stability of the covalent compound: by the charges on the common atom or group. *The Journal of Physical Chemistry A, 109*(29), 6592–6596.
54. Zhou, S., Metcalf, K. J., Bugga, P., Grant, J., & Mrksich, M., (2018). Photoactivatable reaction for covalent nanoscale patterning of multiple proteins. *ACS Applied Materials & Interfaces, 10*(47), 40452–40459.
55. Zhu, D., Sheng, L., Wang, J., Wang, L., Xu, H., & He, X., (2023). Boosting sulfur-based cathode performance via confined reactions in covalent organic frameworks with polarized sites. *Battery Energy*, 20230002.
56. Zoltewicz, J. A., & O'Halloran, J. K., (1975). Kinetics of degenerate solvolysis. Reaction of covalent amino adducts of heteroaromatic compounds in liquid ammonia. *Journal of the American Chemical Society, 97*(19), 5531–5535.

CHAPTER

8 Advanced Techniques in Covalent Bond Characterization

Contents

8.1. INTRODUCTION

Covalent bonding is an essential concept within the field of chemistry, as it plays a critical role in both creation and the long-term viability of molecules. Covalent bonding is the phenomenon in which two atoms possess one pair of electrons, leading to the creation of a robust chemical bond. The stable setup of electrons resulting from covalent bonds is a defining feature that influences the characteristics as well as arrangements of molecules. The fundamental basis of organic chemistry is established by covalent bonds, which serve as the primary structural framework for a significant number of compounds composed of carbon atoms. The formation of intricate and varied molecular structures is facilitated by these chemical bonds, resulting in an extensive array of chemical compounds that are present in both natural and laboratory settings. Covalent bonds aren't exclusively confined to carbon but manifest within other nonmetallic elements, including nitrogen, oxygen, as well as sulfur (Lin et al., 2021).

The comprehension of the properties, along with the reactivity of molecules, is reliant on the characterization of covalent bonds. Chemists may acquire valuable insights through the chemical reactions of compounds and make predictions about their reactivity by means of studying and calculating the characteristics of covalent bonds (Klüter et al., 2010).

The establishment of the molecular framework is a crucial element in the classification of covalent bonds. The study of covalent bonds is an essential aspect that offers crucial insights into the spatial orientation of atoms in a given molecule. Comprehending the molecule's chemical along with physical attributes, along with its conduct in diverse settings, is imperative for acquiring essential knowledge. Scientific researchers are able to precisely measure bond dimensions, bond angles, as well as bond orientations through the use of experimental techniques such as X-ray crystallography as well as spectroscopic methods. The evaluation of bond stability as well as strength is a crucial factor to consider. The bond power concerning a covalent bond has become a determining factor in its strength. The process of describing covalent bonds has significance for researchers as it allows for the determination of bond strength, a key factor for forecasting a compound's stability as well as reaction. Covalent bonds that possess greater strength exhibit a lower propensity to undergo rupture during chemical reactions. Conversely, weaker bonds may experience cleavage, thereby resulting in the generation of novel compounds (Waller et al., 2015; Su et al., 2009) (Figure 8.1).

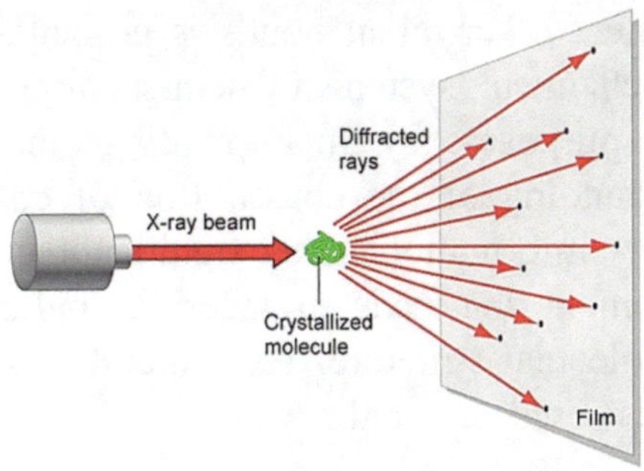

Figure 8.1. Schematic of x-ray crystallography.

Source: Lib guides, Creative Commons License.

The characterization of covalent bonds offers valuable insights into molecular reactivity. The identification of group functions, electron-rich or just electron-deficient regions, as well as potential reactions inside a compound, is facilitated by this technique. The comprehension of these attributes enables chemists to anticipate and regulate chemical conversions, thereby expediting the advancement of novel pharmaceuticals, substances, and accelerators. Moreover, the analysis of covalent bonds enhances comprehension of the electronic configuration of molecules. Spectroscopic methodologies, including nuclear magnetic resonance (NMR) as well as infrared (IR) spectral analysis, furnish insights into the electronic characteristics of covalent bonds, encompassing electron allocation, bond polarity, as well as bond connectivity. The implementation of these methodologies enables chemists to investigate the chemical milieu surrounding individual atoms, thereby facilitating a deeper understanding of molecular characteristics (Matsuda et al., 2020; Liang et al., 2020) (Figure 8.2).

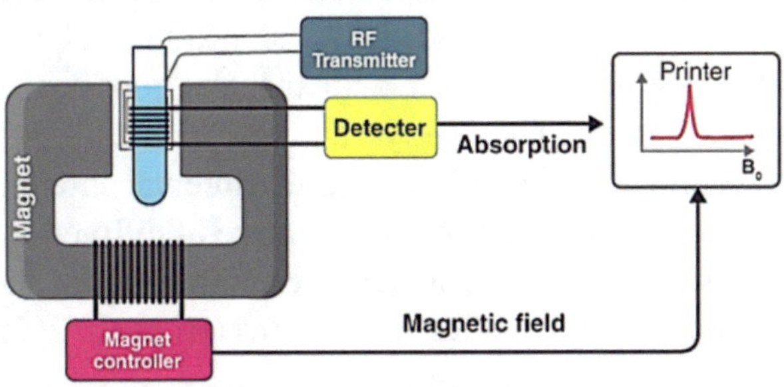

Figure 8.2. Schematic of NMR spectroscopy.

Source: Byju's, Creative Commons License.

Accurate assessment of covalent bonds is crucial for the purpose of rational design for chemical systems. Chemists may attain envisioned characteristics and purposes by manipulating molecular structures through their understanding of the constitution of covalent bonds. The comprehension of this information holds significant importance in fields such as drug development, materials engineering, and catalytic processes, where customized molecular structures are imperative in attaining precise performance attributes (Freccero et al., 2019).

8.2. ADVANCED SPECTROSCOPIC TECHNIQUES

8.2.1. X-ray Crystallography

The fundamental concept underlying X-ray crystallography lies in the fact that the crystal lattice may diffract X-rays, resulting in diffraction patterns that can be utilized to ascertain the atomic positions inside the crystal. Through the examination of the intensity and orientation of diffracted X-rays, scholars are able to reassemble an electron volume map, which offers accurate insights into bond lengths as well as angles within covalent bonds (Cope et al., 1965).

Did You Know?

X-ray crystallography is a widely used technique that allows scientists to determine the three-dimensional atomic structure of covalent compounds by analyzing the diffraction pattern produced by X-rays.

X-ray crystallography is based on the fundamental principles that govern the interaction between X-rays and the crystal lattice. Upon exposure to X-rays, crystals undergo interaction with the electrons that compose the atoms within their lattice. The X-rays that undergo diffraction exhibit a discernible arrangement of beneficial and detrimental interference, which may be recorded through a detector. The structure of diffraction is utilized to compute the arrangement of electron densities within the crystal through the application of intricate mathematical algorithms (Bi et al., 2022).

The utilization of X-ray crystallography allows for the precise analysis of bond lengths as well as angles. Through the analysis of the density of electrons map, scientists are able to quantify the interatomic distances within a covalent bond as well as ascertain the corresponding bond lengths.

Furthermore, the determination of the angles among atoms can be achieved by analyzing the geometric configuration of the atoms that make up the crystal lattice (Lo et al., 2021).

Accurate determination of bond distances and angles is essential in elucidating the structural characteristics of molecules. This technique facilitates scientific inquiry into the fundamental characteristics of chemical bonds, enables the recognition of bonding trends, and permits the assessment of bond vigor and steadfastness. Comprehending the chemical as well as physical features of molecules and their anticipated conduct in diverse circumstances necessitates the acquisition of this crucial information. Although crystallography using X-rays is a potent methodology, it is not exempt from constraints and obstacles. One of the primary constraints involves the necessity for appropriate crystalline specimens. The process of crystallization can pose significant challenges and consume a considerable amount of time, particularly for intricate molecules or just compounds that exhibit a limited propensity for crystal formation. The acquisition of individual crystals of superior quality appropriate for studying X-ray diffraction may present a significant challenge in implementing this methodology. Moreover, X-ray crystallography is predicated on the supposition that the crystal being studied is indicative of the configuration of the molecule in either the solution or just the solid phase. Nevertheless, certain situations may arise in which the crystal lattice may enforce limitations or modify the morphology of the molecule, resulting in possible disparities within the crystallographic configuration and the authentic configuration of the molecular structure within its inherent state (Wang et al., 2022; Whitcombe et al., 1995; Yang et al., 2014).

Interpreting electron density illustrations can pose a challenge, particularly when the number of electrons is indistinct or deficient. The precise estimation of atom places, as well as bond lengths, necessitates meticulous analysis and contemplation of laboratory uncertainties. Furthermore, X-ray crystallography offers stationary representations of molecules, thereby restricting the capacity to investigate dynamic characteristics or momentary conditions.

Notwithstanding the difficulties, X-ray crystallography persists as a fundamental method for the characterization of covalent bonds. The capacity of this technique to furnish accurate data regarding bond lengths, angles, as well as molecular structures makes a noteworthy contribution to our comprehension of chemical bonding as well as the advancement of diverse domains, such as the study of materials, the search for drugs, and catalysis (Müller et al., 2021).

8.2.2. NMR SPECTROSCOPY

The method of NMR spectral analysis is multifaceted in nature and offers significant insights into the molecular makeup, dynamics, as well as interactions of various compounds. This technique leverages the magnetic characteristics of atomic nuclei, particularly their nuclear rotations (Wang et al., 2021).

NMR spectroscopy involves the placement of a sample within a potent magnetic field, which induces the alignment of nuclear spins in either parallel or antiparallel orientation with respect to the field. The application of radiofrequency pulsing can cause perturbation of spins, leading to their precession surrounding the magnetic field's center. A spectrum of NMR records the frequency that the nuclei take in and release energy throughout precession. NMR spectra yield two essential parameters, namely chemical shifts as well as coupling constants. Chemical changes are distinct frequencies that emerge as a result of the shielding or just deshielding impacts of adjacent electron clouds. NMR spectroscopy furnishes data pertaining to the chemical milieu of the nuclei as well as can be associated with the identities of the atoms and their corresponding bonding associates (Azadmanjiri et al., 2020; Sin et al., 2020).

Coupling constants are a result of the magnetic interactions that occur between adjacent nuclei. The splitting patterns observed in the spectra of NMR serve as indicators of atom interaction and the characteristics of chemical bonds. By means of scrutinizing coupling constants, it's possible to ascertain the interconnectivity of chemical bonds present in a given molecule. NMR spectroscopy offers valuable insights into the electron distribution as well as electron density present within bonds of covalent attraction. The magnetized environment of a nucleus is influenced by the electron cloud surrounding it, resulting in fluctuations in chemical shifts. Through the analysis of these shifts, it's possible to deduce information regarding the electron density as well as distribution inside the molecule (de Oteyza et al., 2013; Qu et al., 2021).

8.2.3. Vibrational Spectroscopy (Infrared and Raman)

The field of vibrational spectroscopy comprises two interrelated techniques, namely IR spectroscopy as well as Raman spectroscopy. Both techniques investigate the oscillations of chemical bonds, furnishing significant insights into the robustness of bonds, molecular architectures, and operational groups. The process of infrared spectrum analysis pertains to the assimilation of infrared rays through molecules. Distinct chemical bonds exhibit unique vibrational frequencies, and upon exposure to infrared radiation that corresponds to these frequencies, they undergo absorption, leading to the emergence of characteristic absorbent bands within the spectrum. The spectral bands' intensity offers insights into the bond strength as well as the functional groups' prevalence (Ončák et al., 2011) (Figure 8.3).

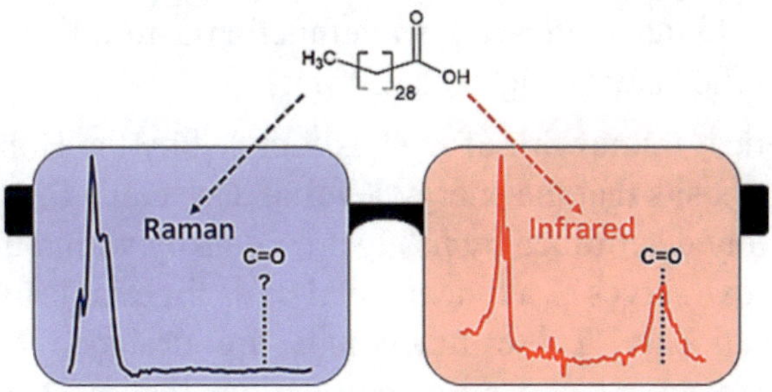

Figure 8.3. Image of Raman and infrared spectroscopy.

Source: ACS publications, Creative Commons License.

In contrast, Raman spectroscopy relies on the phenomenon of inelastic scattered light. When a molecule comes into contact with incoming light, a minute portion of the dispersed light experiences a change in frequency, which corresponds to the energy that is either acquired or forfeited throughout the molecular vibrations. The modes of vibration, along with the bond strengths, are able to be ascertained by gathering data on the frequencies along with the magnitudes of light that is dispersed. The techniques of infrared along with Raman spectroscopy are extensively employed for the purpose of bond analysis in a diverse range of systems, including organic, inorganic, as well as biological. They can be utilized for the purpose of identifying functional groups, ascertaining the existence of particular chemical bonds, and evaluating the conformational alterations in molecules. The techniques above hold significant value as instruments in various domains, including but not limited to pharmaceutical evaluation, materials research, and environmental surveillance (Scarpino et al., 2020; Wang et al., 2017).

8.3. COMPUTATIONAL METHODS

Density Functional Theory (DFT) represents a prevalent computational technique employed in quantum chemistry, which offers a theoretical basis for forecasting and comprehending the characteristics of molecules and materials. The methodology presented provides a pragmatic solution to the Schrödinger formula, which characterizes the dynamics of electrons within a given framework.

The fundamental principle underlying the DFT is the characterization of the electron density, symbolized by ρ(r), that delineates the spatial arrangement of electrons within a given molecule or solid. In contrast to approaches that rely on wavefunctions, the (DFT prioritizes the electron density over individual electron wavefunctions, resulting in improved computational efficiency (Song et al., 2021).

The theoretical framework of DFT is founded by the Hohenberg-Kohn theorem, which posits that the energy level of a system's fundamental state can be exclusively determined by its electron density within the same state. The theorem above serves as a fundamental basis for establishing exchange-correlation functionals. These functionals are designed to incorporate the electrical interactions as well as correlations that exist within a given system. The exchange-correlation function is comprised of two distinct contributions, namely the swap energy as well as the correlation energy. The exchange of energy is a consequence of the measurement mechanical situation of electron swapping, which involves the mutual interchange of positions between 2 electrons. The correlation energy, however, accounts for electron-electron correlations beyond mere exchange interactions (Arzoumanian et al., 2010).

In the context of DFT, the aggregate energy of a given system can be determined by integrating the exchange-correlation function with respect to the number of electrons. The process of energy minimization entails the identification of the number of electrons that reduce the overall energy while adhering to the requirements of the normalization circumstances as well as electron number preservation constraints. The computational methodology of DFT entails the discretization of the number of electrons on a computing grid, followed by the solution of Kohn-Sham equations. These equations constitute a self-consistent collection of equations derived via the Hohenberg-Kohn theorem. The equations above incorporate supplementary non-interacting electrons, referred to as Kohn-Sham orbitals, which replicate the electron volume of the actual system (Li et al., 2020; Wang et al., 2018).

The iterative process of determining the Kohn-Sham orbitals involves an initial guess followed by self-consistent updates until convergence is attained.

Subsequently, the electron density obtained is utilized to compute diverse properties of significance, including but not limited to bond dimensions, bond angles, as well as electronic energies. The accuracy and effectiveness of DFT have rendered it a potent instrument in computational chemistry. This technique facilitates the examination of a broad range of systems, spanning from minute molecules to intricate materials, thereby offering valuable perspectives into their electronic configurations, responsiveness, and characteristics. DFT computations may be executed through diverse numerical techniques, including the plane waves basis set approach, the localized basis set approach, or the pseudopotential approach, contingent upon the particular demands of the system under investigation (Takagiwa et.al 2014; Giummarella et al., 2019).

It is noteworthy that despite the broad applicability and significant outcomes of DFT, it isn't without its constraints. The selection of the exchange-correlation functioning is a critical determinant that can exert a significant influence on the precision of the computed characteristics. Various functionals exhibit distinct strengths and limitations, and their efficacy is contingent upon the nature of the systems under consideration. Furthermore, it is worth noting that the accuracy of DFT may be limited in its ability to capture specific occurrences, such as dispersion effects or highly correlated electron systems. These phenomena may necessitate specialized treatments that go beyond the conventional exchange-correlation functionals (Figure 8.4).

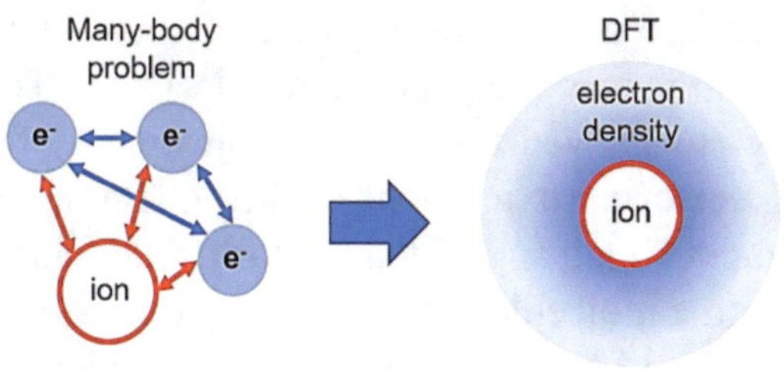

Figure 8.4. Diagram of density functional theory (DFT).

Source: Semantic scholar, Creative Commons License.

8.3.1. Calculation of Bond Lengths, Bond Angles, and Bond Energies

The determination of bond dimensions, bond angles, as well as bond energies seems to be a crucial component of computational chemistry, which facilitates the comprehension of the structure along with the energetic characteristics of molecules by researchers. The precise measurement of these variables is of utmost importance in the investigation of molecular stability, reactions, and physical characteristics. The utilization of DFT as a computational technique is prevalent and provides a robust strategy for computing bond-related characteristics.

Remember

Remember that calculating bond lengths, bond angles, and bond energies using computational methods provides quantitative measures that can help characterize the strength and stability of covalent bonds.

The determination of molecular structure as well as characteristics is significantly influenced by bond lengths, which refer to the interatomic distances between 2 atoms within a molecule. The bond lengths are computed using the DFT approach, which involves minimizing the overall energy for the system compared to the actual positions of the atoms. The optimization procedure entails the successive refinement of the atomic positions till the energy reduction occurs, thereby signifying the attainment of equilibrium bond dimensions (Bagus et al., 2020).

The principle underlying DFT calculations for bond lengths is that the number of electrons determines the overall energy of an entire system. The energy contribution arising from electron-electron relationships as well as correlations is taken into account through the integration of the exchange-correlation functioning over the number of electrons. The minimization of resultant energy is achieved through the adjustment of atom positions, thereby yielding precise approximations of the bond dimensions at a stable state. DFT can compute bond angles that pertain to the spatial configuration of three atoms within a molecule. The energy correlated with various bond angles can be determined by utilizing DFT, which takes into account the relative orientations of atoms as well as their respective electron densities. The optimal bond angle, which results in the lowest energy state, indicates the equilibrium arrangement. Aside from the determination of bond lengths and angles, DFT calculations can yield significant information regarding bond energies. Bond energy pertains to the potency of a covalent connection and denotes the amount of energy necessitated to rupture the bond, thereby generating two distinct atoms. Through the comparison of the aggregate energy for a molecule and that of its individual atoms, DFT has the capability to approximate the bond energy (Zhang et al., 2005; Lo et al., 2021).

The determination of bond energies involves the utilization of DFT, which takes into account the aggregate energy of the entire system in its fundamental state, wherein the atoms are situated at their respective equilibrium states. Bond energy is defined as the disparity between the aggregate energy of a molecule along with the summation of the combined energy levels of its individual constituent atoms. The previously mentioned information holds significant importance in the estimation of reaction energies, comprehension of molecular stability, and exploration of chemical reactions. It's imperative to acknowledge that precise computations of bond dimensions, bond angles, as well as bond energies through DFT necessitate meticulous deliberations. The selection of a particular exchange-correlation function has the utmost importance, as distinct functionals can produce divergent outcomes. The selection of a suitable function is a crucial step for researchers, as it is contingent upon the system being studied and previous validation tests.

DFT computations may encounter convergence challenges, particularly in the case of extensive systems. The attainment of convergence necessitates the optimization of computational variables, including the magnitude for the basis set along with the integration network, to secure reliable and precise outcomes. Insufficient convergence may result in inaccuracies in the computed bond dimensions, bond angles, as well as bond energies (Wijeratne et al., 2018).

8.3.2. Challenges and Considerations in DFT calculations

DFT represents a prevalent computational approach utilized to investigate the electronic structure and features of molecules along with materials. Despite the manifold benefits of DFT, including its computational efficiency and versatility across diverse systems, investigators must confront various challenges and factors that demand attention when undertaking DFT computations (Hu et al., 2022).

The selection for the exchange-correlation functioning is a significant obstacle in DFT computations. The incorporation of electron-electron relationships as well as correlations through calculations is attributed to the exchange-correlation functioning. Numerous functionals are accessible, each possessing unique advantages and drawbacks. The process of selecting the optimal function for a given system and desired property is of paramount importance. It is crucial to select a functional which is approved as well as scored for the particular type of system being studied since various functionals may produce divergent outcomes for bond dimensions, bond angles, as well as bond energies (Fu et al., 2023).

The incorporation of electron correlation constitutes a crucial factor in DFT computations. Although the DFT relies on approximations to elucidate electron-electron relationships, it may not comprehensively encompass intricate correlation effects manifest in certain systems. DFT calculations may encounter difficulties when dealing with systems exhibiting significant electron correlation, including highly correlated materials as well as complexes of transition metals. It is imperative for researchers to acknowledge the limitations as well as exercise prudence when interpreting outcomes derived from DFT computations for these kinds of systems. In certain instances, it may be more appropriate to employ alternative methodologies, like wavefunction-based techniques or hybrid functionals, to achieve a more precise depiction of electron correlation. The careful consideration of convergence seems to be a crucial element in computations using DFT that demands the attention of researchers. Convergence pertains to attaining consistent and precise outcomes concerning the computational parameters utilized in the computations. The parameters above encompass the magnitude for the basis set, integrating grid, and the level of theories implemented. Inadequate convergence has the potential to result in inaccuracies in bond dimensions, bond angles, as well as bond energies. Optimizing computational variables is a crucial step in achieving dependable and precise outcomes. It is recommended that researchers conduct convergence tests to evaluate the stability and the convergence of computed properties, particularly in the case of bigger systems where achieving convergence may pose greater difficulty (Shi et al., 2013; Altaf et al., 2021).

An additional hurdle encountered in DFT computations pertains to the handling of open-shell electron structures, excited states, or just systems with notable dispersion forces. The accurate depiction of such systems can pose a challenge for DFT methodologies. In instances of this nature, it may be necessary for researchers to investigate specialized functionals or alternative computational methodologies, like time-dependent DFT or just post-DFT modifications, in order to attain dependable outcomes. The computational expense associated with performing DFT calculations may also be a factor to consider. Although DFT is typically more computationally economical than wavefunction-based approaches, it necessitates substantial computational resources, especially for high-level computations or large systems. Academic: Achieving practical and effective calculations requires researchers to strike a careful balance between their desired degree of accuracy as well as readily accessible computational resources (Joshi et al., 2019).

8.4. EMERGING TECHNIQUES

Within the dynamic realm of covalent bond evaluation, scholars persistently investigate novel approaches to acquiring a more profound understanding of the essence of chemical bonding. The novel methodologies present distinctive functionalities and opportunities to investigate covalent bonding at the atomic along with molecular scales. By expanding the frontiers of scientific comprehension, these methodologies present intriguing prospects for deciphering the intricacies of chemical architectures and their responsiveness (Yang et al., 2020).

Novel methodologies that surpass conventional bond characterization methods are encompassed within the realm of emerging methods. The utilization of technological advancements and increased computational power has facilitated the development of innovative techniques for visualizing as well as manipulating covalent bonds alongside unparalleled accuracy. The utilization of these methodologies facilitates the investigation of the complex intricacies associated with the formation of chemical bonds, the distribution of electrons, and the dynamics involved. The potential applications of new methods are vast due to their capacity to investigate the complexities of covalent bonds. The utilization of these methodologies presents prospects for significant advancements in diverse domains, such as materials science, nanotechnologies, and pharmaceuticals, ranging from the creation of novel materials with customized characteristics to the clarification of reaction mechanisms as well as catalytic processes. Anticipated progress in the improvement and maturation of nascent methodologies is projected to facilitate substantial strides in the analysis of covalent bonds, thereby furnishing researchers with potent instruments to investigate the boundaries of chemistry and unravel the enigmas of molecular relationships (Görne & Dronskowski, 2019).

8.4.1. Scanning Probe Microscopy (SPM)

Scanning Probe Microscopy (SPM) seems a highly effective and adaptable method that has brought about a significant transformation in nanoscale classification. The technique facilitates the visualization and alteration of areas at a level of atomic or just molecular dimensions, thereby offering significant revelations regarding the composition and characteristics of materials. Atomic Force Microscopy (AFM) as well as Scanning Tunneling Microscopy (STM) are two frequently utilized SPM methods (An et al., 2020).

Both AFM as well as (STM operate on the fundamental principle of scanning a finely pointed probe over the surface of a given sample. AFM is predicated on the detection of forces among the specimen as well as the probe, whereas STM is based on the measurement of the current that travels between the sample as well as the probe. The utilization of these methodologies provides remarkable spatial resolution, enabling researchers to visually perceive individual atoms as well as molecules situated on surfaces (Sanchez-Sanchez & Pomposo, 2014).

SPM exhibits a noteworthy proficiency in imaging as well as manipulation for covalent bonds. This is attributed to its high-resolution capabilities. Through the process of scanning a probe across the specimen's surface, it is possible to identify and evaluate the local interactions that occur between the probe as well as the atoms or molecules present. This facilitates the depiction of covalent bonds along with the assessment of their respective magnitudes and alignments. Moreover, the SPM technique can be employed to investigate the electronic characteristics of covalent bonds, thereby offering valuable information regarding their electronic structure and strength (Mancheño et al., 2019).

SPM facilitates the alteration of covalent bonds, besides its imaging capabilities. By exercising meticulous command over the placement of the probe, it is possible to manipulate, reorganize, or eliminate individual atomic particles or molecules via the surface. This presents opportunities for investigating chemical reactions, fabricating nanostructures, and examining the fundamental tenets of molecular assemblage.

SPM has been utilized in diverse scientific and technological domains, indicating promising prospects for future research and development. Materials science employs this technique to examine surface topography, texture, and the development of thin films. The utilization of SPM is of paramount importance in the production and evaluation of nanoscale structures and devices within the field of nanotechnology. The utilization of nanotechnology is prevalent in the field of biological sciences for the purpose of investigating biomolecules, protein sequences, DNA, as well as cellular frameworks at the microscopic level (Yannacone et.al,2019).

Prospects for the future of SPM appear to be promising. The quality, sensitivity, as well as versatility of SPM techniques are being enhanced through ongoing developments within probe as well as instrumentation technology. This presents novel prospects for investigating intricate structures and phenomena at the atomic as well as molecular scales. The utilization of SPM exhibits significant promise in the progression of our comprehension of chemical reactions, catalysts, surface science, as well as nanoscale phenomena. In addition, the incorporation of other methodologies, like spectroscopy as well as functional imaging, presents intriguing prospects for multifaceted characterization and examination.

8.4.2. Ultrafast Spectroscopy

The scientific method of ultrafast spectroscopy seems a potent tool that enables the examination of molecular dynamics within a remarkably brief timeframe, spanning from femtoseconds (10^-15 seconds) to picoseconds (10^-12 seconds). The present chapter aims to furnish a comprehensive account of ultrafast spectroscopic methods, elucidate their utility in time-resolved investigations of bond creation and cleavage, and evaluate the knowledge they offer regarding bond dynamics as well as reactivity.

Tip

A helpful tip when utilizing ultrafast spectroscopy is to carefully control the time resolution of the technique, as it allows the investigation of fast processes and dynamics of covalent bond formation and breaking on ultra-short timescales.

Ultrafast spectroscopy comprises a variety of experimental techniques that are specifically devised to examine the kinetics of molecular structures with exceptional temporal resolution. The techniques above utilize the basic concepts of spectral analysis, which entail the examination of the electronic along with vibrational characteristics of matter through its interaction with light. In contrast to conventional spectroscopy, ultrafast spectral analysis utilizes ultrashort laser waves to observe phenomena within femtosecond or just picosecond time frames (Gibaja et al., 2021).

Pump-probe spectroscopy is a frequently employed ultrafast spectroscopic technique. This methodology utilizes a dual laser pulse system, wherein a pump pulse is utilized to initiate a targeted molecular process, along with a probe pulse used to observe and record the consequential alterations. Through manipulation of the time delay within the pump as well as probe pulses, investigators are able to discern the temporal evolution of molecular characteristics. Additional methodologies encompass time-resolved fluorescent spectroscopy, transient intake spectroscopy, as well as coherent multifaceted spectroscopy. Every technique provides distinct perspectives on various facets of molecular factors, such as energy transfer, the duration of excited states, and the reorientation of molecules (Sakaguchi et al., 2019; Hassan et al., 2016).

8.4.3. Time-Resolved Studies of Bond Formation and Cleavage

The utilization of ultrafast spectral analysis has brought about a significant transformation in the examination of bond formation along with cleavage procedures, rendering invaluable perceptions into reaction mechanisms. The utilization of ultrafast laser pulses enables investigators to record the brief intermediate states that arise throughout chemical reactions, thereby facilitating direct observation of bond-breaking as well as bond-forming circumstances. Ultrafast spectral analysis has played a crucial role in elucidating the kinetics of bond-splitting reactions triggered by light absorption, particularly in photodissociation research. The methodology above has the capability to monitor the alterations in the molecular structure of the reactants and investigate the transitional states and intermediates that are implicated in the reaction mechanism (Miller et al., 2010; Li et al., 2022).

Ultrafast spectroscopy enables the direct observations of developing bond dynamics during investigations of bond formation. Scholars have the ability to examine the process by which molecules interact, create novel chemical bonds, and progress toward their ultimate end products. This study offers a comprehensive comprehension of the variables that affect the rates of chemical reactions and the degree of selectivity (An et al., 2019).

8.4.4. Insights into Bond Dynamics and Reactivity

The utilization of ultrafast spectroscopy provides distinctive perspectives into the dynamics of bonds and reactivity by providing instantaneous visual representations of molecular mechanisms. This technique enables researchers to investigate the temporal and mechanistic aspects of bond dissociation and association, along with the consequent reorganization of atomic and electronic structures. Ultrafast spectroscopy is a technique that can provide insights into the involvement of excited states as well as transient species within chemical reactions by tracking variations in electronic along with vibrational states. The redistribution of electronic energy within reactant molecules, along with the identification of governing factors that dictate reaction pathways, can be revealed through this process (Wen et al., 2008). Furthermore, ultrafast spectroscopy enables the examination of the impact of extrinsic disturbances, such as variations in temperature as well as solvent surroundings, on the dynamics along with the reactivity of bonds. Through comparative analysis of measurements conducted under varying conditions, researchers can elucidate the intricate interplay within the molecule structure, dynamics, as well as ambient environment (Sun et al., 2018).

Ultrafast spectroscopy provides valuable insights that not only enhance our fundamental comprehension of chemical reactions yet also hold practical implications. They facilitate the advancement of highly effective catalysts, the creation of novel materials exhibiting customized characteristics, and the enhancement of chemical procedures (Martinez-Gonzalez et al., 2017).

Activity 1.1

Imagine you are studying a newly synthesized organic compound with potential applications in optoelectronics. How would you apply X-ray crystallography to determine its molecular structure and understand the arrangement of covalent bonds? Additionally, how would you use ultrafast spectroscopy to investigate the dynamics of the excited states and photoinduced processes involving covalent bonds in this compound?

8.5. SUMMARY

This chapter focuses on advanced techniques used for the characterization of covalent bonds. The chapter begins with an introduction and then explores various advanced spectroscopic techniques, including X-ray crystallography, NMR spectroscopy, and vibrational spectroscopy (infrared and Raman). Computational methods for bond characterization are also discussed, covering calculations of bond lengths, bond angles, and bond energies, as well as the challenges and considerations in DFT calculations. The chapter concludes by highlighting emerging techniques such as SPM and Ultrafast Spectroscopy.

REVIEW QUESTIONS

1. Why are advanced techniques crucial for the characterization of covalent bonds?
2. Explain the principles and application of X-ray crystallography in determining the structure of covalent compounds.

3. How does NMR spectroscopy provide insights into the bonding and molecular structure of covalent compounds?
4. Discuss the use of vibrational spectroscopy, specifically infrared and Raman spectroscopy, in analyzing covalent bond vibrations.
5. What computational methods are commonly used to calculate bond lengths, bond angles, and bond energies in covalent compounds?
6. What are the challenges and considerations that arise in the application of Density Functional Theory (DFT) calculations for covalent bond characterization?
7. Explore the significance and applications of emerging techniques such as Scanning Probe Microscopy (SPM) and Ultrafast Spectroscopy in the study of covalent bonds.

REFERENCES

1. Altaf, A., Baig, N., Sohail, M., Sher, M., Ul-Hamid, A., & Altaf, M., (2021). Covalent organic frameworks: Advances in synthesis and applications. *Materials Today Communications, 28*, 102612.
2. An, D., Cheng, S., Zhang, Z., Jiang, C., Fang, H., Li, J., & Wong, C. P., (2019). A polymer-based thermal management material with enhanced thermal conductivity by introducing three-dimensional networks and covalent bond connections. *Carbon, 155*, 258–267.
3. An, D., Duan, X., Cheng, S., Zhang, Z., Yang, B., Lian, Q., & Wong, C. P., (2020). Enhanced thermal conductivity of natural rubber based thermal interfacial materials by constructing covalent bonds and three-dimensional networks. *Composites Part A: Applied Science and Manufacturing, 135*, 105928.
4. Arzoumanian, H., Castellanos, N. J., Martínez, F. O., Páez-Mozo, E. A., & Ziarelli, F., (2010). *Silicon-Assisted Direct Covalent Grafting on Metal Oxide Surfaces: Synthesis and Characterization of Carboxylate N, N-Ligands on* TiO_2*, 1(1), 6-23.*
5. Azadmanjiri, J., Kumar, P., Srivastava, V. K., & Sofer, Z., (2020). Surface functionalization of 2D transition metal oxides and dichalcogenides via covalent and non-covalent bonding for sustainable energy and biomedical applications. *ACS Applied Nano Materials, 3*(4), 3116–3143.
6. Bagus, P. S., Nelin, C. J., Brundle, C. R., Lahiri, N., Ilton, E. S., & Rosso, K. M., (2020). Analysis of the Fe 2p XPS for hematite α Fe_2O_3: Consequences of covalent bonding and orbital splittings on multiplet splittings. *The Journal of Chemical Physics, 152*(1), 014704.
7. Bi, X., Xu, M., Xie, Z., Li, Y., Tian, J., Wang, Z., & Wang, Z., (2022). A conceptual strategy toward high-reliability metal–thermoplastic hybrid structures based on a covalent-bonding mechanism. *ACS Applied Materials & Interfaces, 14*(44), 50363–50374.
8. Cope, A. C., & Siekman, R. W., (1965). Formation of covalent bonds from platinum or palladium to carbon by direct substitution. *Journal of the American Chemical Society, 87*(14), 3272, 3273.
9. De Oteyza, D. G., Gorman, P., Chen, Y. C., Wickenburg, S., Riss, A., Mowbray, D. J., & Fischer, F. R., (2013). Direct imaging of covalent bond structure in single-molecule chemical reactions. *Science, 340*(6139), 1434–1437.
10. Freccero, R., Solokha, P., De Negri, S., Saccone, A., Grin, Y., & Wagner, F. R., (2019). Polar-covalent bonding beyond the Zintl picture

in intermetallic rare-earth germanides. *Chemistry–A European Journal, 25*(26), 6600–6612.

11. Fu, Q., Xia, Z. Z., Sun, X., Jiang, H. L., Wang, L. L., Ai, S. Y., & Zhao, R. S., (2023). Recent advance and applications of covalent organic frameworks based on magnetic solid-phase extraction technology for food safety analysis. *TrAC Trends in Analytical Chemistry*, 117054.
12. Gibaja, C., Rodríguez-San-Miguel, D., Paz, W. S., Torres, I., Salagre, E., Segovia, P., & Zamora, F., (2021). Exfoliation of alpha-germanium: A covalent diamond-like structure. *Advanced Materials, 33*(10), 2006826.
13. Giummarella, N., Pu, Y., Ragauskas, A. J., & Lawoko, M., (2019). A critical review on the analysis of lignin carbohydrate bonds. *Green Chemistry, 21*(7), 1573–1595.
14. Görne, A. L., & Dronskowski, R., (2019). Covalent bonding versus total energy: On the attainability of certain predicted low-energy carbon allotropes. *Carbon, 148*, 151–158.
15. Hassan, S. U., Zhou, Y., Zhang, L., Shi, Z., Yang, D., Asif, H. M., & Qu, N., (2016). Remarkable enhancement in the nonlinear optical responses of porphyrins realized by combination with polyoxometalates via covalent bonding: a case study. *The Journal of Physical Chemistry C, 120*(14), 7757–7766.
16. Hu, S. Z., Huang, T., Zhang, N., Lei, Y. Z., & Wang, Y., (2022). Chitosan-assisted MOFs dispersion via covalent bonding interaction toward highly efficient removal of heavy metal ions from wastewater. *Carbohydrate Polymers, 277*, 118809.
17. Joshi, T., Chen, C., Li, H., Diercks, C. S., Wang, G., Waller, P. J., & Crommie, M. F., (2019). Local electronic structure of molecular heterojunctions in a single-layer 2D covalent organic framework. *Advanced Materials, 31*(3), 1805941.
18. Klüter, S., Simard, J. R., Rode, H. B., Grütter, C., Pawar, V., Raaijmakers, H. C., & Rauh, D., (2010). Characterization of irreversible kinase inhibitors by directly detecting covalent bond formation: a tool for dissecting kinase drug resistance. *ChemBioChem, 11*(18), 2557–2566.
19. Li, G., Chen, H., Zhang, B., Guo, H., Chen, S., Chang, X., & Li, X., (2022). Interfacial covalent bonding enables transition metal phosphide superior lithium storage performance. *Applied Surface Science, 582*, 152404.
20. Li, Z., Sheng, L., Wang, H., Wang, X., Li, M., Xu, Y., & He, X., (2020). Three-dimensional covalent organic framework with ceq topology. *Journal of the American Chemical Society, 143*(1), 92–96.

21. Liang, R. R., Jiang, S. Y., Ru-Han, A., & Zhao, X., (2020). Two-dimensional covalent organic frameworks with hierarchical porosity. *Chemical Society Reviews, 49*(12), 3920–3951.
22. Lin, X., Wang, J., Ding, B., Ma, X., & Tian, H., (2021). Tunable-emission amorphous room-temperature phosphorescent polymers based on thermoreversible dynamic covalent bonds. *Angewandte Chemie, 133*(7), 3501–3505.
23. Lo, R., Lamanec, M., Wang, W., Manna, D., Bakandritsos, A., Dračínský, M., & Hobza, P., (2021). Structure-directed formation of the dative/covalent bonds in complexes with C 70··· piperidine. *Physical Chemistry Chemical Physics, 23*(7), 4365–4375.
24. Lo, R., Manna, D., & Hobza, P., (2021). Cyclo [n] carbons form strong N→ C dative/covalent bonds with piperidine. *The Journal of Physical Chemistry A, 125*(14), 2923–2931.
25. Mancheño, M. J., Royuela, S., De La Peña, A., Ramos, M., Zamora, F., & Segura, J. L., (2019). Introduction to covalent organic frameworks: an advanced organic chemistry experiment. *Journal of Chemical Education, 96*(8), 1745–1751.
26. Martinez-Gonzalez, A. I., Díaz-Sánchez, Á. G., De La Rosa, L. A., Vargas-Requena, C. L., Bustos-Jaimes, I., & Alvarez-Parrilla, E., (2017). Polyphenolic compounds and digestive enzymes: In vitro non-covalent interactions. *Molecules, 22*(4), 669.
27. Matsuda, T., Kawakami, R., Nakajima, T., & Gong, J. P., (2020). Crack tip field of a double-network gel: Visualization of covalent bond scission through mechanoradical polymerization. *Macromolecules, 53*(20), 8787–8795.
28. Miller, S. G., Bauer, J. L., Maryanski, M. J., Heimann, P. J., Barlow, J. P., Gosau, J. M., & Allred, R. E., (2010). Characterization of epoxy functionalized graphite nanoparticles and the physical properties of epoxy matrix nanocomposites. *Composites Science and Technology, 70*(7), 1120–1125.
29. Müller, P. C., Ertural, C., Hempelmann, J., & Dronskowski, R., (2021). Crystal orbital bond index: Covalent bond orders in solids. *The Journal of Physical Chemistry C, 125*(14), 7959–7970.
30. Ončák, M., Berka, K., & Slavíček, P., (2011). Novel covalent bond in proteins: calculations on model systems question the bond stability. *ChemPhysChem, 12*(17), 3449–3457.
31. Qu, Z., Wang, K., Xu, C. A., Li, Y., Jiao, E., Chen, B., & Wu, K., (2021). Simultaneous enhancement in thermal conductivity and flame retardancy

of flexible film by introducing covalent bond connection. *Chemical Engineering Journal, 421*, 129729.

32. Sakaguchi, M., Makino, M., Ohura, T., Yamamoto, K., Enomoto, Y., & Takase, H., (2019). Surface modification of Fe_3O_4 nanoparticles with dextran via a coupling reaction between naked Fe_3O_4 mechano-cation and naked dextran mechano-anion: A new mechanism of covalent bond formation. *Advanced Powder Technology, 30*(4), 795–806.
33. Sanchez-Sanchez, A., & Pomposo, J. A., (2014). Single-chain polymer nanoparticles via non-covalent and dynamic covalent bonds. *Particle & Particle Systems Characterization, 31*(1), 11–23.
34. Scarpino, A., Ferenczy, G. G., & Keserű, G. M., (2020). Covalent docking in drug discovery: Scope and limitations. *Current Pharmaceutical Design, 26*(44), 5684–5699.
35. Shi, L., Liu, Q., Guo, X., Wu, W., & Liu, Z., (2013). Pyrolysis behavior and bonding information of coal—A TGA study. *Fuel Processing Technology, 108*, 125–132.
36. Sin, Y. Y., Huang, C. C., Lin, C. N., Chih, J. K., Hsieh, Y. L., Tsao, I. Y., & Su, C. Y., (2020). Ultrastrong adhesion of fluorinated graphene on a substrate: In situ electrochemical conversion to ionic-covalent bonding at the interface. *Carbon, 169,* 248–257.
37. Song, X., Zhang, X., Wang, M., Li, X., Zhu, Z., Huo, P., & Yan, Y., (2021). Fabricating intramolecular donor-acceptor system via covalent bonding of carbazole to carbon nitride for excellent photocatalytic performance towards CO_2 conversion. *Journal of Colloid and Interface Science, 594*, 550–560.
38. Su, P., & Li, H., (2009). Energy decomposition analysis of covalent bonds and intermolecular interactions. *The Journal of Chemical Physics, 131*(1), 014102.
39. Sun, S., Samani, M. K., Fu, Y., Xu, T., Ye, L., Satwara, M., & Liu, J., (2018). Improving thermal transport at carbon hybrid interfaces by covalent bonds. *Advanced Materials Interfaces, 5*(15), 1800318.
40. Takagiwa, Y., & Kimura, K., (2014). Metallic–covalent bonding conversion and thermoelectric properties of Al-based icosahedral quasicrystals and approximants. *Science and Technology of Advanced Materials*.
41. Waller, P. J., Gándara, F., & Yaghi, O. M., (2015). Chemistry of covalent organic frameworks. *Accounts of Chemical Research, 48*(12), 3053–3063.
42. Wang, J., Li, J., Gao, M., & Zhang, X., (2018). Recent advances in covalent organic frameworks for separation and analysis of complex samples. *TRAC Trends in Analytical Chemistry, 108*, 98–109.

43. Wang, N., Feng, L., Xu, X. D., & Feng, S., (2022). Dynamic covalent bond cross-linked luminescent silicone elastomer with self-healing and recyclable properties. *Macromolecular Rapid Communications, 43*(7), 2100885.

44. Wang, X., & Ye, N., (2017). Recent advances in metal-organic frameworks and covalent organic frameworks for sample preparation and chromatographic analysis. *Electrophoresis, 38*(24), 3059–3078.

45. Wang, Y., Xiao, Y., Fu, X., Jiang, L., Yuan, A., Xu, H., & Lei, J., (2021). A permanent covalent bond-crosslinked thermosetting polymer with room-temperature autonomous self-healing performance. *New Journal of Chemistry, 45*(46), 21742–21749.

46. Wen, K., Maoz, R., Cohen, H., Sagiv, J., Gibaud, A., Desert, A., & Ocko, B. M., (2008). Postassembly chemical modification of a highly ordered organosilane multilayer: New insights into the structure, bonding, and dynamics of self-assembling silane monolayers. *ACS Nano, 2*(3), 579–599.

47. Whitcombe, M. J., Rodriguez, M. E., Villar, P., & Vulfson, E. N., (1995). A new method for the introduction of recognition site functionality into polymers prepared by molecular imprinting: synthesis and characterization of polymeric receptors for cholesterol. *Journal of the American Chemical Society, 117*(27), 7105–7111.

48. Wijeratne, A., Xiao, J., Reutter, C., Furness, K. W., Leon, R., Zia-Ebrahimi, M., & Chalmers, M. J., (2018). Chemical proteomic characterization of a covalent KRASG12C inhibitor. *ACS Medicinal Chemistry Letters, 9*(6), 557–562.

49. Yang, L. M., & Pushpa, R., (2014). Tuning electronic and optical properties of a new class of covalent organic frameworks. *Journal of Materials Chemistry C, 2*(13), 2404–2416.

50. Yang, Y. X., Fang, Z., Liu, Y. H., Hou, Y. C., Wang, L. G., Zhou, Y. F., & Guan, S. K., (2020). Biodegradation, hemocompatibility and covalent bonding mechanism of electrografting polyethylacrylate coating on Mg alloy for cardiovascular stent. *Journal of Materials Science & Technology, 46*, 114–126.

51. Yannacone, S., Oliveira, V., Verma, N., & Kraka, E., (2019). A continuum from halogen bonds to covalent bonds: Where do λ3 iodanes fit? *Inorganics, 7*(4), 47.

52. Zhang, C., Shu, Y., Wang, X., Zhao, X., Tan, B., & Peng, R., (2005). A new method to evaluate the stability of the covalent compound: by the charges on the common atom or group. The *Journal of Physical Chemistry A, 109*(29), 6592–6596.

INDEX

B

C

D

E

F

G

H

I

K

L

M

Q

R

S

W

X

Z

Printed in the United States
by Baker & Taylor Publisher Services